THE NEW GERMANY
AND THE
NEW EUROPE

PAUL B. STARES
Editor

THE NEW GERMANY
AND THE
NEW EUROPE

THE BROOKINGS INSTITUTION
Washington, D.C.

Copyright © 1992

THE BROOKINGS INSTITUTION

1775 Massachusetts Avenue, N.W., Washington, D.C. 20036

Library of Congress Cataloging-in-Publication data

The new Germany and the new Europe / Paul B. Stares, ed.

    p.   cm.

  Includes bibliographical references and index.

  ISBN 0-8157-8138-5 (alk. paper) — ISBN 0-8157-8137-7
(alk. paper : pbk.)

   1. Germany—Foreign relations—1990–   2. Germany—Relations—
Europe. 3. Europe—Relations—Germany. 4. Europe—Politics and
government—1989–   5. European cooperation. I. Stares, Paul B.
DD290.3.N49 1992

327.43—dc20   92-26403

                                                          CIP

9 8 7 6 5 4 3 2 1

The paper used in this publication meets the minimum requirements of the
American National Standard for Information Sciences—Permanence of
paper for Printed Library Materials, ANSI Z39.48-1948

Foreword

Of the breathtaking changes that have occurred in Europe over the last few years, the unification of Germany commands attention and deserves special consideration. What were already two powerful countries in the heart of Europe have suddenly and quite unexpectedly become one. No other country in Europe is likely to play such a critical role as Germany in shaping the future course of the new Europe. For the countries of Central and Eastern Europe, as well as the former Soviet Union, Germany is seen as a vital source of financial aid and investment as well as a key trading partner needed to overcome the difficult challenges of economic reconstruction. For Western Europe, Germany's active participation in the historic drive toward greater political, economic, and military integration is considered indispensable. So much depends, therefore, on the new Germany.

For these reasons the Brookings Institution embarked on a study to examine the consequences of German unification. The perspectives of twelve scholars from Germany, Great Britain, France, Hungary, Poland, Russia, the United States, and Japan were engaged to provide a wide range of viewpoints. As such this book represents one of the most comprehensive assessments of the implications of German unification. Given that events are still unfolding in Europe in unpredictable ways, it is important to note that the views of the contributors are current as of the time the book went to press in the late summer of 1992.

What is clear now, however, is that the real unification of Germany still has a long way to go. While the country functions as a unitary state, sharp divisions remain along the old boundaries that are as much psychological as physical in nature. These will not be erased for many years and could conceivably grow more pronounced. Germany is also going to great lengths to adjust its foreign and security policy to its new role on the international stage, but Germans, no less than their neighbors and allies, have yet to grow accustomed to this. At the same time, the hope that the end of the Cold War would allow for the reunification of Europe is also far from realization. Again there is a real danger that new barriers will be erected to replace the old. With this concern in mind, two complementary designs are presented as paths toward a more unified Europe.

The editor of the volume is Paul B. Stares, a senior fellow in the Brookings Foreign Policy Studies program. He would like to thank his colleagues in Foreign Policy Studies, John D. Steinbruner, Catherine McArdle Kelleher, Wolfgang H. Reinicke, and Susan L. Woodward, for their valuable support and insights. Charlotte Baldwin Brady, Susanne E. Lane, Caroline Lalire, and Theresa Walker helped to manage the project and steer it through publication.

Emily Chalmers was principally responsible for editing the manuscript, James R. Schneider edited one chapter, and Patricia Dewey provided editorial assistance. The immense task of verifying the factual content of each chapter, including sources in no fewer than six languages, was performed by Melanie Allen, Jon Dyar Boles, Marlin S. Dick, Yuko Iida Frost, Adrianne Goins, Susanne E. Lane, Alexander Ratz, Marion Recktenwald, and Daniel A. Turner. Janelle L. Jameson, Annette D. Leak, Caroline F. Pecquet, Louise F. Skillings, and Ann M. Ziegler provided word processing support. Charlotte Hebebrand helped in proofreading the manuscript. Susan L. Woolen prepared the manuscript for publication, and DoMi Stauber prepared the index. To all of the above, the editor is profoundly grateful.

Brookings would like to acknowledge with gratitude the Fritz Thyssen Stiftung for its financial support throughout the project, which included a conference in Rottach-Egern, Germany, in September 1991 where the original papers of the volume were presented for critical review.

The views expressed in this book are solely those of the individual authors and should not be attributed to the Brookings Institution, to its trustees, officers, or other staff members, or to the organizations that support its research.

Bruce K. MacLaury
President

August 1992
Washington, D.C.

Contents

Part Two: Designs for a New Europe

Part Three: Perspectives on the New Germany

Tables

Figures

Abbreviations and Acronyms

ACCS	Air Command and Control System
ACE	Allied Command Europe
AMF	ACE Mobile Force
APEC	Asian Pacific Economic Cooperation
ATTU	Atlantic-to-the-Urals region
CAP	Common Agricultural Policy
CDU	Christian Democratic Union
CEI	Central European Initiative
CFE	Conventional Forces in Europe Treaty
CIS	Commonwealth of Independent States
CMEA	Council for Mutual Economic Assistance
COCOM	Coordinating Committee on Multilateral Export Controls
CPC	Conflict Prevention Center
CPSU	Communist Party of the Soviet Union
CSBMs	Confidence- and security-building measures
CSCE	Conference on Security and Cooperation in Europe
CSU	Christian Social Union
DM	deutsche mark
DPC	Defense Planning Committee (NATO)
DSU	German Social Union
DVU	German People's Union
EC	European Community
EEA	European Economic Area
EFTA	European Free Trade Association
EMU	economic and monetary union
ERP	European Recovery Programme
ESPRIT	European Strategic Program for Research in Information Technologies
EUREKA	European Research Coordination Agency

FDP	Free Democratic Party
FRG	Federal Republic of Germany
GATT	General Agreement on Tariffs and Trade
GDR	German Democratic Republic
GPGs	General Political Guidelines
HDTV	high-definition television
IAEA	International Atomic Energy Agency
IGCs	intergovernmental conferences
IMF	International Monetary Fund
INFs	Intermediate-Range Nuclear Forces
JESSI	Joint European Submicron Silicon Initiative
JETRO	Japan External Trade Organization
MBFR	Mutual and Balanced Force Reductions
MESU	Monetary, Economic, and Social Union
MTCR	Missile Technology Control Regime
NAC	North Atlantic Council
NACC	North Atlantic Cooperation Council
NAFTA	North American Free Trade Agreement
NATO	North Atlantic Treaty Organization
NBC	nuclear, biological, and chemical
NPD	National Party of Germany
NVA	National People's Army
OECD	Organization for Economic Cooperation and Development
PDS	Party of Democratic Socialism
PHARE	Pologne/Hongorie-assistance à la réconstruction économique
RAF	Red Army Faction
RRF	Rapid Reaction Force
SALT	Strategic Arms Limitation Talks
SAM	Surface-to-Air Missile
SAR	search and rescue
SEA	Single European Act
SED	Socialist Unity Party
SIOP	Single Integrated Operational Plan
SLOCs	sea lines of communication
SNFs	Short-Range Nuclear Forces
SPD	Social Democratic Party
START	Strategic Arms Reduction Talks
TLE	Treaty-Limited Equipment
TR	transferable ruble
VAT	value-added tax
USSR	Union of Soviet Socialist Republics
WEU	Western European Union
WTO	Warsaw Treaty Organization

Federal Republic of Germany

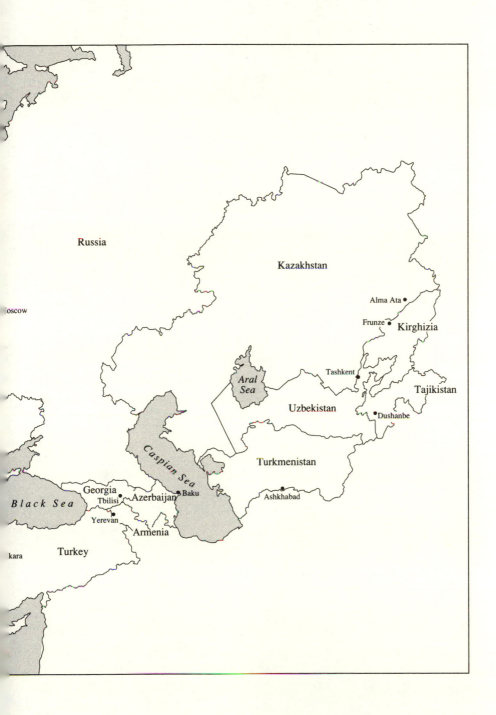

Russia

Kazakhstan

oscow

Alma Ata •

Frunze • Kirghizia

*Aral
Sea*

Tashkent •

Tajikistan

Uzbekistan

• Dushanbe

Caspian Sea

Turkmenistan

Georgia

Black Sea

Tbilisi • Azerbaijan • Baku

• Ashkhabad

Yerevan •

Armenia

kara   Turkey

ONE

Introduction

Paul B. Stares

THE MOST VISIBLE manifestations of the Cold War have virtually disappeared in Europe. The heavily guarded walls and barbed wire fences that once divided the continent, and Germany in particular, have been torn down and their most salvageable elements sold for scrap and souvenirs. In much the same way that the course of old river systems or the earthworks of ancient civilizations can sometimes be detected only from high altitude, so the former contours and residual scars of the Cold War will doubtless fade with time and become increasingly difficult to discern at ground level.

The remarkable changes to the European landscape have taken place so rapidly and often in such confusing circumstances that their full meaning has barely been comprehended, let alone fully assimilated. That the events triggered by the first heroic and largely spontaneous acts of 1989 were wholly unforeseen is not only deeply humbling but also worthy of sober reflection on our sustaining beliefs about the Cold War. More pressing, however, is the need to assess the implications of these changes and the challenges and opportunities they present. While the situation in Europe is still unfolding in unpredictable ways, making such judgments a difficult and even frustrating exercise, the time that has elapsed since 1989 does permit us to more clearly take stock of what has happened and to look ahead, albeit cautiously, to the future.

Observers of the European scene can reasonably disagree on what constitutes the most significant event of the past few years, but the emergence of the unified Germany on October 3, 1990, promises to have the greatest impact on the future course of the new Europe. Indeed, the new Germany, by virtue of its size and geographical position, its growing influence in key international organizations, its economic strength, and its commercial interests in Western and Eastern Europe, can be expected to play a pivotal role. As

1

Elizabeth Pond has cogently observed, "Economically, politically and intellectually, Germany is uniquely a country whose time has come in a continent
whose time has come again."[1]

If the United States is to adapt sensibly to the end of the Cold War and
redefine its world role and foreign policy accordingly, it must have a clear
understanding of the forces and processes at work in the new Europe,
especially the interests and actions of Germany, its most powerful country.
The primary purpose of this collection of essays is to contribute to that
understanding by assessing the consequences and likely implications of
German unification from several different perspectives within and outside
Germany. These assessments also serve as a useful vehicle for presenting
two separate but complementary designs for a new, more unified Europe.

The New Germany: The Challenges of Unification

Beginning with an introductory overview in chapter 2, part 1 of this
volume focuses on how Germany has adapted to unification. The overview
traces the events that shaped the course of German unification and shows
how unexpected it was to all the major participants and how serendipitous
were the internal and external conditions that allowed it to take place so
rapidly. The principal economic, political, and security challenges that have
arisen as a consequence of unification are then outlined for subsequent
chapters to address more fully.

The most striking conclusion that one draws from the chapters in this
section, especially those written by the three German scholars, is that while
the physical barriers separating the two Germanies have disappeared, real
unification is only just beginning. Forty-five years of living under two entirely
different socioeconomic systems has created a sharp divide between the east
and west that cannot be bridged very quickly or very easily, despite a common
language and shared cultural heritage. Unification in the deepest sense means
not just the more obvious integration of the former East Germany into the
Federal Republic's political, military, economic, and legal frameworks—a
process that is already well under way—but also the less obvious but equally
important psychological and behavioral adaptation of all Germans to their
new identity and position. This fact is not generally appreciated outside of
Germany.

As chapter 3 describes in detail, the warm feelings of euphoria and
optimism that followed the breaching of the Berlin Wall have given way to
the cold realization that unification will be more costly—both socially and
economically—as well as more prolonged than anyone imagined. Not
surprisingly, disenchantment with the consequences of unification has grown
within Germany, in the east because the adjustment has been more painful

than expected, and in the west because it has not been as painless as promised. While the economic rebirth of eastern Germany seems assured in the long term, the immediate need to mitigate the human cost of large-scale unemployment while simultaneously replacing the decrepit infrastructure, regenerating the obsolete industrial sector, and cleaning up the ravaged environment will entail massive transfers of public funds from western Germany for many years. At a time when the economy is encountering significant difficulties brought on in part by unification, this burden will continue to drain the already depleted reservoir of goodwill and compassion that the West Germans have traditionally felt toward their eastern counterparts. Simultaneously, continued resentment in the east over the relatively poor standard of living, combined with the easterners' sense that they are second-class citizens with limited political influence within the new Germany, could intensify and prolong the sense of separateness. If there is one certainty in the country, it is that the task of unification will dominate the political as well as the economic agenda for the rest of the decade, if not longer.

Unification and the end of the Cold War have brought relief in at least one important area, however. Having spent over forty years on the front line of the military confrontation in Europe and endured the certain prospect that a war would devastate the country, Germany now finds itself, as chapter 4 observes, encircled by friends and deprived of enemies. In fact, no other country's security has been so profoundly changed by the end of the East-West conflict as Germany's, and no other country has done more to adapt its security posture to the post-Cold War world. As this chapter explains in greater detail, the military forces and infrastructure of the former East Germany have been dismantled or absorbed into the Bundeswehr, while the special terms of unification have led Germany to implement unparalleled reductions to stay within the agreed-on ceilings on military manpower.

Germany has gone to great lengths to reassure its allies and former adversaries that it will never again threaten the peace of Europe not only by accepting limitations on the size of its forces, but also by reiterating earlier commitments renouncing the development of nuclear, biological, and chemical weapons and declaring its borders permanent and inviolable. More importantly, Germany has also championed the logic of cooperative constraints on military power and the value of multinational integration and collective action. Paradoxically, this commitment to multilateralism has created friction with the country's allies as Germany simultaneously endeavors to buttress transatlantic ties through NATO, further West European defense integration through the Western European Union (WEU), and strengthen pan-European security arrangements through the Conference on Security and Cooperation in Europe (CSCE). While Germany sees no contradiction between what it is trying to achieve—if anything viewing these processes as mutually complementary—it nevertheless finds itself in a three-way tug-of-war with the principal supporters of the different institutions. With Germany's involvement critical to all three, its current balancing act will not grow any easier in the years ahead and will likely force some hard choices.

An increasing role in Europe's evolving security arrangements is part of a much larger set of responsibilities that Germany has assumed since unification. After some forty years of living in two midsized powers under the protective embrace of their respective superpower patrons, Germans are not accustomed to their new position of influence or the international expectations that go with it. The recent string of foreign policy crises has given them little time to adjust, and, for many, these crises have represented a rude awakening to the often uncomfortable realities of being a global actor.

First, the Persian Gulf crisis caught the country at a critical juncture in its preparations for unification. Having just gone to great lengths to reassure all concerned that its militaristic tendencies were permanently expunged, Germany suddenly found itself criticized for being too pacifistic and bucking its international responsibilities by not sending military forces to fight with the allied coalition against Iraq, despite the constitutional obstacles to doing so. Not long afterwards, Germany was vilified for throwing its weight around in Europe, or in more coded terms, for being too "assertive" in response to the disintegration of Yugoslavia and for pursuing monetary policies detrimental to its European Community (EC) partners. For Germany, this "damned if you do, damned if you don't" experience was new but hardly surprising, given the legacies of the past and the barely disguised resentment in some countries at its ascendant position.

Chapter 5 examines the conduct of Germany's foreign policy since unification for signs that it has embarked on a new, more assertive course. It finds that although Germany has indeed taken independent initiatives and pursued its national interests, sometimes in an unnecessarily clumsy manner, its foreign policy has been no more unilateralist or self-serving than that of other European powers, notably Britain or France. On the contrary, Germany continues to show a strong preference for working cooperatively within multilateral frameworks. Nevertheless, in the next few years, Germany clearly must become accustomed to the drawbacks that come with a higher international profile and develop the deftness and subtlety appropriate to its new role in the world. At the same time, Europe and the rest of the world must expect and encourage the presence of a more active Germany on the international stage.

The New Europe: Risks and Opportunities

Over forty years of living apart has created not only two very different Germanies but two very different Europes. The western half of the continent enjoys one of the highest standards of living in the world, has well-established democratic institutions, and lives in general tranquility. The level of political accommodation and economic cooperation between states has also evolved to the point where war is considered unthinkable. Indeed, the barriers of the nation-state are being systematically dismantled in the march toward full economic and political union.

Sadly, the same is not true for Central and Eastern Europe, and especially not for the former Soviet Union. Living standards have fallen to perilously low levels as the countries of the region struggle to adapt their economies to the harsh realities of the free market. The new-found democratic freedoms are under immense strain, especially in those countries with no history of self-determination. With the stultifying influence of Soviet rule removed, nationalist sentiments and ethnic rivalries have sprung up with a vengeance, unleashing powerful centrifugal forces and even large-scale civil violence in some countries. The possibility that this general instability could develop into interstate conflict unfortunately cannot be discounted. Furthermore, the renationalization of defense policies in Central and Eastern Europe may also stimulate dangerous new uncertainties about national security, threatening the allocation of scarce resources and the prospects for sustained political and economic cooperation in the region.

Unlike Germany, where the imperatives of political union provide special impetus to economic integration and reconstruction, there is a real risk that the division of Europe will be perpetuated by new, less visible barriers. This risk stems from several sources: fear of mass migration and cheap imports from the east, concern over the financial burden that closer association may generate, and general apprehension that the effort to assimilate the countries of Central and Eastern Europe ("widening") will dilute or even derail the process of political and economic integration ("deepening"). Keeping the fledgling free-market economies at arm's length would be shortsighted and ultimately counterproductive, however, and would almost certainly consign them to prolonged economic impoverishment and political instability—with all the attendant risks that this would bring for Europe as a whole.

As many in Western Europe, especially the Germans, have recognized, the goal must be to integrate the two halves of Europe and progressively bring the East up to the standards and performance of the West. This task requires more than just Western aid, advice, and investment. Central and Eastern Europe must eventually become part of the well-established political, economic, and security arrangements of Western Europe, or the gap will grow even wider. Part 2 of this volume presents two general designs for accomplishing this goal.

Chapter 6 lays out what is termed a "holistic" strategy for unifying the political economy of Europe. As this chapter makes clear, integration cannot be rushed or carried out haphazardly, or the effort will almost certainly be fruitless, if not counterproductive. Rather, integration must proceed from a basic appreciation of the multifaceted nature of a functioning market economy at both the micro and macro level of human interaction, including the legal and administrative, economic, and social and psychological dimensions. This knowledge teaches us that the basic approach to European integration calls for more than fundamental "system transformation" in Eastern Europe to establish the necessary components of a thriving market economy. It also calls for major "systemic reform" of the European Community to allow it to expand its membership without compromising the progress it has already made toward integrating Western Europe.

Chapter 7 lays out an equally comprehensive design for a European cooperative security system. Starting from the premise that the insecurity of states derives from the uncertainty they feel about the offensive potential and aggressive intent of others, cooperative security endeavors to minimize that uncertainty through mutual regulation of the military capabilities and operational practices that fuel such anxieties. More specifically, a cooperative security system would place further limitations on the offensive military potential of European states, make their armed forces more defensive in character, increase the level of mutual transparency in security matters, and promote multilateral integration of national security functions on a pan-European scale. In essence, this is a preventive approach to fostering international security that is in keeping with general trends in Europe.

The Impact of the New Germany: The View from the Outside

By the eve of unification, the two German states had already ascended to positions of considerable power and influence within their respective economic and military spheres. In the process, firm political and economic relationships had been established with allies and trading partners, and, while these were not always harmonious, the overarching frameworks within which the two Germanies operated ensured cooperation and stability. It was not just memories of the past, therefore, that raised apprehensions about the emergence of the new Germany. The prospect that the established pattern of European relations would be radically altered by unification and that Europe's general equilibrium could be jeopardized by the creation of a German superstate made many profoundly nervous. At the same time, the growing interdependence of the world's economies meant that the effects of German unification were likely to be felt outside Europe as well. To assess the current and future impact of unification on Europe as well as Japan, part 3 of this volume provides individual assessments from key regional perspectives.

Chapter 8 examines the impact on Western Europe from a French perspective. German unification has probably affected France more than it has any other country in Western Europe. Not only has the stature France derived from being one of Four Powers responsible for Germany's sovereignty (along with Great Britain, the United States, and the Soviet Union) come to an end, but its grand vision of a Europe led by France with Germany firmly in tow now looks extremely doubtful. Of even greater concern is the possible impact of unification on further West European integration, not only because an increasingly dominant Germany might upset the fragile balance of power within the EC, but also because it might increasingly turn eastward and concentrate on its former sphere of influence. So far, as this chapter makes clear, there are no indications that Germany's commitment to European integration has fundamentally changed or that the unified country will once again seek an independent course in Europe. Recognition that it can't go it alone, however, does not mean that Germany will hesitate to use its already dominant position within the EC and other international organizations to satisfy its interests and concerns.

How German unification has affected the economies of Eastern and Central Europe is the subject of chapter 9. The collapse of the East German market and the higher international interest rates that resulted from unification caused considerable disruption and additional hardship in a region already suffering from severe economic problems. The short-term consequences were not all bad, however, as some countries (notably Poland, Hungary, and Czechoslovakia) benefited from a surge in demand in the German market immediately following unification. Over the longer term, the outlook is still uncertain, as the unexpected costs of unification could divert valuable capital away from rebuilding Central and Eastern Europe, while the likelihood that interest rates will remain high will not help the financial needs of the region. At the same time, Germany offers major opportunities as an export market, especially when the eastern part of the country begins to recover. It also has a direct interest in improving the standard of living in the region in order to prevent political instability that could send still more waves of refugees in its direction. Consequently, Germany now provides the bulk of aid to the region and actively advocates admitting Poland, Hungary, and Czechoslovakia into the EC.

Memories of Germany's aggressive actions in the past caused some concern in Central and Eastern Europe about the impact of German unification on the region's security. This concern was more than offset, however, by the general relief that was felt at the end of the more immediate experience with Soviet domination. As chapter 10 describes, Germany has done much to reassure its neighbors to the east by emphasizing the permanent nature of existing borders and limiting the size of its armed forces. Germany's membership in the various European security organizations, particularly NATO, as well as the continued presence of U.S. forces on the continent have provided additional reassurance. At the same time, the unification of Germany has opened up new opportunities for Central and Eastern Europe to become part of Western security arrangements, something that Germany has encouraged and that the disintegration of the Soviet Union has made somewhat easier. The uncertainty created by the Soviet breakup is now the dominant concern for this region.

The Soviet leadership was as surprised as anyone else by the events leading to the rapid demise of the German Democratic Republic, the Soviet Union's staunchest ally in Europe. The Soviets remained understandably watchful during the ensuing negotiations over the terms of German unification, but they did not actively hinder the final result. In fact, there was considerable optimism that unification would presage a period of close cooperation with the new Germany, helped to a great extent by the considerable amount of economic aid and assistance it had agreed to provide the Soviet Union. With the subsequent collapse of the Soviet Union and the emergence of numerous successor states, the relationship with Germany has become far more complex and more difficult to predict. Accordingly, chapter 11 outlines several alternative futures for the former Soviet Union and the possible consequences they may have for Germany and the West in general.

Finally, chapter 12 assesses the impact that German unification has had on Japan. Given the role the two countries played in World War II, their subsequent rehabilitation as semi-sovereign states with significant constraints on their freedom of action, and particularly their rise to become two of the largest economic powers in the world, Japan watched the unification of Germany with more than a passing interest. Its response was in the main positive, with expectations high that German-Japanese and Japanese-EC relations would improve and promote free trade, joint investment, and even greater security cooperation. However, as this chapter shows, there are valid reasons not to take this prognosis for granted if, as a result of the burdens of unification, Germany turns inward or begins to view Japan, along with the rest of its EC partners, as an economic rival. Growing trade imbalances, Japan's reluctance to help in the reconstruction of Central and Eastern Europe, differences over how to deal with the former Soviet Union, and the difficulties of meeting its obligations in the new world order could all provide additional challenges to improved relations.

The next ten years will be decisive for the new Germany and the new Europe. After decades of being divided, both are confronted with immense problems in fulfilling the promise of real unification and real integration. The end of the Cold War has provided the opportunities to complete this task; the challenge now is to take advantage of them.

Note

1. Elizabeth Pond, "Germany in the New Europe," *Foreign Affairs*, vol. 71 (Spring 1992), p. 115.

Part One

THE NEW GERMANY

The New Germany: An Overview

Catherine McArdle Kelleher

GERMANY WAS REBORN in 1990, a product of the post–Cold War revolutions in Europe and heir to both its middle-aged parent states. Most in the West believed that unification would lead almost immediately to a super West Germany, a larger and more powerful Federal Republic seeking international influence after its release from the dependencies caused by postwar division. To some, Bonn's insistence on European Community recognition of Croatia and Slovenia in December 1991 seemed to confirm the emergence of a German hegemon.

The new Germany is clearly a more visible international force. But since formal unification Germany is still struggling with both the short-term and long-term burdens of economic and social integration and still seeking the greater prosperity and political stability promised in 1990. It is and will continue to be a Germany coping with the legacies of both its parents—their victories and losses, their achievements and failures. And it also stands as the somewhat uneasy heir of the traditions and identities of older, half-forgotten Germanies.

The essays in this volume focus on the implications of German unification across policy sectors, across national and international relationships. This essay attempts to place unification and the policies, problems, and promises of the recent past in a political context. It is not just that German policies in the near future will be dominated for the first time since World War II by domestic politics, or that understanding the process of unification is essential to understanding the range of potential changes in German foreign policy

My appreciation for research assistance to John Occhipinti, and for related research help to Alice Ackermann and Alex Peterhansel. Helpful comments and materials came also from James D. Bindenagel, Elizabeth Pond, Cathleen Fisher, Ullrich Heilemann, Ralf Trapp, and Christian Tuschhoff.

priorities during the next decade. Unification represents not a break with the past but a breaking open of the past. Recent years in both Germanies and the united Federal Republic have been filled with rapid decisions, necessary fixes, and monumental political tasks that could be avoided only at considerable peril and for which there was no right answer or indisputable guidance. For the coming four or five years, the decisions taken for the united Germany, and largely by its "victorious" western German leadership, represent permanency, at least until the country can afford the political luxury of further change and reconsideration.

This discussion begins with an overview of the developments that led to German unification on October 3, 1990, the heritage of postwar German-German relations, and the events that proceeded at such a remarkable pace until formal unification. It then focuses on three crucial political considerations: national security arrangements and relationships, economic unity and its consequences, and domestic political competition and organization. It concludes by considering three problems not yet resolved in unification's absorption with the immediate agenda: how Germans will define their identity, how Germans will relate to their history, and how the unified Germany will understand the new scope and limits of its power.

The Road to Unification

Viewed through the prism of static Cold War history, the road to German unification was a rare sequence of almost serendipitous events that generated a dynamic of its own. In almost every aspect, it was neither predicted nor predictable. The principal actors seemed surprised at almost every turn; painfully devised strategies were overtaken and forgotten time after time. The pace of events was truly dizzying, the outcomes hedged by uncertainty until nearly the end.

In contrast to the frozen divisions of the preceding forty years, unification depended on simultaneous interactive revolutionary change in intra-German relations and in Germany's international context. The motivating force was the democratic revolution in East Germany symbolized by the collapse of the Berlin Wall and then confirmed by the crumbling of the political and economic systems of the German Democratic Republic itself.[1] But by February 1990, many of the leading participants in this revolution recognized that there had to be an external change as well that not only ensured the approval of the four World War II victors still legally responsible for Germany's future but also fostered and legitimized the intra-German dynamic. The formula and substance of the Two plus Four talks were critical parts of the process, but so too were the Conventional Forces in Europe (CFE) agreement, the Conference on Security and Cooperation in Europe (CSCE) negotiations,

NATO strategy changes, new Soviet relations with Eastern Europe, and the German-Polish agreements.[2] German Chancellor Helmut Kohl refers often to the period of internal and external negotiations on unification—late 1989 through July 1990—as a time of unique historical opportunity. He may well be right.

Before Unification: Deutschlandpolitik

The dynamic of unification must be contrasted with its historical antecedents: the policies pursued by West and East Germany toward unification and toward one another. (Such an analysis is, however, clearly biased; far more is known about West German policy than about East German deliberations, and scholars feel far more confident assessing the contradictions in the West between rhetoric and action, public policy and private sentiment.)

West Germany's *Deutschlandpolitik* always began with the formal basis: first on the promise in the federal constitution—the Basic Law of 1949—to work toward unification, and second on Bonn's right and responsibility to speak and act on behalf of all Germans. In the 1950s and 1960s these were critical touchstones; but Bonn's foreign policy tried with diminishing success to gain allied support for their priority while pursuing its "policy of strength" to force Soviet concessions on unification. Konrad Adenauer's demand for progress toward unification before any disarmament, his insistence on the letter of occupation law in the 1958–62 Berlin crisis, and the inflexibility of the Hallstein Doctrine all turned on a vision of a Germany unified on Western terms within the Western framework of alliances.[3]

Time and two events changed both the substance and the tactics of Bonn's *Deutschlandpolitik*. The first turning point came with the building of the Berlin Wall in August 1961 and the failure of the Western allies to respond to this clear rejection of future unity for Germany. The physical division of Germany had been complete since 1953; the borders had been sealed by the East Germans and most normal communication ties broken or made difficult. But the Berlin Wall symbolized a final division, and with the Wall came widespread recognition that only Germany (or perhaps West Germany) had a stake in dismantling it.

West German political circles drew two quite separate lessons for the future, both predicated on keeping the goal of unification and the prospects for change alive during their country's division. Adenauer and Ludwig Erhard stressed the human face of the policy of strength. There were to be greater individual and private sector contacts between East and West Germany and the eventual mounting of social and humanitarian assistance for "the brothers and sisters" to the East. But Bonn would still keep strict political distance from the East German regime: official contacts only at the lowest possible levels to conduct necessary business, and international confrontation and exclusion of the regime whenever possible. In these respects, West German policy was virtually the mirror image of East Germany's and Walter Ulbricht's policy of *Abgrenzung* (demarcation), of gaining legitimacy for East Germany by strict separation from both West Germany and the prospects of a unified Germany in the future.

The second factor was the development of a new Ostpolitik (policy toward the East) within the opposition Social Democratic party (SPD). Reorganized in the late 1950s as a *Volkspartei* (mass party) with a Berlin heart, the new party leadership took up the challenge of promoting change in the East by overcoming the effects of Germany's division. Willy Brandt's proposal for "small steps" and Egon Bahr's concept of change through rapprochement (*Wandel durch Annäherung*) attracted growing elite support. When the SPD entered government—first in a Grand Coalition with the Christian Democratic Union (CDU), then in 1969 in a governing coalition with the Free Democrats (FDP), Ostpolitik became official policy.

The results were substantial: German-German agreements on travel and communications, the *Grundlagenvertrag* (Basic Treaty), and the formula of "two states in the German nation," which demonstrated mutual acceptance of the status quo.[4] In the climate of general East-West détente during the 1970s the option of a unified future was, at least from the perspective of the SPD, preserved and strengthened, if not necessarily made more probable.[5] And intra-German trade, generous Western credits, Bonn's ransoming of East German political dissidents, the strengthening of cultural links, the expanding East-West network of individual and institutional contacts all eased the way.

How much had been gained became clear in the early 1980s, when the new Soviet-American confrontation began and superpower allegiances threatened German-German détente. Both Erich Honecker in East Berlin and Helmut Schmidt in Bonn moved to insulate their détente from the international chill and the double burden of the Soviet invasion of Afghanistan and NATO's INF decision.[6] Schmidt's aim was still to improve human conditions in East Germany and preserve political options for Germany and perhaps also for Europe. Honecker's goals seemed directed at solidifying the legitimacy of the GDR and the Communist party (SED), buttressing against social and economic discontent at home and its Eastern allies and Western opponents abroad. But Honecker's assertiveness on the issue of German-German priorities, even allowing for a weakened Kremlin under Leonid Brezhnev, marked a major new turn. And the independent German-German agenda began to draw criticism in Reagan's Washington and throughout Western Europe.[7]

More insulation was provided when Schmidt's East German strategy was taken up by the new coalition government composed of the CDU, Christian Social Union (CSU), and the FDP that took power in 1982. Chancellor Kohl expressed his willingness to pursue "steady progress," while Franz-Josef

Strauss of the more conservative CSU sponsored a DM 1 billion credit for East Germany from a consortium of West German banks. SPD contacts with East Germany intensified, leading to a series of joint initiatives and even draft treaties on complex and controversial arms control issues. Even the by-now ritual mention of unification was muted. Television transmissions and visits in both directions flowed more freely.[8] East Germany's relative prosperity and the increasing flood of trade, credits, and private loans provided substantial cushions against political disagreements.

The rise of Soviet President Mikhail Gorbachev, however, underscored the general political stagnation and intransigence of the Honecker regime.[9] Soviet "new thinking" on arms control and détente with the West was compatible with the SED's hopes for sustaining the economic gains of German détente. *Glasnost* and *perestroika*, though, threatened the very power base of the SED and its German-German strategy. Gorbachev's agenda tolerated, if not encouraged, not only deviation within the Warsaw Pact but the free expression of differences within socialist systems as long as Soviet security interests were not threatened. It would neither reward nor support East German orthodoxy at home or abroad. By the end of the decade, Moscow's relations with Bonn were in many respects healthier than its relations with East Berlin.

As Poland and Hungary tested the limits of Moscow's tolerance, Honecker and the East German state and party apparatus clung to the status quo. Political dissidence became more vocal; more important, the population began to feel imprisoned and isolated in new ways. As East Germans crowded West German embassies abroad and the West German offices in East Berlin, SED officials did their best to shield their subjects from the winds of change blowing from Moscow and their Warsaw Pact allies. One high-ranking SED official even remarked, "If your neighbor chooses to put new wallpaper on the walls of his house, would you feel obligated to do the same?"[10] With his country's standard of living the highest in the Soviet bloc and his firm belief in the East German model, the aging Honecker publicly indicated that he was not impressed with Gorbachev's reformist orientation.[11] His likely successors in the SED, the group including Egon Krenz, his heir apparent, seemed to promise only more of the same.

The Forces of Unity

Although the story of the road to unification has been well told, it still has not been explained or understood fully.[12] The events recounted here are only those few that had the greatest impact on the shape and pace of unification and on its first years.

THE FIRST PHASE. Following Solidarity's victory in Poland without Soviet opposition, Hungary broke the international status quo in the summer of

1989. Budapest had long decided that its fortunes lay in the West; it now decided to open its border with Austria. The trickle of East Germans fleeing to the West over the Hungarian border grew to a river flowing through all available openings in the East.[13] The rigid SED structure and the now-disabled Honecker reacted badly, demanding support from their unhearing Warsaw Pact allies, offering too few domestic concessions too late, and insisting on face-saving solutions that contained the seeds of their own destruction.[14]

By the time Gorbachev visited East Berlin on October 7, 1989, for the fortieth anniversary of the GDR, Honecker's reign was over. In contrast to Josef Stalin in 1953, Gorbachev was clearly unwilling to use military power to protect East German socialism; any show of force would have ended whatever chance *perestroika* and *glasnost* had in the Soviet Union. Within East Germany itself, the motivating factor was the power of the people, which went unchallenged in successive Monday evening demonstrations in Leipzig and soon thereafter all across the country.

When the SED, now under Egon Krenz, opened the Berlin Wall and the border with West Germany on November 9, 1989, the party apparently saw itself ensuring its own future, buying off East Germans with the promise that they could now travel freely. By releasing pressure and allowing troublemakers to leave, the regime expected a return to stability. But with little confidence that conditions would soon improve, East German citizens left in ever larger numbers.

Talk of unification appeared in November from a variety of sources. Placards in Leipzig changed their democratic-reformist slogan "We Are the People" to "We Are One People." West German flags began to appear, then to dominate.[15] In West Germany, unification leaped to the top of the political agenda. Internationally, the German question began to be discussed sotto voce as a potential and frightening reality, but not one to be officially noticed yet.

The first official airing was Helmut Kohl's 10-Point Plan, presented to the Bundestag on November 28, 1989, without prior notice to either his partners within the governing coalition or the Western allies.[16] Kohl saw himself capturing the high ground, sealing off the issue of unification for the future. What he outlined was the creation of a German confederation after a lengthy process, a situation far from the unity of the past or that foreseen by the constitution.[17]

People power continued to be the driving force behind unification in early 1990—the power of both those who fled to the West and those who stayed behind. Public protests continued despite the now-staggering efforts of the SED to restore calm and attempts by the reformed SED leadership under Hans Modrow to find a German "third way" between socialism and capitalism. The attempt in January by the SED government to retain (or reinstate) the Stasi, East Germany's secret police, prompted popular occupation of Stasi offices. The SED had lost the last traces of its legitimacy and credibility as a vehicle of reform. By January, the party's final contention, that it ensured economic stability, had disappeared, as the scope of the exodus west (more than 2,000 people a day) left manufacturing, health care delivery, and other critical functions at a standstill.

Late January and early February 1990 saw the confluence of more events favoring unity. On January 28, opposition leaders in the all-party East German Round Table "government" established to replace the SED regime persuaded Modrow to advance the date of the first free Volkskammer election from May 6 to March 18. The westward flood of East Germans continued unabated, straining West Germany's resources and public services. Pressed to stabilize the East German situation and to restore West German confidence, the Kohl cabinet decided on February 7 to offer swift monetary union to East Germany, effectively ending the possibility of a free-standing GDR state or economy.[18]

Also favoring unity was the emerging opportunity for external change, for agreement on at least a process of change among the wartime allies who were still both legally and militarily able to influence events in Germany.[19] Late fall 1989 had seen two critical signals. The first was Gorbachev's tolerance of Hungary's unilateral decision to open its border and then his failure to support Honecker. The second was the December 12 speech in Berlin by U.S. Secretary of State James Baker setting forth American preconditions for unification, involving a relatively clear American promise to press Britain and France to agree on unity, and an American green light for German-German discussions.

Early February 1990 saw the intensification of Baker's behind-the-scenes diplomacy and the final round of Baker-Shevardnaze talks on American guarantees of German stability and international good behavior. Baker and later Chancellor Kohl and Foreign Minister Hans-Dietrich Genscher visited Gorbachev and put in place the basic external bargains on which unification was based. Gorbachev reportedly realized that it was too late to slow the course of events he had helped unleash. Moscow stopped denying unification's imminence and attempted to negotiate the best possible outcome for the Soviet Union. During discussions on February 10, 1990, Gorbachev announced that he would not stand in the way of German decisions on German unification.[20] This led to the culmination of Baker's framework—the agreement at Ottawa on a "Two plus Four" forum, rather than the traditionally envisaged "four, then two" process.

THE SECOND PHASE. At this point, the pressures for unification became electoral politics and popular demands in East and West Germany for economic security and stability. The revolutionary power of the streets was no longer sufficient. The allies might still disagree on critical details, but they were now just gatekeepers, not vetoers, and could only await German choices.

What came to be called the "year of elections" began with the first free election in the GDR in March 1990. The vote was to constitute the Volkskammer, but it was widely considered a barometer of East German preferences concerning unification and, at least in West German eyes, a foreshadowing of the general election of the unified Bundestag set for the following December. The power of electoral politics to shape the process of German unification was quickly apparent. Moreover, with the imposition of West German parties on the more diverse East German political landscape, West German party politics in particular was to play a central role.

The Christian Democrats and the Free Democrats were astute in capturing the mood of the East German electorate: unification and prosperity, and quickly. Campaign appearances by the government's leaders turned into events of affirmation as Helmut Kohl received accolades rarely heard in West Germany and Foreign Minister Genscher was hailed for his achievements and his Halle origins. The Social Democrats also had stars—Willy Brandt and Egon Bahr at the pinnacle—and the traditions of interwar political strength in the East and the successes of Ostpolitik. But the SPD's more cautious approach to unification and its warnings about economic sacrifices had little appeal. Its proposed candidate for chancellor, Oskar Lafontaine, was an enigma to the East Germans and hardly a force for party unity in the West.

Organization and financing also determined the campaign. The SED, now turned into the PDS (Party of Democratic Socialism) and led by a mixture of reformers and old guard, retained much of the financial and personal infrastructure of the SED, enabling it to do surprisingly well, especially in Berlin. The Eastern CDU, a former coalition partner of the SED, also had an organizational advantage as well as deep Western pockets. But the SPD and the other former opposition groups that were now divided among splinter parties had neither the time nor the organizational preparation to stage a modern campaign. This contributed to the victory on March 18 of the conservative CDU-led Alliance for Germany, headed by Lothar de Maizière (CDU East).

This pattern continued throughout the string of elections, East and West, that followed and the Bundestag electoral campaign that began almost immediately. Earlier in 1989 Kohl had been losing popularity and support; he now seized the opportunity to ensure that his standing, and that of the CDU, continued to rise in the East. For the first time, he was able to deliver a "chancellor bonus" to his party. Eastern voters saw the Kohl regime, not the opposition, as able to grant their demands and secure their economy. This interaction was clearly key to Kohl's decision on April 23, two weeks before local GDR elections, to grant East German demands for a full German economic and monetary union to begin on July 1, 1990, and to be based on a one-to-one exchange rate.[21] It was not only that the CDU subsequently dominated; it was that the pattern of choice between political and economic criteria was set.

The ongoing Bundestag campaign confirmed the pattern and highlighted the contrast of party styles. Both Kohl and Lafontaine admitted that unification required the resolution of many economic problems and many individual and group sacrifices. But Kohl's message was that the transition would be short and its burdens comparatively light. In particular, he promised that a tax hike would not be necessary to fund unity.[22] In the view of East German voters, Lafontaine failed to come up with alternative concepts and policies. In addition, in sharp contradiction to Kohl, he preached the gloom and doom of economic reality, and the costs to the East, but especially to West Germans. This perspective won him few supporters, particularly among East Germans, who still doubted SPD enthusiasm for unity despite their esteem for Brandt and Bahr. Many of Lafontaine's predictions would be proved correct in 1991, but his message was not what East Germans wanted to hear.

Formal unification was celebrated on October 3, 1990. Trust in CDU optimism was conclusively demonstrated in the October 14 Landtag (state assembly) elections in the five new eastern Länder.[23] The establishment of center-right governments led by the CDU in four of the eastern Länder gave the CDU-FDP a majority in the Bundesrat (which the SPD had controlled since May 1990).[24]

Thereafter, a CDU victory in the December 2 Bundestag election was certain. Aided by the surprisingly strong 11 percent showing of the FDP, stemming from strong support in the east, the Bonn coalition was maintained.[25] The CDU-CSU-FDP won 398 of 662 seats in the newly expanded Bundestag. As expected, the Social Democrats fared poorly, winning only 239 seats. After a court decision in October, the parties in the east had only to win 5 percent of the total vote in the east, not throughout the whole country, to enter the Bundestag.[26] The PDS gained 17 seats and the Alliance '90 list (to which the eastern Greens belonged) 8 seats.

The united Bundestag election capped the formal unification of Germany, itself the result of several phases. The December Bundestag election marked the first all-German democratic vote since the Weimar Republic in the 1930s; Chancellor Kohl had realized his wish to be the first democratic chancellor of a united Germany. Yet by the end of the year it was clear that many problems regarding the unification of Germany remained and were destined to remain in the coming decade.

The Dimensions of Unity

German economic and monetary union (GEMU) has been in place since July 1, 1990, and German political union since the end of 1990, but it is still too early to assess definitively the progress and problems of unification. At best, the experience since 1990 allows only a partial look, an understanding limited to what Germans now think they know about what they have done and what other routes they might have followed. Some of what they believe is only half true, the result of faulty memory caused by the breakneck pace of 1989 and 1990. Most of the major actors and analysts are still too involved in day-to-day policy or still too close to their own actions to have a sense of the broad picture. Much will be left to the clarity of hindsight and the battle of the memoirs.

Assessing the progress of unification is, at its core, about politics, about political confidence and credibility. At issue is Helmut Kohl's performance as the first chancellor of a united Germany and the ability of his coalition to persuade supporters and critics at home and abroad that Germany's future is assured. Government officials not surprisingly tend to stress an optimistic long-term outlook for a Germany now 80 million strong and the third largest market in the world. It is a rich country able to afford both what it will cost to unify and to maintain its role as one of the world's strongest export nations. But ordinary citizens and opposition leaders focus on the overwhelming and often unforeseen burdens of the uncertain present, the problems of finding jobs, providing housing, restraining taxes, and ensuring social justice. Analysts fall somewhere between officials and public. They agree on the favorable longer-term prospects but are overcome by the magnitude and the complexity of tracking present developments. They are fully cognizant of all the short-run dangers but unable to portray adequately the political dynamic now at work or the potential for future benefit.

What follows in this section is yet another partial assessment of how unification has proceeded. The focus is on the integration of defense and security policy, policymaking on economic integration, and the impact of unification on domestic politics.

Unification and Security

Assessing what a united Germany has become is perhaps easiest in discussing security arrangements.[27] Security was at the core of the Two plus Four process; had there not been final, detailed agreement on Germany's alliance membership and the size and armament of its armed forces, unification would not have come until much later, if at all. From the first discussion of unification in December 1990, many saw the American condition for German unity as German membership and forces in NATO.[28] The East German forces, the National People's Army (NVA), were to give way to a unified Bundeswehr with a self-imposed ceiling of 370,000 men.[29] Soviet demands varied throughout the spring of 1990 but eventually translated in the July Kohl-Gorbachev agreements at Stavropol to two principal requirements: assurance of a gradual withdrawal of Soviet forces from East German territory and the implementation of special German undertakings that recognized particular Soviet security interests and that funded the special social and economic burdens of relocating Soviet forces. The new Germany would unilaterally recommit to earlier pledges against producing weapons of mass destruction and against violating existing state borders. East German territory would be a denuclearized zone within NATO and would see assignment only of Bundeswehr soldiers under national (not NATO) command until at least the last Soviet withdrawals by the end of 1994.

SECURITY AND THE NEW BUNDESWEHR. Many of these conditions were fully implemented within a year of unification, a remarkable achievement. The most strenuous and straightforward efforts were those to close the NVA's facilities and to retire most of its personnel and equipment.[30] To oversee this, a new Bundeswehrkommando Ost was established at the former NVA headquarters in Strausberg, staffed by Bundeswehr officers and civilian officials working with remaining NVA staffs. It completed its formal responsibilities on July 1, 1991, and was replaced by Bundeswehr administrative districts in each of the five new states and by normal army, air force, and navy command structures.[31] From the first, West German officers took over most command functions, with only companies and half the battalions headed by former NVA officers.[32] And the first conscripts from East Germany entered the Bundeswehr in January 1991.

Operationally, the integration of approximately half the remaining personnel of the NVA into the Bundeswehr recalls the first years of the Bundeswehr. All of those in higher NVA command posts and officers over age fifty were dismissed during the transition period before October 3, 1990. The remaining 89,000 put on West German uniforms at unification. Of that number about 25 percent, officers and noncommissioned officers, took subsidized early retirement by the end of 1990.[33] Another 25 percent applied for probationary contracts with the Bundeswehr, with final selection to be decided after two years, and for officers after approval by an independent evaluation committee. NCOs stand perhaps the best chance of being hired, given the chronic Bundeswehr shortages in these ranks; there are perhaps twice as many officer applicants (major and below) as are needed.[34] Final strengths in the five new states as of July 1991 were 50,000 military, with 25,000 officers and NCOs and 25,000 conscripts.

Between 1992 and 1994 the major task facing the Defense Ministry will be integrating these personnel into the overall structure of a Bundeswehr with a maximum CFE-approved strength of 370,000 men. Day-to-day integration of the NVA into a restructured Bundeswehr has reflected many of the general takeover problems in German unification. Most former East German facilities are of much poorer quality than those of the Bundeswehr and will be turned over to the federal government's administration for property.[35] West German professionals have found adjustment hard. Few west German conscripts have been assigned to duty in the east and the divide between easterners and westerners dominates in the military as in civilian life. West German military practices and command style have replaced the more formal, isolated, and hierarchical east German patterns. East German officers and NCOs have been retrained, but both are paid less well than their west German counterparts and reportedly feel marginalized.[36] Adjustment to their membership now in NATO forces has added some special symbolic and psychological burdens, shared indeed with the general population in the five new eastern states.[37]

The daily Bundeswehr schedules have been dominated by the rapid pace and cost of change—of personnel separations, closing facilities, retraining and oversight at all levels. Only 17 percent of the armaments inherited from the NVA will be used. At enormous cost, the remainder will either be salvaged for parts or material or will simply be destroyed.[38] Overseeing this process has absorbed as much as 80 percent of the available personnel.[39] The destruction of just 30,000 tons of ammunition in 1991, for example, cost DM 165 million.[40]

In addition, the Bundeswehr suddenly became the landlord of 2,250 NVA properties.[41] Returning the facilities to civilian purposes is also proving difficult. Most new state and local authorities are desperate for the buildings and spaces but lack the funds to convert or to rebuild on any scale.[42] There is also substantial environmental damage, some of it dating back to the Nazi period. Even with the looser environmental regulations that prevail for the five new states, many believe full restoration will take years and enormous sums.

GERMANY'S SECURITY RELATIONSHIPS EAST AND WEST. German efforts to meet Soviet and now Commonwealth of Independent States (CIS) security requirements have required substantial effort. Despite several serious incidents and the unsettled situation in the Soviet Union during 1991, Bonn's policy had generally favorable results. The formal framework was created in the bilateral accords, the Kohl-Gorbachev agreements at Stavropol in July 1990 with later extensions in the formal treaties and continuing German-Soviet discussions in 1991. Involved were agreements on the orderly withdrawal of the Soviet military's Western Group of Forces, and German pledges of $8.4 billion to cover Soviet relocation costs.[43] Germany also recommitted itself to international behavior desired by the former Soviet Union: nonaggression, constraints on armament and armament production, and nonprovocation.[44]

More critical were the informal bases for Soviet-German cooperation: the continuing deep German gratitude to Gorbachev for starting the process that made unification not only possible but acceptable to the Soviet Union, the Soviet and now Russian and CIS recognition that Germany was the most important European partner, and the assumption that Moscow and Bonn were bound together in a "community of fate."[45] And now, with the Soviet Union no more, Germany must strive to forge cooperative relations not only with Russia and Ukraine but also with the other newly independent republics.

Perhaps the most pressing task has been German stewardship with respect to the former Soviet forces withdrawing from the five new states, approximately 337,800 troops, 208,400 family members, 2.5 million tons of matériel, and 115,000 weapons pieces as of October 3, 1990.[46] The united Germany took over responsibility for the support and safety of the forces, Soviet soldiers receiving their monthly pay in deutsche marks and German police providing external security for Soviet personnel and facilities.[47] The withdrawal schedule has proceeded more slowly than anticipated, given the failure for many months to work out arrangements for transit through Poland. But to all appearances it will be completed by 1994. By the end of 1991 the pullout of the Western Group of Forces had proceeded according to the 30 percent a year (1991–93) plan: 110,000 troops, 55,000 family members, 781,000 tons of equipment, and 34,500 weapons pieces were removed.[48] And the pace continues.

Initially there were strains in German-Soviet security coordination at higher levels. What the Soviets considered excessive monitoring of sites and troop movement led to two shooting incidents in summer 1991; new procedures were instituted as a result.

Of continuing concern to both Germans and the CIS states is the morale of Soviet forces, who some have thought are increasingly restive and isolated. As conditions worsened in the Soviet Union in 1991, many observers foresaw greater risk of Soviet defections or refusals to return home to straitened economic conditions and lower social status. To date, despite persistent rumors, few of these fears have materialized, thanks apparently to tight military discipline.[49] Compounding the low morale have been the more than 200 criminal attacks on soldiers and family members of the Western Group of Forces in 1991.[50]

Cynics argue that German efforts to act as broker in Europe for the former republics will change after the final troop withdrawals in 1994. It will then not be in the German interest, they assert, to act in parallel with the former republics, work against their isolation, or take seriously their demands for secure zones on their borders. Those close to Chancellor Kohl argue otherwise, stressing the continuing German and CIS interests in both mutual security and the construction of the common European home.

Germany's demands that the legitimate security interests and the political well-being of the Soviet Union receive appropriate respect and representation have been consistent. At times, there has been a clear public link, as with Chancellor Kohl's pressure for economic aid to Gorbachev before and during the Group of Seven (G-7) meeting in July 1991.[51] Most often, there has been persistent German pressure on all its allies that due attention be given to, for example, CIS sensitivities about security arrangements in central Europe or the need to find a meaningful role for a CSCE that will allow direct Russian participation in European security arrangements.

By far the greatest brokering role the Kohl government has assumed so far has been within NATO. Time and again throughout 1990 and the Two plus Four talks, Kohl and Genscher asserted the need to consider Soviet security interests in all Western efforts to restructure the European order.[52] In 1991 German pressure on these points grew even more intense—in NATO but also within the European Community, the Western European Union, and the G-7. Kohl's personal support of Gorbachev and of massive Western aid continued despite American disagreement and even survived when the Soviet president seemed to side with hard-line and conservative critics of economic reform, armament reductions, or even any engagement with the West. The failed August 1991 coup in Moscow seemed only to reassure Kohl that he should continue his demands for aid by all the European members of NATO.

Germany successfully pushed not only Eastern concerns but several of its own longstanding positions in NATO deliberations on a post–Cold War strategic concept and on plans to reduce and restructure NATO forces. Under pressure of the German unification schedule, NATO's London declaration on July 6, 1990, heralded the organization's adaptation to a changed, more cooperative relationship with the Soviet Union. The risks for the West were now principally instability and uncertainty; the challenge was to develop cooperative peace building with the nations of the East as well as to continue alliance peacekeeping.[53] Nuclear weapons, though still needed, were now a means of "last resort."

In 1991 strong German contributions and official German emphases from the late 1980s decisively influenced key parts of NATO's formal Strategy Review and Force Restructuring program.[54] NATO strategy is to shift away from confrontation and the doctrines of flexible response and nuclear deterrence to a new posture of common reassurance and stability. Fixed forward defense is to be replaced by a maneuver strategy, still designed to defend all of German territory (including the five new states) but putting far greater emphasis on mobility, relatively light armament, and flexible command for rapid reaction. Even before the establishment of the Commonwealth of Independent States, new political conditions meant that the Soviet Union had lost its conventional superiority in central Europe. The warning time to allow counterconcentration by the West suddenly became measurable in weeks rather than days or hours. Nuclear weapons are now to be deemed political weapons, able at most to deter the use of other nuclear weapons. Germany and NATO may still need a residual American nuclear guarantee, but there is no further need for ground-based or short-range nuclear weapons stationed in Europe.

Moreover, to German satisfaction, NATO doctrine no longer names an enemy. The Warsaw Pact is dead. The newly democratizing East European states have received Western reassurances of concern and a new forum, the North Atlantic Cooperation Council, for their security, albeit no formal pledges of alliance. All East European targets have been formally removed from NATO's target base. Targets in the former Soviet Union still remain, as they do in the American Single Integrated Operational Plan (SIOP), but NATO descriptions now emphasize "residual" risks and "potential" capabilities.

From Bonn's perspective, the changes in NATO have given unexpectedly strong support to the Western alliance not only in its core transatlantic functions but also in its present organization. The Kohl government has consistently stressed its commitment to NATO and its American connection as indispensable elements of European security. But even before unification, the government had strongly advocated the evolution of a European security identity within the European Community.[55]

Germany's devotion to an eventual European defense union is in part a response to French desires that a unified Germany of 80 million be firmly embedded economically, politically, and militarily in a unified Europe. The Kohl government has consciously taken Thomas Mann's words to describe its goals: a European Germany, not a German-dominated Europe.[56] Tangible evidence of Germany's commitment was Kohl's decisions in 1991 and 1992 to side with France in proposals to speed up European political union, including one to revive the Western European Union to act as the security agent of the European Community until formal union is reached. Even more deliberate was Kohl's plan to reshape the largely ceremonial Franco-German brigade into what could become the basis of a European rapid reaction corps (the so-called Eurocorps) for use outside Western Europe and perhaps within Europe under orders of the WEU or even CSCE.

Since the democratization of Eastern Europe, Bonn has also tended to treat the CSCE as an important but complementary building block to both the EC and NATO. In the past, Genscher had been among the primary proponents of pan-European solutions, to be associated with existing European and transatlantic structures.[57] CSCE is now seen as one necessary but hardly sufficient mechanism to this end. Clearly it should be transformed into a more permanent organization, strengthened with expanded tasks and capabilities. To the end of his term, Genscher remained publicly optimistic even when, as at the Prague CSCE meeting in late January 1992, his plan to create CSCE peacekeeping units failed in the face of American, French, and British opposition.[58]

But for the foreseeable future, Genscher's successor, Klaus Kinkel, and indeed most German political elites believe that CSCE cannot take on more than a complementary role until some primary issues are resolved. First, stable democracies and viable economies must be established in Eastern Europe and the former Soviet republics. Second, these new democracies, particularly the new republics, must peacefully resolve differences concerning arms control and control of former Soviet forces. Finally, the EC must begin to integrate the new democratic states into the community of peace enjoyed by Western Europe.

The Domestic Security Debate

Unification has added new dimensions to the German debate on the future of German armed forces, a debate that intensified in 1989 in connection with NATO plans for short-range nuclear force (SNF) modernization. The immediate outcome of the SNF crisis was German insistence on domestic political priorities despite American pressure. The longer-term run result was German demands for a broader definition of Western security interests, especially vis-à-vis the Soviet Union, and for the restructuring of Western forces. Moreover, demographic factors and budgetary constraints had already augured for a smaller Bundeswehr. And a CFE agreement would mean newer, lower levels of forces and offensive weapons throughout Europe, including U.S. and Soviet forces deployed outside their borders.

The end of the Cold War rapidly redirected German debate, if not always policy. Nuclear issues retreated far into the background. The 370,000-man Bundeswehr promoted by Kohl and the Bush administration represented perhaps the highest force ceiling talked about in Bonn. Genscher reportedly favored 300,000 and the opposition SPD discussed goals as low as 200,000 to 250,000, as did the Soviet Union. Younger SPD voices also favored a rapid transition to a smaller professional army and an end to conscription.

More radical plans from the past also resurfaced—for instance, that all foreign forces and all nuclear-capable armament be withdrawn from German territory by 1994, roughly the same time foreseen to accomplish Soviet withdrawals. Most of these proposals, however, were lost in the welter of details involved in unification. And in 1990, the year of the election, in the interest of stability and legitimacy, all parties seemingly minimized the number of divisive issues they introduced into campaigns. Traditionally defined security issues, indeed, were hardly mentioned.

The Persian Gulf crisis and external expectations of a German military contribution forced open debate in December 1990. The immediate issue was whether Germany would have a direct role either in an anti-Iraqi intervention force or in a NATO force to support the security of Turkey in accordance with articles 5 and 6 of the North Atlantic Treaty. The Kohl government vacillated, citing constitutional uncertainties and seemingly constrained by both popular opposition and critics within the government. Opposition included those who saw true constitutional prohibitions against such roles except as "blue helmets" under UN command, those who felt a decision to intervene or support militarily was premature because the United States and its allies had not given economic sanctions a full trial, and those who saw parliamentary action as required (and unlikely) before any step could be taken. By December, after its reelection, however, the Kohl government decided to contribute to the cost of the interventionary forces, to provide increased aid to regional allies, and to agree to German deployments in NATO's allied mobile force being sent to Turkey.[59]

At issue in the continuing blue helmet debate are two direct questions: under what political circumstances can or should German forces be used outside German borders, and what constitutional instruments are needed to support a decision to use the forces?[60] The Kohl government has argued that a constitutional amendment is desirable, if not strictly necessary, to allow the use of forces under any legitimate multilateral auspices (not just UN blue helmet or peacekeeping purposes) as the government deems appropriate.[61]

Opposing views have come from both the SPD and the Free Democrats, whose votes are needed for a two-thirds majority to pass a constitutional amendment in the Bundestag and Bundesrat. The Free Democrats support an amendment to allow German participation in any action supported by the UN Security Council. After months of debate and a close party convention vote in late May 1991, the SPD declared its support for constitutional change to allow UN peacekeeping uses only.[62] Any other use except to provide humanitarian assistance—as to the Kurds—would not be allowed. The Kohl government has therefore not yet brought the questions to the Bundestag for a formal vote.

Only slightly below the debate's surface is a more fundamental question: what role will a unified Germany play in world affairs? President Bush, former UN Secretary General Perez de Cuellar, and other officials have called on Bonn to take more direct responsibility, to use not just its financial resources but its political and military capabilities in the interests of global security. There have been repeated suggestions that the Federal Republic, along with Japan, be added to a reformed, restructured UN Security Council. These matters, however, have rarely surfaced in German public discussion, which has been completely absorbed with unification or the fate of the former Soviet Union. But in 1991 and 1992, as Gorbachev's tenuous union began to crumble and the violence in Yugoslavia intensified, debate concerning the direction of united Germany's foreign policy intensified.

Whatever else happens, unification has as yet not brought significantly reduced defense spending.[63] Initially the Kohl government announced a 16 percent reduction in 1991 to be followed by an additional DM 1.5 billion, or 3 percent, cut in each of the next three years, but the government immediately set the proposal aside. Overall, the Defense Ministry plans to cut back spending by DM 43.7 billion by 2005, scrapping major procurement projects entirely and scaling back many others. But the 1992 and 1993 defense budgets are to remain above DM 50 billion, much too high for many in the Bundestag.

Critics of Defense Ministry proposals, both in the coalition and among parliamentary opposition parties, call for more extensive budgetary and force cuts, indicating that the size of the Bundeswehr in the next century could be significantly smaller than the 370,000 favored by the Defense Ministry. And it is clear that there will be further weapons reductions, especially since the fiscal difficulties of the Federal Republic mean that defense cuts are needed to fund domestic initiatives.

Unification and Economic Integration

Economic issues have clearly dominated the immediate agenda of unification for political leaders and public alike. From the beginning, the integration of East Germany into the economy of the West has been marked by political promises, unanticipated economic realities, and dashed optimism.

Almost from the outset, the Bonn government promised that no Germans would be made worse off by unification. Chancellor Kohl himself set economic prosperity and equal living standards as the benchmarks of unification's success, perhaps to be accomplished in as few as five to ten years. In addition, West Germans were assured that unification would be affordable and that no tax increases would be necessary. These promises are crucial to understanding popular economic expectations and demands as well as government policies to meet them.

Aside from their usefulness as campaign promises, Kohl's optimistic guarantees stemmed from his confidence in the robust West German economy. In mid-1990 the economy was growing 4 percent annually, inflation stood at 2.3 percent, unemployment was declining, and Bonn's $55 billion trade surplus represented a larger share of GNP (4.3 percent) than that of even Japan (1.8 percent).[64] It was thus assumed that the continued robustness of the West German economy would ensure the affordablity of unification.

THE COLLAPSE OF THE EAST GERMAN ECONOMY. Following the July 1, 1990, conclusion of the German Economic and Monetary Union, the East German economy began to falter. And soon after the government's reelection in December 1990, with registered unemployment soaring above a million, and a million more working part time, it was apparent that Kohl's promises of a speedy and painless transition would not be fulfilled. By February 1991, when the government announced a DM 46 billion tax increase package, including a one-year unity surcharge on income and corporate taxes, it had become apparent as well that the unification would also be costly for west Germans.

By July 1991, the first anniversary of the GEMU, the collapse of the east German economy was fully expected. Despite financial transfers from Bonn of more than DM 200 billion, eastern Germany would not be spared the slow and arduous economic restructuring faced by other former communist states in Europe, including privatizing thousands of state-run firms, settling disputes over property ownership, repairing dilapidated infrastructure, and overcoming a shortage of managerial skill. The only real question was how long it would take for the economy of the new Länder to reach bottom.

Unemployment in the five new states stayed at 1 million; 2 million more people were working part time. As more enterprises closed in the autumn of 1991, unemployment increased, bringing the total in the east to 11.8 percent.[65] In an annual report released in late October, the five leading German economic institutes concluded that the eastern German economic collapse had almost reached bottom and predicted a 10 percent recovery in 1992.[66] But in line with the complaints voiced by the Bundesbank throughout the year, the report was critical of the government's deficit spending and painted a gloomy picture for the future of the overall economy.

THE SLOWING OF THE WEST GERMAN ECONOMY. In the final months of 1991 the west German economy stagnated. By the time the new tax increases took effect on July 1, 1991, the government's deficit spending had driven inflation above 4 percent—a critical psychological threshold for an electorate with memories of the runaway inflation under the Weimar Republic. Hoping to protect the value of the mark, the Bundesbank raised its interest rate and warned against both deficits and inflation. By the close of the year, growth in the west German economy had slowed to 3.2 percent, the result of a depressed world economy and weakened demand for German exports, the tight monetary policy of the Bundesbank, and the deflationary impact of new tax increases (equaling 1.5 percent of GNP).[67]

The end of the west German boom highlighted a much deeper problem. Unification has, in effect, created a dual German economy with inverse interactions. When east Germany languished in virtual depression, west Germany boomed. And Kohl's attempts to keep his promises to both constituencies made the problem worse. Seeking to improve the standard of living in the new Länder, the government oversaw huge transfers to the east. Trying to appease west Germans, Kohl delayed raising taxes, allowing the mounting budget deficit to accelerate inflation and forcing the intervention of the Bundesbank. Ultimately, the cost of unification, in the form of interest rate hikes and the belated tax increase, ended the west German boom. By making public resources and private investment increasingly scarce, Kohl's action brought fears that a prolonged economic slowdown would follow and would further inhibit the economic transition in the east.

The constant reminder of the end of the boom is what Germans find uncomfortably high unemployment rates. Special government subsidies for short-time work have ended; joblessness jumped sharply in 1992, with more than 306,000 newly registered east German unemployed in January.[68] The east has 20 percent of Germany's total population; yet it accounts for only 8 percent of total GDP and has a per capita GDP only one-third that of western Germany. Industry has been hardest hit by closures. At most, only 20 to 30 percent of the existing east German industrial plant will survive. Net migration east to west has been one-half million since summer 1989; rates have varied widely but are again on the rise.

To be sure, almost 1 million new jobs or training opportunities have been created, and some 350,000 east Germans have become commuters, taking up jobs in border areas or in western Germany. Some regions, such as Saxony, are experiencing a miniboom in new construction. And there is even reason for cautious optimism at signs of improving business confidence and economic activity in eastern Germany.[69]

But the overall outlook for the German economy has remained poor. Leading economic forecasters have scaled back their growth prognoses for 1992 and beyond. Analysts at the Institut der Deutschen Wirtschaft in Cologne project real growth of only 1.5 percent to 2.0 percent for 1992, blaming overly generous pay raises, investment-retarding interest rates, and the tax increase for the gloomy outlook.[70] The government's own forecast for economic growth matches the institute's expectations, and sees overall German unemployment increasing to 8 percent in 1992 (in the east to about 17 percent). And it predicted an overall German inflation rate of 5 percent.[71]

IMPLICATIONS. Efforts by the government to resist terming the economic slowdown a recession miss the deeper implications of a less energetic west German economy. From the beginning, successful economic integration was predicated on a continuing west German boom. Although west German economic support for the east would be painful and unavoidable, many experts assumed it would be tolerable if growth in eastern Germany would accelerate to 10 percent and the west German economy would grow by an average of 3 percent from 1992 to 1995.[72]

Moreover, there is a growing feeling that for the foreseeable future, Germany economically is a nation united yet apart. Some analysts and some recent wage settlements suggest parity in east and west German wages by 1994. But many analysts, especially critical west Germans, point to the huge gap in relative productivity. Economic reconstruction by the end of the 1990s had a nice electoral ring, but independent analysts and officials privately suggest a far longer period, the most pessimistic counting in decades or even generations.[73] And this is without considering what impact the more than 1 million claims for restitution of property lost since 1933 will have on the pace and surety of economic activity.

Gloomy statistics and expert projections suggest only part of the story. From the moment the Berlin Wall came down, economic policy has been guided by political choices, not technical economic choices. The timing of German economic and monetary union, the choice of the currency conversion rates, the scope and timing of the second German treaty, all reflected political calculations or bargains struck by the Kohl government. Implementing unification has itself highlighted the effects of basic political processes that may in the end be more important for policy outcomes and political choices than the specifics of employment or currency adjustment.

First is the continuing sense of relative economic deprivation in both east and west. West Germans have only begun to face significant real cuts in their standard of living and levels of disposable income. But the real measuring stick for the present is set by their perceptions of the future and the past. For the future, it is what might have been had unification costs not intervened—not precise calculations but certainly the sense of having foregone better and less constrained choices. The past standard is set by memories (now distorted) of what west Germans suffered and achieved to create their economic miracle and what ungrateful and perhaps underachieving east Germans now seem to demand as an automatic right.

The east Germans' sense of deprivation is perhaps simpler to understand but more pervasive and probably longer lasting. At first they had considerable misinformation about their relative status—the effects of images on West German television, the rich array of consumer goods in West German stores, the many choices from travel to entertainment that seemed to come so easily to the self-assured West Germans. But soon a sense of deprivation arose from east Germans' real lack of individual and group economic security, the increasing feeling of personal risk, and the withdrawal of the social safety net. Government services and relative entitlements—day care centers, work-related recreational opportunities, housing guarantees—have been cut. But more telling have been the changes in personal relations, the new competition for the remaining jobs at downsizing enterprises, the tensions from layoffs in two-worker families, the search for affordable arrangements for aging relatives or single-parent families.

A contributing factor has been the constant lowering of expectations. To be sure, the transition to capitalism was expected to be marked by substantial unemployment. But both east and west Germans believed that the economic transformation of the GDR could be handled quickly and affordably, given the economy of the Federal Republic. Hence, east Germans were not prepared to accept economic reality when it became apparent in the winter of 1990–91 that they were in for a full-blown, drawn-out depression. West Germans also rankled at the realization they had no choice but to pay dearly to ensure the speed of the transition in the east and dampen its human costs.

Partly to blame for these misplaced expectations were interacting self-hypnoses, primarily the confident tenor of Kohl's electoral promises throughout 1990 and the willingness of the electorate in both east and west not to hear or believe bad news. The opposition Social Democrats did not strike the right tone; the electorate heard only nay saying and fumbling efforts to present an alternative program. The public opposition of the Bundesbank and the warnings of its president, Karl Otto Pöhl, about fiscal peril could have been more dramatic and clearly signaled by bank decisions. However critical or convinced that Kohl's decisions were fatally flawed, most opponents did not persist in public comment or present alternative policies, even when the GDR's economic system collapsed.

Confusion also stemmed from a dearth of reliable economic data about the east and a lack of adequate models against which to gauge the dizzying stream of events and political pressures. Officials often simply did not know the baseline for their projections. What most turned to instead was a talisman more than a model: the successful economic reconstruction of West Germany from 1947 to 1955. The legend of the economic miracle (*Wirtschaftswunder*) seemingly blinded most Germans to what, in hindsight at least, should have been economic common sense: that the integration of the GDR into West Germany's social market economy (*soziale Marktwirtschaft*) would be slow and painful for all.[74]

In sum, the inability of political leaders to meet the popular expectations they encouraged explains much of the current economic situation in the united Federal Republic. Germans in both west and east have long measured their own status in economic terms and assessed the success of their respective regimes in terms of economic achievements and world economic standing.[75] Bonn's economic policies since 1990 are thus closely related to Germans' fundamental fears, frustrations, and hostilities about unification. East Germans fear unemployment, the loss of occupational identity, an inability not only to advance but indeed even to hold onto what they had so painfully achieved under the GDR. Many see themselves as victims or those forced to sacrifice—first to the East German system because they were in the wrong place at the wrong time, then to a unification process and a free market that promised equity and prosperity but has delivered neither. Unification has brought fewer jobs and higher prices, more expensive rents and fewer automatic social services, greater economic competition and fewer outlets for their goods.[76]

West Germans see themselves burdened with both the tasks and the costs of change, neither of which they can deny. It is not just the new higher taxes, the reallocation of public programs and attention, the slowing of economic growth, and the shrinking of government subsidies. It is the continuing disorder and change in what was the basic political and economic consensus in a successful West Germany, the reorientation to an unsettled national economic agenda, and the risks of inflation and deficit. To be faced are the incessant demands for east German equity now, the needs of those east Germans who came westward to seek opportunity, and the uncomfortable passivity of many of those left behind.

New Politics in the New Germany

Chancellor Kohl's decision in April 1990 to proceed with the economic and monetary union on terms other than those recommended by financial experts and the Bundesbank began the new politics of the new Germany. The next several months witnessed political vacillation and indecision, a chancellor buffeted by events and surprises, a governing coalition and an opposition mired in the problems of statemaking. The muddle on taxes is perhaps the best illustration of what happened—first a firm government pledge against new taxes, then new taxes in early 1991, then in early 1992 the possibility of extending the extraordinary taxes or raising new levies.

Kohl's credibility was temporarily saved by external events. Germany's financial pledge to the United States to aid the Persian Gulf effort and transfers to Moscow in exchange for the pullout of Soviet troops from eastern Germany seemingly provided good, if not totally real, reasons for raising taxes. Few Germans however accepted Kohl's February 1991 announcement of new taxes at face value. The "tax lie," as it became known, was the start of months of political and economic disaster for the chancellor.

But the problems facing the government in Bonn are not just economic. The difficulty is not just integrating the east economically into the Federal Republic but combining two essentially heterogeneous societies. After forty years of communist rule and many unresolved shadows from the Nazi past, east Germans differ in fundamental ways from west Germans. Their lives remain focused far more on home and locality; their expectations and consumption patterns reflect a different time scale and modes of economic behavior. They seem bemused by or even disdainful of west German life styles. Even their reading habits differ.

German unity thus places the Kohl government and indeed the entire German political class in a dilemma. They must find answers to three pressing difficulties: how to devise policies that will be acceptable to both east and west Germans whose socioeconomic values are not just different but sometimes in conflict; how to devise standards of equity for the treatment of fellow citizens at very different levels of economic activity and productivity; and how to prevent new cleavages in societies that have only begun to grow together. The wrong solutions could well lead toward political disaster, domestically and even internationally.

FASHIONING COMMON POLICIES. The prospects for facing these challenges are not improved by the clear shadows surrounding the future of Germany's party system. The enduring east-west disparities in the Federal Republic indicate that traditional party loyalties may weaken because of heightened attention to regional or specific Länder interests. East and west wings may emerge within parties, replacing the traditional dominance of Right-Left distinctions, or the intersection of north-south, Catholic-Protestant identities. A more extreme effect of east-west cleavages may be the appearance of regionally based parties. The significance of Land-Bund relations is enormous, especially as the central government takes on greater burdens and powers.

In February 1992, Länder and national interests clashed vividly. Kohl succeeded in increasing the value-added tax from 14 to 15 percent (a second VAT rate, for items such as groceries, remains at 7 percent).[77] The SPD had tried to block the legislation in the Bundesrat, but the Brandenberg delegation broke party ranks, supported the increase, and contributed to the government's victory. This vote may signal a shift from party politics to regional politics.[78]

The future of the existing parties also seems clouded. One illustration came early in the 1991 debate over where to locate the new seat of government. According to the Unification Treaty, the capital of the united Germany is Berlin, but the treaty left unresolved whether the seat of government (*Hauptstadt*) would stay in Bonn. As the Berlin-Bonn debate unfolded, it became clear that the issue could not be decided along party lines.[79] To fashion a clear majority, politicians including Hamburg's mayor, Henning Vorscherau, and Heiner Geissler, proposed various compromise plans.[80] But when the issue came up for debate in the Bundestag on June 20, resolving it was left to a free (nonparty) vote.

Eleven hours of impassioned debate ensued, with more than a hundred deputies addressing the Bundestag. Speaking from the wheelchair he has been forced to use since the assassination attempt against him in 1990, Interior Minister Wolfgang Schäuble delivered one of the most emotional and influential speeches of the debate, urging his colleagues to vote for Berlin because the location of government "has to do with the future of Germany."[81] The vote was close but Berlin won out 338–320. Two weeks later, the matter came to a free vote in the Bundesrat, which voted 38–30 to remain in Bonn, at least temporarily.

More telling than the closeness of the contest was that voting cut across party lines. Because the SPD and CDU were very much divided on the issue, strong support by the smaller Free Democrats party and the Party of Democratic Socialism made the difference.[82]

Perhaps only the debate on abortion rights in eastern and western Germany has matched the symbolic value and emotion surrounding the Berlin-Bonn choice. Yet there have been other indicators of new regional alignments, especially on economic and tax policies. Given the disparity of interests between east and west Germans, traditional disciplined party politics in the Federal Republic is in for major changes. This is seen most clearly in the CDU, whose Länder party organizations, east and west, have blamed their poor electoral showings in 1991 and 1992 on the government's unification policies. If the economies in the eastern Länder controlled by the CDU do not improve in the next three years, CDU politicians in power there will attempt to distance themselves from Kohl. But the SPD faces similar criticism and resistance, especially given the obvious fissures in the party and in the national leadership.

Politics in Germany, particularly in the next three years, may experience two important changes resulting from unification. First, the federalist character of the Federal Republic may have to be renegotiated as both the SPD and the new states in the east attempt to wield influence in Land-Bund cooperative projects on revenue sharing, and even on decisions such as the surrender of sovereignty under the Maastricht Treaty. Second, when regional factions of parties believe their interests are better served by breaking with the main party, they can be expected to do so. The national party organizations will have to restructure to be far more responsive to the interests of their counterparts in the Länder.

Moreover, many issues at the national level of politics are simply not amenable to or appropriate for intracoalition bargaining or party jousting. In 1992, for example, the so-called asylum issue bedeviled both Kohl's coalition and its opposition. At question was the fundamental right of political asylum guaranteed to all under the Federal Republic's Basic Law. Disruptions in the Middle East, economic despair in southern Europe, and civil war in Yugoslavia have generated a surge of petitions for asylum: some 35,000 (more than 11,000 from former Yugoslavs) in January 1992 alone. The flood overwhelmed the already beleaguered asylum review process, which frequently took a year to consider petitions. And it increased the anger, especially among the German Right and the have nots in both eastern and western Germany, about the rights and comforts accorded to asylum seekers.

The asylum issue was complex, and the answers by no means certain. Was a constitutional limitation—and therefore all-party agreement to constitutional change—necessary? Was working on limitations desirable, given such other unresolved constitutional issues—allowing the army to fight outside Germany, for example, or legalizing abortion, or creating proportional electoral representation—resulting from unification? Was reform of the process of petition itself still possible? And which level of government, which parties, were to be responsible for the failures of the past and the defense of asylum seekers against attackers?

In the end, Kohl bungled his handling of the asylum issue. His demand for a constitutional change produced political gridlock and strengthened the hand of the right-wing parties he sought to preempt. The failure to reach cabinet closure further divided the FDP and encouraged stonewalling in the SPD along generational and regional lines. The result was an increased loss of credibility for the national decisionmaking institutions and their leaders.

One traditional political solution for dealing with crises would be to create either a formal or informal grand coalition, a government involving at least the CDU and the SPD. This worked well in the mid-1960s after the collapse of the Erhard government. But a grand coalition would not only require CDU-SPD agreement on basic principles but also that the parties be able to command obedience from all the party leaders of state governments. In the next five years that is by no means a certainty in any of the present political parties.

THE FUTURE OF THE CDU. The problems for the CDU began even before the announcement of new taxes. In the January 20, 1991, Landtag election in Hesse, a slight gain by the SPD and losses by the CDU and FDP, compared with the results of the previous election in 1987, enabled the formation of a Red-Green (SPD-Green) coalition in Wiesbaden.[83] Landtag elections are considered a barometer of broader party standing in Germany, so the losses by the CDU and the FDP were widely interpreted as signals of west German uneasiness with government policies on unification and indeed began a downward slide in CDU fortunes.

The spring of 1991 witnessed the rapid deterioration of the east German economy and a series of political setbacks for the coalition. In the east, thousands demonstrated against Bonn, pelting Kohl with rotten eggs when he visited in early May. In the west, voters continued to display their growing displeasure with the government at the ballot box. In April, Kohl was personally embarrassed when the CDU was voted out of office in his home state of Rhineland-Palatinate. The SPD continued its success by capturing an absolute majority in the May Hamburg election. More than just damaging in their reflection of west German dissatisfaction with Kohl, these elections also gave the Social Democrats a controlling majority in the Bundesrat, the council of state government delegations, and hence the potential to block Bundestag legislation.

Support for the CDU has returned to about 40 percent of all voters, although in 1992 the party continued to have trouble in both state elections and regional caucuses. The state elections in spring 1992 in Schleswig-Holstein and Baden-Württemberg showed substantial CDU losses, most disturbingly to small right-wing parties. The forced resignation of Defense Minister Gerhard Stoltenberg over arms export scandals exposed CDU fissures in Bonn. There is once again speculation that Kohl's leadership may be in question. But this is nothing new for the chancellor, who has frequently been the target of the CDU's anxieties whenever the party's future seemed bleak.[84]

But even after the 1991 Hamburg election, CDU General Secretary Volker Rühe made clear that this was no simple minor slide for the party. In an interview with *Der Spiegel*, Rühe referred to the "catastrophic situation" of the CDU.[85] In the west, he said, the party had only 660,000 members, 78,000 fewer than in 1984. In the east, Rühe estimated membership at 80,000 to

100,000. Considering this, and the sluggish economic transition in the east, the CDU's majority in four of the five new Länder is by no means secure.[86]

It is conceivable that by the end of 1994 (by which time new elections must be held in the eastern Länder) the Christian Democrats could lose their majorities in all but the conservative and Catholic south. The rallying-round effect of unification may simply have allowed Kohl and the CDU-CSU old guard to avoid making the changes necessary for continued success. But Kohl's skill as a politician and party leader ought not be underestimated. He may once again resist the forces of change and be the CDU candidate in 1994, as he says he will be.[87]

A different concern for the CDU is its ties to the legacy of the eastern CDU as a bloc party under the SED. Although all parties suffer from revelations of Stasi connections, allegations that current east German CDU politicians had ties to the Stasi are the most frequent and often the most painful. Charges of collaboration forced Lothar de Maizière to resign as Kohl's deputy. At its December 1991 party congress held in Dresden, the CDU sought to overcome this setback and rejuvenate the party by electing Minister of Women and Youth Affairs Angela Merkel to succeed Maizière.[88] But the CDU has since been shaken by further charges of Stasi connections, most dramatically those that forced Thuringia's Minister President Josef Duchac to step down and be replaced by Kohl's choice, a west German.

THE FUTURE OF THE SPD. Fortunately for the Christian Democrats, the situation of the SPD is even worse. The leadership of Germany's oldest political party remains unable to unify it. Under Hans-Jochen Vogel during much of the 1980s, and under Oskar Lafontaine in 1989 and 1990, the Social Democrats proved themselves divided and fractious. In 1991 the SPD began to rebound, capitalizing on the government's absorption with the east and the public's perception of CDU failure. Following its victory in Hesse, it elected a new party leader, Björn Engholm, minister president of Schleswig-Holstein, who on a number of occasions has outpolled Kohl when Germans were asked for whom they would vote were a direct election of the chancellor held.[89]

Engholm soon found his leadership tested by party division. The Bremen party congress in May 1991 was split over moving the seat of government to Berlin and over the future role of the Bundeswehr, especially in blue helmet peacekeeping operations. Engholm came out strongly in favor of the Bundeswehr's participation, effectively turning the issue into a vote of confidence, which enabled the measure to pass.[90]

Certainly, the SPD is not alone in its division on these issues or in its quandary about matters of equity, division, and accountability. Yet, the continuing discord among the party leaders (Engholm, parliamentary leader Hans-Ulrich Klose, and Oskar Lafontaine) means Engholm now stands in the middle of a debate on how the SPD can best position itself for the 1994 Bundestag election. Essentially, Engholm must decide if the SPD can afford to be passive, taking advantage of the Bonn coalition's economic problems, or articulate its own policy recommendations and push for them in the Bundesrat.[91]

The state elections in 1992 showed the SPD has also suffered losses in credibility with the voters. And it has its own Stasi problem: Manfred Stolpe, minister president of Brandenburg, for example, has had to fend off accusations that he once reported to the Stasi.

THE FUTURE OF THE SMALLER PARTIES. The proliferating divisions within the major German political parties stem mostly from the burdens of unification. Their self-absorption and their increasingly apparent inabilities to agree on any decisive initiatives have meant new opportunities for smaller political groupings. But they too face divisions and uncertainties.

Probably under the greatest pressure are the Free Democrats, the sometimes uncomfortable coalition partner of the CDU. They disagree strongly with Kohl on many aspects of economic and fiscal policy and have managed to extract critical concessions and to force some policy changes on these matters. But despite their new strength in the east, they see no credible way to leave the governing coalition before the 1994 elections, if then.

In early 1992, for example, FDP resistance focused on the asylum issue.[92] The Christian Democrats argued that changing article 16 of the constitution was necessary to stem the tide of what they considered economic, not political, refugees. Although many in the FDP agreed with Kohl on the severity of the refugee influx, the Free Democrats, like the SPD, contended that constitutional change was unnecessary.[93] In the past, such disputes have led to speculation, even from party leader Otto Graf Lambsdorff, that the Free Democrats might leave the Bonn coalition. Following the Rhineland-Palatinate election in 1991, for example, accusations flew in both directions in the coalition as to who was responsible for the state of affairs in Germany in general and the loss in Kohl's home state in particular. But in the midst of the asylum controversy, Lambsdorff reaffirmed the FDP's intention to stick with Kohl.[94]

In the longer run, what matters most for the liberals is simply to be included in Bonn. As Jürgen Möllemann, the FDP's young and popular economics minister and designated successor to Lambsdorff, has said, "It is not so important, whether the CDU or the SPD is our partner. It is much more important that we remain partners of one of the two parties."[95] For the FDP, saving itself from blame for Germany's current economic troubles, especially in the east, may prove more important than loyalty to a sinking CDU coalition.

But the FDP stands at a generational crossroads. Hans-Dietrich Genscher was the most popular politician in the Federal Republic, but age and poor health forced the end of his political career. The choice of his successor, Klaus Kinkel, revealed major divisions in the party. It remains to be seen if the new generation of the FDP, represented by Kinkel, Möllemann, and Bundestag parliamentary group leader Otto Solms, can continue to maintain the FDP's perennial 10 percent national support and attractiveness as coalition partner. In addition, after 1994 and foreseeable party realignment, the FDP may find it difficult to maintain its hold on the foreign ministry or its critical influence over foreign policy.

The clear alternative to the FDP in terms of a coalition with the Social Democrats is the Greens. Inclusion in coalition governments with the SPD in Hesse and Lower Saxony offers the Greens an opportunity to demonstrate ability to govern and not just criticize. In fact, collaboration with the Social Democrats, a source of tension in the ranks of the Greens, has been made easier by the victory of the pragmatic Realos faction at the chaotic Green party congress held in Neumünster in April 1991.[96]

The new smaller directorship ought to make party decisionmaking easier, further enhancing the appeal of the Greens as a coalition partner. Indeed, Oskar Lafontaine, in observing the developments at Neumünster, speculated favorably on an SPD partnership in Bonn with the Green party, while Björn Engholm spoke of a potential "traffic light" (Red-Yellow-Green, SPD-FDP-Green) coalition.[97]

But for such scenarios to come to life, the Greens must fare better in the next Bundestag election than they did in 1990. In 1994 the old 5 percent electoral vote threshold for entry into the Bundestag will be back in place, so the west and east Greens and Alliance '90 will probably need to run a united campaign. Appeals to protect ecology are attractive in an east beset by environmental damage unaddressed since the 1930s. But until pressing economic problems such as inflation and unemployment are on their way to being resolved, the problems of environmental damage will be relegated to the political background, inhibiting the Greens' ability to win support.[98] And holding together sufficient nationwide support in the splintered far Left of the German political spectrum in both east and west may prove difficult.

In addition to a new party founded by the former Green Fundis, there is also the Party of Democratic Socialism, the former SED, under the leadership of Gregor Gysi. Owing much to the preelection alteration of the 5 percent clause, the PDS was able to win seats in the current Bundestag. Nevertheless, Gysi's party does not appear to have a bright future in the united Germany. Support has declined in eastern Germany since the 1990 Volkskammer election, dropping to less than 15 percent after the October 1990 Landtag elections and to less than 10 percent after the Bundestag election.[99] And given that communist parties have never done well in western Germany, there was never much chance the PDS would do well there.[100]

Since June 1990, Gysi has consistently tried to build party unity while blasting the established parties' responsibility for the "vulgar and antisocialist form" of unification.[101] He has guided the PDS through financial scandal and

Stasi scandals, and he has finally crafted a party platform that includes support
for constitutional rights to employment and basic health care and opposition
to allowing the Bundeswehr to operate outside NATO territory.

Although many east Germans are sympathetic to these views, the PDS
will find it difficult to win enough voters nationwide to maintain its Bundestag
seats after 1994. When Gysi was reelected head of the party in December
1991, PDS membership had stabilized at 180,000.[102] Most east Germans who
are dissatisfied with the course of unification are not looking further Left than
the SPD for alternative policies. And they are mostly not looking Left at all.
The PDS is also in difficulty because the deterioration of economic conditions
is leading radicals, particularly among the young, to turn to the far Right,
not the far Left.

Right extremism remains for now more a political embarrassment and a
potential political threat than a political crisis.[103] According to most accounts,
Right extremism in the east stems from the high unemployment and social
insecurity.[104] In particular, these conditions are causing a "sinking self-
confidence" among the young, leading them to turn to neo-Nazi activity.[105]
In addition to rallies and marches, there have been an increasing number of
violent attacks on foreigners, Soviet troops, and Jewish institutions. And in
an apparent attempt to win public support, neo-Nazis have also focused their
attacks on the sex shops and gay bars that have moved into many east German
cities since unification.

Presently, there are about 2,000 active right-wing extremists in the east.
About 1,200 live in Saxony, with the highest concentration in its capital
Dresden. But more alarming is that in addition to active members, there may
be as many as 15,000 neo-Nazi sympathizers in Saxony alone, with thousands
more scattered among the other eastern Länder. The organizers, however,
often seem to be west Germans.[106]

The future of the right-wing parties is still unclear. Both the Republikaner,
with some 11 percent of the vote in Baden-Württemberg, and the German
Peoples' Union (DVU) with more than 5 percent in Schleswig-Holstein scored
major upsets in the spring 1992 state elections. But at least some of
the support seems to be true protest votes, expressions of fundamental
dissatisfaction with the indecision of the major parties and the gridlock of
party politics as usual. The hostility to asylum rights and the related "hatred
of foreigners," however, are still potent rallying points, especially for the 10
percent or more of all west Germans seeking a scapegoat for the burdens of
unification.

Unification: Still Growing Together

The *Hauptstadt* debate and the asylum debate revealed another critical
dimension of unification: the number of unresolved questions. Most if not all

are aspects of questions debated at least since the Peace of Westphalia in 1648, issues that have been rallying cries in revolution after revolution and the focus of numerous wars, including two in this century, and of the Cold War. Who are the Germans? What is their fatherland? What is the relation between the German cultural and linguistic communities and the creation of states that express that community or govern Germans? To what part of Europe do the Germans belong, east or west or middle Europe, or do they have their own Sonderweg (special or unique path)? For much of the past forty years, these issues have been settled by the reality of division, by the commitment of political elites in both Germanies to the values espoused by their Great Power protectors, and by what seemed in the short run the impossibility of unification.

For most West Germans, as years passed, the issues became less relevant and the sense of lost history less acute. Bonn after Konrad Adenauer was firmly in Western Europe, the Europe eventually of the European Community and part of the transatlantic compact based on shared American-European values.[107] State loyalty and social identification resulted from individual choices to be or to remain West German. Especially in the first decades of the Federal Republic, economic achievement and the economic miracle were the principal sources of civic pride.[108] To this were added pride in the strength of democracy in the Federal Republic, the fulfillment of constitutionalism and the rule of law, and the humanitarian outreach on the basis of universal human rights to Eastern Europe and to the Third World. In Jürgen Habermas's formulation, West Germans developed civic patriotism—a non-nationalist self-understanding that was pragmatic and bound to a legitimized common interpretation of past, present, and future.

In East Germany, there were similar forces promoting group esteem and state adherence, if not civic loyalty. Unquestionably, by the late 1960s, East Germany's pride in its economic achievements was palpable. Whatever their party status or social standing, East Germans trumpeted their achievements vis-à-vis West Germany (that had "everything handed to it by the West"), their Warsaw Pact allies, who were doing less well in terms of GNP and living standards, and even the Soviet Union. And they usually believed more was to come, that the promises of socialism would be realized through German industry and resourcefulness. The other pillar of East German identity was antifascism, that in contrast to West Germans they had been cleansed of the Nazi past and were safe from the return of fascists in capitalist clothing.

Germany's unification brings all these sources of identity into question, yet does not guarantee definite answers soon. There have been more than enough speeches and exhortations: every electoral campaign has called for reform and sacrifice but also promised the benefits of participation in a united Germany and the prospects for all German citizens to join with the best heritage of the past to build a common future. For many absorbed in the day-to-day realities of integration, Willy Brandt's often quoted formulation is reassuring and enough: "What belongs together is now growing together." Yet reality may well be different, as is shown by three matters that are still unresolved and that involve both opportunity and risk for the process of unification in the next decade.

The Legitimate Dimensions of National Identity

At every point since unification, east and west Germans have acknowledged their Germanness and in some sense the inevitability of the process in which they are now involved. What they also feel, however, is difference, often stressing their own superiority in terms of the "others," those "over there," or even their individual alienation from policies designed to safeguard the rights of citizenship and property or guarantees of social and economic justice. But it is not politically correct either to note these differences directly or discuss the mutual suspicion that exists.

In Habermas's terms, much of what West Germans identify with is the economic success of the Federal Republic. Their "deutsche mark nationalism" is based on forty years of economic growth and a unique economic self-confidence. The longing to share in the "deutsche mark identity" explains why so many East Germans fled to the West, but that economic identity will never provide a sufficient basis for a new sense of state identity. Moreover, some mourn the passage of the social and cultural community of the GDR and its replacement with a materialist, capitalist west German culture imbued with promises of economic gain but not equality or social justice. Often they particularly miss the closeness and significance of family and workplace ties that provided both psychic defense against the SED state and the human glue in the niche society East Germany truly had become.

West Germans feel similar alienation but for different reasons. In the main, they knew less about the East Germans than vice versa before unification. Their knowledge often came from occasional trips or family visits or official contacts. Many Western assumptions about East Germans and unity were too simple. They imagined a group of Germans "just like us" who would return to normal behavior once the SED regime disappeared. Alternatively, East Germans were "not at all like us," but it was West Germans' duty to bring them to full citizenship and prosperity, to overcome the legacy of history and the intervening forty years. Similarly, many Westerners were shocked when they began to realize in the spring of 1990 that a unified Germany would not just be a West Germany plus five new states, somewhat backward but with firm prospects.

The problem remains how to define and ensure the legitimate sources of a common identity. The successful pattern of the West German past is simply not available. Whatever the issue, the level of economic satisfaction and identification in both east and west is declining, not increasing. Achievements in the west are "held back" by the east; in the east's eyes, the west is not granting the east its due. The prospects may be bright, but they are still too distant and are less certain than before.

Pride in citizenship, in democratic participation, may be a substitute. So too is Germany's role as the model democracy and source of advice for the newly democratizing East European states—advice on everything from relations between civilian structures and the military to the organization of savings banks. But pride in citizenship has its own disquieting potential, principally definition of identity against those who would enter Germany from outside—refugees, Gypsies, perhaps Poles, Russians, or Ukrainians if their economies continue to deteriorate.

Another source of identity might be east and west German adoption of the same groups of national heros. A 1991 poll showed that more than 60 percent of the citizens from both parts of Germany chose as "great Germans" four quite different historical figures: Konrad Adenauer (89 percent), Martin Luther (77 percent), Bismarck (68 percent), and Friedrich II (60 percent).[109] The controversy about the reburial of Friedrich the Great in Potsdam may be proof that historical honors may be simply that, a source of abstract pride and historical interest, just as in an ordinary country.[110] But before history can be used positively, its darker chapters must be dealt with. In this task, both east and west Germans must come to grips with a past tainted by Nazi and Stasi oppression. But there are also brighter historical chapters, the foremost being the democratic revolution of 1989. In fact, this may be the defining moment in German history, for it gave legitimacy to democracy in Germany.[111]

Which German History?

Soon after the capitulation of the Third Reich, Germans began the painful process of coming to terms with National Socialism and its crimes. Their streets still cluttered with the ashes and rubble of the war just lost, Germans were led by the allied victors through denazification. In West Germany, this began with the Nuremberg trials and focused on the installation of political pluralism. The arguments about the past turned most often on the distinctions between individual and collective guilt. But in East Germany, the Soviet occupiers simply replaced the Nazi state with another oppressive system. According to the socialist line, the Nazis had victimized not Jews but communist martyrs. Similarly, the Soviets' "Great Patriotic War" was fought against not totalitarian but capitalist imperialism. In short, the Soviet Union and its SED allies ensured that East Germans did not debate their past openly. Instead, they were simply given the socialist catechism and declared free of guilt or history. All Nazis were assumed to have fled to West Germany.

To be sure, weighing history was by no means a simple task in the budding democracy of the Federal Republic. It took a new generation of Germans and the tumultuous summer of 1968 to force open debate and far-reaching educational reform. And even after this, questions remained. For example, in the mid-1980s the themes to be included in a national history museum set in the Reichstag became subjects of public debate. Old wounds were also reopened when the Kohl government appeared sympathetic to conservative historians who sought to minimize the crimes of National Socialism. Indeed, the ensuing *Historikerstreit* (historian's debate) reminded Germans just how much their national consciousness was shaped by their past.[112]

Certainly, in forty years of debate in the Federal Republic, few questions of German history were laid to rest. But it is perhaps more important that they were discussed openly and frequently, at least allowing West Germans to come to grips with their past. It is precisely this sort of national dialogue about history that still needs to take place in the east and needs to be reflected in the integration process.

There are a few aids in the recent GDR past that may help. In the 1980s the Honecker regime did allow fragments of German history to invade SED dogma. For example, in cities across the GDR, Martin Luther's birthday was commemorated with official celebrations in 1983. The Prussian past was also not completely obliterated, illustrated by the historical exhibitions in East and West Berlin and in 1986 by the restoration of the famous equestrian statue of Frederick the Great to its traditional post on Berlin's Unter den Linden. But these events could not substitute for the kind of public discourse necessary to deal with the more recent past.

By forcing east Germans out of the security of the niche society they had created for themselves, unification compels them to deal openly with their history. The task is perhaps more difficult for them than it has been for west Germans. The former citizens of the GDR must reflect on the Nazi past and on the Stasi legacy as well. But unification not only compels the easterners to ponder history, it once again throws the westerners into debates they hoped were closed. Even at the practical level, history cannot be avoided as the integration of the former GDR into the Federal Republic proceeds. For example, when state-owned property is privatized in eastern Germany, the government must decide just who the former owners are and how they will be compensated (presumably on the basis of the circumstances under which the property was lost or expropriated).

Moreover, given the depth and breadth of the Stasi network, it is clear that a replay of Nuremberg is neither possible nor desirable. But the release of Stasi files on individuals and the prosecution of GDR border guards means there must be some coming to terms with the crimes not only of citizens against citizens but of the upper and middle levels of the SED leadership as well.

If the experience of West Germany is any guide, the challenges of national identity and history eventually will be met in the united Germany. Thereafter, Germans will be able to turn outward, confident that past has been dealt with sufficiently to move ahead. But it will take time, leadership, and civic courage.

German Concepts of International Power

Probably the third unresolved question in unification is what will now be German ideas on the uses of power in international interactions. Until the most pressing disparities between east and west are met, Germany will remain rather inward looking. Unless the most pessimistic forecasts are correct, however, the challenges of unification will be met within the decade. Thus the question remains, how will the united Germany, with a population of 80 million and with the third largest economy in the world, wield the power it possesses?

Recalling the past will provide one limit on German power. For Germans, this means being aware of how the united Germanies of the past grew expansionary and being careful not to let a democratic united Germany blunder into the same mistakes. The historical experiences of Germany's neighbors also establish limits. German policies will be scrutinized as never before for proof that the unified German state can be trusted to circumscribe its power and limit its geopolitical aspirations. Many of these enduring fears came into play as the Two plus Four talks took place in 1990. The results were arrangements reaffirming present German borders, limiting the size and armament of the Bundeswehr, and restricting the military use of eastern Germany by NATO forces. Moreover, given German attitudes and the fact that Germany is a signatory of the Nuclear Nonproliferation Treaty, a united Germany in possession of nuclear weapons seems highly unlikely.

But even if German public opinion were to change and the Federal Republic were to forgo its commitments, German power would still be inhibited. These final limits are economic but also political. As the framers of European unity had hoped, the German economy, its industry and monetary system, is now inextricably tied to the economics of the rest of the European Community. Germany's political commitment to European political union is unchallenged. Germany would be highly sensitive to unified European economic sanctions if not political sanctions in response to unacceptable demonstrations of power.

One of the most striking developments in the 1980s was how both Germanies came to publicly exhibit new concepts of power. These became evident not only in their behavior toward each other but also in their relations with their superpower allies. Equally striking at least for West Germany was the style of approach it used and advocated in multilateral forums, formal and informal, European and global.

Two West German leaders were particularly identified with this international style: Helmut Schmidt and Hans-Dietrich Genscher. Schmidt was perhaps most forceful in asserting the "German Model," the superiority of economic achievement, of successful domestic socioeconomic policies and reforms as the basis for international standing. In or out of office, Schmidt did not hesitate to criticize others when they relied on what he considered the failed legacies of power politics—Mr. Reagan's attack on Libya, Mrs. Thatcher and the war in the Falklands, Mr. Gorbachev's vacillations vis-à-vis both the West and his right wing.

Genscher was in many respects only a brilliant tactician, using his sense of timing, the prevailing winds, and European internal dynamics to pursue Germany's interests. Yet he also evolved a set of basic foreign policy precepts that went beyond merely making a virtue of a divided Germany's dependencies. In various coalitions, he consistently asserted the superiority of multilateral solutions; of progressive, cooperative steps that expand rather than limit the list of participants in diplomatic negotiations and European security arrangements; and of a spectrum of nonmilitary methods to be used creatively and patiently before force is invoked. Most fundamentally, he molded the image of Germany as a major participant in world affairs, unable and unwilling to act alone except in the service of universally accepted principles (for example, to provide humanitarian food aid to the Soviet Union in 1989 and 1990), and perhaps not even then.

The original structure of West Germany was established with foreign democracies as its model. Its relations with other states were shaped by its participation in the West's multilateral organizations. But once all the tasks associated with unification are accomplished, the new Federal Republic may well become a model for other nations, the multilateral styles of Schmidt and Genscher poised to shape the future of world politics in the image of the democratic, united Germany.

Notes

1. Terms such as "East Germany" and "GDR" are used here for convenience even though I am aware that this may perpetuate conceptual blinders.

2. The Two plus Four talks refer to the negotiating forum established at the Ottawa Open Skies summit in mid-February 1990, in which the two Germanies and the four wartime allied powers—France, the Soviet Union, the United Kingdom, and the United States—explored and agreed to German unification.

3. The Hallstein Doctrine, set down in 1955 and abolished only in 1967, stated that Bonn would withhold or withdraw diplomatic recognition from governments, with the exception of the Soviet Union, that recognized the German Democratic Republic.

4. For more on the Basic Treaty see Ernest D. Plock, *The Basic Treaty and the Evolution of East-West German Relations* (Boulder, Colo.: Westview Press, 1986).

5. However, from the point of view of some in the GDR, these policies actually served to solidify and deepen the East-West division.

6. For an account of Schmidt's and Honecker's efforts to establish a German minidétente, see Wolfram F. Hanrieder, *Germany, America, Europe* (Yale University Press, 1989), pp. 209–19.

7. For an account of postwar U.S.-German relations, see W.R. Smyser, *Restive Partners: Washington and Bonn Diverge* (Boulder, Colo.: Westview Press, 1990).

8. Indeed, West German television became not only a window on the West but also an essential feedback mechanism for East Germans about what was happening and what was significant in their own country. This phenomenon would play a crucial role in the revolution of 1989.

9. For more complete accounts of the impact of Gorbachev's policies on the GDR see Karen Dawisha, *Eastern Europe, Gorbachev and Reform: The Great Challenge*, 2d ed. (Cambridge University Press, 1990); and Michael J. Sodaro, *Moscow, Germany, and the West from Khrushchev to Gorbachev* (Cornell University Press, 1990).

10. Remarks made by Kurt Hager, chief SED ideologue, in an interview with the German magazine *Stern*, published April 9, 1987. Cited in F. Stephen Larrabee, "Eastern Europe: A Generational Change," *Foreign Policy*, no. 70 (Spring 1988), p. 58. To this, Larrabee prophetically countered, "But the demonstrations in East Berlin in June and August 1987 suggest that the calls for greater *glasnost* may eventually have an impact in the GDR as well."

11. See, for example, William Echikson, "Hard-Liners Shrug Off Soviet Reform," *Christian Science Monitor*, January 24, 1989, p. 3.

12. See manuscripts in preparation on German unification by Stephen F. Szabo, Elizabeth Pond, and Daniel Hamilton, as well as Elizabeth Pond's path-breaking first volume *After the Wall: American Policy Toward Germany* (Twentieth Century Fund, 1990) and the comprehensive and useful Michael A. Freney and Rebecca S. Hartley, *United Germany and the United States* (Washington: National Planning Association, 1991).

13. By mid-August 1989, three months after the opening of the border to Austria, more than 200,000 East Germans were camped out in Hungary, hoping to get exit permits. Repudiating previous agreements with East Germany, the reform Budapest government allowed all claimants free passage in mid September. See Jim Hoagland, "Hungary Had Soviet Approval," *Washington Post*, September 17, 1989, p. 1, and Leigh Bruce, "Hungarian Tells of Meeting with Kohl on Opening Border," *International Herald Tribune*, September 24, 1990, p. 5. According to Bonn interview sources, the actual date for the September border opening was the subject of secret Hungarian-German discussions in the chancellor's office in late August 1989. The East German Stasi learned of this through its bugging system and confronted Hungarian Prime Minister Miklos Nemeth about his betrayal. Reportedly only then did Kohl learn that his office had been bugged.

14. For example, in September 1989 the SED reluctantly gave its consent to Czechoslovakia to allow East German refugees congregated at the West German embassy in Prague to flee to the West. To save face, East Berlin insisted that the emigrants be transported by train via the GDR (instead of directly into Bavaria) to create the legal fiction that the refugees were departing from East Germany. But this move backfired: the sight of their fellow citizens passing through GDR train stations only served to incite more East Germans to flee.

15. For more thorough coverage of the German revolution, see, for example, Pond, *After the Wall*, pp. 12–20.

16. See Pond, *After the Wall*, pp. 22–23. For a detailed, insider's view of the Kohl government's policymaking regarding unification, see Horst Teltschik, *329 Tage: Innenansichten der Einigung* (Berlin: Wolf Jobst Siedler Verlag, 1991).

17. According to Horst Teltschik, Kohl's chief national security adviser, the chancellor intended that movement toward German unity should occur in cooperation with the GDR and be consistent with the "overall European process as well as with East-West relations." The initial warm reception of Kohl's speech by the SPD came as a surprise to Teltschik. See Teltschik, *329 Tage*, pp. 55–58.

18. See Teltschik, *329 Tage*, pp. 130–32.

19. For a more thorough consideration of the external influences favoring unity and corresponding documentation, see Karl Kaiser, *Deutschlands Vereinigung: Die internationalen Aspekte* (Bergisch Gladbach: Gustav Lübbe Verlag, 1991).

20. Teltschik, *329 Tage*, pp. 137–43.

21. More specifically, GDR citizens could exchange an average of 4,000 eastern marks (6,000 for retired persons, 2,000 for children) at a rate of one to one and the rest of their savings at two to one.

22. Although opposition leaders have successfully exploited the government's apparent tax lie, Kohl and his finance minister, Theo Waigel, had publicly admitted in September 1990 that the costs of unification might require a tax increase, albeit only as a last resort. See Marc Fisher, "Kohl Concedes Unity Linked to Tax Rise," *Washington Post*, September 19, 1990, p. A16.

23. The Christian Democrats were the strongest party in four of the five races, winning an absolute majority in Saxony and leading the coalition with the FDP in Mecklenburg–Western Pomerania, Saxony-Anhalt, and Thuringia. The SPD placed first only in Brandenburg, establishing a coalition government with the FDP, Greens, and the former opposition groups on the Alliance '90 list.

24. Landtag elections held on May 13, 1990, in North Rhine–Westphalia and Lower Saxony led to a majority in the Bundesrat of 27–18 in favor of the SPD-led delegations.

25. For a complete analysis of the Bundestag election see Klaus von Beyme, "Electoral Unification: The First German Elections in December 1990," *Government and Opposition*, vol. 26 (Spring 1991), pp. 167–84.

26. On September 29, 1990, the second chamber of the Federal Constitutional Court in Karlsruhe, ruling on a case initiated by the PDS, Greens, and Republicans, declared unconstitutional the application of the 5 percent clause—that is, that a party would be seated in the Bundestag only if it won 5 percent of the total national vote. The court argued that given the rapidity of unification, the 5 percent clause put smaller parties at an unfair disadvantage. Thus it recommended that for the December election lawmakers amend the electoral law to create, in essence, two separate constituencies, eastern and western, in which the 5 percent restriction would be applied. See "Karlsruhe Judges Declare Election Rules Invalid," *Week in Germany*, October 5, 1990, p. 2. For comment on this, see von Beyme, "Electoral Unification," pp. 173–74.

27. For a more detailed account of defense policy in the united Germany, see the essays by Hilmar Linnenkamp and Harald Müller in this volume and Catherine M. Kelleher and Cathleen Fisher, "The Federal Republic of Germany," in Douglas J. Murray and Paul R. Viotti, eds., *The Defense Policies of Nations: A Comparative Study*, 3d ed. (Johns Hopkins University Press, forthcoming).

28. Speech by U.S. Secretary of State James Baker before the Berlin Press Club, December 12, 1989. This and other important speeches dealing with German unification can be found in Lawrence Freedman, ed., *Europe Transformed: Documents on the End of the Cold War* (St. Martin's Press, 1990).

29. For an assessment of the new Bundeswehr and its role in the united Germany see Geoffrey Van Orden, "The *Bundeswehr* in Transition," *Survival*, vol. 33 (July–August 1991), pp. 352–70.

30. Before the Berlin Wall fell, the NVA numbered 170,000; by October 3, 1990, defections and attrition left 89,000 military and 47,000 civilian personnel. The East German border guards were disbanded at unification. See "The Federal Armed Forces in United Germany," MoD-Fürungsstab briefing delivered at the Brookings Institution, May 10, 1991, p. 13.

31. See comments made by German Defense Minister Gerhard Stoltenberg at formal disbandment, "Bundeswehrkommando Ost Aufgelöst," *Süddeutsche Zeitung*, July 2, 1991, p. 6.

32. "Federal Armed Forces," p. 5.

33. "Federal Armed Forces," p. 13.

34. Concerning the question of former NVA officers, see, for example, David C. Morrison, "Germany Merges Its Militaries," *National Journal*, April 20, 1991, p. 933; and "Federal Armed Forces," p. 14.

35. Concerning the quality of NVA facilities, see the Soviet publication, *New Times*, Nikita Zholhver, "Bundeswehr Marches East," no. 13 (April 2–8, 1991), pp. 20–21. By the end of 1991, 1,487 of the former NVA properties, covering more than 15,000 acres, were simply turned over to the federal government, with an additional 539 sites to be turned over in 1992. "Die meisten Waffen werden zerstört," *Frankfurter Allgemeine Zeitung*, February 1, 1992, p. 2.

36. Zholkver, "Bundeswehr Marches East," pp. 20–21.

37. In a survey commissioned by the Rand Corporation and conducted by the German polling firm Infratest in October-November 1991, it was found that east and west Germans have significantly different views regarding the United States and German membership in NATO. For example, on a scale of 0 to 2.5, west Germans were more sympathetic toward the United States than east Germans by 2.1 to 1.6. Also, by the end of 1992, 64 percent (down from 69 percent in the previous year) of west Germans thought that NATO membership was essential for German security, compared with 35 percent (down from 43 percent) of east Germans. This and other survey data are in Ronald D. Asmus, "Germany in Transition: National Self-Confidence and International Reticence," statement prepared for Subcommittee on Europe and the Middle East, Committee on Foreign Affairs, House of Representatives, January 29, 1992. For a less recent, but more detailed public opinion study see Asmus, *German Perceptions of the United States at Unification* (Santa Monica: Rand, 1991).

38. "Die meisten Waffen werden zerstört," p. 2.

39. From remarks made by General Jörg Schönbohm at the Atlantik Brücke conference in Berlin in April 1991. Much of NVA equipment cannot be used: some was given away to the eastern Europeans; some was donated for humanitarian purposes (for example, to help provide the Soviet Union with food); and some was sent to the Persian Gulf for the resupply of former Soviet clients as part of the German contribution. East Germany's MiGs were, however, retained for training purposes.

40. "Die meisten Waffen werden zerstört," p. 2.

41. "Die meisten Waffen werden zerstört," p. 2.

42. State and municipal governments in the new Länder have also received at no cost 16,000 of the 100,000 construction vehicles and trucks inherited from the NVA. "Die meisten Waffen werden zerstört," p. 2; and "Federal Armed Forces," p. 11.

43. See German Information Center, "Focus on German Support for the Transition to Democracy and Market Economy in the Former Soviet Union," Position Papers of the German Embassy, Washington, June 1992. This includes DM 7.8 billion for the construction of 36,000 housing units in the republics. According to Colonel Strelnikov, head of Moscow's delegation to the German-Soviet commission for troop withdrawal, 55,000 members of the Russian army do not have homes to which to return. By the end of 1991, only 2,000 new apartments were completed; Tomas Morgenstern, *Neue Zeit*, November 27, 1991, p. 4, in "Details of Soviet Troop Withdrawals Reported," in Foreign Broadcast Information Service, *Daily Report: West Europe*, December 2, 1991, pp. 18 (Hereafter FBIS, *West Europe*.)

44. The formal agreements were signed in September 1990.

45. See Marc Fisher, "German-Soviet Friction Masked by Mutual Needs," *Washington Post*, April 23, 1991, p. A10.

46. Figures supplied by the Russian embassy in Berlin and published in Marc Fisher, "Red Army Radio Aims at Germans," *Washington Post*, March 8, 1992, p. A28. At the MoD-Führungsstab briefing (see note 32) the official figures provided were 245 garrisons, 482 depots, 1 million tons of ammunition, and 2.6 million tons of equipment.

47. Zholkver, "Bundeswehr Marches East," p. 20. In a surprisingly favorable article, the *New Times* reported that Soviet privates receive approximately DM 25 a month; West German privates receive DM 400 a month.

48. Fisher, "Red Army Radio," p. A28. Slated for withdrawal in 1992 are 100,000 troops, 60,000 family members, 780,700 tons of matériel, and 33,600 weapons pieces. For a more precise breakdown of the troops and equipment removed in 1991, see the figures supplied by Colonel Strelnikov, head of Moscow's delegation to the German-Soviet commission for troop withdrawal, in Morgenstern, "Details of Soviet Troop Withdrawals Reported," p. 18.

49. Official figures say about 200 Soviets have sought asylum. It is not clear if this figure also includes those who are AWOL and family members who have asked to remain. A Soviet general told Marc Fisher of the *Washington Post* that more than 500 Soviet soldiers had deserted. See "German-Soviet Friction Masked by Mutual Needs."

50. Morgenstern, "Details of Soviet Troop Withdrawals," p. 18.

51. Concerning Kohl's presummit 1991 visit to Kiev to underscore the point, see " 'The Soviet Union Must Not Split'—Gorbachev," *Financial Times*, July 6–7, 1991, p. 3.

52. See Anne-Marie Le Gloannec, "Change in Germany and Future West European Security Arrangements," in Gary L. Geipel, ed., *The Future of Germany* (Indianapolis: Hudson Institute, 1990), pp. 129–40.

53. London Summit Declaration, meeting of the North Atlantic Council, London, July 5–6, 1990. See also communique from the NATO foreign ministers meeting in Turnberry on June 8, 1990.

54. See, for example, Defense Minister Stoltenberg's Kommandeurtagung remarks of June 13, 1990, reprinted in *Bulletin*, no. 76, June 14, 1990, pp. 653–67; and Ulrich Weisser, *Toward a New Security Structure in and for Europe: A German Perspective* (Santa Monica: Rand, August 1990) for the types of German arguments heard in NATO discussions. See as well, Ronald D. Asmus, *German*

Unification and Its Ramifications (Santa Monica: Rand, June 1991), especially chapters 5 and 6.

55. For the Kohl-Mitterand declarations of December 1990, see Presse-und Informationsamt der Bundesregierung, *Bulletin*, no. 144 (December 11, 1990), pp. 1513–14.

56. See Asmus, *German Unification*, pp. 49 and following. Asmus cites Genscher as referring to Germany's crucial role in the building of a new Europe: "This historical task means the beautiful fulfillment of the Germans' European mission."

57. See, for example, Genscher's January 31, 1990, speech at Tutzing on CSCE institutionalization; and the "six building blocks" from the DGAP address printed in *Europa-Archiv*, vol. 15 (1990), pp. 473–78.

58. See "Foreign Ministers Hold News Conference," FBIS, *East Europe*, February 3, 1992, p. 7.

59. According to official accounts, the Federal Republic paid about $11.5 billion, mostly to the United States, to offset the costs of Operation Desert Storm, and in-kind contributions to Britain, Israel, Turkey, and other coalition states. See T. Enders and M.J. Inacker, "The Second Gulf War and Germany," paper prepared for the Center for National Security Studies, Los Alamos, New Mexico, October 1991, pp. 13–15.

60. See Stephan-Andreas Casdorff, "Bundeswehr vor dem Neubeginn," *Süddeutsche Zeitung*, April 5, 1991; and Frank Drieschner, Thomas Kleine-Brockhoff, and Ulrich Stock, "Eine Armee zum Schießen," *Die Zeit*, February 22, 1991, pp. 17–19.

61. The CSU also contends that constitutional amendment is not necessary. See also Defense Minister Gerhard Stoltenberg (CDU) to UN Secretary General Perez de Cuellar, *Tageszeitung* (Berlin), June 26, 1991, p. 2.

62. The Bremen SPD *Parteitag* was essentially split until new Chairman Björn Engholm asked that the party conference reject an absolute prohibition of the external use of German troops and support rather a constitutional change allowing use only after a UN vote for strictly peacekeeping purposes. See Katharine Campbell, "SPD Backs German Role in UN Force," *Financial Times*, June 1-2, 1991, p. 2. For further intraparty disputes, see Martin E. Süskind, "Blauhelm-Beschluß der SPD auf dem Prüfstand," *Süddeutsche Zeitung*, June 13, 1991, p. 4.

63. See Giovanni de Briganti, "Germany Reverses Plan to Reduce Defense Spending," *Defense News*, July 15, 1991, p. 4. The Federal Republic's defense budget has not however increased, although unification has enlarged the Bundeswehr in territory covered and personnel. This suggests that funds formally approved for West Germany have been diverted, which can be interpreted as a reduction of defense spending. See "Die Bundeswehr verringert ihre Rüstungsausgaben drastisch," *Frankfurter Allgemeine*, January 13, 1992, p. 34; and Quentin Peel, "Bundeswehr Set for Radical Cutback," *Financial Times* February 20, 1992, p. 3.

64. Norbert Walter, "Strengths, Weaknesses and Prospects of the German Economy," in Geipel, ed., *Future of Germany*, p. 48.

65. Leslie Colitt and Andrew Fisher, "Bundesbank Assailed over High Interest Rates," *Financial Times*, January 10, 1992, p. 2.

66. Quentin Peel, "Germany Given Grim Warning on Economy" and "German 'Wise Men' See No Rising Star in East;" and the editorial comment, "Some Angst in Germany," *Financial Times*, October 22, 1991, pp. 1, 2, 20.

67. Norbert Walter, "A Year of Transition," *Financial Times*, January 3, 1992, p. 9.

68. "Arbeitslosenzahl in Ostdeutschland im Januar um *300000* gestiegen," *Handelsblatt*, February 6, 1992, p. 1.

69. Quentin Peel, "Signs of Upturn in East Germany Fail to Lift Gloom," *Financial Times*, February 25, 1992, p. 3. In late January 1992 the government reported that it expects a 10 percent economic growth rate in the new Länder during 1992. See "Government Expects Growth for New Länder," in FBIS, *West Europe*, January 24, 1992, p. 11.

70. Christopher Parkes, "German Economic Confidence Declines," *Financial Times*, January 4–5, 1992, p. 2.

71. See "Government Expects Limited Economic Growth," FBIS, *West Europe*, January 22, 1992, p. 9; Reinhard Uhlmann, "Unsicherheiten," *Handelsblatt*, January 27, 1992, p. 2; and "Arbeitslosenquote steigt auf 8%," *Handelsblatt*, January 23, 1992, p. 1. Economics Minister Jürgen Möllemann contended that long-term investment would be retarded unless the inflation rate (high by German standards) was brought below 4 percent. New SPD Bundestag Chairman Hans-Ulrich Klose criticized the government, however, blaming the inflation problem on the high value added tax rates implemented by the coalition. "Möllemann: Wir müssen runter von 4% Inflation," *Handelsbatt*, February 14–15, 1992, p. 1.

72. *Deutsche Bank Letter*, July 1, 1991.

73. In "Christmas in July? The Economics of German Unification Reconsidered," *RWI-Papiere*, no. 27 (November 1991), p. 8, Ullrich Heilemann cited another analyst's estimate of thirty-five years.

74. A psycho-cultural explanation for this phenomenon is that Germans, especially west Germans, had become confident, to the point of arrogance, in the Federal Republic's economic prowess—what Jürgen Habermas has termed "DM nationalism." See "Yet Again: German Identity—A Unified Nation of Angry DM-Burghers?" *New German Critique*, no. 52 (Winter 1991), pp. 84–101.

75. See Gabriel A. Almond and Sidney Verba, *The Civic Culture: Political Attitudes and Democracy in Five Nations* (Princeton University Press, 1963); and Almond and Verba, *The Civic Culture Revisited* (Boston: Little Brown, 1980).

76. For one of the most complete analyses of the economic impact of the GEMU see George A. Akerlof and others, "East Germany in from the Cold: The Economic Aftermath of Currency Union," *Brookings Papers on Economic Activity* (1991), pp. 1–105. The authors argue that eastern Germany is in a state of great depression caused by a wage-driven "price-cost squeeze" among formerly state-owned businesses and a reduction in demand for east German goods. Although this situation will eventually be improved by the in-migration of capital and modern technology and the out-migration of labor, the government could quicken the pace by subsidizing employment bonuses designed to save jobs and making existing firms attractive for privatization.

77. See, for example, "Bonner Steuerstreit beigelegt," *Neue Züricher Zeitung*, February 16–17, 1992, p. 16.

78. For more on this possibility see Torsten Riecke, "Im Streit zwischen Bund und Ländern droht der Föderalismus auf der Strecke zu bleiben," *Handelsblatt*, February 13, 1992, p. 4.

79. This phenomenon had been foreshadowed during the May 1991 SPD Bremen party congress when a vote on the issue split delegates 203–202 in favor of Bonn.

80. Vorscherau's plan called for moving the office of the federal president, the Bundesrat, the Foreign Ministry, and foreign embassies to Berlin, while the chancellory, all other ministries, and the Bundestag would remain in Bonn. Geissler proposed moving the Bundestag to Berlin but leaving the government in Bonn. "Die Doppelhauptstadt Droht," *Der Spiegel*, June 10, 1991, p. 8.

81. *Deutscher Bundestag, Stenographischer Bericht, Plenarprotokoll*, 12/34, June 12, 1991, pp. 2746–47.

82. The SPD voted 126–110 for Bonn; the CDU-CSU voted 164–154 for Bonn; the FDP voted 53–26 for Berlin; the PDS voted 15–1 for Berlin; and the Greens–Alliance '90 voted 6–2 for Berlin. For a more complete summary see Klaus Dreher, "FDP und PDS gaben den Ausschlag," *Süddeutsche Zeitung*, June 22–23, 1991, p. 2.

83. The SPD received 40.8 percent of the vote (40.2 percent in 1987) and 46 seats; the Greens 8.8 percent (9.4 percent in 1987) and 10 seats; the CDU 40.2 percent (42.1 percent in 1987) and 46 seats; and the FDP 7.4 percent (7.8 percent in 1987) and 8 seats. The SPD governed in coalition with the Greens from late 1985 until 1987, when the coalition broke down over different attitudes toward protecting the environment. The CDU-FDP government was formed after the subsequent election. See "SPD, Greens Win in Hessen," *Week in Germany*, January 25, 1991, p. 2.

84. For an account of CDU politics up to German unification, see Clay Clemens, "Helmut Kohl's CDU and German Unification: The Price of Success," *German Politics and Society*, no.22 (Spring 1991), pp. 33–44.

85. "Die Lage ist katastrophal," *Der Spiegel*, July 8, 1991, pp. 23–25.

86. According to a 1991 poll, had new Landtag elections been held in the eastern Länder, the CDU would have lost its control of the governments to the SPD in Western Pomerania, Saxony-Anhalt, and Thuringia and would have been forced to form a coalition with the FDP in Saxony. Meanwhile, the SPD would have increased its support in Brandenburg enough to form an absolute majority there. See "Die SPD steigt in der Wählergunst," *Frankfurter Allgemeine Zeitung*, July 12, 1991, p. 2. Given that Berlin is already governed by a CDU-SPD grand coalition, it could also slip out of Christian Democratic hands after new elections.

87. David Goodhart, "Kohl Vows to Be Party Candidate for Chancellor in 1994 Election," *Financial Times*, August 8, 1991, p. 2.

88. For details on the party congress, see "CDU Manifesto Views Unity as Challenge," FBIS, *West Europe*, December 19, 1991, p. 7. See also Wolf Ullmann, "An Easterner Is Elected CDU Deputy Chairman," *German Tribune*, December 22, 1991, p. 4.

89. "Erdrutsch im Osten: SPD klar vorn," *Der Spiegel*, May 13, 1991, pp. 64–73.

90. Katherine Campell, "SPD Backs German Role in UN Force," *Financial Times*, June 1-2, 1991, p. 2. The SPD remained divided, however, on whether and how the Basic Law needed to be amended to allow Bundeswehr participation outside the NATO area.

91. This question is discussed in "Glänzende Position," *Der Spiegel*, August 12, 1991, pp. 25–27.

92. "Im Bonner Asyl-Streit ärgert sich die FDP über die Union," *Frankfurter Allgemeine Zeitung*, February 13, 1992, p. 1.

93. More than 250,000 refugees, most from Eastern Europe (especially Yugoslavia) sought political asylum in Germany in 1991. See David Marsh, "Asylum-Seekers Cost West $7 bn Last Year," *Financial Times*, March 4, 1992, p. 3.

94. "Lambsdorff bekennt sich zu der Bonner Koalition," *Handelsblatt*, January 7, 1992, p. 3.

95. "Genscher als Kanzler?" *Der Spiegel*, May 20, 1991, pp. 18–20.

96. For a more complete analysis of the Neumünster Congress, see "Mühselige Wurstelei," *Der Spiegel*, May 6, 1991, pp. 20–21.

97. "Mühselige Wurstelei," pp. 20–21.

98. See, for example, Wolfgang Stock, "Das Bündnis 90 fürchtet 'den Anschluß' durch die Grünen," *Frankfurter Allgemeine Zeitung*, January 22, 1992, p. 4.

99. The PDS still has fewer than 200,000 members, most of them in eastern Germany. According to one survey, many of these members have remained mostly out of continuing solidarity. See Knut Pries, "Eine Geschichte von Rechtfertigungen," *Süddeutsche Zeitung*, June 20, 1991, p. 6.

100. In the three Landtag elections in West Germany in 1991, the PDS did best in Hamburg, where it won just 0.5 percent of the vote.

101. "Gysi mahnt Geschlossenheit an," *Süddeutsche Zeitung*, June 22–23, 1991, p. 6.

102. "PDS strafft Führung—Gysi wiedergewählt," *Das Parlament*, December 20–27, 1991, p. 17.

103. In a speech to Roman Catholic church leaders, Kohl expressed his outrage over the "shameless appearance" of east German neo-Nazis, warning his countrymen to be wary of "old demons." "Kohl Warns of 'Old Demons,' " *Financial Times*, June 24, 1991, p. 2.

104. See, for example, Stephan-Andreas Casdorff, "Dresden ist Hauptstadt der Rechtsextremisten," *Süddeutsche Zeitung*, June 15–16, 1991, p. 9.

105. See "Bis zu 2000 Rechtsextremisten im Osten," *Süddeutsche Zeitung*, June 12, 1991, p. 5.

106. "Bis zu 2000 Rechtsextremisten im Osten," p. 5. See also Casdorff, "Dresden ist Hauptadt," p. 9; and John Tagliabue, "The Dresden Scene: Sex Shops and Neo-Nazis," *New York Times*, June 13, 1991, p. A16.

107. For the American view of this, see Catherine M. Kelleher, "U.S. Foreign Policy and Europe, 1990–2000," *Brookings Review*, vol. 8 (Fall 1990), pp. 4–10.

108. See Almond and Verba, *Civic Culture*, p. 103.

109. Emnid poll published in *Der Spiegel*, August 12, 1991, p. 33. Respondents were given three other names on the same list: Friedrich Ebert, the SPD hero (43 percent), Friedrich Barbarossa (40 percent), and Karl Marx (34 percent).

110. Thus, in the same *Spiegel* poll, while 65 percent declared they placed a positive value on Prussian history, 41 percent were indifferent as to whether Kohl participated or did not participate in the reburial of Frederick the Great. *Der Spiegel*, August 12, 1991, pp. 32–33.

111. Should the Germans' search for identity lead them to the revolutionary acts of individual courage in search of democracy that were so much a part of the revolution of 1989, they will find themselves on the path started at Schloss Hambach in 1832 and in St. Paul's Church in 1848.

112. The *Historikerstreit* (historians' debate) erupted in 1986 when Jürgen Habermas criticized publications by Ernst Nolte and Andreas Hillgruber for, in his opinion, their trivializing of the Nazi Holocaust. For more on this, see Charles S. Maier, *The Unmasterable Past: History, Holocaust, and German National Identity* (Harvard University Press, 1988).

THREE

The Political Economy of the New Germany

Michael Kreile

WHEN THE UNITED Germany celebrated its first anniversary on October 3, 1991, there was neither exuberant rejoicing nor a display of DM nationalism. Collective soul-searching, measured satisfaction, frustration, and concern predominated, and the intensity of these mixed feelings was more pronounced in east than in west Germany. For it has become increasingly obvious that within the one Germany now coexist two societies divided by forty-five years of separate histories, by disparate levels of economic development, and by mentalities shaped by the distinct social systems in which the people have grown up, lived, and worked. The gap between the two parts of the country is therefore not simply a matter of differences in living conditions arising from economic dualism; it also reflects differences in collective experiences. The corresponding psychological distance between west Germans and east Germans has not been narrowed by the process of unification. On the contrary, the collapse of the east German economy that followed the introduction of economic and monetary union, and the large-scale unemployment that is part of the painful transition to a market economy, have frustrated the hopes of those citizens who saw themselves as victims of history and felt entitled to prompt redress. As unification produces a boom in the west and a bust in the east, it is not surprising that discontent, insecurity, emotional instability, and resignation have spread among east Germans.[1] The avenues of opportunity that the demolition of the wall had apparently opened up now seem to lead often into blind alleys. The east Germans expected the most from unity, and they now must bear the brunt of adjustment.

The west Germans, in comparison, have followed the unification process as more or less benevolent spectators, eager not to be disturbed in their material comfort and their mental habits. Relatively modest tax increases are already considered sacrifices, indicating that support for unification was predicated on the assumption that unity would not cost much. In an opinion poll conducted in May 1991, 84 percent of the west Germans interviewed expressed positive feelings—such as solidarity and a willingness to help—toward the east Germans. Among the east Germans, 41 percent expressed positive feelings toward their western counterparts; 45 percent had negative feelings about them. However, 55 percent of the west Germans felt unduly burdened by the additional taxes required to finance the costs of unity, and 80 percent felt that the east Germans expected and asked for too much from the west. Conversely, 76 percent of the east Germans polled believed that their expectations were justified and that the west Germans owed them more help.[2]

Many west Germans, ordinary citizens and politicians alike, are slow to realize that while the Federal Republic has kept its name, it is no longer the same entity. In this respect, the decision to move government and parliament to Berlin was a salutary act of consciousness-raising. For the task of integrating the two societies is enormous and will dominate the political agenda for at least a decade. Inevitably, the integration process will be fraught with political and social tension as east Germany undergoes a profound transformation on several levels. The transition from a one-party dictatorship to a pluralist democracy has already been completed at the level of political institutions, but it also needs to take root in the political culture and patterns of behavior. A discredited judiciary subject to party orders must be reformed into an independent organ of the *Rechtsstaat*.[3] The conversion of a centrally planned economy protected from global competition into a viable free market economy will require the wholesale restructuring of industry as well as the rebuilding and modernization of the rundown infrastructure. An egalitarian society organized by an oppressive but paternalistic state is giving way to a more stratified society in which a "welfare state" does not insure its citizens against all possible misfortunes, thus exposing individuals to more risks as well as more opportunities. Future social integration will depend largely on the successful transformation of the east German economy, the equalization of living conditions across the territorial divide, and the assimilation of value systems.

Since the reference system is basically west German, the entire integration process is highly asymmetric and an inevitable source of grievances and conflicts. The inhabitants of the "accession territory" (a gem of west German bureaucratic jargon to denote the five new Länder) complain that they are "second-class Germans" and feel colonized by the influx of west German managers, civil servants, and professors (appointed to evaluate university departments). In a way, German unity is a huge experiment in social engineering. Triggered by the peaceful revolution in the GDR but designed and financed by the West, it is being carried out—and suffered—by the east Germans in the hope that it will work. The integration of east Germany is clearly more difficult than was the integration of millions of refugees and expellees into West German society in the 1950s. No party questions the fact that it will require a massive redistribution of resources in favor of the east ("sharing" in the words of President Richard von Weizsäcker) to ease the strain of transition and facilitate economic restructuring. However, the makers of public policy are faced with a dilemma, as the requirements of political stability may well come into conflict with the imperatives of economic adjustment. How the transfer of resources is to be financed has become one of the most contentious issues of domestic politics, involving both antagonism among social groups and the problem of burden-sharing among levels of government.

The topic of this chapter could easily become a multiyear research project. It also carries the temptation to indulge in prophecies tainted, according to the scholar's temperament, by wishful thinking or thoroughgoing pessimism. But as social scientists have not distinguished themselves by their ability to anticipate the revolutions in Central and Eastern Europe, restraint in forecasting the outcomes of a complex process of social change may be in order. Thus, the purpose of this chapter will be to offer an account of the political and economic developments in Germany since the introduction of economic and monetary union and to analyze some key aspects of the politics and economics of the unfinished "real" unification. The first section sketches out the legal and institutional framework within which east Germany has been incorporated into the west German political system and highlights some of the problems of political and administrative integration. The second section takes up a question raised in the political and academic debate on unification, namely, whether the dynamics of west German politics led to a premature and ill-advised decision in favor of economic and monetary union. Here, the argument will be that there was no viable alternative, since the East Germans had sealed their country's fate with their vote of March 18, 1990. The third section reviews the adjustment crisis of the east German economy and shows the effect of this crisis on the labor market. Subsequently, it examines the functions of public policy, which have been expanding in response to the deepening crisis in the east, in the restructuring of the east German economy, with particular emphasis on the Treuhandanstalt, the privatization agency that may become a sort of state holding company against its will. The final section discusses the challenge posed to German federalism by the financing of unity, and the conclusion provides an interim assessment of the process of political and economic integration.

The Institutional Framework of German Unity: The Transfer of a Political System

The orderly disappearance of the GDR left no institutional void. Accession to the Federal Republic under Article 23 of the Basic Law simply extended the West German constitutional framework to East Germany. The GDR had already adopted the "economic constitution" of the Federal Republic when the treaty creating economic, monetary, and social union between the two German states entered into force. Both acts had been preceded by the alignment of the East German electorate with the West German party system, which was demonstrated by the Volkskammer elections of March 18, 1990. The dissolution of the East German state and the transfer of West German political institutions have been managed with remarkable efficiency as far as the legal groundwork and the merger of organizations are concerned. As was to be expected, however, political and administrative integration have met with a host of obstacles that derive from the legacy of socialism, a lack of organizational resources in the east, and differences in east and west German mentalities.

Unification and Its Aftermath

The period since the beginning of the peaceful revolution in the GDR can be divided into three phases. During the first phase, between the mass demonstrations in East Germany in October 1989 and the Volkskammer elections in March 1990, the dynamics of the political upheaval created growing pressure for unification, a movement that was accelerated by what Lehmbruch describes as "the irruption of the West German party system and its competitive action logic into the political system of the GDR."[4] The second phase was marked by the negotiations conducted between the two Germanies—and within their respective political arenas—on the conditions and procedures of the two-stage unification process completed on October 3, 1990, the "Day of German Unity." During the third and present phase, which began with the first all-German Bundestag election on December 2, 1990, the economic and financial consequences of unification have dominated the domestic political agenda as the ongoing crisis compels the government to adjust its policies.

In order to understand the dynamics of the unification process, it is useful to look back on some key developments of the first phase.[5] Antigoverment demonstrations and the mass exodus of East Germans through Hungary to the West forced the resignation of Erich Honecker, Communist party (SED) chairman and head of state, on October 18, 1989. Shortly afterward, on November 9, the Berlin Wall was opened, and, in the aftermath of these events, a new but still SED-dominated government was formed by Hans Modrow, the reform-minded party secretary of the Dresden area.[6] The new government held together what was left of executive power as the ruling party disintegrated. Although committed to a program of far-reaching political and economic reforms, the Modrow government was unable, for lack of capacity and will, to organize the transition to a market economy. Nor was it prepared to dismantle the "Stasi" state security apparatus, the hated instrument of internal spying and oppression. With popular protest mounting and government authority decaying, the parties of the "ancien régime" accepted the invitation of the churches to form a Round Table with representatives of the opposition groups in an effort to stabilize the situation.[7] The Round Table, first convened on December 7, 1989, became an instrument of political control vis-à-vis the Modrow government, then an emergency legislature, and, toward the end, an election campaign forum. It set the date for the first free elections (May 6, 1990) and forced the government, with the help of demonstrators, to dissolve the Office of National Security, a renamed and slimmed-down version of the Stasi. However, in spite of the power struggle pitting the opposition groups against the revamped SED-PDS (now the Party of Democratic Socialism, or PDS), the leaders of the civil-rights movement, mostly new-left intellectuals and church activists, shared one essential objective with their adversary: the preservation of the GDR as an independent state. On this crucial issue, they found themselves increasingly out of step with the hundreds of thousands of East Germans demonstrating in the streets. The slogan "We are the people" gave way to "We are one people," and calls for rapid unification grew louder as the crisis in the GDR deepened.[8] At the end of January 1990, the Volkskammer elections were advanced to March 18, and the Round Table groups and parties which were not represented in the Modrow cabinet joined his "government of national responsibility."

By early February, when the government of Chancellor Helmut Kohl offered to open negotiations on economic and monetary union, most political forces in East Germany, including the PDS, had rallied to the idea of German unity. The issue then resolved itself into the questions of speed, terms, and procedure over which the election campaign was being fought. As Elizabeth Pond observed, "The takeover by West German parties of the East German campaign seemed to attract rather than repel East German voters. They knew the Western politicians better than they knew their own formerly reclusive politicians, and they certainly trusted them more."[9] The eastern Christian Democratic Union (CDU), the former bloc party leading the conservative Alliance for Germany, had been recognized by the western CDU as a sister party only after some hesitation,[10] whereas the newly founded Social Democratic Party (SPD) (initially the SDP), which had no embarrassing associations with the past, had quickly received the support of the party of Willy Brandt and Oskar Lafontaine. The colorless three-party Alliance of Free Democrats could do no better than to rely on the popularity of the Halleborn Hans-Dietrich Genscher.[11]

Accession under Article 23, advocated by the "Alliance for Germany," was advertised not only as the fast track to unity but as the fastest route to economic prosperity. The clear-cut victory of the conservatives[12]—a bitter surprise for the SPD, which had been expected to win an absolute majority—

demonstrated that the majority of the voters did not want an ill-defined "third way" between socialism and welfare state capitalism and did not care about drafting a new all-German constitution, as the Round Table had demanded, on the basis of parity.[13] To suggest, as Habermas has, that the GDR fell victim to a strategy of destabilization initiated by Chancellor Kohl in order to obtain a kind of rapid *Anschluss* completely overlooks the internal erosion and paralysis of the East German state.[14] If there was an external factor of destabilization, it was the existence of a prosperous and democratic West Germany that could hardly renege on its constitutional commitment to re-unification. Polemical terms such as *Anschluss* or annexation are certainly valid as expressions of disapproval, but they also imply, unwittingly or not, that the East Germans were unable to exercise their right to democratic self-determination.

The Grand Coalition government formed by Lothar De Maizière of the CDU in April 1990 took up negotiations on economic and monetary union with West Germany on April 27. On May 18, the State Treaty on the Establishment of Monetary, Economic, and Social Union (MESU) was signed in Bonn; it entered into force on July 1. On July 6, formal negotiations on the Unification Treaty opened in East Berlin. The treaty was signed on August 31, approved by large majorities of both parliaments on September 20, and came into effect on September 29, with the accession of the GDR becoming effective on October 3. During the previous weeks, the FDP, SPD, and CDU had held their unification congresses. On October 14, the state legislatures were elected in the newly created East German Länder. The first all-German Bundestag election of December 2 confirmed Chancellor Kohl and his con-servative-liberal coalition.

In the end, laying the institutional foundations of German unity had taken less than nine months, although the process required negotiations at several tables. The Unification Treaty, in particular, involved controversies within the Bonn and Berlin coalitions. In West Germany, the government had to come to an agreement with the SPD opposition, since the May 1990 state elections in Lower Saxony had given a majority in the Bundesrat (the chamber of Länder representatives) to the SPD-led Länder governments, and since constitutional amendments require a two-thirds majority in both chambers.[15] Moreover, the law governing the first all-German Bundestag election was declared unconstitutional by the Constitutional Court on the grounds that applying the 5 percent rule and the provision on joint lists to the whole of Germany violated the principle of equality of opportunity by putting GDR-based parties at a disadvantage.[16] The amended electoral law applied the 5 percent clause separately to a western and an eastern district.

In the election campaign, the costs of unity and the appropriate methods of financing them were a central theme. The government coalition firmly denied that it would be necessary to raise taxes, while the SPD accused the governing parties of deceiving the voters. At the end of February 1991, with expenditures for the east moving beyond the limits envisioned by wishful thinkers, the government had to adopt a package of tax increases made necessary, it was awkwardly explained, by the German contribution to the Gulf War. The SPD seized on the "tax lie" in the Rhineland-Palatinate election campaign and, on April 21, inflicted a resounding defeat on the CDU, which had governed the state for forty-four years. Although the outcome of the election was probably determined more by state politics than by the tax issue, it greatly strengthened the SPD's position at the national level. Having won the Hesse election in January, the SPD now regained the Bundesrat majority it had lost in the state elections in eastern Germany. Meanwhile, plant closures and soaring unemployment in the east provoked social protest, a situation the Red Army Faction (RAF) terrorists tried to exploit by assassinating Treuhand Chairman Detlev-Karsten Rohwedder. In March, the government reacted to the continuing decline of the east German economy by launching a new program for economic recovery, noting that an extraordinary situation requires unconventional means.[17] However, the decline of the east German economy continued during 1991 and the upturn expected for 1992 is unlikely to reverse employment trends before 1993.

Legal and Constitutional Foundations

The most important documents establishing the legal framework of German unity are the State Treaty on Monetary, Economic, and Social Union (MESU), the Unification Treaty, and last but not least, the Final Settlement regarding Germany (the Two plus Four Treaty), in which the Four Powers granted the united Germany full sovereignty. The State Treaty on MESU was explicitly designed as a first significant step toward state unity under Article 23 of the Basic Law, although it did not anticipate political unification taking place within a few months.[18] It not only made the deutsche mark the sole legal tender in both German states, transferring responsibility for "domestic and external monetary policy in the extended Deutsche Mark currency area to the Deutsche Bundesbank," but also extended the West German "economic constitution" to East Germany.[19] The social market economy was adopted as the common economic system of the union.[20] The GDR assumed the obligation to introduce a market-based banking system, a social security system along West German lines, and West Germany's labor legislation and budget structures. West Germany pledged DM 22 billion in 1990 and DM 35 billion in 1991 to the east German budget, as well as start-up financing for the social security system of DM 5.75 billion in 1990–91. These transfers would enable the east German government to stay within the borrowing ceilings set by the treaty.[21]

The Unification Treaty, a monument of legal perfectionism with appendices of several hundred pages, set the rules under which the GDR joined the Federal Republic.[22] Through accession under Article 23, the Länder Brandenburg, Mecklenburg-Pomerania, Saxony, Saxony-Anhalt, and Thuringia became Länder of the Federal Republic, and the eastern district of Berlin became part of the Land Berlin. Amendments to the Basic Law were kept to a minimum: Article 23, for instance, was repealed in order to avoid giving the impression that the Federal Republic might lay claim to additional "other parts of Germany" that could avail themselves of the accession option.[23] The distribution of voting rights in the Bundesrat was modified and the system of revenue-sharing was subject to a special transition regime applying to the new Länder (see "Financing German Unity").

The SPD, the trade unions, the leaders of the East German civil rights movement, and many intellectuals would have preferred unification under Article 146 of the Basic Law, which allowed an all-German constituent assembly to write a new constitution that would be approved by referendum. This procedure, they argued, would have satisfied the East Germans' aspirations for a transition that respected their dignity and would have offered an opportunity to introduce into the constitution provisions such as the right to work, a ban on lockouts, the protection of the environment as a goal of the state, and elements of direct democracy.[24] Since the balance of political forces was not favorable to those who wanted to embellish the Basic Law, they had to settle for a consolation prize. The option to draft a new constitution was kept open by a modified Article 146, while Article 5 of the Unification Treaty stipulated that the governments of the two contracting parties could recommend that the legislative bodies of the united Germany take up within two years the questions of constitutional amendments and the application of Article 146.

The treaty also extended almost the whole corpus of federal law to the new Länder and introduced a myriad of transitional regulations covering everything from pyrotechnic products and the appointment of judges to drivers' licenses and allotment gardens.[25] Moreover, the treaty specified which East German laws and regulations would remain in effect.[26]

In the negotiations leading to the State Treaty on MESU, one of the most controversial issues involved ownership rights to property expropriated and nationalized between 1945 and 1949 in the Soviet Occupation Zone and later in the GDR. In a joint declaration, the two governments laid down the terms on which they were able to reach agreement. The Unification Treaty incorporated this declaration as well as two East German laws regulating special investments and open property issues.[27] For the federal government, the basic problem was reconciling the protection of private property provided by Article 14 of the Basic Law with the legitimate ownership rights or rights of use of those East Germans who had acquired expropriated property, as well as with the need to promote private investment. The De Maizière government and the Soviet Union insisted that these rights should not be reversed with respect to land expropriated by the Soviet authorities between 1945 and 1949, when land reform nationalized some 30,000 square kilometers. In spite of strong opposition among the coalition parties, the Kohl government agreed. An all-German parliament would later decide on compensation payments. This last provision was challenged as unconstitutional but was eventually upheld by the Constitutional Court.[28]

For ownership claims after 1949, the following terms applied: restitution of property would take precedence over compensation, but it should not impede or prevent investment. Real estate and buildings for which restitution claims were made could be sold to investors only if the proposed projects secured or created jobs, satisfied needs for housing, or provided the infrastructure for such projects, and only when authorized by the municipal or district authorities.[29] In these cases compensation would be mandatory, as it would be if restitution were determined to be against the public interest or would significantly damage an enterprise.[30] As will be shown, these regulations created a Pandora's box of implementation problems.

Undoubtedly the immediate transfer of federal law to eastern Germany guaranteed the uniformity of the legal system and assured the certainty of the law. However, applying the laws and regulations of a highly developed *Rechtsstaat*-cum-welfare state to the east is bound to be a difficult process— and therefore a source of confusion, inequities, and discontent, as long as the public administration and judiciary in the new Länder suffer from a lack of well-trained personnel.

The Expansion of the West German Party System

At first glance, the all-German party system appears to be an enlarged reproduction of the West German system, with some minor variations. The 12 million additional voters registered for the Bundestag election of December 1990 did not fundamentally alter the overall balance of political forces in the Parliament. The conservative-liberal coalition captured 54.8 percent of the vote nationwide, the same percentage it carried in West Germany in 1987, with the CDU winning 36.7 percent, the CSU 7.1 percent, and the FDP 11 percent. The SPD received only 33.5 percent of the vote nationwide, down from its 1987 total of 37 percent in West Germany, its worst showing since 1957. The West German Greens, who had been unable to join forces with their eastern counterparts, allied themselves with the civil rights alliance Bündnis 90, but missed the 5 percent threshold with 3.9 percent and did not win any seats. Thanks to the Constitutional Court ruling introducing separate 5 percent thresholds for the western and eastern districts, the PDS with just 2.4 percent of the overall vote (but 11.1 percent of the east German vote, as compared with 0.3 percent in western Germany obtained 17 of the 662 seats

Table 3-1. *Election Results in East Germany, 1990*
Party shares in percent of valid votes

Party	Volkskammer, March 18	State Parliaments,[a] October 14	Bundestag, December 2
Vote-turnout (percent)	93.4	69.1	74.7
CDU	40.8	43.6	41.8
DSU	6.3	2.4	1.0
FDP[b]	5.3	7.8	12.9
SPD	21.9	25.2	24.3
Bündnis 90/GRÜNE[c]	4.9	6.9	6.0
PDS	16.4	11.6	11.1
Other parties	4.4	2.5	2.9

Source: Wolfgang G. Gibowski and Max Kaase, "Auf dem Weg zum politischen Alltag: Eine Analyse der ersten gesamtdeutschen Bundestagswahl, vom. 2, Dezember 1990," *Aus Politik und Zeitgeschichte*, B 11–12/91 (March 8, 1991), pp. 3–20.

a. There was no election in East Berlin.
b. Volkskammer election: Bund Freier Demokraten.
c. Separate lists in Volkskammer election; various joint lists in state elections.

in the Bundestag. Moreover, the joint eastern list of Bündnis 90 and the Greens won eight seats on the basis of 6 percent of the eastern and 1.2 percent of the nationwide vote.[31] Whether or not the separate 5 percent clause is repealed for the 1994 Bundestag election, it is clear that the PDS will remain confined to the role it is already playing, namely, that of a regional party.

The outcome of the 1990 election also indicates that the SPD is in a bad starting position if it intends to pursue the option of a "Red-Green coalition" at the national level. Unless the voters turn against the CDU and the FDP decides to switch coalitions, the SPD is unlikely to return to power. This situation, of course, strengthens the FDP's hand, since its arch-rival within the governing coalition, the CSU, has been weakened by German unity. The CSU's attempt to nurture a subsidiary in the east, the German Social Union (DSU), has failed. The option of expanding the CSU beyond the borders of Bavaria, which is put forward now and then out of frustration, is not very promising, as trying to compete with the CDU would basically create a zero-sum situation.[32]

The results of the 1990 East German elections alone seem to confirm a high degree of similarity between the east and west German party systems that is broken only by the existence of the PDS in the east (table 3-1). The conservative-liberal camp, it is true, is strengthened by the fact that the major parties on the left of the political spectrum, the SPD and the PDS, are not possible coalition partners. However, the east German electorate's acceptance of the west German party system should be interpreted neither as an expression of structural homogeneity nor as proof of successful political integration. Electoral behavior in east Germany displays distinctive features with respect to voters' party identification and the social makeup of the parties themselves.[33] Analyses of the Volkskammer election of March 1990 have stressed the "issue orientation" of the east German voter, who appears to be the quintessential rational voter.[34] The election was largely a plebiscite on rapid unification, and the CDU was considered the party most competent to deal with the problems of economic transformation.[35] The same motive probably explains the large number of votes the CDU received in the Land and Bundestag elections. If the "issue voting" hypothesis is correct, east German voters are much more likely to change their party preferences than are their west German counterparts, since only 20 percent of east German voters identify with a particular party (as opposed to almost two-thirds of the west German voters). This assumes, of course, that the voter's perceptions of the issues and the parties most competent to deal with them will change markedly.

One of the biggest surprises of the east German elections has been the fact that, among workers, the CDU is by far the strongest party, a finding that runs counter to traditional assumptions regarding political cleavages. Industrial regions such as Saxony and Thuringia have become CDU strongholds, whereas the SPD draws the smallest percentage of its support from these two states.[36] In the absence of a strong entrepreneurial middle class, the FDP looks more like an employees' party. The PDS draws its electoral support primarily from the political-administrative class of the former communist regime, and the shadow of its SED past limits its prospects of becoming a catalyst for social protest.[37] With east German society undergoing a profound transformation characterized by a steep decline in employment and important shifts between economic sectors, the emerging cleavages may lead to changes in voter alignments that cannot be predicted with any confidence. The evolution of the party system will also be affected by the process of interest group formation as membership in trade unions and business associations shapes political preferences and loyalties.[38]

At the level of individual parties, the political integration of the eastern components is a function of party organization, access to leadership (and cabinet) positions, and ability to influence policy formulation. Low memberships and a lack of political professionalism among the eastern party organizations account for their relatively modest role within the CDU and the SPD. In September 1991 the eastern SPD, which had to begin from scratch, numbered only 29,400 members, as opposed to 897,000 in the west, but the Bonn headquarters is striving to build a strong party organization in the east by 1994.[39] The CDU is clearly in a better position, but its metamorphosis from a bloc party into the eastern branch of the chancellor's party has not been without friction. The peculiar combination of organizational continuity and imported legitimacy that characterizes the former bloc parties is a source of both strength and weakness.[40] An established party organization is an asset in election campaigns and may facilitate recruitment efforts. But the new members do not necessarily harmonize with the old members, and the dissatisfaction with political parties in general has taken its toll. By summer 1991, the eastern CDU had lost 30,000 of the 130,000 members it claimed in 1990, and out of the 21,000 newcomers it had gained in 1990, some 4,000 had already left; membership in the west, however, stood at 650,000.[41] The FDP stands out due to the fact that the party now has more members in the east (92,000) than in the west (70,000).[42] This development has changed the social composition of the membership, with the percentage of the self-employed middle-class decreasing, and it is likely to add a social note to economic liberalism. The party's new secretary-general, Uwe Lühr from Halle, is the only FDP member of the Bundestag elected directly to his seat. The fairly weak representation of the east German politicians in the federal government—three out of nineteen ministers and four out of thirty-three parliamentary secretaries of state—is probably a transitory phenomenon. Due to the scarcity of qualified and well-known politicians in eastern Germany, a number of top positions in Länder governments have been filled with pioneers from the western part of the country, including three state governors, Kurt Biedenkopf in Saxony, Werner Münch in Saxony-Anhalt, and Bernhard Vogel in Thuringia.[43] There can be no doubt that this transfer of personnel promotes political integration, but it is equally clear that integration will have been completed only when such migration becomes a two-way street.

The Reconstruction of Public Administration

West German civil servants are among the winners from unification, as they are benefiting from an "image revolution." Business leaders and liberal economists who used to complain about the burdens of bureaucracy have recently discovered the value of a smoothly functioning public administration. The lack of it in eastern Germany is currently considered one of the main obstacles to investment. In the case of public administration, institutional integration is a particularly difficult task. Public administration in the east cannot simply be adjusted to accommodate the methods of the west; rather, it must be reconstructed in order to eliminate the structural incompatibility that exists between the two models of public administration.

The centralized administration of the socialist state, which was subject to tight control by the party hierarchy, is being replaced by a differentiated system in accordance with the tenets of federalism and municipal self-government.

An authoritarian and often arbitrary administration lacking many features of efficient bureaucratic and legal organization, such as administrative records, must be transformed into a service-oriented administration mindful of the protection of citizens' rights, which are provided by administrative courts.[44] An unfamiliar and highly complex system of laws and regulations needs to be implemented by administrative personnel who do not have the appropriate training and experience. Specialized administrative bodies that did not exist under socialism, such as tax offices, administrative courts, and municipal land registries, are being built from scratch. One example of implementation problems linked to deficiencies in the current east German administrative infrastructure is provided by the inability of the local authorities to cope with the flood of property restitution applications consequent to the Unification Treaty. Since land registers often have not been kept properly, it is difficult to sort out competing claims. Moreover, when west German lawyers threaten east German officials with liability suits on behalf of their clients, local authorities sometimes hesitate to release the antirestitution certificates. The authorities may also be faced with a conflict of interest when the land in question can be used for municipal purposes.[45] Finally, in cases of litigation, the overburdened courts pose another obstacle.

Public administration in eastern Germany is also weak because of the small size of administrative units at the local and the district level. The average number of inhabitants in the eastern districts is 60,000, considerably lower than the 150,000 in the western districts; 87 percent of the municipalities belonging to districts have fewer than 2,000 inhabitants.[46] Such fragmentation calls for a reform of territorial organization.

The most demanding and difficult tasks, however, lie in the area of personnel policy. Since the East German administration was characterized by overstaffing, relatively low levels of professionalism, and recruitment policies based on political loyalty—"politicized incompetence," as Derlien judges harshly—personnel are being cut, retrained, and scrutinized for political misdeeds (for example, Stasi activity) simultaneously.[47] Given the mistrust of the population toward the SED-dominated judiciary, this sector is being screened particularly thoroughly, and estimates suggest that up to 50 percent of judges and public prosecutors will be removed.[48] Meanwhile, the administration of justice relies heavily on personnel from the western Länder. Training and retraining of personnel take place on a large scale. Administrative assistance from the federal government, the western Länder, and local authorities plays a vital role in the reconstruction process; in August 1991, 14,000 civil servants and public employees from the west were working in the east, mostly on temporary assignments.[49] The strong involvement of western Länder, which are acting as temporary "godfathers" to their eastern counterparts, testifies to the federation's capacity for integration and contrasts favorably with their posture on financial matters.

Monetary and Economic Union: Politics versus Expertise?

In the domestic political and academic debate, the rapid introduction of monetary and economic union has been read (and criticized) as a textbook example of electoral politics overriding economic expertise. The decision was made, it is said, against the advice of most economic experts and over the objections of the Bundesbank, whose reputation for autonomy was thereby damaged.[50] The collapse of the east German economy and the dramatic rise in unemployment—foreseeable effects of an economic "shock therapy" that combined radical trade liberalization with a drastic revaluation of the currency—could have been avoided, it is argued, if a strategy of gradualism had been adopted.[51]

A detailed review of the academic debate on monetary and economic union is certainly beyond the scope of this chapter, and available sources do not permit an accurate account of the decisionmaking process. It is nevertheless possible to offer some observations that qualify the argument just outlined. First, expert opinion was more divided than is currently assumed, and it was partly based on status quo assumptions, which were quickly overtaken by events. Second, although the Bundesbank was initially snubbed by the federal government, which failed to consult it before launching its proposal on MESU, an appropriate division of roles between the government and the central bank prevailed during the preparation of economic and monetary union. Third, the alternative to MESU and political unification that had been envisaged was hardly feasible.

According to then Interior Minister Wolfgang Schäuble, the first discussion of economic and monetary union took place in the chancellor's office in mid-December 1989. Schäuble himself proposed it as a step toward German unity and a measure to stem the flow of emigrants from the GDR. Most of the participants in the discussion felt, however, that the time was not yet ripe for such a major initiative.[52] In an opinion dated December 16, 1989, the Scientific Advisory Council to the federal Ministry of Economics outlined the reforms required for a transition to a market economy in East Germany and called on the authorities there to make their country attractive for direct investment. West Germany would provide economic aid for public infrastructure investment (primarily for measures that were also in its interests, such as those preventing cross-border environmental damages) but was advised not to support an arbitrarily fixed exchange rate for the ostmark (OM). The council concluded that the prospects for economic activity in the east would improve rapidly if the task of integrating the two German economic spaces could be tackled soon under the roof of a common state. The transition to a market economy in East Germany, with the deutsche mark as the all-German currency, would mobilize private capital flowing eastward and make extraordinary transfers of public funds conceivable.[53]

In a special opinion submitted on January 20, 1990, the Council of Experts based its recommendations on the explicit assumption that the political status quo would not immediately change and advocated limited technological and financial assistance as the Federal Republic's contribution to economic reform in the GDR. Like the Advisory Council, the Council of Experts stressed that the task of closing the economic gap between the two territories would change completely in a unified Germany. However, the council did not envisage monetary union.[54] Public discussion of economic and monetary union was stimulated by a proposal put forward by Ingrid Matthäus-Maier, SPD spokeswoman on finance, on January 17. The proposal initially met with a cool reception from the federal government, but by February 6 Kohl had changed his mind without heeding the Bundesbank's recommendation for a gradual approach to the convertibility of the ostmark.[55] Alarmed by the turn of events, the Council of Experts sent Kohl a letter expressing strong reservations about such rapid monetary integration. The introduction of the deutsche mark would offer the East Germans the illusion that they would soon be catching up with West German standards of living. The gap between eastern and western incomes would provoke wage demands that were out of step with productivity increases. East German firms would suddenly be exposed to international competition they would be unable to match. Monetary integration, the council warned, was no substitute for the necessary economic reforms the GDR had not yet introduced.[56] This letter again reflected the assumption that the two Germanies would continue to exist for some time.[57]

In a widely discussed article, President of the German Institute for Economic Research Lutz Hoffmann predicted formidable adjustment problems if monetary and economic unification were undertaken prematurely. Eliminating the buffer function provided by exchange rates in transactions between economies with substantial productivity differences would deprive East German industry of an instrument for becoming competitive. Early unification could lead to as many as 2.5 million to 3 million unemployed. Lutz argued that only by temporarily maintaining two German states with separate economies could the rapid process of catching up take place in the GDR at costs acceptable to both sides.[58] But his predecessor, the finance senator from Hamburg Hans-Jürgen Krupp, came out in favor of monetary union, which he considered less risky and expensive than a fixed exchange rate involving high support costs. Krupp maintained that monetary union would also raise productivity by motivating the work force and eliminating supply bottlenecks.[59] Hans Willgerodt of the University of Cologne published a detailed opinion commissioned by the chancellor's office, arguing that the introduction of the deutsche mark was to become the lever for reforming the whole economic system.[60] The think tank of the German Federation of Industry also advocated early monetary union and rejected gradualism as an appropriate strategy for the transformation of the East German economy.[61]

Horst Siebert, president of the Kiel Institute of World Economics, called East Germany a "new frontier" and German integration a "positive supply-side shock" not only for the country itself but for Europe and the world economy as well.[62]

The variety of these opinions suggests that the debate among economists was characterized by a high degree of uncertainty as to the actual effects of monetary and economic union. Not surprisingly, the government tended to value economic expertise according to its political utility and placed its hopes on the expected psychological boost monetary union would give the East German economy. Faith is important for success, Gerhard Fels and his coauthors declared.[63] As noted, some observers felt that the autonomy of the Bundesbank had been diminished in the decisionmaking process leading to MESU. Helmut Hesse, a member of the Central Bank Council, deplored not only the federal government's failure to consult with the Bundesbank before making an offer to the East German government, but also its decision against the OM 2 to DM 1 conversion rate recommended by the Bundesbank and the minister of finance. As a higher conversion rate would bring with it the danger of rising inflation, the Bundesbank had, some believed, been deprived of its leadership role in its very own domain.[64]

However, taking the political context into account, it is clear that economic and monetary union did not belong primarily to the realm of monetary policy but rather to the domain of high politics, where the chancellor's responsibility for setting the guidelines of government policy came into play. Otherwise, the Bundesbank would have retained implicit veto power over unification policy. Its president, Karl Otto Pöhl, was therefore entirely correct when he unenthusiastically declared that the decision on economic and monetary union was a political decision of the federal government for which the federal government alone would have to take responsibility.[65] Moreover, the State Treaty on MESU was negotiated by Hans Tietmeyer, the chancellor's representative "on loan" from the Bundesbank Directorate. At the technical level, however, the preparation of monetary union was in the hands of the Bundesbank. The conversion rate that was finally adopted—OM 1 to DM 1 for wages, pensions, and rents and up to OM 4,000 per person in cash or bank accounts; 2 OM to 1 DM for other financial assets and liabilities[66]— was called by Norbert Kloten, another member of the Central Bank Council, a by-and-large defendable political decision.[67] Despite this decision, however, unification did not weaken the Bundesbank's commitment to price stability, although the environment in which the central bank operates has become more complicated. Its institutional autonomy has been left intact, which will not be the case with a European central bank.

Undoubtedly the gloomier predictions regarding the effects of MESU on the east German economy have been largely vindicated by subsequent developments, as the following section describes. Does this mean, however, that a viable alternative existed that would have made for a less costly and painful transformation? Maintaining eastern Germany as a separate economy relying on a realistic exchange rate to protect both domestic and external markets was perhaps a theoretically attractive option. But this would have required not only the reintroduction of border controls, but also the propping up of a disintegrating state with economic aid from the Federal Republic.[68] Stabilizing East Germany when its citizens had individual and collective exit options would have been an exceedingly difficult task. To put it bluntly, the continued existence of two Germanies was an alternative that could have been realized only by an unholy alliance between West Germany and the Soviet Union.

The East German Economy in Transition

The authors of a study by the International Monetary Fund on the economic issues of German unification have formulated the question that will dominate German economic policy for the next years:

> The regional imbalances that characterize many advanced industrial econo-
> mies have long frustrated economic policy-makers. The large gaps in our
> understanding of these imbalances prompt the question: Will the evolution of the
> east German economy over the next decade reveal a new economic miracle—
> *Wirtschaftswunder*—or the emergence of another regional problem within the
> European Community?[69]

In terms of economic geography, unification has added a large but structurally weak region to the Federal Republic. The relative backwardness of the east German economy is at the root of a protracted crisis of adjustment that is reflected in the polarized pattern of economic developments in the united Germany.

Economic Dualism and Structural Crisis

East Germany entered MESU with an old and partially obsolete capital stock, a poorly motivated work force, an inadequate infrastructure, and record levels of environmental pollution. According to various estimates, the size of the two economies differed by a ratio of between 8:1 and 10:1. East German productivity was estimated at 35–40 percent of the West German level.[70] Due to the emigration of 343,000 citizens in 1989, East Germany lost 220,000 qualified workers, and an additional 238,000 citizens had left by the end of June 1990.[71] Foreign trade was conducted primarily with the countries of the Council for Mutual Economic Assistance (CMEA) and, in particular, the Soviet Union. In 1988 CMEA countries accounted for more than two-thirds of East Germany's total foreign trade, with the USSR's share reaching 56 percent of that total, or over one-third of all foreign trade. Fourteen percent of industrial output was exported to socialist countries.[72]

The unification of the two German economies immediately revealed the lack of competitiveness of East German firms. The collapse of East Germany's economy occurred almost overnight. In July 1990 alone, industrial output fell by 35 percent, and by early 1991 it had declined to one-third of its 1989 level.[73] East German consumers turned to Western goods, and "in an over-reaction probably caused by the 'attractiveness of novelties,' even thoroughly competitive east German products were crowded out of the market."[74] As a result of the disintegration of the CMEA and the transition of the Central and East European countries to trade in convertible currencies, exports to the region (including the Soviet Union), which had been expected to keep east German industry afloat, also declined. Moreover, high wage increases before and after July 1, 1990, "placed the majority of East German firms in a severe price-cost squeeze," as Akerlof and his coauthors have stressed.[75] A number of chemical and metallurgical plants also had to be closed for environmental reasons.

The contraction of the east German economy was followed by a surge in unemployment. At the end of 1991, roughly 1.1 million people, or 12 percent of the total labor force, were jobless, and 1.2 million were working short time (full-time workers whose hours have been reduced due to economic difficulties).[76] Contrary to original expectations, a massive inflow of private west German and foreign investment has not materialized. Several barriers to investment have been identified: difficulties in finding adequate commercial sites and premises, a problem linked in part to the issue of ownership and restitution claims; an inefficient telecommunications system and other deficiencies in the public infrastructure; requirements obligating investors to take on overstaffed work forces; hidden environmental problems; and the anticipation of more generous state investment subsidies.[77] According to a survey conducted by the Ifo Institute, West German firms (including the federal post office and railways) planned to invest DM 25 billion during 1991 in the new Länder, with an expected increase to DM 36 billion in 1992.[78] Yet, statistics show that between DM 150,000 and DM 250,000 is required to create one new job.[79]

The development of incomes and consumer demand in east Germany has been largely uncoupled from the decline in production and employment levels, by the "social flanking" of the adjustment process through massive transfer payments to the east. According to the Bundesbank, in 1991 public funds amounting to DM 140 billion (or about two-thirds of the east German GNP) were transferred to the east.[80] The hunger of east German consumers for western goods turned into a bonanza for west German trade and industry: during the twelve months following the beginning of MESU, west German deliveries of goods and services to east Germany amounted to DM 130 billion. The stimulus to west German economic growth (the "unification dividend") came to 2.3 percent. Moreover, the growing number of immigrants and commuters improved supply-side conditions in the old Länder.[81] Indeed, even today emigration to the west has not subsided. No longer dramatized and requiring little in the way of registration, it is estimated to have amounted to 382,000 persons between the last quarter of 1989 and the last quarter of 1991.[82] The impact of unification on Germany's external situation needs to be mentioned only in passing. The high current account surpluses, a constant source of complaints from West Germany's trade partners, were rapidly eliminated by steeply rising imports. As a result, the countries of the European Community also received a stimulus equivalent to about 0.5 percent of aggregate GNP of the EC countries in 1990.[83]

What are the prospects for the east German economy taking off into self-sustained growth? On the basis of recent analyses, they are rather bleak, or at best uncertain, at least in the short term. A joint report published by the German Institute for Economic Research and the Kiel Institute of World Economics in June 1991 described the situation of the east German manufacturing industry as follows:

> Except in a few isolated cases East German enterprises are faced with the extremely arduous task of regaining the domestic market and finding new export markets from all but scratch. In most cases they lack both suitable products and production processes and the necessary distribution channels and sales expertise. . . . East Germany must come to terms with the fact that it will have to reconstruct its industrial base anew. . . . In this period of fundamental structural change . . . it is all but impossible accurately to predict future trends.[84]

The adjustment problems of east German firms are often aggravated by the fact that wage increases are outrunning productivity improvements obtained by shedding surplus labor. The prospects for growth are much brighter in the construction industry, where output is rising dramatically due to public investment in infrastructure. The craft professions are expanding as well. In general, however, the demand for private services has been subdued, given the overall employment situation and income development.[85]

According to the Council of Experts, the economic upturn expected in 1992 will yield an increase in the east German GDP of 7.5 percent, following a decline of 16.5 percent during the second half of 1991.[86] It should be kept in mind, however, that the upturn will start from a very low level of production and that it will be sustained by transfer payments from west German public budgets.[87]

The Labor Market and Union Strategy

The transition to a market economy and the outbreak of structural crisis have caused a revolution in the east German labor market, or better, in the state of employment. The socialist system prided itself on providing full employment and not treating labor as a commodity. But full employment was made possible only by overstaffing (by Western standards), and it contributed to the poor productivity record. The employment rate in West Germany in 1988 was 64 percent (27.4 million persons), whereas the employment rate in East Germany amounted to 83 percent (9 million persons).[88] The difference in female employment is particularly striking: 90 percent of East German women between the ages of 25 and 60 were employed in 1989, whereas only 60 percent of West German women in this age group belonged to the work force. East German women also contributed 40 percent to the household income of couples.[89]

The magnitude of the decline in employment that has taken place in east Germany is staggering, even when the artificial nature of full employment in the former centrally planned economy is taken into account. In 1990–91, employment losses totaled 3 million persons, while the labor force decreased by 1.9 million persons.[90] In May 1992, the number of unemployed came to 1.15 million, while the number of short-time workers was 435,000, down from almost 2 million in the second quarter of 1991.[91] The labor force decreased as a result of early retirement, emigration, and commuting to west Germany. In May 1992, about 405,000 people were involved in job creation programs. Adding up the number of those covered by short-time work, early retirement, training and job-creation programs, and unemployment benefits results in the finding that over 3 million people draw their income from the federal labor office or the federal budget. This situation is in stark contrast with labor market conditions in West Germany, where employment gains of 1.5 million and an increase of 1.7 million in the labor force were registered in 1990–91.[92]

According to Council of Experts estimates, employment in east Germany will decrease to 6.5 million persons by the end of 1992, with 900,000 working short time.[93] Needless to say, an employment crisis of these proportions is a formidable challenge to labor market policy. The problem is exacerbated by the regional concentration of declining industries, such as shipbuilding on the Baltic Sea coast and chemical and brown coal industries in Saxony-Anhalt. Given the preexisting regional differences within the east German economy, an increase in the north-south development gap with a concomitant impact on employment can be expected.[94] And as long as high levels of open or disguised unemployment persist in east Germany, the labor market is likely to be more politicized than in the western part of the country.[95] Although the social "safety net" provided by the welfare state will probably prevent large-scale social unrest, political pressures for subsidizing employment are bound to become stronger. At the same time, the growth of public sector employment could be determined in part by considerations of labor market policy.

In a way, the trade unions have already anticipated a politicized labor market with subsidized employment in their wage policies for east Germany. The unions have in fact come under attack for promoting wage levels that are completely divorced from productivity levels.[96] But this is the result of a deliberate union strategy accommodated by employers who, at least in the case of managers of state enterprises, have had no experience in collective bargaining and are disposed to social pacification, given the disparities in living standards between the two parts of Germany. The first freely negotiated collective agreements were aimed at maintaining real incomes and providing protection against layoffs. Subsequent agreements have provided for the gradual adjustment of wages and salaries to west German levels, in some cases by 1994. The same applies to working hours and employee benefits.

According to the unions, wage policy for east Germany cannot be productivity oriented. First, investors should not act on the assumption that east Germany will remain a low-wage country; second, large-scale emigration can be prevented only by reducing the income gap between eastern and western Germany; and finally, workers should not simply earn enough to live on but should also have reasonable prospects for the future.[97] Significantly, the contracts provide for the upward adjustment only of pay governed by collective agreements, while extra pay and allowances (which in west Germany account for wage drift of up to 20 percent) are not included.[98] Income development as a social consideration seems also to have been a guideline for setting wage policy,[99] because unemployment benefits, pay for short-time work, and income support for participants in training programs are linked to the wage levels set by collective agreements.[100]

The departure from a productivity-based wage policy can be explained by the logic of organizational interests. A dual labor market with low wages in the east would alter the existing balance of power between capital and labor to the disadvantage of the unions. Moreover, the tasks of organization-building and recruitment (or maintaining the membership inherited from the communist trade union organization) require a wage policy that produces tangible results.[101] However, union experts recognize that, in the long run, if west German wage levels are to be achieved in east Germany, west German productivity levels must also be met. As most of the firms that are not yet privatized are unlikely to reach such productivity levels in the short term, at least temporary external cofinancing of higher wages is required in order to avoid plant closures.[102] In other words, the negative impact of wage policy on employment should be averted by subsidies granted by the Treuhandanstalt or out of the federal budget.

This wage subsidy proposal, incidentally, should not be confused with the employment bonus scheme put forward by George Akerlof and others who have criticized the contract introducing wage parity in the metalworking industry within four years:

> Such contracts represent an absence of any social contract between government and workers. Any employment bonus plan . . . must be made with the understanding, implicit or explicit, that the government is giving bonuses to protect jobs, and that unions in turn should show wage restraint in order to maintain the viability of those jobs.[103]

The debate triggered by the Akerlof proposal has been inconclusive so far, as economists are divided on wage subsidies and the Ministry of Economics is opposed to such support.[104]

Another instrument of labor market policy, the employment and training companies, was born amid controversy but has been making headway under pressure from the unions, governments of the east German Länder, and employers' associations. The function of these companies is to employ laid-off workers for purposes such as cleaning up plant sites or dismantling obsolete equipment and, at the same time, to offer them opportunities for further training or retraining. These firms are organized locally as "holding companies," established at the Land level by the state government, unions, employers, chambers of industry and commerce, and the Treuhandanstalt, which reluctantly agreed to 10 percent participation.[105] Wages and salaries are provided by the federal labor office under job-creation programs that normally finance jobs for one to two years. Small- and medium-sized enterprises have complained about unfair competition, especially when the employment companies became active in the construction sector.[106] Of course, the risk exists that these companies may perpetuate themselves as an expensive substitute for unemployment. But as long as the east German labor market remains depressed, subsidized employment is an instrument to prevent the emergence of poverty-stricken regions.

Restructuring the East German Economy: The Expanding Functions of the State

The key issue in the current economic policy debate about the future of the east German economy is the appropriate division of functions between the market and the state. The fact that market forces have been slow in propelling the east German economy out of its slump is either blamed on defects in underlying conditions or taken as proof that the state must commit itself to a more interventionist industrial policy. The debate, which focuses on the role of the Treuhandanstalt in particular, has become more intense as unemployment rises and entire regions face the threat of deindustrialization. "Many untidy departures from *Ordnungspolitik*" are inevitable in the transformation of a planned economy,[107] and in eastern Germany, these deviations have become a matter of degree and duration. As the controversy surrounding the employment and training companies shows, stressing the "social" in the "social market economy" may involve sacrificing opportunities such as rapid modernization, with the terms of the trade-offs determined in the political arena.[108] Such considerations notwithstanding, the political dynamics of German unity have forced the state to assume almost immediately a higher profile in the restructuring of the east German economy than was originally envisaged by the federal government, which had placed great reliance on an eastward rush of private capital.

Logically enough, the government has meanwhile implemented a wide range of direct and indirect measures designed to promote investment in the new Länder, including investment subsidies, special depreciation allowances, tax concessions, and low-interest loans as direct incentives for fixed capital formation. In order to improve general conditions for investment, local infrastructure projects by local authorities receive massive support. Labor market policy measures also make an important contribution to restructuring, as they provide opportunities for training and retraining—in spite of the high uncertainty regarding future labor demand—and alleviate social hardship. Moreover, exports to the former Soviet Union have been secured by export credit guarantees that totaled DM 9.7 billion in October 1991.[109] And public procurement regulations now allow for exceptional preferences for east German suppliers.[110] Finally, the east German Länder will receive DM 6 billion between 1991 and 1993 out of the structural funds of the European Community.[111]

As far as direct investment promotion is concerned, "the most important form of support is the tax-free bonus for investment in equipment," which in 1991 covered 12 percent of investment costs and in 1992 will cover 8 percent. It can be topped with a subsidy under the Improvement of Regional Economic Structures program, to a maximum of 23 percent.[112] Adding special depreciation allowances can raise the subsidy to more than 50 percent of the firm's investment costs.[113] The most popular instruments of direct investment so far have been the European Recovery Programs (ERPs) that provide loans at subsidized interest rates and loan guarantees to small- and medium-sized enterprises.[114] An obstacle to investment created during the unification process has been removed by the legislature with the Law to Eliminate Obstacles, of March 1991, which amends the property restitution regulations in favor of investment promotion.[115] As regional aid for the new Länder now claims priority, special aid for Berlin and the areas along the former intra-German border will be phased out by 1994. The extent to which the funds allocated for infrastructural investment are spent will depend largely on the local authorities.

The importance of this panoply of programs notwithstanding, the key actor in the economic transformation of east Germany is undoubtedly the Treuhandanstalt. Created under the Modrow government as a trust for the administration of public property, the "Treuhand" was given its current mandate by the Volkskammer in June 1990 under the Law for the Privatization and Reorganization of Nationally Owned Property, which has been amended and incorporated by Article 25 of the Unification Treaty. The agency's primary task is to restructure and privatize the former nationally owned enterprises, which have been reorganized under federal corporation law. Treuhand operates under the supervision of the Ministry of Finance and, on policy matters, under the Ministry of Economics. It started out with responsibility for more than 9,000 companies, 20,000 retail trade outlets, 7,500 hotels and restaurants, and several thousand pharmacies, libraries, and other enterprises that employed a total of 3 million workers. It owns 2.3 million hectares of farm land and 1.9 million hectares of woods, administers the property of the former Communist party, and provides municipalities with the nationally owned property they need for local projects.[116] Birgit Breuel, a former CDU finance minister from Lower Saxony, is Treuhand's chief executive, and the staff has grown to about 3,000. Most of the directors in the Berlin head office and the fifteen regional offices are west German managers.

Treuhand sees itself as a managerial technocracy that deals with companies and not as an agency in charge of industrial or structural policy. Given its strategic position and the range of its tasks, however, the decisions or non-decisions it makes inevitably produce political fallout. It is up to the agency to negotiate the terms under which companies are privatized, to determine which companies are viable candidates for restructuring, and to liquidate those companies that are determined to be unsalvageable. As an agency directing the transformation of the whole industrial sector, Treuhand is to some degree an inherently political institution. Not surprisingly, it is also the ideal scapegoat, drawing attacks from dissatisfied would-be investors, union leaders denouncing the "job-killers," politicians lamenting the lack of parliamentary control, and municipalities waiting for the assignment of property. And the agency tends to find itself saddled with an increasing number of new responsibilities.

According to the Treuhand philosophy, privatization is the best way to restructure a company. The agency's statistics on privatization as of the end of November 1991 show that almost 5,000 enterprises had been privatized and that their proceeds amounted to DM 16 billion. Investments pledged by the new owners totaled over DM 105 billion, and the number of jobs secured was 900,000.[117] In addition, 20,000 wholesale and retail trade firms as well as hotels and pharmacies had been sold. The Unification Treaty and the law establishing Treuhand specify how the proceeds from these privatizations should be used. However, these provisions were probably based on the assumption that proceeds from the sale of the companies to private investors would be high.[118] In fact, the proceeds cover only a fraction of Treuhand's expenditures. To enable the agency to service eastern Germany's corporate debt and to finance restructuring operations and other activities, such as social plans to protect employees in case of plant closures, Treuhand was authorized to borrow up to DM 25 billion in 1991 and DM 30 billion in 1992.[119] Moreover, by the end of 1991, Treuhand had granted DM 28 billion in liquidity credit guarantees and bridging finance to keep enterprises afloat after the introduction of economic and monetary union. Otherwise, there would be no shipyards nor chemical, steel, or textile companies in the new Länder today.[120] In addition, by the end of 1991, 800 firms with 150,000 employees had been closed. The approach to liquidation is deliberately cautious and Treuhand has negotiated an agreement with the largest German unions to provide severance pay out of its own funds for firms unable to finance a social plan that protects laid-off workers. In cases where plant closures result in mass layoffs, Treuhand, the Land in question, and the federal authorities are committed to labor market policy measures designed to limit the damage to the region. To coordinate the agency's activities with the economic and labor market policies of the eastern Länder, "Treuhand economic cabinets" have been established.[121]

As the Treuhand still owns thousands of companies—some of which are unlikely to find buyers in the near future—the unions, the SPD, and the governments of the eastern Länder (regardless of their political composition) continue to press for a more active role for the agency in the restructuring of companies. As the metalworkers' union has argued, the bride should be dressed up before being given in marriage. IG Metall Chairman Franz Steinkühler has called for an active industrial policy, the creation of an industrial holding company, company-controlled restructuring, and the creation of competitive locations, since such sites will not emerge as a result of market forces.[122] SPD Chairman Björn Engholm advocates maintaining viable core areas of industry, such as shipbuilding in Mecklenburg-Pomerania, brown coal mining and steelworking in Brandenburg, and the chemical industry in Saxony-Anhalt.[123] Although so far the proposals have not been very specific, they recall the less-than-successful Italian industrial policy of the seventies; their common denominator seems to be open-ended subsidizing of companies and even sectors with uncertain prospects.[124] It is also worth considering that a policy of interventionism aimed at the conservation of uncompetitive locations can hardly be maintained for long under the rules of the European single market, and any subsidization policy must be subject to thresholds and a phasing-out schedule. In the medium term, Treuhand's future is that of a giant holding company that must walk a tightrope between "socially compatible" modernization and the preservation of nonviable industrial structures.

Financing German Unity: Federalism under Stress

Compared with the task of restructuring and revitalizing the east German economy, the fiscal consequences of German unity are certainly less challenging. But they have become the main bone of contention in party politics and threaten to upset the institutional balance of German federalism. By and large, fiscal policy has been guided by a muddling-through approach along the lines of "a problem postponed is a problem half-solved." The preferred instrument of financing has been increased public sector borrowing rather than tax hikes and spending cuts, which have made only modest contributions to the unification budget. The financial burden of unification is not distributed equally among either social groups or between territorial authorities. In particular, the reaction of the western Länder to German unity is a study in financial self-preservation. But the financial constitution of the Federal Republic was not designed to cope with a fiscal shock of this magnitude.

The Basic Law provides for an elaborate system of intergovernmental financial relations "based on joint taxes and vertical and horizontal revenue sharing."[125] According to Article 106, "the Federation and the Länder shall share equally the revenues from income and corporation taxes." Their respective shares from the value-added sales tax (VAT) are "determined by federal legislation requiring the consent of the Bundesrat." Both sides "have an equal claim to coverage from current revenues of their respective necessary expenditures," but uniform living standards within the Federal Republic must be ensured. VAT revenues must be reapportioned whenever the ratio of federal revenues to expenditures becomes substantially different from that of the Länder. An outside observer might expect that unification would activate this mechanism, but, as will be discussed, the western Länder effectively blocked this possibility.

VAT revenue is distributed among the individual Länder on a per capita basis. Horizontal revenue-sharing is designed to "ensure a reasonable equalization between financially strong and financially weak Länder, due account being taken of the financial capacity and financial requirements of communes and associations of communes," according to Article 107. (Communes are administrative districts similar to American counties.) Under the system of fiscal equalization, the poorer western Länder receive transfers from the richer ones "so that no Land falls below 95 percent of the average per capita revenue of all eleven Länder."[126] Financially weak Länder can also obtain "complementary grants" from the federal government. Conflicts over the distribution of revenue have become an ongoing feature of German federalism and tend increasingly to involve the Constitutional Court.[127]

As soon as the State Treaty on MESU took shape, the west German Länder moved to protect their coffers. On May 16, 1990, the federal government and the Länder reached an agreement that excluded eastern Germany from the fiscal equalization mechanism. The inclusion of the future east German Länder in horizontal revenue-sharing would have drastically increased the volume of transfers from richer to poorer Länder, which in 1989 stood at DM 3.5 billion. According to various estimates, west-east transfers would have reached DM 20 billion to DM 30 billion and even the poorer western Länder (with the possible exception of Bremen) would have become payers instead of recipients. To cover eastern Germany's financing requirements, the German Unity Fund was set up and subsequently incorporated into the Unification Treaty. Between 1990 and 1994, the fund will provide a total of DM 115 billion to eastern Germany, with payments reaching DM 35 billion in 1991 and decreasing to DM 10 billion in 1994. The federal budget contributes DM 20 billion to the fund, and DM 95 billion is borrowed in the capital market. Debt servicing is shared equally by the federal government and the Länder, which pass on 40 percent of their share to their communes. At the same time, distribution of the VAT revenues to the federal government and the Länder (65 to 35 percent) will remain unchanged until 1992.[128]

When the Unification Treaty was negotiated, the western Länder insisted that their financial contributions to German unity should not exceed their obligations under the German Unity Fund.[129] The clause inserted in the treaty by the western Länder excludes the eastern Länder from horizontal fiscal equalization until the end of 1994 (Article 7 of the Unification Treaty). Thus the constitutional provision on the reapportioning of VAT shares does not apply to the eastern Länder until then. Moreover, it was agreed that, until 1994, the eastern Länder would receive only a graduated percentage of the average per capita VAT shares of the western Länder. The eastern Länder were allocated 85 percent of the German Unity Fund's budget, and the remaining 15 percent was reserved for federal government expenditures in the east.[130] Critics have argued that, with the transitional rules for public finance laid down in the Unification Treaty, the federation has placed itself in a financial bind.[131] Bonn's chief negotiator, however, has pointed out that alternative solutions would not have won a majority support in the Bundesrat. The large western Länder had taken out additional insurance against the possible risks of unification.[132] For Länder with more than 7 million inhabitants, the number of Bundesrat votes was raised from five to six, so that the four largest Länder continue to hold a blocking minority of twenty-four out of sixty-eight votes on constitutional amendments, which require a two-thirds majority in both chambers.

Although the unification process required three supplementary federal budgets in 1990, the Kohl government assumed that unity could be financed from the dividends of growth, savings on expenditures (such as subsidies to intra-German border regions) that had been related directly to the East-West split, and a limited temporary increase in public sector borrowing. The government's stubborn refusal to acknowledge that tax increases might be necessary was determined in part by wishful thinking and political expediency, but it was also an attempt to save the supply-side fiscal policy practiced since 1982. It was only in early 1991 that fiscal policy began to reflect the reality of the situation. To raise additional revenue, the following measures were taken: social security contributions were increased by 1.5 percent; a 7.5 percent surcharge on income and corporation tax liabilities was introduced for one year, from mid-1991 to mid-1992; and the mineral oil and the tobacco tax were raised substantially. Together with some other measures, this package was expected to increase revenue by DM 31 billion in 1991 and DM 40 billion in 1992.[133]

In order to relieve the financial plight of the eastern Länder, the federal government decided to transfer to them its 15 percent share of the German Unity Fund budget. In addition, it launched the "Upswing East" program, which provides DM 24 billion for the two-year period 1991-92. The western Länder, for their part, agreed to end discrimination against their eastern counterparts in the allocation of Länder VAT revenue. In September 1991, the federal government announced its intention (subject to Bundesrat approval) to transfer DM 2.45 billion in structural aids from the weaker western Länder (in fact all of them are defined as weak, with the exception of Baden-Württemberg and Hesse) in order to finance an increase in its contribution to the German Unity Fund of DM 5.9 billion a year between 1992 and 1994).[134]

As 1991 tax revenues in the eastern Länder reached only about 30 percent of western levels, only massive transfers of public funds from the west have enabled the eastern Länder and communes to afford per capita spending that approached western levels—91.5 percent in 1991—without incurring heavy debts. The transfers have also flowed into infrastructure projects, investment subsidies, labor market policy measures, and increases in old-age pensions (since January 1, 1992, a uniform pension system has existed in Germany). Other costs of unity include the credit-financed Treuhand activities, loans from the ERP Special Fund, and the Debt Processing Fund, which manages the debt of the east German state budget and offsets claims awarded to lending institutions with the introduction of monetary union.[135] In 1990, transfers from public budgets (including the special funds) to eastern Germany came to DM 48 billion. According to the Council of Experts, in 1991 total net public transfers (according to the definition of the term), amounted to DM 113 billion, or about 4 percent of Germany's GNP, and are expected to rise to DM 145 billion in 1992.[136] It is quite instructive to see how the different institutions shared the bill: the federal government made a net contribution of DM 47 billion to the 1991 transfers, the Länder provided DM 5 billion, the German Unity Fund DM 31 billion, the ERP Special Fund and the European Community DM 7 billion, and the federal labor office DM 23 billion.[137]

The costs of unity have driven up public sector borrowing, which in 1991 came to DM 135 billion. If borrowing by the two railway corporations is included (the western Bundesbahn and the eastern Reichsbahn), the federal post office, and Treuhand, the figure reaches DM 155 billion, or 5.5 percent of GNP. In 1992, the enlarged public sector is expected to borrow about DM 200 billion in the capital market.[138] Thus far, the capital market has been able to accommodate higher public sector borrowing without crowding out private investors.[139] But there can be no doubt that this relatively painless method of financing German unity simply extends the bill into the future, burdening public budgets with rising interest payments.

In terms of public finance, however, unification came at the best possible moment. Since entering office in 1982, the Kohl government had pursued a strategy of fiscal consolidation. The federal deficit had been reduced from 4.1 percent of the GNP in 1982 to 0.4 percent in 1989. Public expenditure as a share of the GNP declined from 52.1 percent in 1982 to 46.8 percent in 1989. It rose to 52 percent for Germany as a whole in 1991.[140] Given the extraordinary problems caused by German unity, there is no reason to dramatize these figures. After all, the federal government has taken corrective action, however limited, to deal with new fiscal realities. Moreover, financial planning in the medium term limits the growth of federal expenditure to an average of 2.3 percent a year by 1995 and envisions a reduction in net federal borrowing from DM 45 billion in 1992 to DM 25 billion in 1995.[141] A determined effort to bring federal deficits under control is all the more necessary, as a long list of budgetary risks can be anticipated but not quantified. These include the costs of compensating former owners of confiscated or nationalized property in the GDR, repairing the ecological damage left over from the years of socialism, moving the Parliament and government from Bonn to Berlin, and covering the export credit guarantees granted to the Soviet Union.

The policy of providing huge transfers of public funds to eastern Germany has been faulted for supporting consumption too generously, as only one-third of the money has been invested in infrastructure.[142] But, without this income support for the victims of the adjustment crisis, the transition to a market economy could produce social dynamite. In addition, public services must be adequately financed to prevent an aggravation of location disadvantages in the east from further polarizing east-west economic and social development. The costs of unity have also raised the issue of fairness in burden-sharing among social groups. In the west, this issue is highly divisive politically, as the tax cuts introduced between 1986 and 1990 have favored higher income groups, while the measures taken to finance the costs of unity have fallen more heavily on lower income groups.[143] Calls for wage discipline are therefore likely to remain unheeded unless fair burden-sharing takes precedence over the clientela politics of the governing coalition. The resistance offered by the western Länder to more equitable burden-sharing among levels of government is only the most conspicuous example of how the anxiety of key institutional actors to maintain the status quo works against effective national solidarity.

The reordering of fiscal priorities as well as the reform of revenue-sharing will be a difficult process, because the fiscal immobility that characterizes relations between the federal government and the Länder will be reinforced by the logic of party competition as long as the SPD-controlled Bundesrat majority challenges the conservative-liberal government coalition.[144] Nevertheless, by 1995 Germany will need to generate a new federal financial constitution. Some experts have suggested that the time has come to strengthen the legislative powers of the Länder and to grant them more fiscal autonomy.[145] As "the Europe of the regions" approaches, they argue, the diversity of living conditions in the united Germany should be interpreted as a national virtue rather than as a shortcoming that must be remedied.[146] These ideas have served the vested interests of the west German Länder well. However, if the federal government remains the primary source of funds for the eastern Länder, unity will become a potent force behind centralization.[147] The Constitutional Court will also most likely be called on to ensure that the principle of the "uniformity of living conditions" is not seriously weakened.

Conclusion

The economic and political unification of Germany was driven by popular revolt against an oppressive regime and a decaying economic system. The political dynamics of the East German upheaval offered the West German government a strategic opportunity to channel the East Germans' urge for economic prosperity into the institutional framework of economic and monetary union as the first stage to national unity. East Germany has thus become a laboratory where the "social market economy" will have to prove its dynamism as well as its capacity for economic and social integration. The structural dualism resulting from different political strategies for economic development has made for a painful transition to a market economy in eastern Germany. The dimensions of the adjustment crisis indicate that economic and social integration will probably require between one and two decades, if not a generation. For an extended transitional period, eastern Germany will therefore remain an economic region supported by massive transfers of government funds, where labor market developments are determined largely by political decisions. This may violate the precepts of liberal economic doctrine, but political integration and the legitimacy of the new order will be in part a function of the standardizing of living conditions between the two parts of the country.

Within a few years, however, it may no longer be useful to treat eastern

Germany as a separate economic unit. A differentiation of economic development may by then have resulted in the emergence of a diversified modern industrial structure in some regions of Saxony and Thuringia, whereas Mecklenburg-Pomerania will be lucky if it manages to catch up with the Schleswig region. Berlin will develop a "headquarters" economy, thriving not only on infusions of public money, but also on the private capital that will be attracted by the city's new prestige. This process, in turn, will bolster the economy of Brandenburg. As the economic transformation and the breakup of an egalitarian society produce winners and losers, the social divisions that develop could undermine the sense of identity that was rooted in the experience of socialism.

Political and social integration in general are being facilitated by the institutional framework of the German polity. The party system has taken the lead in the process of political integration, although the parties have not yet mobilized sufficient political support for the redistribution effort required by economic and social integration. Neither have the western Länder risen to the challenge posed by German unity. Nevertheless, the federalist system provides criteria for redistribution which, if necessary, will be strengthened and enforced by the Constitutional Court. Federalism is already proving to be a good recipe for mobilizing regional energies in eastern Germany. As far as public finance is concerned, there is no doubt that Germany can "afford" unity. The open question is whether the strength of vested interests and the increase in conflict over burden-sharing between social groups will allow for the implementation of economic policies that promote growth without compromising internal and external monetary stability.

In fact, German policymakers face a whole range of difficult choices linked to the process of integration. Should the lengthy procedures of the Rechtsstaat, for instance, be allowed to slow down the rapid modernization of the transportation infrastructure? Do the interests of property owners deserve more protection than the jobs of industrial wage earners? To what extent should economic efficiency be sacrificed to social pacification? How much income redistribution from western Germany to eastern Germany is compatible with election politics? These questions highlight only some of the domestic issues that have emerged since unity. No doubt, for all its new weight, Germany has become a more ordinary European country where miracles are not just around the corner.

Notes

1. See Hans-Joachim Maaz, "Psychosoziale Aspekte im deutschen Einigungsprozeß," *Aus Politik und Zeitgeschichte*, B 19/91, May 3, 1991, pp. 3–10, especially p. 5. Walter Friedrich and George Turner, "Lädiertes Selbstwertgefühl der Ostdeutschen wieder aufbauen," *Handelsblatt*, August 2-3, 1991, p. 1.

2. "'Wessis' meinen, daß sie genug für den Osten täten. Umfrage im Auftrag des Bundesarbeitgeberverbandes Chemie zur Stimmungslage in Ost und West," *Handelsblatt*, June 7–8, 1991, p. 4.

3. *Rechtsstaat* can be defined as a constitutional state.

4. Gerhard Lehmbruch, "Democracy and Economic Performance: Prospects for a United Germany," paper prepared for the IPSA Round Table, Seoul, May 22–24, 1990, p. 3. Lehmbruch, "Die improvisierte Vereinigung: Die Dritte deutsche Republik," *Leviathan*, vol. 18 (December 1990), pp. 462–86.

5. For an excellent account see Elizabeth Pond, "A Wall Destroyed: The Dynamics of German Unification in the GDR," *International Security*, vol. 15 (Fall 1990), pp. 35–66.

6. The government included representatives of the bloc parties Christian Democrats (CDU), National Democrats (NDPD), Liberal Democrats (LDPD), Democratic Peasants' Party (DBD), but all the important ministries were controlled by the SED. CDU and LDPD left the Democratic bloc on December 4, 1989. See Gert-Joachim Glaessner, *Der Schwierige Weg zur Demokratie* (Opladen: Westdeutscher Verlag, 1991), pp. 103–35.

7. Uwe Thaysen, *Der Runde Tisch. Oder: Wo blieb das Volk?* (Opladen: Westdeutscher Verlag, 1990).

8. See Thaysen, *Der Runde Tisch*, p. 83.

9. Pond, "A Wall Destroyed," p. 65.

10. Wolfgang Schäuble, *Der Vertrag. Wie ich über die deutsche Einheit verhandelte* (Stuttgart: Deutsche Verlagsanstalt, 1991), pp. 23–24.

11. Bund Freier Demokraten.

12. Alliance for Germany: 48 percent; Alliance of Free Democrats: 5.3 percent; SPD: 22 percent; PDS: 16.4 percent; Bündnis 90: 2.9 percent. See Dieter Roth, "Die Wahlen zur Volkskammer in der DDR. Der Versuch einer Erklärung," *Politische Vierteljahresschrift*, vol. 31 (September 1990), p. 372, table 1.

13. Thaysen, *Der Runde Tisch*, p. 148, pp. 195–96.

14. Jürgen Habermas, *Die nachholende Revolution* (Frankfurt/M.: Suhrkamp, 1990), p. 211.

15. See the account by Schäuble, *Vertrag*, pp. 101–22, pp. 209–28.

16. Christine Landfried, "Das Wahlrechtsurteil vom 29. September 1990 zur 5%-Klausel für die ersten gesamtdeutschen Wahlen," *Gegenwartskunde*, no. 4 (1990), pp. 461–70.

17. Helmut Kohl, "Gemeinschaftswerk Aufschwung-Ost," *Bulletin*, no. 25, March 12, 1991, p. 177.

18. The treaties are published in a paperback edition, *Die Verträge zur Einheit Deutschlands*, Beck Texte (Munich: Beck, dtv, 1990); and Leslie Lipschitz and Donogh McDonald, eds., *German Unification: Economic Issues* (Washington: International Monetary Fund, 1990), p. 9.

19. *Report of the Deutsche Bundesbank for the Year 1990* (Frankfurt/M., 1991), p. 1.

20. Art. 1, par. 3, of the State Treaty, in *Die Verträge zur Einheit Deutschlands*, p. 2.

21. See Art. 28, State Treaty, in *Die Verträge Zur Einheit Deutschlands*, p. 14.

22. Published in *Die Verträge zur Einheit Deutschlands*, pp. 43–585.

23. Article 23 was repealed within the Unification Treaty, which was ratified on August 31, 1990.

24. See, for example, Habermas, *Die nachholende Revolution*, pp. 216–17, and

the discussion "Verfassungsrechtliche Wege zur deutschen Einheit," *Zeitschrift für Parlamentsfragen*, vol. 21 (July 1990), pp. 333–54.

25. Annex I to Unification Treaty, in *Die Verträge zur Einheit Deutschlands*, pp. 81–483.

26. Annex II to Unification Treaty, in *Die Verträge zur Einheit Deutschlands*, pp. 485–565.

27. *Die Verträge zur Einheit Deutschlands*, pp. 567–85. See also Schäuble, *Vertrag*, pp. 250–64.

28. Decision of April 23, 1991, see *Entscheidungen des Bundesverfassungsgerichts*, vol. 84 (Tübingen 1992), p. 90.

29. Gesetz über besondere Investitionen in der Deutschen Demokratischen Republik, Par. 1 and 2, *Bundesgesetzblatt 1990/II*, pp. 1157–58.

30. Gesetz zur Regelung offener Vermögensfragen, §§ 4, 5, published in *Die Verträge zur Einheit Deutschlands*, pp. 575–76.

31. Wolfgang G. Gibowski and Max Kaase, "Auf dem Weg zum politischen Alltag. Eine Analyse der ersten gesamtdeutschen Bundestagswahl vom 2. Dezember 1990," *Aus Politik und Zeitgeschichte*, B 11-12/91, March 8, 1991, p. 3.

32. Jürgen W. Falter and Siegfried Schumann, "Konsequenzen einer bundesweiten Kandidatur der CSU bei Wahlen. Eine in die unmittelbare Vergangenheit gerichtete Prognose," *Aus Politik und Zeitgeschichte*, B 11-12/91, March 8, 1991, p. 44.

33. Ursula Feist, "Zur politischen Akkulturation der vereinigten Deutschen. Eine Analyse aus Anlaß der ersten gesamtdeutschen Bundestagswahl," *Aus Politik und Zeitgeschichte*, B 11-12/91, March 8, 1991, pp. 22–23.

34. Roth, "Die Wahlen zur Volkskammer in der DDR," pp. 388–91.

35. Max Kaase and Wolfgang G. Gibowski, "Deutschland im Übergang: Parteien und Wähler vor der Bundestagswahl 1990," *Aus Politik und Zeitgeschichte*, B 37-38/90, September 14, 1990, p. 24.

36. Gibowski and Kaase, "Auf dem Weg," p. 6. In Saxony, the CDU obtained 49.5 percent in the Bundestag election, and the SPD got 18.2 percent. In Thuringia the figures were 45.2 percent and 21.9 percent, respectively.

37. In the Bundestag election, the PDS obtained 24.8 percent in East Berlin against 9 percent in Saxony and 8.3 percent in Thuringia. Gibowski and Kaase, "Auf dem Weg," p. 6. See also Kaase and Gibowski, "Deutschland im Übergang," pp. 24–25.

38. Kaase and Gibowski, "Deutschland im Übergang," p. 25.

39. Data communicated by telephone from SPD headquarters, December 3, 1991.

40. Gerhard Lehmbruch, "Institutionentransfer im Prozeß der Vereinigung: Zur politischen Logik der Verwaltungsintegration in Deutschland," Wolfgang Seibel and others, eds., *Verwaltungsreform und Verwaltungspolitik im Prozeß der deutschen Einigung* (Baden-Baden: Nomos, forthcoming).

41. "Rühe: Wechsel in der Ost-CDU," *Der Spiegel*, no. 34 (August 19, 1991), p. 16.

42. Hans Jörg Sottorf, "Standortbestimmung. Ost-Mitglieder verändern Profil der FDP," *Handelsblatt*, August 15, 1991, p. 2.

43. According to Hans-Ulrich Derlien, "Integration der Staatsfunktionäre der DDR in das Berufsbeamtentum: Professionalismus und Säuberung," Seibel and others, eds., *Verwaltungsreform*, p. 10. Out of a total of forty-seven East German state ministers (minister-presidents not counted) fifteen came from West Germany.

44. Wolfgang Seibel, "Zur Situation der öffentlichen Verwaltung in den neuen

Bundesländern," Beitrag zur kommunalpolitischen Konferenz der Gewerkschaft Öffentliche Dienste, Transport und Verkehr am 6./7. Juni 1991 in Berlin, p. 9.

45. Schäuble, *Vertrag*, p. 258.

46. Seibel, "Zur Situation," p. 3.

47. Derlien, "Integration der Staatsfunktionäre," p. 4.

48. Heinz Boschek, "Personalhilfe aus dem Westen verhinderte einen gravierenden Rechtspflegenotstand. Überprüfung von Richtern und Staatsanwälten in den neuen Bundesländern läuft schleppend—Vertrauenskrise," *Handelsblatt*, August 16–17, 1991, p. 5.

49. "Kräftiger Aufschwung in der zweiten Jahreshälfte Schäuble zieht Zwischenbilanz," *Handelsblatt*, August 14, 1991, p. 1.

50. Lutz Hoffmann, "Preise, Politik und Prioritäten," *Frankfurter Allgemeine Zeitung*, February 2, 1991, p. 13; Lehmbruch, "Institutionentranfer," p. 15; and Hans-Hermann Hartwich, "Der Weg in die deutsche Währungsunion 1990 - Eine zeitgeschichtliche Skizze über die Beziehungen zwischen Bundesregierung und Bundesbank," *Gegenwartskunde*, no. 2 (1991), pp. 157–70.

51. Hoffmann, "Preise, Politik und Prioritäten."

52. Schäuble, *Vertrag*, pp. 21–22.

53. *Wirtschaftspolitische Herausforderungen der Bundesrepublik Deutschland im Verhältnis zur DDR*, Gutachten des Wissenschaftlichen Beirats beim Bundesministerium für Wirtschaft, (Bonn: Bundesministerium für Wirtschaft, 1989), pp. 9–11.

54. See *Jahresgutachten des Sachverständigenrates 1990/1991 zur Begutachtung der gesamtwirtschaftlichen Entwicklung*, Deutscher Bundestag. Drucksache 11/8472, pp. 276–305. The Council of Experts is an independent body. It is not attached to any ministry or department.

55. See "Die Ostdeutschen Bürger Wollten die D-Mark Sofort," *Frankfurter Allgemeine Zeitung*, June 29, 1991, p. 4.

56. See *Sachverständigenrat 1990/1991*, pp. 306–08.

57. *Sachverständigenrat 1990/1991*, p. 172.

58. Lutz Hoffmann, "Wider die ökonomische Vernunft. Eine rasche wirtschaftliche Vereinigung mit der Bundesrepublik erschwert den Aufholprozeß der DDR," *Frankfurter Allgemeine Zeitung*, February 10, 1990, p. 15.

59. "Krupp: Ohne eine rasche Währungsunion wird es für beide Seiten sehr schwierig. Gespräch mit dem Hamburger Finanzsenator - Keine Leistungsbilanzprobleme," *Handelsblatt*, February 9–10, 1990, p. 12.

60. Hans Willgerodt, *Vorteile der wirtschaftlichen Einheit Deutschlands* (Cologne: Institut für Wirtschaftspolitik, 1990), p. 8.

61. Institut der deutschen Wirtschaft (Gerhard Fels and others), *Sozialverträgliche Ausgestaltung der deutsch-deutschen Währungsunion* (Cologne: Deutscher Instituts-Verlag, 1990).

62. Horst Siebert, "Die Politik muß auf den Markt setzen - Wer ist der Ludwig Erhard der 90er Jahre?" *Handelsblatt*, June 13, 1990, p. 7.

63. Institut der deutschen Wirtschaft, *Ausgestaltung*, p. 48.

64. Helmut Hesse, "Bundesbank wurde auf ihrem ureigensten Gebiet die Führungsrolle genommen. Nicht nur im Ausland Zweifel an Autonomie der Währungshüter—Mit 1:1 sind Inflationsgefahren in dreifacher Weise verbunden," *Handelsblatt*, May 28, 1990, p. 11.

65. Hartwich, "Der Weg," p. 167.

66. For a more detailed description of the mechanics of the conversion, see Garry J. Schinasi and others, "Monetary and Financial Issues in German Unification," in Lipschitz and McDonald, eds., *German Unification*, pp. 144–54; and *OECD Economic*

Surveys, Germany 1990/1991 (Paris: Organization for Economic Cooperation and Development, 1991), pp. 53–60.

67. Norbert Kloten, "Die deutsch-deutsche Wirtschafts- und Währungsunion," *Der Bürger im Staat*, vol. 40 (June 1990), p. 91.

68. For a more thorough treatment of the issue, see Hans Willgerodt, "Gegen eine Dolchstoßlegende," *Frankfurter Allgemeine Zeitung*, April 13, 1991, p. 13; and Erhard Kantzenbach, "Ökonomische Probleme der deutschen Vereinigung. Anmerkungen zur jüngsten Wirtschaftsgeschichte," in *Hamburger Jahrbuch für Wirtschafts- und Gesellschaftspolitik*, vol. 35 (1990), pp. 307–28.

69. Donogh McDonald and Günther Thuman, "East Germany: The New *Wirtschaftswunder*," in Lipschitz and McDonald, *German Unification*, p. 78.

70. *Geschäftsbericht der Deutschen Bundesbank für das Jahr 1989* (Frankfurt/M.: 1990), p. 10; and Holger Schmieding, "Währungsunion und Wettbewerbsfähigkeit der DDR-Industrie," *Kieler Arbeitspapier*, no. 413 (Kiel: Institut für Weltwirtschaft: 1990), p. 9.

71. *Geschäftsbericht 1989*, p. 10; and "Die Lage der DDR-Wirtschaft zur Jahreswende 1989/90," *DIW-Wochenbericht*, 6/90, February 8, 1990, p. 72.

72. "Gesamtwirtschaftliche und unternehmerische Anpassungsprozesse in Ostdeutschland," *DIW-Wochenbericht*, 12/91, March 21, 1991, p. 126.

73. George A. Akerlof and others, "East Germany in from the Cold: The Economic Aftermath of Currency Union," *Brookings Papers on Economic Activity*, 1: 1991, p. 5; "Economic Trends in 1991/92—Western Industrialised Countries: The Business Cycle Bottoms Out," *Economic Bulletin*, vol. 28 (September 1991), p. 6.

74. "One Year of German Monetary, Economic, and Social Union," *Monthly Report of the Deutsche Bundesbank*, vol. 43 (July 1991), p. 22.

75. Akerlof and others, "East Germany," p. 13.

76. *Jahresgutachten des Sachverständigenrates 1991/92 zur Begugutachtung der gesamtwirtschaft-lichen Entwicklung* Deutscher Bundestag, Drucksache 12/1618, p. 396, tables 84*, 85*.

77. See *Sachverständigenrat 1990/91*, pp. 65–66.

78. "Export Schwächerer Motor für Kunjunktur als erhofft," *Handelsblatt*, December 20/21, 1991, p. 5.

79. "Micro and Macroeconomic Adjustment Processes in East Germany," *Economic Bulletin*, vol. 28 (August 1991), p. 6.

80. "Die Westdeutsche Wirtschaft unter dem Einfluß der Ökonomischen Vereinigung Deutschlands," *Monatsberichte der Deutschen Bundesbank*, vol. 43 (October 1991), p. 19.

81. "One Year of German Monetary, Economic, and Social Union," p. 18. For the "unification dividend" see "Vereinigung wirkt positiv auf Weltwirtschaft. Ergbnisse einer ökonometrischen Simulationsstudie," *DIW-Wochenbericht*, 32/91, August 8, 1991, p. 451. Total growth of GNP was 4 percent between July 1990 and June 1991.

82. "Gesamtwirtschaftliche und unternehmerische Anpassungsprozesse in Ostdeutschland," *DIW-Wochenbericht*, 12-13/92, March 19, 1992, p. 133.

83. "One Year of German Monetary, Economic, and Social Union," p. 26.

84. "Micro and Macroeconomic Adjustment," p. 8.

85. "Gesamtwirtschaftliche und unternehmerische Anpassungsprozesse in Ostdeutschland," *DIW-Wochenbericht*, 51-52/91 (December 19, 1991), pp. 712–37, esp. pp. 712, 719–31.

86. *Sachverständigenrat 1991/92*, p. 160, table 44.

87. "Konjunkturlage," *Monatsberichte der Deutschen Bundesbank*, vol. 43 (December 1991), p. 37.

88. *Geschäftsbericht der Deutschen Bundesbank für das Jahr 1989*, p. 10; and "Erwerbstätigkeit und Einkommen von Frauen in der DDR," *DIW-Wochenbericht*, 19/90, May 10, 1990, p. 265. Some sources provide the figure of 9.8 million for total employment in 1989 (for example, *Sachverständigenrat 1991/92*, p. 95).

89. "Vereintes Deutschland—geteilte Frauengesellschaft?" *DIW-Wochenbericht*, 41/90, October 11, 1990, pp. 575–76.

90. *Sachverständigenrat 1991/92*, p. 107, table 30.

91. "Konjunkfurlage," *Monatsberichte der Deutschen Bundesbank*, vol. 44 (June 1992), p. 36.

92. *Sachverständigenrat 1991/92*, p. 96, table 24.

93. *Sachverständigenrat 1991/92*, p. 163, table 45.

94. See Eckhardt Bode and Christiane Krieger-Boden, "Sektorale Strukturprobleme und regionale Anpassungserfordernisse der Wirtschaft in den neuen Bundesländern," *Die Weltwirtschaft*, no. 2 (1990), pp. 91–93.

95. "Economic Trends in 1991/92," p. 11.

96. "Öffnungsklauseln in Tarifverträgen und Differenzierung der Gehälter verlangt. Beirat des Wirtschaftsministers Kritisiert Lohnpolitik der Sozialpartner," *Handelsblatt*, August 9–10, 1991, pp. 1, 5.

97. Franz Steinkühler, "Die Tarifpolitik ist nicht die Ursache der Krise. Der 1. Vorsitzende der IG Metall zur gewerkschaftlichen Lohnpolitik in den neuen Bundesländern," *Handelsblatt*, July 22, 1991, p. 4. On the migration argument see Akerlof and others, "East Germany," p. 46.

98. "WSI: Lohnniveau in neuen Ländern wird überschätzt. Sachsens Metaller verdienen effektiv nur 40% der Gehälter ihrer bayrischen Kollegen," *Handelsblatt*, July 29, 1991, p. 3.

99. WSI-Arbeitsgruppe, "Zur wirtschaftlichen und sozialen Entwicklung in den ostdeutschen Ländern," *WSI-Mitteilungen*, vol. 44 (May 1991), p. 282.

100. Akerlof and others, "East Germany," p. 61.

101. On the organization of the DGB in the new Länder, see Peter Seideneck, "Die soziale Einheit gestalten. Über die Schwierigkeiten des Aufbaus gesamtdeutscher Gewerkschaften," *Aus Politik und Zeitgeschichte*, B 13/91, March 22, 1991, pp. 3–11. In October 1991, DGB membership in East Germany came to 4.4 million. "DGB hat 4,4 Millionen Mitglieder im Osten," *Handelsblatt*, October 18/19, 1991, p. 8.

102. WSI-Arbeitsgruppe, "Zur wirtschaftlichen und sozialen Entwicklung," p. 282.

103. Akerlof and others, "East Germany," p. 82.

104. See, for example, Erhard Kantzenbach, "Lohnsubventionen für Arbeitsplätze," *Wirtschaftsdienst*, 7/1991, pp. 326–27; Horst Siebert, "Brauchbares Konzept der Qualifizierungsgutscheine," *Handelsblatt*, June 3, 1991, p. 8; "Allgemeine Lohnsubventionen—Kein Ausweg aus der Beschäftigungskrise in Ostdeutschland," *DIW-Wochenbericht*, 36/91 (September 5, 1991), pp. 511–13; and *Sachverständigenrat 1991/92*, pp. 242–43.

105. "Anpassungsprozesse," p. 161.

106. "Die Treuhandanstalt hat keinen Auftrag für eine Industrie-und Strukturpolitik," *Handelsblatt*, July 19–20, 1991, p. 5; "Die IG Metall hat mit Bedenken Zugestimmt," *Handelsblatt*, July 18, 1991, p. 1; and Elmar Pieroth, "Vorrang für die Infrastruktur," *Frankfurter Allgemeine Zeitung*, May 25, 1991, p. 13.

107. See Lipschitz and McDonald, *German Unification*, p. 15. They define *Ordnungspolitik* as "a clear institutional framework within which the free play of market forces guides the economy."

108. Pieroth, "Vorrang," p. 13.

109. "Anpassungsprozesse," p. 139.

110. "Promoting Economic Activity in the new Länder," *Monthly Report of the Deutsche Bundesbank*, vol. 43 (March 1991), pp. 15–26; "Micro and Macroeconomic Adjustment," pp. 16–18; *Handelsblatt Supplement*, "Investieren in den neuen Bundesländern," July 5–6, 1991; and "Sonderregelungen für alle Bundesbeschaffungen Erlaß aus dem Bundeswirtshafts-ministerium zur Bevorzugung von Ost-Unternehmen," *Handelsblatt*, August 13, 1991, p. 1.

111. "EG hilft beim Aufbau der Marktwirtschaft in den neuen Ländern," *EG-Information Extra*, no. 4 (1991), pp. 4–7.

112. "Micro and Macroeconomic Adjustment," p. 17.

113. *Handelsblatt Supplement*, July 5–6, 1991, p. 14.

114. "Micro and Macroeconomic Adjustment," p. 17.

115. Klaus Kinkel, "Das Hemmnisbeseitigungsgesetz ebnet den Weg für Investitionen. Die Eigentums- und Vermögensregelung zwischen Rückgabeanspruch und Investitionsbedarf - Elf Gesetze geändert, ein neues eingeführt," *Handelsblatt Supplement*, July 5–6, 1991, p. 7.

116. Birgit Breuel, "Der Auftrag der Treuhandanstalt," *Wirtschaftsdienst*, vol. 71 (April 1991), pp. 163–65.

117. Birgit Breuel, "Die Treuhand will Dienstleister, aber nicht allen zu Diensten sein. Investoren haben die Erhaltung von 800,000 Arbeitsplätzen zugesagt," *Handelsblatt*, December 13/14, 1991, p. 7. Deutsche Bank, *Deutschland-Thema*, no. 68 (December 19, 1991). The number of Treuhand companies increased as large enterprises were divided into smaller units.

118. *Sachverständigenrat 1990/91*, pp. 230–31.

119. Treuhandanstalt, *Auftrag, Zwischenbilanz, Grundsätze*, (Berlin: June 1991), p. 11; David Goodhard, "So Much to Do, So Little Time," *Financial Times*, April 9, 1991, p. 23; "Erschreckend niedrig. Die Treuhand schafft ihr Plansoll nicht. Die tatsächlichen Zahlen werden unter Verschluße gehalten," *Der Spiegel*, no. 34 (August 19, 1991), pp. 102–03. "Obergrenze für Kredite. Kabinett stimmt Gesetzentwurf zu," *Handelsblatt*, December 12, 1991, p. 9.

120. Treuhandanstalt, *Auftrag*, p. 11. Out of the DM 28 billion allocated, 24 billion had been used by enterprises. Communication by Treuhandanstalt, January 7, 1992.

121. Treuhandanstalt, *Auftrag*, pp. 18–19. For a critical assessment of Treuhand activities see Jan Priewe and Rudolf Hickel, *Der Preis der Einheit* (Frankfurt/Main: Fischer, 1991), chap. 6.

122. " 'Ohne eine vernünftige Industriepolitik wird Ostdeutschland zur Wüste werden' " *Handelsblatt*, July 9, 1991, p. 4.

123. "Aktive Industriepolitik in den neuen Ländern gefordert," *Handelsblatt*, July 31, 1991, p. 4; Harry Maier, "Integrieren statt zerstören. Für eine gemischtwirtschaftliche Strategie in den neuen Bundesländern," *Aus Politik und Zeitgeschichte*, B 29/91, July 12, 1991, pp. 3–12. On the debate in general, see Roland Sturm, *Die Industriepolitik der Bundesländer und die europäische Integration* (Baden-Baden: Nomos Verlag, 1991), pp. 102–17.

124. For a thorough discussion of future Treuhand strategy, see *Sachverständigenrat 1991/92*, pp. 226–32.

125. Arthur B. Gunlicks, "Introduction," *Publius*, vol. 19 (Fall 1989), p. 8.

126. Gunlicks, "Introduction," p. 8.

127. See Rüdiger Voigt, "Financing the German Federal System in the 1980s," *Publius*, vol. 19 (Fall 1989), pp. 109–12.

128. Peter Gottfried and Wolfgang Wiegand, "Finanzausgleich nach der Vereini-

gung: Gewinner sind die alten Länder," *Wirtschaftsdienst*, vol. 71 (September 1991), p. 460. See also *Sachverständigenrat 1990–1991*, p. 210.

129. Schäuble, *Der Vertrag*, pp. 177–84.

130. See Article 7, Unification Treaty, in *Die Verträge zur Einheit Deutschlands*, pp. 46–47.

131. See, for example, Rolf Peffekoven, "Deutsche Einheit und Finanzausgleich," *Staatswissenschaften und Staatspraxis*, no. 4 (1990), p. 490.

132. Schäuble, *Der Vertrag*, p. 184.

133. See *OECD Economic Surveys*, Germany (Paris: Organization for Economic Cooperation and Development, 1991), pp. 65–67.

134. *Sachverständigenrat 1991/92*, pp. 146–50; Ullrich Heilemann, "Christmas in July? The Economics of German Unification Reconsidered," *RWI-Papiere*, no. 27 (November 1991), pp. 39–41.

135. *Sachverständigenrat 1991/92*, pp. 131–36.

136. *Sachverständigenrat 1991/92*, pp. 135–36, 185. Net transfers in a narrow sense are defined as gross transfers (from territorial authorities, German Unity Fund, ERPEC, Federal Labour Office) minus tax revenues raised in eastern Germany, minus tax revenue due to higher growth in the west, reduction of division-related expenditure, and so on.

137. *Sachverständigenrat 1991/92*, pp. 135–36.

138. *Sachverständigenrat 1991/92*, pp. 138, 165.

139. "Die öffentlichen Haushalte in Deutschland 1991/92: Anhaltend hohe Finanzierungsdefizite trotz Steuererhöhungen," *DIW-Wochenbericht* 38/91, September 19, 1991, p. 547; and Heilemann, "Christmas in July?" p. 16.

140. "One Year of German Monetary, Economic, and Social Union," p. 29.

141. *Sachverständigenrat 1991/92*, p. 149.

142. *Sachverständigenrat 1991/92*, p. 185.

143. "Steuerentlastung 1986/90 und Steuerbelastung 1991: Umverteilung der Einkommen von unten nach oben," *DIW-Wochenbericht*, 14/91, April 4, 1991, p. 180.

144. Gerhard Lehmbruch, "Die deutsche Vereinigung. Strukturen und Strategien, *Politische Vierteljahresschrift*, vol. 32 (December 1991), p. 599.

145. See, for example, Peffekoven, "Deutsche Einheit und Finanzausgleich," p. 503.

146. Joachim Jens Hesse and Wolfgang Renzsch, "Zehn Thesen zur Entwicklung und Lage des deutschen Föderalismus," *Staatswissenschaften und Staatspraxis*, no. 4 (1990), p. 567.

147. Fritz W. Scharpf, "Föderalismus an der Wegscheide: eine Replik," *Staatswissenschaften und Staatspraxis*, no. 4 (1990), pp. 582–83.

FOUR

The Security Policy of the New Germany

Hilmar Linnenkamp

FROM 1949 TO 1989, the security of a divided Germany was in the hands of the World War II victors. Nowhere else in the world were so many foreign troops stationed, so many foreign nuclear weapons stored, and so many war plans developed and exercised, decade after decade. The two Germanies—children of the East-West confrontation—understood themselves to be role models for their respective worlds. Implicitly alluding to the fact that West Germany had become a sovereign state by joining NATO in 1955, Chancellor Helmut Kohl went so far as to call integration with the West one of the reasons for the statehood of the Federal Republic of Germany.[1]

For more than twenty years, the German nation remained a silent entity behind the screens of the two governments. It was only in the early 1970s that East German party chief Erich Honecker undertook to strike a final blow to that notion by declaring that a separate "socialist nation" existed on the territory of the then German Democratic Republic. This rhetorical construct proved to be an empty shell when, in 1989, the East Germans took to the streets, shouting "We are the people." As the German people began to make decisions for themselves, they rushed to economic and national unity in months, not the years or decades that many had expected.[2] But unity required the consent of Germany's allies and neighbors. To their lasting credit, the Four Powers complemented the benign attitude of Germany's neighbors to the west and the east, especially Poland, by engaging in the Two plus Four talks and allowed the united Germany to be integrated into the new European order of peace and security.

This marriage of national will and international accommodation makes German unity the symbol of a new era. European security in this era no longer rests precariously on the military preparedness of two opposing blocs, but rather on the more stable conditions of mutually beneficial interdependence among nation-states that need no external enemies in order to define and defend their identity.

Encircled by Friends, Deprived of Enemies

How can the new Germany, under such circumstances, redefine its security? History sometimes offers ironic answers. The once-threatening Soviet forces close to the old West German border—Chancellor Helmut Schmidt used to impress American audiences by mentioning that Soviet tanks were deployed a mere thirty miles from his home in Hamburg—have now become a fact of everyday life on German territory. Military forces in Europe are currently crossing international—mainly German—borders, but only to be redeployed at home or dismantled. As they withdraw, they serve an extremely important political function, confirming that war must not be fought in Europe and that peace must be based on negotiated and verified reductions of national military arsenals. It is no coincidence that Germany, the most prominent symbol of change in European security relations, has agreed in the Two plus Four Treaty to reduce the military component of its national security structure to a greater extent than any other NATO member.

Europe's military forces serve other functions as well. As traditional power structures disintegrate and ideology falters, national idiosyncracies have re-emerged, and secession—or at least disintegration—looms. The former Soviet Union and Yugoslavia are cases in point. The central authorities see the armed forces as the guarantors of state unity, despite the disciplinary problems that develop among conscripts of different and often antagonistic nationalities. The armed forces, however, face psychological and organizational challenges in moving away from their traditional role of securing borders against foreign aggression and engaging instead in domestic security. This phenomenon is not completely unknown in Western Europe—although their situations differ, the United Kingdom and Turkey are relevant examples. In Germany, however, there are no domestic security tasks for the military. Germany's security requirements will always derive from what it is obliged and willing to contribute to the efforts of NATO and other international security institutions. Integration was not merely the starting point for German sovereignty in 1955; it will very likely remain the cornerstone of German security policy in the decades to come.

What the new Germany's security policy will be depends largely on the answers to two questions: what is the German vision of Europe, and what role will Germany play in that future Europe? While it is easy to recall Thomas Mann's famous dictum that Germany should strive for a European Germany rather than a German Europe, it is not nearly as easy to define a "European Germany." Many commentators are suspicious of the political consequences of such a formula, which appears to diminish the newly achieved national grandeur of the economic giant and allow it to hide comfortably behind multinational decisionmaking structures in the European Community or the Conference for Security and Cooperation in Europe (CSCE).[3] Others know well that history did the Germans a favor in 1989–90 that must be answered by firmly integrating Germany's huge economic might, growing political importance, and residual military powers into European structures. In doing so, Germany will rid itself of a depressing historical burden: its neighbors' collective memories of a powerful Germany in the heart of Europe striving for predominance and going its own way instead of cooperatively mastering a common future.

German Defense since Unification

Since their founding in the early 1950s, the Bundeswehr and German defense policy have not experienced changes as dramatic as those that have occurred since October and November of 1990. German unification brought with it an entirely new framework for the German armed forces, within which their functions and purpose will be determined.

Uniting and Streamlining German Forces

The driving factor behind the recent change has been the decline of the East-West conflict. The liberation of the peoples of Central and Eastern Europe from communist rule and Soviet domination did not immediately affect Germany, especially the GDR. Having served as the most strategically important front-line state in the Soviet Union's hegemonic structure, the GDR was the last to fall, but its revolution was the shortest and most spectacular. The extremity of its position also made the GDR's departure from the past total, and the country traveled the longest distance possible by giving up not only its sovereignty but also its well-equipped, highly trained, and extremely combat-ready force, the National People's Army (NVA). It is true that for a few months in early 1990, members of successive East German governments hoped that the NVA would remain a separate entity while East Germany moved on its slow and deliberate journey toward eventual German unity.[4] In July 1990, however, with the Two plus Four talks nearing resolution and with the deal struck in the Caucasus by Kohl and Soviet President Mikhail Gorbachev a reality, it became clear that the two Germanies would soon become a united federal state with a single military organization, the Bundeswehr, with a peacetime strength of no more than 370,000 soldiers,[5] a reduction of more than 40 percent in the combined troop strength of the former West German Bundeswehr (495,000) and NVA (170,000).

Thus, it was not only the dissolution of a decades-old army (with its own peculiar mix of Prussian veneer and communist interior) that required the German postunification government to embark on a major restructuring of German forces. It was also the ceiling that had been placed on the peacetime strength of the Bundeswehr, a reduction that went well beyond all the planning hypotheses of the preceding decades. Never before had the West German political or military leadership been confronted with the need to reduce its military potential so drastically. Until well into the 1980s, the standard problem in NATO had been inducing German governments to share what used to be called "the equitable burden of common defense." For example, when East-West relations began to sour after the period of Ostpolitik and détente, the Brandt and Schmidt administrations raised the troop strength of the Bundeswehr from its 1970 level of 460,000 to 490,000 in 1980. In 1984, Defense Minister Manfred Wörner set a long-term planning goal that would maintain the 1955 peacetime strength of 495,000 men (including, as well, a few women)—a remarkable decision, since the drastic shrinkage of the conscript pool due to the declining birth rate after the mid-1960s pointed toward gradual reductions. Moreover, it was not until 1989 that the idea of extending the period of mandatory military service from fifteen to eighteen months was given up. The final reduction to twelve months turned out to be a consequence, ironic at first, of German unification. Had the NVA not decided to reduce its period of mandatory service, the Bundeswehr might have retained its fifteen-month obligation for some time.

The ceiling on the all-German military is the single most important factor in current German defense planning. However, apart from the tasks of integrating the remnants of the former NVA into the Bundeswehr and reducing the combined force to 370,000 by 1994, German defense policy must also deal with other less immediate but no less substantial consequences of the strategic and political landslides of 1990: the Treaty on Conventional Forces in Europe (CFE), the Two plus Four Treaty specifications, and the internal changes in NATO. All three developments deserve attention before long-term German force planning is discussed.

CFE CONSEQUENCES. The CFE treaty signed at the November 19-21, 1990, CSCE summit was finally submitted for ratification after seven months of disturbing reinterpretations by the Soviet Union.[6] At the time it was drafted, the treaty would have had only minimal effects on the capabilities of the Bundeswehr. Some 600 tanks, little more than 10 percent of the fleet, would have been scrapped, but no Armored Combat Vehicles (ACVs), artillery, aircraft, or helicopters. However, by the time of the summit, the German military arsenal had expanded dramatically through the inclusion of the NVA following unification on October 3, 1990. As a result, Germany is required to do more disarming in all categories of treaty-limited equipment (TLE) than any other Western country; in fact, its obligations are second only to the former Soviet Union's.[7]

Until the demise of the Soviet Union in 1991, however, the political and strategic impact of the CFE treaty appeared to be of much greater importance than these reductions. Politically, the treaty set, for the first time since German rearmament, upper limits to the number of major weapons systems Germany could field, something that has always been an important Soviet objective. Although all other parties to the treaty also agreed to ceilings, most of those countries, particularly the former Warsaw Treaty Organization (WTO) members and Germany itself, were not likely to reach them.

Strategically, the CFE treaty reversed more than forty years of Soviet conventional superiority over NATO. After implementing the treaty provisions, the Soviet Union would have been left with no more than one-third of all European forces. Yet with the dissolution of the WTO, the treaty's original goal of achieving quantitative parity in Europe has lost its strategic meaning. The Soviet Union, after all, has been deprived of her allies and is not yet encircled by friends, to say the least. For those involved in the business and culture of force comparisons, this strategic reality cannot be ignored, especially by Germany which, as the nation closest to the threats from the dense military buildups of both alliances, has relied to a considerable extent on balance assessments. Force comparisons, moreover, used to play a major role in the political battles between the public, the government, and Parliament. Thus, the new situation in Europe is bound to change dramatically public attitudes toward defense and, in particular, affect arguments in favor of a sustained security policy effort.

TWO PLUS FOUR TREATY EFFECTS. The terms of the Two plus Four Treaty are extremely advantageous for Germany and NATO.[8] To summarize the most important effects on Germany's future security status, it is appropriate to refer to some of the articles of the "Treaty on the Final Settlement with Respect to Germany" signed in Moscow on September 12, 1990.[9]

Articles 6 and 7 give the united Germany full sovereignty over its internal and external affairs. The Four Powers terminate their responsibilities relating to Berlin and Germany as a whole, and all related Four Power institutions are dissolved. Article 6 states explicitly, "The right of the united Germany to belong to alliances, with all the rights and responsibilities arising therefrom, shall not be affected by the present treaty." Few in the West would have expected this unequivocal concession only a few months after the beginning of the Two plus Four negotiations.

A second and no less surprising benefit to the security of the new Germany is set out in Article 4: Germany and the Soviet Union will "settle by treaty the conditions for and the duration of the presence of Soviet armed forces" in eastern Germany and Berlin, "as well as the conduct of the

withdrawal of these forces, which will be completed by the end of 1994."
Again, very few had considered a negotiated withdrawal of Soviet forces
from Germany a feasible outcome, especially given the fact that NATO
would be strengthened by the presence of a united Germany as a full
member.[10]

Compared to these historic improvements to Germany's position in Europe,
the conditions that limit and qualify German unity seem light. First, Germany
will abide by the commitments made by both German states to renounce the
manufacture, possession, and control of nuclear, biological, and chemical
(NBC) weapons. The "rights and obligations arising from the Treaty on the
Non-proliferation of Nuclear Weapons of 1 July 1968 will continue to apply
to the united Germany" (Article 3). Second, both German governments
declared on August 30, 1990, at the CFE negotiations in Vienna that the
united Germany would reduce the personnel strength of its armed forces to
370,000 (ground, air and naval forces combined) within three to four years.
No more than 345,000 would belong to the ground and air forces (Article
3). Third, as long as Soviet forces remain in Germany, only German territorial
defense units will be stationed on the territory of the former GDR. The armed
forces of other countries cannot be stationed there or carry out any other
military activity. Once the Soviet forces have withdrawn completely, German
armed forces may be deployed in any part of the country, although the
restrictions on deploying foreign armed forces, nuclear weapons, and nuclear
weapons delivery systems in the former GDR will remain in effect (Article
5).

NEW NATO ROLES. During the Two plus Four process, NATO also began
to rethink its political and strategic future. One of the results was the London
Declaration on a transformed North Atlantic Alliance, which was made public
on July 6, 1990. It envisioned "a united Germany in the Atlantic Alliance of
free democracies and part of the growing political and economic integration
of the European Community . . . an indispensable factor of stability, which
is needed in the heart of Europe."[11] NATO at the same time extended "the
hand of friendship" to the Eastern countries that had been its adversaries
during the Cold War. Furthermore, the declaration set out fundamental
changes in the Western military posture and strategy that will deeply influence
NATO and German defense policies.

—NATO will field smaller, restructured active forces that will be highly
mobile and versatile, allowing NATO leaders maximum flexibility in deciding
how to respond to a crisis. Increasing reliance will be placed on multinational
corps made up of national units.

–NATO will scale back the readiness of its active units, reducing training
requirements and the frequency of exercises.

–NATO will rely more heavily on the ability to build up larger forces if
and when they are needed.

In accordance with those goals, NATO defense ministers also agreed to establish a Rapid Reaction Corps under British command. Much to the disappointment of the French government, Germany has agreed to play a major role in that endeavor. The tug-of-war between the transatlantic conception of European defense put forward by Great Britain and the U.S. and the European vision stressed by France leaves Germany walking a tightrope. Either German defense policy continues to honor its traditional commitment to NATO integration by joining in activities such as the Rapid Reaction Force, or it supports the French line of developing a separate European defense identity as part of the movement toward European political union. For the time being, however, it appears that a revamped NATO along the lines discussed at the summits in London in 1990 and Rome in 1991 will remain Germany's first resort in defense and security matters.

NATO also stated in the London declaration that political and military changes in Europe have rendered its forward defense posture invalid. The layered defensive deployment of NATO troops on West German soil has likewise become obsolete. As a result, all NATO countries involved in the Central European theater have begun to reduce their forces and withdraw from the Allied Forces Central Europe (AFCENT) region, particularly from Germany. The classical dimensions of space, force, and time, which logically determine defensive requirements and capabilities, must be thoroughly reassessed in terms of the changing security environment. NATO's new strategy, adopted in November 1991 at the Rome meeting of heads of state and government, will allow the alliance to develop new policies based on that reassessment.

Together, these factors have been conducive to a major reorientation of German defense planning. In fact, this planning process is similar to what occurred at the NATO summits in London in 1990 and Brussels in 1991, when detailed decisions were made on a multinational force and the specifics of a Rapid Reaction Corps before the political and strategic guidelines had been agreed on. It is no coincidence that no German Defense White Paper has been published or even announced and that no new Defense Policy Guidelines have been issued since 1985.[12] Because German force planning for the 1990s is still influenced much more by the dynamics of intra-German affairs than by a reassessment of the international security environment, it is necessary to take a closer look at the projected structure and deployment of the Bundeswehr before considering the larger context of security threats and options.

Current Force Planning for the 1990s

With the end of the East-West military confrontation and the obsolescence of NATO's forward defense posture, new and more political criteria will be applied to German force planning. While Germany must maintain an appropriate level of forces within the future alliance structure, it must at the same time take into account the historically rooted perceptions of its neighbors. Active German participation in the arms control process will therefore remain an indispensable element of force planning.

A second planning criterion results from the requirement that Germany be able to participate effectively in crisis management measures in Europe. In the German view, the central goal of NATO's political strategy must be to promote peaceful cooperation and crisis prevention in Europe. However, since these goals cannot be assured, the armed forces must be highly flexible and mobile in order to contribute to crisis management and resolution through military escalation and de-escalation.

The success of NATO's crisis management efforts will depend largely on the level of multinational solidarity. While NATO has long valued its multinational forces, including such specialized units as the ACE Mobile Force and the Standing Naval Forces in the Atlantic and Channel, they have become an even more important element in NATO strategy. From a German perspective, these kinds of forces offer three basic benefits. First, they have always been the visible expression of the participants' will to act in concert; because of this, they send out a very strong political signal. Second, multi-national integration increases the level of collective involvement in organizational and operational planning and thus establishes some mutual control. Third, multinational units foster political integration. The Rapid Reaction Corps established in Brussels and the "Eurocorps" that France and Germany recently proposed may well be the precursors of a European force.[13]

Specifically, three basic structural requirements are driving German army, navy, and air force planning. First, Germany, like any other country, must have at its disposal a basic military force tasked with safeguarding the nation's sovereignty. This includes territorial units for training, logistical support, and liaison between military and nonmilitary security institutions. All these tasks are confined to Germany's national territory, requiring a central command organization with relatively large peacetime staffs.

Second, Germany must have a military force that can be augmented and reconstituted with warning for defensive operations in the unlikely event that a large-scale military conflict develops in Central Europe. These forces will include primarily army—and, to a lesser degree, air force and navy—units with a reduced peacetime strength at category B or C level, according to traditional NATO standards. Until recently, it was assumed that forces of this kind could be mobilized within a few months, at least as long as Soviet troops were still on German territory, but warning time is likely to increase to almost a year after the withdrawal of Soviet troops from Germany and Poland.

Third, in the future Germany will need its own rapid response units for minor conflicts or crisis management on short notice in Central Europe and as Germany's contribution to multinational missions along Europe's borders, especially in NATO's southern region. Rapid response units will include highly mobile ground forces, rapidly deployable air force units, and the bulk of naval assets. The primary characteristics of these forces will be that they are ready at all times, fully manned and equipped, and mobile with organic support.

With this basic force structure, the Bundeswehr should be able to safeguard Germany's sovereignty and meet the NATO requirements with highly mobile standing forces for flexible crisis management and the elements of a large reconstitutable force. Moreover, these same forces will enable Germany to respond to the needs of collective security structures outside the alliance framework—namely, the United Nations or a European security organization.

According to the Two plus Four Treaty, Germany's reduced peacetime forces will be distributed as follows: army, 255,400; air force, 82,400; and navy, 32,200. Over the long term, there will be a slight shift in favor of the army, which is ultimately expected to reach 260,000; the air force will have 83,800 and the navy 26,200.

The reduction and reform of the German Army will be primarily carried out by consolidating the Field Army and the Territorial Army. In terms of manpower, this approach is highly economical. There will be three territorial corps commands, two of which will replace the three current autonomous Field Army corps commands and three autonomous Territorial Army commands, including their respective headquarters and subordinate command, control, and support elements in the western part of Germany. Below the three territorial corps commands will be eight consolidated military district/division commands plus two division commands for operational planning tasks. The military district/division command echelon will remain the point of reference and contact for the state governments and authorities as before. This structure, designed to cover all of Germany, will at the same time replace the twelve separate division commands and six military district commands presently in western Germany. The army will consist of twenty-eight brigades (compared to forty-eight in 1990) with varying levels of operational readiness. These twenty-eight brigades will break down into twenty-three mechanized brigades, three mobile air brigades, one mountain infantry brigade, plus the Franco-German brigade. Eight brigades will probably be fully operational (Category A), and the remaining twenty will have lower readiness levels.

The new air force is reorganizing into northern, southern, and eastern areas of responsibility, reducing its combat aircraft by about one-third, and deactivating some parts of its ground-based air defenses. The total number of aircraft will diminish to fewer than 500. With its new structure and modernized reconnaissance assets and fighter aircraft, the air force will be able to preserve its reconnaissance capabilities and strengthen its overall air defense component. However, this shift in focus will be made at the expense of attack capabilities.

The new navy structure provides for a long-term peacetime strength of 26,200. The drawdown of the naval forces, scheduled to be completed by the year 2005, will have the greatest impact on the Baltic Sea component, reducing the inventory of units afloat to about ninety, or by almost 50 percent. The Navy Structure 2005 plan calls for a reduction of the airborne platforms by one Tornado fighter/bomber wing, which will be transferred to the air force. The future navy will focus on securing the sea lines of communication (SLOCs) and the capability for maritime presence on the flanks, putting more emphasis on ocean-going units, including the necessary command/control and support assets. In doing so, it shifts its attention toward the North Sea, concentrating the unavoidable cuts on the forces and installations located in the Baltic.

As has been discussed, special arrangements and provisions apply to military deployment on the territory of the GDR. The Bundeswehr will station about 50,000 soldiers in the eastern part of Germany, but the NATO allies will not station any troops or conduct any training activities there. On October 3, 1990, a regional command was established in the eastern part of Germany, the *Bundeswehrkommando Ost*, or Federal Armed Forces Command East. This was a temporary joint headquarters staffed by personnel from all services and reporting directly to the Bundeswehr's vice chief of staff. It oversaw the disbanding of the NVA, assumed responsibility for destroying NVA matériel, and helped facilitate the withdrawal of Soviet troops. On July 1, 1991, this command ceased to exist and has since been replaced with three regular command structures.

—The army's territorial command in Potsdam will oversee two military district commands in Leipzig and Neu-Brandenburg. The territorial command will also serve as a corps command, while the military district commands will serve as divisional headquarters. This combination of territorial and operational-tactical command structures will soon be the pattern for all of Germany. The following army units are planned: six mechanized brigades and two home defense regiments, plus command and control, combat support, combat service support, and medical units.

—The air force has established a division command in Eggersdorf that will provide command and control for the ground-based and airborne air defense forces, one air transport wing, one radar control command, five communications sectors, one training battalion, and one service regiment. No offensive forces will be stationed in eastern Germany.

—The navy has established a naval command in Rostock that will oversee two transport battalions, two communications groups, two coastal radar stations, one Search and Rescue (SAR) field office, and depots. In addition, two naval bases will exist in Warnemünde and in Peenemünde, but no combat forces will be stationed there.

Given the breakup of the Soviet Union and all the problems that have ensued, and considering the uncertainties of NATO's force posture plans in the light of the drastic changes in Europe's military map, it is not very likely that the basic concept of German force planning just described will hold beyond the 1994 planning horizon. Skeptics argue that financial, demographic, and political reasons are almost certain to drive the Bundeswehr down to a small professional military of 200,000 to 250,000 between 1995 and 2000. Radical cuts in projected new equipment are also being considered, and conscription may be given up in the not-too-distant-future as the ideological construct of the citizen-soldier becomes obsolete along with the possibility of major wars in an eventually civilized Europe.

The Changing Security Environment

In the short period between 1985 and 1990, Europe changed more than it had at any time during the previous four decades. The depth and momentum of change can, in retrospect, be explained by the backlog of decisions that the Soviet Union and the Eastern European countries had long avoided making. In domestic as well as foreign policy, the former East bloc governments had followed the rigid ideological course of their hegemonic power, precluding more than token exchanges of ideas, people, and technology.[14] For its part, the West gradually but only partially loosened its confrontational defensiveness. In 1967 NATO offered a second avenue of cautious accommodation and cooperation with the dual strategy of defense and détente set forth in the Harmel Report. The 1975 Helsinki accord notwithstanding, the Soviet Union did not fully react to NATO's offer for almost twenty years, adhering instead to policies that promoted military buildup in Central and Eastern Europe, adversarial competition with the U.S. strategic posture, and ideological stagnation. When it finally became clear in the first half of the 1980s that these policies would have to be changed, Gorbachev's leadership and the courage of the peoples in Central and Eastern Europe initiated the collapse of the Soviet system with its double hegemony of Communist party rule and domination of the region. Europe has changed profoundly as a result.

Europeanization

The gradual dissolution of the WTO has had a direct bearing on the autonomy of all the countries that used to be labeled East European but which now deserve to be differentiated into "Central" and "Southeastern" European states. They are no longer mere objects of Soviet or post-Soviet policy. The indirect consequence for the West is that, as the former enemy's internal structure collapses, the NATO countries have also begun to act more independently. Three features of the growing self-determination of the European nation-states should be kept in mind.

First, the United States and the former Soviet Union are becoming less important in the affairs of European countries. This does not mean that either country is losing interest in Europe—quite the contrary. But as the former Soviet glacis states change sides ideologically, Europe is no longer the symbolic battlefield of the East-West conflict, as it was during the Cold War era. The war of ideas has been called off, and the former protagonists in Washington and Moscow are fighting fierce battles on their respective domestic fronts. The role models no longer exist; the simple convictions and economic blueprints of theorists from Karl Marx to Milton Friedman have been shattered, although this is obviously more true for the Marxists than for the Monetarists. The responsibility for determining the right mix of laissez-faire market economics and welfare economics is in the hands of the individual European governments and multilateral institutions such as the European Community.

Second, the admission of a united Germany to the community of European states indicates that the principal security problem in Europe, as the Harmel Report called it, no longer exists. The war begun by Germany and the division of the country had been the rationale for the U.S. and Soviet presence in Central Europe. Their presence brought with it not only military confrontation between the victorious powers of 1945, but also powerful political influences on their respective European clientele. These influences have always been mutually dependent and reinforcing, and the withdrawal of Soviet forces from Eastern Europe will thus weaken the relevance of a continuing U.S. presence in Western Europe. The pacifying effect of America's involvement in Europe is bound to fade.[15] Self-determination is likely to extend beyond its customarily defensive meaning to the pursuit of national interests outside the traditional alliances. This option is not open to Germany, however, as the Two plus Four agreement has clearly revealed.

Third, the emerging community of European countries has undertaken the task of finalizing the political map of Europe. The Four Powers have not only led the unified Germany forward toward a sovereign future but also made possible the German-Polish territorial agreement mentioned in the Two plus Four Treaty and concluded in a binding international treaty between Germany and Poland. Disputes in other areas of the European continent will no longer involve overwhelming U.S. or Russian interference. Both powers are essential partners of European security, as they have been since the 1975 Helsinki CSCE accord was signed, but they are no longer benign or brutal pacifiers. The European Community's effort to play a major role in resolving the Yugoslav crisis is a clear indication of growing European self-determination. This effort, despite its lack of success to date, still finds support in the United Nations.

The Europeanization of what remains of the military confrontation is unfolding. While the first CFE agreement does not set ceilings for indigenous or stationed troops, it does limit former Soviet armaments radically and so compels the former Soviet Union to restructure its entire military apparatus. Of even greater importance to the strategic landscape between the Atlantic and the Urals is, of course, what might be called the "race of unilateralism." Since December 1988, when Gorbachev announced before the UN General Assembly that Soviet troop strength would be reduced by 500,000, almost all partners of the new European security area have pledged to disarm. Not even the staunchest skeptics of arms control, the British and the French, have remained firm believers in their old dogmas. Even before the manpower ceilings agreed to in CFE IA, both governments indicated their intention to withdraw major portions of their troops from the former West Germany, their Central Front ally.

It is not necessary here to go into greater detail with regard to unilateral reductions of other East and West European military establishments that paralleled the CFE negotiations and the agreement to reduce the Bundeswehr. Suffice it to say that the end of the Cold War, the healing of Europe's division, and last but not least, domestic pressures will drive force levels down still further. Multilateral arms control negotiations and agreements will be desperately needed, however, since conspicuous adherence to agreements and treaties will always be a major source of confidence and trust. Conversely, increasing force levels or military readiness above and beyond agreed thresholds would, under a strict verification regime, be undeniable indications of hostile intentions or at least of escalatory policies.

Not the least important feature of the emerging military situation in Europe will be, in the language of operational planners, the "thinned-out battlefield." The drastic reductions in foreign troop deployment, especially in Germany, and the complete withdrawal of what used to be Soviet forces from the former WTO glacis states will force military staffs everywhere to adapt to a new strategic and operational situation. Future arms control negotiations (the Forum on Security Cooperation) may well be confronted with the difficult task of having to tackle military doctrine as well as force structures and deployment options.

Threats and Options

At a time when confrontation is developing into cooperation, NATO has included the former WTO countries in the North Atlantic Cooperation Council (NACC), jointly proposed by U.S. Secretary of State James A. Baker III and then Foreign Minister Hans-Dietrich Genscher in October 1991 and mandated at the North Atlantic Council meeting in Brussels at the end of the year. Since common security has become the hallmark of pan-European politics, it seems outdated, to say the least, to talk about the remaining threats to European countries or current perceptions of potential adversaries. Politicians and diplomats (not only those of German origin) often talk as if military competition in the traditional East-West context had receded solely to the arcana of U.S.-Soviet strategic nuclear arsenals and their perennial mutual neutralization. This view is shortsighted, however. Europe still hosts enormous military capabilities, conventional and nuclear, and is likely to do so for some time, even after the conclusion of arms control agreements such as the CFE treaty. What will these capabilities mean in the future? Can we expect them to become gradually obsolete? Or do they serve vital functions for the nation-states and the alliances or groups of nations now, and will they continue to serve these functions in five or ten years? What is Germany's role? And what are the prospects of building regional cooperative structures to replace the simple bipolar order that was the result of the last and most devastating war in Europe?

The leaders of the former Soviet Union—and certainly those of the European and North American countries—may never have intended to fight a major war in Europe. Mutual fears that political crises could escalate into military action have nevertheless fueled a decades-long competition in arms and military readiness—a competition that in itself carried the serious risk of perpetuating and even strengthening mistrust between the main actors as well as their clients. This classical security dilemma, so much a part of the old structure and displayed in its most extreme form in the confrontation between the two Germanies, seems to be disappearing. A disarmament race began at least two years before the Vienna CFE agreement, as governments in Moscow, Washington, Warsaw, and Bonn and other European capitals rushed to anticipate the treaty.

Nevertheless, the formidable military capabilities that remain in place may, at critical junctures, once again appear threatening to countries in the region. It is therefore necessary to consider the remaining risks posed by the latent military capabilities still in Europe. What are the potential threats? With the exception of Germany, West European NATO members will hardly be perceived by any Eastern country as militarily threatening. The same can safely be assumed of former Central and East European WTO members vis-à-vis Western Europe. Hence, as players in what is left of the security game, only the United States, the Commonwealth of Independent States (CIS) or Russia, and Germany are left.

Eastern Europe is confronted with the uncertainties and instabilities of the post-Soviet developments to their east. No longer does the offensive potential of the former Soviet Union appear threatening enough to demand that military contingencies be taken into consideration. This may well change, however, in the long term. Some proposals envisage a special security arrangement for a group of European countries in the form of a neutral belt, ranging from Finland in the north to Yugoslavia in the south, which might be able to provide reassurance against possible threats. Still, most of these countries, if not all of them, prefer their security interests to be connected to those of the West. After all, they no longer see themselves as part of a European East. For them, potential military threats could come only from their eastern neighbors.[16] Vaclav Havel's and Lech Walesa's visits to NATO Headquarters in the first half of 1991 were a clear, though rhetorically cautious, indication of this feeling. Toward the end of 1991, however, Russian President Boris Yeltsin introduced even his own country as an applicant for NATO membership.

What residual fears there were of a Soviet threat after the dissolution of the WTO have now ceased to exist. The breakdown of central power since the August coup in Moscow has meant not only that the Soviet Union disappeared from the international political arena but that a military threat—conventional or nuclear—against the West by any CIS member is inconceivable in the immediate future.

As has been well known for decades, the United States and the Soviet Union (and now perhaps even Russia) have appeared incapable of extricating themselves from the costly and not necessarily stabilizing modernization race in the area of nuclear strategic systems. The mutual threat of annihilation is still working, and the recent START agreement has not changed this fact. Even though the nuclear confrontation is becoming increasingly unreal, it may still be the backbone of a residual deterrence in the minds of those who do not feel comfortable ruling out man's inclination to use force. Because the threat of using force will be an important domestic issue in the former Soviet Union for some time to come, controlling the nuclear arsenal after Soviet disintegration has become a prominent item on the international agenda.

As the previous threats receded, a new element in traditional European security perceptions began to take shape in 1990: the military power of a unified Germany. Even with the steep reductions in the Bundeswehr, German forces, measured in the usual categories of defensive and offensive capabilities, will clearly be strong enough to justify a neighbor's military assessment of German "invasion capabilities." The fact that these capabilities can be directed towards western and southern as well as northern and eastern neighbors indicates the complexity of German defense policy, for no neighboring country will ever accept a truly national German defense policy. Only in the context of multinational alliances and organizations can Germany's security needs be fulfilled. Thus, it is not surprising that the Soviet Union eventually consented to Germany's membership in NATO.

The common perception of the remaining military threats in Europe, however, must not obscure the spectrum of nonmilitary challenges affecting many regions and peoples. Future security arrangements will need to move beyond the traditional task of perpetuating mutually assured risks of aggression to cope with at least two areas of major conflict—ethnic and economic.

The end of the repressive Soviet hegemony over Central and Eastern Europe and, in 1991, the end of the Soviet Union itself have brought old rivalries, deeply rooted in national sentiments, and unsolved territorial disputes "back to the future."[17] Eastern and Southeastern Europe is not yet the zone of security and cooperation that the Helsinki process has been encouraging and promoting for almost twenty years. The ethnic strife and religious tension that have long been part of the history of these regions were only temporarily buried under the false future and the grim reality of communism. Large-scale migration may turn out to be one consequence of these conflicts, and such movement rarely adds to the domestic stability of the recipient countries. Economic disparities and social unrest frequently accompany ethnic conflict. It is clear from this picture that the usual instruments of security policy fail when they are applied to the resolution of such disputes. A new security order in Europe must therefore allow for comprehensive conflict prevention and crisis management, since military instruments will rarely be appropriate in such endeavors.

While the military-strategic and ideological divisions of Europe are fading away, huge economic disparities remain. Europe and Germany are still divided in an economic sense, although this fact has only recently become apparent. Not only is the actual level of vital supplies in the former CMEA countries and Yugoslavia far below Western standards, but also the short- and medium-term prospects for economic recovery in the area look very grim indeed, largely due to the systemic decay of capital stock and comparatively low productivity levels in communist economies, as well as the immense ecological damage caused by irresponsible production processes in almost all economic sectors. For Europe to develop into a single zone of cooperation and security, it will undoubtedly need to bridge the technological and welfare gaps between the European Community members and the backward economies of Eastern and Southeastern Europe. In fact, this bridging task must not be restricted to aiding the economies of the former communist states but must also include the regulation of competitive conflict between Western states or groups. In the future, NATO could well become a transatlantic institution for balancing the traditional security interests and the competitive power of American or European partners. This prospect will give a new accent to the alliance's familiar West-West role.

Had it not been for Iraq's August 1990 attack on Kuwait, the diminishing East-West conflict in Europe might have postponed the perception of common military threats to the European order for some time. To be sure, there is no need simply and simplistically to replace the Eastern threat with a newly discovered southern enemy; neither Algeria, Egypt, nor Syria is threatening Europe.[18] But terrorism and ruthless aggression in disregard of international law have become facts of political life, and any European security system will have to deal with such menaces.

Consequences for German Security Policy

There have always been issues in the German security debate that cause heated domestic arguments as well as irritation among Germany's allies. Since West Germany joined NATO, the issue of nuclear weapons in Europe and in particular on German soil has become the most contentious political subject. In contrast, conventional disarmament never raised as much partisan debate. Yet in the future, as nuclear concerns recede and as the scope of conventional arms control is enlarged to include coordinated arms export control, the government and opposition may well be driven further apart by the pressure of their respective constituencies.

During the ten-year period that began in the mid-1970s, when the West German strategic community—a group neither too powerful nor particularly vocal—found itself at the forefront of a doctrinal debate about the general notions of stability and defensiveness, a specifically European approach to the concept of an "alternative defense" emerged.[19] It now appears that the security environment of the 1990s is at the same time both receptive and adverse to these earlier ideas.

Setting the framework for future German security policy, the Two plus Four Treaty bans Soviet forces from German soil but does not say much about a Western presence in Germany. NATO's future and that of any evolving European defense concept is thus left to West-West bargaining and common policy formulation. The debate has hardly begun in Germany, where more attention has been given to the options for German participation in non-NATO contingencies. These options have not yet been clearly defined, but they deserve consideration in this chapter.

Nuclear Weapons

Will Germany one day be free of nuclear weapons? This possibility is no longer completely unimaginable, since the Two plus Four Treaty stipulates that the former GDR will remain nuclear free after all Soviet forces withdraw, taking with them the nuclear weapons whose existence was never acknowledged during the Cold War. Thus, what had been one of the anathemas of West German security policy was silently buried: its desire not to be assigned a special status that would relegate it to a minor security role.

This concern has been replaced by a deeper logic influencing the nuclear status of the new Germany.

First, ceding positions that cannot be maintained is likely to yield greater benefits for all sides than forcing a maximum advantage. The competitive, zero-sum perception of international relations is, at least in the East-West context, being replaced by a more cooperative view, a paradigmatic change that rewards the "heroes of the retreat."[20] To be sure, Gorbachev was more a hero of that kind than Kohl or other Western leaders, but accepting the non-nuclear status of parts of Germany does in fact represent a withdrawal from longstanding tenets of security policy.

Second, giving eastern Germany a special status in conventional terms as well, so that no foreign troops will be stationed there after 1994, recalls an idiosyncratic element of German security policy that has existed since the early 1950s. To the extent that Germany as a nation-state—apart from its position as an integrated member of the Western communities—has once and for all renounced possession of NBC weapons, its peacetime military responsibilities in the former GDR are purely national. It thus fits the historical legacy of German security policy to associate truly national duties with a non-nuclear posture.

With regard to the necessity of having nuclear weapons stationed in Europe as part of NATO's deterrence potential, the current German leadership appears firm in supporting a continued U.S. nuclear commitment to the continent, with land deployment widely distributed among European NATO countries. It is less clear, however, whether the major opposition party, the SPD, will support the deployment of air-delivered nuclear missiles on West German soil.[21] The 1990 London summit formula that defines nuclear weapons as "truly weapons of last resort" does not, for all its unifying rhetoric, indicate an unequivocal change of doctrine in favor of the two widely debated residual functions nuclear weapons could serve in a less confrontational international environment. The first of these is nuclear counterdeterrence, or deterring the use of nuclear weapons by others; the second, often called "existential deterrence," invests nuclear weapons with the largely symbolic power of reminding a potential enemy of the ultimate horrors of war even in the age of "smart" weapons and "surgical strikes."

There was, of course, wide agreement in all quarters of German public opinion on the desirability of getting rid of all Short-Range Nuclear Forces (SNFs) rather than just the missiles mentioned in the Comprehensive Concept of NATO in 1989 (and several times since). No intense debate, however, has developed concerning procedures for removing substrategic arsenals from Europe. Until the summer of 1991, most experts within and outside the German government favored negotiations on missiles but not necessarily on nuclear artillery, which could be withdrawn from NATO's arsenal even without a formal treaty.[22] President Bush's September 27, 1991, announcement of a unilateral withdrawal of all nuclear artillery and short-range missiles eventually ended the debate, adding another example to the list of surprising U.S. initiatives on European arms control—not unlike the aircraft and helicopter proposals for the Vienna CFE talks, which opened two weapons categories to reductions of a size never before conceived feasible in NATO.

Yet apart from this debate on substrategic weapons, there is, from a German perspective, an increasingly important European dimension to nuclear issues. France, for many years, continued to develop its nuclear forces along largely traditional lines: twenty HADES missile launchers were to become operational in 1992, and a new command structure has been developed for French missile forces. According to a recent government decision, the missiles will not be deployed, but the modernization of long-range weapons is well underway even under conditions of budgetary stress. Traditionally, French governments have distanced their own nuclear doctrine from NATO's, a policy that has recently led to skepticism from President Mitterrand about the last-resort formula of the London summit. French officials displayed a similar skepticism during the November 1991 strategy summit in Rome, which subsequently issued a communiqué that did not include the last-resort formula.

The French position presents German defense and security policy in the nuclear field with two major challenges. First, a fatal, if understandable, strategic mindset has developed in Germany, which holds that the range of a nuclear system defines its deterrence value. From the time of the debate on Intermediate-Range Nuclear Forces (INFs) in 1987 until the establishment of the Comprehensive Concept in 1989, a battle cry united right-wing conservatives and left-wing peace movement activists: the shorter the range, the deader the Germans.[23] Indeed, with respect to the nationality of their likely victims in Europe, the HADES missiles would have been no better than the LANCE or Follow-on-to-LANCE for the Germans. It can be argued, however, that this brand of chauvinist angst has distracted Germans from the main issue. Instead of drawing a cynical distinction between German and non-German fatalities, analyses of the utility of short-range nuclear weapons should have shown that these systems no longer play an important role in NATO military strategy. This has been especially true since 1986, when NATO agreed on General Political Guidelines (GPGs) for the use and follow-on use of nuclear weapons, and is even more true in the context of a last-resort strategy. Such reasoning may in the end have contributed to the U.S. decision to scrap land-based short-range systems altogether.

The second challenge lay, until recently, in France's insistence on HADES, which raised serious questions about whether and how nuclear strategy could ever become part of a European defense identity as it has been envisioned by the intergovernmental process of deepening EC political integration. German defense policy could well contribute to bridging the seemingly insurmountable gap between official NATO strategy and French nuclear philosophy. While France argues that the NATO last-resort formula increases the alliance's distance from the French strategic concept, Germany could seize the opportunity to reinterpret NATO's intentions in light of the changing strategic environment in Central Europe. As military threats to territorial integrity give way to cooperative interdependence, nuclear arsenals will become anachronistic symbols of the past. However, they may still reach into the present rather than becoming obsolete at once. It is in Germany's interest to demilitarize NATO's strategy, including its nuclear components, as much as possible. Operational options for nuclear weapons are not at the forefront of German policy, but rather techniques for the cooperative management of residual anachronisms—including nuclear strategy—as part of the political unification of the European Community, and eventually also of all European countries. Close Franco-German cooperation in this management process is an absolute necessity, and consultations on nuclear policy beyond the bilateral 1986 agreement may serve as an element of that process. If France had gone forward with HADES deployment, the German government would probably have been induced simply to close the book on Franco-German nuclear consultations.

Arms Control and Defense Doctrine

Since October 3, 1990, the day of German unification, Germany has feared being singled out as a "special case" in the multilateral processes of the post-Cold War era. Before the 1992 CFE IA Agreement resulted in manpower ceilings for the other twenty-one participants, no other country had undertaken to restrict the peacetime strength of its forces. No other European country has committed itself by international treaty to establishing a nuclear weapon-free zone on its territory. The reasons for "singularizing" Germany are well known and obvious to all partners. In order to unite the divided nation and solve the core problem of European security, it was necessary to make special arrangements to mitigate the concerns of the former Soviet Union about giving up the strategic position it had held in Central Europe for over forty years.

What has happened to the European arms control paradigm in recent years? For more than fifteen years, beginning in 1973 with the Mutual and Balanced Force Agreement (MBFR) negotiations in Vienna, "balance" was the catchword of conventional arms control. Collective numerical equalities were intended to reflect a putative stability between NATO and WTO postures in Europe. The German perspective on the East-West rhetoric of the 1970s had it that détente was to materialize in the collective and balanced restraint of the respective military potentials of both alliances. Until at least 1985, when Gorbachev entered the scene and began to rewrite the script of the European drama, the confrontational aspects of East-West relations dominated arms control policies. Yet two developments turned the traditional paradigm of confrontational balance into a new paradigm of cooperative restraint. First, confidence-building (as contained in the Stockholm 1986 CSBM agreement) and real disarmament (as demonstrated by the 1987 INF Treaty) extended the scope of European arms control beyond the "balance" orientation of the MBFR talks. Second, and even more important, a concept of mutual and cooperative security gained ground in the Soviet Union, changing its traditional perception of the West as an existential threat to the security of the country and its increasingly unwilling allies. Its own excessive armament, conventional and nuclear, came to be regarded as a double threat to Soviet interests: first, as a mechanism that reinforced the classical security dilemma; and second, as an economic burden that was likely to become unbearable in the long run. The logical consequences of this change of perception were meaningful arms control negotiations within the CFE framework that had as their objectives adequate defensive capabilities for both sides—still within the NATO and WTO context—and reductions in destabilizing offensive capabilities.

Yet when the CFE treaty was concluded in November 1990, the European world had already changed, and the treaty had assumed a different meaning.[24] It became an epilogue to the extinct confrontational structure of European relations rather than the hallmark of a new Europe. Germany's singular position thus appears to be a transitory, if symbolic, phenomenon of European security. German unification needed the close cooperation of the sometimes forgotten World War II alliance and required that German military capabilities be restrained.

It appears that cooperative restraint rather than confrontational balance will become the driving force behind future arms control policies. Beyond reducing TLE items and military manpower, a process of force restructuring has begun in both West and East. NATO forces in Europe, as well as former Soviet forces on their own territory, are being reorganized to reflect the new cooperative security. Had it not been for the complete breakdown of the Soviet Union, forward defense might well have become a Soviet preoccupation after 1994, only a few years after NATO's reformulation of its own understanding of this strategic and operational principle. Defense dominance, a concept born during the second half of the 1970s in Western—most visibly German—circles, resembles the peace movement's critique of the destabilizing elements of NATO's doctrine and armaments and has become a common denominator in the endeavors to restructure armed forces.[25] Originally, the concept put forward the possibility of unilaterally changing the rules of the strategic game, which was after all considered a noncooperative one. Any country that could satisfy its defensive needs by restructuring, rearming, and redeploying its own forces in such a way as to render an enemy's offensive capabilities useless and obsolete would simultaneously break out of the vicious security dilemma without having to wait for the other side. Now, however, defense dominance has become a concept whereby both sides opt for what since 1986 have gradually become known in Soviet terms as defense sufficiency, crisis stability, and dissuasion stability, resulting in benefits that far exceed those produced by one-sided restructuring.[26]

However, while East-West deterrence and defense unfold favorably in this direction, and even the nuclear strategic relationship between the United States and the CIS or Russia may soon contain mutually acceptable defensive elements, a clearly less encouraging trend is evident in the international environment with regard to offensive forces.[27] While threat perceptions along the East-West divide are fading in Europe, many so-called Third World countries have been rearming—to a large degree by taking advantage of the vast proliferation of weapons, technology, and expertise of the Northern industrial countries—and are often involved in bitter conflicts. Cooperation in the North is likely to be driven not only by the need to find ways to manage the new East-West relations but also by the need to join forces against certain actors in the not-so-new world disorder. State actors are only part of the picture; other organizations and institutions are becoming increasingly influential. Drug cartels, terrorist groups, and violent minorities are hardly enemies to be fought on classical military battlefields, but respect for international law requires responsible countries and groups of countries to provide ways to enforce international standards and agreements. Doing so will involve necessarily military means, which must be effective, readily deployable, and sustainable even in remote areas. Global interests preclude limiting military capabilities to purely defensive needs.

Thus it comes as no surprise that, according to their interests and capabilities, the United States, NATO, major European countries and, to some extent, Russia, Ukraine, and Kazakhstan cannot afford to take defensive restructuring to the extreme but feel compelled to retain high-mobility offensive forces for possible use outside East-West theaters. For its part, Germany has not historically been receptive to such reasoning but, due to the changing international environment, will need to define its proper role as a member of NATO, the EC, security institutions such as the CSCE, and, most of all, the United Nations.

Furthermore, it is not surprising that arms control in the context of continuing world disorder has assumed a nontraditional meaning, extending the scope of its policies to include coordinated efforts to restrict, reduce, and ban arms exports to areas of instability and crisis. Again, cooperative restraint is the name of the game, but the difficulties involved are enormous. Since exports of complete weapons systems represent only a part of the critical transfer of military capabilities these days—the part that is comparatively easy to define and control—intrusive agreements and verification procedures will have to be negotiated among the major suppliers of modern technology.

German experience with legal and not-so-legal loopholes in arms and dual-use technology exports suggests that a "technology control regime," which is a logical extension of the existing Missile Technology Control Regime (MTCR), will remain only one element in a broader approach to limiting the spread of arms.[28] Such an approach acknowledges that supply-side arms control will never be able to stop the spreading global demand for arms. Arms export controls will therefore remain a minor contribution to stabilizing crisis areas.

The dissolution of the Soviet Union adds a new dimension to the arms control formula of cooperative restraint. It is in fact very likely that the negotiations under way between the members of the CIS on the future of the former Soviet military will lead to agreements similar to many traditional arms control treaties and will be based either on the East-West model of mutual defensive sufficiency structures and CSBMs or on the North-South model of nonproliferation and technology control.

Foreign Forces in Germany: The Future NATO Posture

For more than thirty years, NATO allies stationed much of their conventional potential in the Federal Republic. Although concrete withdrawal plans have not been finalized, particularly by the United States, it seems likely that when the former Soviet forces leave Germany at the end of 1994, no more than about 100,000 NATO soldiers will remain in Germany, or roughly one-quarter of the foreign Western contingent that was stationed there during the 1970s and 1980s. This massive decrease is not a consequence of the CFE I negotiations or the CFE IA agreement establishing national ceilings on manpower. Rather, this reduction has grown out of a fundamental reassessment of the European security situation. Great Britain and the United States, which will be cutting their respective forces by slightly more than half, remain committed to supporting Germany's military security with substantial land and air forces. France originally intended to withdraw its forces almost completely, leaving only its contribution to the Franco-German brigade behind. Recently, however, in the context of the October 14, 1991, Kohl-Mitterand plan to increase the WEU's significance, the withdrawal was quietly reduced by half.

These essentially unilateral decisions have produced two important effects. First, in spite of its own force reduction, Germany is assuming increased responsibility for the military preparedness of what is still called NATO's Central Region. This responsibility, however, will continue to be carried out within the framework of multilateral integration set out by NATO in the summer of 1990 and reinforced by the Rome summit in November 1991.

Second, while forces from the U.S. and Great Britain—along with small contingents from Belgium, Denmark, and The Netherlands—that had been deployed with the Germans along the intra-German border are now being reorganized to provide a more flexible defense of NATO territory, French defense policy with regard to Germany finds itself in a serious dilemma. French operational reserves have always been an important element in the defense of the Central Front. Had NATO's forward defenses ever been endangered by deep incursions of WTO forces into Germany, the French First Army would have been prepared to cooperate closely with integrated NATO commands. When forward defense along the intra-German border ceased to exist, this support function lost its traditional meaning. Completely new cooperative arrangements were necessary to organize a common defense among those NATO countries involved in Central Front contingencies, but nothing of this sort happened until late 1991. In fact, France felt excluded from the common task of reorganizing European defense when multinationality (vaguely introduced at the July 1990 London summit and then with more details at the Brussels Defense Planning Committee meeting in 1991) became the new catchword for the restructuring of the allied posture in the new Germany. The announcement that the Franco-German brigade would be the nucleus of a European corps clearly served as a reminder of the continued operational role of French forces in Central Europe.

However, a political question lies behind these efforts at military and operational restructuring. Is the French government willing to accept the idea that the much-heralded objective of a "European defense identity" could well—and perhaps ought to—develop within NATO? Acknowledging this possibility would make determining this identity more than just a routine item on the agenda of WEU meetings or another issue in the European Community's discussion of political union. Serious proposals from across the Atlantic have argued for a stronger European component of the common security organization.[29] Such proposals have not always met with the attention in Europe they deserve, unlike less sensible diplomatic interventions from the United States warning the Europeans against undue haste in the pursuit of more autonomy or self-determination in defense and security matters.[30]

The framework that NATO provided for German security policy is changing drastically, but thus far the considerable force reductions have not been accompanied by a weakening of political commitments. Germany may well gain relative weight in the new defensive posture of NATO's Central Front as well as in the strategic reserve forces such as the Rapid Reaction Corps. It is still unlikely, however, that this change will translate into a more active out-of-area role for German military and security policies, given the constitutional responsibility of German defense forces to abstain from what many neighbors experienced as "power politics" after the less peaceful nineteenth-century process of national unification. The debate over the new role of the united Germany and its armed forces in European and world affairs has just begun.

Employment Options for German Forces

The Persian Gulf crisis of 1990–91 reopened the debate begun ten years earlier about the possible participation of German forces in out-of-area conflicts. The fundamentalist revolution in Iran, the second oil crisis, and the buildup of U.S. command structures and plans for Persian Gulf contingencies had led to NATO consultations on the possible commitments of its members. A rather limited constitutional debate took place in West Germany during that period, resulting in a decision by the Federal Security Council (the cabinet committee for defense and security matters) that the Basic Law legally barred German forces from engaging in military actions other than those required for the defense of German or other NATO members' territory. Yet in 1990, two important factors changed the scope of the German debate considerably. First, the United Nations became deeply involved in the response to Iraqi aggression, with the Security Council assuming responsibility for managing the crisis. Second, German unification altered the framework of the domestic debate by forcing a drastic reassessment of the new Germany's role in world affairs.

It has now become clear that the domestic political irritation over NATO's support of Turkey as a neighbor of Iraq was highly detrimental to Germany's standing in the Western community. Sending German ACE Mobile Force (AMF) components to southeastern Turkey was clearly completely legitimate under the terms of the NATO treaty. With regard to the legal aspects of Bundeswehr commitments in areas outside NATO's responsibility, however, a consensus is emerging on four basic criteria for future action:

—Any war of aggression, or the support of it, is forbidden by Article 26 of the Constitution. Under Article 87 only defensive actions are allowed.

—The obligations of the Federal Republic of Germany arising from UN membership must be honored. Financial and logistical support of the Gulf coalition, minesweeping and minehunting operations, and more recently transportation and expertise for UN efforts to eliminate NBC weapons in Iraq are considered international duties.

—While the conduct of foreign policy remains the prerogative of the executive branch of the government, formal approval by Parliament will probably be sought if and when Germany considers contributing military contingents to UN or European peacekeeping or peace-enforcing activities.

—There will be no substantive change in those articles of the Basic Law that pertain to the role of German forces. Instead, the law will be clarified by additional wording that reflects current common understanding. Such wording will probably allow German forces to take part in multilateral activities in accordance with and in defense of international law.

The envisaged level of parliamentary involvement in governmental decisions on international affairs is extremely important, for it reflects a fact that is not given sufficient attention in the German debate. After all, when the international responsibility of a country as powerful as Germany is called upon, a political decision is needed, not just a legalistic interpretation of constitutional clauses that are necessarily rooted in historical circumstances. The long-established tendency in West German foreign policy to revert to the Basic Law as an instrument for circumventing political decisions on delicate foreign policy issues must have been irritating to other countries. A consensus now seems to have been reached on replacing the hermeneutic capabilities of legal advisers with the responsibility delegated to elected representatives.

No consensus, however, exists thus far on which political principles should govern the actual decisionmaking process on German participation in out-of-area conflicts. While it is true that no national interests other than the defense of German territory or that of NATO allies—according to Article 51 of the UN Charter—will be protected by military force, it is not at all clear which conditions must be met for German troops to participate in collective military actions. Several questions will have to be answered in the near future. First, is Germany prepared to provide combat forces—beyond traditional blue helmet peacekeeping contingents—if a UN command structure as envisaged in Chapter VII of the UN Charter has been established, or would an enforcement mechanism such as that developed during the Gulf conflict provide a sufficient rationale for direct German military involvement? Second, under what conditions would Germany participate in a West European rather than a UN intervention force? Would it be necessary first to establish a collective security system based on the CSCE, perhaps as an explicitly regional organization along the lines set out in Articles 52 and 53 of the UN Charter, before German forces could be committed?[31] Or would the common foreign and security policy the European Community has in mind be an instrument for transferring the burden of a purely national decision to a supranational authority?

These seemingly pressing questions confronting German security policy may well fade in light of the growing unrest and instability in Eastern and Southeastern Europe, especially the fierce internal conflict and rapidly decreasing central authority in Yugoslavia and the former Soviet Union. But such developments are not amenable to the military element of conciliatory foreign intervention. The fact that foreign and security policy seem to be demilitarizing (not so much due to the rational intentions of international players but simply as a result of the force of events) will have some influence on the German debate over employment options for Germany's forces.

It is all too clear, however, that intrastate relations and domestic policies do not necessarily follow a pattern of demilitarization. Organizations of collective defense (such as NATO) or even organizations of collective security (such as the United Nations and, in its incipient form, the CSCE) do not have treaty mandates or the legitimacy granted by international law to intervene by military force against a party perceived as violating the law within its own borders. This enforcement vacuum has in part been filled with diplomatic gestures such as Germany's and the EC's recognition of Slovenia and Croatia as sovereign states. It is no coincidence that such cautious German unilateralism, while annoying to some EC countries caught in their own geopolitical past, is the only conceivable form of national foreign policy open to the new Germany. No German military element will be able to take part in anything other than a collective multinational force for some years to come.

A New Security Policy

In his address to the Aspen Institute Berlin on June 18, 1991, Secretary of State Baker pointed to what seems to be the most important general issue of European security:

> Perhaps the most striking phenomenon across all of Europe today is the combined and simultaneous devolution and evolution of the nation-state. While the nation-state remains by far the most significant political unit, its political role is being increasingly supplemented by both supranational and subnational units. In other words, some of the nation state's functions are being delegated "upward" and others "downward."[32]

As a born-again nation-state, Germany faces the challenge of having to create its own view of the common future of Europe. This view, however, is bound to be based on Germany's past and present role in European affairs and its aspirations toward a peaceful and prosperous future.

German security policy has traditionally dealt with three international axes along which confrontation, competition, and cooperation had to be managed: the East-West, West-West, and North-South. The principal players—with the exception of the Soviet Union—are still around, but the rules of the game have changed over the past two decades. Twenty years ago, far-reaching transformations of the international system were initiated, but they remained overshadowed by the inability of the Soviet Union to give up its ideological fixation and rigid internal and external autocratic structures. The transformations did finally take place, however, and they set a new European agenda. First, Ostpolitik—West Germany's series of treaties with the Soviet Union, Poland, Czechoslovakia, and the GDR, as well as the Four-Power Berlin Agreement—began to break down enemy images on both sides of the East-West divide, but without resolving the ideological confrontation or reducing the mutually perceived need to maintain large military arsenals. Second, the strategic and economic predominance of the United States began to erode.

The end of the Bretton Woods world financial system and the nuclear-strategic equality granted to the Soviet Union by the SALT I/ABM Treaty symbolized a decline in American power long before the declinist debate began at the end of the 1980s. Third, the Western world began to reflect on nonmilitary and long-term threats to its security. The first oil crisis reminded both governments and people of their dependence on other countries, and the first Club of Rome report on the limits of growth in 1972 brought the increasing scarcities of vital resources to the attention of the expansionist Western industrial societies.

German security policy has reacted to these transformations by cooperating with the Western communities and promoting East-West and North-South dialogue and accommodation. There have been no major changes in German foreign and security policies since the early 1970s, due in part to the predictable foreign policy consensus of a long-divided and precariously situated country that represented the epitome of the Cold War confrontation, and in part to the continuous challenge posed by the issues of Ostpolitik, Western cooperation, and global threats. All three of these issues will remain with us.

Yet simply continuing traditional German policies is no option for the 1990s. With the end of the Cold War and the unification of Germany, two fortunate developments have occurred. First, Germany, even more than other West European countries, has been deprived of the old enemies that for so long served as negative reinforcement of the identity and self-image of the real German democratic republic. Second, Germany is now surrounded by friendly countries that, in their economic and political relations with Germany, are increasingly developing into dependents or competitors rather than remaining stabilizing enemies or tutelary friends.

What is Germany's reaction to the continuing challenges in East-West relations? To be sure, enormous military capabilities are left over from the period of mutual distrust and balanced suspicion. Russia will remain a great military power, but as the CFE accord demonstrates, cooperative approaches to managing existing threat potentials are being worked out. Transparency and confidence-building are the principal means of reducing the uncertainty and improving the predictability of state behavior—prerequisites to finally breaking out of the vicious cycle of the security dilemma.[33] A further consequence that has not been sufficiently discussed is the gradual evolution of defensively oriented arms control negotiations into a mechanism for cooperative defense planning among neighboring countries or regions. Why not open up a country's defense planning to those countries that need to understand the precautions taken on the basis of military threats perceived as emanating from their territory? In the long run, such an approach could well create a dynamic process of de-escalation of mutual defensive preparations, adding operational logic to the already existing economic and social pressure to further reduce military arsenals. Germany has been active in this regard during the last two years, establishing extensive military and academic exchanges with its eastern neighbors. The procedure is completely in line with NATO's new openness to contacts and consultations with Eastern countries and has also been institutionalized in the NACC. Cooperative relations with former WTO countries are not likely to be preludes to NATO's eastward expansion, however. The NACC has in fact focused on communication among member states rather than on consultations regarding outside threats. Collective security, not collective defense, is the logic behind this project.

German security policy must meet two more challenges to any new Ostpolitik. Europeans are becoming aware of the "other division" of Europe, which is characterized by the enormous economic and social gap between West and East. As German President Richard von Weizsäcker said during the meeting of the Council of Foreign Ministers of the CSCE on June 19, 1991: "Military considerations must not continue to monopolize the notion of security. . . . The true dangers of the future do not lie in issues of military power or governmental force but are the result of the disappointment of citizens and societies about basic rights that have not been granted, economic injustice, and social insecurity."[34] It is not surprising that large-scale migration may be one consequence of such a state of affairs. To overcome the huge economic disparities and avoid the concurrent threat of poverty-driven migrations, German policy must be conceived as an integral element of a common EC foreign and security policy. The traditional concept of a national security policy has, in the interdependent Europe of our times, lost its meaning. Only in concert with its Western partners can the new Germany successfully deal with the remaining challenges along the East-West axis.

What is Germany's reaction to the continuing need for West-West coordination and understanding? Germany achieved unity on the basis of its willingness to remain firmly anchored in NATO. Traditionally, military coordination within NATO has included not only operational defense planning but burden-sharing as well. There will be a relative decline in the U.S. share of the European defense burden. With other than Soviet threats to Western security interests remaining, however, Germany will be asked to assume a greater share of the collective responsibilities of the Western communities, at least in the context of the United Nations and its peacekeeping and peace-enforcing activities. It is likely that Germany's contributions to these tasks will be made as part of a multilateral European endeavor. Progress toward a common foreign and security policy of the twelve would certainly be accelerated if the European Council could develop a well-coordinated CSCE and UN policy.

Yet all these military security issues are of secondary importance to future West-West relations. Just as with East-West relations, the ability of governments to manage economic competition and cooperation is likely to have the most profound influence on the prospects for long-term sustained prosperity in the Northern industrial states. In this context, trade negotiations and agreements that eliminate barriers to the free flow of commodities, technology, or capital are instruments of stability and a peaceful order. Germany will play a prominent role in shaping the emerging Euro-Atlantic community—a role that will require discarding some cherished elements of EC policies, such as the large subsidies to agrobusiness and the aerospace industry.

Finally, the fundamental nonmilitary threat to modern industrial societies emanates from the internal and inevitable functional disparities between the Northern economies and their Third World dependents. While liberal democracy and capitalism have won the battle against authoritarian communism and centralized economies, enemies still exist: "We may have won the Cold War, which is nice—it's more than nice, it's wonderful. But this means that now the enemy is us, not them."[35] History has not ended. Economic and technological progress always enshrine their dialectic contraries—overpopulation, poverty, famine, and unmanageable risks. Even in the well-protected industrial societies of Europe, North America, and Japan, the nuclear, chemical, and genetics industries produce large-scale dangers that defy scientific assessment and preclude reliable damage limitation in the event of serious accidents.[36] Thus, security has become a major preoccupation of civil society as well, but it has not stirred up the necessary concern among political establishments. The most dangerous examples of neglect are the nuclear power plants in Eastern Europe and the former Soviet Union, where dozens of Chernobyls still operate on the brink of disaster, as German environmental studies have shown. Traditional Rapid Reaction Forces and their command structures, logistics, and reconnaissance and surveillance capabilities still receive far greater attention in security policy circles than do the nonexistent European or, for that matter, CSCE task forces for damage limitation in case of nuclear accidents. Such forces would be in desperate need of early-warning and monitoring satellites, huge transport and engineering capabilities, specialized equipment and training for NBC surveillance and decontamination, and medical services of previously unknown flexibility and quantity.

There is a more general way to express such concern, however. The uneven distribution of global poverty and risk may lead to dangerous militarization of the conflicts between the world's privileged classes (the rich countries) and its proletariat (the poor countries). But still more pressing is the fact that economic injustice and social insecurity are irrevocably tied to the massive restructuring taking place east and south of the wealthy Western countries. Contagion is likely—the borders are open, after all. No single country, including one as rich and powerful as Germany, is likely to be able to deal constructively with such transnational risks—one more (and perhaps the most important) reason for a new German security policy that restrains national power and shares burdens and responsibilities in an international environment that has recently been friendly to Germans but continues to pose immense challenges to all peoples. May the Germans defend on that front.

Notes

1. Address given to the North Atlantic Assembly on May 20, 1985, in Stuttgart. See Presse- und Informationsamt der Bundesregierung, *Bulletin*, no. 56 (May 21, 1985), p. 474.

2. See Stanley Hoffman, "A Plan for the New Europe," *New York Review of Books*, January 18, 1990, pp. 18–21. Hoffman envisages German unification occurring toward the end of the 1990s "if the two German electorates so wish." Chancellor Kohl had a similar time frame in mind when he announced his 10-Point Plan for German unification in the Bundestag on November 28, 1989.

3. See, for example, Dan Diner, *Der Krieg der Erinnerungen und die Ordnung der Welt* (Berlin: Rotbuch Verlag, 1991). Karl-Heinz Bohrer, coeditor of *Merkur*, continually attacks what he calls "German provincialism." See his "Provinzialismus (VI). Europrovinzialismus," in *Merkur*, vol. 45 (November 1991), pp. 1059–68.

4. See Michael J. Inacker, "Eine wahre Volksarmee nach einem halben Jahr? Legenden und Wahrheiten über die Nationale Volksarmee nach dem Umbruch in der DDR," in *Aussenpolitik*, vol. 42 (January 1991), pp. 31–36. On May 2, 1990, the chief of staff of the NVA, together with Soviet and Polish staff members, presented then Defense Minister Eppelmann (currently a member of the Bundestag for the CDU) and the participants of a Commanders Conference the outline of a new NVA force structure as well as specific plans for the "Drushba 90" Command Post Exercise. Reprinted in Ministerium für Abrüstung und Verteidigung, *Militärwesen: Zeitschrift für Militärpolitik und Militärtheorie*, Sonderheft, May 10, 1990, pp. 38–48.

5. See the relevant documents in Adam Daniel Rotfeld and Walther Stützle, eds., *Germany and Europe in Transition* (Oxford: SIPRI/Oxford University Press, 1991).

6. See, for example, "CFE Parties Approve U.S.-Soviet Treaty Settlement," in *Arms Control Today*, vol. 21 (July–August 1991), pp. 22 and 30.

7. According to the Ministry of Defense, Bonn, Germany would reduce MBTs by 42%, ACVs by 64%, and artillery by 42%. See *KSE-Vertrag: Anlage 2–3*, November 20, 1990.

8. See Gilbert Gornig, "Die vertragliche Regelung der mit der deutschen Vereinigung verbundenen auswärtigen Probleme," *Aussenpolitik*, vol. 42 (January 1991), pp. 3–12.

9. Full text in Rotfeld and Stützle, *Germany and Europe*, pp. 183–86.

10. The liquidation of not only the Warsaw Treaty Organization but also of NATO seemed a more appropriate way out of the old confrontational structure of East-West relations. See, for instance, the comment of a Soviet participant during a conference held in Potsdam on February 8–10, 1990, reported in Rotfeld and Stützle, *Germany and Europe*, p. 82.

11. Full text in Rotfeld and Stützle, *Germany and Europe*, pp. 150–52.

12. An independent panel of experts has studied in rather general terms the policy and force structure issues the German armed forces are facing. See Unabhängige Kommission für die künftigen Aufgaben der Bundeswehr, *Die künftigen Aufgaben*

der Bundeswehr—Abschlußberichte und Empfehlungen (Bonn: Ministry of Defense, September 1991).

13. The text of the Kohl/Mitterrand message to the chairman of the European Council is published in *Bulletin*, no. 117 (October 18, 1991), pp. 929–31.

14. This was not true, however, for dissident movements organized after 1975, such as Charter 77 in Czechoslovakia and Solidarity in Poland.

15. That function was clearly outlined in the influential article by Josef Joffe, "Europe's American Pacifier," *Foreign Policy*, no. 54 (Spring 1984), pp. 64–82.

16. A recent and concise analysis is presented by Hans-Joachim Giessmann, "Die Sicherheitspolitik in Mittel-Osteuropa," in Reinhard Mutz, Gert Krell, and Heinz Wismann, eds., *Friedensgutachten 1992* (Hamburg/Münster: Lit-Verlag, 1992), pp. 196–206.

17. A good commentary can be found in Secretary of State Baker's speech at the Aspen Institute Berlin on June 18, 1991, "The Euro-Atlantic Architecture: From West to East," reprinted in U.S. Department of State, *Dispatch*, vol. 2 (June 24, 1991), pp. 439–43.

18. See Volker Matthies, "Neues Feindbild Dritte Welt: Verschärft sich der Nord-Süd-Konflikt?" in *Aus Politik und Zeitgeschichte*, Beilage zur Wochenzeitung, *Das Parlament*, no. 25/26 (June 14, 1991), pp. 2–6.

19. See, for example, Christian Krause, *Defensive Verteidigung in Europa— gestern und heute*, Study 36 (Bonn: Abteilung Außenpolitik- und DDR-Forschung, Forschungsinstitut of the Friedrich Ebert Foundation, February 1990); see also Dieter S. Lutz, "Security Partnership and/or Common Security?" in *Coexistence*, vol. 24, no. 3 (1987), pp. 271–307.

20. I borrow this expression from an article by Hans Magnus Enzensberger, "Die Helden des Rückzugs. Brouillon zu einer politischen Moral der Macht," in Frank Schirrmacher (Hrsg). *Im Osten erwacht die Geschichte. Essays zur Revolution in Mittel- und Osteuropa* (Stuttgart: Deutsche Verlags-Anstalt, 1990), pp. 151–58.

21. Even Karl Kaiser, who is associated with conservative SPD security policy, has argued that stationing such missiles in Germany is politically unfeasible. See his "From Nuclear Deterrence to Graduated Conflict Control," *Survival*, vol. 32 (November/December 1990), pp. 483–96, as well as his "Alte Bedrohungen sind gewichen, neue entstanden," in the *Frankfurter Allgemeine Zeitung*, February 13, 1992, pp. 9–10. A thorough discussion of the 1990–91 debate on substrategic nuclear weapons is presented by Matthias Dembinski in "Nukleare Rüstungsdynamik und Rüstungskontrolle in Europa nach Ende des Ost-West-Konflikts," HSFK-Report 2/1991, Frankfurt, July 1991.

22. See, for example, Catherine M. Kelleher, "Short-Range Nuclear Weapons: What Future in Europe?" *Arms Control Today*, vol. 21 (January–February 1991), pp. 17–21. See also William D. Bajusz and Lisa D. Shaw, "The Forthcoming 'SNF Negotiations' " *Survival*, vol. 32 (July–August 1990), pp. 333–47.

23. The most comprehensive and thoughtful account of the German debate has been given by Catherine M. Kelleher, "The Debate over the Modernization of NATO's Short-Range Nuclear Missiles," Stockholm International Peace Research Institute Staff, *SIPRI Yearbook 1990: World Armaments and Disarmament* (Oxford: Oxford University Press, 1990), pp. 603–22.

24. See Ivo H. Daalder, *The CFE Treaty: An Overview and an Assessment* (Washington: Johns Hopkins Foreign Policy Institute, 1991).

25. A state-of-the-art overview of defense dominance and conventional stability concepts is given in Reiner K. Huber, ed., *Military Stability. Prerequisites and*

Analysis Requirements for Conventional Stability in Europe (Baden-Baden: Nomos Verlagsgesellschaft, 1990).

26. For definitions of the whole range of stability concepts see a Working Group I report in Huber, *Military Stability*, pp. 259–63.

27. Sam Nunn, "Strengthen Anti-Missile Defense," *International Herald Tribune*, August 1, 1991, p. 4.

28. For a critical view on the Missile Technology Control Regime see Benoit F. Morel, "Proliferation of Missile Capability," *Disarmament*, vol. 14, no. 3 (1991), pp. 21–43.

29. See, for example, *The United States & NATO in an Undivided Europe: A Report by the Working Group on Changing Roles and Shifting Burdens in the Atlantic Alliance* (Washington: Johns Hopkins Foreign Policy Institute, 1991).

30. In February 1991, the U.S. government had warned the Europeans against uncoupling European defense from NATO's integrated structures. See "Amerika befürchtet seine Ausgrenzung," *Frankfurter Allgemeine Zeitung*, April 9, 1991, p. 7.

31. An interesting view on the feasibility of collective security in Europe is presented by Charles A. Kupchan and Clifford A. Kupchan, "Concerts, Collective Security, and the Future of Europe," *International Security*, vol. 16 (Summer 1991), pp. 114–61.

32. Secretary of State James Baker, "The Euro-Atlantic Architecture," p. 439.

33. This idea has been brilliantly explained in an article by Ernst-Otto Czempiel, "Eine Institution, die Ungewißheit verringert," *Frankfurter Allgemeine Zeitung*, August 21, 1990, p. 8.

34. Speech of President Richard von Weizsäcker addressed to the CSCE Council of Foreign Ministers in Berlin, June 19, 1991, *Bulletin*, no. 72 (June 22, 1991), pp. 579–81.

35. Irving Kristol in his contribution to "Responses to Fukuyama," *National Interest*, no. 16 (Summer 1989), p. 28.

36. A thorough sociological critique of the built-in risks of modern industrial societies is given by Ulrich Beck in *Gegengifte. Die organisierte Unverantwortlichkeit* (Frankfurt: Suhrkamp, 1988) and his earlier *Risikogesellschaft. Auf dem Weg in eine andere Moderne* (Frankfurt: Suhrkamp, 1986).

FIVE

German Foreign Policy after Unification

Harald Müller

STEREOTYPES ABOUND concerning the new Germany, principally because of its history. Twice in this century, Germany has been a destabilizing and destructive force in Europe. Some trace this behavior to the geostrategic imperatives of Germany's location at the center of the European continent, while others see its roots in the German national character. Either way, it has fostered the expectation that a unified Germany will quickly revert to an assertive unilateralism aimed at expansion and ultimately the triumphant domination of a trembling Europe from Berlin.

It is the thesis of this chapter that this prognosis is mistaken. In order to establish a fair standard of comparison to the policies pursued under the government of Chancellor Helmut Kohl, we must go back to the beginning of the century. Thirty years after Bismarck presided over the first unification of Germany, his successors had become the leaders of the most dynamic and economically powerful country in Europe. Driven by high ambitions, fear of encirclement, and a fateful feeling of having been deprived of a well-deserved "place in the sun" of world power, William II's governments pursued a confrontational course that brought Germany into conflict with practically every major neighbor.

This chapter analyzes the newly united Germany for indications that the country could follow a similar course today. It starts with a short review of the politics of unification, records the intra-German debate on the new German identity and foreign policy strategy, and then briefly describes the most important foreign policy challenges for Germany since unification: the Gulf War and the ensuing debate on Germany's "global responsibility," including the steps taken on sensitive export controls; the relationship with Poland and Czechoslovakia and German policy during the Yugoslav crisis; and Germany's efforts to shape the architecture of European security after the Cold War and its contribution to the further integration process of the European Community. The chapter concludes by summarizing the characteristics of the new German foreign policy identity.

Prelude: The Road to Unification

That Kohl single-mindedly steamrollered over the rest of Europe to unification without due consultation with his partners is a myth that sticks in many minds. In fact, this is a misrepresentation of what actually happened between November 1989 and October 1990.

It took the government three weeks to make up its mind which course to follow. During those weeks, the slogans in the streets of East Germany had changed from "We are the people" to "We are one people." For the East Germans, two weekends of visits to West German cities glittering with wealth in the pre-Christmas period had eliminated any thought of an independent "third way," and, through the broken Wall, streams of immigrants started to arrive in West Germany.

When Kohl announced his 10-Point Plan on November 28, 1989, after only brief, last-minute consultations with his allies, he was not aiming at unification. Rather, he proposed a protracted process of confederation, with "federation" as a remote and vague long-term goal. One-third of his plan was devoted to embedding intra-German rapprochement into the process of West European integration and all-European accommodation. If necessary, Kohl was even willing to propose a moratorium on political union to the Soviets in order to gain their blessing for a rapprochement between the two German states.[1]

He adapted his course toward unification as events unfolded during the next eight weeks. One important reason was his two encounters with East German Minister-President Hans Modrow, who declared during the second meeting that his country was virtually bankrupt and painted an economic picture much worse than what the West German government had imagined. In addition, Kohl was almost overrun by masses of sympathizers in Dresden in December 1989, something that had never happened to him in West Germany. And public opinion polls—now possible for the first time in East Germany—revealed that between 2 million and 4.5 million East Germans were literally sitting on their luggage, ready to enter West Germany if change did not come. After the reality of the situation had sunk in, Kohl and Foreign Minister Hans-Dietrich Genscher acted determinedly. Unity had become not a matter of choice, but an economic and political necessity. They now believed that they had to accelerate the process by opening up the prospect of prompt economic unity; otherwise, stability in Central and Eastern Europe could be lost for good. They still believed, however, that political unity was a mid-term prospect, to be achieved no sooner than within three to five years.[2]

Kohl's course was soon vindicated by the March elections in East Germany, in which all the winning parties endorsed unification and the Christian Democratic Union (CDU) won because it was seen as the force most capable of achieving unification quickly.

Once it became clear that unification would become a reality far sooner than had been expected, domestic considerations entered the picture. Kohl's party started at a disadvantage compared to the main opposition party, for the CDU's counterpart in East Germany was tainted by its collaboration with the old regime. To overcome this handicap, Kohl was forced to present himself as the "father" of German unity. Domestic political considerations also dictated that unity come before the year-end elections, which would then be all-German, making Kohl an almost certain winner.[3]

The first factor driving unification, therefore, was the behavior of the East Germans, which neither the East nor the West German government could control. The second, following from the first, was simple election politics. The third important factor was the growing concern about the stability of Soviet President Mikhail Gorbachev's government. Kohl and his colleagues believed that the "window of opportunity" for unification would be open only while Gorbachev remained in power. The uncertainty of the situation in the Soviet Union indicated that it would be better to seize the opportunity sooner rather than later. Thus, when the first signals emerged from Moscow at the end of January indicating that there was no real opposition to unification, the German leaders understood that they could set their own timetable.[4]

From early 1990 on, Kohl and Genscher took the goal of unification (first economic and then political) so seriously that they easily overruled the usual neocorporatist process of consensus-building between ministries, bureaucracies, and nongovernmental organizations. The concerns of the ministries and the Bundesbank were put aside, and business associations were rarely consulted on unification's political aspects.[5]

From the beginning of January on, Germany often used the European Community and NATO to convey their views and to rally support. The government placed the utmost importance on anchoring the unification process firmly in both Western institutions, as announced in Kohl's 10-Point Plan. In the first quarter of 1990 alone, there were twenty-nine meetings on German unity at the head of state and ministerial level with the country's European partners.[6] This process was all the more important as Germany could have been tempted to accept neutrality as a condition of unification. Indeed, even some inside the country—including in the opposition parties—seemed willing to pay this price. The Soviet Union also played with this card, though it never really attempted to trump.

On the basic issue, however, the Germans were crystal clear and very firm. Because the Kohl government felt that unity must be achieved quickly, it did not wait for permission to pursue the policies of unification. Not only was the situation vis-à-vis the East German emigrant situation extremely volatile, but the increasing instability of the Soviet Union raised the possibility that the window of opportunity might soon close. There was no time for a protracted and possibly controversial discourse on the pros and cons of unification. The immediate reactions of the European allies had not been entirely positive, especially the biting remarks from London and a hastily arranged visit by French President François Mitterrand to the ailing East German government on December 20–22, 1989. But Kohl and Genscher, after making sure they had the backing of Washington, proceeded on the assumption that unification was the right course. Whether they wanted to or not, the European allies would have to fall in line.[7]

From then on, however, every step of the unification process was carefully coordinated with the Western allies. For them, the basic condition of unification was that Germany remain in NATO and the EC—something the German government also desired. When the decisive Kohl-Gorbachev meeting took place in July 1990, Kohl acted on the understanding that he had a broad mandate from the West to negotiate. What he brought home was a Soviet concession on the main point: membership of a united Germany in NATO. Two of the concessions he made in return—reaffirmation of Germany's renunciation of nuclear weapons and a ceiling on troop strength—were no doubt welcomed by Germany's Western neighbors and had been cleared in advance with the United States. The one concession that was somewhat controversial to Kohl's Western allies—the agreement not to station NATO troops or nuclear weapons in the eastern part of Germany after unification—did not detract from the security or solidarity of the alliance. In short, when Kohl paved the way for the Two plus Four Treaty, he did not breach the mandate given by the Western alliance. He acted in line with the plan he had announced earlier in the year, and no one should have been surprised that he took advantage of the unique opportunity that arose.[8]

Overall, the story of unification cannot be offered as proof of Germany's relentless unilateralism. On the contrary, given that the highest national interests were at stake, the unification process was embedded in an astonishing web of consultations and mutual adjustments. That the German government took advantage of opportunities that presented themselves, accelerated the unification process when the urgency of the situation became clear, and was unwilling to entertain arguments about a political goal that had received Western support throughout the Cold War period can hardly be seen as a sign of exceptional unilateralism, pushiness, or power politics.[9]

The Public Debate on Germany's New Foreign Policy

It was the criticism of German policy during the Gulf War that forced the German political establishment to reluctantly re-examine its existing foreign policy. This task was complicated by the fact that two powerful and opposing forces were at work. On the one hand, Germany was expected to assume new responsibilities on the international level that would be in keeping with its more powerful position; on the other, it was expected to downplay its newly acquired power—or at least to demonstrate a willingness to actively dilute it—in order to assuage growing fears of an assertive and potentially dangerous German giant. In the internal debate on Germany's new foreign policy, these fears were widely acknowledged and became a guiding concern in the formulation of that policy. This open-mindedness and sensitivity differed markedly from German reactions to such criticisms in the past.

The policy adopted by the German government had four major components. The first was to pursue vigorously the integration of Germany into the principal international organizations to which it belonged, notably the European Community, the West European Union (WEU), NATO, and the Conference for Security and Cooperation in Europe (CSCE), with an emphasis on building a stronger, more inclusive institutional structure for the latter. Transatlantic relations and the U.S. military presence in Europe were not to be compromised in the process. This strategy, which can best be described as "self-containment by integration," was designed to soothe fears that Germany would once again become a "loose cannon" in Europe by demonstrating that its freedom of action was firmly circumscribed. The strategy, however, required more than a general commitment to greater integration; special initiatives intended to enhance institutional growth (and with it German entanglement) were needed. This explains German efforts to bolster the CSCE, its determined pursuit with France of European political union, and its support for the predominantly U.S. proposals to reform and strengthen NATO.[10]

The second component to the new German foreign policy was the strong emphasis placed on nonmilitary instruments. These were intended to mitigate the fear among Germany's neighbors that the country's economic power would translate into added political influence, which would inevitably turn into military pressure. These instruments included the following: economic assistance (for Central and Eastern Europe, the Soviet Union, and developing countries), arms control measures, environmental agreements, and creative proposals for institutional evolution.[11] At the same time the military component of Germany's "self-containment" policy included such open steps as reaffirming the country's renunciation of all nuclear weapons and limiting the united Germany's armed forces to 370,000 troops, even though no other European country had made a similar commitment. When it became clear in the debate on Germany's "new responsibility" that an out-of-area role for the Bundeswehr was inevitable, the government also worked hard to enhance the integration of German troops within NATO. The new NATO concept of a multinational corps was willingly accepted, but German troops were to participate in out-of-area missions only in a multilateral framework.

The third component of the government's strategy was a carefully selected set of initiatives to show that Germany was responding adequately to calls for it to assume a higher profile on the international stage. Thus, Germany took the lead in asking for international aid for Central and Eastern Europe and the Soviet Union, arguing that a "welfare wall" would hurt German and Western security interests.[12] Germany participated in efforts to help the Kurds in Iraq, in the process pushing the limits of what was possible under the consensus interpretation of the constitution. At the same time it initiated an internal debate on changing the constitution to allow German soldiers to participate in out-of-area missions and proposed reforms in the United Nations, asserting the UN's right to intervene in cases involving significant violations of human or minority rights and to impose sanctions when global ecological security is threatened by national policies.[13] Furthermore, Germany developed new criteria for development assistance that would make aid contingent on the recipient's respect for human rights, evolution towards democracy and a market economy, and restraint in weapons procurement.[14] International environmental policy initiatives were similarly enhanced, most notably with a program for saving tropical rain forests and a "climate convention" at the Environmental Summit in Rio in June 1992, another sign that environmental policy ranks almost as high on the German foreign policy agenda as economic and security policy.[15] In all these cases, the German government took great pains to emphasize its commitment to a multilateral approach. The one exception was its policy toward the Yugoslav republics of Croatia and Slovenia, the strongest example to date of German leadership in joint EC foreign policy. While Germany tried to pursue this policy in a multilateral framework, it did so with an unusual amount of arm-twisting and muscle-flexing.

The final component of the strategy was designed directly to reassure neighbors, friends, and potential enemies that Germany would not, for example, seek a new Rapallo, turn neutral, or revive the old style of power politics by explaining how Germans saw the world and why the new Germany was different from the country that wrought havoc on an earlier Europe.[16] Part of this campaign consisted of speaking openly about the past and emphasizing that Germany had learned from history. German leaders pointed to the stable roots of democracy in their country and to German opposition to a revival of nationalism in Europe.[17] They made European integration the centerpiece of German foreign policy, explaining that Germany was not interested in power politics but preferred to follow what Genscher termed a "policy of responsibility." As German President Richard von Weizsäcker put it,

> Of course, the united Germany carries, with its population, its economic power, and its central geographical location, a certain weight in Europe. But it

has become—in the old FRG—a totally and completely Westernized country and will remain so after unification. Germany has irrevocably evolved by constitution, basic values, and way of life into a democratic society of citizens that can stand up in every way to a comparison with the other Western democracies. And externally, it has shown far fewer national reservations and more readiness to integrate than many other European countries.[18]

The new German foreign policy strategy also reflected German public opinion. Polls taken in 1990 showed that Germans agreed with the principles put forward by this policy. Most important, the integrationist strategy was embraced by a majority of the population. About half of the respondents— more in east Germany—put even greater weight than before on European integration, while only a small minority considered it less important. And, while NATO was seen as the best guarantee for peace in Europe by two-thirds of West Germans but only one-third of East Germans, two-thirds of the respondents from both Germanies supported continued German membership in the alliance. Fewer than one-fourth preferred neutrality (table 5-1). In other words, the government was on firm ground with its emphasis on institutional entanglement.

To no one's surprise, Kohl's party was closest to his own line of policy. Some 53 percent of the supporters of the coalition between the CDU and the Christian Social Union (CSU) held that European integration had become more important than before, and 85 percent supported a united Germany's continued membership in NATO.[19] Integration, a stronger emphasis on transatlantic links (as compared to the CSCE),[20] and drawing Central and Eastern Europe and the Soviet republics into the realm of market economy and democracy were the pillars of the conservative strategy. The CDU emphasized not only Germany's global responsibility but also the normalization of relations with its European partners, which would keep it from being singled out as a "special case." Consequently, the party devoted much attention to the possibility of allowing the Bundeswehr to participate in out-of-area operations. This issue was important for another reason: it was one of the few serious disagreements between the CDU and the opposition parties over foreign policy.[21]

The CDU's Bavarian partner, the CSU, by and large followed the same line, but with some notable differences. The CSU maintained a more geopolitical and less institutional line of foreign policy reasoning, and its pronouncements had a more nationalistic tone. In 1991, CSU Chairman and Minister of Finance Theo Waigel declared that the main task of German foreign policy was "to represent German interests effectively on the international level, together with our partners and friends"; exactly how the partners and friends could be persuaded to express German interests was not made clear.[22] NATO and German-American relations received even more attention in the CSU

Table 5-1. *German Opinions on European Integration and German Unification, 1990*
Percent

| Category | Will German unification make the process of European integration more or less important?[a] | | |
	More important	Less important	Unchanged
Total Germany	49	12	38
West Germany	47	13	40
East Germany	56	11	31

| Category | What is the best guarantee for peace?[a] | | |
	NATO	Neutrality	Undecided
Total Germany	57	28	15
West Germany	64	21	15
East Germany	31	51	16

| Category | Should a united Germany be a member of NATO?[b] | | |
	Yes	No	Undecided
Total Germany	66.8	24.7	8.5

Source: Hans-Joachim Veen, "Die Westbindungen der Deutschen in einer Phase der Neuorientierung," *Europa-Archiv*, vol. 46, no. 2 (1991), pp. 38, 40.
a. September 1990.
b. June 1990.

than in the CDU. In early 1992, the CSU began to place stronger emphasis on the importance of national interests, including in its platform a demand that the friendship treaty between Germany and Czechoslovakia be renegotiated to give more weight to the property claims of ethnic Germans who had emigrated from Czechoslovakia.[23] This policy culminated in the May 1992 announcement of the CSU-led government of Bavaria that it would vote against the German-Czechoslovak friendship treaty in the Bundesrat, the upper chamber of Parliament.

The Free Democratic party (FDP), to which Genscher belonged, concentrated on supporting its "star" member of the government. As a consequence, it was the most institutionalist and least unilateralist or nationalist of all the German parties. This corresponded to the desires of FDP voters: 56 percent believed in the increasing importance of European unification, and 83 percent wanted NATO membership for a united Germany.[24] The FDP valued the rapid expansion of CSCE institutions significantly more than its conservative partners did. Arms control and arms reductions, including a comprehensive test ban treaty, were listed as more important than German participation in out-of-area operations under the auspices of the United Nations. The FDP also took a more explicit stand against nationalism and German hegemony in Europe.[25] While the CDU did not see a contradiction between power and responsibility,[26] the FDP wanted Germany to choose responsibility over power.[27]

The Social Democrats (SPD) agreed with the government's main foreign policy principles, creating a problem for itself as the opposition party. The SPD consequently sought a distinct profile by supporting bolder steps toward disarmament,[28] more sympathy for the CSCE, more skepticism toward (though not outright opposition to) NATO, and highly restrictive conditions for out-of-area missions for the Bundeswehr. Otherwise, the SPD supported the goal of a United States of Europe (and multilateralism in general) and asked for a radical reform of the United Nations to make it a collective security system free of privileges for individual states. The SPD's agenda was not, however, entirely free of unilateralist and nationalist overtones. These were expressed in the party's claim that Germany has a singular role to play in international "peace politics," its insistence that Germany had no alliance obligations during the Gulf War, and its desire to revoke all special rights of the Western powers that remained in Germany after unification, even those based on bilateral treaties and agreements.[29] The party's positions reflected the attitudes of its voters. Some 47 percent believed that the importance of European unification had increased; 35 percent preferred neutrality as the best guarantee for peace; and 58 percent supported membership in NATO, giving the SPD the highest level of support for neutrality and the lowest level of support for NATO of all the major German parties.[30] Mirroring the differences among its voters, the party itself was somewhat split. The left wing, led by Oskar Lafontaine, Heide Wieczorek-Zeul, Herman Scheer, and others, was more openly skeptical of NATO, pacifistic, and nationalistic, while the center-right, under Björn Engholm, Johannes Rau, Hans-Jochen Vogel, and Hans-Ulrich Klose, was more in line with the mainstream German foreign policy.

Green voters agreed with the other parties in their support for European unification (48 percent) but were unique in that only one-third supported continued German membership in NATO.[31] Dissolving NATO had long been a popular goal of Green members,[32] but a growing minority of the party had begun to view NATO membership as a way to control German power ambitions.

Other parties, such as the Party of Democratic Socialism (PDS) and the right-wingers (the Republicans, the National Party of Germany [NPD], and the German People's Union [DVU]), deviated from the norm in their fundamental opposition to NATO (mainly the PDS) or to the European Community (the right-wing extremists) but played no role in the debate. The main conclusion that can be drawn from this brief analysis is that an astonishing degree of consensus existed on the most decisive questions of foreign policy and even on details of strategy—for example, the link between economic and political union in the EC, the relentless push toward further institutionalizing the CSCE, and Yugoslavia. Thus a consistent feature of the foreign policy debates in the Bundestag in 1990–91 was the difficulty party leaders had in explaining why their party differences remained important.[33]

The Gulf War and German Policy

German policy during the Gulf crisis has been perceived as lackluster, weak, pacifistic, and neutralist, among other things. In fact, Germany's policy was not very different from that of its most important allies. Early on, Kohl condemned Iraqi dictator Saddam Hussein's invasion of Kuwait and declared solidarity with alliance efforts. The Germans supported the UN Security Council initiatives, offered financial support for troop deployment during the fall of 1991, and opened German territory for overflight, logistic, and material support for U.S. transport and resupply activities.

There were, however, three major weaknesses in the German position. The first was simply a lack of commitment. It is important to understand that, by the time the situation in the Gulf had evolved into a crisis, Germany was deeply involved in making unification a reality. The process of unification not only absorbed public attention and psychic energy but tied down the best brains in the government. Most ministries were working overtime to complete the complex legal formulas for the internal unification treaty. The foreign ministry was preoccupied with the Two plus Four Treaty and the integration of the German issue into the CSCE process that would culminate in the Paris agreements. The Defense Ministry had the extremely delicate task of working to integrate the former East German Army into the Bundeswehr, and the Foreign and Defense Offices were also involved in finalizing the Treaty on Conventional Forces in Europe (CFE), which was of great importance to the security of the united Germany. That the first all-German election campaign was under way did not help either.[34] Top-level bureaucracies and political leaders were left with little time to address world policy issues.

The second weakness of the German position stemmed from the fact that war fitted neither the political needs nor the mood of the people. One of the most nagging problems of German diplomacy was reassuring the world that a united Germany would be nonmilitaristic and peaceful. Germany was also seeking to establish a security system in Europe that would exclude war as a practical instrument of policy. The prospect of a war in the Persian Gulf was at odds with both efforts. During the last months of 1990, neither German diplomacy nor the internal debate was able to reconcile the political needs emerging from the unification process with the increasing probability of an armed clash in a distant desert. Consequently, German statements on the crisis concentrated on mediation, peacemaking, compromise, and diplomatic efforts to prevent war rather than on the possibility of military intervention. Because they failed to grasp the reality of the situation, the German public and the government itself were mentally unprepared for the real fighting in 1991.[35]

The third weakness consisted of the constitutional impediments to direct participation in the operations of the U.S.-led coalition. The German political establishment held that, according to the terms of the existing constitution, German soldiers were not permitted to participate in these operations. Early in the conflict, German leaders had made this clear to the alliance, although they had also indicated that they were working to change the situation.[36] This statement may have created the unrealistic expectation that the legal barrier could be removed before hostilities began (or ended) in the Gulf. Some of the criticism of Germany was certainly based on disappointment at the fact that what the alliance had taken as a promise was not fulfilled in time.

At the beginning of the crisis, several hundred Germans were hijacked by Iraqi authorities and used as hostages. The German government came under heavy domestic pressure to strike a deal with Saddam Hussein to liberate the hostages, and this pressure increased as a stream of elder statesmen from other countries went to Baghdad and succeeded in freeing some of their fellow citizens. Then Willy Brandt, Germany's principal elder statesman, felt obligated to do the same. The German government at first opposed the idea, fearing that Brandt's trip would be interpreted as a breach by Germany of the EC agreement to hold firm on the hostage issue. When it was no longer possible to resist the domestic pressure, Kohl asked Brandt to wrap a "European mantle" around the visit by inviting a conservative and a liberal from two other European countries to make the journey with him. Brandt refused and went to Baghdad with, as the government put it, the leadership's tolerance, but not its support. While Kohl was not completely happy with Brandt's activities (which included, in addition to hostage-freeing, discussing the substance of the Gulf conflict with Hussein), he would not criticize Brandt, who returned on November 9, 1990, with 175 hostages from 11 countries, among them 131 Germans. Genscher himself defended Brandt against foreign criticism at a conference of European ministers.[37]

Meanwhile, the question of German participation in the Gulf War was fully under way. During the fall, it was decided that Germany had to support the alliance's effort financially. The initial contribution was DM 3.3 billion for the U.S., together with supplies of military equipment and munitions. Among the supplies were sixty Fuchs special armored carriers re-equipped specifically for the desert environment, the best equipment available for field intelligence on chemical munitions.[38] A minesweeping unit with 7 ships and 570 sailors was also deployed in the eastern Mediterranean, but U.S. suggestions to send the unit to the Suez Canal were rejected due to the constitutional limitations on German troop maneuvers. In addition, German territory was opened without restriction for U.S. resupply efforts.[39]

The German government did respond to the Turkish request for assistance from the alliance, however; eighteen Alpha Jet fighters and 212 German soldiers were deployed to Turkey.[40] The decision was highly controversial. The SPD claimed that the government risked making the German soldiers pawns of Turkish President Turgut Özal's ambitious politics (a point that was also of concern to Genscher) and that Germany would be drawn into the war. The SPD threatened a constitutional suit. Legal experts in the FDP doubted whether an attack on Turkey in retaliation for the alliance's actions would constitute the kind of attack on a NATO ally that justified German support, while the CDU and Ministry of Defense maintained that it would. Only an order from Kohl created a unified government position supporting the U.S.-led coalition.[41] However, according to the government, the German soldiers in Turkey would not engage in active combat unless the government decided the issue separately, and only a clear-cut case of aggression against Turkey would convince the government to give the order to fight.[42]

This development showed clearly that the government itself had had second thoughts about the matter. First, it was concerned about domestic stability, particularly in the new states in eastern Germany, where opposition to war was much stronger than it was in western Germany. Second, the failure of the U.S. to consult with its allies before making its decision in October to send more troops to Saudi Arabia raised fears that the U.S. was irrevocably moving toward combat that could involve Germany.[43] Thus, Kohl and Genscher issued strong statements in the first two weeks of January 1991. Genscher stated, "The determination to maintain international law must not automatically lead to a war. Everything must be done to give diplomacy a chance. He who does not want to shoot must talk." They also supported Mitterrand's single-handed attempt at last-minute mediation, resisted U.S. proposals to add ground troops to the air defense units in Turkey, and declined to move the units closer to the border.[44]

On the eve of the war, Kohl once again emphasized Germany's interest in a peaceful solution to the crisis, but he rejected appeasement. Germany, he reaffirmed, was not neutral in the conflict and fully supported the alliance's efforts.[45] He repeated this theme throughout the fighting,[46] along with expressions of hope for an early peace and more appreciation for Gorbachev's attempts at mediation than was heard from other European leaders.[47]

The attacks on Israel ushered in another period of embarrassment for Germany. The contribution German companies had made to Iraq's missile and chemical arsenals raised the horrifying specter of Jews once again becoming victims of German poison gas. The government responded immediately with expressions of solidarity with Israel, DM 250 million in humanitarian aid, special Fuchs armored vehicles for antichemical warfare, and Patriot air defense missiles. A stream of German politicians from all parties and with the explicit support of the government visited Israel in a show of solidarity.[48] Another financial contribution of $ 5.5 billion was granted to the war effort in order to enhance the visibility of the German commitment to the coalition. Germany added Roland and Hawk anti-aircraft missile units with about 800 troops to protect the airfields in Turkey where the ACE Mobile Force (AMF) was deployed.[49]

Meanwhile, the domestic debate on the war raged on. The SPD, led by Lafontaine, condemned the deployments to Turkey, argued against the use of force, and opposed Germany's financial contributions.[50] Demonstrations took place in the major cities; the largest occurred in Bonn on January 26, 1991, attracting around 200,000 participants.[51] The number of conscientious objectors rose from 22,197 in January 1991 to 30,000 in February 1991, an increase of 26 percent from the second half of 1990, when the total number of conscientious objectors had fallen by 5 percent.[52]

The center-right in the SPD, led by Klose, the future chairman of the SPD caucus in the Bundestag, and Klaus Matthiesen, a minister in North Rhine-Westphalia, asked for German solidarity with the war effort. Some prominent members of the German left, such as Green members Petra Kelly, Joschka Fischer, Micha Brumlik, and Bundestag Deputy Konrad Weiss, pointed out Germany's responsibility for Israel's security. Singer Wolf Biermann and writer Hans Magnus Enzensberger, not renowned for their conservatism, compared Hussein with Hitler and declared that the alliance's operations were a "liberation from evil."[53] The FDP supported Genscher's line, which offered qualified support for the alliance, while the CDU stood behind Kohl. The CSU criticized the government for not offering the alliance more support, as well as for not using the opportunity to demonstrate Germany's new importance on the world scene.[54]

Interestingly enough, public opinion in Germany did not deviate from the general Western pattern. About 60 percent of Germans believed that it was right to fight Hussein, though this percentage was lower in eastern Germany. A majority thought that it was right to offer financial help and to deploy troops to Turkey, though a majority in eastern Germany opposed both moves.[55] Thus, the government kept in line with the majority view.

Despite the many claims on its energy and finances, Germany was on the right side during the Gulf War, and its contributions to the alliance were heavy. Before the end of the war, the German taxpayer's share amounted to more than DM 16 billion (not including the costs of the deployment in Turkey and the eastern Mediterranean), or one-third of the annual defense budget. Germany had deployed as many as 3,200 soldiers in connection with the war.[56] As Kohl rightly put it, "We have dedicated ourselves to the side of freedom, law, and justice during the Gulf conflict, using such means as were available in accord with our constitution."[57] But even these strong statements did not help abate the criticism from abroad. Germany's behavior was proof that, while the Germans had experienced considerable difficulty accepting the use of force as a legitimate instrument of policy even in such an extreme case, they had accepted it, though not without heated debate and controversy and only in a multilateral and international-legal context.[58] Nevertheless, at the end of the war, the international and domestic debates on Germany's future role intensified.

The Debate on Out-of-Area Missions

The Gulf War had made it obvious to Germany's political establishment that the country's global military role was the key issue in the debates on the "new responsibility" and, ultimately, Germany's national identity. While it was generally accepted that military security had lost its priority to such issues as environmental security, east-west migration, and economic stability and that Germany must give priority to such issues and the corresponding nonmilitary instruments, it was also acknowledged that the united Germany's military role had to be more clearly defined.

After World War II, West Germany's position on engaging in military activities was based on an unequivocal interpretation of ambiguous legal language. The constitution, or Basic Law, permitted Germany to participate in systems of collective security but precluded the Bundeswehr's involvement in any but defense activities—including defense within an alliance—unless explicitly authorized elsewhere in the constitution. According to this interpretation, UN missions could be placed under the heading of "collective security." However, the time-honored interpretation was that missions outside the area covered by the North Atlantic Treaty were not legitimized by the constitution. This interpretation had been confirmed by a cabinet decision of the pre-1982 coalition government, which consisted of the SPD and FDP, shortly before its breakup and was reaffirmed by the new Kohl government shortly after it took power.[59]

The new debate triggered by the Gulf War began with the premise that the consensus position was no longer tenable, a belief opposed only by the PDS, the Greens, and the left wing of the SPD. Their principal objections were based on an old-fashioned Marxist-Leninist critique of Western imperialism, on radical pacifism, and on the deep mistrust of what some critics perceived as the global ambitions of the new, assertive Germany.[60] A sizable majority of the political establishment agreed that a change in Germany's policy toward international military involvement was needed. It was also generally agreed that such a revision would mean amending the constitution rather than just changing the way it was interpreted, for two reasons. First, simply reinterpreting a long-held policy would seriously compromise German credibility. Second, the Bundeswehr might be called on to join a UN mission while a constitutional suit against the government's decision permitting such participation was under way, a situation that would be unfair to the soldiers.[61] At this point, however, agreement ended. The CDU/CSU held that a change was needed not for legal but for political reasons.[62] The FDP and the SPD maintained that such a change was required for substantive legal reasons; a new policy, they felt, could not be based on the present Basic Law.[63]

But no one could agree on what the change should entail. The only compromise the left wing of the SPD was willing to accept was participation in UN peacekeeping operations. Even then, German involvement would require a ceasefire, the consent of the warring parties, a mandate by the UN Security Council, operational control by the UN, and the participation of other European governments. This compromise, won by a relatively small 230–179 majority during the SPD convention in May 1991, was possible only because the new leader, Engholm, made support for the agreement a vote of confidence in his leadership. This demonstrates how strong the resistance of the left was to any enlargement of the Bundeswehr's role.[64] The SPD refused to sanction German participation in combat missions under Chapter VII of the UN Charter, with or without operational control by the UN Military Staff Committee. It gave as reasons fears that German soldiers might become pawns of superpower (principally U.S.) interests; the idea that military force, rather than being a legitimate and useful instrument of policy, is a cure worse than any conceivable disease; and the belief developed as consequence of Germany's history that the country should not take an active role in any military operations.[65]

There were some dissenting voices in the SPD right and center factions, however. The new caucus leader, Klose; the party leader, Engholm himself; Foreign Policy Speaker Norbert Gansel; and possibly a majority in the Bundestag caucus would no doubt have preferred a broader mandate for all UN operations.[66] Unequivocally, however, the SPD objected to accepting a WEU mandate as the single justification for sending German troops on out-of-area operations.[67]

The FDP followed Genscher, who before the Gulf War had promoted exactly what the SPD agreed on in its aftermath: confining the Bundeswehr's out-of-area missions to blue helmet peacekeeping activities. After the war, however, Genscher switched to supporting all Chapter VII UN missions. Genscher's primary aim was to avoid challenging the generally reluctant attitude of the Germans toward military involvement. The participation of German soldiers in NATO or WEU out-of-area units was also to be confined to cases for which a UN mandate existed. If the constitution were to be changed, Genscher believed, the missions mandated by the change would require explicit UN authorization.[68] FDP members accepted the position of their most prominent foreign policy specialist without demurring. They argued for a well-considered change in the constitution and against rushing into a hasty compromise. In addition to a Security Council mandate, the FDP wanted fighting missions restricted to those that included other EC members, as well as a joint EC force for UN missions and a Bundestag vote on each decision to deploy German troops under a specific mandate in order to limit both the scope of the amendment and the power of the executive.[69]

The CDU, with Kohl at the top, made it clear from the beginning that it would not be content with changing the constitution to legitimate blue helmets missions only. For a time, the party pondered the argument that the constitution would not need changing at all if a multilateral framework were made available that would satisfy the "collective security" stipulation. At the time of this writing, the CDU leadership has avoided the expression "change," preferring "clarification" of the law, a term based on a rather broad interpretation of "collective security." Beyond UN missions, the CDU sees NATO out-of-area operations or similar missions conducted under the aegis of the WEU as falling under this label.[70] As CDU Foreign Policy Speaker Hans Stercken put it, neither the UN nor the CSCE is strong and reliable enough to provide security in and out of the area. For this reason, German participation in bodies with a real capability for effective action must be secured.[71]

The CDU was far more anxious to terminate the special constraints on Germany and reduce the chance that Germany would once again embark on a unilateral path by eliminating all impediments to German participation in a common European defense than it was to accept military restraints derived from the country's past.[72] The CSU was even more outspoken in this respect, and some on the right wing of the CDU/CSU coalition would certainly have preferred to put Germany on an equal footing with its partners France and Great Britain by eliminating all constitutional restraints and allowing German military actions to be guided by international law and national interest. But those holding this view were aware that majority support for their position was lacking, even within their own party. For example, CDU arms control spokesman Karl Franz Lamers strongly emphasized nonmilitary means of preserving peace and security and stated that military instruments were not the most important priority by far in German policy.[73]

The question is still under consideration, and no end is yet in sight. All relevant parts of the political establishment see that a change is necessary, but the divergences remain so large that it is uncertain whether any position can attract the two-thirds majority needed for constitutional change. However, new Minister of Defense Volker Rühe has indicated that, for the time being, public opinion will not tolerate any but peacekeeping activities, so that any clarification in the law must be confined to permitting only these missions. Full participation in Chapter VII actions remains a long-term objective.[74] In the meantime, the government has, with great care and sophistication, provided more leeway under the present interpretation. It decided, for example, to send German minesweepers to the Persian Gulf after the war ended, and 7 ships with 570 sailors operated in Gulf waters from April through July 1991.[75] Clearing the Gulf of remaining Iraqi mines was justified as serving humanitarian purposes, but it sent German soldiers on duty out of the NATO area—and thus set a precedent. When Iraqi action against the Kurds was in full swing, Germany set up camps in Turkey and Iran and established a supply operation from Iranian soil, again employing the Bundeswehr. This involved as many as three daily flights by Transall military transport aircraft in Turkey and the deployment of twenty military helicopters in Iran.[76] Germany also offered the UN Special Commission tasked with finding and destroying Iraq's weapons of mass destruction heavy transport helicopters flown by German pilots. And finally, German military medical personnel became part of the UN mission in Cambodia.[77] To the government's credit, in none of these cases has the opposition dared object to such an overtly humanitarian mission. The SPD was also concerned that a constitutional challenge might end with a court opinion that permitted this sort of activity—and perhaps collective security operations as well—without a change in the constitution, completely undermining the SPD's position in the debate. In any case, the German public became accustomed to at least the idea of German soldiers participating in UN missions.[78]

Today, it is unlikely that the CDU position, which would permit German forces to join NATO and WEU operations not covered by a UN mandate, will ever command a majority. Not only does such a concept run counter to majority opinion in German political parties, but it would also be unpopular; any attempt to engage German soldiers in out-of-area activities is likely to face stiff objections from the German people. Under these circumstances, the most that can be expected is a bill proposing German participation, together with its EC partners, in all UN operations—in effect the FDP position—which might split the opposition and attract enough votes.

Eliminating Irresponsibility: The Reform of Export Policy

Germany has acquired a reputation as the world's most prominent supplier of equipment for the production of weapons of mass destruction to developing countries.[79] Certainly Germany is not the only sinner, and its fairly restrictive export policy on military hardware is often overlooked abroad. But it is also true that German companies share a disproportionate amount of the responsibility for having supported nuclear projects in Pakistan and South Africa, chemical weapons programs in Libya and Iraq, and missile programs in Argentina and India.

The overly liberal philosophy dominating foreign economic policy during the last few decades has made the country the favorite spot for the illegal acquisition activities of threshold nuclear countries. Among the many German engineering, machinery, and chemical companies were those willing to circumvent or breach the law for a sizable profit. The controlling agencies, badly understaffed and underequipped, were often unable to keep track of the deals, may have misunderstood others, and sometimes lacked the authority to intervene because of legal loopholes—for example, they were often not supplied with accurate lists of items requiring special export licenses, and some transactions were even exempted from reporting requirements. The poor quality of the law reflected the attitude of the political leadership. Germany, limited to exercising its power economically and with a rather provincial outlook on world politics, gave commercial gain a higher priority than more general foreign policy and security considerations.[80]

This changed, however, toward the end of the 1980s, in part due to an adjustment of bureaucratic power that gave the Foreign Office a stronger position vis-à-vis the commercially minded Ministries of Economics and of Research and Technology, and in part due to a series of scandals involving German supplies to the "usual suspects" of world politics. These scandals directed the attention of the German public, parliament, and leadership to export policies and, from about 1988 on, led to changes in the relevant laws, regulations, and administrative procedures. After the revelations of German support for the Rhabta chemical weapons plant in Libya, the speed of these changes was accelerated considerably.

The unification process added further urgency to the issue of export control reform. The government and the opposition both agreed that a reaffirmation of Germany's renunciation of all biological, chemical, and nuclear weapons was necessary to smooth the unification process and would become a cornerstone of the foreign policy of the united Germany. (This reaffirmation was in fact included as Article 3.1 of the Two plus Four Treaty).[81] A consistent and efficient export control policy, furthermore, would provide proof that Germany took its new responsibility seriously. In addition, the unified Germany was not content, as it had been in the past, to acquiesce passively to nonproliferation policies designed by others. It wanted to promote such policies actively as a priority on its global security agenda; export controls, therefore, were viewed as indispensable to the credibility to this effort.[82] Although CDU and FDP deputies close to industry made some initial attempts to delay and water down the legislation, strong government pressure overcame these pockets of resistance.[83]

Between 1989 and the spring of 1991, five major changes were made in export law and twenty-six to export regulations. As of this writing, nearly forty changes in regulations have been made and another major legal reform has been completed as a consequence of the Gulf War.

—More than 400 staff positions have been added to the export control office, customs, intelligence services, and the export control desks of the Foreign, Economics, and Finance Ministries during a time when frugality in staff politics has been the rule because of the burdens of unification.[84]

—The penalties for both unauthorized arms and dual-use civilian arms exports have been doubled, many misdemeanors changed to felonies, and the two-year minimum jail sentences made nonsuspendable.

—Previously, prosecutors had to prove that nonlicensed exports were actually detrimental to German security and foreign policy interests or to world peace. The first revision of the law makes it sufficient for such exports to "endanger" these interests. The bill presently under consideration eliminates even this condition and thus lowers the burden of proof needed against lawbreakers.

—Along with direct participation in arms export deals that violate German law, support for such deals, intent to violate export law, violations resulting from the exporter's neglect to adhere to the law, and even the use of persuasion in illegal export deals are all equally punishable. In a major revolution of German legal philosophy, the law's extraterritorial provisions have been extended to cover trade transactions involving products that previously were not subject to customs regulations, as well as German participation in weapons production abroad. This change reflected the far-reaching definition of "technology transfer," which includes everything from blueprints to human knowledge.

—Companies are now legally obligated to nominate an "export-responsible executive" who will be held personally accountable for any illegal actions by the firm. This change has institutionalized in the boards of industrial enterprises a substantial interest in avoiding illegal export deals.

—Intelligence, licensing, customs, and police operations have been authorized to exchange information that can be used in the prevention and early investigation of illegal exports. A register of potential exporters of militarily sensitive items, their skills, past contacts, and ongoing exports is being created and will be updated annually.

Additional legislation adopted in January 1992 creates even stiffer penalties for unlicensed exports, makes deals through middlemen and fake companies illegal, and authorizes courts to order the confiscation of receipts not just for net profits but for gross income from exporting. Companies deemed "unreliable" can be ordered to shut down. These new regulations also make it obligatory for companies to apply for licenses for items not listed as requiring them if the companies suspect that these items may be used in military projects. Since "export by neglect" is already a punishable crime, companies— and particularly their export-responsible executives—are under pressure to acquire the necessary knowledge.[85]

However, one major stumbling block did develop between the opposition and the government, postponing the bill for one year. The government wished to give the Customs Crime Office, the main investigative body for export crimes, the authority to eavesdrop, wiretap, and open the mail of individuals and firms under suspicion for export crimes, shortcutting the more exacting requirements local prosecutors must observe. The opposition balked at this invasion of privacy, and even the government parties shared some misgivings about possible violations of civil rights. Otherwise there was consensus on the new policy, with the SPD even criticizing the government for not going far enough.[86]

As proof of its good intentions in the area of arms exports, Germany has cooperated with the UN Special Commission to control Iraqi disarmament, and the government has been prompt in investigating firms accused of participating in Iraq's various weapons programs. These investigations have enabled the commission to extract an admission from Iraq that its uranium enrichment program was larger than had been estimated.[87]

Of course, enthusiasm among industry leaders for this change of heart and policy was not unequivocal, but remarkably enough, there was no significant opposition. The major industrial associations understood that the commercial success of German enterprises could be seriously undermined if the label of "merchants of death" stuck and were particularly concerned about possible hostile reactions from the U.S. Congress. Consequently, despite occasional warnings against going too far and a few more vigorous protests against additional bureaucratic burdens by the associations of small exporters, industry has in general welcomed the changes. The associations have prepared briefing brochures on the new rules and advised their members to be exceptionally careful to avoid questionable export deals. The major companies, after installing their export-responsible executives, issued internal rules requiring employees to notify the boards immediately of any suspicions that ongoing deals might lead to the support of military activities in a recipient country.[88]

A distinctly changed declaratory policy corresponds to these internal changes. Since unification, Germany has used major international forums to confirm its commitment to nonproliferation policy, from the Fourth Nuclear Non-Proliferation Treaty (NPT) Review Conference in Geneva[89] to the Conference on Disarmament. It has promoted the creation of a conventional arms register at the United Nations.[90] In the summer of 1990, the cabinet decided to follow a policy that would require a country to accept full International Atomic Energy Agency (IAEA) safeguards before nuclear-related items could be delivered, a position West Germany had fought against for two decades. Germany continued to push until this principle was adopted by all major suppliers in April 1992 and has supported any major initiative to strengthen international export control organizations, including the Australian Chemical Exporters' Group, the Missile Technology Control Regime (MTCR), and the revived Nuclear Suppliers Group. Germany has also been anxious to persuade its European partners to adopt commensurately strong legislation before 1993. Concerns over competitiveness, once an impediment to more determined export controls, have now become a driving force behind Germany's external efforts in this field.[91]

These changes in export control policy are probably the most valid proof that the German political establishment takes Germany's new global responsibility seriously. The changes have been expensive in terms of competitiveness, and some of them run counter to time-honored legal principles and governmental policy. That these steps were taken and received broad political support shows that Germany is willing to make some sacrifices in order to uphold its avowed principle that "only peace, not war, must emerge from German soil."

From Distrust to Good Neighborliness: Warsaw and Prague

The litmus test for the direction of Germany's foreign policy was and no doubt remains its relationship to Poland and Czechoslovakia, the eastern neighbors that suffered most from German aggression in this century and who took the fiercest revenge after World War II against people of German origin. This relationship is far more significant than Germany's ties to the successors of the Soviet Union. Germany's leading role in providing aid to the former Soviet Union, support for its timely admission to international economic and political organizations, and persistent requests for more Western aid to the troubled area can be and have been interpreted as a new Rapallo, or an attempt to reach an agreement with the Russian colossus on dividing up Central and Eastern Europe. Germany's rapprochement with Poland and Czechoslovakia, in contrast, can be seen only as the expression of a willingness to be a "good European citizen." As the years 1990–92 have proved, however, this rapprochement has not been an easy endeavor for either side.

With respect to German-Polish relations, three problems stood out: borders, minorities, and the accounting for the past. Understandably, the issue of borders made the Poles the most nervous. The Warsaw Treaty of 1971 had confirmed the Oder-Neisse line as the official border between the two countries, but the final legal settlement of the issue was to be resolved when Germany was once again united. Thus, when the German unification process began gathering steam, this stipulation came immediately to the minds of the members of the new Polish government. Polish Prime Minister Tadeusz Mazowiecki tried desperately to extract a binding commitment from Kohl that Germany's borders would not be questioned, but Kohl's reply stayed the same: only the united, sovereign Germany could finally settle the issue. While his position was legally correct, it did nothing to stop either the parliaments or the governments of the two German states from making unambiguous statements, something that was not lost on Poland, Germany's allies, or Kohl's domestic opponents.

The reasons behind Kohl's hesitation were purely domestic.[92] He did not intend to change the border, only to keep the vote of the Silesian immigrants for his Bavarian partners in the CSU. The CSU, alarmed by the disturbingly good showing the Republicans had made in the elections for the European Parliament in June of 1989, feared losing its absolute majority in Bavaria, the seat of its political power. The CSU became quite vocal on the subject of Poland and argued against the quick conclusion of a border treaty. Behind the scenes, the Bavarians urged Kohl to delay the inevitable treaty until after the Bavarian and, if possible, the all-German elections (scheduled for December 1990).[93] Kohl wanted the Poles to give up their claims for reparations and to guarantee the rights of the German minority in Poland in return for border recognition.[94] He was, however, under increasing pressure from all the Western allies, particularly the French, and calls for a resolution of the issue were heard within Germany.[95] Genscher's September 1989 address to the UN General Assembly all but promised there would be no change in the German-Polish border, in virtual defiance of Kohl's authority. CDU Interior Minister Wolfgang Schäuble made a similar statement in Washington in February 1990.[96] Thus, when the CSU made the border issue a matter of choosing between unification and Bavarian interests, Kohl did not hesitate to choose unification.

In early 1990, the question was whether to sign the border treaty at the same time as the more complicated friendship treaty, which would take more time to conclude. The CSU wanted the treaties signed simultaneously. But in the final months before unification, Kohl made his priorities clear: in mid-June, in a strong speech to the Bundestag, he declared frankly that the border treaty was necessary to achieve unification. Following this speech, both German parliaments confirmed that the united Germany would accept the current border as permanent.[97] The border was confirmed in the Two plus Four Treaty, and a formal Polish-German border treaty was signed on November 14, 1990, and ratified along with the friendship treaty.[98]

The second major issue in German-Polish relations was minority rights. The communist regime in Poland had refused to recognize ethnic Germans in Poland as a minority, instead suppressing and harassing them. This caused an upsurge of immigration to West Germany once the borders became more permeable. Poland was extremely reluctant to acknowledge minority rights that would permit its German citizens to organize cultural and political activities or groups. Some problems, such as bilingual geographical names, could not be resolved.

The third major issue in Polish-German relations was "mutual accounting," or compensation, for Poles forced to work for the Germans in World War II and for nationalized property of Germans in Poland. This last problem was connected to the question of whether Silesians who had immigrated to Germany would be able to purchase land they had owned in Poland.

The friendship treaty, signed in June 1991 and ratified together with the border treaty, guaranteed rights to the German minority in Poland in accord with CSCE standards. Annual meetings of the heads of government, foreign ministers, and high-level officials of both countries were agreed on.[99] Poles who had been forced to work for the Germans during World War II were promised limited compensation through a foundation set up by the German government. Other issues were postponed for future settlement.[100] Some ex-Silesian deputies in the Bundestag voted against the treaty, which received almost unanimous support after Kohl himself delivered a spirited defense to the deputies.[101]

Polish-German relations remained strained even after the conclusion of the treaties, especially in the border areas, where they are anything but amicable. A heavy influx of Polish workers in 1990 led to anti-Polish feelings in eastern Germany, and in several localities, east German right-wing youths have attacked Polish tourists. As a sign of goodwill, both governments abolished visa requirements in 1990. While Kohl and Genscher were taking some domestic risks in making this decision, there was no serious opposition.

Matters were slightly less difficult between Germany and Czechoslovakia because the border was not in question. Yet negotiations on the complicated issues of minority and property rights were protracted.[102] The issue of the rights of the German-speaking minority in Czechoslovakia was as difficult to resolve as it had been in Poland.

The CSU made itself the voice of the many Germans from the Sudeten region of Bohemia who had settled in Bavaria after World War II. The Sudeten Germans and the CSU requested an immediate halt to the selling of state-owned property in Czechoslovakia, resettlement rights for the emigrants in the Sudeten area, and compensation for expropriations of German property after World War II. The Czechoslovak government understandably balked; President Vaclav Havel had already taken the bold step of apologizing for the forced expulsion of Germans after the war, provoking furious protests from nationalists and Communists. The Czechoslovak government argued that the damage the Germans had done to them far surpassed any injustice they had committed against the Germans. Prague was particularly worried about the allegations by the Sudeten association and the CSU that Germany had never been at war with Czechoslovakia (and thus owed no reparations) and that the Munich agreement was not invalid from the beginning, but only in the result. This fine legal difference was meant to make the claims of the Sudeten Germans claims by German citizens rather than claims by subjects of the Czechoslovak state. The enormous insensitivity of putting this issue back on the agenda not only proved how desperate the Bavarian CSU was to save its dwindling power as a provincial party in a larger nation-state but helped to thoroughly exacerbate German-Czechoslovak relations after a fairly good start.[103] The CSU insisted on an exchange of letters and, anticipating that the Czechoslovaks would refuse this suggestion, on a Bundestag resolution supporting its positions.[104]

As in the Polish case, Kohl at first hesitated. For some months he took no action on the treaty finalized by Genscher and his Czechoslovak counterpart Jiri Dienstbier in October 1991.[105] Only in January 1992, under pressure from Prague, Genscher's ministry and party, and the opposition, did Kohl agree to sign the treaty. The CSU's outspoken protest was silenced in a short, rough meeting of the coalition. The language of the treaty was not to be changed, nor would the proposed exchange of letters take place confirming that reparations and compensation for expropriations would not be regulated by the treaty. A resolution was also added reaffirming the goals of the treaty rather than the peculiar claims of the Sudeten association.[106] The decision to sign the treaty in February was unanimously welcomed by all Bundestag parties. The treaty was endorsed by the Bundestag in May, together with a friendship treaty with Hungary and with the strong support of all parties. Again, the CSU speaker was the most critical. The treaty was finally endorsed by the Bundesrat in June 1992 despite the opposition of CSU-governed Bavaria.[107]

This was the difficult part in establishing good relations. In all other areas, the German government has proved the best supporter of the interests of the Central and Eastern Europeans. Germany put up more than 25 percent of all aid going to the region, in addition to some 50 percent for the Soviet Union and its successor states. Debt forgiveness for Poland reached 70 percent of the total the Poles owed German lenders.[108] In spite of demands that economic resources be concentrated in the Eastern part of the country, the German government emphasized that an "economic iron curtain" at the Oder and Neisse would not serve German security interests.[109]

Kohl and Genscher were also stubborn in their support for the timely association of Hungary, Poland, and Czechoslovakia with NATO and the EC. The Germans asked their allies to open the prospect of eventual EC membership to the Central and East Europeans at a time when others were quarreling about the contradictions between "widening" and "deepening" the Community. Kohl proposed a regular consultation mechanism that would symbolize the firm prospect of future membership.[110] Remarkably, the Germans also agreed on a joint Czechoslovak-German initiative for enhancing the institutionalization of the CSCE [111] and opened a new consultation process between the foreign ministers of France, Poland, and Germany.[112]

Overall, this case shows some determination to come to grips with the unpleasant legacy of German history. Bonn's strategy was to clear up the most pressing issues, with due regard to the German interests involved, and to focus on helping the three Central and East European countries accelerate the process of economic reconstruction and timely integration into the Western world. Kohl once more proved that, even when sensitive foreign policy issues were involved, he was not above calculating the electoral impact of the small share of the vote belonging to the stubborn members of the immigrants' associations. The CSU showed that it was willing to carry its point to the extreme but toed the line after Kohl's rebuffs.[113] Genscher's position demonstrated that there was another side to the domestic equation, represented by the vast majority of Germans who preferred to lay the disputes of the past to rest and to establish as viable a relationship with their eastern neighbors as they had with France.[114]

Assertive Peacemaking? The Case of Yugoslavia

The one situation in which German foreign policy exhibited a high profile and provoked the most concern was the Yugoslav crisis. This policy, however, developed only during the crisis. Until the summer of 1991, German policy had been in line with EC and U.S. priorities, which were aimed at keeping Yugoslavia intact. Germany was particularly concerned about the consequences of a forced breakup of Yugoslavia on the Soviet Union. Thus, when the EC's European Council requested that Slovenia's and Croatia's declaration of independence be suspended for three months, Kohl was in full agreement. He warned only that, in the long run, Yugoslavia could not be kept united by military force.[115]

In July, however, the German position changed in response to two developments. First, Genscher came under sudden and unexpected domestic pressure to revise the existing policy on Yugoslavia, not because Germany had any geopolitical interest in the Balkans but because the German political parties had agreed that the violence in Yugoslavia threatened European stability, and that the main culprit was Serbian President Slobodan Milosevic and the Serb-dominated Yugoslav People's Army.[116] Then came the failed coup in the Soviet Union, which the prevailing policy had been largely aimed at preventing. The coup made the dissolution of the Soviet Union seem increasingly inevitable, no matter what happened in the troubled Balkan country.

Genscher, not accustomed to drawing fire from all sides, hastily changed positions and overshot the mark. He now vowed that Germany would unilaterally recognize Slovenia and Croatia. No discussion of Croatia's treatment of its Serb minority accompanied the initial decision. After a few days, the German position changed again. Unilateral recognition was withdrawn and replaced with relentless pressure within the EC for mediation. However, Germany made its request for recognition of the breakaway republics by the West a matter of policy.[117] The Germans wanted the EC to act in concert to exert increasing pressure on Serbia and the Yugoslav People's Army to stop the advances and, in particular, the shelling of civilian targets. Germany believed that recognition of Slovenia and Croatia should be a joint act by the EC, a position it held as late as November.[118]

In addition to requesting EC recognition for the two republics, Germany pursued other multilateral possibilities for an end to the violence. Genscher, who was presiding over the CSCE Council as well as the WEU at the time, invoked the freshly established CSCE "crisis mechanism." The CSCE participants expressed their concern over the Yugoslav situation, established that the allegedly "internal affair" was a matter that concerned European security, and gave an all-European mandate to the EC's efforts at peacekeeping and mediation.[119] For the Germans, this was an important step; Serbia's argument that intervention in Yugoslavia lacked legitimacy was clearly refuted, and the Paris Charter was made the basis for action on the situation. The initiative to bring the matter before the UN Security Council provided added legitimacy and offered a further method of trying to maintain peace should the EC mediation efforts fail.[120] The German government had to overcome considerable French and British misgivings, however, before the matter could be dealt with in New York. It was presumably Bonn's success in convincing Belgium, which was also on the Security Council at that time, to move unilaterally that persuaded Paris and London to go along.

Germany also put Yugoslavia on the WEU agenda, primarily because this was another way to demonstrate the urgency of the situation for European security, but also because involving the WEU was a way to please the French. Within the WEU framework, the discussion focused quickly on the possibility of sending peacekeeping forces to the troubled country. But here again, the Germans suffered from the same handicap they had during the Gulf War in being prevented by the constitution from sending German troops abroad. As a consequence, Germany's chances of success appeared considerably weaker within the WEU than within the EC and CSCE.[121]

Throughout this period, Germany tried to convince its partners to increase pressure on Serbia through economic sanctions. In July, economic aid was summarily suspended for all of Yugoslavia; weapons deliveries were halted, and an oil embargo was later instituted. From then on, the Germans tried to direct sanctions at the perceived culprit, Serbia. Finally, in early December, Germany suspended the bilateral German-Yugoslav transport agreement, but only for Serbia and Montenegro, sending a strong signal that Germany was now willing to take unilateral steps.[122] Yet despite all its attempts to utilize multilateral frameworks to somehow resolve the crisis, Germany was encountering frustrating resistance from some of its European partners. Bonn understood the reluctance of some countries where minority conflicts could become severe to take an early stand on the side of secessionists. But as Serbia's aggressive policy became clearer between October and December

1991, the German government determined to wait no longer for its allies to take action. In early December, Germany promised to recognize Slovenia and Croatia before Christmas.[123] In contrast with Genscher's earlier statement, the new declaration made clear to both countries, particularly Croatia, that recognition would be offered only if minority rights were guaranteed.[124]

Thus, Germany offered unilateral recognition only after it had become clear that there was little chance of achieving a common EC position on the issue. The government was encouraged by the willingness of several other EC members to recognize the breakaway republics, including Italy, which initially had been one of the most fervent promoters of maintaining Yugoslav unity. Thus, while Germany would be acting outside the EC framework, it would not be operating in complete isolation from its EC partners.[125] On December 11, on the basis of a report of one of Germany's leading international lawyers, the cabinet decided to recognize Slovenia and Croatia, reasoning that in October the EC Council of Foreign Ministers had given the Serbs two months to stop fighting and accept the terms of the plan negotiated by Lord Carrington.[126] If the EC members failed to act after imposing this deadline, they would in effect be condoning Serbian aggression.[127]

As Bonn had expected, Germany's announcement sent shock waves through the EC. France in particular did not want a split on the eve or in the immediate aftermath of the crucial Maastricht summit and thus indicated its willingness to act. Mitterrand proposed adopting a common set of criteria for the recognition of new countries, which the Germans and the French began drafting. However, Germany was now fully committed to recognition of the two republics.[128] Thus, on December 16, with an unusual amount of arm-twisting and muscle-flexing, Germany persuaded its eleven EC partners to agree to a five-member commission that would establish whether Slovenia and Croatia met the new criteria. Formal recognition would be granted by January 15, 1991.[129]

Germany had achieved a major diplomatic success. Bound by Kohl's word, Germany itself extended recognition to Croatia and Slovenia on December 23, delaying only the exchange of ambassadors (the last formal step in establishing regular diplomatic relations) until January 15. Germany's action, however, was not the formal procedure agreed on by the EC, as Mitterrand correctly argued. Driven mainly by its open commitment to recognize the republics and by domestic considerations, Germany's clumsy behavior nevertheless demonstrated that it was determined to take the lead on this issue. Singlehandedly, it overcame the reluctance of all its EC partners in the fight for recognition of Slovenia and Croatia—in the face of the avowed opposition of the UN Secretary-General and the U.S. government.

Much speculation surrounds Germany's motives. An unfortunate historical analogy has been drawn between this recent German policy and the alliance between Nazi Germany and the Croatian Ustasa regime in World War II. It is safe to say, however, that this historical association played no part whatsoever in Germany's considerations. Indeed, the German government repeatedly acknowledged Germany's abhorrent historical role and, on these grounds, expressed understanding for the Serbs' refusal to allow German soldiers to join a European peacekeeping force.[130]

Germany was in fact influenced by two major and two minor considerations. First, the Germans were actively working for a stable and peaceful security system in Europe. They were aware that many unsolved ethnic and territorial issues in Central and Eastern Europe and the former Soviet Union could lead to violence that would immediately affect German security, if only in the form of waves of refugees. Bonn feared that a military victory for the Serbs in Yugoslavia would serve as a signal to ambitious leaders and groups in the region, especially in the former Soviet Union, which increasingly resembled the decaying Yugoslavia. For Germany, asserting the principles of the Paris Charter—renunciation of the use of force, respect for the inviolability of established borders, and respect for human and minority rights—had an importance that extended far beyond the Yugoslav case. This consideration, above all else, explains the determination of the German government to insist on its position despite U.S., UN, and some European opposition.[131]

Second, the German government saw in the Yugoslav conflict the pitting of democracy and self-determination against the ambitions of Europe's last hard-line totalitarian leader, a man willing to use violence to bolster his small empire against change. Germany was struggling to abolish the remnants of communist totalitarianism in eastern Germany, and the leadership had a strong interest in denying success to Milosevic and his army. Because of the unstable situation in the former communist countries in general, success for the Communists in Yugoslavia might have sent encouraging signals to the remaining hard-liners in other countries, particularly since communism in Serbia was closely entwined with the century's other dangerous ideology, nationalism.[132] The Germans feared that their recognition of Slovenia and Croatia would lead the Serbs to escalate rather than de-escalate hostilities. But the Germans also believed that withholding recognition as a concession to the Serbian leadership would be the equivalent of appeasement and could result in an even more intransigent policy in Belgrade.[133]

Third, domestic pressures played an important role. All parties, from right to left, and a majority of the public were unwavering in their sympathies for the republics struggling for independence.[134] Millions of Germans had travelled as tourists to the mountains of Slovenia and the beaches of Croatia, and the shelling of Dubrovnik, Zadar, Sibenik, and Split destroyed places they had come to cherish. The Bavarian CSU had even deeper sympathies for the Catholic trans-Alpine republics—sympathies that were centuries old and had little to do with the ugly World War II episode. Last but not least, half a million Croats in Germany urged their host government to act.[135]

Fourth, after the criticism suffered during and after the Gulf War, the German government felt compelled to show the kind of leadership which, as everybody was impressing upon Bonn, came with unification. Kohl and Genscher perceived the EC and the West as divided, undecided, disinterested, and largely irresponsible on the issue of Yugoslavia. They believed it was incumbent on Germany to provide the leadership that was otherwise lacking, and they supplied it until their goal of recognition was finally achieved.

Why did the government place so much emphasis on recognition? First, because recognition would finally move the problem out of the legal grey zone of "meddling in internal affairs" and make it a legitimate international concern open to all the instruments of policy available in the international community. Second, recognition of the republics was a signal to the Serbs that their expansionist goals were at odds with the wishes of the international community. Third, recognition was one of the few instruments besides economic sanctions available to the Germans. Still unable to participate in any military action, the government naturally focused on the means at hand.

What are the lessons of the Yugoslav case? First, although it showed that the German government was willing to pursue unilateralism in every instance, it also made clear that the leadership had, in the end, concentrated its best energies on multilateral approaches to the problem.[136] Second, it was the first time the Germans had shown some willingness to take the lead on an issue they felt strongly affected their interests. Third, it demonstrated that they had considerable problems with political style in this unusual role. Even an old hand such as Genscher overdid the arm-twisting techniques, and the active pursuit of a separate path toward recognition even after the Western allies had declined, on December 16, to fall in line was an unnecessary and counterproductive strategy and demonstrated that leadership skills must be learned. But it was probably not a sign that German foreign policy would in the future be aggressive and defiant. The insistence on the Paris Charter principles, which was at the heart of the German position, was completely in line with the Federal Republic's tradition of nonviolent, peaceful foreign policy.

Shaping Europe's Security Architecture

To the German political establishment, West European integration is one of the three pillars of European security architecture, along with NATO and the CSCE. Depending on the political camp, one or the other receives more sympathy and support (the government parties favor NATO, while the SPD leans toward the CSCE), but in principle both are viewed as indispensable to further EC integration.[137]

Germany is placed in a dilemma by periodic requests to choose among these institutions—or at least to prioritize them—when in fact the Germans see them as intricately interwoven. In each case, the alleged choice involves relations with one or more of the country's important allies. The European integration process, for instance, is at the heart of the Franco-German relationship. German support for NATO is essential to German-American and Anglo-German relations. At first, promoting the further institutionalization of the CSCE created a bridge between Bonn and Moscow in the transitional period between 1985 and the disintegration of the Soviet Union. This joint effort has now developed into an important point of cooperation between Germany and the Central and East European states, at least as long as they are not full members of NATO and the Community. Because of this sensitive interrelation between specific bilateral relations and the institutional question, Germany has been careful to share its politically visible initiatives with each of these partners. Mitterrand and Kohl have, as will be discussed later, moved the EC/WEU process along with several proposals at critical junctures, and a unique working meeting of German and French ambassadors resulted in the proposal for the CSCE crisis mechanism.[138] Germany and Czechoslovakia have made joint proposals for the CSCE, and the foreign ministers of Germany, Poland, and France held an unusual meeting (which will be repeated) to discuss the future of Europe. Finally, Genscher and Baker jointly proposed the North Atlantic Cooperation Council (NACC) that was created at the end of 1991.[139]

A telling example of Germany's dilemma was the reaction provoked in the United States, Great Britain, and elsewhere by the Franco-German initiative for a joint military force that would evolve into a European corps. In the summer and fall of 1991, considerable irritation developed between Germany and France; they were divided by the Yugoslav crisis, opposing positions on agricultural subsidies and GATT, and contradictory priorities for Maastricht. The French were also still having difficulty adjusting to the reality of German unification.[140] It was therefore essential to give something to the French, since keeping the Franco-German relationship viable and amicable had long been one of the key doctrines of German foreign policy.[141] Thus, Chancellor Kohl decided—after briefing the Americans but without consulting the Foreign or Defense Ministry—to move on the issue.[142] The French had made a European defense identity a matter of high priority, and the joint initiative would draw them closer to the common defense.[143] In addition, it would give more perspective to the political union that was the goal of Maastricht and to which, in the German view, a common security policy was indispensable. Kohl also wished to foster European integration by preparing common positions before submitting proposals to full NATO deliberations.[144] Predictably, the reactions from abroad were not overly positive, and, in the domestic debate, the SPD expressed concern that NATO might be sacrificed to an undesirable binationalism.[145]

The main thrust of German diplomacy on this issue thus changed from making Paris happy to showing London and, in particular, Washington that Germany's intention was not to weaken NATO or to try to undermine America's commitment to Europe; rather, it was to give the time-honored U.S. request for a "European pillar" an operational meaning and to strengthen the alliance. Kohl, Genscher, and former Defense Minister Gerhard Stoltenberg repeatedly confirmed their interest in the presence of U.S. troops in Europe. This policy was no doubt genuine, for in Bonn's view, NATO and the U.S. presence are indispensable to European stability and provide reassurance in the wake of German reunification.[146] This view is shared by the mainstream of the SPD and a few Greens, although it is opposed by the SPD left and the Green majority.

To underline this policy principle, the Germans made it clear that the operational, organizational, and command aspects of the new joint force would not compromise the efficiency of the established NATO structure. Rather than duplicating or even replacing NATO, the new initiative would complement it, since the WEU's activities should be conspicuously different from NATO's. The Germans used the Franco-German study on an air/sea transport component and a WEU agency to process satellite data as examples of the type of structure they wanted to create.[147] Rather than being withdrawn from NATO assignments, German units would have a dual function, and the "divisibility of common security" would be avoided at all costs. Communication between the WEU and NATO would be strengthened by moving WEU headquarters to Brussels.[148]

Germany wanted to preserve NATO but also had a definite interest in adapting the alliance to the changed circumstances. Its new strategy, which was driven by this interest, advocated eliminating forward defense and relegating nuclear weapons to "weapons of last resort." The Germans were also keen to start negotiations on Short-Range Nuclear Forces (SNFs) early on and asked for the largest possible reduction in SNFs in Europe. Support for total elimination of short-range nuclear weapons in Germany and a no-first-use strategy came not only from the opposition parties but from the government as well, with the exception of the Defense Ministry.

Germany also argued that NATO should be opened to the East as soon as possible. The hostile relationship that had existed between East and West was to be bridged quickly, and ways were to be found to associate Central and Eastern Europe and the Soviet Union with the Western alliance. It was with this purpose in mind that Genscher joined Baker in proposing the NACC. The proposal was a lucky coup for German diplomacy, as it added a German-American initiative to the many joint initiatives with France and linked NATO to the CSCE.[149] The German preoccupation with building up the CSCE process had for some time caused disagreement—and, at times, mistrust—between Bonn and Washington. Some in the U.S. saw this preoccupation as another sinister attempt to weaken NATO, when in fact the German approach was influenced by six considerations:

—that all-European confidence-building was essential in the post-Cold War period;

—that Europe needed instruments immediately to deal with emerging political and security crises;

—that it was essential to intensify the political dialogue with former WTO members on all issue areas;

—that isolation of the Soviet Union must be avoided at all costs;

—that even under the best of circumstances, the former WTO countries would not be granted full membership in either the EC or NATO in the immediate future;

—that NATO had no mandate in Central and Eastern Europe and was thus unable to carry out essential security functions in that area.

For these reasons, Genscher had pressed hard to introduce at the 1990 Paris summit at least the rudimentary elements of joint institutions charged with overall security tasks. When the Council of Ministers, the High-Level Group, the Conflict Prevention Center, and the Election Observation Center were finally created with fairly limited mandates, the German authorities made it clear that they regarded what to others was a far-reaching concession as only a rather mild beginning.[150]

Consequently, in the first half of 1991, the Foreign Ministry pressed discreetly but insistently for additional institutions—most prominently a crisis mechanism that would put the first modest constraints on the consensus decisionmaking principle prevailing in the CSCE. French support for the plan was secured, and an agreement on the mechanism was finalized during the Berlin meeting in the summer of 1991. However, Kohl and Genscher again emphasized during the conference that they regarded their achievement as just another small step on the long road toward institutionalization; the new mechanism, as well as the Conflict Prevention Center, needed an expanded mandate and increased authority.[151]

Germany also actively supported both the installation of a conflict settlement procedure (the Valetta mechanism) and authorization for the CSCE to monitor the compliance of member states with human and minority rights standards and to use violations of these standards as a legitimate reason for diplomatic intervention. In such cases, the veto rights of the countries concerned would not apply.[152] The reasoning behind these positions was that strengthening human and minority rights standards was an essential prerequisite to avoiding major upheavals and violence in Central and Eastern Europe. After the failed coup in the Soviet Union, the assertion of CSCE rights to diplomatic intervention when democracy and constitutional procedures are jeopardized in member states—one of Genscher's major achievements during his term as president of the Council of Ministers in 1991—must be seen in the same light. In fact, Germany supports further institutionalization of and stronger authority for the CSCE, including a European Security Council and CSCE peacekeeping forces.[153]

The mainstay of German security policy is multilateralism. It envisions a Europe whose countries are bound together by multiple memberships in overlapping organizations and where decisions on national security (such as troop strength), defense planning, and key foreign policy issues are all embedded in multilateral institutions and constrained by legal obligations. Binding regulations concerning the preservation of democracy, respect for human and minority rights, and the settlement of disputes will prevent the outbreak of violent conflicts. In this Europe, the EC, NATO, and the CSCE all have a role to play in maintaining peace and stability.

Shaping EC Integration

The policy of integration with the European Community that Bonn was pursuing served three purposes.[154] First, it was aimed at allaying the fear that the unified country might re-embark on dangerous paths in foreign policy[155] by demonstrating Germany's determination to maintain and even voluntarily strengthen the mechanisms of "self-entanglement."[156] Its second goal was to keep intact the close Franco-German relationship that, despite the insecurity in Paris, had led to a variety of joint integration-promoting initiatives. Finally, multilateral integration was seen as the best means of ensuring Germany's stability, counteracting the tendency toward renationalization in other countries, and preventing it in Germany itself.

Germany's support for the timely association and eventual membership of the Central and Eastern European countries (where nationalism, exacerbated by the desperate economic situation, was rising) must be seen in this strategic perspective.[157]

Germany, in fact, saw no great contradiction between "deepening" and "widening" the Community, as did some of its partners. Since the strategic aim was to preserve stability in Europe and to build a new and lasting order, the Germans saw "deepening" and "widening" as parts of a single process. "Widening" was seen as needed to exploit fully the benefits of long-term political and economic stabilization provided by the Community, particularly for Central and Eastern Europe.[158] The government agreed that accession was not a short-term possibility, preferring to open the prospect of accession to the Eastern countries.[159] The German conclusion was not to have a "closed shop," but to accelerate the present integration process. Because preserving the existing EC process of reaching agreement by consensus made the decisionmaking process too cumbersome to accommodate new members, Germany pushed for acceptance of majority voting even if this meant that

Germany itself would at times be forced to submit to decisions it did not particularly like.[160] The Kohl/Genscher approach to the deepening/widening debate enjoyed broad support. Indeed, one of the objections to the Maastricht agreement was that it gave no clear signal on EC membership to Central and Eastern Europe.[161]

Immediately after the fall of the Berlin Wall, the government had made unification within the framework of the European integration process a priority. Only after it became clear that the movement toward unification must be accelerated did Bonn consciously uncouple the two processes. Given the internal and external pressure to move forward, the German leadership deemed it unwise to subject key decisions on unity, such as economic union and East German accession to the usually protracted deliberations of the European Council, the highest EC decisionmaking body.[162]

That this strategy was not met with enthusiasm by Germany's partners, especially France, did not surprise the German leadership. As an antidote, Kohl suggested in April 1990 that he and Mitterrand submit a joint proposal to the council on opening a second track in the European integration process. The proposal put forward bold steps toward a political union to parallel those already being taken toward European economic and monetary union. Two intergovernmental conferences (IGCs) would simultaneously advance both goals. Political union, including integrated foreign, security, and defense policies would serve to further entangle Germany. The timely connection of the Kohl-Mitterand initiative with the extraordinary EC summit in April 1990 helped to clear the air on the subject of unification, and, for the first time, all Germany's partners unequivocally welcomed the drive toward German unity. New prospects for accelerated European integration had helped to overcome previous misgivings.[163]

At the same time, the Germans indicated that they might be willing to relax their resistance to far-reaching concessions in the monetary field. Giving up the deutsche mark for the sake of European integration would be a terrible sacrifice but would, it was hoped, convince the partners that Germany was not willing to act solely in its own interests. The proposition was highly controversial; the Bundesbank itself had grave misgivings. President Karl-Otto Pöhl led a stubborn struggle against the government's policy and eventually resigned before the Maastricht agreement was signed. The lower echelons of the Finance Ministry and elements within the governing parties were also opposed to a single European currency, including FDP leader Otto Graf Lambsdorff, who responded to the Maastricht treaty with a biting speech in Parliament.[164] The closer the agreement on monetary union came, the more widespread and outspoken was opposition to it.[165] Yet the government stuck to its commitment, this time for purely political reasons.

On the other hand, Germany's concession on monetary union was far from unconditional. The government formulated three conditions on which it would not waver: the European bank would be as independent as the Bundesbank; its charter would make monetary stability the first and foremost goal for the operations of the new organization; and only those countries meeting certain criteria for budgetary discipline would be allowed to participate.[166] Later, at the Luxembourg summit in the summer of 1991, under heavy domestic pressure, Kohl added a fourth condition: throughout the "second phase" of economic and monetary union, before authority over monetary matters was transferred to the central bank, there would be no "grey zone" of shared authority. Monetary decisions would rest with the individual countries alone.[167] The new European currency was to be as stable as the deutsche mark. In the words of Finance Minister Theo Waigel: "[Germany] will bring the German currency order to Europe."[168]

This parallel approach to political union was important to the Germans because they believed that progress had to be made to put future expansion on a sounder footing. Only a high level of regulation of the important political issues would prevent the Community from being shattered by the likely diversity of interests and opinions once eighteen or twenty-five countries were participating. The government wanted to avoid a situation in which EC members would cash in on the deutsche mark without making appropriate concessions that would help to facilitate Germany's strategic goals on European stability. Kohl and Genscher thus explained repeatedly that they would not submit to the German Parliament an agreement on economic and monetary union without an adequate agreement on political union.[169]

Germany's vision of political union was predicated on its new multilateral security and foreign policies. First, these policies would put further restraints on the country's potential military might. Second, they were in the interests of the French, who otherwise had numerous objections to the political priorities set up in Maastricht, especially to the increased powers of the European Parliament and to monetary union. Bonn had in fact used the security issue largely to intervene, along with France, in the process leading to Maastricht whenever it appeared to slow down or stop altogether.[170]

Other issues on which Germany sought progress were internal security, notably the fight against drug trafficking and organized crime; a common approach to asylum and immigration; and the environment.[171] One of the crucial points was the enhancement of the rights of the European Parliament. The Germans saw an enhanced European Parliament as a further commitment to the principles of democracy—one of the pillars of the new European order— and as an important step toward supranational as opposed to intergovernmental decisionmaking. Pursuing their own interests at the same time, the Germans pressed for the addition of eighteen new German seats for representatives of the new citizens in the eastern part of the country.[172]

A last principle pursued by the German government throughout the process was "irreversibility," which was to be achieved through the binding language and fixed timetables insisted on by the German negotiators. This, again, served to further several strategic goals at once: it underlined the German determination to adhere to its policy of permanent self-containment through integration; it made European integration more predictable and therefore more stable; and it ensured that the sacrifice of the deutsche mark would not be for a short-term, incidental political constellation.[173]

Throughout the process leading to Maastricht—and during the conference itself—Germany showed a willingness to compromise. Though the bold Dutch draft was far closer to what the Germans wanted than its weaker Luxembourgian predecessor, Bonn would not fight for it. Kohl and Genscher did not want to confront the French, especially since there was no chance of winning Great Britain's support for either draft of the treaty. The Germans' reluctance to offer Dutch Foreign Minister Hans van den Broek the backing he had expected for his proposal exacerbated existing tensions between him and Genscher.[174] As Maastricht approached, Kohl warned the Bundestag that they could not fight for absolutes and that Germany would have to be satisfied with compromises in matters of internal security, the rights of the European Parliament, social policy, and immigration.[175]

This attitude characterized Germany's approach during the final stages of negotiation. Despite an earlier understanding that Germany would be given eighteen additional seats in the European Parliament, German negotiators agreed to postpone a decision on the matter. The rights of the European Parliament were not expanded according to Bonn's wishes, but Kohl and Genscher did not press the point. Progress on the issues of common asylum and immigration policy was not great, despite the domestic importance of the issue, but the Germans were content with the meager compromise.[176]

The priority placed on self-containment, European integration, and stability in German foreign policy strategy was proven at Maastricht. For Germany, it was far more important to make visible progress toward integration than it was to let the summit fail by pressing certain issues. In this respect, Germany's leniency at Maastricht will have far more lasting effects on Europe than its tough stance on the recognition of Croatia and Slovenia.

Conclusion: New Assertiveness or Self-Contained Leadership?

The picture that emerges from the foreign policy debate and the events discussed in this chapter deviate from the image of Germany presented by the non-German media. Germany has certainly not adopted an assertive, go-it-alone approach. A considerable degree of unilateral activity was visible during the Yugoslav crisis and temporarily during the process of unification. To a lesser degree, national interests were also strongly expressed during the negotiations with Poland and Czechoslovakia and the setting of conditions for European monetary union. Despite a policy style that was somewhat clumsy, at least during the Yugoslav crisis, German unilateralism was no greater than that of other European countries. In fact, it could be argued that it has been less unilateral than the style and goals of British and French foreign policy.

The cases discussed above demonstrate, by and large, a very strong preference not only for multilateral instruments in pursuing a foreign policy strategy, but for multilateralism as the genuine goal and substance of national strategy. Germany sees the strengthening of institutions in Europe and worldwide as a primary objective of its foreign policy. Self-containment is well embedded in this strategy, which also includes European integration, the continued presence of the United States as a European power, and the deepening and strengthening of CSCE institutions.

Germany also maintains a strong preference for economic, political, and diplomatic instruments, arms control, and dispute settlement as the preferred means of security policy. This preference contrasts sharply with a reluctance or, depending on the political camp, an open refusal to consider military means as a legitimate instrument of foreign policy. This stance was most visible during the Gulf War and can be observed in the ensuing debate on out-of-area missions for the Bundeswehr. By and large, this attitude serves as a healthy brake on any far-reaching ambitions that could emerge, although it also has the disadvantage of impeding a frank and prejudice-free discussion of the meaning of "global responsibility." The solution lies, again, in entangling German military activities in multilateral institutions.

The debate on the "new responsibility" has not ended, however. Germany has not yet fully developed a new foreign policy identity, but its awareness of the global as opposed to the strictly European reach and purposes of its foreign policy has risen. An empirical analysis of Germany's foreign policy since unification thus presents a rather encouraging picture of a fairly rational approach to foreign policy issues that is strong and self-confident yet peaceful and multilateral. Germany is a maturing (though not yet completely mature) upper-middle power. And it has indeed developed all the attributes of the "trading state": a high degree of interdependence that makes multilateralism the most cost-efficient way of dealing with external issues; a democratic system wherein efficiency and rationality usually reign over domestic discourse; a welfare state that gives the majority of citizens the desire as well as the power to request economic gains and environmental health as primary goals of the state and to demand that foreign policy serve these purposes or at least not work against them; and the instruments and institutional maturity that enable the state to pursue its goals successfully by other than military means. Looked at from this angle, the identified attributes of current German foreign policy should not come as surprise, for they rest on a fairly solid societal, political, and institutional basis.

All things being equal, there is no discernible reason why Germany's foreign policy should not evolve further in this direction. Before the picture grows too rosy, though, a few caveats are in order, as all things may not be equal in the future.

First, as discussed above, Germany has shown signs of a new assertiveness. To this must be added its strong drive to be treated equally with its major European partners, evidenced by its application for German as a working language in the EC, open embarrassment at the British and French efforts to deal with the issue of Soviet nuclear weapons in ostensibly non-German forums, and anxious efforts to create a role for itself on this issue. In short, an anxiety not to be excluded from its well-deserved place in the diplomatic sun has become a part of German foreign policy for the time being. There is nothing wrong with these individual attempts at assertiveness, which may be only temporary phenomena. But if they continue and become an overriding concern, in the long run they will hinder the enlightened multilateralism that has become a hallmark of German foreign policy.

Second, Germany has demonstrated its desire to exorcise memories of the dark side of its history and to re-establish itself as a country like any other. Again, this is an understandable goal, but it could lead to a lack of sensitivity to the fears and the perceptions of other countries, particularly Germany's near neighbors. A full awareness of the shadow cast by its past has become a remarkable quality of German foreign policy during the last twenty-five years. Germany's task now will be to balance its leadership role with the degree of humility and modesty necessary to maintaining the course of self-containment.

Third, some new nationalistic overtones have emerged on the right, most notably in the foreign policy conventions of the Bavarian CSU. These manifestations are not abnormal by European standards, and they do differ from past German nationalism. It is unclear whether they reflect the Bavarian party's attempts to hold on to the votes of the right or to develop a special profile to make up for its loss of influence, or whether they actually reflect a new national feeling on the German right.

Fourth, the potential for unpleasant right-wing developments lingers among an estimated 5 to 25 percent of the population (depending on which polls, criteria, and methodology are used). This percentage falls fully within European standards, and rightist gains in federal and most regional elections have in fact been far below those of nationalists or protofascists in France or Italy. Yet because of Germany's location, strength, and history, the potential for such developments deserves to be watched.

Fifth, right-wing potential must be contained because of the tendency toward violent action among young, lower-class Germans, which has already found ugly expression in the recent outbursts of violence against immigrants. Sentiments against foreigners run high in Germany, and an artificial nationalism serves as a source of otherwise unattainable self-esteem for many of those people who have suffered the most from the rapid economic changes and social costs of unification. Foreigners exacerbate uncertainty and fear of the future in those already deprived. Consequently, uncontrolled immigration to the West might be the only identifiable factor that could fundamentally alter the character of German society and the course of its foreign policy.

Sixth, on the other side of the political spectrum, a strange version of national pacifism often combined with a conscious or unconscious anti-Americanism has emerged on the German left. The danger of this position is a certain lack of understanding of the importance of comprehensive multilateralism to Germany's future. The international organizations that serve as indispensable instruments of political stability and German self-containment are despised, distrusted, and rejected. The devaluation and denigration of these organizations may, in a worst-case scenario, unwittingly pave the way for those who want to replace them not with peaceful coexistence but with a revival of German power.

It is crucial to keep these caveats in perspective. They are possibilities that have a low probability of leading to fundamental change, side-factors in the mainstream evolution of a big trading state. Whether they come true in spite of our present expectations and prognosis depends on the intricate interaction between domestic developments and the international environment.

How Germany evolves is not contingent only on the Germans. Much depends on how the united country is treated by its partners, friends, and neighbors. Not all reactions to German policy since the fall of the Wall have been expressions of enlightenment and wisdom. The overreaction to the alleged "new assertiveness," the insinuations about sinister motivations in the Yugoslav crisis, the disdain over the quite justified desire to make German a working EC language, the ostensible *Schadenfreude* at the German embarrassment during the Gulf War are all cases in point. The more Germany's partners accept Germany as a "normal state"—with all due regard for its past and potential—and the more they join the Germans in their emphasis on multilateralism, the better the chances will be that Germany will stay on a steady course.

Notes

1. See Horst Teltschik, *329 Tage. Innenansichten der Einigung* (Berlin: Siedler, 1991), pp. 48–58, and 83.
2. Teltschik, *329 Tage*, pp. 87–92, 103–04, 108, 118, and 128; and " 'Das war wie eine Ohrfeige' " *Der Spiegel*, February 19, 1990, pp. 19–32.
3. Beate Kohler-Koch, "Die Politik der Integration der DDR in die EG" in Beate

Kohler-Koch, ed., *Die Osterweiterung der EG: Die Einbeziehung der ehemaligen DDR in die Gemeinschaft* (Baden-Baden: Nomos, 1991), pp. 7–22, especially pp. 11–13.

4. Teltschik, *329 Tage*, pp. 120–21.

5. Kohler-Koch, "Integration," pp. 13–16.

6. Kohler-Koch, "Integration," p. 19. Teltschik, in *329 Tage*, gives an impressive and detailed account of the many consultation processes that took place in 1990. No one who reads this report by one intimately involved in the memorable politics of that year can claim that unification was a purely German affair.

7. Teltschik, *329 Tage*, passim.

8. Teltschik, *329 Tage*, pp. 291, 307, and 313–45.

9. For an excellent overview and empathic interpretation, see Elizabeth Pond, *After the Wall: American Policy toward Germany* (New York: Priority Press, 1990).

10. See Helmut Kohl, "Die Bedeutung der Westeuropäischen Union für die gemeinsame Sicherheitspolitik," Presse- und Informationsamt der Bundesregierung, *Bulletin*, no. 11 (January 31, 1992), pp. 77–79, Hans-Dietrich Genscher, "Eine Vision für das ganze Europa," no. 14 (February 6, 1991), Helmut Kohl, "Fundamente und Strukturen einer gemeinsamen europäischen Zukunft," no. 60 (May 29, 1991), p. 474, Hans-Dietrich Genscher, "Perspektiven gemeinsamer Politik kooperativer Sicherheit in Europa," no. 81 (July 12, 1991), p. 656; Speech of German Foreign Minister Hans-Dietrich Genscher addressed to the General Assembly of the United Nations; Gerhard Stoltenberg, "Bericht der unabängigen Kommission für die künftigen Aufgaben der Bundeswehr," no. 104 (September 26, 1991), pp. 825–30, and 832, Helmut Kohl, "Zeitwende und neue Herausforderungen," no. 114 (October 17, 1991); and Helmut Kohl, "Der Weg zur Europäischen Union ist unumkehrbar," *Das Parlament*, December 20/27, 1991, p. 3.

11. Kohl, "Die Bedeutung der WEU," pp. 74–75.

12. Helmut Kohl, New Year's Address, *Bulletin*, no. 1 (January 2, 1991), especially p. 3.

13. Stoltenberg, "Bericht der Unabhängigen Kommission," p. 832; and Hans-Dietrich Genscher, "Die Vereinten Nationen stärken Weltinnenpolitik und Friedensvölkerrecht," Presse- und Informationsamt der Bundesregiergung, *Stichworte zur Sicherheitspolitik*, June 1991, pp. 10–12.

14. Carl-Dieter Spranger, "Neue politische Kriterien deutscher Entwicklungszusammenarbeit," *Bulletin*, no. 113 (October 16, 1991), pp. 893–94.

15. Helmut Kohl, "Die Rolle Deutschlands in Europa," *Bulletin*, no. 33 (March 22, 1991), p. 244; and Kohl, "Fundamente und Strukturen," p. 477.

16. Kohl, "Fundamente und Strukturen," p. 475; and Kohl, "Verpflichtung der Bundesrepublik Deutschland zu Toleranz und Gewaltlosigkeit," *Bulletin*, no. 132 (November 22, 1991), p. 1075.

17. See Kohl, "Zeitwende," p. 901; Kohl, "Der Weg zur Union," p. 3; and Kohl, "Unterwegs zu einem versöhnten Europa," *Stichworte*, May 1991, pp. 17–19.

18. See the description of Mitterrand's official visit (September 18–20, 1991) to Germany in *Bulletin*, no. 103 (September 25, 1991), p. 818.

19. Hans-Joachim Veen, "Die Westbindungen der Deutschen in einer Phase der Neuorientierung," *Europa-Archiv*, no. 2 (November 10, 1991), pp. 38 and 40.

20. See Hans Stercken, "Die Außen- und Sicherheitspolitik des souverän gewordenen Deutschland," *Stichworte*, September 1991, pp. 16–18.

21. For party positions, see the statements in Außenpolitischer Kongreß der CDU, "Deutschlands Verantwortung in der Welt," CDU-Dokumentation 17, Bonn, May 15, 1991, part 1.

22. Außenpolitischer Kongreß der CSU, *Manuskript der Rede des Vorsitzenden der CSU, Dr. Theo Waigel* (Munich, June 1, 1991).

23. "CSU verlangt größere Rolle für Deutschland," *Süddeutsche Zeitung*, January 13, 1992, p. 1, and Udo Bergdoll, "Bonn kann sich Geduld leisten," p. 4.

24. Veen, "Westbindungen," pp. 38 and 40.

25. FDP Bundeshauptausschuß, "Liberale Außenpolitik für das vereinte Deutschland," Hamburg, May 25, 1991, pp. 3–5; see also Hermann Otto Solms, "Sozial- und Friedensengagement für Deutschland und Europa," *Das Parlament*, December 6, 1991, p. 5; and FDP, *Das liberale Deutschland, Programm der FDP zu den Bundestagswahlen am 2. Dezember 1990* (St. Augustin: Liberal Verlag, 1990).

26. See Außenpolitischer Kongreß, "Deutschlands Verantwortung," p. 5.

27. FDP Bundeshauptausschuß, "Liberale Außenpolitik," p. 3

28. See Horst Ehmke, "Ein Krieg in Europa muß undenkbar werden," *Das Parlament*, November 30, 1990, pp. 1–2; and Norbert Gansel, "Reformen in der europäischen Sicherheitspolitik gefordert," November 15/22, 1991, p. 5.

29. Vorstand der SPD, Referat Öffentlichkeitsarbeit, "Außen-, Friedens- und Sicherheitspolitik. Beschlüsse des Parteitages der SPD," Bonn, SPD, 1991.

30. Veen, "Westbindungen," pp. 38, 40.

31. Veen, "Westbindungen," pp. 38, 40.

32. See Gerd Poppe, "Osteuropa den Weg in die EG bahnen," *Das Parlament*, November 15/22, 1991, p. 8; see also the statement by Antje Vollmer, spokeswoman for the Greens in the Bundestag, "Gelingt eine gerechte Zukunftsordnung?" November 30, 1990, p. 3.

33. See Johannes L. Kuppe, "Wenig Differenzen zwischen Regierung und Opposition," *Das Parlament*, November 15/22, 1991, p. 1; and Karl-Heinz Reith, "Große Herausforderungen an der Jahrtausendwende. Regierung und Opposition stimmen in vielen Fragen überein," December 21/28, 1990, p. 1.

34. Thomas Kielinger, "The Gulf War and the Consequences from a German Point of View," *Aussenpolitik*, no. 3 (1991), pp. 241–50, especially pp. 243–44.

35. Kielinger, "Gulf War," pp. 244–46.

36. Statement of Foreign Minister Hans-Dietrich Genscher on the meeting of the WEU and EPZ with respect to the situation at the Gulf, *Bulletin*, no. 102 (August 25, 1990), p. 858.

37. "Im Geiselbasar von Bagdad," *Der Spiegel*, November 5, 1990, pp. 18–20; " 'Da muß noch was drauf,' " November 12, 1990, pp. 18–24; and "Fortgang der Krise am Golf: Die Politik der Bundesrepublik; die Brandt-Mission," *Archiv der Gegenwart*, no. 23 (November 12–23, 1990), pp. 35055–57.

38. Statement of Foreign Minister Genscher, p. 858; "'Das wird ein schwieriges Jahr' " *Der Spiegel*, January 28, 1991, pp. 22–23, and "Mogelpackung aus Bonn," September 24, 1990, p. 16.

39. Helmut Kohl, "Fünf Jahre EUREKA," *Bulletin*, no. 73 (June 25, 1991), p. 591; and " 'Wir müssen erwachsen werden,' " *Der Spiegel*, August 20, 1990, p. 121.

40. "Innenpolitische Entwicklung: Diskussion über den Bündnisfall; Entsendung deutscher Kampfflugzeuge in die Türkei," *Archiv der Gegenwart*, no. 2 (January 17/28, 1991), p. 35278.

41. "Schwieriges Jahr," pp. 16–19; "Die Deutschen an die Front," *Der Spiegel*, February 4, 1991, pp. 18–19, and " 'Den Ernstfall nicht gewagt' " February 11, 1991, p. 26.

42. Statement of government spokesman Dieter Vogel, *Stichworte*, January 1991, pp. 22–23.

43. "Schwieriges Jahr," p. 23.

44. " 'Der will schlicht überleben' " *Der Spiegel*, January 7, 1991, p. 19, " 'Der Himmel schließt sich,' " January 21, 1991, p. 20, and "Innenpolitische Entwicklung," p. 35278; and Kohl, New Year's Address, p. 2; "Bemühungen der Bundesregierung zur friedlichen Lösung der Golfkrise," *Bulletin*, no. 2 (January 10, 1991), pp. 5–6.

45. Statement of Chancelor Helmut Kohl on the situation in the Gulf region and in Lithuania, *Bulletin*, no. 4 (January 15, 1991), pp. 1–3; and Statement of Chancellor Helmut Kohl on the Gulf War, no. 6 (January 19, 1991), pp. 35–36.

46. Helmut Kohl, "Solidarität mit dem Staate Israel und den Partnern und Verbündeten," *Bulletin*, no. 7 (January 24, 1991), pp. 37–38, and Policy statement of Chancellor Helmut Kohl addressed to the German Bundestag, "Unsere Verantwortung für die Freiheit," no. 11 (January 31, 1991), pp. 61–62.

47. Statement of Hans-Dietrich Genscher on the most recent developments in the Gulf region, *Bulletin*, no. 20 (February 23, 1991), pp. 137–38.

48. "'Die totale Beistandschaft' " *Der Spiegel*, February 11, 1991, pp. 32–33; Kohl, "Solidarität," pp. 37–38.

49. Kohl, Policy Statement, pp. 61–62; and "Bundeswehr im Mittelmeer," *Stichworte*, February 1991, p. 32.

50. " 'Den Ernstfall nicht gewagt' " *Der Spiegel*, February 11, 1991, pp. 25–27; see also the speech of then leader of the SPD caucus Hans-Jochen Vogel, "Mäßiger Start in schwieriger Zeit," *Das Parlament*, February 8/15, 1991, pp. 4–5.

51. "Operation Wüstensturm; zweiter Golfkrieg—Alliierte gegen Irak: Friedensbemühungen," *Archiv der Gegenwart*, no. 2 (January 17/28, 1991), pp. 35266–67.

52. "Zahl der Kriegsdienstverweigerer auf rund 30 000 gestiegen," *Stichworte*, March 1991, p. 46.

53. "Schwieriges Jahr," pp. 23, 28; Hans Magnus Enzensberger, "Hitler's Wiedergänger," *Der Spiegel*, February 4, 1991, pp. 26–28, and Peter Glotz, "Der ungerechte Krieg," February 25, 1991, p. 38.

54. "Die Deutschen an die Front," pp. 18–22.

55. EMNID-poll on the Bundeswehr and the Gulf War, *Stichworte*, February 1991, pp. 36–37; "Angst vor dem Krieg am Golf," *Süddeutsche Zeitung*, January 29, 1991, p. 10, and "Uneinig über die deutsche Rolle am Golf," February 19, 1991, p. 10.

56. "Bush spricht mit Mulroney, Mitterrand, Walesa, Özal und Waigel," *Archiv der Gegenwart*, no. 6 (March 11-26, 1991), pp. 35468–69; and "Bedeutender Beitrag der Bundesrepublik Deutschland zur Unterstützung im Golfkrieg," *Stichworte*, February 1991, pp. 19–22.

57. Statement of German Chancellor Helmut Kohl addressed to the Bundestag, *Bulletin*, no. 28 (March 14, 1991), p. 209.

58. As is so often the case, the differentiated German position has been best expressed by President von Weizsäcker. See, for example, his interview "Der Golfkrieg weist nicht in die Zukunft," *Die Zeit*, February 8, 1991, p. 3.

59. See Robert Leicht, "Wann darf der Helm blau oder grün sein?" *Die Zeit*, December 6, 1991, p. 9; and Kielinger, "Gulf War," p. 244.

60. "Bundeswehr: tolerant, charakterfest," *Der Spiegel*, June 3, 1991, pp. 20–23.

61. See Außenpolitischer Kongreß, "Deutschlands Verantwortung," pp. 9–10.

62. "Bundeswehr: tolerant, charakterfest," pp. 20–23.

63. "Wir müssen erwachsen werden," pp. 121–23.

64. "Bundeswehr: tolerant, charakterfest," pp. 20–21.

65. *Stichworte*, "Diskussion in den Parteien um UN-Einsatz der Bundeswehr," March 1991, p. 42.

66. "SPD: In den Wolken," *Der Spiegel*, February 4, 1991, p. 37; "Außenpolitik: Normale Rolle," March 11, 1991, pp. 22–23; and "Ein Dolch mit Monogram," March 25, 1991, pp. 21 and 24.

67. Gansel, "Reformen in Sicherheitspolitik," p. 5.

68. Interview with Hans-Dietrich Genscher, " 'Ich habe Kurs gehalten,' " *Der Spiegel*, February 4, 1991, p. 24; "Den Ernstfall nicht gewagt," pp. 23 and 25; and Genscher, "Eine Vision," p. 91.

69. FDP Bundeshauptausschuß, "Liberale Außenpolitik," p. 8; and "Beschluß des Bundeshauptausschusses der F.D.P. vom 25.05.91 in Hamburg (Auszug)" *Stichworte*, June 1991, p. 39.

70. Pressemitteilung, CDU (Bonn, May 31, 1991); Kohl, "Die Rolle Deutschlands," p. 243; and Kohl, statement to the Bundestag, pp. 208–09; "Diskussion um UN-Einsatz," p. 42.

71. Stercken, "Die Außen- und Sicherheitspolitik," pp. 16–18.

72. Außenpolitischer Kongreß, "Deutschlands Verantwortung," pp. 9–10; and "Außenpolitik: Normale Rolle," pp. 22–23.

73. See Lamers's statement in the *Rheinischer Merkur*, May 10, 1991, p. 6.

74. Interview with Defense Minister Volker Rühe on state and development of the Bundeswehr, *Stichworte*, May 1992, pp. 31–32.

75. Kohl, "Fünf Jahre," p. 591.

76. Statement of Foreign Minister Hans-Dietrich Genscher on the state in Iraq and the situation of the Iraqi refugees, especially the Kurds, *Bulletin*, no. 38 (April 18, 1991), p. 278, and Kielinger, "Gulf War," p. 247.

77. "Möglichst unauffällig: Die ersten deutschen Soldaten sind im UNO-Einsatz—in Kambodscha," *Der Spiegel*, June 1, 1992, pp. 125–28.

78. "Bundeswehr: tolerant, charakterfest," pp. 20–23; and "Beschluß des Bundeshauptauschusses der F.D.P.," pp. 40–41.

79. Most pointedly the attack by Lally Weymouth, "Third World Nukes: The German Connection," in the *Washington Post*, December 13, 1991, p. A29.

80. See Harald Müller, *After the Scandals: West German Nonproliferation Policy*, PRIF Reports, no. 9 (Frankfurt: PRIF, 1989).

81. Karl Kaiser, *Deutschlands Vereinigung. Die internationalen Aspekte*, Document 50 (Bergisch Gladbach: Lübbe, 1991), p. 263.

82. Kohl, "Unsere Verantwortung," p. 62.

83. See "Behinderungen durch kontrolle befürchtet," *Woche in Bundestag* (November 2, 1989, p. 43; and "Herstellung von ABC-Waffen härter bestrafen" (May 23, 1990), p. 39.

84. Bundesministerium für Wirtschaft, Dokumentation 311: *Die Reform von Außenwirtschaftsrecht und -kontrolle* (Bonn: BMWi, 1991).

85. "Maßnahmen der Bundesregierung zur Verbesserung der Exportkontrollen," *Bulletin*, no. 15 (February 8, 1991), p. 97.

86. "Die Telefonüberwachung bleibt ein Streitpunkt," *Woche in Bundestag* (September 4, 1991), p. 42, "Mithorchen nur unter Regie des Staatsanwalts" (October 16, 1991), p. 43, and "Praktikabilität des Telefonabhörens umstritten" (December 11, 1991), p. 38.

87. "Moralische Verpflichtung für die Sicherheit des Staates Israel und seiner Bürger," *Bulletin*, no. 8 (January 26, 1991), pp. 45–46; and "German Inquiry Shows Iraq Got More Centrifuge Parts," *Nucleonics Week*, no. 3 (January 16, 1992), pp. 7–8.

88. Based on Christian Schlupp, "Impressionen aus der Bonner Außenwirtschaftsszene nach Gesprächen im BMWi, kanzleramt, BMF und mit dem BMVg," unpublished.

89. See the speech of Foreign Minister Hans-Dietrich Genscher concerning the adherence of the united Germany to its NBC renunciations, given at the Fourth Review Conference of the Parties to the Treaty on the Non-Proliferation of Nuclear Weapons, Geneva, August 23, 1990.

90. Helmut Schäfer, "Konventionelle Rüstungskontrolle und Waffentransfer," *Bulletin*, no. 54 (May 17, 1991), pp. 429–31.

91. Personal communication with officials from several West European foreign ministries.

92. This has been confirmed by Teltschik in *329 Tage*, pp. 14–15, 30.

93. " 'Fünf minus x' " *Der Spiegel*, October 8, 1990, p. 95, and "Bonn-Warschau: Ersatzlose Preisgabe," October 29, 1990, pp. 80–85.

94. Teltschik, *329 Tage*, p. 125.

95. Teltschik, *329 Tage*, pp. 111 and 164–5; and "EG: Nur Lippenbekenntnisse," *Der Spiegel*, March 19, 1990, p. 200.

96. Speech of Foreign Minister Hans-Dietrich Genscher addressed to the General Assembly of the United Nations, September 27, 1989, *Bulletin*, no. 98 (September 28, 1989), p. 849; Wolfgang Schäuble, *Der Vertrag. Wie ich über die deutsche Einheit verhandelte* (Stuttgart: DVA, 1991), pp. 59–60.

97. Statement of Chancellor Helmut Kohl on the German-Polish treaties, *Bulletin*, no. 96 (September 9, 1991), p. 762, and Decision of the German Bundestag on the German-Polish border, no.79 (June 22, 1990), p. 684; Teltschik, *329 Tage*, pp. 192 and 270–72; and "Da muß noch was drauf," p. 25.

98. Kohl, statement on German-Polish treaties, *Bulletin*, no. 96 (September 9, 1991), pp. 761–66.

99. "Vertrag zwischen der Bundesrepublik Deutschland und der Republik Polen über gute Nachbarschaft und freundschaftliche Zusammenarbeit," *Bulletin*, no. 68 (June 18, 1991), pp. 541–46.

100. See the interview with Janusz Reiter, Polish ambassador to Bonn, "Keiner will der Ossi scin," *Der Spiegel*, June 17, 1991, pp. 34–37, and "Diplomatie: Dreck aus dem Kamin," May 6, 1991, pp. 24–26.

101. Helmut Kohl, "Unterwegs zu einem versöhnten Europa," *Bulletin*, no. 75 (July 2, 1991), pp. 605–06.

102. "Sudetendeutsche: Schmuggel wie früher," May 20, 1991, pp. 62–68.

103. Werner A. Perger, "Störfaktor Bayern," *Die Zeit*, January 24, 1992, p. 6.

104. "CSU schürt Streit um den CSFR-Vertrag," *Frankfurter Rundschau*, January 18, 1992, pp. 1, 2; and "Kohl und Genscher über Abkommen mit der CSFR einig: 'Vertrag bleibt unverändert' " *Süddeutsche Zeitung*, January 20, 1992, p. 1.

105. "Zeittafel: Tschechoslowakei," *Europa-Archiv*, no. 21 (1991), p. Z 233.

106. "Nachbarschaftsvertrag mit Prag wird nicht geändert: CSU muß zurückstecken," *Süddeutsche Zeitung*, January 22, 1992, p. 1.

107. Berthold Kohler, "Deutsche Unverschämtheit und slawische Schwäche," *Frankfurter Allgemeine Zeitung*, January 23, 1992, p. 3; "Debatte des Deutschen Bundestages über die Freundschafts- und Partnerschaftsverträge mit der CSFR und mit Ungarn," *Das Parlament*, May 15, 1992, pp. 2–6; and "Ratifizierung im Bundesrat: Verträge mit Prag und Budapest perfekt," *Süddeutsche Zeitung*, June 27/28, 1992, p. 5.

108. Genscher, "Eine Vision," p. 94; Helmut Kohl, "Aufgaben deutscher Politik in den neunziger Jahren," *Bulletin*, no. 56 (May 22, 1991), p. 445; and Karen E.

Donfried, "International Assistance to Eastern Europe," Washington, Congressional Research Service, December 23, 1991, p. 7.

109. Dirk Holtbrügge, "Westliche Hilfe ist kein Zauberelixir. Möglichkeiten der Unterstützung des Systemtransfers in der UdSSR durch die westlichen Industrieländer," *Osteuropa*, no. 1 (January 1992), pp. 41–45, especially p. 44. Kohl's address to Bundestag, pp. 210–11.

110. Statement of Chancellor Helmut Kohl on the NATO summit in Rome, on the EC summit in Maastricht, the Middle East peace conference, and the visits to Brazil and Chile, *Bulletin*, no. 124 (November 7, 1991), pp. 986–89; Kohl, "Zeitwende," p. 901; and Communiqué of the WEU Council of Ministers on June 27, 1991 in Vianden, Luxembourg, *Stichworte*, July 1991, p. 18.

111. "Außenpolitische Aktivitäten Genschers," *Archiv der Gegenwart*, no. 8 (April 9–22, 1991), pp. 35528–29.

112. Wolfgang Schäuble/Günther Krause, "Der Einigungsvertrag als Fundament für die Vollendung der Einheit Deutschlands," *Bulletin*, no. 92 (September 3, 1991), p. 735.

113. Perger, "Störfaktor Bayern," p. 6.

114. Hans-Dietrich Genscher, "Beide Verträge sind Elemente gesamteuropäischer Architektur," *Das Parlament*, May 14, 1992, p. 2. For a commentary by Kohl, see "Im Bewußtsein der europäischen Idee als Werte- und Kulturgemeinschaft," *Bulletin*, no. 45 (May 4, 1991), p. 335.

115. Statement of Chancellor Helmut Kohl on the results of the European Council meeting in Luxembourg, June 28-29, 1991, *Bulletin*, no. 78 (July 9, 1991), p. 635; and Helmut Kohl, "Chancen einer säkularen Veränderung für die Sicherung der Zukunft Europas," no. 136 (November 28, 1991), p. 1110.

116. See Genscher's key speech, "Für Recht auf Selbstbestimmung," *Das Parlament*, November 15/22, 1991, p. 7; and " 'Drei Tage Lang am Telefon,' " *Der Spiegel*, July 8, 1991, p. 128; and "Gansel-Bericht fordert Anerkennung Sloweniens und Kroatiens; Föderation souveräner Staaten vorgeschlagen," *Archiv der Gegenwart*, no. 14, (June 28–July 7, 1991), pp. 35795–97.

117. See Statement of Chancellor Helmut Kohl on the situation and development in the Soviet Union and Yugoslavia, *Bulletin*, no. 94 (September 5, 1991), p. 752. A very clear statement was given by Chancellor Kohl in Berkeley, *Bulletin*, no. 102 (September 20, 1991), p. 813.

118. Kohl, address to Bundestag, p. 987; and Genscher, "Für Recht," p. 7.

119. "Kommunique des KSZE-Krisenmechanismus über eine Mission nach Jugoslawien, Prag, 3. Juli, 1991," *Europa-Archiv*, no. 21 (1991), pp. D534–36; "Kommunique des KSZE- Krisenmechanismus, Prag, 8./9. August, 1991," pp. D541–42; "Kommunique des KSZE-Krisenmechanismus, Prag, 3./4. September, 1991," pp. D546–47; and "Kommunique des KSZE-Krisenmechanismus, Prag, 10. Oktober, 1991," pp. D556–58.

120. Genscher, Address to UN, p. 829.

121. Hans-Dietrich Genscher, "Die EG sollte Kroatien und Slowenien Assoziierung anbieten," *Die Welt am Sonntag*, December 1, 1991, p. 9.

122. Kohl, address to Bundestag, p. 987; and "Verkehrsabkommen außer Kraft: Flugverkehr mit Jugoslawien gestoppt," *Süddeutsche Zeitung*, December 10, 1991, p. 2.

123. Discussion between Chancellor Helmut Kohl and the President of Croatia, *Bulletin*, no. 140 (December 10, 1991), p. 1144.

124. "Kohl sagt völkerrechtliche Anerkennung Sloweniens und Kroatiens zu,"

Archiv der Gegenwart, no. 26 (December 15–31, 1991), p. 36348. and "Perez bringt Bonn nicht von Anerkennungskurs ab," *Frankfurter Rundschau*, December 14, 1991, p. 1.

125. "'Friedensmission in Kroatien praktisch gescheitert': EG-Beobachter fordern gewaltsames Vorgehen gegen jugoslawische Armee," *Süddeutsche Zeitung*, December 4, 1991, p. 1.

126. "Zur Unterstützung für Kroatien und Slowenien: Bonn hat Anerkennung beschlossen," *Süddeutsche Zeitung*, December 16, 1991, p. 2.

127. Genscher, "Die EG sollte Assoziierung anbieten."

128. "EG-Außenminister offerieren Anerkennung jugoslawischer Republiken; Bonn erkennt Slowenien und Kroatien an," *Archiv der Gegenwart*, no. 26 (December 15–31, 1991), pp. 36349–50; and "EG will Kriterien für Anerkennung festlegen," *Süddeutsche Zeitung*, December 11, 1991, p. 2.

129. "Die Mitgliedstaaten der EG einigen sich auf Richtlinien zur Anerkennung neuer Staaten: Beschluß der Außenminister," *Frankfurter Allgemeine Zeitung*, December 18, 1991, p. 3.

130. Genscher, "Für Recht," p. 7; and Kohl, "Chancen einer Veränderung," p. 1110.

131. Kohl, Statement on the Soviet Union and Yugoslavia, p. 752; Statement of Foreign Ministry on Yugoslavia, *Bulletin*, no. 103 (September 25, 1991), p. 823; Genscher, "Für Recht," p. 7; Genscher, "Die EG sollte Assoziierung anbieten," p. 9; and Kohl, Address to Bundestag, p. 987.

132. Genscher, "Für Recht," p. 7.

133. "Diplomatie: Die Frist läuft ab," *Der Spiegel*, December 9, 1991, pp. 25–27.

134. See the Bundestag debates, "NATO-Debatte im Bundestag," *Das Parlament*, November 15/22, 1991, p. 5; "Außenpolitik," *Das Parlament*, December 6, 1991, p. 9; for the attitude expressed in newspapers from *Die Welt am Sonntag* to the *Frankfurter Rundschau*, see, for example, the editorial by Johann Georg Reißmüller, "Absurditäten statt Politik," *Frankfurter Allgemeine Zeitung*, December 18, 1991, p. 1.

135. See Chancellor Kohl's statement in Berkeley, p. 816.

136. See Genscher's justifications in "Die EG sollte Assoziierung anbieten," p. 9; and Kohl, Statement on NATO and EC Summits," p. 987.

137. Kohl, "Unsere Verantwortung," pp. 72–74; Genscher, "Perspektiven," pp. 656–57; and Kohl, "Die Rolle Deutschlands," p. 44.

138. Conference of German and French ambassadors, May 16/17, 1991, *Bulletin*, no. 56 (May 22, 1991), pp. 447–48.

139. Joint declaration of German Foreign Minister, Hans-Dietrich Genscher, and U.S. Secretary of State, James A. Baker, on European-Atlantic security issues, *Stichworte*, October 1991, pp. 15–17 and 32–33.

140. " 'Ein bißchen unheimlich' " *Der Spiegel*, July 22, 1991, p. 18.

141. Joint statement of Chancellor Helmut Kohl and President Francois Mitterrand on Yugoslavia, *Bulletin*, no. 103 (September 25, 1991), p. 819.

142. "Eine historische Entscheidung," *Der Spiegel*, October 21, 1991, pp. 18–20.

143. Richard von Weizsäcker, "Perspektiven der europäischen Einigung im Geiste der Humanität," *Bulletin*, no. 127 (November 13, 1991), p. 1027.

144. Kohl, Statement on NATO and EC Summits, pp. 986–87.

145. Gansel, "Reformen," p. 5.

146. Kohl, "Unsere Verantwortung," pp. 72–74; Gerhard Stoltenberg, "Zukunfts-aufgaben der Bundeswehr im vereinten Deutschland," pp. 215–16; and Kohl, "Die Rolle Deutschlands," p. 245; and Hans-Dietrich Genscher, "Eine Stabilitätsordnung für Europa," *Stichworte*, May 1992, p. 8.

147. Genscher, "Perspektiven, pp. 656–57.

148. Kohl, Statement on NATO and EC summits, pp. 485–87; Stoltenberg, "Zukunftsaufgaben," p. 215; Kohl, "Die Rolle Deutschlands," p. 444; Kohl's statement in Berkeley, p. 812; and Message from Chancellor Helmut Kohl and President Francois Mitterrand to the current head of the European Council, Ruud Lubbers, on a common European foreign and security policy, *Bulletin*, no. 117 (October 18, 1991), pp. 929–31, and Kohl, "Der Weg zur Union," p. 3.

149. Speech of President Richard von Weizsäcker addressed to a joint session of Congress on April 30, 1992, *Stichworte*, May 1992, pp. 3–9, and Joint Declaration of Genscher and Baker, pp. 15–17.

150. "Die Bedeutung der WEU," pp. 77–79; and Genscher, "Eine Vision," p. 92.

151. First meeting of the CSCE Council of Foreign Ministers, June 19/20, 1991, *Bulletin*, no. 72 (June 22, 1991), pp. 577–84; see also Kohl's remarks in Washington, "Deutsch-amerikanischer Beitrag zu Stabilität und Sicherheit," *Bulletin*, no. 58 (May 28, 1991), p. 458.

152. Third meeting of the CSCE on the Human Dimension of the Conference, *Bulletin*, no. 100 (September 18, 1991), pp. 798–99; and First Meeting of CSCE Council, pp. 577–84.

153. Kohl, Statement on NATO and EC Summits, p. 985; Third Meeting of CSCE Council, pp. 798–99; and Stercken, "Die Außen- und Sicherheitspolitik," p. 14.

154. A concise statement on the policy by Chancellor Kohl is his statement on NATO and EC Summits, pp. 985–89.

155. "Ergebnis in Maastricht völlig offen: Tauziehen um die Europäische Währungs-union," *Süddeutsche Zeitung*, December 10, 1991, p. 1; and "Spätestens 1999 beginnt Europas Währungsunion," December 11, 1991, p. 29.

156. Kohler-Koch, "Integration," pp. 18–19; "Sondergipfel in Dublin," *Archiv der Gegenwart*, no. 10 (April 25-May 10, 1990), pp. 34470–71; and "EG: Auf den Müllhaufen," *Der Spiegel*, May 7, 1990, p. 186.

157. Genscher, "Eine Vision," pp. 92–93.

158. Kohl, "Die Bedeutung der WEU," pp. 77–79; see also von Weizsäcker, "Perspektiven," p. 1027.

159. Helmut Kohl, "Im Bewußtsein der europäischen Idee als Werte- und Kulturgemeinschaft," *Bulletin*, no. 45 (May 4, 1991), p. 335.

160. Kohl, "Der Weg zur Union," p. 3; and Kohl, "Chancen einer Veränderung," p. 1111.

161. "Der Gipfel von Maastricht: Regierungserklärung und Debatte am 13. Dezember, 1991," *Das Parlament*, December 20/27, 1991, pp. 1–9.

162. "EG: Nur Lippenbekenntnisse, p. 200.

163. "Sondergipfel in Dublin," pp. 34470–71; and "EG: Auf den Müllhaufen," p. 186.

164. Kohler-Koch, "Integration," pp. 18–19.

165. Otto Graf Lambsdorff, "Keine Währungsexperimente," *Das Parlament*, December 20/27, 1991, p. 5; and "Es gibt kein Zurück," *Der Spiegel*, December 9, 1991, pp. 124–31.

166. Kohl, "Fundamente und Strukturen," p. 475.

167. Kohl, Statement on European Council meeting," p. 635.

168. Kohl, "Der Weg zur Union," pp. 3 and 6; Theo Waigel, " 'Wir bringen die deutsche Währungsunion nach Europa' " *Das Parlament*, December 20/27, 1991, p. 6, "Ergebnis in Maastricht," p. 1, and "Spätestens 1999," p. 29.

169. Kohl, "Die Rolle Deutschlands," pp. 245–46.

170. "Vorschlag Deutschlands und Frankreichs zu einer gemeinsamen Außen- und Sicherheitspolitik," *Stichworte*, February 1991, pp. 10–11; "Die sicherheitspolitische Zusammenarbeit im Rahmen der gemeinsamen Außen- und Sicherheitspolitik der Politischen Union," *Stichworte*, May 1991, pp. 16–20; Kohl, "Die Rolle Deutschlands," p. 247; and Joint Message of Chancellor Helmut Kohl and President Francois Mitterrand to the current President of the European Council, Giulio Andreotti, *Bulletin*, no. 144 (December 11, 1990), pp. 1513–14.

171. Kohl, "Der Weg zur Union," p. 3; Kohl, "Chancen einer Veränderung," p. 1111; Kohl, "Die Rolle Deutschlands," pp. 245–46; Kohl, Statement on NATO and EC Summits, p. 987; and Meeting of the European Council in Rome, *Bulletin*, no. 149 (December 21, 1990), pp. 1555–56.

172. Kohl, "Chancen einer Veränderung," p. 1111, and "The European Summit," *New York Times*, December 9, 1991, p. 10.

173. "Ergebnis in Maastricht," p. 1 and "Spätestens 1999," p. 29.

174. "Die Zeit ist nicht reif," *Der Spiegel*, October 14, 1991, p. 19.

175. Kohl, "Chancen einer Veränderung," p. 1111.

176. O. Ulrich Weidner, "Geteilte Zustimmung zum Ergebnis von Maastricht," *Das Parlament*, December 20/27, 1991, p. 1; and Kohl, "Der Weg zur Union," p. 3.

Part Two

DESIGNS FOR A NEW EUROPE

SIX

Toward a New European Political Economy

Wolfgang H. Reinicke

EUROPEANS STAND AT the beginning of an era that will define the new political and economic architecture of their continent. The end of the Cold War has both provided the opportunity and shown the pressing need to "unite" Europe on the basis of the rule of law, democratic political systems, and the principles of the market economy.[1] But while the formal division of Europe has ended, the magnitude of the difficulties of transforming the economic and political systems of Central and Eastern Europe and integrating them into the political economy of Western Europe is only beginning to emerge.[2] A failure to effectively address the economic and political legacies of the Cold War, however, could further divide Europe along social and economic lines, with costly and even dangerous consequences for the West. This has manifested itself in the rising threat of authoritarianism, ethnic conflict, socially destabilizing migration, and the potential loss of profitable investment opportunities and lucrative export markets. If Europeans want to ensure that the ideological and military division of Europe is not replaced by an economic and social one, they need to develop a strategy for the formation of a new European political economy. While other initiatives are needed, particularly in the security sphere (see chapter 7), the primary goal should be to integrate the former East bloc into the market economy of Western Europe. Since the European Community embodies this market economy and contributes significantly to the high standard of living and political stability in Western Europe, it is the most logical institutional vehicle for transforming the East. In fact, its founders saw it from the outset as an all-European institution.[3]

This chapter benefited from the comments of Ullrich Heilemann and Lilly Gardner-Feldmann. The author gratefully acknowledges the assistance of Lyle Goldstein, Andreas Luge, Marion Recktenwald, and especially Dan Turner. Caroline Pecquet assisted with typing the chapter.

This basic goal of European "unification" presents some major challenges to all concerned, most obviously to the countries of Central and Eastern Europe that are undergoing painful if historic changes, but also to Western Europe—in particular to the EC's aspirations for greater political and economic integration, as articulated most recently at the Maastricht summit. The renewed debate between "widening" and "deepening" the Community has not only captured the complexity of these challenges but also highlighted the urgency of developing an adequate response. The immediate task, then, is to develop a strategy that will satisfy the need to integrate the East with the West without compromising the Community's achievements or its future plans. The purpose of this chapter is to identify the central principles and policies that should inform such a strategy and, more specifically, to underscore the need for what is termed a "holistic" approach to bringing about the required changes in Western, Central, and Eastern Europe—and ultimately a unified political economy.

Analytical Framework

The creation of a unified European political economy presents different challenges to the countries and institutions involved, but the principal burden of adjustment undoubtedly falls on the countries of Eastern Europe. As many have correctly argued, the primary goal of this adjustment process must be the introduction of an economic system based on private property and the free exchange of goods, services, labor, and capital—a market economy.

However, this essay argues that although the free interaction of economic interests is important, it is only one element of a market economy. In defining a market, much of the utilitarian tradition, including classical and neoclassical economics, specifies an almost idealized state where rational, self-interested economic actors interact independently of legal, political, or other constraints. In addition, these actors are minimally affected by social relations, history, traditions, ethnic allegiances, or other factors. The market is a differentiated sphere of modern society unrelated to the broader political, social, and historical environment in which it is embedded.[4]

However, a market economy is more than a loosely structured agglomeration of individual economic actors freely expressing their economic preferences and generating *Pareto superior* or even optimal outcomes for themselves and the economy at large. Rather, a modern market economy is the principal form of social organization governing advanced industrial democracies. It is a complex organization based not only on the interaction of individual economic preferences, but on social relationships and patterns of behavior, legal norms and mechanisms, and political forces and institutions, all of which interact in a structured manner to produce the relatively consistent behavior characteristic of any large institution. Moreover, any change in the economic circumstances under which individuals interact will also have a major impact on the political, legal, and social structures in which economic activities are embedded. In other words, change in one area cannot be separated from change in the others; on the contrary, it may often be the cause. Finally, the institutions of a market economy and the transactions they undertake depend on the presence of collective goods such as trust, which cannot be provided by market processes themselves. The social organization of trust is an important element of a market economy, and economic theory has not been able to cope with it.[5]

The purpose of employing this holistic concept of a market is both analytical and methodological.[6] From an analytical perspective, only a holistic conception of a market economy is likely to capture the complexity and uniqueness of the system transformation required in Central and Eastern Europe. Similar approaches have been used by scholars studying the transformation from feudalism to capitalism in Europe during the sixteenth and seventeenth centuries.[7] Although several aspects vary, the challenge to East European societies is similar in scope, demanding not merely economic reform but a transformation that permeates all spheres of society. A holistic approach to system transformation in Central and Eastern Europe also takes into account the close interdependence among the legal, economic, social, and political aspects. Indeed, from a holistic perspective, a market economy is best perceived as an organic system that forms a social whole and is highly dependent on its constituent parts. The full relevance of the individual elements can therefore only be evaluated in the context of the system as a whole.

From a methodological perspective, using the concept of the market economy as the central focus of the analysis provides a common framework of inquiry for the larger issue this essay addresses—the emergence of a new political economy of Europe. Much of the discussion about the new Europe has concentrated on Central and Eastern Europe and neglected Western Europe, where market mechanisms are firmly established and widely accepted as the dominant form of social organization. However, the structures, rules, and norms that define West European markets—and in particular the European Community market—will need to change in order to cope with the transformation and integration of Central and Eastern Europe. Thus the size, shape, and structure of the political economy of the new Europe will be determined not only by a process of system transformation in Eastern Europe but also by systemic reform in the Western half of the continent. A holistic concept of the market establishes a common frame of reference to examine the necessary political, economic, and social changes. Ultimately, the degree to which each market is willing and able to undergo such changes will determine the extent to which both markets can be integrated and the degree to which the division of Europe can be overcome.

A holistic strategy of system transformation or systemic reform is based on two principles. First, transformation or reform must take place in at least three dimensions of social organization: the legal and administrative, the economic, and the social and psychological. Economic interactions, the most visible characteristics of an economy, are most closely associated with the wealth-generating potential of market exchange. However, all market interactions are firmly embedded in a set of administrative rules and regulations governed by political forces. In addition, any market economy relies on a set of social and psychological norms and the respective institutions that have internalized the norms that create individual behavioral patterns characteristic of and essential to the functioning of a market economy. Finally and most important, the three dimensions of social organization are organically linked and interdependent, and a strategy to either create a market or adjust an existing one to new internal or external conditions must consider them as a whole.[8]

The second principle demands that transformation or reform permeate all levels of society, from the major political and economic institutions to midlevel organizations and, finally, families and individuals. If the strategy fails to reach all members of society, the market economy will lack both a social base and the social support that is essential on both the supply and demand sides. On the supply side, the institutional structure will become fully functional only if it is adequately equipped with trained personnel who understand the dynamics of a market economy and adhere to a professional ethic that commits them to its functioning. On the demand side, a large part of the population must be aware of the complexities and difficulties of system transformation and reform. Unless the process of change is supported by a sufficiently large number of people and the organizations that represent them, the necessary consensus will never be attained or will disintegrate under stress. Combining these two dimensions generates a matrix that delineates the multiple policy domains of a strategy of system transformation and systemic reform (see table 6–1).

Eastern Europe: The Challenge of System Transformation

Because the market economy has long been the dominant form of social organization in Western industrial democracies, it is considered something almost "natural." Observers tend to focus on its most obvious attributes such as private property, a price system for allocating scarce resources, and other economic characteristics. At the same time, many of its supporting but less

Table 6-1. *A Holistic Strategy of System Transformation and Systemic Reform*[a]

Level of social structure	Three market dimensions		
	Legal/administrative	*Economic*	*Social/psychological*
Macro	Legislative structure Judicial system Bureaucracy	Efficient labor and capital markets Convertible exchange rates Free trade	Educational system Religion Mass media
Micro	Interest-pressure groups (unions, business associations)	Private-competitive enterprise system Free price system	Family Peer groups Schools Voluntary associations

a. The characteristics defining the various market domains are by no means exhaustive and are for illustrative purposes only. Similarly, in reality the dividing lines between the various domains are more fluid, and additional levels of the social structure could be introduced.

visible structural elements are taken for granted by the public and policymakers alike. The primary task facing policymakers, once a market economy has been established, is managing it and, if necessary and politically feasible, reforming the management process.

None of the countries of Central and Eastern Europe, however, has ever experienced a modern market economy for any sustained period of time. The challenge to these countries, therefore, is not the systemic reform of their economies through the refining or reorienting of current macro- or microeconomic policies, but the total transformation of their system into a market economy. The political, economic, and social structures that have governed these societies for the last forty years must be dismantled. In the economic dimension alone, this implies the dismantling of many of the vertical control hierarchies that enabled the state to use distribution as the primary mechanism of allocating scarce resources and economic output. These hierarchies must be replaced with thousands of horizontal market linkages that will make information easily available and allow sellers and buyers to interact freely.[9] There is no need here to elaborate on the prerequisites for the successful creation of a market economy, as many valuable reform proposals have addressed the various economic structures in need of transformation. However, as the holistic approach suggests, the economic dimension of the market cannot be separated from the larger structure of which it is a part. It may thus be useful to elaborate on the other two dimensions and examine the implications of the interdependence of the three dimensions for a strategy of system transformation.

In the legal and administrative dimension, a modern market economy depends not only on private property and free prices that enable exchange, but on a complex and differentiated network of administrative organizations to structure that exchange. At the macro level, their function is often administrative, ensuring smooth and efficient market interactions and supported by laws and regulations. For example, most labor markets in advanced industrialized countries have a network of employment offices that provide not only unemployment benefits but support in the form of career counseling, aptitude tests, and information on job opportunities. In addition, most countries offer vocational training and retraining to smooth the transition process during periods of industrial restructuring and adjustment.

At the microstructural level, legal and administrative organizations often perform the function of interest aggregation and intermediation, providing information to policymakers and representing the interests of particular groups in the market. For example, chambers of commerce, unions, trade and business associations, and consumer groups are all vital elements of a modern market economy. In the labor market, these organizations often smooth adjustment periods by offering technical advice and expertise, physical space, and financial support for training programs. At both the macro- and microstructural levels, these measures are vital to the functioning of labor markets, allowing demand and supply to clear at relatively low levels of unemployment.[10]

Reflecting the importance attached to decisionmaking by individuals and groups as both consumers and producers, market economies also rely extensively on networks of representative institutions. But such a decisionmaking structure results in permanent conflict at all levels of society and across many issues. Thus, market economies have established elaborate mechanisms of conflict prevention and resolution based on a legal framework that includes commercial codes, antitrust legislation, arbitration procedures, and consumer safety and protection standards. This legal framework in turn relies on an adequate judicial apparatus (in both institutional and human capital terms) to implement and enforce laws and procedures. Centrally planned economies, on the other hand, have relied largely on mono-organizational structures of social organization. As a result, conflicts among producers and consumers were rare and mechanisms for conflict resolution almost nonexistent. These mechanisms must now be created before the economy can function efficiently.

In the social and psychological dimension, a strategy of system transformation must take into account the market's reliance on certain types of behavior. For example, the introduction of a market economy will require the acknowledgment of the spontaneity and unpredictability of market decisions and the acceptance of market developments as processes over which individuals and the society at large have limited influence, even in such key areas as production, investment, and distribution. This is not to say that unpredictability did not exist in the command economies of Central and Eastern Europe, but it was considered a sign of confusion and treated as the exception—as something sick or pathological.[11] Thus an essential task during the creation of a market economy is to establish the social legitimacy of risk and spontaneity in everyday life. This legitimacy can be established only when individuals shed the "learned helplessness" that is a reflection of state and party monopoly over political, economic, social, and cultural life. In turn, individuals must acquire the skills to deal with the insecurities that the unpredictability of a market economy generates.

Entrepreneurship, innovativeness, creativity, independent decisionmaking, the acceptance of responsibility for one's own actions, and self-confidence are some of the characteristics that make up the social and psychological foundation of a market economy. For a market economy to act as the principal mode of social organization, individuals must understand how it works, identify with it, and benefit from it. Only then will it have the integrative attributes that it has had in the Western industrialized economies.[12] In addition, individuals will have to come to terms with some of the consequences of a market economy. Social acceptance of the unemployment and wide income differentials associated with the rise of a middle class and a new managerial elite will lead to major adjustments in the social stratification of Central and East European societies.

Merely recognizing the importance of these dimensions alone, however, will not suffice to create a market economy. While it is important to adopt a commercial code and consumer protection laws, they will function only if they are fully implemented and their effectiveness is monitored. Similarly, while some Central and East Europeans may make social and psychological adjustments, such changes need to take root in society at large, not just in a narrow new elite. Unless these changes are actively promoted, it will be years before they permeate all levels of society.[13] What is required, then, is not only an elaborate design of system transformation but also a scheme of system maintenance to manage the economy's development in all three dimensions.

The previous discussion has several implications. First, it shows that a modern market economy relies not just on its ability to exchange goods and services or labor and capital, but also on a legal and administrative framework within which these exchanges are embedded and a social and psychological foundation upon which the exchanges are based. Second, the previous discussion suggests that a market economy is not only a multidimensional institution, but one in which the dimensions are organically linked. This organic interdependence has significant policy implications, for if progress in one dimension of a market depends on parallel progress in the others, then it is important to develop a strategy of simultaneity. Viewed from a different perspective, the capacity of a system to truly absorb economic transformation depends on its ability to institute legal and administrative and social and psychological changes to sustain it.

Such a strategy would not necessarily slow the course of economic change, as many have suggested it would. What it does mean, however, is that economic transformation that takes place in a legal and administrative and social and psychological vacuum is likely to stall or require reorientation at a relatively early stage in order to allow the other spheres to catch up. Such an effect can already be observed in Central and Eastern Europe, in particular in the slowdown in privatization programs and the recent changes in Poland's economic policies. To allow for more simultaneous progress, resources must be relatively evenly distributed across all three market dimensions. Ignoring the need for uniform progress and enforcing economic transformation without taking into account the organic linkages not only will cause setbacks or even collapse, but can destroy the initial achievements and undermine societal and political support for continued change.

The previous discussion has further policy implications. The first and most important involves the appropriate speed for implementing system transformation, a central determinant of which is the availability of necessary resources. A holistic strategy requires a broad range of resources, not just the financial capital essential to stabilization programs that focus almost entirely on the economic dimensions of a market. A holistic strategy also relies on vast amounts of human capital—in the form of knowledge and experience—to generate progress in the legal and administrative and social and psychological spheres. Unless these nonfinancial resources are sufficient to complement the financial means, capital must be reallocated to recruit more human resources. Moreover, the nature of the required social and psychological change suggests that it is likely to evolve primarily as an endogenous process of social evolution specific to each country. Foreign capital in whatever form, though providing necessary support, may be only a limited contribution.

The above suggests that a holistic strategy is likely to favor a gradual or piecemeal approach to system transformation. For this reason, advocates of economic "shock therapy" believe that the gradualist approach contains certain built-in obstructive or even destructive tendencies. The more time the opponents of change have at their disposal, these critics argue, the greater the risk that the transformation process will be retarded or even reversed. Such criticism is well taken if time alone is considered the key factor in the success of system transformation. However, when uniform progress replaces time as the central factor, the gradual approach appears far more likely to succeed. In fact, seen from the holistic perspective, it is the shock therapy approach that is piecemeal and gradual, as it concentrates its efforts only on the economic dimension of a market. In addition, the emphasis that critics of the gradual approach place on the risk that increasing opposition to reform will undermine the transformation effort is not very convincing. First, a strategy that relies on a surprise effect to overcome resistance to change is equally, if not more, risky.[14] Second, it is true that opposition often develops during system transformation. But before drawing any conclusions about the appropriateness of an unpopular policy, it is necessary to determine the source of the opposition. Does the opposition indicate such a powerful resistance to transforming a command economy into a market economy that it can be outmaneuvered only by the application of shock therapy? Or is the resistance directed at the shock therapy itself—as much of it has been—calling for a change in strategy?

In discussing the merits of these two approaches, it is also important to keep the ultimate objective of system transformation in mind. This objective is not simply privatization and economic stabilization, but a market economy that will improve the living standards of East European societies by generating long-term, sustainable economic growth. Seen from this perspective, privatization and stabilization are necessary but insufficient conditions that can be met only if large segments of society identify with the system transformation and have the incentive to participate in and support it—that is, if transformation also occurs in the social and psychological dimension of a market.[15]

Given this more realistic assessment of the time and resources needed for system transformation, policymakers must be highly selective, targeting components of a market economy with a high strategic payoff from a functional as well as a structural perspective. For example, the transformation of the telecommunications sector is likely to have great functional value, as industries, businesses, and households will all benefit from it. Moreover, a modern telecommunications system may also become an important tool to facilitate system transformation in other areas such as education—which in turn plays a vital role in transforming the social and psychological dimension. Other sectors of strategic importance are energy and transportation, but in general, the greater the diffusion and demonstration effect of transforming one specific sector of the economy, the higher its strategic value.

The financial sector is of particularly high strategic value in both structural and functional terms. The absence of an efficient mechanism for financial intermediation is generally considered to have been one of the principal causes of the collapse of the Central and East European economies,[16] and the history of economic development attests to the fact that a working financial system is indispensable to a market economy.[17] A stable financial system will not only facilitate and serve the transformation process in other areas of the economy, but it may well be a precondition for their success.[18] Current developments in Central and East European financial markets provide an excellent context for the application of the holistic approach to system transformation.[19]

Finally, a holistic strategy must take the political context and any constraints it imposes into consideration. The extent to which system transformation can be undertaken at any particular time—whether by shock therapy or by a holistic approach—depends upon the capacity of the political system to design and carry out such a transformation, and in particular on the degree of legitimacy accorded the government. Western politicians and bureaucrats are accustomed to advocating policies in a stable democracy where the government's legitimacy is generally high. However, the legacy of single-party rule in Central and Eastern Europe is a lack of trust in government officials and political institutions and the absence of a shared sense of national identity. This lack of legitimacy and national consensus places constraints on the speed with which the new governments can enact major changes, in particular those of "shock therapy" magnitude. If transformation is enforced faster than the emerging democratic systems can absorb it, it is likely to undermine and damage the fragile trust that has developed in the new political elites, causing a political backlash and raising the possibility of a return to authoritarian or even totalitarian forms of government.[20]

A gradualist approach is more likely to avoid this latent conflict between an emerging market economy and democracy during the process of system transformation. First, a holistic strategy allows the market economy to evolve at a slower pace, leaving more time for the new political institutions to establish their legitimacy and enhancing the capacity of the political system to keep up with the many changes. Second, by avoiding some of the economic and social hardships of shock therapy, the holistic approach itself is likely to contribute to the government's growing legitimacy, strengthening both the political institutions and the government's power to continue with the transformation process.

A holistic approach to system transformation makes clear the complexity of the process, generating a more realistic set of expectations regarding the resources and time necessary to establish even the most basic foundations of a market economy in Central and Eastern Europe. One consequence of considering only the economic aspects of market formation has been the emergence of a gap between what the majority of the region's citizens expect from the transformation and what can realistically be achieved in such a short period of time. The "expectation gap" that has emerged in these countries has led to disillusionment and frustration, weakening domestic political support for systemic change.

As a result, the likelihood that system transformation in Eastern Europe will come to a halt or even be reversed has increased since late 1990, especially during 1991. In macro-political terms, the countries of Central and Eastern Europe had, until recently, made considerable progress in establishing the basic institutions of democracy and the rule of law. However, because

Table 6-2. *Industrial Output in Central and Eastern Europe and the Soviet Union, 1986–91*

Percent change over the same period of the preceding year

Country or area	1986	1987	1988	1989	1990	1991 Jan.– March	1991 Jan.– June	1991 Jan.– Sept.	1991 Jan.– Dec.
Bulgaria	4.7	6.0	3.2	−0.3	−12.6	−21.0	−29.1	−28.1	−27.3
Czechoslovakia	3.2	2.5	2.1	0.8	−3.5	−10.5	−14.3	−19.8	−23.1
Hungary	1.9	3.5	−0.3	−2.5	−4.5	−8.7	−14.2	−16.6	−19.1
Poland	4.7	3.4	5.3	−0.5	−24.2	−5.5	−9.3	−11.0	−11.9
Romania	7.3	2.4	3.1	−2.1	−19.0	−17.0	−16.6	−17.7	−18.7
Yugoslavia	3.9	0.6	−0.7	0.9	−10.3	−21.1	−17.4	−18.3	−20.7
Central and Eastern Europe	4.6	3.2	3.3	−0.1	−18.9	−13.7	−15.6	−17.7	−19.1
Soviet Union	4.4	3.8	3.9	1.7	−1.2	−5.0	−6.2	−6.4	−9.0[a]

Sources: United Nations, *Economic Survey of Europe in 1991–1992* (New York: UN Economic Commission for Europe, 1991), table 3.2.6, p. 64, and table B.11, p. 302; United Nations, *Economic Bulletin for Europe*, vol. 43 (Geneva: UN Economic Commission for Europe, November 1991), table 1.3.2, p. 26; OECD, *Main Economic Indicators* (Paris: December 1989), p. 166; and *Neue Zürcher Zeitung*, December 25, 1991, p. 11.

a. Goskomstat projection (*Izvestiya,* July 18, 1991).

the transition to a market economy is still at an early stage and numerous complications have cropped up, the record so far is mixed at best.[21] Briefly, throughout the 1980s industrial output had been stagnating in most Central and East European countries. However, starting in 1989, Hungary, Poland, and Romania experienced negative industrial growth rates for the first time. During 1990 and 1991, industrial output collapsed in all Central and East European countries, declining at double-digit rates (see table 6–2).

As a result, unemployment is rising dramatically. Between December 1990 and December 1991, unemployment in Bulgaria rose from 1.7 percent to 10.7 percent, in Czechoslovakia from 1 percent to 6.6 percent, in Hungary from 1.7 percent to 8.3 percent, and in Poland from 6.1 percent to 11.5 percent. Official government estimates project double-digit unemployment rates for most of the region's countries by the end of 1992 (see table 6–3).

These economic statistics lie at the root of the deteriorating societal and political climate across Central and Eastern Europe that currently threatens the transformation process. An EC survey conducted in the fall of 1991 showed that at least 50 percent of the population in every Central and East European country believed that the economic situation had deteriorated during the previous twelve months.[22] The outcome of the poll is even more troubling on a microstructural level, for over 60 percent of those surveyed also believed that their household finances had worsened over the last twelve months, with the exception of Romania, which had just entered into the process of system transformation.[23] Confidence is declining with respect not only to the

Table 6-3. *Unemployment in Central and Eastern Europe, 1989–92*
Percent of the labor force

Country	Dec. 1989	Dec. 1990	1991 March	1991 June	1991 Sept.	1991 Dec.	Dec. 1992[a]
Bulgaria	0.0	1.7	3.5	6.0	8.8	10.7	17.8
Czechoslovakia	0.0	1.0	2.3	3.8	5.7	6.6	12.6
Hungary	0.3	1.7	3.0	3.9	6.1	8.3	13.0
Poland	0.1	6.1	7.1	8.4	10.4	11.5	16–18
Romania	n.a.	1.3	0.7	1.6	2.4	3.1	n.a.
Yugoslavia	12.2	13.6	14.2	14.7	15.2[b]	19.6	n.a.

Sources: United Nations, *Economic Survey of Europe in 1990–1991* (New York: UN Economic Commission for Europe, 1991), table 2.2.14, p. 59; United Nations, *Economic Survey of Europe in 1991–1992* (New York: UN Economic Commission for Europe, 1992), table 3.2.9, p. 68.; OECD, *OECD Economic Outlook*, vol. 50 (Paris, December 1991); and various issues of Foreign Broadcasting Information Service, *Daily Report*.
n.a. Not available.
a. Forecasts based on government projections.
b. August 1991.

economy, but also to the political system, a development that is beginning to erode the legitimacy of the governing elite. According to the EC survey, at least half the population in almost every Central and East European country felt some dissatisfaction with the results of democracy.[24] In another poll conducted in Poland during the summer of 1991, 71 percent of the respondents agreed that "corruption in Poland today is a major problem," and over half thought it was as bad now as it had been under the communist regime.[25] In fact, the Poles' frustration with the deteriorating economic conditions and the inability of the political system to address the issues has manifested itself in active opposition; for example, the number of strikes increased sharply during 1990 and 1991.[26] Even more threatening to the political transformation process, however, is the increasing political apathy. For instance, in April of 1991, 50 percent of Poles surveyed did not intend to cast a ballot in the fall elections. By July this figure had risen to the 63 percent that did in fact not vote in the elections.[27]

Other Central and East European countries are exhibiting similar social and political tendencies, and as in Poland, this discontent is reflected in voter apathy and declining government support.[28] The September 1990 local elections in Hungary drew a turnout of less than 30 percent and a poll in January 1990 revealed that only 64 percent of those polled would go to the polls for a general election.[29] As a result the current government has warned the public against growing antidemocratic sentiment and an increasing willingness to accept an authoritarian leader as the price of an economic miracle. The situation is not very different in the other countries of the region.[30]

The inability to maintain public support and the generally deteriorating economic situation shed additional doubt on the long-term viability of current transformation strategies. No strategy, however promising its eventual outcome, will succeed unless the transition period can be managed successfully and the outcome of the transition is sustainable. The failure of the transformation process, however, would not only have serious internal, social, economic, and political repercussions for each country, but would also jeopardize the efforts of other countries to transform their social systems. Besides posing a threat to the stability of the entire region, such a failure would also preclude its speedy integration into the all-European political economy and dilute the EC's role as the external anchor of political and economic stability.

While it is probably too late to reduce the "expectation gap" that has emerged in Central and Eastern Europe, a holistic approach could help prevent it from becoming wider. More important, however, by emphasizing both the multidimensional nature of a market economy and acknowledging the political constraints on system transformation, a holistic approach is more likely to provide a sustainable foundation for the emerging market economy by reducing the risk of both policy failure and the loss of political legitimacy of the governing elite.

Western Europe: The Challenge of Systemic Reform

Systemic reform in West European markets—and in particular the single European market—will play a decisive role in facilitating and shortening the process of system transformation in Central and Eastern Europe. Because this reform cannot be separated from an overall strategy of European unification, policymakers must ensure that it does not undermine what West Europeans have achieved since World War II in the context of the European Community. The EC, therefore, should have a leadership role in the process of systemic reform.

First, the EC has a historic responsibility to embrace the countries of Central and Eastern Europe. In principle, Article 237 of the Treaty of Rome opens the possibility of full EC membership to every democratic European state. Second, since overcoming some initial doubts both at the Community level and among current members, the Community has made clear that it is unwilling to risk its own political and economic integration process by considering alternative structures of future European architecture. As Italy's foreign minister, Giannni De Michelis stated, "It is basically up to the Europeans to manage the establishment of peace and restoration of unity to their continent, and the European Community (EC) will be the core around which the new balance is fashioned."[31] The decision by the Community and the European Free Trade Association (EFTA) countries to form a European

Economic Area (EEA), as well as the applications for membership of Austria, Sweden, Finland, and Switzerland, are clear indications that an alternative intergovernmental or supranational organizational—with the possible exception of a military-security arm—is no longer viable. According to Commission President Jacques Delors, "It is difficult to see what would be gained from wasting more than thirty years of successful experience to create a completely new organization."[32]

Third, the European Community has a strong political interest in supporting the transformation in Central and Eastern Europe. The formation of democratic political regimes based on market economies will contribute to the stability and prosperity of the entire European continent. A failure of the transformation process, however, would have considerable negative consequences not just for the fledgling democracies but for the Community as well. Instability on the EC's periphery could spill over into its territory or draw its members into conflicts. Continued economic disparities could set off mass emigration from East to West, precipitating a nationalistic counter-reaction in the EC member countries and threatening the ongoing process of deepening the Community. A failure of the transformation process would also result in a loss of the investment and other economic opportunities for the EC that have developed with the sudden opening of Central and Eastern Europe, including many of the resources that have already been allocated. And failure of system transformation would create new political and economic barriers.

Fourth, for the countries of Central and Eastern Europe, the European Community is the anchor of political and economic stability in Europe. It is a magnet in the new European architecture and the central focus of the new democracies in establishing foreign relations because of its geographic proximity, success in peacefully managing interstate relations, and the possibilities for political and economic aid as well as open export markets. The failure of the transformations would thus not only destabilize the region but delegitimize the Community as the center of political and economic authority in the new Europe. It is thus in the general interest of the Community and its members to develop a strategy that will allow the EC to cope with the political, economic, and social challenges emanating from the process of system transformation in Eastern Europe.

However, two factors have complicated the debate over the exact course of such a strategy. First, the EC itself is in the midst of a systemic reform process laid out long before the events in Central and Eastern Europe unfolded. The two intergovernmental conferences (IGCs), one on political, and one on economic and monetary, union concluded at the Maastricht summit in December 1991 had originally been intended to lay the institutional foundations that would govern the current twelve members of the Community beyond the completion of the single market program. Although it is not often publicly acknowledged, the developments since the fall of 1989 have diminished the political importance of the two IGCs as the EC members struggle to redefine their positions in the emerging Europe. For example, Germany's increasing political weight in Europe since unification undoubtedly influenced the negotiations leading up to the Maastricht summit. The summit itself and the ratification process, as the Danish referendum of June 2, 1992, demonstrated, can no longer be separated from the process of unification. The German government's basic support for European integration has not changed, but there is little doubt that the country will use its new strength to influence the future architecture of Europe according to its own interests, possibly accentuating current differences among the members.[33]

German unification has also led other members to re-evaluate their positions on the issues negotiated at the two IGCs. One way to weaken Germany's newly gained power is to accelerate the path toward political and economic integration, enhancing the Community's character as an autonomous political entity and diluting the strength of individual states. This option is an attractive one for France, which is especially concerned about Germany's future role in the Community. The events in Eastern Europe and the Soviet Union have also had an impact on the two IGCs and the Maastricht summit. In order to constructively use its political and economic power in the vacuum that the collapse of the East bloc has created, the Community now perceives that it must strengthen its internal cohesion and political capacity. This has increased the pressure on individual member states to work toward a successful conclusion of the IGC on political union and on matters of joint foreign policy in particular.[34]

The second factor complicating the development of a strategy of European "unification" involves the differences among current EC members on the integration of the Central and East European countries into the Community. Since its inception, France has considered the Community a means of balancing German power with that of other member states. German unification had already disturbed this balance and threatened the special Franco-German relationship that in many ways is the foundation of the Community itself. To maintain the traditional balance of power on the European continent, France initially attempted to stop and later to at least slow down the process of German unification.[35] When the countries of Central and Eastern Europe eventually join the EC, the center of gravity in Europe will shift even more toward Germany, further weakening the French position. The French response to this challenge so far has been mixed and has at times even appeared confused.[36]

Some members of the EC's "southern tier," in particular Portugal and Spain, have also expressed reservations about embracing the countries of Central and Eastern Europe, offering three reasons for their reluctance. First, the Southern members of the Community have profited from membership in the EC and fear that this may change if the Eastern region is linked closely to the EC. During the 1980s the EC turned from the East to the South for supplies of industrial imports stimulating economic growth. With Spain's entry to the EC and the French economy's reorientation to the South, a new pole of economic growth and development emerged. Second, Southern member countries continue to depend on the EC for funds to facilitate the economic and industrial restructuring of their economies that will bring them into compliance with EC laws and regulations. These structural funds amount to between 1.6 and 2.1 percent of the GNP of the poorer EC member states. As Portugal's secretary of state for foreign affairs and cooperation, Durao Barroso, has stated, "The countries of the South should in no way be penalized, especially the less advanced among them."[37] Third, the Mediterranean members—including France—consider migration from the Maghreb countries and political instability in the Middle East just as threatening as a mass exodus of refugees from the East and would prefer to see additional funds allocated to North Africa and greater attention given to promoting peace in the Middle East.[38]

Germany, however, has been a strong advocate of providing large-scale support for Central and Eastern Europe and accelerating its integration into the Community, as is clearly reflected in the credits and grants that Germany has made to the countries of the region. At the end of December 1991, 20.4 percent of all G-24 assistance to Eastern Europe came from Germany[39] or 0.5 percent of Germany's GDP at 1991 prices, compared with 0.1 percent and 0.08 percent for the United States and Japan respectively. If one considers the contributions by EC members alone—which at the end of December 1991 totaled approximately Ecu 11.4 billion—Germany's share rises to 54.8 percent.[40]

Several factors explain Germany's position. First, since Central and Eastern European integration can only strengthen its overall position in Europe, it is not surprising that Germany would support such a policy. Second, as an immediate neighbor, Germany is the Western country most threatened by political and economic instability and the possibility of large-scale emigration. Third, given Germany's historical links to the countries of the region and the fact that the East German economy was once firmly embedded in their economic network, Germany is also likely to benefit most from EC support of the region. Finally, Germany has pledged to reciprocate Hungarian, Czechoslovak, and Polish support during the summer and fall of 1989 by publicly supporting their calls for eventual EC membership.[41]

But while Germany is the most outspoken supporter of Community support for Central and Eastern Europe, it is not alone. For their own reasons, Denmark, Italy, and the United Kingdom also strongly support the idea of widening the Community.[42] Both Denmark and Italy are also expected to gain from a shift of political and economic power toward the center of Europe. The membership of the three Baltic states (as well as Poland) will open up new opportunities, and Denmark, with its historical ties and geographic proximity, will be one of the primary beneficiaries. Great Britain, however, favors greater EC engagement in Central and Eastern Europe and a clear commitment to membership in order to slow down or even undermine the current integration process within the Community itself.[43] The differing interests of EC members in the integration of Central and Eastern Europe have found their expressions in the renewed debate over whether to widen or deepen the Community. Should the Community focus on geographic expansion by allowing new countries to become full members? Or should it continue on its present course toward political and economic integration without accepting any new members?

While this debate may have been relevant in the immediate aftermath of the democratic revolutions in the fall and winter of 1989, it is largely academic today. As the economic legacy of over four decades of central planning was exposed during 1990 and 1991, it became clear that, given their current problems, full economic integration of the Central and East European states into the Community would have severe social, economic, and political consequences. It is unlikely that any of the region's governments could survive the economic shock therapy being applied in the former GDR, and neither they nor their Western counterparts have the resources to adequately cushion these societies from a too-sudden exposure to the world economy. In addition, the vast structural differences between the economies in Central, Eastern, and Western Europe would threaten the economic integration process among current EC members. Therefore, from an economic perspective, while the two concepts of widening and deepening are not incompatible, they should be implemented sequentially.

In the short term, therefore, an EC strategy must be geared toward facilitating system transformation in Central and Eastern Europe and initiating the long process of integration into the Community by strengthening the association agreements concluded at the end of 1991. In the medium term, if it wants to remain at the center of the new European political economy, the EC must strengthen its own economic and political capacity by accepting the current EFTA countries as full members. In the long term, the EC must fully integrate the Central and East European countries into its institutional framework, substantially widening the EC in the process. This raises questions, however, about its future institutional structure.

Strengthening the Association Agreements

In the short term, the association agreements between the EC and Czechoslovakia, Hungary, and Poland provide the central mechanism through which the EC hopes to facilitate system transformation in Central and Eastern Europe and pave the way for its eventual integration into the Community.

While the agreements differ in their specifics, they are structured around a common framework with six components: political dialogue, the "four freedoms" (free movement of goods, services, capital, and labor), economic, cultural, and financial cooperation, and the Association Council, Committee, and Parliamentary Commission.[44]

The primary purpose of the association agreements is to support and stabilize system transformation. Its centerpiece is a series of measures aimed at providing the three countries with direct economic aid and indirect trade assistance but only if their economies are brought into line with the laws and regulations of the Community according to the principle of *acquis communautaire*. In addition, these agreements offer the countries of Central and Eastern Europe a forum for political dialogue, opening the possibility of cooperation on matters of foreign policy through the Association Council. The agreements are contingent on the willingness of the three countries to meet certain political and economic prerequisites: adherence to the rule of law, respect for human rights, creation of a multiparty system with free and fair elections, and economic liberalization that encourages a market economy.

Since the full agreements must be ratified by national parliaments and therefore will not take effect for some time, a provisional agreement covering the commercial aspects (over which the EC enjoys jurisdiction) came into force on March 1, 1992.[45] The Community requested authorization to open negotiations on similar agreements with other East European countries in early September 1991, and negotiations have since started.[46] These agreements are clearly unprecedented in the history of the EC's relations with nonmember countries and indicate the strength of Western Europe's ties to the region as well as its support for the difficult transformations going on there.

Despite the generally positive character of the association agreements, however, several issues that have not been adequately addressed may ultimately jeopardize their original intent. First, as discussed at greater length elsewhere, the history of the negotiations raises the question of whether the agreements in their current form will receive the necessary parliamentary support. Among EC member countries, strong protectionist resistance has led to the near-collapse of negotiations on several occasions.[47] This resistance has not yet subsided, raising the possibility that the accords will be derailed at the national level. On the Central and East European side, Czechoslovakia, Hungary, and Poland have consistently charged that the accords are unfairly biased toward Community interests. In light of the increasing economic difficulties in the region, these governments are coming under increasing domestic political pressure not to concede to the Community. In addition, once the significance of the agreements becomes clear to the people of the region, they may be unwilling to relinquish their newly gained independence to the EC.

Second, four aspects of the agreements should be reconsidered.[48] The first relates to the debate over a membership clause. According to the initial mandate of the Community, the objective of the agreements is "to create a climate of confidence and stability favorable to political and economic reform and to establish political relations that reflect common values."[49] Hungary, Poland, and Czechoslovakia all argued that this confidence and stability would be substantially enhanced by an EC commitment to eventual membership.[50] But while the preamble to the agreement mentions future membership as a hypothetical possibility and acknowledges the desire of the three countries to join the Community, nowhere in the argeement does the Community make a firm commitment to accept these countries. According to Pablo Benavides, the commission's chief negotiator, "This is not an entrance ticket. It's a kind of trial run [to see] if they would like to become members."[51] This failure to resolve the membership issue in a constructive way suggests that some of the EC members do not fully appreciate the symbolic importance membership in the Community has for the transformation process itself. And while EC membership for the new democracies may be a long-term reality, it is certainly not a short-term threat. A guarantee of membership does not imply unconditional acceptance; the Community can establish a list of primarily economic targets that must be met prior to the granting of full membership status.

Both parties would benefit from such a policy approach, which would provide the Eastern countries with a clear perspective on their future status in Europe (and the requirements for attaining that status), and force the West Europeans to develop a more coherent long-term strategy for the future of the entire continent. At the same time, the Western countries would be reassured that integrating Central and Eastern Europe into the Community would not undermine its achievements.

The second element that the Community must reconsider in the association agreements is its approach to trade. The Community must open its markets to more of the exports that are essential to economic growth in Central and Eastern Europe. While the association agreements favor the transforming economies, they restrict access to EC markets for Central and East European exports except industrial goods, which have a limited competitive advantage. Most Central and East European countries have a comparative advantage in agricultural products, textiles, and coal and steel, but it will be some time before the markets for these products are opened. In agriculture, for example, the process of liberalization is based on reciprocity.[52] The disappointment over this "hidden" asymmetry was best summarized by Czechoslovak Minister of Economy Vladimír Dlouhý: "When we started our political changes and then the economic reforms, we had a lot of support from West European political circles. But now, when we are really coming to the terms of that support, only cool-blooded economic facts are put on the table."[53]

Community members, therefore, must reconsider their position on market access for Central and East European economies in those product categories where the Eastern enterprises can compete. Considering the share of EC imports from Central and Eastern Europe as part of total EC imports in these three product categories, the overall effect of liberalization on the EC is likely to be very small, for the shares range from 1.41 percent of agricultural products to 2.55 percent of coal and steel.[54] But measuring the same quantities as a percentage of total exports from the region to the EC shows how important further market liberalization is to those countries: these percentages range from 11.7 for coal and steel to 16.4 for agricultural products.[55]

The third element that has not been adequately addressed by the association agreements is financial support. The Community has pledged such support but has declined to include protocols in the general framework of the agreements that would commit it to specified amounts or set priorities for the various elements of the agreement.[56] The cooperative aspects of the agreements are of little political value to the three countries without a solid financing plan.

Finally, in their current form, the agreements place a disproportionate weight on the "four freedoms." Taken together, these freedoms amount essentially to the establishment of free market conditions within the Central and East European countries. This effort is supported by macrofinancial assistance in the form of a stabilization fund and loans by the G-24 and international financial institutions. With the exception of the privatization programs, less emphasis is placed on the microeconomic aspects of system transformation, such as industrial restructuring and labor market reform, and little attention is given to the legal and administrative and social and psychological dimensions. For example, between January 1990 and December 1991 over one-third (35.9 percent) of total G-24 cumulative commitments went toward macrofinancial assistance, with another 25.7 percent allocated to export credits and investment guarantees that must be repaid in full. These figures compare with 2.0 percent for social infrastructure and services and 7.9 percent for economic infrastructure and services, including such items as the environment and training.[57]

Macroeconomic stabilization is, of course, important during the process of system transformation. But a large discrepancy exists between the amounts of financial assistance provided to the micro- and macroeconomic levels of a market economy and to the economic dimension as opposed to the legal and administrative and social and psychological dimensions. As discussed earlier, in order for system transformation to succeed, including macroeconomic stabilization itself, this systemic imbalance must be corrected by redistributing more resources to the microeconomic level and legal and administrative and social and psychological dimensions of the emerging market economies. In the context of the association agreements, this reality implies that more resources should be spent on what the agreements call "economic and technical cooperation," which includes such specific issues as investment protection and industrial norms and standards as well as broader aspects such as modern transportation and distribution systems, telecommunications, the environment, and adequate health care and training.[58]

The Community should also greatly expand the "political dialogue" envisioned in the association agreements. First and foremost, expanded political dialogue would allow market participants in the West—legislators, regulators, administrative personnel, and interest associations among others— to share their expertise with officials in Central and Eastern Europe. Given that there is likely to be less resistance from current EC members to intensified political dialogue and cooperation, this element of the association agreements could become the primary mechanism for integrating all countries of Eastern Europe on an equal basis. Even under favorable circumstances, the Community is unlikely to radically open its markets to exports from Eastern Europe in the short term. It is also fair to assume that the vast financial, technical, and human resources required to support the process of system transformation will not be available in the short term. These two factors and the fact that the social-psychological dimension of system transformation requires money, time, and experience suggest that a strategy of association that relies disproportionately on the rapid establishment of a market economy as the principal stabilizing factor in Central and Eastern Europe today is, at the very least, questionable.

Political dialogue and cooperation would allow countries to be integrated on an equal basis as soon as they have met the initial conditions set out in the association agreements. Currently, differences in economic structure, degree of economic development, and previous experience with systemic reform—as distinct from system transformation—will allow some Central and East European countries to transform their economic systems faster than others over the next decade. If the EC structures its new relationship with Central and Eastern Europe primarily around economic issues, it will soon be forced to emphasize the differences among these countries rather than their similarities, raising questions about the integrative and stabilizing attributes of the economic dimension of association.

If the Community shifts its focus toward a greater emphasis on economic cooperation and intensifies the political dialogue, the EC should reconsider the idea of an affiliate membership proposed by EC Commissioner Frans Andriessen in the spring of 1991.[59] The principal advantage of an affiliate membership is that it would provide a more flexible strategy for the integration of new members and would thus be better able to deal with the increasing number and diversity of potential applicants. The degree to which economic and political integration can be separated from each other is limited, of course, but as an immediate response, such a separation may be the only way to produce some visible examples of the stabilizing effect of integration.

In the short term, the Community is aware that it cannot risk its own political and economic cohesion by fully absorbing Central and Eastern Europe into its institutional network and arrangements. Lack of financial resources, budgetary constraints, and the current economic slowdown in Western Europe make it difficult for the Community to take on a much larger role in Eastern Europe—especially in the economic realm—without risking a domestic backlash. The challenge for the Community is to find the right balance between what is necessary for the stability of Central and Eastern Europe and what is possible for the continued cohesion of Western Europe. Affiliate membership provides such a balance and is a satisfactory response to membership issues. In addition, it would require a financial protocol that allows all participants to develop a comprehensive strategy for European unification.

Widening and Deepening—I

In the medium term, the EC must strengthen its own economic and political capacity to respond to the challenge that system transformation in Central and Eastern Europe poses to the continent. Two interrelated systemic reform steps are necessary. First, the EC must strengthen itself politically and economically by accepting the EFTA countries as full members as soon as possible. However, this step will have its full effect only if the Community simultaneously reforms its own decisionmaking apparatus through continued deepening, especially in the legal and administrative and social and psychological dimensions.

While the Central and East European countries are not ready for full EC membership, the EFTA countries are. Indeed, including the EFTA countries as members would increase the economic and political capacity of the Community and enable it to better face the challenges emerging from the East. First, the EFTA and EC could closely coordinate their assistance to the region, pooling the available resources and avoiding the inefficiencies and waste that often occur during data gathering, fact-finding, and project evaluation there. Second, the EFTA members would raise the average per capita GNP of the Community from $13,547 to $16,370. Using the recent Italian proposal to allocate 0.25 percent of Community GDP to Central and Eastern Europe, annual resources available from the Community would increase from $11.9 billion to $13.7 billion if applied to each country on an equal basis.

Third, a Community enlarged by the EFTA countries would increase the market access granted to Central and Eastern Europe in the association agreements.[60] The applications for EC membership by Austria in June 1989,

Sweden in July 1991, Finland in March 1992, and Switzerland in May 1992 raise serious doubts about the long-term viability of the EFTA. If successfully concluded, the EEA agreement should be considered the first and decisive step toward the integration of the EFTA countries by 1995.[61] Such a timetable is realistic, for the EEA agreement resolves half the negotiating points that would arise between the EC and EFTA during membership negotiations.[62] In addition, the differences in the political and economic systems of the EC and EFTA are minimal compared with those between the EC and Central and East European countries and should allow for a smooth and rapid integration into the Community.

The second step of systemic reform that the EC must implement is the further deepening of the political and economic integration process. As with system transformation in Eastern Europe, this will only succeed if it follows a holistic approach. The most recent manifestation of this reform is the adoption of the Single European Act in February 1986, which provided a blueprint for the deep integration of the national economies of the member states. The prospect of continued deepening in the economic realm led to calls for similar reforms in both the legal and administrative and the social and psychological spheres of the emerging single market.[63]

The two IGCs on political and economic and monetary union, which began in December of 1990 and were completed a year later at the Maastricht summit, were aimed at moving the Community forward in these dimensions. The principal goal of the Conference on Monetary and Economic Union was to agree on an institutional and administrative structure as well as some macroeconomic policy principles that would govern the single market. In principle, such an agreement was reached at Maastricht. If the Council of Ministers determines that some or even all of the signatories can meet the economic conditions set out in the document, a monetary and economic union governed by an independent central bank could be created as early as January 1, 1997, but no later than January 1, 1999.[64]

If this decision is fully implemented, the implications will be profound. For the union to be operational and effective, member states will have to give up sole management of their national economies in return for a share in the collective management of the European economy. One of the principal reasons why members are likely to agree to this requirement is that, from an economic perspective, it represents a logical extension of the Single European Act. Politically, the decision can be rationalized by the fact that, in the area of monetary policy, most states have already lost their policymaking autonomy and sovereignty to Germany. Economic and monetary union would actually allow them to regain some of that autonomy by sharing sovereignty in the newly created European Central Bank.

But the implications of the Maastricht decision reach far beyond the issue of monetary policy. For the union to be credible and effective, states will also have to give up much of their individual capacity to influence the employment level in their economies. More specifically, macroeconomic intervention to reduce unemployment will have to be decided on at the European level and will require a "common European position" on the necessity, purpose, effectiveness, and timing of such intervention.[65] In addition, the escape clause in the Maastricht treaty negotiated by Britain has opened the possibility for all countries to renege on their commitment, even though Britain is the only country likely to make use of this option. This has given the agreement a provisional flavor.[66] Both examples indicate that the real challenge of implementing the agreement is much greater than is currently perceived and will penetrate deeply into the politics of both the individual member states and the emerging European market economy as a whole.

The holistic approach can illuminate the complex dynamics of European integration and point to some other policy steps necessary in order for the continued deepening of the Community to succeed. EC policymakers, member states, and domestic interest groups that advocated the initial integrative steps are likely to support additional reforms. This likelihood follows from the holistic argument presented earlier that unless systemic reform in one dimension is accompanied by similar adjustments in other dimensions, the initial reform measures will stall and possibly even be reversed with substantial economic and political costs not only to those that initiated systemic reform but to society as a whole.

By targeting those narrow areas where systemic reform can be initiated without major political resistance, policymakers can set in motion a much more far-reaching process than was initially envisioned. The European Commission and other forces supporting European integration have consistently made use of such a strategy, as the dynamics of European integration during the 1980s and early 1990s indicate. With the signing of the Single European Act, member states committed themselves to partial systemic reform by pledging to integrate their economies primarily at the microeconomic level, including the legal and administrative dimension. Only a few years later the advocates of closer European union won increased support for their proposed macroeconomic integration, and complete economic and monetary union, once considered improbable, began to seem an almost logical and even necessary extension of the EC 92 program to most member states.

Different countries had different interests in this process, of course. But the ensuing debate largely avoided the question of whether the single market should be governed by a common macroeconomic policy, focusing instead on the principles such a policy should follow and how they should be implemented. To some degree, the Maastricht agreement has resolved that debate, but, as indicated above, it did not address many obstacles to economic and monetary union. Moreover, new problems resulting from conflicting political, economic, and social interests are likely to emerge. In particular, the implications of European macroeconomic management for individual countries is likely to create political obstacles to economic deepening or to increase pressure for changing the conditions set at Maastricht. This concern has been expressed most strongly by the Bundesbank's Central Bank Council: "The Maastricht decisions do not yet reveal an agreement on the future structure of the envisaged political union and on the required parallelism with monetary union. Future developments in the field of the political union will be of key importance for the permanent success of the monetary union."[67] The treaty also had immediate political ramifications in the negotiation of the European Commission's new five-year budgetary plan.[68]

The social and psychological aspects of European integration will also become obstacles to deeper economic integration. The IGC on political union was aimed at securing some specific advances in systemic reform and initiating further steps toward political union, but it did not fully meet those goals. In the field of social policy, most members agreed to establish a European Social Charter that would ensure the member states that further integration would not lead to competition among different national social policy regimes, eroding long-established labor market principles and the rights of individual workers. But the refusal of Great Britain to join the agreement forced the other eleven member states to conclude a separate agreement in a unique procedure that raises questions about the future of a common European legal dimension.[69]

In the psychological dimension, the decision to establish a "citizenship of the union," which among other things confers the right on all citizens of EC member countries to vote and to stand as candidates at municipal elections in their countries of residence, is an important step toward generating higher awareness and a better understanding of European integration at all levels of society.[70] The idea of a European citizenship is based on the belated recognition that in the early 1990s, European economic integration has progressed to the point that the general public can no longer be excluded from the process of decisionmaking. While the fact that many Europeans were both unaware of and uninterested in European integration may have helped overcome earlier impediments to integration, excluding the public now would be detrimental to the Community.

European citizenship, however, must not only generate greater interest in Europe itself; it must also be accompanied by the right to translate those interests into policy decisions. To ensure popular representation at the all-European level, the Conference on Political Union also aimed at strengthening the legislative power of the European Parliament at the expense of the Council of Ministers, where most of the power is currently lodged. In this respect Maastricht failed, for the European Parliament continues to be excluded from all central decisionmaking and is relegated to the role of merely issuing position papers and calling for hearings.[71] The European Parliament gave its approval to the Maastricht agreement in order to ensure continued progress on the road to European integration,[72] but it also sharply criticized the failure to reduce the democratic deficit.[73] As a sign of its dissatisfaction, the Parliament presented a long list of necessary improvements and has indicated that it is unlikely to ratify any new international treaties—especially on the incorporation of new members—unless some of its concerns are addressed in a new IGC.[74]

Most government leaders hailed the Maastricht summit as a major success, and some went so far as to describe its outcome as an "irreversible process toward a European Union."[75] Implicitly, such a statement relies on the holistic approach to systemic reform, stressing the economic and political costs each country and the Community as a whole would incur if the process were to come to a halt or even be reversed. But European integration is not some inevitable fully determined process. Just as with system transformation in Central and Eastern Europe, systemic reform in the Community is unstable during the transition phase and vulnerable to political forces that try to undermine it. These forces, which have taken a clear anti-European position, have found their expression in the recent success of nationalist, mostly right-wing movements and political parties in EC member states. Their popularity will continue to rise unless all Europeans are given the right to participate in the decisions that shape political and social union. Europeans will reject deeper economic integration unless they believe that they can exchange their social contract at the national level for a European social contract without giving up the rights and responsibilities they have acquired.

To make such a judgment, however, the European public must also develop a better understanding of European integration. The outcome of the June 1992 Danish referendum confirms that efforts by policymakers to address the social and psychological dimension of European integration at the Maastricht summit were too few and came too late. The voters defied the 84 percent majority in the Danish Parliament, the major industrial associations, the unions that believed a "no" vote would mean more unemployment, and the powerful agricultural lobby that feared Denmark's exclusion from the Common Agricultural Policy (CAP). The Danish vote was at least as much a rejection of the political elite made out of personal anger, confusion, and insecurity as it was a decision against the goals of European integration. From a holistic viewpoint, then, the compromise of Maastricht failed because its architects disregarded the social and psychological dimension of systemic reform.

Even before the Danish referendum, the debate on the implications of Maastricht in other European countries indicated that this lack of attention to the social and psychological aspects of European unification was a problem throughout Europe. For example, the German public's sudden wariness of the agreement on economic and monetary union points to the fact that German popular support for closer European integration does not run very deep and can easily be shaken even though Germany is usually considered to be among its most ardent supporters.[76] The Germans are particularly concerned about the future of the deutsche mark, which has remained the symbol of German economic strength and political power despite the difficulties encountered during the process of German unification. In France, however, where President François Mitterrand has decided in the wake of the Danish vote to hold a referendum as well, the debate has centered largely around the implications of European citizenship for French sovereignty.[77]

Whatever the particular concern of each country, from the holistic perspective, the debate on the benefits and costs of European integration that has erupted in many member states is beneficial to the process of European integration.[78] Successfully resolved, this debate will eliminate many of the suspicions and insecurities among Europe's citizens and clarify the purpose, scope, and limits of European union. In addition, it will force all political parties to define their positions more clearly and require those political forces that oppose European integration to develop realistic alternatives for responding effectively to the challenges emanating from Central and Eastern Europe and the former Soviet Union and for addressing the process of global economic integration.

Broad social support will also be required to develop a common European foreign and security policy. Pressure for systemic reform in this area has increased over the last three years, and the issue was in fact pushed to the top of the agenda of the Conference on Political Union once it became clear that the United States would not assume a leadership role in the system transformation of Central and Eastern Europe. The Community's lack of institutional and technical mechanisms to deal with security crises largely explains its less-than-successful intervention in Yugoslavia. But while the EC's handling of the Yugoslav crisis can be considered a foreign policy failure, it does not mean there is no EC foreign policy at all, nor does it mean that EC foreign policy has failed to meet other challenges in Central and Eastern Europe and the former Soviet Union. For example, in response to the recent developments, member states have established common political criteria for countries seeking associate member status as well as for the recognition of former Soviet republics. The association agreements are also a clear indication of the willingness of member states (including Denmark) to cooperate in matters of foreign and security policy.

Nevertheless, the Yugoslav crisis illustrates that current institutional mechanisms for European foreign policy formation are inadequate to meet the more serious challenges posed by the system transformation taking place to the east. More specifically, the crisis displayed the weaknesses of a system that continues to reach decisions on the basis of unanimity among members. The same weakness was exposed by the negotiations over the association agreements, which were obscured by narrow national economic interests rather than guided by an overall strategy to unify the divided Europe. To some, the Maastricht summit also fell short of its original goal of establishing a framework for a common foreign and security policy. Policy issues related to the CSCE process, arms control and disarmament, nuclear nonproliferation, and the economic aspects of security—including controls on arms exports— will become subject to a procedure that may lead to decisions based on a qualified majority.[79] The new procedure has come under fire as being more likely to block common action than to encourage it, and member states can still exercise individual veto power.[80]

The commitment by the West European Union (WEU) to developing a common foreign and security policy with some limited provision for majority voting was largely responsible for the outcome of the Danish referendum.[81] The debate, which evolved around Denmark's independence on issues of foreign and security policies, was fueled by a parallel discussion over Danish membership in the WEU.[82] Denmark currently is not a member of the WEU and wants to preserve the Community's civilian image. But the decision of the nine Maastricht participants to develop the WEU into a European defense component strengthened Danish suspicions and ultimately its resistance to transferring more power to Brussels.

This question of how much policymaking authority should be transferred to Community institutions is one of the most politically sensitive issues in the debate over systemic reform, but so far it has been largely avoided by the member states. Policymakers tend to refer to the principle of subsidiarity as a solution to this problem. The Maastricht agreement has attached increased importance to the concept of subsidiarity by including it under the basic principles of the treaty. According to Article 3b of the Principles, "In areas which do not fall within its exclusive competence, the Community shall take action, in accordance with the principle of subsidiarity, only if and in so far as the objectives of the proposed action cannot be sufficiently achieved by the Member States and can therefore, by reason of the scale or effects of the proposed action, be better achieved by the Community."[83]

But while this principle sounds convincing in theory, it does not work in practice. As the Danish referendum shows, national constituencies may differ on the question of what problems should or should not be solved at the domestic level. Determining under what circumstances EC action should override the principle of subsidiarity is thus not a technical matter but a highly political question that often depends on domestic political circumstances and is sometimes influenced by historical legacies. In addition, what action the Community can initiate under the principle of subsidiarity is also open to interpretation, since such action "shall not go beyond what is necessary to achieve the objectives of this treaty."[84] These objectives, however, are so broadly defined that they do not provide any clear guidelines.[85]

The Danish referendum points to the urgent need for the EC to develop an operational definition of subsidiarity and specify a set of criteria that will trigger its application. In developing such criteria, governments must use the current debate to engage their constituents in a discussion that weighs the potential costs and benefits of further integration or disintegration. However, it is important that this discussion not only consider the economic aspects of European integration but also outline the legal and administrative and political implications of continued integration, in particular the required systemic reforms.

Broadly speaking, it is necessary to distinguish between two sets of systemic reforms, structural-institutional and functional-operational. In the area of structural-institutional reform, the policy outcomes of both IGCs showed that European integration has reached the stage where continued progress through intergovernmental negotiations can only be limited and will lead to vague results that are open to interpretation. In addition, even though a compromise had been reached, the nature of the ratification process, which requires unanimity, allowed 0.65 percent of the European Community's eligible voters—one-half of Danes who voted—to block the treaty.[86]

To serve the public good, any political decision-making authority must take policy steps opposed by some of its constituents. If member states continue to structure the Community's policymaking process around the principle of unanimity, they defy this basic political axiom and undermine the Community's ability to serve the European public good. This cannot be in the members' interest.

The principle of unanimity has consistently distorted the Community's policy agenda and weakened its European and global policy. First, if the European Commission knows in advance that a member will make use of its veto right, it will not put even very important issues on the agenda.[87] Second, those issues that do get on the agenda are subject to a lengthy bargaining process that can easily be biased by the unanimity requirement. Unresolved aspects of a policy measure may be omitted, altering the original mandate and postponing full implementation. Individual countries may not want to join an agreement or may ask to opt out at a later date, as the United Kingdom did at the Maastricht summit. Third, obstacles to unanimous agreement may simply be negotiated away so that all member countries can agree.

If the Community is to develop into an effective decisionmaking body that promotes common European interests at home and abroad, it must make two changes in its decisionmaking process. First, member states must relinquish their veto power in most policy areas, and qualified majority voting must become the principal decisionmaking mechanism in the Council of Ministers.[88] Second, the Council of Ministers should delegate some of its executive power to the European Commission in order to strengthen that body's authority not only to implement existing policy but to make and implement new policy decisions. The following division of labor could exist between the council and the commission: having made a decision on the general terms of a policy, the council could refer the matter to the commission, which would work out the technical details and subsequently implement the policy. Transferring a substantial amount of power from the council to the commission, however, would increase the Community's democratic deficit and further reduce the meaning of European citizenship. Thus the shift in the balance of power toward the commission must be matched by a substantial strengthening of parliamentary control. The European Parliament must have the full legislative powers which so far have been monopolized by the Council of Ministers. In addition, to ensure greater accountability of the commission to the European electorate, the Parliament must have direct influence over the appointment of the president as well as the commissioners.

To enable the Community to meet the challenge both at home and in Central and Eastern Europe, its functional-operational capacity must also be enhanced in two ways. First, in those policy areas over which the Community currently has partial authority, jurisdiction should be absolute and additional policy areas should come under EC jurisdiction. Unless this transfer of autonomy takes place, institutional reform is of little real significance. Second, the Community can only become fully operational in these policy areas if it has control over the financial resources that national budgets have allocated for their implementation. This requires a transfer of budgetary and taxing authority in these policy domains from the national to the European level.

Widening and Deepening—II

In the long term, however, further consideration of systemic reform is required. Until the fall of 1989, two objectives dominated the EC policymaking agenda: continued deepening among members and the possible inclusion of some EFTA countries. While the EC should continue to pursue these objectives, it must realize they are no longer ends in themselves, but a means of stabilizing system transformation in Central and Eastern Europe in the short run and, in the long run, of facilitating a new policy goal: the unification of Europe, with the EC at its core.

If the EFTA countries do join the EC by the second half of this decade, followed by Central and Eastern Europe, membership will rise from the current twelve to twenty and possibly thirty countries. If the Community wants to meet the challenge of increased membership and remain the political and economic nucleus of the new Europe, avoiding "the risk of being geographically marginalized and becoming somewhat like an enlarged Bene-lux," it must undergo even greater systemic reforms.[89]

The internal debate on how to cope with the Community's eventual enlargement has only just begun and will require a new IGC to be concluded by the end of 1995 when some or all EFTA countries may join the Community and Central and East European countries will begin submitting their applica-tions. The purpose of this conference would be to agree on a European architecture to accommodate the realities of the new Europe. Although in many ways this IGC would continue the work of the last two, by focusing on further deepening the Community, it would concentrate not on West European but on European unification—in particular, the incremental integra-tion of Central and Eastern Europe.

While most EC member countries are open to discussing a new European architecture, not all of them are likely to subscribe to the strategy outlined above. As has been mentioned, Britain, which currently holds the EC presidency, and Denmark, which may take on the presidency in January of 1993, both support widening the Community in part because they hope that it will undermine other countries' efforts to deepen the EC. As the debate that erupted in the wake of the Danish referendum has shown, both countries consider further deepening an unacceptable threat to their nation's sovereignty. They are thus unlikely to sponsor a conference to achieve both goals.[90]

But the argument that further deepening compromises a country's sover-eignty is not well founded and in fact defies one of the EC's most basic principles: sovereignty is not indivisible.[91] Even if the Community receives complete jurisdiction in some policy areas, taking on some of the function of federalism, members will retain their autonomy in other areas. The increasingly popular concept of a "Europe of regions" has gained quasi-institutional standing since the formation of the Committee of the Regions at the Maastricht summit, suggesting that in some cases sovereignty may actually be devolved to lower levels of social organization than the nation-state in a more deeply integrated Europe.[92] In this context it is interesting to note that the British government strongly opposes any move toward the further independence of Scotland within the European Community.[93] This raises the question of whether the British government's campaign against Brussels is based on a genuine belief in the decentralization of political decisionmaking or whether this belief stops at the level of the nation-state and thus serves to solidify and protect the British government's own power. In addition, the divisibility of sovereignty is the analytic foundation of the concept of subsidiarity, which relies on the presence of multiple layers of autonomy, making the institutional role of the Community of the Regions an urgent policy matter.

Finally, Webster's dictionary defines sovereignty as "freedom from external control," a definition that does not give the nation-state a monopoly on the

concept. On the contrary, the increasing interdependence of national economies has left the nation-state increasingly incapable of providing such
freedom. From this perspective, European integration in some policy areas
could allow countries to regain some of the freedom they have lost. EC
member states would, for instance, regain some control over the conduct of
monetary policy, which Germany has dominated for the last decade. In
addition, EC members would be able to collectively preserve some of their
decisionmaking power in the international arena, where no single European
country—not even a unified Germany—could compete with the United States
or Japan. By pooling their sovereignty, EC members therefore will be able
to collectively preserve some of the sovereignty that individually they have
lost. It is this projection of external strength that will allow for greater
diversity within the Community.

How many countries will continue to subscribe to the notion that
sovereignty is divisible and press ahead with deeper integration is an open
question. One response to the possibility that some countries will favor a
greater degree of integration than others in a specific policy domain has
gained renewed momentum since the Danish referendum. This is the concept
of "Europe à la carte." Europe à la carte would allow countries to choose
from a menu that offers differentiated degrees of integration within various
policy areas. Clearly this is an attractive option, as it resolves one of the
most divisive issues in the EC. This paper in fact has employed the concept
of Europe à la carte twice: first, when it advocated the notion of affiliate
membership for Central and East European countries; and second, when it
suggested that not all current EC members may be able to join the EMU by
January 1, 1999. In both cases, however, the "menu" choices were considered
a transitional stage. In the case of the Central and East European countries
the affiliate members will eventually join the EC; in the case of economic
and monetary union allocating an additional Ecu 10.7 billion to the structural
and cohesion funds would make little sense if it were not for the purpose of
facilitating economic and monetary union among all members.[94] As long as
the concept of L'Europe à la carte is understood as a menu of transitional
options, it may well be an ingenious response to the multiple challenges that
Europe faces—in particular to the dual pressure of widening and deepening.

To consider it as a lasting structure, however, would contradict a holistic
approach to European integration, as it permanently divorces economic from
legal and administrative and social and psychological integration. This has
been understood by the EFTA countries, which have realized that their status
is not only untenable in the long run but may even be disadvantageous. They
have responded by agreeing to form the EEA and are pressing ahead with
their drive toward full membership. Ironically, just as these countries are

applying for membership, one option that was suggested for Denmark in response to the referendum was to return to an EEA status.

Conclusion

Clearly no blueprint has been drawn up for the new European political economy. One reason why the European Community has been so successful is because it has not developed a fixed master plan geared toward a single goal. Given the cultural, ethnic, and linguistic diversity of the European continent and the powerful political and economic interests that would feel threatened by some grand European design, a scheme that finalizes any future structure of the Community is doomed to failure. At the same time, however, the challenges brought forth by the end of the Cold War require at the very least a structured and well-balanced response.

This chapter has outlined some of the policy parameters that should guide a European response to these challenges. First, it is important to recognize that both Eastern and Western Europe will have to adjust if Europe is to become a politically and economically integrated entity with the Community at its core. This paper has examined the nature and extent of these changes using a holistic concept of a market economy, an approach that has important policy implications. It conditions policy choices along the lines of economic, political, and social rationality and exposes the risks of developing strategies of system transformation strictly on the basis of economics. The holistic approach also reveals the complexity of creating a market economy in Central and Eastern Europe and of reforming the European market economy. And finally, it reveals that systemic reform in Western Europe faces many obstacles and requires some institutional realignment within the European Community that may be difficult to achieve without the strong support of the member states.

The societies of Central and Eastern Europe face a historic challenge. At present, the benefits of system transformation continue to outweigh its costs, but the margin has narrowed considerably since the spring of 1991. A breakdown of system transformation is unlikely to return the region to its earlier status quo but would most likely destabilize it, precipitating crises that threaten the stability of the entire continent and the cohesion of the European Community.[95] As a result, the EC has been propelled into a powerful but precarious position. To avoid regressing to the traditional balance of power, the EC will have to form the core of the new European political economy. As such, the Community, particularly individual member states, bears considerable responsibility for the success or failure of establishing democracy and a market economy in Central and Eastern Europe. Judging from the response to date, the Community and its members have yet to publicly acknowledge the magnitude of the challenge and the potential implications of a failure of system transformation for both East and West.

Notes

1. Unification refers to transforming two systems, divided during the Cold War, into a common political, economic, and security system, but not necessarily into a single state.

2. Eastern Europe refers to Albania, Bulgaria, Czechoslovakia, Hungary, Poland, Romania, Yugoslavia and its successor states, and possibly the three Baltic republics. It does not refer to the successor states of the former Soviet Union.

3. For more on the historical background, see Wolfgang H. Reinicke, *The New Europe: The Challenge of System Transformation and Systemic Reform*, Occasional Paper (Brookings, forthcoming).

4. See, for example, Marc Granovetter, "Economic Action and Social Structure: The Problem of Embeddedness," *American Journal of Sociology*, vol. 91 (November 1985), pp. 481–510; and Fred Block and Margaret Somers, "Beyond the Economistic Fallacy: The Holistic Social Science of Karl Polanyi," in Theda Skocpol, ed., *Vision and Method in Historical Sociology* (Cambridge University Press, 1984). See also Albert O. Hirschman, "Against Parsimony, Three Easy Ways of Complicating Some Categories of Economic Discourse," *Economics and Philosophy*, vol. 1 (April 1985), pp. 7–21, and "Rival Interpretations of Market Society: Civilizing, Destructive, or Feeble?" *Journal of Economic Literature*, vol. 20 (December 1982), pp. 1463–84; and N. Kaldor, "The Irrelevance of Equilibrium Economics," *Economic Journal*, vol. 82 (December 1972), pp. 1237–55.

5. See James S. Coleman, "Introducing Social Structure into Economic Analysis," *American Economic Review*, vol. 74 (May 1984), pp. 84–88.

6. For more on holism as a scientific method, see Paul Diesing, *Patterns of Discovery in the Social Sciences* (Chicago: Aldine-Atherton, 1971); and George Dalton and Jasper Kocke, "The Work of the Polanyi Group: Past, Present and Future," in S. Ortiz, ed., *Economic Anthropology* (University Press of America, 1983). The concept of holism was coined by General the Right Hon. J.C. Smuts in a book entitled *Holism and Evolution* (Greenwood Press, 1973). Later, scholars working primarily in economics adopted the notion of holism for their work. According to Allan G. Gruchy, "The term 'holistic' has been selected because it called attention to what is most characteristic in the new economics: Its interest in studying the economic system as an evolving, unified whole or synthesis, in the light of which the system's parts take on their full meaning." Allan Gruchy, *Modern Economic Thought: The American Contribution* (Prentice-Hall, 1947), as cited in Philip A. Klein, "A Reconsideration of Holistic Economics," in John Adams, ed., *Institutional Economics, Contributions to the Development of Holistic Economics* (The Hague: Martinus Nijhoff Publishing, 1980), pp. 45–58.

7. Karl Polanyi, *The Great Transformation: The Political and Economic Origins of Our Time* (Beacon Press, 1944); Fernand Braudel, *Civilization and Capitalism, 15th–18th Century*, 3 vols. (Harper and Row, 1981–1984); for an analysis of how social norms were changing with the introduction of capitalism and the market economy and how it affected the political debate, see Albert O. Hirschman, *The*

Passions and the Interests: Political Arguments for Capitalism before Its Triumph (Princeton University Press, 1977).

8. This rather brief description is not to imply that market economies cannot differ widely among themselves. To the contrary with the end of the overarching East-West ideological conflict, more substantive differences in the institutional structure and the standards and norms among Western industrial democracies are now coming to the fore.

9. A similar but opposite change is required for the transformation of the polity where close *horizontal* relationships among the bureaucratic and political elites existed, which enabled them to exercise the vertical control over the economy. They must be replaced by *vertical* organizational forms in order to transmit and aggregate the interests of all factions of society.

10. The opening of the societies in Eastern Europe has led in some cases to the emergence of many groups and organizations. These groups could become vehicles for the transmission of ideas and interests to government, as well as the basis for society's self-organization. Both outcomes are essential aspects of a market economy. However, such groups have not yet become an organic entity. To the contrary these organizations contribute to the ongoing social disintegration occurring in the region. Moreover, they only constitute a narrow segment of the society. Many people, previously forced to participate in social life, now refuse to engage in it. Lena Kolarska-Bobińska, "Civil Society and Social Anomy in Poland," *Acta Sociologica*, vol. 33 (1990), pp. 277–88.

11. Tadeusz Mazowiecki, "Polens schwieriger Weg in die Normalität," *Frankfurter Allgemeine Zeitung*, August 24, 1991.

12. George Dalton, ed., *Primitive, Archaic, and Modern Economies: Essays of Karl Polanyi* (Beacon Press, 1968).

13. In most East European countries new educational structures have not yet been implemented. In Poland a new law is currently being discussed. Hungary began educational reform in 1985, advocating decentralization and autonomy for the system, but the reform was not very effective. A new law is being planned for 1992. See Gerhard Huck, "Neudefinition der Bildungsinhalte," *Das Parlament*, August 16 and August 23, 1991. However, besides implementing new structures and laws that may replicate Western systems, staff has to be trained in curriculum development and the management of educational systems, including both schools and universities, so that each country can develop its own system based on its history and tradition.

14. Charles E. Lindblom, *The Intelligence of Democracy: Decision Making through Mutual Adjustment* (Free Press, 1965).

15. In fact the high levels of state ownership and control in France, Italy, and several other West European countries suggest that large-scale privatization is not even a necessary condition for the establishment of an effective market economy.

16. See, for example, Institute of International Finance, *Financial Sector Reform in Central and Eastern Europe* (Washington, January 1991).

17. For the role of the financial system in economic development see Rondo E. Cameron, ed., *Banking in the Early Stages of Industrialization: A Study in Comparative Economic History* (Oxford University Press, 1967) and *Banking and Economic Development: Some Lessons of History* (Oxford University Press, 1972); and Charles P. Kindleberger, *A Financial History of Western Europe* (George Allen and Unwin, 1984). For the role of financial markets in the post-World War II economies, see Jacques Polak, *Financial Policies and Development* (Paris: Organization for Economic Cooperation and Development, 1989); *Financial Systems and Development*, Policy and Research Series, no. 15 (Washington: World Bank, October 1990).

18. E. Gerald Corrigan, "The Role of Central Banks and the Financial System in Emerging Market Economies," *Federal Reserve Bank of New York Quarterly Review* (Summer 1990), pp. 1–7; Lawrence J. Brainard, "Reform in Eastern Europe: Creating a Capital Market," *Federal Reserve Bank of Kansas City Economic Review* (January–February 1991), pp. 49–58; Thomas H. Hanley and others, *Banking in Eastern Europe: A New Market Opens Up* (New York: Salomon Brothers, 1991); Alan H. Gelb and Cheryl W. Gray, *The Transformation of Economies in Central and Eastern Europe: Issues, Progress, and Prospects*, Policy and Research Series, no. 17 (Washington: World Bank, 1991); "Gelingen der Reformen im Osten setzt leistungs-fähiges Bankensystem voraus," *Handelsblatt*, September 30, 1991.

19. See Reinicke, *The New Europe*.

20. Adam Michnik, "The Two Faces of Europe," *New York Review of Books*, July 19, 1990, p. 7.

21. United Nations, Economic Commission for Europe, *Economic Survey of Europe in 1989–1990* (New York: United Nations, 1990); and United Nations, *World Economic Survey 1991* (New York: United Nations, 1991).

22. Commission of the European Communities, *Central and Eastern Eurobaro-meter: Public Opinion about the European Community*, Ten Countries Survey-Autumn 1991, no. 2 (Brussels: January 1992), annex figure 2.

23. Commission of the European Communities, *Central and Eastern Eurobaro-meter*, annex figure 3.

24. Commission of the European Communities, *Central and Eastern Eurobaro-meter*, annex figure 8.

25. "Corruption Still a Problem in Poland," *RFE/RL Daily Report*, no. 150 (August 8, 1991), p. 3.

26. From January to June 1990 the main statistical office reported 91 strikes in Polish factories. This number rose to 159 during the second part of 1990. During the first six months of 1991, 271 strikes were registered, see "GUS Releases Data on Production, Deficits, Pay," Warsaw PAP, July 23, 1991, in Foreign Broadcast Information Service, *Daily Report: East Europe,* July 24, 1991, p. 18. (Hereafter FBIS, *EEU*.)

27. "Poles Losing Interest in Elections," Warsaw PAP, July 22, 1991, in FBIS, *EEU,* July 23, 1991, pp. 22–23. A close aide of Walesa commented on this trend as follows: "People feel more and more threatened by the future . . . support for the reforms is falling continuously. Eventually this might reach a critical point and turn into a general strike or such a level of apathy that people will stop taking part in public life." See "Walesa Adviser Najder on Threat to Reform," Warsaw ZYCIE WARSZAWY, July 26, 1991, in FBIS, *EEU,* August 2, 1991, pp. 27–29.

28. "Somber Mood Grips Hungary," *Journal of Commerce*, January 15, 1991, p. 10a; "The Dilemmas of Freedom," *Financial Times*, December 27, 1990, p. 10.

29. Peter Falush, "Hungary's Reform in Low Gear," *World Today*, vol. 47 (April 1991), pp. 57–59. In a recent by-election less than 17 percent of the voters cast ballots, "Hungarian By-Election Marked by Apathy," *RFE/RL Daily Report*, no. 152 (August 12, 1991), p. 2.

30. On the Czech case, see "Heavy Going Slows the Pace of Race to Reform Czechoslovakia's Economy," *Financial Times*, March 26, 1991, p. 2. On Bulgaria and Romania, see "KNSB Demands Higher Minimum Subsistence Level," Sofia Khorizont Radio Network, August 1, 1991, in FBIS, *EEU*, August 2, 1991, p. 13; "Trade Union Views on Privatization Bill Reported," Bucharest REALITATEA, July 23, 1991, in FBIS, *EEU*, July 26, 1991, pp. 25–26.

31. Gianni De Michelis, "Reaching Out to the East," *Foreign Policy*, no.79

(Summer 1990), pp. 44–55, quotation on p. 44; see also "In Stufen auch zur Politischen Union," Deutsche Bundesbank, *Auszüge aus Presseartikeln*, no. 43 (June 11, 1991), pp. 7–8.

32. As quoted in *Liberation*, September 6, 1991, pp. 21–23.

33. So far the outcome of Germany's efforts has been mixed. The disagreements among EC members over the timing and conditions attached to recognizing the Yugoslav republics as independent states and the nature of the compromise reached by the European Community are clear manifestations of this influence. On other occasions, however, Germany has been more careful in applying its increased political weight—as, for example, at the Maastricht summit where German negotiators accepted an agreement that fell far short of their original goals, especially on political union.

34. See, for example, Luis Planas Puchades, *Report on Community Enlargement and Relations with other European Countries*, A3–0077/91 (Luxembourg: European Parliament, March 1991).

35. This position was confirmed by Francois Mitterand's surprise meeting with Mikhail Gorbachev in Kiev and the French position during the initial rounds of the 2 + 4 negotiations. During the meeting in Kiev he warned West Germany not to push for unification with East Germany as it would upset the delicate balance in Europe and the process of European integration, see "Mitterand, in Kiev, Warns Bonn Not to Press Reunification Issue," *New York Times*, December 7, 1989, p. A21. The first shift in the French position at least on Germany was indicated when Mitterand and German President Richard von Weizäcker traveled together through East Germany in September of 1991 even before political unification had occurred.

36. See Reinicke, *The New Europe*.

37. As quoted in "Aid to Eastern Europe, USSR Raise Concern," Lisbon RDP Commercial Radio Network, December 11, 1991, in FBIS, *West Europe (WEU)*, December 17, 1991, p. 34 (Hereafter, FBIS, *WEU*); see also "Portugal Seeks Greater Unity within the EC," *Financial Times*, October 10, 1991, p. 1.

38. See for example "Mittelmeeraum befrieden," *Europa Forum*, May 1991.

39. This does not include assistance from international financial institutions such as the IMF and EBRD. Commission of the European Communities, *Scoreboard of G-24 Assistance: Summary ECU Tables and Graphics* (Brussels, April 1992).

40. The data for GDP are from Commission of the European Communities, *Annual Economic Report 1991–92*, *European Economy*, no. 50 (Luxembourg, December 1991), statistical annex, table 5, p. 218.

41. The German government was particularly grateful to Hungary. At a meeting on August 25, 1989, Hungary's premier Miklós Németh revealed to Chancellor Kohl that the country had made a decision to reopen its border with Austria. According to an account of the meeting, the leaders then discussed aid for Hungary and associate membership in the EC. A similar exchange took place between Czech and German officials after the Czech embassy was filled with East Germans. See Jim Hoagland, "Europe's Destiny," *Foreign Affairs*, vol. 69 (America and the World 1989/90), pp. 33–50. As to Poland, the Polish-German treaty explicitly mentions German support for Poland's membership in the EC; see also Géza Jeszenszky, "Eckpfeiler ungarischer Europapolitik: EG-Mitgliedschaft und gesamteuropäische Zusammenarbeit," in Gerhard Eickhorn, ed., *Ungarn und Deutschland im künftigen Europa* (Bonn: Europa Union Verlag, 1991), pp. 30–34; and "Bonn soll Warschau die Wege ebnen," *Handelsblatt*, June 17, 1991.

42. For the British position, see, for example, "EC 'Should Expand Trade with E Europe'" *Financial Times*, July 5, 1991, p. 16. According to Danish Foreign

Minister Uffe Ellemann-Jensen, "We [Denmark] want to enlarge it [the EC] with new member states: the EFTA (European Free Trade Association) countries and countries in central and eastern Europe," as quoted in "New World Order Requires Wider and Deeper EC," *Financial Times*, April 25, 1991, p. 2.

43. "Major Urges EC to Admit East European States," *Financial Times*, September 13, 1991, p. 1; and "Major: EG nach Osten öffnen," *Süddeutsche Zeitung*, September 13, 1991.

44. Commission Des Communautes Europeennes, Communication de la Commission au conseil et au Parlement, *Accords d'association avec les pays d'Europe centrale et orientale: cadre général*, COM(90) 398 final (Bruxelles, August 1990). For the European Parliament's position see Christa Randzio-Plath, *Report of the Committee on External Economic Relations on a General Outline for Association Agreements with the Countries of Central and Eastern Europe*, European Parliament, Session Documents A3–0055/91 (Luxembourg, March 1991).

45. "EC Signs Treaties with Poland, Hungary, CSFR," Warsaw PAP, December 16, 1991, in FBIS, *EEU*, December 27, 1991, p. 1.

46. "Delors: Slow East European Integration into EC," Paris AFP, September 6, 1991, in FBIS, *WEU*, September 6, 1991, p. 3.

47. For more see Reinicke, *The New Europe*.

48. For an expanded discussion of these aspects see Reinicke, *The New Europe*.

49. Commission Des Communautes Europeennes, Communication de la Commission au conseil et au Parlement, *Accords d'association avec les pays d'Europe centrale et orientale: cadre général*, COM(90) 398 final (Brussels, August 27, 1990), quotation on p. 2.

50. "Europe's Reluctant Empire-Builders," *Financial Times*, December 2, 1991, p. 15.

51. As quoted in "EC Paves Way for Free Trade with E Europe," *Financial Times*, November 23/24, 1991, p. 2.

52. "Czech Prime Minister Views EC Association Plan," Prague Federal Television Network, December 13, 1991, in FBIS, *EEU*, December 16, 1991, pp. 10–11.

53. "Europe's Reluctant Empire-Builders," *Financial Times*, December 2, 1991, p. 2. But even if the community reduces its current quantitative restrictions in these sectors, considerable problems are likely to remain. If EC standard antidumping and safeguard clauses continue to apply, exports from Eastern Europe will be subject to penalties. The use of undervalued exchange rates to increase the competitiveness of their exports in world markets will trigger antidumping actions by the Community. According to a representative of the German steel industry, it would be better for the countries of Eastern Europe to maintain the old trade and cooperation agreements, as "the alternative would be antidumping suits, 'because in our perspective everything which comes from there is either being dumped or subsidized,'" see "Die versprochene Öffnung der Märkte stösst oft an Quoten und Kontingente," *Handelsblatt*, July 29, 1991.

54. For more information see Reinicke, *The New Europe*, appendix table 14.

55. See Reinicke, *The New Europe*, appendix table 14.

56. "Poland, Hungary, and Czechoslovakia Initial EC Agreements," *RFE/RL Daily Report*, no. 223 (November 25, 1991), p. 6.

57. Commission of the European Communities, *Scoreboard of G-24 Assistance: Summary of ECU Tables and Graphics* (Brussels, April 1992).

58. Commission Des Communautes Europeennes, Communication de la Commission au conseil et au Parlement, *Accords d'association avec les pays d'Europe centrale*

et orientale: cadre général, COM(90) 398 final (Brussels, August 1990), annex pp. 1–5.

59. For more see Reinicke, *The New Europe*.

60. EFTA is already negotiating trade agreements with Poland, Hungary, and Czechoslovakia that closely resemble the trade components of the association agreements.

61. For more on the EEA agreement see Reinicke, *The New Europe*.

62. "Westeuropäer bilden Freihandelszone vom Nordkap bis zum Mittelmeer," *Süddeutsche Zeitung*, October 23, 1991.

63. Proposals to reform the Community go further back than the signing of the Single European Act. However, their success was limited, and it was not possible to get any sweeping reform. For an overview, see Werner Weidenfeld, ed., *Nur verpasste Chancen? Die Reformberichte der Europäischen Gemeinschaft*, Mainzer Beiträge zur Europäischen Einigung, Band 2 (Bonn: Europa Union Verlag, 1983); see also the discussion in Roy Price, ed., *The Dynamics of European Union* (Croom Helm, 1987).

64. The exact time for the creation of the monetary union is determined by the Council of Ministers based on a qualified majority decision. If that majority cannot agree on a date by the end of 1997, the starting date is fixed for January 1999, see *Treaty on European Union* (Luxembourg: Office for Official Publications of the European Communities, 1992), Article 109j, pp. 40–42, and "Protocol," p. 190. For a discussion of the conditions, see Reinicke, *The New Europe*.

65. Taking the incongruent political business cycles in EC member states into account, the harmonization of a position on macroeconomic interventions seems particularly difficult to achieve.

66. The acceptance of the escape clause may also have set a precedent for other countries on other issues, perhaps severely undermining the cohesion and credibility of the EC policymaking and its decisions.

67. "The Maastricht Decisions on the European Economic and Monetary union," *Monthly Report of the Deutsche Bundesbank*, vol. 44 (February 1992), pp. 43–52, quotation on p. 51; see also "Kohl Faces Tough Line on EMU from Bundesbank," *Financial Times*, January 29, 1992, p. 1; and "Family Quarrel at the Bundesbank," *Financial Times*, January 29, 1992, p. 12.

68. For more on the five-year budget plan, see Reinicke, *The New Europe*.

69. Article 117 of the Treaty of Rome was supplemented by an agreement that was signed by eleven of the twelve member states, see *Treaty on European Union* (Luxembourg: Office for Official Publications of the European Communities, 1992), pp. 197–201. However, the eleven members will be able to use the institutions of the Community to formulate and implement policy. In other words, the European Commission will develop directives that will be agreed on with a majority of forty-four (instead of usual fifty-four) votes.

70. Citizenship of the union will come into effect on or before December 31, 1994. The same principle will be applied for elections to the European Parliament, see *Treaty on European Union* (Luxembourg: Office for Official Publications of the European Communities, 1992), Article 8a-e, pp. 15–16.

71. The only real change occurred in the European Parliament's ability to partake in the election of the European Commission president and its members.

72. A vote that would have called for a new summit to renegotiate the treaty failed by one vote. "Das EG-Parlament billigt Maastrichter Vertragsreformen," *Frankfurter Allgemeine Zeitung*, April 8, 1992; and "Ein klares Ja zu Maastricht," *Das Parlament*, April 10, 1992.

73. European Parliament, *Report of the Committee on Institutional Affairs on the Results of the Intergovernmental Conferences*, A3–0123/92/Part I–III (Luxembourg, March 1992). In fact, given that some decisions in the Council of Ministers are now made on a majority basis, which reduces the control of individual national parliaments even further, one could argue that the democratic deficit has increased.

74. For a summary of the list, see "Ja zu Maastricht," *Europa Forum*, April 6–10, 1992. See also "Europaparlament fordert Verbesserungen," *Das Parlament*, December 20/27, 1991.

75. See "Leaders Address Bundestag on Maastricht Summit," Hamburg ARD Television Network, December 13, 1991, in FBIS, *WEU*, December 13, 1991, pp. 6–11, and "Mitterand Discusses Maastricht, USSR, Issues," Paris TF-1 Television Network, December 15, 1991, in FBIS, *WEU*, December 16, 1991, pp. 15–22.

76. "Ein Wechsel auf Europas Zukunft," *Die Zeit*, December 13, 1991; "Beschränkt belastbar," *Der Spiegel*, February 10, 1992, pp. 20–22; "Opposition to Maastricht Accords Stiffens," Dusseldorf *Wirtschaftswoche*, February 14, 1992, in FBIS, *WEU*, February 26, 1992, pp. 6–7. In this context it is interesting to note that the final decision to replace the deutsche mark with the European currency unit is due in late 1997 shortly before the next general election in Germany. The strong performance of the deutsche mark in the aftermath of the Danish referendum confirmed that point.

77. "Further on Mitterand's Comments on Maastricht," *Le Monde* January 12–13, 1992, in FBIS *WEU*, January 14, 1992, p. 23; "French Prepare for Debate on Maastricht," *Financial Times*, April 23, 1992, p. 3; "Verfassungskorrektur für 'Maastricht' in Paris," *Neue Zürcher Zeitung*, April 24, 1992; "Divisions Ease Path in France for EC Treaty," *Financial Times*, May 13, 1992, p. 3. On Mitterand's decision to hold a referendum, see "Mitterand Raises the Stakes," *Financial Times*, June 4, 1992, p. 4.

78. Although he has been the target of most criticism, Jacques Delors, the president of the European Commission, has publicly emphasized the need to engage the public in the debate over European Union. But with the exception of Great Britain, politicians have avoided the issue for the most part. On Delors, see "Final Uphill Push for the Treaty," *Financial Times*, April 23, 1992, p. 16.

79. For the procedure, see *Treaty on European Union* (Luxembourg: Office for Official Publications of the European Communities, 1992), Title V, Article J.3.

80. Günther Nonnenmacher, "Nach Maastricht wird es ernst," *Frankfurter Allgemeine*, December 12, 1991. The decisionmaking procedure has also been criticized by the commission's president. According to Delors, "We will need to get back to the drawing board and devise simple, effective evaluation and decisionmaking procedures." See "1992: a Pivotal Year," Address by Jacques Delors, president of the European Commission, to the European Parliament, *Bulletin of the European Communities*, Supplement 1/92 (Luxembourg, 1992), quotation on p. 9.

81. Britain, Ireland, and Portugal also resisted this move.

82. "Danish Referendum Frays Brussels Nerves," *Financial Times*, March 31, 1992, p. 2; "Lone Dane in Maastricht Campaign," *Financial Times*, May 18, 1992, p. 3; and "WEU Row Fuels Danish Debate on EC Treaties," *Financial Times*, February 21, 1992, p. 3.

83. *Treaty on European Union* (Luxembourg: Office for Official Publications of the European Communities, 1992), quotation on pp. 13–14.

84. *Treaty on European Union*, p. 14.

85. The conflict that erupted over the inclusion of the word "federal" in the preamble of the treaty and its subsequent rephrasing to "resolved to continue the

process of creating an ever closer union among the peoples of Europe, in which decisions are taken as closely as possible to the citizens in accordance with the principle of subsidiarity" is a case in point.

86. See Reinicke, *The New Europe*, appendix table 16.

87. The European Commission even has the right to withdraw a proposal during a Council of Ministers meeting if it becomes clear that it will fail the unanimity test. The most recent such withdrawal took place when Andriessen proposed the affiliate membership option.

88. According to Article 100 of the Treaty of Rome, the council shall act unanimously on a proposal from the commission. This article was amended with the implementation of the Single European Act in 1986. With a few, though important, exceptions the countries agreed to adopt the measures designed to approximate the legal, regulatory, and administrative aspects of the single market by a qualified majority vote. Decisions that would be exempted from qualified majority voting, for example, would be new memberships or matters related to national or European military security.

89. Karlheinz Neunreither, "The Constitutional Debate in the European Community: Towards which Europe? How to Govern it?" Paper presented at the *Conference on the New European Architecture*, International Political Science Association, Research Committee on European Unification.

90. It is not sure, however, whether Denmark will be able to take on the presidency in January 1993 pending its future status in the Community. Belgium, which would follow Denmark in July 1993, may thus take over as early as January 1993.

91. The divisibility of sovereignty is one of the initial principles on which the Community is built. See Europe Federalists' Union, *European Federation Now* (Paris: Union européenne des fédéralists; distributed by the American Committee on United Europe, New York, 1951).

92. The Committee of the Regions is composed of 189 members representing the "regional and local bodies" in Europe and has an advisory status, being consulted by the council and the commission, see *Treaty on European Union*, Article 4, section 2, p. 14, and Article 198 a-c. In the long run, such a committee could well develop into a second legislative chamber representing the subnational interests.

93. "Hurd Attacks Opposition Proposals for Scotland," *Financial Times*, February 29/March 1, 1992, p. 1.

94. The proposal was made in the Delors II proposal for the years 1992–97. See Commission of the European Communities, *From the Single Act to Maastricht and Beyond: The Means to Match Our Ambitions*, COM (92) 2000 (Brussels, 1992), p. 36.

95. Ralf Dahrendorf, *Betrachtungen über die Revolution in Europa* (Stuttgart: Deutsche Verlags-Anstalt, 1990).

SEVEN

Cooperative Security in the New Europe

Paul B. Stares and John D. Steinbruner

PERHAPS THE GREATEST PARADOX of the Cold War is that it brought Europe one of its longest periods of peace. The price, however, was extreme and ultimately unsustainable. For over forty years the continent remained partitioned into two heavily armed camps, with one deprived of basic human rights and consigned to increasing economic backwardness. Although the danger that the military confrontation might suddenly turn into outright hostilities rarely became acute, it also never entirely disappeared. As President Lyndon B. Johnson once remarked, it was a "restless peace . . . shadowed by the threat of violence."[1] No country in Europe could realistically escape that shadow. Participation in one of the military alliances virtually guaranteed involvement in a war whose destructive effects were unlikely to remain geographically contained, especially if nuclear weapons were employed. At least in this respect, Europeans shared a common fate.

Although the demise of the Cold War has brought a shared sense of relief from the danger of an all-consuming conflagration, it has not produced—again paradoxically—a shared sense of security. A cursory review of the new Europe reveals major variations in the prospects for peace and stability across the continent.

The countries of Western Europe clearly feel the most secure now that the threat of a massive attack by the Warsaw Treaty Organization (WTO) has vanished. What residual fears existed about the Soviet Union's latent offensive military capabilities—excepting concerns about the safety of its nuclear

The authors gratefully acknowledge the assistance of Alf Hutter, Marion Reckten-wald, and Adrianne Goins in the preparation of this chapter. Useful comments and suggestions were also received from Ivo Daalder, Jonathan Dean, Wendy Silverman, and a specially convened group of government and nongovernment experts who reviewed an earlier draft of the paper.

weapons—have also dissipated with that country's political demise. With war among the countries of Western Europe long judged to be unthinkable by virtue of over forty years of political, military, and economic cooperation— a trend, moreover, that shows every sign of continuing—the prospects for a lasting peace in the region have never looked better. Only the most ardent pessimists worry about old animosities and rivalries resurfacing to make war a real possibility once again.[2]

Farther eastward the outlook is decidedly different. The fledgling democracies of Eastern and Central Europe face a far more unpredictable future than their Western neighbors, without many of the benefits that the West enjoys as a hedge against uncertainty. Although the previously dominant concern that the Soviet Union might reverse its policy of benign disengagement and seek to regain control of the region through coercion or force has now subsided, the new situation is hardly more comforting, for several reasons.[3] First, the disintegration of both the Soviet Union and Yugoslavia may presage further assertions of self-determination and independence in the region. Not only could such challenges lead to violent clashes and even open civil war, as Yugoslavia has tragically demonstrated, but they could also have serious international repercussions. Besides the possibility that an internal conflict might spill across national borders or precipitate a massive, socially destabilizing exodus of refugees into adjoining countries, separatist movements could draw in similar ethnic factions in nearby countries. The potential for friction or even outright hostilities cannot be dismissed under such circumstances. Cross-border passions are also sure to be inflamed if the minorities of adjoining nations are mistreated or violently suppressed in their efforts to seek greater autonomy or incorporation. Here the possibility of direct external intervention on their behalf becomes more real.

Second, strong nationalist sentiments in the newly emancipated states could foster the revival of irredentist claims that had been effectively suppressed under Soviet rule. Although the inviolability of existing borders has been one of the cornerstones of numerous bilateral and multilateral agreements among Eastern and Central European countries since the end of the Cold War, this general commitment may start to unravel now that Soviet power has crumbled. A series of messy and divisive boundary disputes could be triggered that, at a minimum, increase tension in the region as well as concern about the sanctity of national borders. More worrisome is the possibility that force may be threatened or even used to support the realignment of territorial boundaries.

Third, the dismantling of the WTO and the creation of many new European actors with independent armed forces has injected new uncertainties into the security calculations of countries in the region. Although the WTO's command arrangements were designed to ensure Soviet hegemony more than collective defense, they did help to dampen regional rivalries and bring a degree of predictability to military activities in the region. The Conventional Forces in Europe (CFE) agreement setting ceilings on force levels and the Vienna accords establishing confidence- and security-building measures (CSBMs) for the Atlantic-to-the-Urals (ATTU) region are in their own ways intended to achieve the same effect, but these arms control initiatives were originally conceived with the old East-West confrontation in mind. As will be discussed, some of these measures are still relevant; others, however, have now been brought into question by the new reality of Central and Eastern Europe and the former Soviet Union.

The situation in the former Soviet Union represents a more volatile mixture of the same basic problems that confront Central and Eastern Europe.[4] The long-suppressed ethnic disputes that have erupted are already having violent repercussions in several of the former Soviet republics. Further unrest, fueled by a combination of surging nationalist sentiment and deepening economic austerity, is considered almost inevitable and may lead to additional splintering of the new independent states. Given the intermixing of nationalities and ethnic groups inside the former Soviet Union, such unrest is likely to spill over into or directly embroil other states. Relations between the former republics of the Soviet Union could also be seriously strained by the territorial disputes that have emerged in several areas. Since many of the borders lack the legitimacy that derives from prolonged international recognition, the resolution of such disputes does not promise to be easy or immediate. As in Central and Eastern Europe, the possibility that force may be threatened or used in such circumstances cannot be ruled out, especially now that the former Soviet Union's centralized military control structures have collapsed. The concomitant rise of independent national armies, moreover, adds to the uncertainty of the situation.

This brief overview makes the qualitative change in the European security environment since the end of the Cold War readily apparent. From NATO's perspective, the previously dominant need to deter and defend against deliberate aggression has now given way to the more general task of engaging its former adversaries in the collective task of building a durable peace for Europe as a whole. Achieving this fundamental goal will depend largely on the fortunes of the many democratic experiments under way in the East, which are intimately related to the parallel process of economic regeneration. Establishing a solid economic foundation is of paramount importance to the fragile democracies, as a catastrophic drop in living standards would likely provide fertile breeding grounds for authoritarianism and extreme forms of nationalism, with potentially dangerous consequences. A massive infusion of Western capital investment, financial aid, and technical assistance is clearly needed to help reconstruct shattered economies and bring stability to the region, in much the same way that the U.S.-sponsored Marshall Plan helped Western Europe after World War II. While the newly unified Germany has already shown great initiative in this area (and assumed most of the financial burden), the help of others is clearly needed.[5]

The Marshall Plan, however, was not the only reason why the postwar reconstruction of Western Europe proved so successful. A key factor was undoubtedly the framework of international security guarantees centered around the North Atlantic Treaty, with its explicit commitment of U.S. military assistance to the defense of Western Europe. Although NATO was designed first and foremost to contain Soviet expansionism, it also provided general reassurance about West Germany, particularly after the country began rearming in the 1950s. Deliberately harnessing West Germany's military potential to NATO's integrated command system and limiting its power to the defense of the Western alliance effectively resolved a recurring source of instability and uncertainty in Europe.[6] As NATO gradually expanded to include most West European countries, it also helped to dampen regional rivalries and build confidence in the peaceful intentions of its members. This development undoubtedly facilitated the parallel process of political accommodation and economic cooperation that culminated in the commitment to a European Union at the Maastricht summit in December 1991.

The long-term goal for the countries of Central and Eastern Europe, as well as for the former Soviet Union, must be to attain the same level of confidence about national security that Western Europe enjoys. The incentives are clear and compelling. Unless fundamental uncertainties about national security are resolved, the process of democratization and economic reconstruction will almost certainly be compromised, if not derailed entirely, by the diversion of scarce resources from domestic to military programs and the inhibiting effect of insecurity on economic cooperation and political accommodation in the region. Furthermore, as long as doubts about the stability of this part of Europe persist, the region will have difficulty attracting much-needed foreign capital and assistance.

This chapter proposes the establishment of a cooperative security system designed to extend Western Europe's peaceful condition to the continent as a whole.[7] As the first part of this chapter makes clear, the basic idea of cooperative security eschews many of the attributes of traditional thinking about national security. Yet it is not so radical a departure as to be either inconceivable or impractical. Indeed, many of its essential components are already in place or currently taking shape. The second part of the chapter shows that establishing such a security system is more the extension and consolidation of an existing process than the adoption of a completely novel scheme. It is important to note at the outset that the concept of cooperative security described here is directed primarily at reducing the classical threat of interstate violence. At the same time, however, it can help in the prevention and resolution of other threats to peace and stability in Europe.

As in the economic sphere, Germany has played an important role in fostering and implementing the basic ideas of cooperative security.[8] The New Thinking that characterized the security policy of the former Soviet Union likewise reflected an acceptance of its underlying logic and associated operating principles.[9] The new Germany, however, by virtue of its geographical position, its influence in key international organizations such as NATO, the Coordinating Committee for Multilateral Export Control (COCOM), and the EC, its economic strength and commercial interests in both Western and Eastern Europe, and its strong ties to the United States (and increasingly to the countries in the East) can and should play a pivotal role in promoting the transition to a true cooperative security regime in Europe.

Premise and Principles of Cooperative Security

The underlying premise of cooperative security is that the insecurity of states derives directly from the uncertainty they feel about the aggressive intent of others. Although the level of uncertainty depends largely on the quality of political relations between these states, the military potential to coerce or physically occupy others is a common source of international suspicion and rivalry. Unilateral attempts by a state to reduce the level of uncertainty by increasing its own military capacity and preparedness to counter such threats can be costly and ultimately counterproductive, however.[10] In particular, improvements to a state's military capabilities may not only stimulate offsetting responses from other states concerned about a possible adverse impact on their own security but also encourage them to maintain forces at high states of combat readiness in peacetime. Besides increasing the risk of accidents, such conditions heighten the pressure for states to respond rapidly in a severe crisis to avoid falling victim to a potentially devastating attack. Given the inherent difficulty of distinguishing offensive from defensive military preparations, the danger of intentions being misunderstood and a crisis escalating inadvertently grows accordingly. Such conditions could, moreover, increase the incentives for either side to take pre-emptive action if war is considered unavoidable and imminent.

Seeking security through a coalition of states jointly dedicated to deterring and resisting aggression by a common adversary has the comparative advantage over unilateral solutions in being more efficient and less costly, while also promoting cooperation among its members. Coalition-building, however, can lead to the creation of antagonistic military alliances that are caught in essentially the same security predicament as independent state actors. NATO and the WTO are cases in point. While Europe remained at peace for over forty years, the military standoff was extremely wasteful and solidified the economic and social division of Europe. Furthermore, despite the outward appearance of stability, the confrontation in central Europe was also arguably extremely volatile in a severe crisis.[11]

Collective security based on an international commitment to resist the threat or actual occurrence of aggression is another option for reducing uncertainty about national security. By focusing on the general threat of international aggression rather than on aggression by a specific state, collective security has the advantage over military coalitions of being nondiscriminatory and nonconfrontational except when invoked. One weakness of collective security arrangements, however, is that they require the mobilization of sufficient international opposition during or immediately following an act of aggression, something the international community has not always been predisposed or organized effectively to do at that stage.[12] For this reason, collective security has not inspired confidence as a reliable system for safeguarding national security.

In contrast, the basic idea of cooperative security is to minimize the uncertainties that states feel about national security through the mutual regulation of the military capabilities and operational practices that fuel such anxieties. It is, in essence, a preventive approach to dealing with the international insecurities that flow from offensive military capabilities. But just as preventive health care cannot preclude the need for remedial emergency treatment, so a cooperative security regime cannot preclude, as a residual guarantee to its members, the need for a credible mechanism to resist international aggression. Thus, while cooperative security enshrines the core principle that the only truly legitimate use of military force is to protect national territory and its citizenry, exceptions are made for collective security endeavors. With systematic constraints on offensive forces in place, collective security guarantees are easier to convey, since they are less likely to be invoked. A cooperative security regime must also be inclusive in order to be effective and acquire general legitimacy. Traditional coalition-type security arrangements directed at a specific country or group of states are not compatible with the general principle of including all states willing to uphold the rules.

Cooperative security arrangements are not a substitute for other political and economic initiatives designed to build international trust and confidence. Nor can they resolve the root causes of international disputes, although, as has been indicated, a commitment to cooperative security can facilitate such a process.[13] Over time, the goal of a cooperative security regime is to diminish the probability of deliberate interstate aggression until it becomes virtually inconceivable. Cooperative security, therefore, can be seen as a transitional process toward what has been labelled a "security community" or "peace community" within which the threat of war has for all intents and purposes disappeared.[14]

General Design

A cooperative security regime would exhibit the following general design features, which must be viewed as mutually reinforcing.

OFFENSIVE REGULATION. The overall military capacity of states would be restricted by mutual agreement to enhance the performance of missions clearly associated with the defense of national territory and inhibit the projection of power beyond it. Although this ideal probably cannot be categorically and unambiguously achieved, it is certainly possible to make military establishments conform more closely with it than they now do. Several basic methods can be utilized to achieve this goal. The first is to set ceilings on the size of forces so as to make the aggregate firepower available to contiguous states as nearly equal as possible. Traditionally, a successful offensive against an opponent of equal strength has required a substantial margin of advantage in firepower at the point of attack, and eliminating that advantage has been the principal means of establishing defensive force configurations. This equalization, calculated between NATO and the WTO, was understandably the primary guiding principle of the CFE treaty.

Unfortunately, however, basic firepower equalization between individual countries is not a feasible criterion, given the large differences in size and historical patterns of military development. In order to adjust to this unavoidable fact, ceilings on the size and aggregate firepower of deployed forces must be supplemented by rules regulating the density of deployments (the concentration at given points along the perimeter of national territory), the rate of movement (the number of units that are allowed to be relocated in a given period of time), and the alerting and mobilization of reserve forces. These rules can be designed to prevent an immediately threatening offensive concentration by one state against another, even in instances where their overall capabilities are substantially different.

Logically, limits on the offensive capacity of national armed forces should also be extended to the regulation of military research and development and the diffusion of related technology. The goal here is the same: to inhibit the exploitation of technology in ways that might convey a meaningful offensive advantage to a state or be perceived as such by others. Similar incentives apply to constraining military-industrial capacity and international transactions of weaponry, support equipment, and technical expertise.

DEFENSIVE RESTRUCTURING. Military forces can be reconfigured in ways that clearly de-emphasize their inherent offensive capabilities without compromising their legitimate defensive functions. While armed forces and their weapons admittedly have dual applications, the necessary support infrastructure for prosecuting offensive operations can be identified and defined as a matter for practical restructuring. Considerable attention has already been focused on what a more obviously defensive force structure might look like.[15]

Likewise, the associated "software" of military forces—their doctrine, training, and operational procedures—can also be redesigned to emphasize a predominantly defensive orientation.

MUTUAL TRANSPARENCY. Since cooperative security is about building trust and confidence among states, rules and standards must be developed to facilitate the collection, collation, and dissemination of relevant information. More specifically, states would be obligated to disclose to others in standardized form a minimum amount of security-relevant data and also to accept agreed-upon procedures for remote and on-site inspection. Optimally, the inspection arrangements should be organized along multilateral lines. While some if not all states may want to continue using their own technical and nontechnical means of gathering intelligence, these should also be subject to greater regulation to reduce—and preferably to avoid altogether—the friction and suspicion that have been associated with such activities in the past.

FUNCTIONAL INTEGRATION. To the fullest extent possible, a cooperative security regime would foster multilateral integration of national security-related tasks not just to promote greater efficiency but also to build mutual confidence. As a practical matter, functional integration typically entails extensive exchanges of information and personnel to allow states to coordinate their respective activities effectively. Though the confidence-building benefits of such transactions are hard to quantify, their underlying value is indisputable, as the day-to-day workings of large international organizations such as NATO and the European Community demonstrate. The web of institutional commitments, operating procedures, personal relationships, and information flows that evolve in international organizations also has a constraining effect on the latitude of members to engage in activities that might threaten others. This, for example, has always been one of the hidden functions of NATO's integrated military command.[16] Functional integration, however, must be carried out in an inclusive and nondiscriminatory way for the reasons outlined earlier.

Operational Incentives

The formation of a regulated and therefore more predictable security environment is the most compelling incentive for adopting the principles and practices of cooperative security. Lower force levels, reduced operational readiness, greater functional integration, and moderated technical development can also significantly reduce costs and increase efficiency. And with forces at lower readiness, the likelihood of dangerous accidents and unauthorized military activity is also reduced. Cooperative security, moreover, permits international attention to be redirected to other issues that demand resolution without security concerns becoming an impediment.

Forces structured for defensive operations and maintained at lower readiness levels are less likely to be perceived as hostile, decreasing the risk of destabilizing and potentially dangerous interactions during an international crisis. Likewise, the constraints on the movement and concentration of forces function as an early warning system, alerting states to unusual activity and offering the opportunity for collective response. A calculating opponent denied the advantage of surprise and facing the prospect of international opposition is obviously more readily deterred. In addition, the crisis management arrangements that naturally complement a cooperative regime—from established channels of communication to dispute resolution mechanisms—further reduce the danger of a serious crisis escalating into conflict. In the event that hostilities do break out, the same consultation and coordinating mechanisms allow for prompt international reaction and, if necessary, the implementation of collective security arrangements. In the process, the likelihood of the conflict spreading or escalating is also reduced.

Implementing Cooperative Security in Europe

As will become evident, the key elements of a cooperative security regime are already taking shape in Europe. Implementation, then, is more a matter of refinement, consolidation, and extension of an existing process than the introduction of a radically new idea.

Offensive Regulation

Though conceived in a different era and designed essentially to stabilize the now-defunct military confrontation between NATO and the WTO, the CFE 1 agreement signed in 1990 still serves a useful and important function. Once the participating countries (including the successor states of the Soviet Union, which had to reach a separate agreement on dividing up the military entitlements under CFE), begin to implement the treaty, the number of weapons capable of being employed offensively in the ATTU region will be reduced significantly over the next several years.[17] By placing ceilings on key categories of weapons, the CFE treaty helps to legitimate the unilateral reductions taking place in Europe and to establish a legal barrier to future rearmament. The extensive monitoring and verification arrangements to ensure compliance also enhance confidence and set valuable precedents for further arms control initiatives. At the same time, the Stockholm and Vienna I and II accords will, among other things, further limit the potential for surprise attack in Europe by placing significant constraints on the size and frequency of major military exercises. In addition, statutory requirements for providing advance notification will limit the possibility that such exercises can be used to hide offensive preparations.[18]

The CFE and CSBM agreements represent substantial progress toward regulating offensive military capabilities in Europe, but alone they cannot be considered satisfactory. Even with the expected unilateral cuts in defense spending, Europe will be left with large residues of military forces. In some countries, certain categories of Treaty Limited Equipment (TLE) may actually increase, and redistributing equipment to stay within subregional ceilings will substantially improve the quality of the weaponry in others.[19] In general, all signatories will be free to modernize their arsenals as well as to produce, import, or export treaty limited weaponry. CFE 1 is also silent on the mobilization of reserves and does little to constrain paramilitary forces or the support systems necessary for prosecuting offensive operations.[20] More significant, however, is that with the breakup of the WTO and the Soviet Union, the CFE entitlements bear little or no relationship to the emerging strategic environment and latent security concerns of this part of Europe. In fact, the CFE agreement promises to accentuate several militarily significant asymmetries in Central and Eastern Europe, most notably between the newly unified Germany and its neighbors to the east and between Russia and the other former republics of the Soviet Union.[21] How important these asymmetries become clearly depends on the future political and economic evolution of this region, but their mere existence could create a source of friction and uncertainty. The current CSBM regime can help to alleviate this problem, but it too has its limitations—in particular, the high military exercise thresholds and the loophole created by the exemptions for alerting and mobilizing forces.[22]

To address these shortcomings, several complementary initiatives have been proposed. First, the planned force levels under CFE 1 can be reduced further and extended to cover all the participants in the Conference on Security and Cooperation in Europe (CSCE) rather than just the original signatories to the CFE agreement. The easiest method of accomplishing this would be to have all countries agree to reduce their arsenals by the same percentages in existing TLE categories and military manpower.[23] While attractive for its relative simplicity, this method would do little to redress the force imbalances mentioned earlier and could conceivably exacerbate them.[24] Another way to deal with this problem is to avoid the all-European format and conduct future negotiations at the subregional level.[25] While this suggestion also has its attractions in terms of negotiability, it represents a departure from the underlying intention to create all-European security arrangements.

A more logical approach is simply to adopt a completely new criterion for determining national military holdings—one that is both universally applicable and capable of commanding general legitimacy. Since the goal of cooperative security is to limit forces to levels sufficient for the defense of national territory, the length of border to be defended becomes a logical basis for establishing national force levels. As a follow-on agreement to CFE I, a commonly accepted standard of force density (defined as the amount of manpower and associated equipment needed to defend a given segment of border) can be established and then applied to calculate national entitlements. An initial application of this approach to CSCE states, using as the basic unit of account a single brigade of standard size and structure for every 100 kilometers of border, produces major asymmetries between certain countries. However, applying different force density standards to specific regions in much the same way that the CFE agreement set zonal ceilings for different parts of the ATTU region produced more practical results. Figure 7-1 illustrates the resultant force levels for all CSCE states in four different density zones. Figure 7-2 illustrates permitted force levels under CFE I converted into the same units of account. Table 7-1 presents the tabulated results with the percentage variation.

These density rules illustrate the general principle and can be determined differently. Deviations from the accepted norm can also be permitted to adjust for local imbalances or special conditions between certain states. National holdings, for example, can be weighted according to the number of neighboring countries or scaled upwards for those countries sharing borders with non-CSCE states. Whatever methodology is accepted, however, the ceilings on active forces must be complemented by restrictions on reserve military strength and paramilitary formations in order to prevent states from circumventing the restrictions.

Conspicuously absent from these calculations is any reference to U.S. forces based in Europe and, for that matter, to any other military forces deployed beyond national borders. Since such forces are not subject to the same force density rules as resident national forces, special conditions need to be applied. As is the case today in NATO, the deployment of forces on foreign soil would require, at a minimum, the permission of the host country. The legitimacy of such deployments could also be enhanced by the official approval of the CSCE. Ultimately, however, their presence in a cooperative security regime is justified only if they form part of a multilateral arrangement for collective security and peacekeeping operations.

National military entitlements based on certain force density standards limit the scope of offensive operations but by themselves do not preclude localized concentrations of military force that pose an offensive threat. Thus, restrictions on the movement and concentration of ground forces are also desirable. The normal peacetime locations of ground force units can be disclosed, as they are under CFE I, and movements away from these garrisons can be constrained by rate (number of units allowed to move in a given amount of time) and with rules for advance notification, as they are already to a certain extent by the Vienna CSBM accords.[26] These movement constraints, as part of larger zonal restrictions for each country, would effectively cap the level of forces in prescribed geographical areas at any given time. While special dispensation may be required for military exercises, they can also be subject to size constraints and rules for prior announcement, again as they are under the various CSBM accords. Similar restrictions governing or even banning military activity within a specified distance of national borders can be reached as well.[27]

The scope for offensive operations can also be inhibited by specific restrictions on the logistical or combat support equipment necessary to project and sustain military forces over long distances, particularly beyond national borders. The most commonly cited candidates include "operational" bridge-laying equipment (as distinct from smaller tactical bridging equipment), fuel pipe-laying facilities, self-propelled Surface-to-Air Missile (SAM) batteries, and large mobile field hospitals.[28] Such equipment, of course, is not unequivocally offensive in nature and can be used for defense operations as well. However, since defenders can more easily exploit comparable civilian facilities on their home territory and prevent attacking forces from using them, such restrictions on balance favor the defense.

With air power such a potent military instrument, there is a clear need to limit its use for offensive purposes. Major obstacles, however, lie in the way of meaningful constraint. The inherent flexibility and responsiveness of air power make it equally attractive for defensive missions and difficult to constrain operationally. Although some combat aircraft are clearly more suited for prosecuting offensive missions such as long-range interdiction and defense suppression, even those designed primarily for air defense and close air support can be used to support offensive operations, as was demonstrated during the recent Gulf War. For some nations, air forces also represent the only means of carrying out strategic retaliation and, as a result, typically enjoy considerable prestige within national military organizations. It is not surprising, therefore, that little progress other than limits on the overall number of combat aircraft and some CSBM provisions have been acceptable at the negotiating table.

The principle of subceilings for certain categories of combat aircraft with certain size or payload characteristics is one possible method of limiting tactical air power. An alternative approach to limiting platforms capable of being used for offensive purposes is to focus on the air-delivered munitions with the most threatening features. For purposes of limitation, it may be possible to define the technical parameters of precision-guided munitions capable of attacking fixed and hardened targets such as airfields, command and control centers, and air defense sites, all of which are obvious targets for pre-emptive action. Constraints can be placed on the development, production, and deployment of such munitions, sparing those needed to repulse an attack, such as air-to-air, anti-armor and antipersonnel weapons. Such constraints clearly do not preclude the capacity for offensive air operations using conventional "dumb" or jury-rigged precision munitions,

Figure 7-1. *The CSCE Balance with CFE*

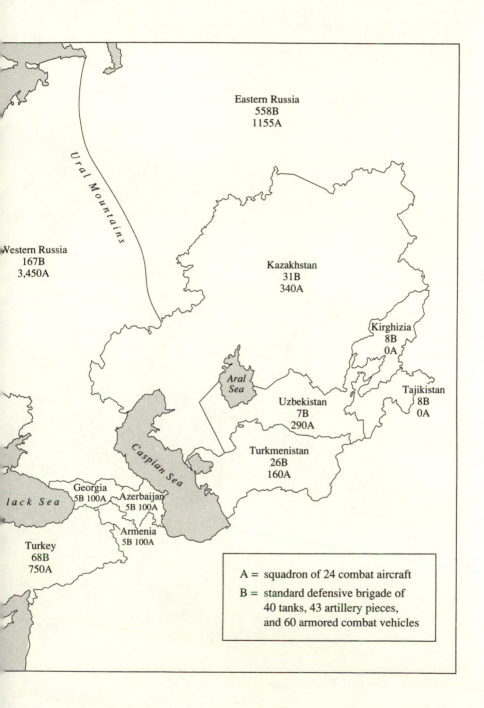

Eastern Russia
558B
1155A

Ural Mountains

Western Russia
167B
3,450A

Kazakhstan
31B
340A

Kirghizia
8B
0A

Aral Sea

Uzbekistan
7B
290A

Tajikistan
8B
0A

Caspian Sea

Turkmenistan
26B
160A

Georgia
5B 100A

Azerbaijan
5B 100A

Black Sea

Armenia
5B 100A

Turkey
68B
750A

A = squadron of 24 combat aircraft

B = standard defensive brigade of
40 tanks, 43 artillery pieces,
and 60 armored combat vehicles

Figure 7-2. *The CSCE Balance with Equal Force Density*

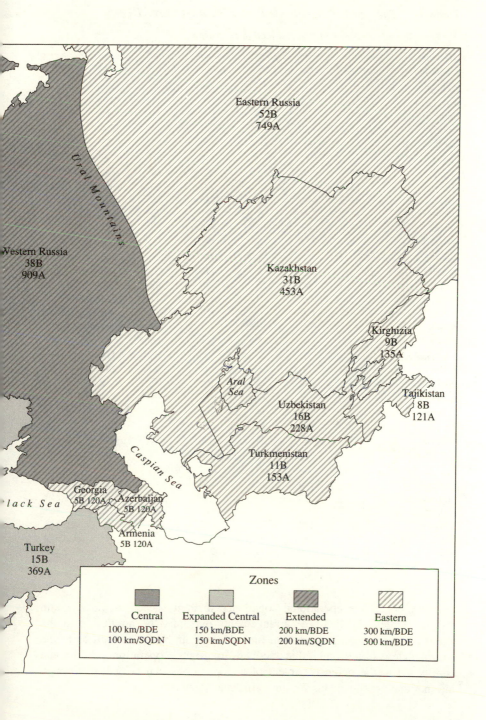

Eastern Russia
52B
749A

Western Russia
38B
909A

Ural Mountains

Kazakhstan
31B
453A

Kirghizia
9B
135A

Aral Sea

Tajikistan
8B
121A

Uzbekistan
16B
228A

Turkmenistan
11B
153A

Caspian Sea

Georgia
5B 120A

Azerbaijan
5B 120A

Black Sea

Armenia
5B 120A

Turkey
15B
369A

Zones

Central	Expanded Central	Extended	Eastern
100 km/BDE	150 km/BDE	200 km/BDE	300 km/BDE
100 km/SQDN	150 km/SQDN	200 km/SQDN	500 km/BDE

Table 7-1. *The CSCE Balance: CFE versus Equal Force Density*

Country (by new zones)	With CFE[a]		Equal force density		Percent change, BDEs[d]	Percent change, aircraft	Defensive perimeter (km)[e]
	Defensive BDEs[b]	Combat aircraft[c]	Defensive BDEs	Combat aircraft			
Central			(100 km/BDE, SQDN)				
Austria	8	54	15	348	81	544	1,450
Belgium	11	232	7	179	−32	−23	745
Britain	31	900	17	417	−44	−54	1,738
Czechoslovakia	32	345	18	420	−45	22	1,750
France	42	800	21	512	−49	−36	2,135
Germany	75	900	24	576	−68	−36	2,400
Hungary	23	180	13	300	−46	67	1,250
Italy	45	650	23	540	−50	−17	2,250
Netherlands	17	230	5	121	−70	−47	505
Poland	39	460	18	439	−53	−5	1,830
Switzerland	26	289	8	192	−69	−34	800
Expanded central			(150 km/BDE, SQDN)				
Albania	4	95	5	120	25	26	610
Belarus	42	260	13	316	−69	22	1,975
Bulgaria	37	235	9	207	−77	−12	1,295
Estonia[f]	4	110	5	120	25	9	470
Greece	43	650	10	251	−76	−61	1,570
Latvia[f]	4	180	7	158	65	−12	990
Lithuania[f]	18	70	6	150	−66	114	935
Moldova	5	50	6	144	20	188	900
Portugal	8	160	5	130	−33	−19	815
Romania	35	430	12	286	−66	−33	1,785
Spain	26	310	11	266	−57	−14	1,665
Turkey	68	750	15	369	−77	−51	2,305
Ukraine	93	1,090	24	570	−75	−48	3,560
Yugoslavia[g]	63	489	14	337	−78	−31	2,105
Extended			(200 km/BDE, SQDN)				
Denmark	9	106	5	120	−44	13	638
Finland	17	118	11	270	−35	129	2,250
Iceland	0	0	5	120	n.a.	n.a.	845
Norway	7	100	12	293	74	193	2,445
Western Russia	167	3,450	38	909	−77	−74	7,572
Sweden	23	470	11	254	−54	−46	2,120

but they do reduce operational confidence in their success against certain military targets. CSBM-type arrangements may also be applicable to the storage of munitions and aviation fuel close to air bases, as well as to the use of external fuel tanks that facilitate long-range operations. Additional confidence in the defensive intent of air operations can be gained through international arrangements for air traffic management.

Table 7-1. *(Continued)*

Country (by new zones)	With CFE[a]		Equal force density		Percent change, BDEs[d]	Percent change, aircraft	Defensive perimeter (km)[e]
	Defensive BDEs[b]	Combat aircraft[c]	Defensive BDEs	Combat aircraft			
Eastern			*(300 km/BDE; 500 km/SQDN)*				
Armenia	5	100	5	120	0	20	975
Azerbaijan	5	100	5	120	2	20	1,515
Eastern Russia	558	1,155	52[h]	749	−91	−44	15,598
Georgia	5	100	5	120	0	20	1,130
Kazakhstan[f]	31	340	31	453	2	33	9,445
Kirghizia[f]	8	0	9	135	18	n.a.	2,810
Tajikistan[f]	8	0	8	121	5	n.a.	2,525
Turkmenistan[f]	26	160	11	153	−59	−4	3,193
Uzbekistan[f]	7	290	16	228	127	−21	4,755

Sources: "FACTFILE: Weapons in Europe before and after CFE," *Arms Control Today*, vol. 21 (January–February 1991), p. 29; The International Institute for Strategic Studies, *The Military Balance 1991–1992* (Brassey's, 1991); "CFE Military Analysis: Post-CFE USSR Forces by Republic," *ViennaFax*, vol. 2 (November 25, 1991), p. 2; "HLWG Meeting on 25th May 1992: Chairman's Summary," NATO Press Release (92)50, Brussels, May 25, 1992; Department of Defense, *Military Forces in Transition, 1991* (U.S. Government Printing Office, 1991), p. 51; *The Times Atlas of the World: Comprehensive Edition* (Houghton Mifflin, 1967), plate 16, p. 51; and "Treaty on Conventional Armed Forces in Europe," *Arms Control Today*, vol. 21 (January–February 1991), pp. CFE Supp. 7-CFE Supp. 16.

a. Data reflect legal ceilings under CFE for signatories and current holdings for nonsignatories. The following CSCE members are excluded from this table: Canada, Cyprus, Ireland, Liechtenstein, Luxembourg, Malta, Monaco, San Marino, The Holy See, and the United States.

b. A standard defensive brigade has 40 tanks, 60 armored combat vehicles (ACVs), and 43 artillery pieces. We begin with the assumption of 40 tanks per brigade. The ACV-to-tank ratio of 1.5 and the artillery-to-tank ratio of roughly 1.1 are the ratios that best "fit" the force levels allowed by CFE. "Fit" here is determined by taking weighted geometric means, which in this case is equivalent to the ratios of the sum of ACVs to the sum of tanks, and the sum of artillery to the sum of tanks. Actual CFE numbers of tanks, ACVs, and artillery for a given country are then divided by their respective "standard" 40/60/43 numbers, yielding the number of standard brigades each weapon category could form. The country's final brigade count is the arithmetic mean of these three separate brigade counts.

c. The CFE definition of combat aircraft is used throughout. One standard, tactical squadron (SQDN) has 24 aircraft.

d. Discrepancies in percent change calculations are due to rounding.

e. Defensive perimeter considers a relatively smooth-lined military perimeter for defense of national territory rather than the often twisting official borderlines. One-fifth of a country's coastline is counted toward its total defensive perimeter (one-half if its coastline accounts for 75 percent or more of its defensive perimeter). A country may have a minimum of 5 brigades and 120 aircraft regardless of defensive perimeter.

f. Force levels "with CFE" in the Baltic states, Kazakhstan, Kirghizia, Tajikistan, Turkmenistan, and Uzbekistan reflect former Soviet equipment based there as of Fall 1991.

g. Bosnia-Herzegovina, Croatia, Slovenia, and Yugoslavia are members of the CSCE. However, because many borders within the former Yugoslavian state remain in dispute, the military balance among the new states is not calculated here.

h. Russia might be allowed to deploy additional forces facing non-CSCE states such as China.

A truly comprehensive cooperative security regime in Europe also cannot exclude naval activities. While naval forces (with the exception of amphibious units) have so far not been the subject of conventional arms control negotiations at the insistence of the West, such forces cannot justifiably be omitted. At a minimum, CSBMs should be applied to the size, notification, and observation of major naval exercises.[29] More ambitious global control regimes can also be designed that involve tonnage limits, force ratios, and the structural composition of navies.[30]

Finally, in keeping with the general thrust of regulating offensive conventional military capabilities, a cooperative security regime aims to continue the process already underway of reducing nuclear weapons in Europe and redefining their essential purpose as weapons of last resort. Weapons stored on foreign territory must be progressively withdrawn and European stockpiles reduced further, again in line with current strategic arms reductions.[31] Hopefully, a treaty banning chemical weapons can also be negotiated along with additional constraints to buttress the current biological weapons convention.

Defensive Restructuring

The regulation of offensive military capabilities can be complemented by further reducing uncertainty about military intentions through the restructuring of national forces in ways that are clearly more defensive in orientation. While this transformation has already begun, particularly among former WTO armies, the general reduction in conventional forces has at the same time led to the development of more flexible and rapidly deployable forces in other countries (notably within NATO) to compensate for the lower force densities. While defensive in purpose, these rapid deployment forces can be viewed as incompatible with the overall intent of a cooperative security regime. This problem can be alleviated through many of the constraints mentioned earlier and by integrating these forces into multilateral frameworks that constrain unilateral actions. Through role specialization, moreover, countries would not possess all the necessary components to project military force offensively.[32] It is also important to note that while military forces cannot be structured in ways that deprive them of all offensive potential, as Johan Jorgen Holst argues, "It is a question of emphasis rather than a choice among absolutes . . . . [T]he organizational structures within which [military forces] will function, the doctrines developed for their potential, and the patterns of training will shape perceptions of the relative emphasis on defensive and offensive operations."[33] These perceptions can be enhanced by greater openness and the exchange of relevant military information.[34]

Mutual Transparency

Great strides have already been made toward achieving mutual transparency in Europe. Besides the greater openness that has attended the democratization of Central and Eastern Europe, various international agreements now permit or demand new levels of intrusiveness and disclosure from the signatories. The extensive and complex on-site inspection regimes of the Intermediate-

Range Nuclear Forces (INF) and CFE treaties are obvious cases in point. The Stockholm/Vienna CSBM accords have also made a major contribution, especially with respect to the notification and inspection of military exercises, annual exchanges of information on the peacetime location and structure of military forces, deployment of major weapons systems and equipment, and national military expenditures. Fact-finding visits to military air bases have also been arranged, as well as international seminars to exchange information about national military doctrine.[35] Moreover, provisions have been made for states to request information about "unusual military activities" in neighboring countries. Finally, the Conflict Prevention Center, with a supporting communications system linking the capitals of all CSCE countries, has been established in Vienna to exchange information and generally assist with the implementation of the CSBM provisions.[36]

An agreement to permit aerial inspection has also been reached as a result of the Open Skies negotiations.[37] An Open Skies regime will provide valuable additional information, especially for the Europeans, over a much broader area than is currently covered by ground inspection arrangements, most notably beyond the Urals.[38] Such a regime, however, should not preclude or necessarily replace bilateral aerial inspection agreements of the type reached between Hungary and Romania in 1991.[39]

Although the trends are positive, cooperative security in Europe will ultimately depend on the creation of an information regime more transparent and inclusive than the one currently taking shape. States are now willing to accept much higher levels of intrusion and more demanding disclosure rules, but national military establishments still remain relatively closed and secretive. Despite the very real breakthroughs of recent years, the emerging inspection and monitoring arrangements continue to reflect traditional patterns of thinking and behavior. Since they were largely conceived at a time when adversarial perceptions and national suspicions dominated, the resultant arrangements for ensuring compliance with the new accords understandably bear the hallmark of that era. Thus, the CFE and CSBM agreements are multilateral in scope, while the associated inspection and observation arrangements are organized along national lines. Since the original aim of these agreements was to reduce competition and friction between the two military blocs, NATO has also become the organizational focus for sharing information and determining compliance among the North American and Western European signatories.[40] Nevertheless, with no real strategic intelligence-gathering assets of their own, the European members of NATO remain heavily reliant on the United States for information relevant to their security, something that has long been a source of friction in the alliance.[41] For the Central and East European countries, the situation is much worse. The collapse of the WTO has left them with no coordinating mechanism commensurate to NATO and without the intelligence support the Soviet Union once provided.

With these shortcomings in mind, several initiatives can be taken to establish an information regime that more closely conforms to Europe's cooperative security needs.[42] In the short term, the current CSBM notification and inspection arrangements can be tightened up with respect to alerting requirements for military exercises (as indicated earlier) and extended where practicable to cover large-scale air and naval activities. National notification requirements can also be broadened to include basic research activities, weapons production schedules, and significant military infrastructure plans. Some degree of national security classification is necessary but can be limited to technical and operational details. With these expanded information disclosure requirements, a regularly updated CSCE data base should be established, as some have already suggested.[43] The most logical host organization is the Conflict Prevention Center, although it would need to markedly increase its support staff above the current level.[44]

Efforts should also be made to make the inspection and monitoring arrangements multinational rather than national. There are numerous precedents for this, including the Armaments Control Agency of the Western European Union (WEU) and the International Atomic Energy Agency (IAEA).[45] The initial phase of CFE implementation will be too early for such a transition, which may be possible, however, in later stages and for follow-on agreements.[46] One idea is to establish permanent missions with small multinational staffs on the territory of each participating country to replace visiting inspection teams. Multinational inspections can also be implemented from the outset under an Open Skies agreement.

Over the long term, a compelling argument can be made for developing a CSCE satellite monitoring capability with the necessary data analysis and dissemination facilities. Standard objections to regional monitoring arrangements of this type maintain that they duplicate other means, are too expensive given the level of technical performance required of them, and liable to abuse.[47] As argued earlier, however, access to information is quite uneven in Europe, and while states are free to develop whatever additional technical means of verification they want at the national level, all should have access to a minimum level of information in order to feel reassured about the intentions of others. Such access would hopefully also reduce the incentives to engage in potentially provocative espionage activity. It is conceivable that regular ground inspection teams and aerial overflights will eventually be viewed as anachronisms from an era when confidence in state behavior was understandably low. But satellite overflight has the advantage of being less obviously intrusive and therefore more politically sustainable over the long term.[48] The cost, while substantial, is not beyond what the countries that would be most involved can afford, and the expense can be further justified if the system is expanded to monitor other areas, such as the environment, as well as activities beyond Europe. As for the possibility of abuse, special security regulations can be established to safeguard access to data and control its dissemination.

Functional Integration

The organizational framework of a functionally integrated and inclusive cooperative security regime is already taking shape in Europe. As a result of the November 1990 Paris Charter and the July 1992 Helsinki summit, the CSCE process is being institutionalized and strengthened through a parliamentary assembly, a permanent secretariat, an election monitoring center and, as already noted, the Conflict Prevention Center, all in different European capitals. Regular meetings have also been instituted between the foreign ministers and other senior officials of member states to discuss, among other things, human rights, arms control, crisis management, and peacekeeping. While there has been considerable skepticism about the effectiveness of an organization that can only reach decisions on the basis of consensus among the more than fifty participating countries, the CSCE has nevertheless steadily expanded its role and legitimacy as the only truly pan-European security forum.[49]

At the same time, a separate but overlapping institutional arrangement is taking shape under NATO sponsorship. Former members of the WTO, including the successor states of the Soviet Union, have joined with NATO members to form the North Atlantic Cooperation Council (NACC). Designed as part of NATO's efforts to reform its image and "extend the hand of friendship" to its former adversaries, the NACC serves to increase the level of cooperation with and provide general reassurance to the countries of Central and Eastern Europe without conveying the security guarantees of full membership. Besides annual NACC meetings at the ministerial level, more regular contacts have also been established with the permanent representatives or liaison missions of its non-NATO members at the Brussels headquarters of the alliance.[50]

In parallel with these developments, the European Community has also taken significant steps to extend its competence into the security and defense sphere. As agreed at the EC's 1991 Maastricht summit, the WEU has been designated as the institutional vehicle to develop a European security and defense identity in areas complementary to NATO.[51] These plans represent a further strengthening of the "European pillar" of the Western alliance, although over the long term the WEU's membership is likely to be enlarged as new states join the EC, presumably including those of Central and Eastern Europe. This may again create a source of friction with NATO.

The growing level of cooperation in security matters among all European states is encouraging but falls short of what is needed for a truly inclusive cooperative security regime. As has been discussed, the level of confidence about security remains much higher for Western than for Central and Eastern Europe, not just because old animosities are long buried and the threat of external attack has dissipated, but also because the Western countries continue to enjoy the general reassurance that comes with the mutual security guarantees of NATO and, to a lesser extent, WEU membership. In accordance with the general cooperative security design, the collective defense commitments of NATO should be replicated in the form of a more inclusive collective security commitment by all CSCE states.[52] The CSCE, however, has no military arm or planning element capable of buttressing such a commitment, even if it can make its decisionmaking process more effective. NATO, in contrast, has the only working military organization capable of mounting a collective security or peacekeeping operation in Europe, but its current members remain understandably reluctant to enlarge the alliance and extend security guarantees to a region that is still quite unstable.

NATO's long-term future is also in question. As the process of economic and political deepening continues in the EC, the desire to build a credible European defense organization from the nucleus of the WEU will inevitably gain momentum. In the process, the compromise reached at Maastricht preserving NATO's primacy in European defense will come under stress. This could happen sooner rather than later if the U.S. commitment to Europe (embodied by the physical presence of its ground forces) is seriously eroded, or if the Europeans become disenchanted with America's attempts to use NATO as an instrument for preserving its hegemony in Europe. Many of NATO's institutional assets could wither away as a consequence.

The immediate impediments in the way of a cooperative security organization point to the need for interim initiatives that allow progress toward this goal to continue without causing undue friction between the various security-related institutions. With this in mind, the CSCE's role in negotiating further arms control measures, conflict prevention, and mediation—as well as its established function of promoting human rights—should be progressively strengthened. At the same time, NATO can take a more active role in promoting military cooperation and managing military operations throughout Europe, with the NACC acting as the principal coordinating mechanism. In the process, the alliance should become less obviously an organization for the defense of Western Europe. In the short term, military-to-military contacts can be strengthened through personnel exchanges and even joint maneuvers. Liaison officers can be exchanged not only between allies, as they are now, but between military units in sensitive areas. In addition to changing the standard assumptions about NATO's crisis management exercises, former WTO members should also be encouraged to participate in order to foster mutual understanding about common concerns.[53]

There are also areas where real functional integration can be developed. Multinational verification and monitoring is one that has already been proposed; the development of an integrated civil-military air traffic control system for Europe is another. The object here, besides safer and more efficient air space management, is to alleviate concern over the inherently preemptive potential of tactical aircraft armed with advanced conventional munitions. The continuous monitoring function of air traffic control can provide the additional reassurance against preemptive strikes that has traditionally been offered by the air defense systems of the two Cold War alliances, with their integrated networks of early warning radars and command centers. It is also worth noting that considerable informal cooperation took place along the boundaries of the two systems to reduce the risk of accidents and misunderstandings. With NATO embarking on an expensive overhaul of its air command and control system—the Air Command and Control System (ACCS) program—and the Central and East European countries looking to reorganize their own systems in the wake of the WTO's demise, the opportunity exists to foster functional linkages that will internationalize military air traffic control in Europe.[54]

Military integration can also be fostered for peacekeeping duties and disaster relief work. Units from different countries can train together, develop common operational practices, procure common equipment, and be on permanent call for deployment. Fully integrated forces of this kind are not unknown. NATO's ACE Mobile Force (AMF) has traditionally acted as the alliance's "fire brigade," and the Nordic countries have also created a standing force for U.N. peacekeeping operations. In addition, a larger Rapid Reaction Force is currently being created by NATO for the traditional purpose of defending alliance members. As a consequence of the decision taken by NATO foreign ministers in Oslo, on June 5, 1992, NATO forces may one day be used for peacekeeping missions under the auspices of the CSCE.[55]

A wider and more elevated pan-European role for NATO would serve two purposes. It would help give NATO the new legitimacy and relevance it needs to sustain public support over the long term, and it would allow the WEU to develop within the CSCE and NATO as a regional subgrouping with narrower but compatible security responsibilities. Conceivably, many of the facilities that NATO has established for the purpose of defending Western Europe could be transferred to WEU control. The United States could actively foster this outcome rather than continuing to appear openly resistant to change. Although the United States would not be part of this organization, its commitment and presence in Europe would be maintained through its association with NATO and the CSCE.

Conclusion: Toward a Global Security Regime

Creating long-term peace and security in Europe cannot be seen solely as the responsibility of Europeans. Certain non-European powers have legitimate interests and also important roles to play in fostering the process, including traditional powers such as the United States, Canada, and also, as the world becomes increasingly interdependent, Japan. Conversely, European security cannot be seen as a purely European problem, for many of the challenges to the continent's security lie beyond its borders and require a collective response. Regional conflicts that threaten Europe's economic interests or pose the risk of mass migration of socially destabilizing proportions, direct military threats rising from the proliferation of weapons technology, political or religiously motivated terrorism, and last but not least, environmental disasters all call for a pan-European response.

The principles and practices of cooperative security, also have applications outside of Europe. Despite regional differences, the incentives are equally compelling to create a global security regime with Europe as the principal model. Thus, commensurate restrictions on military force levels and operational practices would be extended to other major regional powers, most notably Japan, India, and China. Greater transparency and functional integration would likewise be core features of the global regime. To buttress these restrictions, however, worldwide controls must be adopted on the transfer of arms and the proliferation of weapons technology. All arms sales, as well as trade in militarily sensitive technologies, need to be internationally licensed and monitored for compliance with the overarching force level restrictions. Moreover, along with deep reductions in nuclear weapons deployments, other weapons of mass destruction must be successively phased out and eventually prohibited. While a regime of this scope clearly represents an ambitious undertaking, the underlying imperatives demand a solution of this magnitude.

Notes

1. Lyndon B. Johnson, "Remarks in New York City before the National Conference of Editorial Writers," October 7, 1966, reprinted in *Public Papers of the Presidents of the United States: Lyndon B. Johnson, 1966*, book 2 (Washington: Government Printing Office, 1967), p. 1126.

2. A notable example is John J. Mearsheimer, "Back to the Future: Instability in Europe after the Cold War," *International Security*, vol. 15 (Summer 1990), pp. 5–56. For dissenting views see the correspondence of Stanley Hoffmann and Robert O. Keohane, as well as John J. Mearsheimer's response, in "Back to the Future, Part II: International Relations Theory and Post-Cold War Europe," *International Security*, vol. 15 (Fall 1990), pp. 191–99. See also Stephen Van Evera, "Primed for Peace: Europe after the Cold War," *International Security*, vol. 15 (Winter 1990/91), pp. 7–57.

3. This section draws on several sources: Christopher Smart, *The Emerging Security Structures of East Europe: Girding for Europe's Next Wars*, HI-4126-RR (Indianapolis, Ind.: Hudson Institute, September 1990); Christoph Royen, "Potential

Conflict Constellations in Relations between the Countries of Central Eastern Europe and the Neighboring Successor States of the USSR" (Ebenhausen: Stiftung Wissenschaft und Politik, March 1992); and Joseph A. Yager, *Prospects for Nuclear Weapons Proliferation in a Changing Europe* (McLean, Va.: Center for National Security Negotiations, February 1992).

4. See Joan DeBardeleben, "Madly Off in All Directions: The Dark Side of the USSR's Independence Bandwagon," *Peace and Security*, vol. 6 (Winter 1991/1992), pp. 2–4; Stephen Van Evera, *Managing the Eastern Crisis: Preventing War in the Former Soviet Empire*, DACS Working Paper (Massachusetts Institute of Technology, Defense and Arms Control Studies Program, January 1992); and Shlomo Avineri, "The Return to History: The Breakup of the Soviet Union," *Brookings Review*, vol. 10 (Spring 1992), pp. 30–33.

5. See "Genscher Calls for Quick, Pragmatic Aid to CIS at Washington Conference," *The Week in Germany*, January 24, 1992, p. 1; and W.R. Smyser, "U.S.S.R.-Germany: A Link Restored," *Foreign Policy*, no. 84 (Fall 1991), pp. 130–31.

6. The Brussels Treaty and the subsequent Paris agreements of 1954, establishing the WEU, were directed even more at preventing Germany from threatening the peace of Europe. See Paul B. Stares, *Allied Rights and Legal Constraints on German Military Power*, Occasional Paper (Brookings, 1990).

7. Some of the ideas presented here are drawn from earlier publications. See John D. Steinbruner, "Revolution in Foreign Policy," in Henry J. Aaron, ed., *Setting National Priorities: Policy for the Nineties* (Brookings, 1990), pp. 65–109; and John D. Steinbruner, "The Consequences of the Gulf War: Forging the New World Order under a Forced Schedule," *Brookings Review*, vol. 9 (Spring 1991), pp. 6–13.

8. See Stephen F. Szabo, *The Changing Politics of German Security* (St. Martin's Press, 1990), pp. 70–73, 88–94; Dieter S. Lutz, "Security Partnership and/or Common Security?" *Coexistence*, vol. 24 (1987), pp. 271–307.

9. See Michael MccGwire, *Perestroika and Soviet National Security* (Brookings, 1991), pp. 179–186; and Marian Leighton and Robert Rudney, "Non-Offensive Defense: Toward a Soviet-German Security Partnership?" *Orbis*, vol. 35 (Summer 1991), pp. 377–93.

10. This is often referred to as the "security dilemma," in which actions by one state to improve its security are perceived by others as having been made at their expense. An independent search for security, therefore, is likely to cause a negative reaction, producing no lasting improvement in security and, quite probably, a net loss. See Robert Jervis, "Cooperation under the Security Dilemma," *World Politics*, vol. 30 (January 1978) pp. 167–214.

11. See Bruce G. Blair, "Alerting in Crisis and Conventional War," in Ashton B. Carter, John D. Steinbruner, and Charles A. Zraket, eds., *Managing Nuclear Operations* (Brookings, 1987), pp. 75–120; Paul B. Stares, *Command Performance: The Neglected Dimension of European Security* (Brookings, 1991), pp. 121–25; and John D. Steinbruner, "The Prospect of Cooperative Security," in John D. Steinbruner, ed., *Restructuring American Foreign Policy* (Brookings, 1989), pp. 107–09.

12. For a general critique of collective security see Josef Joffe, "Collective Security and the Future of Europe: Failed Dreams and Dead Ends," *Survival*, vol. 34 (Spring 1992), pp. 36–50. For a more positive prognosis, see Charles A. Kupchan and Clifford A. Kupchan, "Concerts, Collective Security, and the Future of Europe," *International Security*, vol. 16 (Summer 1991), pp. 114–61.

13. It is worth noting that cooperative security differs somewhat from earlier ideas of "common security," although both concepts proceed from shared beliefs about the

security predicament of states and the futility of independent solutions. See The Independent Commission on Disarmament and Security Issues, *Common Security: A Blueprint for Survival* (Simon and Schuster, 1982) (otherwise known as the Palme Commission Report), p. 12. The authors state: "In the modern age, security cannot be obtained unilaterally. . . . The security of one nation cannot be bought at the expense of others. The danger of nuclear war alone assures the validity of this proposition. . . . We face common dangers and thus must also promote our security in common." See also Richard Smoke, "A Theory of Mutual Security," Working Paper 11-Brown University, Center for Foreign Policy Development, November 1990). Common security, however, evolved during the stalemate of the Cold War with a prescribed course of action to establish a less dangerous and less burdensome basis for peaceful coexistence between two ideologically opposed and very different socioeconomic systems.

14. The term "security community" was coined by Karl W. Deutsch and others in *Political Community and the North Atlantic Area: International Organization in the Light of Historical Experience* (Princeton University Press, 1957). The term "peace community" can be found in Eckhard Lübkemeier, "Security and Peace in Post-Cold War Europe," in Armand Clesse and Lothar Rühl, eds., *Beyond East-West Confrontation: Searching for a New Security Structure in Europe* (Baden-Baden: Nomos Verlagsgesellschaft for the Institute for European and International Studies, 1990), pp. 183–201. Western Europe, the Nordic countries, and North America are three areas generally considered to have reached this evolutionary stage. While it is recognized that the peaceful status of these regions derives largely from shared values, established democratic institutions, and growing economic interdependence, an agreement that addressed key security concerns is also a factor. In North America, it was the Rush-Bagot agreement, which limited naval forces on the Great Lakes and by extension largely demilitarized the U.S.-Canadian border; in Western Europe it was the Brussels Treaty establishing the WEU and the 1954 Protocol on Forces of the WEU, which set force ceilings for Western European forces as well restrictions on West Germany's rearmament.

15. There is indeed a voluminous body of literature on defensive force structures. See, for example, Jonathan Dean, "Alternative Defence: Answer to NATO's Central Front Problems?" *International Affairs*, vol. 64 (Winter 1987–88), pp. 61–82; and Robert Neild, "Non-Offensive Defence: The Way to Achieve Common Security in Europe," Background Paper 25 (Ottawa, Ontario: Canadian Institute for International Peace and Security, January 1989). For an interesting historical perspective on this debate, see Marion William Boggs, "Attempts to Define and Limit 'Aggressive' Armament in Diplomacy and Strategy," *University of Missouri Studies*, vol. 16, no. 1 (1941).

16. This view was evident during the debate over West Germany's rearmament and its accession to the alliance. See Stares, *Allied Rights and Legal Constraints*, pp. 15–17.

17. For details of the division of Soviet military entitlements, see "HLWG Meeting on 25th May 1992: Chairman's Summary," NATO Press Release (92)50, Brussels, May 25, 1992. See also Robert Mauthner, "European Arms Cuts Pact Signed," *Financial Times*, June 6/7, 1992, p. 2. For a comprehensive assessment of the CFE Treaty see Ivo H. Daalder, *The CFE Treaty: An Overview and an Assessment* (Washington: Johns Hopkins Foreign Policy Institute, 1991). For other valuable commentaries see Jonathan Dean, "The CFE Negotiations, Present and Future," *Survival*, vol. 32 (July/August 1990), pp. 313–24; Lee Feinstein, "The Case for

CFE," *Arms Control Today*, vol. 21 (January/February 1991), pp. CFE Supp. 2-CFE Supp. 4; and Robert Leavitt, "Next Steps for European Conventional Arms Reductions," *Arms Control Today*, vol. 21 (January/February 1991), pp.12–16; Catherine Guicherd, *Treaty On Conventional Armed Forces in Europe (CFE): A Primer*, CRS Report for Congress, 90–615F (Washington: Congressional Research Service, December 1990); Gilles Andreani, "The Paris Summit: A Disarmament and Security Assessment," *Disarmament*, vol. 14, no. 2 (1991), pp. 1–10; Michael Moodie, "The Treaty on Conventional Armed Forces in Europe," *Disarmament*, vol. 14, no. 2 (1991), pp. 11–23; and Tadeusz Strulak, "The Treaty on Conventional Forces in Europe–A Polish View," *Disarmament*, vol. 14, no. 2 (1991), pp. 24–31.

18. See CSCE, "Vienna Document 1992 of the Negotiations on Confidence- and Security-Building Measures," CSCE/WV.31/Rev. 1, Vienna, February 28, 1992; Michael Z. Wise, "European Security Group Adopts New Rules to Limit Threats," *Washington Post*, March 5, 1992, p. A32; John Borawski, "The Vienna Negotiations on Confidence- and Security-Building Measures," *RUSI Journal*, vol. 135 (Autumn 1990) pp. 40–44; Bruce George, M.P., "The Negotiations on Confidence- and Security-Building Measures: The Vienna Agreement and Beyond," *NATO Review*, vol. 39 (February 1991), pp. 15–20; Victor-Yves Ghebali, *Confidence-Building Measures within the CSCE Process: Paragraph-by-Paragraph Analysis of the Helsinki and Stockholm Régimes*, UNIDIR Research Paper 3, UNIDIR/89/14 (New York: United Nations, March 1989); and John Borawski, *Security for a New Europe: The Vienna Negotiations on Confidence- and Security-Building Measures 1989–90, and Beyond* (London: Brassey's, 1972).

19. John D. Morrocco, "NATO Plans Call for Boosting Number of Combat Aircraft under CFE Treaty," *Aviation Week and Space Technology*, vol. 135 (July 15, 1991), pp. 26–27.

20. Jonathan Dean, "CFE: A Good First Step," *Arms Control Today*, vol. 20, (December 1990), p. 3. The Vienna II CSBM agreement, however, does provide reporting requirements for the activation of reserve forces as well as limits on the size of exercises involving such forces. See CSCE, "Vienna Document 1992 of the Negotiations on Confidence- and Security-Building Measures."

21. See Daalder, *The CFE Treaty*, pp. 22–24.

22. Jonathan Dean, "Some Characteristics and Requirements of a European Security System," paper presented to the Conference on Cooperative Security in the New European Order, Brookings Institution, April 8–10, 1991. The Vienna II accords have helped to close these loopholes, however.

23. Jenonne Walker, "New Thinking about Conventional Arms Control," *Survival* vol. 33 (January/February 1991), p. 60. See also Ivo H. Daalder, "The Future of Arms Control," *Survival*, vol. 34 (Spring 1992), pp. 51–73.

24. Walker, "New Thinking about Conventional Arms Control," p. 60. Special accommodation would also have to be made for the inclusion of the neutral states.

25. Fred Chernoff, "Arms Control, European Security, and the Future of the Western Alliance," *Strategic Review*, vol. 20 (Winter 1992), p. 26.

26. See the useful discussion of this topic in Kurt Gottfried, ed., *Towards a Cooperative Security Regime in Europe* (Cornell University Peace Studies Program, August 1989), pp. 106–08.

27. Walker, "New Thinking about Conventional Arms Control," p. 59.

28. Walker, "New Thinking about Conventional Arms Control," p. 59; and Dean, "The CFE Negotiations."

29. See John Borawski, "Oceanic Overtures: Building Confidence at Sea," *Arms*

Control Today, vol. 20 (July/August 1990), pp. 18–21; Andrei E. Granovskiy, "Necessity of Including Naval Armaments in Disarmament Negotiations," *Disarmament*, vol. 14, no. 1 (1991), pp. 155–67; Douglas M. Johnston, "Naval Arms Control: The Burden of Proof," *Disarmament*, vol. 14, no. 1 (1991), pp. 168–82; Gwyn Prins, "The United Nations and Naval Power in the Post-Cold-War World," *Disarmament*, vol. 14, no. 1 (1991), pp. 183–215; and James Eberle, "Global Security and Naval Arms Control," *Survival*, vol. 32 (July/August 1990), pp. 325–32.

30. See Steinbruner, "Revolution in Foreign Policy," pp. 81–83; and Johan Jorgen Holst, "Arms Control in the Nineties: A European Perspective," *Daedalus*, vol. 120 (Winter 1991), p. 107.

31. See Daalder, "The Future of Arms Control," pp. 55–57.

32. See Ivo H. Daalder, "Arms Control in the Post-Cold War Era: The Need for a Cooperative Approach," draft Occasional Paper, University of Maryland, Center for International Security Studies at Maryland, March 1992, p. 35.

33. Holst, "Arms Control in the Nineties," p. 99. See also the special edition on nonoffensive defense in Europe in *Bulletin of Atomic Scientists*, vol. 44 (September 1988), pp. 12–54; R.K. Huber, "A Model Analysis on Some Basic Properties of a Militarily Stable European Security System," Report No. Bericht-Nr. S-9005 (Neubiberg, Germany: Institut fur Angewandte Systemforschung und Operations Research (IASFOR), September 1990); and Dieter S. Lutz, "SIA and Defensive Zones," *Bulletin of Peace Proposals*, vol. 20, no. 1 (1989), pp. 71–80.

34. The construction of large-scale fortifications along national borders, for example, which is sometimes equated with defensive restructuring, would not be desirable. Despite their defensive advantages, they would suggest fears of hostile intent and generally strike a discordant note at a time when borders were becoming more permeable. If further defensive confidence were needed, nonobtrusive terrain modification systems, prechambering of roads and bridges, and rapidly deployable obstacle systems would be more acceptable. For a very useful discussion on the military value of barrier systems see Joshua M. Epstein, *Conventional Force Reductions: A Dynamic Assessment* (Brookings, 1990), pp. 67–72.

35. See Admiral Dieter Wellershof, "First Successful Step in CSBM Negotiations: The Military Doctrine Seminar," *NATO Review*, vol. 38 (April 1990), pp. 10–16; and Peter Almquist, "The Vienna Military Doctrine Seminar: Flexible Response vs. Defensive Sufficiency," *Arms Control Today*, vol. 20 (April 1990), pp. 21–25. Regular visits to airbases and military contacts have now been instituted by the Vienna II CSBM agreement.

36. Charter of Paris for a New Europe, signed November 21, 1990 (Washington: Commission on Security and Cooperation in Europe, 1990).

37. See Patrick E. Tyler, "Agreement Will Open Skies to Reconnaissance Flights," *New York Times*, March 21, 1992, p. 4. For more details, see "Open Skies Treaty Completed," *Focus on Vienna*, no. 27 (March 1992), pp. 1–2, 9–14.

38. One senior U.S. official also expressed the belief that under an Open Skies regime it will also be easier for the United States to share sensitive intelligence, especially that gained from satellites, with its allies. Interview.

39. See paper presented by Marton Krasznai of the Hungarian Ministry of Foreign Affairs to seminar on confidence-building measures, Henry L. Stimson Center, Washington, July 25, 1991.

40. NATO has set up a Verification Coordinating Committee with support staff to manage the alliance verification effort. Interview.

41. See Stares, *Command Performance*, pp. 87–100. The traditional problem associated with sharing intelligence among allies has apparently improved—for

example, during the Gulf War U.S. satellite imagery was shown to a meeting of the Defense Planning Committee at NATO headquarters. Interviews.

42. See Lynn Davis, Project Director, Project on Arms Control, "An Arms Control Strategy for CSCE: Helsinki 1992," Santa Monica, Rand Corp., March 23, 1992, pp. 13–14.

43. See Ivo H. Daalder, "The Role of Arms Control in the New Europe," *Arms Control*, vol. 12 (May 1991), pp. 20–34; and Holst, "Arms Control in the Nineties." Holst suggests establishing a CSCE military yearbook containing all the declared information, pp. 99–100.

44. See Robert Mauthner, "New World Watchdog in Search of Bark and Bite," *Financial Times*, March 24, 1992, p. 21.

45. See James A. Schear, "Compliance Diplomacy in a Multilateral Setting," in Michael Krepon and Mary Umberger, eds., *Verification and Compliance: A Problem-Solving Approach* (Ballinger, 1988), pp. 264–68; and Jozef Goldblat, *Agreements for Arms Control: A Critical Survey* (London: Taylor and Francis Ltd. for Stockholm International Peace Research Institute, 1982), pp. 95–111.

46. Apparently NATO is considering the formation of multinational inspection teams for the reduction phase of CFE implementation. Interview.

47. See Allan S. Krass, *Verification: How Much is Enough?* (Philadelphia: Taylor and Francis for Stockholm International Peace Research Institute, 1985), pp. 234–38. Assembly of Western European Union, Technological and Aerospace Committee, *Observation Satellites—a European Means of Verifying Disarmament: Symposium: Rome, 27th–28th March 1990: Official Record* (Paris: Office of the Clerk of the Assembly of WEU, 1990); Mr. Lenzer, Rapporteur, *Observation Satellites—A European Means of Verifying Disarmament—Guidelines Drawn from the Symposium*, report submitted on behalf of the Technological and Aerospace Committee, Assembly of Western European Union, Document 1230 (Paris: Assembly of WEU, May 1990). For a discussion of the technical requirements see Rear Admiral Sir Peter Anson Bt CB, "The Verification of Conventional Arms from Space: An Assessment of European Capability," Matra Marconi Space, Portsmouth, England.

48. It would still be desirable, however, to maintain some short-notice ground or aerial inspection capability for special contingencies.

49. The CSCE has begun to amend its decisionmaking rules to deal with this problem. See Mauthner, "New World Watchdog"; Robert Mauthner, "US Says CSCE Could Use Nato Force," *Financial Times*, February 26, 1992, p. 2; and Michael Bryans, "The CSCE and Future Security in Europe," A Report of a Two-Day Conference Held in Prague, December 4–5, 1991, Working Paper 40, Canadian Institute for International Peace and Security, Ottawa, March 1992.

50. For the most comprehensive discussion of the NACC and NATO's growing ties with the countries of Central and Eastern Europe, see Stephen J. Flanagan, "NATO and Central and Eastern Europe: From Liaison to Security Partnership," *Washington Quarterly*, vol. 15 (Spring 1992), pp. 141–51. See also William Drozdiak, "NATO States, Ex-East Bloc Meet for Talks," *Washington Post*, March 11, 1992, pp. A11, A16; Carey Goldberg, "NATO's Chief Hails Russian Partnership," *Los Angeles Times* (Washington edition), February 26, 1992, p. A3; and Theresa Hitchens, "NATO-East Europe Body Hits Snag," *Defense News*, March 9, 1992, p. 21.

51. See "Declaration on Western European Union," Council of the European Communities, Commission of the European Communities, *Treaty on European Union*, signed in Maastricht on February 7, 1992 (Luxembourg: Office for Official Publications of the European Communities, 1992), pp. 242–46.

52. For similar suggestions see Richard H. Ullman, "Enlarging the Zone of

Peace," *Foreign Policy*, no. 80 (Fall 1990), pp. 111–15; Harald Müller, *Beyond CSCE: Institutionalizing European Security*, draft PRIF Report, Frankfurt, November 1990. It is worth mentioning here that the Commonwealth of Independent States signed a Treaty on Collective Security at Tashkent on May 15, 1992. See "Treaty on CIS Collective Security Published," *Rossiyskaya Gazeta*, May 23, 1992, first edition, p. 2, in Foreign Broadcast Information Service, *Daily Report: Central Eurasia*, May 26, 1992, pp. 8–9.

53. NATO's political-military exercises to test crisis management procedures were suspended temporarily to review the standard scenarios and existing procedures. A new exercise is planned for 1993. Interview.

54. See Leif Klette, "The European Air Traffic Crisis: NATO's Search for Civil and Military Cooperation," *NATO Review*, vol. 39 (February 1991), pp. 24–29.

55. Robert Mauthner, "Nato Agrees Europe Peacekeeping Role," *Financial Times*, June 5, 1992, p. 4. See also Paul Beaver, "JDW Interview" of NATO Secretary General Dr. Manfred Worner, *Jane's Defence Weekly*, July 11, 1992, p. 32.

Part Three

PERSPECTIVES ON THE NEW GERMANY

EIGHT

The Implications of German Unification for Western Europe

Anne-Marie Le Gloannec

ON THE DAY THAT Germany was finally united, President Richard von Weizsäcker announced, "For the first time, we Germans are not a point of contention on the European agenda. Our unity has not been inflicted on anybody; it is the result of a peaceful agreement."[1] Indeed, Germany's unification took place with the consent of its neighbors and allies, in sharp contrast to the German unity won by Bismarck with "blood and iron" in 1871. While many European governments appeared to be ambivalent about German unification, public opinion in Western Europe hailed the liberation of East Germany and the peoples of Central and Eastern Europe as a triumph of freedom.

The European Community also did much to assuage concerns about Germany and facilitate unification. The Federal Republic's membership in the EC helped reassure those countries that feared the new Germany would once again embark on an independent course with ominous consequences for the rest of Europe. In the process, the EC received an added boost with the decision to buttress further economic and monetary integration with political union.

It is not entirely true, however, that Germany has ceased to be a point of contention. History—both recent and more distant—still haunts the minds of many. Divided or united, Germany has always been a great power or a pawn at the core of Europe and has always exerted a decisive influence on the continent. As a great power, it was too strong not to seek domination, but it was too weak to dominate for long. While the "Yalta system" temporarily solved the German question by dividing the country and incorporating its two halves into antagonistic alliances, unification has raised the concern that a sovereign Germany will now dominate the continent. As *Der Spiegel* asked rhetorically in 1989, are the Germans finally "getting what they sought in vain to obtain with two world wars?"[2]

Among West European states, apprehension over German unification has been more evident in the Netherlands, Denmark, Great Britain, and France than in Italy and Spain.[3] Political uneasiness, however, has been most obvious in Great Britain and France, the two West European powers that shared responsibility for Berlin's security and Germany's future. In Great Britain, the Chequers Conference in March 1990 and the Ridley affair in July 1990 actually stirred diplomatic waters. In France, President François Mitterrand tried in vain to put a brake on reunification and even prevent it by entering into an old-style "alliance de revers" with the Soviet Union, the GDR, and Poland, even traveling to Kiev and Leipzig and upholding Poland's position on the issue of the Oder-Neisse border.[4] But the French president eventually resorted to a more constructive policy by rallying Chancellor Helmut Kohl's support for a European union. Great Britain in turn sought reassurance within NATO, which it saw as a way of constraining Germany and enhancing Great Britain's status; France looked to the EC to play this role.

It is not just memories of the past, however, that cause the new Germany to loom large in all the schemes designed to establish a new order on the European continent. Germany is now too powerful not to play a central role. Unification and the demise of the inner and outer empires of the Soviet Union have removed traditional international constraints. Old dilemmas have vanished, including the need to import security from the United States at the cost of sovereignty and the desire to accommodate the Soviet Union at the cost of commitments to the Western alliance. This does not mean that Germany no longer needs to rely upon allies—above all the United States— or participate in security arrangements within NATO, the West European Union (WEU), or the Conference on Security and Cooperation in Europe (CSCE) to prevent potential conflicts. Nor does it mean that Germany no longer has to worry about potential trouble east of its borders or that the country is not constrained by new vulnerabilities or liabilities. What it means is that the political, geographical, and symbolic boundaries of German power have expanded. Geographically, both unification and the demise of the Soviet empire have shifted Germany's center of gravity eastward, situating the country again at the heart of the continent and at the crossroads of its flows and interactions. Germany is now the country in Europe surrounded by the greatest number of neighbors. Politically as well as geopolitically, the united country has regained its sovereignty and may become more powerful than ever, especially if its important partners to the east and west fare badly for any reason.

All seem to agree that Germany's power must be constrained in some way, but opinions differ on how to limit it. Supporters and opponents of the treaty reached at Maastricht establishing a European union point to Germany's increasing power and influence to support their arguments for or against European integration. While advocates of the treaty argue that integration and shared decisionmaking processes will limit Germany's influence, opponents contend that Germany will dominate even an integrated Europe, as no crucial decision can be adopted without its consent; as a result, the European community will increase rather than limit Germany's role.

The purpose of this chapter is to assess Germany's future role and the influence the united country is likely to have on Western Europe and, in particular, on the process of European integration. Such assessments are laden with uncertainties. For example, by the spring of 1992 the nature of the apprehension about Germany had changed considerably. The combination of a German economy weakened by the expense of reconstruction in the east, a public shaken by the wave of strikes in the west, and the poor showing made by the main political parties at the by-elections in April 1992, triggered foreign concern over Germany's weaknesses rather than its putative strengths. Awareness also grew that instabilities in the eastern and southeastern parts of Europe could have a significant bearing on Germany's political evolution, especially if political crises and military turmoil in the region foster mass immigration to Germany—a possibility that is already becoming a reality as a result of the Yugoslav civil war.

Despite the uncertainties, however, it is still possible to reach some conclusions about the impact of German unification on Western Europe. First, it is useful to compare the Federal Republic's economic power and political influence in Western Europe prior to unification with what has happened since. Second, the attitudes of the German public and the political establishment toward the country's new international status and responsibilities provide another useful indicator of Germany's future course. And finally, it is important to examine the challenges that are the most likely to affect Germany's role in key institutions such as the EC and NATO, as well as its relationship with its West European partners. Germany's role in the new Europe does not rest in its hands alone; what happens will depend greatly on whether its interests—in terms of stability and influence—are met by existing arrangements and by its partners, especially France, Germany's closest European ally.

German Economic Power and Political Leadership prior to Unification

Before the five Länder of the former GDR joined the Federal Republic, the West German economy was already the most powerful in the European Community. In both production and trade, the FRG had consolidated its position over the years, increasing its share of the EC's GNP and total trade from the time the Common Market was established until unification. According to an EC study, it produced 27 percent of the Community's GNP and accounted for 25 percent of total intra-Community trade. In fact, West Germany had become the world's major exporter and the main source of imports for all EC members except Ireland, which drew most of its imports from Great Britain. Similarly, West Germany had become a major exporter of direct investments, ranking fourth behind the United States, Great Britain, and Japan at the end of the 1980s. One-half of these investments were concentrated in Europe. France, Austria, Spain, and Great Britain attracted the bulk of German investments in Europe, although investment in Portugal and Ireland had also grown to above-average levels.[5]

In other areas as well, West Germany had become a pivotal country long before unification. The Federal Republic has for some years been the major net contributor to the EC's budget. In such areas as tourism, student exchange, and emigration West Germany before 1989 was "at the center of [a] network of multiple flows . . . [and took] part in *all* types of movements, often with a prominent role."[6] A pivotal country for all EC members, it also became increasingly a focal point for both the northern and southern countries on the EC's periphery as Western Europe grew more cohesive and its relations with the North and the South more dense.[7] Furthermore, Germany had already become the juncture between East and West for trade and emigration.[8]

In many respects, Germany's preeminent economic position within Europe has defied rational expectations. The rise in production and exports and the growth of structural surpluses has promoted prosperity in Germany, but its high prices—due in part to rising labor costs and a strong currency—should, on the face of it, have curbed exports and checked production. The answer to this apparent contradiction lies in the notion of a "virtuous circle."[9] For many years Germany has specialized in the production of high-quality equipment and chemical products that have remained in almost limitless international demand regardless of price. Far from hindering exports, the strong currency and higher prices have led to increased growth, higher wages, and ultimately internal stability. External growth and internal stability have thus complemented one another. In fact, Germany's entire socioeconomic system has been adapted to meet international demand—and has benefited from it.

But Germany's increasing wealth has brought disadvantages to its partners: "The corollary of a permanent improvement in the FRG is deterioration in the partner countries."[10] In trade, in particular, German surpluses have meant deficits for others. In fact Germany has been "the sole beneficiary among the major EC members, and the primary beneficiary from EC trading arrangements among all members as measured in terms of balance-of-trade surpluses."[11] In the 1970s and 1980s, these imbalances threatened to undermine the cohesion of the European Community. Wolfgang Hager, for instance, called them "a potential timebomb." For the system to last, "the weak have to be either bribed or forced to continue playing a game they lose."[12] Thus, under the guise of financial contributions from the EC budget or through direct loans, such as one to Italy in the 1970s, Germany helped countries with balance-of-trade deficits to continue playing by the rules of the game.

At the same time, the Federal Republic of Germany has continued to constrain the fiscal policies of the West European countries, largely because of the increasingly close intra-Community trade relations and stricter monetary rules—the Snake in the 1970s and, from 1979 on, the European Monetary System (EMS).[13] A system of fixed parities has compelled the other members of the Snake and of the EMS to pursue tight monetary policies in spite of their growing trade deficits with the Federal Republic. In other words, as trade relations have developed within the EC framework and as monetary policies have fallen into line, Germany's commercial, financial, and monetary partners have had to adopt the latter's deflationary policy, in spite of their own deficits.

However, the gains and losses that accrue from Community arrangements cannot be measured simply in terms of trade surpluses and budget contributions, nor in fact do they lend themselves to cost-benefit analyses. In particular, it is impossible to calculate the dynamic gains from trade or structural advantages: "To the extent that theories exist in the field of trade economics, both static and dynamic variants yield hypotheses which are the opposite of generally received wisdom: they suggest that Germany profited less than others from the formation of the Common Market. . . In the field of macro-economics, including exchange rates, there is a general consensus that the EC/EMS has benefited everyone. But no exceptional benefit for Germany can be credibly proven."[14]

In any case, whatever its gain may have been, Germany has come to dominate the European economies, so that the relationship with its partners is now asymmetrical. First, as the hub of all kinds of commercial and financial networks, the anchor of monetary stability, and for economic and monetary frameworks, Germany has retained a kind of veto power over all EC enterprises. Nothing can be done without Germany's support, a factor that sometimes irritates its partners. Second, Germany shapes decisions in more subtle ways, especially through the German model of economic and industrial organization. In the 1970s, many believed that this model could not be successfully imitated by others, for two reasons. If other countries successfully copied the German model, "one might wonder whether the formula could still be applied to the Federal Republic. The latter would be compelled to share with others its position on export markets."[15] And, the model's success appeared to rest, at least in part, on German social and cultural traits, which made its adoption by other countries questionable. By the 1980s and early 1990s, however, the original skepticism about the applicability of the German model had changed, and other countries had come to consider some of its characteristics worth adopting. For example, closer cooperation between banks and industry, vocational training, and consultations and co-decisions that gather employers and trade unions around the same table have all been advocated by successive contemporary French governments. Cooperation between banks and industry is also being introduced in France as a way of avoiding both nationalization and reprivatization. Many have begun to realize that Germany's success not only rests on macroeconomic balances but also is rooted in microeconomic performances that are worth imitating.

At the same time that Germany's microeconomic processes are being held up as an example, its larger economic and political arrangements are also being viewed as a general blueprint for the European Community. The future European bank, for example, has been patterned on the Bundesbank, and others are arguing that the German system of shielding decisions on monetary policy made by the Bundesbank in Frankfurt from the direct political influence of Bonn should be applied to the Community. Germany's political organization, particularly the devolution of power between Bund and Länder, is also being held up as a model in the context of European Community discussions on subsidiarity.[16]

The increasing acceptance of the German model has certainly eased the problems associated with German dominance within the Community. Those countries that accept Germany as a model more easily accept the country's position. There has been very little talk of France leaving the EMS, for instance, while Great Britain accepts both the German model and the European Community, if only half-heartedly.[17] On the whole, "Germany's quiet influence in the EC has grown largely by virtue of its ideological leadership."[18]

Germany's economic dominance, however, has not translated into political leadership within the European Community. Only once in the thirty-year history of the Common Market and the EC has the Federal Republic taken the initiative, and that only recently, when Germany and France created the EMS. A number of international and domestic factors account for this lack of German leadership. The most important is the Federal Republic's political system, in particular its limited chancellorial authority; the sectorization of policy responsibilities among individual German ministries, which undermines overall policy coherence; Bund-Länder dynamics, with their ongoing power struggles (especially after the signing of the Single European Act, when the Länder tried to win back powers devolved by Bonn to Brussels and now again during the ratification process of the Maastricht treaty); and, last but not least, party politicization, for instance in agriculture.[19] As a result, "no clear framework of action reflecting national interests" has been established. For while the Federal Republic has been able to successfully defend sectoral interests—in agriculture or the textile industry, for example—it has been much less able to frame EC policies and take initiatives. Paradoxically, the

EC's dominant economy is a "vague actor," as Bulmer and Paterson have dubbed it.[20]

Second, the European Community itself reduced the likelihood that West Germany or any other member would become a hegemonic power by creating an area of shared prosperity and peace based on the resolution of old disputes between former enemies. West Germany did not seek political power, in part because it was not expected to do so and in part because it was constrained by the written and unwritten rules of the system. At best it shared initiatives with other governments, mainly the French, with which it devised the EMS and launched the two intergovernmental conferences (IGCs) that led up to the Maastricht summit, but also with the Italians, resulting in the ill-fated proposal put forward by Foreign Ministers Hans-Dietrich Genscher and Emilio Colombo. Indeed, French-German relations were looked upon as "a convenient substitute for German leadership."[21]

The Federal Republic's limited sovereignty—both in the symbolic and more tangible legal and political sense—also had an indirect bearing on its position in the Community. As part of a divided nation, at the front line between two conflicting military systems, it had to import its security from the United States and seek accommodation with the Soviet Union; it also had to ensure its own survival and alleviate the tension that might have hampered the development of intra-German governmental relations and societal ties. In addition, it had to work within frameworks designed at the end of World War II to deter or contain Soviet aggression and prevent a German revival. As such, these frameworks could not be challenged, and while they constrained Germany, they also assured it of protection against the Soviets. Within the given frameworks, West Germany would become NATO's main European pillar and the most important European ally of the United States.

Nevertheless, these frameworks limited the expansion of German power, perpetuated Germany's subordinate status, and anchored the present in the past. Within these frameworks, the country would forever play second fiddle to the United States. Germany's influence in the East was also constrained by the European divide, limiting its relations with East Germany and Central and Eastern Europe and providing its partners with some leverage. The postwar status granted to Great Britain and France was derived in part from Germany's division and diminution. Both countries became quadripartite powers and permanent members of the UN Security Council—positions ensuing from the fact that they had been among the victors. In spite of the increasing imbalance that Germany's economic dominance fostered in Franco-German relations and within the European Community, France maneuvered to reinforce its position by reaching for limited nuclear power and partial independence, a strategy strengthened by its presence in Berlin, the geographical core of Germany, and by its position as one of the authorities responsible for Germany's future.

The Economic and Political Impact of Unification on the EC

According to major German and foreign economic institutes, unification will have a short-term adverse effect but a long-term positive impact on Germany's position within the Community. Although the incorporation of the old East German Länder involves enormous costs that have reduced the overall performance of the German economy in the EC, this setback is expected to be temporary. Over the long term, the reconstruction of eastern Germany will provide a boost to the economy. According to estimates by the Industrial Bank of Japan, the share of the united Germany in the Community's GNP will increase—despite the collapse of production in the former GDR from the sudden and almost complete liberalization of the economy in 1990–91—from a combined total of 25 percent for both Germanies in 1985 to 28 percent in 1995 and 30 percent in the year 2000.[22]

Trade should also expand. After declining in 1991, exports are expected to resume, and the surge in imports resulting from a boom in consumption in the five new Länder in 1990–91 will presumably abate.[23] Thus the trade surpluses that shrank drastically in 1991 as Germany's partners profited from the opportunities in eastern Germany will rise again from 1992 on, though at a much lower rate than before unification. German investments abroad have not been affected by capital flows to the five new Länder, however. On a yearly basis, the united Germany is still a net exporter of investments: in 1991, the outflow of direct investments abroad remained about the same as in 1990.[24] Fiscal constraints remain, however. With the public budget strained by the costs of reconstruction in eastern Germany, and with more money in circulation since unification, the Bundesbank has not modified its tight policies. A series of interest rate increases in 1990 were passed on to Germany's partners, perpetuating the imbalances between Germany and other EC countries.

Overall, once the upheavals of 1989–91 subside, Germany's pivotal role will undoubtedly increase. Various factors point in this direction: the growth in Germany's export and import capacities, in terms of goods, capital, and labor; the integration of the EC through the single market, the Schengen agreement (which would abolish border controls between all the signatories to the treaty of Rome except Italy), and the Maastricht treaty; and, last but not least, the resumption and the development of relations of all kinds between the EC and the former members of the Soviet inner and outer empire. Even in terms of demography, the Federal Republic may turn out to be much more dynamic than is often assumed. Although the united Germany accounts for only 23 percent of the EC's total population (as compared with West Germany's 19 percent before unification) and its natural population growth is modest, it attracts numerous emigrants, many of German origin, as well as asylum seekers.

In the political realm, unification has cleared away many of the impediments that prevented West German governments from assuming a more decisive leadership position within the European Community, but for some time it was not clear that the German leadership was ready to exploit its new position and become more assertive. Both before and after the U.S.-led intervention during the Gulf War, the German government lacked clarity, hesitating either to publicly support U.S. policy or take direct action to uphold Turkish security. It did, however, contribute decisively to the military success of the Western coalition.[25] In stark contrast, a few months later Germany launched a series of initiatives—both unilaterally and together with other EC members such as France—designed to influence the reaction of the Community and the United Nations to the Yugoslav crisis. These actions were motivated by Germany's assessment of the future of Yugoslavia, which differed radically from that of Great Britain and France. These countries adhered to the fiction that the status quo in Yugoslavia could be maintained and advocated withholding recognition of the breakaway states of Slovenia and Croatia. Germany, Austria, and, to a certain extent, Belgium and Denmark took heed of the centrifugal forces undermining the Yugoslav federation and advocated early recognition in order to pressure Serbia into desisting from further aggression against the secessionist states.

Frustrated over the EC's failure to act, the German government threatened more than once to bypass the Community and unilaterally recognize both states. This breach showed that members of both the Christian Democratic Union (CDU) and the Christian Social Union (CSU) were eager to defend their stance at any cost, even if this meant breaking away from EC frameworks. German unilateralism on the issue, however, was softened by the fact that Germany recognized Slovenia and Croatia only after the other members of the Community had signaled that they were moving toward recognition.[26] Germany also launched a series of proposals with France. First, in September 1991, they suggested that a buffer force be set up between the warring factions in Croatia; in April 1992, they put forth a plan for sending the UN peace mission stationed in Croatia to Bosnia-Hercegovina. But these initiatives may have been directed more at patching up differences between the two countries than at finding solutions to the crisis.

This pattern of assertiveness and cooperation in German foreign policy can be observed in other areas. With little prior consultation, Germany requested an increase in its representation in the European Parliament through a change in the status of the eighteen East German observers invited to Strasbourg in 1990 that would make them permanent representatives. The Kohl government also requested that German be made an official language of the Community. It pressed for the installation of the future European bank in Frankfurt or Bonn, a move that would turn either city into a major financial center. It called for a redistribution of the contributions to the EC budget.

And, last but not least, the Bundesbank decided to increase interest rates just after the signing of the Maastricht treaty.[27] All these steps raised concern about what came to be called the "new German assertiveness."[28]

To be fair, some of these initiatives are the logical continuation of previous policies. The ill-timed rate increase, for example, proved that the Bundesbank responds first to German economic concerns even though its actions have consequences for all the European economies simply because of Germany's economic dominance. The increase has been justified economically, serving as a warning against both the government's policy of financing unification with increased public deficits and the wage demands of the trade unions. It is also politically logical, since the Bundesbank is not accountable to any German or European polity. But the rate hike nevertheless demonstrated that Germany's economic interests are the Bundesbank's primary consideration.[29] It is less obvious, however, whether Germany's other demands reflect a new sense of national purpose or just the leadership's willingness to be more assertive.[30]

At the same time that Germany has shown signs of more independent behavior, the German government has also worked with the country's partners (mainly the French) to further EC integration and to devise a new European architecture. The first indication of this trend toward cooperative action was spelled out on November 28, 1989, in Chancellor Kohl's 10-Point Plan for unifying the two Germanies within the EC framework. This was followed in April 1990 by the Kohl-Mitterrand proposal to the EC to convene two IGCs that would further European integration. This move did not signal a passive acceptance of integration, however, for Kohl wanted to shape the agenda for the conferences. As a corollary to economic and monetary union (EMU), he insisted on greater political integration that would lead to a common foreign and security policy and a European defense identity. He also asked that the European Parliament's authority be increased and advocated including in Community affairs such matters as justice, immigration, and asylum policy.[31] While the success of democracy in Germany has turned the country into the champion of the European Parliament, some of its reasons for promoting a full-fledged political union are practical as well as idealistic. The Bundesbank, for instance, has repeatedly emphasized that a monetary union requires, among other things, a close political union to foster the convergence of economies. Placing immigration and asylum policy on the Community agenda may also help the federal government impose changes in immigration laws.

As far as the European architecture is concerned, the German government has put forward a number of proposals to strengthen and broaden the role and scope of action of all security organizations on the continent—NATO, the WEU, and the CSCE. While the government stresses the "complementarity" of these security organizations, it has focused on those best suited to promoting

German interests. For example, it is acutely aware of the necessity of stabilizing the eastern part of the continent, a concern that guided the joint U.S.-German proposal in the fall of 1991 to set up the North Atlantic Cooperation Council (NACC). The NACC is intended to promote, in the absence of a security guarantee, greater cooperation among NATO, the new democracies of Central and Eastern Europe, and the successor states to the Soviet Union. In January 1992, Genscher suggested using NATO to coordinate Western assistance in the destruction of nuclear weapons in the Commonwealth of Independent States (CIS), although he emphasized that Germany would not seek to gain access to sensitive information in the process. Genscher's suggestion was a response to the earlier French proposal to convene a conference of the four nuclear powers in Europe—the United States, Great Britain, the CIS, and France—to discuss this same topic, a proposal that clearly excluded Germany and attempted to short-circuit NATO. Similarly, he proposed that the West provide financial support to scientists in the former Soviet Union to prevent them from selling their expertise to countries seeking to develop nuclear weapons, a proposal that was eventually accepted by the international community.

A staunch advocate of pan-European arrangements, Genscher openly discussed in September 1991 his ideas for strengthening the CSCE, including endowing it with a Security Council and special forces for peacekeeping (blue helmets) and fighting ecological disasters (green helmets). Together with France, in February 1992 he also put forward the idea of setting up an arbitration tribunal within the CSCE. Before he left office, however, Genscher had become more supportive of West European defense schemes, reflecting a general trend toward the "Europeanization" of German security policy.[32] For although Germany has played a central role in revamping NATO's doctrine and in increasing cooperation with former members of the Warsaw Treaty Organization (WTO), some within the country have criticized the lack of boldness in these reforms. At the Bundeswehr commanders' convention in Leipzig in May 1992, Inspector-General Klaus Naumann asked for a "more European NATO" in which the United States would have a less decisive influence.[33] An increasing number of politicians and government officials have also voiced similar criticisms and shown an increasing willingness to further West European and Franco-German military cooperation.[34] While the chancellor used to be a fairly lonely voice, he recently gained support from the new Minister of Defense Volker Rühe and the recently appointed Minister of Foreign Affairs Klaus Kinkel.

One manifestation of this growing interest in military cooperation is the Franco-German corps, which was formalized in May 1992. Although still limited in scope and aims, the corps is to encompass about 35,000 troops and will have three missions: the defense of Western territories in line with

NATO and WEU commitments; peacekeeping and peace enforcement; and humanitarian actions. It is hoped, however, that it will eventually become the nucleus of a European corps. The two governments look upon it as a means of both strengthening NATO and furthering the goal of a European defense identity as conceived at Maastricht, objectives that both the United States and Great Britain have criticized as being mutually contradictory. Whether or not NATO and a European defense identity come into conflict with one another, however, Franco-German military cooperation certainly strengthens Franco-German relations in general and also gives Germany more room to maneuver with the United States.[35]

Public Attitudes toward Germany's New International Status and Future Role

Unification has changed how Germans define their identity, their interests, and their role in the world.[36] Understanding these changes not only helps explain the sometimes contradictory aspects of German policy since unification but also provides some indication of Germany's future behavior.

If opinion surveys conducted in the wake of unification can be believed, Germans have confidence in their own achievements and do not look to the quadripartite powers—the United States, Great Britain, and France—for direction. In a poll published in early 1990, only 6 percent of Germans questioned said they considered the United States a model, while 8 percent said France, and only 2 percent Great Britain. Switzerland and Sweden obtained the highest ratings, with 40 percent and 29 percent, respectively.[37] A Rand survey made public in January 1992 showed similar results, with Germans giving themselves high marks in overall terms, especially in the areas of social justice, broad-based affluence, culture, and even technology and science.[38]

More striking is the shift in the Germans' appreciation of their country's role in Europe. In October 1990 a mere 29 percent of East and West Germans advocated a greater role for their country, but 43 percent supported it in December 1991; in both cases, more West Germans than East Germans took this stand.[39] The Rand survey confirmed these findings: 59 percent of those interviewed advocated greater responsibilities for Germany, and 64 percent considered Germany the country most likely to play an increasingly important part in world politics by the year 2000. Some 43 percent named Japan, 27 percent the United States, and 26 percent the USSR; the European Community, however, was seen by 82 percent as destined to play a greater role.[40] These figures seem to indicate that Germans expect to see their country play a greater role within both the EC and international frameworks.

The surveys nevertheless display an ambiguous picture of German attitudes toward international cooperation. Germans still approve of keeping their country in NATO, as the Rand survey indicates (64 percent of west Germans and 35 percent of east Germans support this idea; over the last decade, such approval has varied from 62 percent in 1981 to 87 percent in 1985). Yet support for a continued U.S. military presence and for the deployment of nuclear weapons has eroded: a growing majority of Germans favor the withdrawal of U.S. forces, and a high percentage advocate giving Germany a greater say over nuclear weapons deployed on its territory. Germans increasingly question the necessity of deploying U.S. troops and nuclear weapons on German territory, although insisting on continued membership in NATO. As outlined above, in 1990 a slight majority of 53 percent of all Germans favored a complete withdrawal of U.S. troops, but in 1991 the figure increased to 57 percent.[41] Only 48 percent of respondents support a common European currency, 44 percent political union, and 40 percent a common defense. The Allensbach Institute has corroborated these data: 26 percent of the respondents favor a common European currency and 49 percent oppose it, while only a minority look forward to the creation of a single European market.[42]

Ambiguous as the findings seem, a clear conclusion may be drawn: Germans still show a preference for working within international frameworks, but those frameworks should be loose or limited. This trend has been more evident since the conclusion of the Maastricht agreement in December 1991. Some 75 percent of Germans interviewed in the spring of 1992 thought that "Bonn could not afford to pay for European union while the costs for German unity were mounting."[43] The German press also vented strong criticisms against Kohl's compromise on monetary union at Maastricht. The widely read *Bild Zeitung* wept over "unsere schöne DM" (our beautiful DM) while the *Süddeutsche Zeitung*, a liberal daily, strongly attacked the chancellor's move.[44] Unfortunately, all the details of the decision have not yet been made clear, and some of them must still be hammered out, while the full consequences of economic union remain unclear not only in Germany but in the other EC member countries. Still, the fierceness of the often very emotional reactions has led some to wonder whether Germans have become more resistant to change because they fear that their welfare, independence, and pride are at stake; or whether, as the German philosopher Jürgen Habermas has argued, the deutsche mark is the symbolic manifestation of the German national consciousness.[45] In this context it is also worth noting that members of the CSU expressed dismay at the Maastricht agreement, while Kohl's CDU showed signs of nationalistic stirrings as it struggled to devise policies toward Yugoslavia outside the EC framework.[46] As a result, Chancellor Kohl himself may have deemed it domestically wise to recognize Slovenia and

Croatia a little ahead of other Community members in order to appease those conservatives critical of the government's policy.

Despite these indications of a willingness to take a more independent line in the future, the evidence that Germany will continue to work within international institutions remains powerful. Kohl, in particular, wants to further Germany's entanglement in the EC by promoting the integration process of the EC itself. In doing so, he belongs to those Germans who interpret the history of their country in terms of the *Sonderweg*, that particular, singular path Germany has followed from the nineteenth century through World War I and eventually to the rise of Nazism and World War II. This "German catastrophe," as the German historian Friedrich Meinecke called it, caused the country's ideological and political isolation and its encirclement by unfriendly neighbors. Seen in this light, Germany's integration into international frameworks offers a guarantee against a return to such a calamitous course. To that extent, Kohl may well be considered the true heir to the first chancellor of the Second Republic, Konrad Adenauer. Some Germans, however, draw other conclusions from this interpretation of German history. The teachings of the past have paradoxically led them to revive the idea of the *Sonderweg*. According to them, Germans now know the horrors of war better than anyone else and thus have a special mission to fulfill in working for peace. During the Gulf War, their views caused a domestic debate with those who believed that universal values sometimes have to be defended at the cost of peace.[47]

Such arguments permeate the debate over whether or not the Bundeswehr should intervene in troubled regions outside the NATO area. The federal government has so far interpreted the constitution, or Basic Law, restrictively, limiting possible military actions to the designated geographical area. However, this restriction weighs heavily on German diplomacy, as its Gulf War and Yugoslav policies have demonstrated. As a consequence, Germany is heading toward a revision of guidelines for out-of-area actions. It faces two separate kinds of criticism, first from those who oppose intervention outside the NATO area, and second from those who question whether an appropriate institutional framework for such intervention exists. For the latter, intervention may take place, but only in those forums that have the international legitimacy to define peace actions. While Genscher favored working through the United Nations, an informal coalition of liberals—including the Free Democratic Party (FDP) leader Otto Graf Lambsdorff, conservatives such as Defense Minister Volker Rühe, and members of the Bundeswehr such as Klaus Naumann—advocate the possibility of WEU interventions.[48] At the moment consensus is more likely to be reached for humanitarian actions (as in Cambodia, for instance) than it is for peacekeeping actions, let alone peace enforcement. And even if such a consensus expands to include further options, it will be nearly impossible to muster military missions in those sensitive areas where the Wehrmacht fought during World War II. Germany must rely upon others to fight in these regions—and may indeed someday need their help.

Future Challenges

As Germany's identity and interests change in the wake of unification and the country grows more powerful, many wonder if Europe can adjust sufficiently to accommodate its new status and if the integrating frameworks that formerly contained Germany will still be able to do so. The challenges are multiple. The EC, more than NATO, was created as a Community of equals that would balance out imbalances. Now that Germany is changing, can the Community still regulate growing imbalances? Meanwhile, Germany's environment is also changing. The disintegration of the Soviet empire and concomitant disappearance of the Soviet threat, along with the partial withdrawal of the United States, have loosened the traditional NATO framework. And despite recent agreements, the EC's efforts to integrate further may be halted or delayed as the Community widens to increase its membership. The Community faces three basic challenges: furthering its integration, redefining its security policy and developing appropriate security arrangements, and creating an effective mechanism for incorporating new members.

Integration

At the same time that the EC has made German unification more acceptable to its members by providing the institutional framework to constrain the Federal Republic and keep it firmly anchored in the West, unification has also accelerated integration within the Community itself. While the Single European Act launched a new stage in the creation of the single market by 1993, unification triggered a new stage in political integration. The decision of the Community's three main actors—Kohl, Mitterrand, and Jacques Delors—and of the Community's two main bodies—the European Commission and the Council of Ministers—to organize two IGCs on economic, monetary, and political union was a direct response to unification and the possible delay it might cause to European integration. Germany thus acted as a catalyst to further integration. In turn, Germany has apparently pledged its willingness to abide by the rules of the game within the Community, on the grounds that an increase in power calls for increased limitations of power. Further integration was the price of unity: German and European unification were expected to go hand in hand.

Yet integration as a means of binding Germany to Europe is now being questioned by German and non-German critics who believe that the success of such a tactic is not assured and that the cost is too high. Some of Germany's partners wonder whether integration is in fact the best way to mitigate Germany's dominance, or whether it will only make the unified country more powerful. This latter assumption in part fueled the Danish rejection of the Maastricht Treaty in June 1992 and has caused concern in Great Britain and France among such opponents of the treaty as former Prime Minister Margaret Thatcher, former French Defense Minister Jean-Pierre Chevène-ment, and former Minister of Social Affairs Philippe Seguin. Governmental policies in these two countries toward European integration have been ambiguous at best. For the past twelve years, the French president has looked upon Europe as a way to tie down Germany—both the pacifist Germany of the 1980s, which was supposed to be looking eastward, and the united Germany of today—and to ensure France's competitiveness and position. In practice, this has meant as much integration as possible and as little as necessary. In other words, there has been much integration in the economic field, where Germany dominates, and little in other areas, where France could retain some independence, power, or prestige within the Community and internationally.

Consequently, the French government has not taken up all German requests to further political union, in particular those to enhance the authority of the European Parliament; it opposes Germany's demand to increase its parliamentary representation; and it tried for a while to limit Franco-German military cooperation, advocating a common defense identity without putting forward concrete proposals. France's participation in the Gulf War, its efforts to boost the role of the UN Security Council, where it holds a permanent seat, and its call for a conference of the four nuclear powers in Europe can be seen in the same light. Great Britain has championed a parallel strategy. While it sought to enhance its power, just as France did, by sending troops to the Gulf in early 1991 and by convening a UN Security Council summit at the beginning of 1992, it has relied primarily on its ties with the United States, its position within NATO, and the possible enlargement of the EC to balance Germany. As such, Great Britain wants to refurbish NATO as little as possible to avoid redefining both its own and Germany's positions.

Can the Community's "existence and policies help dampen a rising hegemon's national aspirations so that they remain acceptable to the less powerful states, without at the same time appearing too burdensome to the hegemon?" A united Germany may be "satisfied with certain arrangements (including monetary union, if it is on German terms) but unwilling to extend them further. Its government, absorbed by the costly 'rehabilitation' of the former East Germany and by calls for aid in Central and Eastern Europe, could become less willing to pay large sums to the Common Agricultural Policy (CAP) and to regional funds, its industrialists and bankers less willing to cooperate and merge with others, its diplomats less eager to seek a European legitimacy."[49] Germans may frown at both the aims and costs of integration; some of the latest moves mentioned earlier, such as the call for redistributing contributions to the EC budget, express Germans' dissatisfaction with current rules and can be interpreted as a demand for a readjustment of the old balance of losses and rewards. Furthermore, more stringent commitments in the context of economic, monetary, and political union or increased contributions to the EC budget will upset Germany's domestic balances between Bund and Länder and among the government, Parliament, and public opinion, in addition to further straining the financial system. Such demands may also disrupt the intra-EC balance, since contributions to the EC budget have always been conceived not only in financial terms but also as part of a broader package—financial, commercial, economic, and political—that weighs many factors. In this framework, dominance entails costs to assuage political concern among partners.

Last but not least, the debates over the ratification of the Maastricht treaty evidence a chasm between public opinion and the government in a number of signatory countries, primarily Denmark and Germany. While the treaty will certainly be ratified by the German Parliament in spite of unfavorable public opinion, the SPD opposition is insisting on a parliamentary vote in 1996, before the third phase of an EMU is launched, while some are asking for a referendum. Two factors account for this alienation. First, the possible outcome of an EMU remains unclear. Individual countries will no doubt accrue some losses, such as dwindling decisionmaking power at the national level and increased budgetary contributions, but the potential gains are much less certain. While the creation of a common currency and a central bank by 1999 is intended as a compulsory matter, the last stage of EMU may not be launched if Germany does not fulfill the budgetary and inflationary criteria for entry. Second, the debate has been fueled in part by the discrepancy between the specific national and international frameworks and the open-endedness of the integration process. An open-ended Community is abstract in the long run, offering nonspecific rewards in terms of peace and prosperity, not to mention cooperation. As far as its future structure is concerned, it is a new subject of international law more comparable to the Holy Roman Empire than to the United States. Open-endedness, however, may be a disturbing concept for the people of all twelve member countries. Roger de Weck, a leading journalist formerly with the weekly *Die Zeit*, is right in thinking that "there are many irrational things in the European Community, yet there is no rational alternative to the Community."[50] But rationality alone is not likely to mobilize the support of constituencies or to generate legitimacy, all the more as, at the same time, the public identity is still defined in national terms and the role of the European Parliament remains limited. This is the reason why the greater part of the political, economic, and intellectual establishments in Germany argue for the democratization of the Community. This is also the reason why some intellectuals in France, drawing the opposite conclusion, extol the virtues of the nation-states.[51]

Security

The second challenge concerns future European security arrangements. Until the 1989–91 upheavals, one of the tasks NATO had to perform—besides containing the Soviet Union and providing a basis for the American presence in Europe—was that of tying in Germany. As a hegemon outside Europe, the United States had equalized the European powers by burying the enmities that had led to two world wars. It pacified Europe even though it provoked hostility in those countries that resented their loss of sovereignty, and it became the umbrella under which the EC could be established.[52] For these reasons, Western governments wanted the united Germany to remain in NATO, for a Germany outside NATO would have caused concern, especially among the East and West Europeans, and a NATO without Germany would have been deprived of personnel, logistics, and space. While the Western governments were adamant, so were the Germans, who regard NATO as a provider of collective defense, a channel for U.S. support that was much valued during the unification process, and a safeguard against a renationalization of defense policies in Europe.

Yet NATO is undergoing changes as a consequence of the withdrawal of both superpowers—or, more precisely, of the almost complete withdrawal of a Soviet Union that has ceased to exist and of the partial withdrawal of the United States in the wake of the Gulf War and its own domestic problems. As a result, most of NATO's traditional functions are changing. With the collapse of the inner and outer Soviet empire, threats have given way to risks and containment to the necessity of both devising a means to ensure that a threat is not reconstituted in the successor states and designing ways to help stabilize and reconstruct them, thus tying them in. One of NATO's new mandates is to assist the successor states in abiding by arms reduction agreements and commitments to which the Soviet Union or Russia subscribed by destroying weapons and preventing their dissemination.

Is NATO obligated to perform all these roles, and if so, to what extent? NATO members have different points of view, according to the importance they attach to other political priorities—such as the necessity to keep the United States in Europe and to balance it; the need to hem Germany in or to increase its power; the desire to further European political integration or to sustain independence or cooperation within NATO according to the forum they think they can best manipulate: NATO, the WEU, the CSCE, or the United Nations. As Germany, Great Britain, and France all aim at maximizing their security and power, they resort to different strategies that are undergoing important changes. The most dramatic of all may well turn out to be the gradual Europeanization of Germany, as indicated earlier.

Franco-German military cooperation may serve a number of purposes. It is intended to prevent the nationalization or renationalization of defense policies, both German and French. A future Germany outside NATO might renationalize its defense in the absence of significant European arrangements; on the other hand, it might give added impetus to such arrangements, considering that the Europeans fear Germany's independence. As Josef Joffe contends, it might even want to develop nuclear weapons in order to enhance its security.[53] In any case, the dissolution of NATO would be either a recipe for disaster—a recreation of nineteenth century Europe—or for success—but only if it promoted a European defense community. The French government has long hesitated between the search for independence and the promotion of European integration. To conceal ambiguities, Mitterrand and Kohl put forward in 1990 a broad vision of a European defense identity. Yet the notion remained abstract until the fall of 1991, and, in practice, the French government even contradicted its own intention, announcing in July 1990 the withdrawal of French troops from Germany, as though the stationing of French troops accrued from victors' rights and not from bilateral agreements. The French president wanted to preempt any future German demands that French troops withdraw, while the German chancellor wanted the French troops to remain. The misunderstanding was partly mended in October 1991, when both agreed to enlarge the Franco-German brigade and support turning the WEU into the security arm of the European Community, a decision formalized at the bilateral summit in La Rochelle in May 1992.

The Franco-German corps and possible Eurocorps will allow the continued deployment of French troops on German territory, as well as the stationing of a limited number of German troops in France, and is thus a political signal of the willingness of the two countries to act together. In the medium term, it may help the German government overcome the public's reluctance to see the deployment of German troops beyond NATO areas. In the long term, it may eventually contribute to the stability of the continent, according to the missions defined at La Rochelle. If it facilitates the definition of a European foreign and security policy, it may also consolidate the European Union. Last but not least, it may strengthen the European pillar of NATO while at the same time increasing Germany's margin of maneuverability with the United States. For this very reason, the Franco-German initiative met resistance in the United States as well as in Great Britain, the Netherlands, and Denmark. As hostile to increasing NATO's political role as the French government is (and the president is more opposed to it than Pierre Joxe, his minister of defense), it still sees NATO as performing important functions—providing, for instance, logistics and information for overseas operations. NATO's political function, however, is a point of contention. Mitterrand criticizes, among other things, the institutionalization of links with the former communist countries through the NACC and of ties with the CSCE through the direct use of NATO troops, leaving to the German government the delicate task of mending Franco-American rifts.

Franco-German military cooperation, strengthened as it is by other cooperative ventures, does not preclude friction. Besides the differences over nuclear weapons in the former Soviet Union, France has made no attempt to revamp the UN Security Council to reflect the unification of Germany, and it only moved to discard the short-range Hades missile (in June of 1992). On both subjects, German criticism has been restrained but not altogether absent; debates in Parliament in the fall of 1991 echoed the country's uneasiness, and while Chancellor Kohl has publicly stated that a seat in the UN Security Council is not at issue, public rumors and outside pressures, such as Japan's or Italy's suggestion to give the EC a permanent seat on the Security Council, will probably combine to moot the question.[54]

Enlargement

Finally, the very question of providing help to the former members of the Soviet empire will bear on Germany's relations with its Western partners, particularly in the European Community. The old specter of Rapallo is gone, as the Federal Republic is no pariah and the former Soviet Union has little to offer. Certainly, relations between Germany and countries east of its borders are not free of historical memories, and cultural affinities remain, in particular with Central and Eastern Europe, an area where states can be defined as latecomers, just as the German state was. The myth of complementarity between Germany's technology and Russia's natural resources has also persisted. Yet rather than providing an area of opportunity for Germany, Central and Eastern Europe is seen as a source of potential troubles of all kinds: political, economic, social, and military.

The closest, richest Western neighbor to the new democracies, Germany is vulnerable to virtually all developments in these countries. Politically and even militarily, it might be drawn into turmoil should Soviet troops stationed on its soil be involved in or become an instrument of blackmail. Socially, it is already the main refuge for asylum-seekers fleeing troubled areas. Some 260,000 of them came in 1991, two-thirds from the east and the southeast of Europe, as well as 220,000 Central and East Europeans of German origin.[55] Politically, it may well be called upon to become involved in a number of countries; yet, in some others, even in those where German investments are needed, such as Poland or Czechoslovakia, the possibilities are marred by the past. Financially, its budget is strained and it is overcommitted, though some of the credits granted to the former Soviet Union are linked to the agreement on Germany's unification and Soviet troop withdrawal. Germany contributes more than half of all the EC aid granted to Central and Eastern Europe within the PHARE Program, excluding the CIS. As a result, both the government and opposition have resisted further commitments, including increased contributions to the EC budget, despite the fact that these could be used to fund foreign aid to Central and Eastern Europe. In any case, Germany does not have the capacity to shoulder all the burdens of stabilizing and reconstructing these countries.

Almost all German politicians, analysts, or journalists insist on the urgency of reconstructing Central and Eastern Europe—"the second European reconstruction" after the rebuilding of Western Europe in the post–World War II era—and of integrating it into the European Community.[56] Thus Germany seems ready once more to alter the Community by promoting enlargement, now that it has catalyzed integration. This policy, however, could have very different outcomes. On the one hand, Central and Eastern Europe could actually draw Germany closer to the EC and its main partners within the EC. The immensity of immigration problems, the implications of the freedom of movement within the Community granted by the Schengen agreement, and, last but not least, the necessity faced by the German government to change its constitution to restrict immigration (a move opposed by the Social Democrats [SPD]) all explain why, at the Maastricht summit, Kohl suggested a common European policy toward immigration.[57] On the other hand, while this task may bring Germany and Eastern Europe closer together, it may drive a wedge between Germany and its Western neighbors, especially France, as well as between Germany and the countries of the Southern tier. Part of the budget increase requested by the European Commission should be redirected toward the poorer states of Southern Europe, a demand harshly criticized by German commentators: "While the Minister of Foreign Affairs Genscher warns that the West cannot fare well in the long run if the East suffers, the current presidency in Lisbon shouts back that the EC is here for Portugal, not for Poland."[58]

The French government has displayed a stiff resistance to granting Central and Eastern European countries access to both the European Community and European markets. In 1991, it devised the grand scheme of a European Confederation, which was put forth rather vaguely by Mitterrand in a New Year's address on December 31, 1989, and later hammered out, in June 1991, in Prague. Its flaw was to exclude the United States from the European Confederation and the Central and East European states from the European Community. Although the European Commission deemed association treaties with Central and Eastern Europe a reasonable transitional solution both politically and economically, the French government fought a rearguard battle against allowing agricultural exports from these countries into the Community. In the winter of 1991–92, however, Germany and France drew closer to each another. Mitterrand displayed some flexibility during an official visit to Berlin and the new Länder in September 1991, emphasizing that sound candidates for the EC would be considered. And twice in 1991–92 the French and German foreign ministers met their Polish colleagues in Weimar and Bergerac. Chancellor Kohl, while continuing to advocate early accession of the Central European states to the European Community, has indicated that a line should be drawn after the entry of Poland, Czechoslovakia, and Hungary into the EC.

Enlargement nonetheless raises very practical problems. Can the EC, for instance, afford as new members the established democracies of the European Free Trade Association (EFTA) and the new democracies of the former Soviet empire and, at the same time, meet the challenge of Maastricht to construct an EMU and a political union, both of which are under dispute? Can the EC both widen and deepen, remaining open-ended in terms of finality and borders? Excluding the Central and East European countries would be detrimental to the whole continent, however; Serbia's aggression against Croatia and Bosnia-Hercegovina has certainly shown the weakness of the EC in this region. Thus the Community faces a dilemma, as Pierre Hassner has noted: "It must both offer a pole of stability and sacrifice, or at least temporarily run the risk of sacrificing part of its stability for the benefit of the whole continent. To that extent it cannot avoid opening itself, in a progressive, controlled manner."[59]

A Europe à la carte could provide the answer. While the "inner core" of the Community shrinks to encompass the members of an EMU, a combination of association treaties and political consultations could tie the new democracies to the Community, mitigating the economic shocks and political transition. Yet some potential members of the looser association, such as Italy, dislike this idea because it could relegate them to the economic and political periphery of Europe. In addition, some members of the inner core question the feasibility of multiple arrangements that would allow, for instance, Denmark to remain a member of the Rome Treaty without adhering to the Maastricht arrangements. Thus the success of any such formulas devised by the European Commission is not guaranteed. They also may not address the problem of balancing the pressures from Central and Eastern Europe and the demands from Southern Europe. Europe could become fractured instead of turning into a flexible body. Dissatisfaction could grow in Germany if it is forced to bear the brunt of immigration from the East. Combined with the uneasiness Germans feel about the Maastricht agreement and their irritation at the increased financial demands from Southern European countries, this dissatisfaction could well reinforce nationalistic trends resulting in withdrawal, disruption, or arrogance that would be detrimental to Europe's future. As a country that will play a decisive role in shaping the continent, Germany needs to legitimize its power, but as a country too weak to master instabilities on the continent, it needs to obtain support from partners and allies, primarily France and the European Commission.

Much depends also on how Germany's partners respond to its interests and concerns. They may, on the one hand, want to use Germany's increasing dominance as an argument for tying the country into European frameworks, as Chancellor Kohl seems willing to do. On the other hand, there is some danger that Germany's partners, particularly Great Britain and France, could use fears of German domination in Europe as leverage to gain concessions from Germany. Such a strategy could be counterproductive, however, and produce unwanted reactions in Germany. West European countries in particular must be sensitive to Germany's concerns about Central and Eastern Europe and demonstrate a willingness to accommodate its interests for the good of European cooperation as a whole. A failure to respond might drive a wedge between Germany and its partners and also foster instabilities in Eastern Europe. This is especially true for France. As in the past, the Franco-German relationship will remain vital to European cooperation, but the course of this relationship depends on the future political leadership in the two countries. Although it is not likely in the near term, especially if Jacques Delors is elected president, new leaders could conceivably come to power who attach less priority to the importance of Franco-German cooperation. Another factor will be the extent to which the many economic, technological, and cultural cooperative ventures are pursued. While the French government is promoting such ventures, France and Germany are still some way from sharing a common view toward the East, yet it is only through cooperation and integration that the challenges instability poses to the continent will be met.

Cooperation and integration will not preclude Germany's growing influence in Europe. By changing its relative weight and status, unification has certainly increased Germany's ability to influence Europe. But Germany will not become a new hegemon, for it remains too weak to meet Europe's challenges alone. Paradoxically, this weakness may become an instrument of influence. Genscher often quoted Thomas Mann's statement that a European Germany is preferable to a German Europe, a view shared by most Germans. The terms of the proposition, however, are not mutually exclusive: as Germany imposes its problems and priorities on its partners, it will necessarily Germanize Europe.

Notes

1. Richard von Weizsäcker, Statement made during the *Staatsakt* in Berlin on October 3, 1990. Cf. text in *Der Tagesspiegel*, October 4, 1990. Quoted by Josef Joffe, "The Security Implications of a United Germany," in International Institute for

Strategic Studies, *America's Role in a Changing World*, Adelphi Papers, no. 257 (London, Winter 1990/91), pp. 84–91.

2. Gordon Craig, "Zu groß für Europa," *Der Spiegel*, November 13, 1989, pp. 183–87.

3. Public opinion in the countries of the southern tier looks more favorably on Germany probably because the recent past has been less traumatic than in the other countries mentioned. One should add that, inside individual countries, there are differences between public opinion and establishment. France provides such a blatant example: political and intellectual elites expressed outspoken concern over Germany's unification while the public welcomed it without, however, concealing its worries over Germany's increased power. See, for example, Ingo Kolboom, *Vom geteilten zum vereinten Deutschland. Deutschland-Bilder in Frankreich,* Arbeitspapiere zur internationalen Politik, no. 61 (Bonn: Forschungsinstitut der Deutschen Gesellschaft für Auswärtige Politik, April 1991), pp. 44–68.

4. At the Chequers Conference, a group of experts on German affairs was convened at Margaret Thatcher's request, and they were misleadingly reported to have raised concern. Cf. Charles Powell, "What the P[rime] M[inister] Learnt about the Germans," *Independent on Sunday,* July 15, 1990, p. 19; and Timothy Garton Ash, "What We Really Said about Germany," *Independent,* July 17, 1990, p. 7. Monetary Union was conceived as "a German racket designed to take over the whole of Europe with the French behaving like poodles to the Germans." Nicholas Ridley in an interview with Dominic Lawson, "Saying the Unsayable about the Germans," *Spectator,* July 14, 1990, p. 8. For overviews of European opinions, see Günter Trautmann, ed., *Die häßlichen Deutschen: Deutschland im Spiegel der westlichen und östlichen Nachbarn* (Darmstadt: Wissenschaftliche Buchgesellschaft, 1991), and Andrei S. Markovits, "Die deutsche Frage. Perzeptionen und Politik in der europäischen Gemeinschaft," in Ulrike Liebert and Wolfgang Michel, eds., *Die Politik zur deutschen Einheit: Probleme, Strategien, Kontroversen* (Opladen: Leske and Budrich, 1991), pp. 321–41.

5. See M. Wortmann, *Country Study on the Federal Republic of Germany* (Brussels: Commission of the European Communities, April 1991), pp. 10, 11, 21. This investment has mainly taken the form of takeovers of foreign companies rather than the establishment of affiliates abroad, a mode of operation which entails two consequences. First, growth through takeovers is no substitute for exports and, second, acquired companies may own technological and R&D competencies. In other words, German direct investments abroad do not reduce export surpluses and may strengthen the country's competitive edge.

6. Federico Romero, "Cross-border Population Movements," in William Wallace, ed., *The Dynamics of European Integration* (London: Pinter Publishers for the Royal Institute of International Affairs, 1990), pp. 188–89 (emphasis in original).

7. Per Magnus Wijkman, "Patterns of Production and Trade," in *The Dynamics of European Integration*, p. 100.

8. Wijkman, "Patterns," p. 104.

9. According to Bernard Keizer, *Le modèle économique allemand. Mythe et réalités*, Notes et études documentaires, nos. 4549–4550 (Paris: La Documentation Francoise, December 1979), pp. 132–44.

10. Bernard Keizer, "La République fédérale d'Allemagne: puissance extérieure," in *Statistiques et Etudes financières*, hors série (Paris: Ministère de l'Economie, Direction de la prévision, 1980), p. 35.

11. Andrei S. Markovits and Simon Reich, *The New Face of Germany: Gramsci,*

Neorealism and Hegemony, Working Paper Series 28 (Harvard University, Center for European Study, 1991), p. 26.

12. Wolfgang Hager, "Germany as an Extraordinary Trader," in Wilfrid L. Kohl and Giorgio Basevi, eds., *West Germany: A European and Global Power* (Lexington Books, 1980), pp. 5 and 15–16. In the 1970s, Italy and France left the Snake and President Mitterrand considered this move again in 1983 though the French franc eventually stayed in the EMS.

13. A vast body of literature has over the years amply demonstrated the fact that the West German economy put constraints on its environments. Cf. Christian Deubner, Udo Rehfeldt, and Frieder Schlupp, "Deutsch-französische Wirtschaftsbeziehungen im Rahmen der weltwirtschaftlichen Arbeitsteilung; Interdependenz, Divergenz oder strukturelle Dominanz?" in Robert Picht, ed., *Deutschland, Frankreich, Europa. Bilanz einer schwierigen Partnerschaft* (Munich: Piper, 1978), pp. 91–136; Michael Kreile, "West Germany: The Dynamics of Expansion," in Peter Katzenstein, ed., *Between Power and Plenty: Foreign Economic Policies of Advanced Industrial States* (University of Wisconsin, 1978), pp. 191–224; and Keizer, *Le modèle économique allemand. Mythe et réalités*.

14. See, for example, Wolfgang Hager, "Costs and Benefits from the Common Market: Problems of Measurement," in Wolfgang Wessels and Elfriede Regelsberger, eds., *The Federal Republic of Germany and the European Community: The Presidency and Beyond* (Bonn: Europa Union Verlag, 1988), pp. 125–42, especially p. 140; see also Helen Wallace, "Making Multilateral Negotiations Work," in Wallace, *The Dynamics of European Integration*, p. 225.

15. This analysis of the German model and the evolution of the concept is taken from Anne-Marie Le Gloannec, "Le Sens de la puissance allemande," in Zaki Laïdi, ed., *L'ordre mondial relâché. Sens et puissance après la guerre froide* (Paris: Presses de la Fondation Nationale des Sciences Politiques, 1992), pp. 45–67, especially p. 51.

16. However, federalism is being strained by unification. Cf. Quentin Peel, "Germany's F-word," *Financial Times*, December 11, 1991.

17. In France, leaving the EMS has been advocated by only very few, somewhat marginal, economists. See, for example, Alain Cotta, *La France en Panne* (Paris: Fayard, 1991). In the United Kingdom, application to the EMS foreshadowed a new policy towards the EC.

18. See Markovits and Reich, *The New Face of Germany*, p. 32. Both authors' argument is, however, different from mine—as they solely rely upon a cost-analysis that is, as explained below, extremely limited.

19. Simon Bulmer and William Paterson, *The Federal Republic of Germany and the European Community* (London: Allen and Unwin, 1987), pp. 20–22; see also by both authors, "European Policy Making in the Federal Republic—Internal and External Limits to Leadership," in Wessels and Regelsberger, *The Federal Republic of Germany and the European Community: The Presidency and Beyond*, p. 231.

20. Bulmer and Paterson, *The Federal Republic and the European Community*, p. 3.

21. Helen Wallace, "*The Federal Republic of Germany and Changing Coalition Habits—The Paradox of Partnership*," in Wessels and Regelsberger, *The Federal Republic of Germany and the European Community: The Presidency and Beyond*, p. 280. The Federal Republic could expand its power elsewhere, in NATO or through Ostpolitik.

22. Data are cited in "Prévisions à long terme et handicaps initiaux," *Regards Sur*

L'Économie Allemande, Bulletin économique du CIRAC, no. 1 (March 1991), p. 13.

23. A recent study published by the EC Commission shows Germany's unification is responsible for a 0.4 percent growth in the EC in 1990 and for 0.6 percent in 1991, those countries that benefited most being Spain, France, Denmark, and Belgium-Luxemburg. Cf. "Die EG hat an der deutschen Einheit bestens verdient," *Süddeutsche Zeitung*, June 1, 1992.

24. "Les investissements directs allemands à létranger," *Regards sur l'économie allemande*, Bulletin économique du CIRAC, no. 3 (April 1991), p. 16: DM 9.976 billion for the first five months of 1991 compared with DM 11.086 billion for the first five months of 1990.

25. For a good analysis of Germany's perceptions and policy during the Persian Gulf War see Karl Kaiser and Klaus Becher, "L'Allemagne et le conflit irakien," in Nicole Gnesotto and John Roper, eds., *L'Europe occidentale et le Golfe* (Paris: Institut d'Etudes de sécurité, Union de l'Europe occidentale, 1991), pp. 41–73.

26. The compromise that was reached on December 16, 1991, spelled out that secessionist republics should be recognized if they met a catalogue of principles. A commission then concluded whether or not they did meet such principles. The FRG decided that Slovenia and Croatia met the conditions anyway and announced its decision to recognize both states by January 15, 1992.

27. Cf. Christopher Parkes and David Waller, "Politics Comes to the Finanzplatz," *Financial Times*, January 24, 1992.

28. Cf. Christoph Bertram, "Eine Macht ohne Augenmaß? Im Ausland weckt die Bonner Jugoslawienpolitik alte Zweifel," *Die Zeit*, January 3, 1992; Dieter Schröder, "Der deutsche Alleingang," *Süddeutsche Zeitung*, December 22–23, 1991; Josef Joffe, "Ist Bonn Wilhelminien?" *Süddeutsche Zeitung*, January 24, 1992; Daniel Vernet, "Le retour de la 'question allemande,' " *Le Monde*, December 22–23, 1991; Hans W. Maull, "Assertive Germany: Cause for Concern," *International Herald Tribune*, January 17, 1992.

29. Incidentally, this move proved the soundness of the Maastricht agreement to set up a European Bank.

30. Representatives of fourteen chambers of industry and commerce in East Germany explained in early 1992 that the use of English and French constituted a language barrier and hindered competition. Cf. "Für mehr Deutsch in Brüssel," *Frankfurter Allgemeine Zeitung*, January 29, 1992. For a critical, humorous comment, see Klaus-Peter Schmidt, "Chauvi spitzt seine Zunge. Die Deutschen wollen, daß Europa auch deutsch spricht," *Die Zeit*, July 26, 1991.

31. Cf. Joachim Bitterlich (a counselor to the chancellor for foreign affairs), "La politique communautaire et occidentale de Bonn: un examen de passage pour l'Allemagne unie," *Politique Étrangère*, January 24, 1992, pp. 833–47, especially pp. 838, 841.

32. See, for example, "Rede von AM Genscher vor dem Zentrum Innere Führung der Bundeswehr am 7. April 1992 in Koblenz zum Thema 'Eine Stabilitätsordnung für Europa' " Presse- und Informationsamt der Bundesregierung, *Stichworte zur Sicherheitspolitik*, May 1992, especially pp. 7–8.

33. See "Bleibt es bei Blauhelm-Missionen? Kohl: Auch deutsche Soldaten müssen notfalls kämpfen," *Frankfurter Allgemeine Zeitung*, May 13, 1992. For other analyses of NATO reform, see, for example, Hilmar Linnenkamp, "Rom-nur ein Zwischengipfel? NATO noch ohne Antwort auf neue Frage," *Der Tagesspiegel*, November 6, 1991, as well as Uwe Nerlich, "Einige nichtmilitärische Bedingungen

europäischer Sicherheit," *Europa Archiv*, no. 19 (October 10, 1991), pp. 547–57. Oskar Lafontaine has also suggested extending NATO. See "SPD streitet über NATO-Kozept," *Süddeutsche Zeitung*, January 15, 1992.

34. See, for example, "Die Union will die NATO-Strategie ändern. Herausragende Aufgabe ist Krisenvorsorge und Krisenbewältigung," *Frankfurter Allgemeine Zeitung*, October 17, 1991.

35. Another example of Franco-German cooperation is the new structure called RISKAUDIT set up by IPSN and GRS, two institutes specializing in nuclear safety, to tackle safety problems in Central and Eastern Europe.

36. Unification may also introduce subtle yet important changes in the decisionmaking process. It may strengthen the Bund to the prejudice of the Länder. Conventional wisdom notwithstanding, the increase in the number of Länder may weaken federalism, at least as long as differences in interests exist in eastern and western states. Reconstruction in eastern Germany is essentially funded by the Bund—since the eastern Länder do not have the means while the western Länder object to increased spending: this tends to deprive the Länder of a say in the reconstruction process though regional authorities are fighting back to retain or to obtain power. The future composition of the Bundesbank is not yet settled—the central government suggests cutting down representation while all the states insist on being represented. In any case, if federalism were to weaken in Germany, the central government might strengthen its hold and harmonize or arbitrate interests a little more easily and eventually articulate them more clearly in international forums.

37. Peter Meroth, "Deutschland 2000: Der Staat, den wir uns wünschen," *Süddeutsche Zeitung Magazin*, January 4, 1991, pp. 8–15, especially pp. 8–9.

38. Ronald D. Asmus, "Germany in Transition: National Self Confidence, International Reticence," in *U.S.-German Relations*, Hearing before the Subcommittee on Europe and the Middle East of the Committee on Foreign Affairs, 102 Cong. 2 sess. (Government Printing Office, 1992), p. 20.

39. Dr. Renate Köcher, "Aufwind für die Bonner Koalition. Die Europabegeisterung der Deutschen kühlt sich ab "Der Allensbacher Monatsbericht," *Frankfurter Allgemeine Zeitung*, January 15, 1992 (polls by Allensbach Institute).

40. Asmus, "Germany in Transition," pp. 24–25.

41. Asmus, "Germany in Transition," pp. 15–17.

42. Joseph Fitchett, "Mood Shift in Germany: Growing Nationalism Is Tracked by Poll," *International Herald Tribune*, January 30, 1992.

43. "Germans Dubious on EC Unity, Poll Finds," *International Herald Tribune*, June 4, 1992.

44. Dieter Schröder, editor-in-chief of the *SDZ*, "Keine Mark für Maastricht," *Süddeutsche Zeitung*, December 7–8, 1991.

45. Jürgen Habermas, "Nochmals: Zur Identität der Deutschen: Ein einig Volk von aufgebrachten Wirtschaftsbürgern?" in Habermas, *Die nachholende Revolution*, (Frankfurt am Main: Suhrkamp, 1990), p. 210. For a background argument of a similar vein, cf. Harold James, *A German Identity 1770–1990* (Routledge, 1989).

46. See Karl Lamers, a CDU representative in Parliament, expert on foreign policy, in an interview with this author in September 1991. See also "In der Unionsfraktion zeichnet sich eine Haltungsänderung zu Jugoslawien ab," *Frankfurter Allgemeine Zeitung*, September 27, 1991.

47. This controversy opposed Wolf Biermann, Hans Magnus Enzensberger, Peter Schneider, and others to Peter Glotz, for example. For a good analysis, see Dan Diner, *Der Krieg der Erinnerungen und die Ordnung der Welt* (Berlin: Rotbuch

Verlag, 1991). For a more ambiguous analysis, see Jürgen Habermas, *Vergangenheit als Zukunft* (Zürich: Pendo Verlag, 1990).

48. See, for example, the interview of Bundeswehr Inspector General Klaus Naumann with Rolf Clement of DLF Interview der Woche DLF, January 5, 1992, in *Stichworte*, January 1992, pp. 45–46; "Lambsdorff auch für WEU-Einsätze. Der FDP-Vorsitzende zur Arbeit der Koalition," *Frankfurter Allgemeine Zeitung*, April 24, 1992; and interview of Defense Minister Rühe with *Welt am Sonntag*, April 5, 1992, in *Stichworte*, April 1992, pp. 46–47.

49. Robert Keohane and Stanley Hoffmann, *The New European Community: Decisionmaking and Institutional Change* (Westview Press, 1991), pp. 30–32.

50. Roger de Weck, "Ein Wechsel auf Europas Zukunft," *Die Zeit*, December 13, 1991.

51. According to some French intellectuals, the EC displays two weaknesses; as a judiciary producing norms and regulations, the EC is deprived of political functions, a failing that will be reinforced when the German economic model is adopted by the Community since German monetary policy bypasses political decisions. See, for example, Pierre Rosanvallon, "Bruxelles, tu nous étouffes!" *Le Nouvel Observateur*, February 6–12, 1992, pp. 26–27.

52. Josef Joffe, "Europe's American Pacifier," *Foreign Policy*, no. 54 (Spring 1984), pp. 64–82.

53. Joffe, "Europe's American Pacifier," pp. 78–79.

54. "Bundestag gegen Frankreichs 'Hades'-Raketen," *Süddeutsche Zeitung*, November 8, 1991, and "Kohl ist die unsichtbare Nummer 16," *Süddeutsche Zeitung*, January 31, 1992.

55. "Im vergangenen Jahr fast 260.000 Asylbewerber in Deutschland. Die Mehrheit kam aus Ost- und Südosteuropa/220.000 Aussiedler," *Frankfurter Allgemeine Zeitung*, January 4, 1992.

56. Nerlich, "Einige nicht militarische Bedingungen."

57. A change in the Constitution is presented as "required" by the Community. On the necessity of a common policy vis-à-vis the East, cf. Karl Kaiser, "Die deutsch-amerikanischen Sicherheitsbeziehungen in Europa nach dem Kalten Krieg," *Europa-Archiv*, no. 1 (January 10, 1992), pp. 7–17.

58. Winfried Münster, "Die EG hält weitere Enttäuschungen bereit. Mit der bisherigen Europa-Mystik sind die Interessenkonflikte nicht mehr zu überdecken," *Süddeutsche Zeitung*, February 10, 1992. Gerhard Wettig's call, for instance, for enlargement at the cost of integration can be deemed dubious and even dangerous. See Gerhard Wettig, "Security in Europe: A Challenging Task," *Aussenpolitik*, vol. 43, no. 1 (1992), pp. 3–11.

59. Pierre Hassner, "Construction européenne et mutations à l'Est," paper presented at a conference on "Identité et diversité dans l'Europe démocratique," May 23–25, 1991.

NINE

Economic Implications of German Unification for Central and Eastern Europe

András Inotai

ECONOMIC RELATIONS with Germany have traditionally played a prominent part in the economic development strategies of Central and East European countries. Despite the division of Germany and the former Soviet Union's domination of the region after World War II, the German connection remained an important one, and it became increasingly vital to the reforming economies in the 1980s.

After the Soviet Union, the former East Germany was the most important trading partner within the now-defunct Council for Mutual Economic Assistance (CMEA). In 1989, East Germany accounted for 9.8 percent of total Soviet trade and 4.5 percent of total Polish trade. Long-term cooperation and specialization agreements with East Germany played a fundamental role in shaping the pattern of economic and technological development within the CMEA. While East German trade with the Soviet Union remained primarily interindustrial, trade with the smaller and more developed member countries— Hungary, Poland, and Czechoslovakia—had a relatively high level of intraindustry specialization.[1]

At the same time, West Germany maintained its leading position as the major trading partner of all Central and East European economies. Since the 1960s, it has accounted for 20 to 35 percent of their trade with the Organization for Economic Cooperation and Development (OECD). In 1989, its share was 16 percent of total Polish and Hungarian imports and 15 and 12 percent, respectively, of the two countries' total exports. Many resources essential to growth, including credits, other financial transfers, and, most important, modern technology have always been provided by western Germany.

In the year prior to unification, Poland and Hungary's cumulative imports from the two Germanies surpassed imports from the Soviet Union, while exports to East and West Germany nearly equaled exports to the Soviet Union. After the collapse of the CMEA in 1990 and 1991, the unified Germany became the leading foreign trade partner for Czechoslovakia as well as for Poland and Hungary.

Given Germany's economic importance, unification and some of its ramifications cannot help but influence the future of the Central and East European economies. Moreover, the collapse of East European economic cooperation within the CMEA and the political and economic breakdown of the Soviet Union make an analysis of potential developments resulting from unification extremely timely. It seems certain that German unification will have a significant impact on the speed and pattern of market economy reforms and on the future role of the new democracies in the all-European framework.

This paper is divided into four sections. The first deals with the short-term economic impact of German unification, while the second is dedicated to some medium-term implications. The third section discusses some strategic challenges facing both Germany and the Central and East European countries in shaping their relations. The final section summarizes some fundamental lessons that can be drawn from the experience of unification as it affects economic reforms in Central and East European countries.

Short-Term Impacts

The currency union implemented on July 1, 1990, produced three dramatic changes between the former East Germany and its traditional CMEA partners: trade relations collapsed, large trade deficits emerged, and historically shaped structural interdependencies with substantial economic and social implications broke down.[2]

Prior to the currency union, 70 percent of East German trade was with the CMEA and 37 percent with the Soviet Union.[3] Thus, East Germany was substantially more dependent on trade with this economic area than was Poland or Hungary. And unlike these countries, East Germany's dependence on the CMEA did not decline during the 1980s. This strong CMEA orientation was accompanied by a dramatic decline in international competitiveness in most product markets.[4]

East German trade with the CMEA declined substantially in 1990 and 1991, but imports from Central and East European countries had already started to decline sharply just before the currency union. In the first half of 1990, European CMEA exports had amounted to 53 percent of total East German imports. But these exports decreased rapidly in the second half of 1990—from DM 11.8 billion to DM 3.8 billion, or by almost three-fourths, to 19 percent of total imports. While European CMEA exports to eastern

Table 9-1. *Foreign Trade of East Germany, January 1990–June 1991*

Area	Amount (millions of DMs)			Share (percent)		
	1990		1991	1990		1991
	Jan.–June	July–Dec.	Jan.–June	Jan.–June	June–Dec.	Jan.–June
Total exports	22,738	23,609	12,871	100	100	100
Intra-German	3,927	4,347	4,403	17	18	34
CMEA Europe	14,066	15,745	5,515	62	67	43
Other	4,745	3,517	2,953	21	15	23
Total imports	21,105	19,512	29,363	100	100	100
Intra-German	7,851	13,475	19,965	37	69	68
CMEA Europe	11,088	3,766	3,672	53	19	13
Other	2,166	2,271	5,727	10	12	20

Source: Statistisches Bundesamt, "Händel, Gastgewerbe, Reiseverkehr," Fachserie 6, Reihe 6: Innerdeutscher Warenverkehr (Wiesbaden, June 1990, December 1990, June 1991).

Germany increased slightly to DM 3.7 billion in the first half of 1991, they accounted for a yet smaller 13 percent of total imports (table 9-1). At the same time exports from western to eastern Germany more than doubled, rising from DM 7.9 billion to DM 20 billion, or from 37 to 68 percent of total east German imports (table 9-1).

In the first half of 1991, exports from the Soviet Union to eastern Germany, backed by special German-Soviet agreements, represented 42 percent of the level reached in the first half of 1990. Poland's exports to eastern Germany fell to 29 percent, Czechoslovakia's to 26 percent, Hungary's and Romania's to 14 percent, and Bulgaria's to 4 percent of the level reached one year before. At the same time, all the European CMEA countries, with the exception of Romania, substantially increased their exports to western Germany. Moreover, the growth rate of Polish, Czechoslovak, and Hungarian exports rose faster than western Germany's demand for imports. Eastern Germany's share of total German imports from the European CMEA region, calculated according to the artificial—and, for eastern Germany, favorable—exchange rate fell from 52 to 23 percent in one year. Those countries experiencing the greatest decline were Czechoslovakia (from 51 to 16 percent), Hungary (from 48 to 7 percent), and Bulgaria (from 73 to 9 percent) (table 9-2).

Several factors explain this dramatic market loss. After the currency union and the liberalization of trade between eastern and western Germany, many Central and East European products disappeared overnight, along with some well-established products manufactured in eastern Germany. West German deliveries to eastern Germany increased more than fivefold between the first

Table 9-2. *Foreign Trade of the European CMEA Countries
with Germany, January–June 1991*
January–June 1990 = 100

Country or area	Total	West Germany	East Germany	East German share (percent)	
				Jan.– June 1990	Jan.– June 1991
Exports by Germany	94.7	97.6	40.3	5.43	2.31
CMEA Europe	69.0	104.4	39.3	54.4	31.0
Soviet Union	60.4	75.5	49.9	58.7	48.4
Poland	134.5	172.2	62.4	34.4	15.9
Czechoslovakia	64.9	138.6	17.8	61.0	16.7
Hungary	71.8	114.2	16.4	43.4	9.9
Romania	46.9	78.2	21.4	55.2	25.1
Bulgaria	29.9	62.6	11.2	63.7	23.9
Imports by Germany	115.5	120.7	31.4	6.01	1.64
CMEA Europe	75.9	122.5	33.3	52.2	22.9
Soviet Union	71.4	115.6	41.9	59.9	35.2
Poland	93.0	132.6	28.5	38.0	11.6
Czechoslovakia	81.1	139.1	25.8	51.2	16.3
Hungary	82.0	126.2	14.2	48.0	6.8
Romania	62.6	92.3	14.0	37.9	8.5
Bulgaria	33.5	115.3	4.0	73.4	8.6

Source: Statistisches Bundesamt, *Aussenhandel*, Fachserie 6, Reihe 1 Zusammenfassende Übersichten für den Aussenhandel (Wiesbaden, June 1990, June 1991).

quarter of 1990 and the second quarter of 1991. Indeed, one month's exports for June or July 1991 amounted to 50 percent of total 1989 exports. In the first half of 1991, Eastern Germany's total imports from outside the country totaled only 26.5 percent of those from western Germany, while imports from ex-CMEA countries reached just 18.4 percent of imports from western Germany.

The uncompetitiveness of many CMEA products and changing east German consumption patterns, supported by psychological motives and an increase in financial transfers, contributed to the sometimes economically unreasonable preference for more expensive and not necessarily better west German goods. This may explain why the seemingly favorable exchange rate of 2.34 DM to 1 transferable ruble (TR) was unable to stimulate imports from CMEA countries.[5] In addition, a number of formerly state-owned east German enterprises reduced production or closed altogether, causing demand for well-known products to decline or vanish altogether. Particularly harmful was the disappearance of most of the former East German foreign trade companies that had provided popular goods with well-established retail channels.[6] The collapse of the CMEA further diminished export possibilities, but it was not, as is often claimed, the primary reason for the catastrophic developments in export trade with eastern Germany. German unification and the period of preparation for it preceded the breakdown of the CMEA system by several months; the serious decline in CMEA exports to eastern Germany came at a time when other CMEA trade channels were still performing relatively well.

The collapse of the CMEA played a much more direct role in the decline of exports from eastern Germany to Central and Eastern Europe. These exports increased between the first and the second half of 1990 from DM 14.1 billion to DM 15.7 billion, or by 11 percent. Despite the impact of unification on trade, eastern Germany's exports remained very much oriented to the CMEA market. The CMEA's share even grew during 1990 from 62 to 67 percent. However, in the first half of 1991, exports declined by almost two-thirds, from DM 15.7 billion to DM 5.6 billion. Nevertheless, the European CMEA still remained the main export area for east German products. Reorienting export trade from the East to the West proved to be much more successful in Poland or Hungary than it did in an eastern Germany heavily financed by the former West German budget.

The decline in exports from eastern Germany was not confined to the CMEA region, however. Other export markets did not show signs of retraction, but east German exports to these markets also declined—by more than 38 percent between the first half of 1990 and the first half of 1991, 19 percent of it between the second half of 1990 and the first half of 1991 alone. The west German market, moreover, provided no substantial impetus to export growth. Exports from eastern to western Germany grew by 12 percent in the first full year of currency union (July 1990 to June 1991), falling considerably short of export growth in Poland, Hungary, Czechoslovakia, and even Bulgaria (see tables 9-1 and 9-2).

Although German analyses tend to blame the sharp decline in east German exports to Eastern and Central Europe on the collapse of the CMEA, the main causes for this downturn were self-inflicted. The currency union and the uniform exchange rate drastically increased export prices of east German products, reducing their competitiveness. In addition to a 300 percent revaluation, already uncompetitive wages in eastern Germany have continued to increase. The decline of the east German production and trade system has added to the export problems.

Germany guaranteed the fulfillment of existing bilateral trade agreements in 1991. Due to the collapse of the east German import market, this guarantee supported exports from eastern Germany to the CMEA but not CMEA exports to eastern Germany. As the financial costs of unification climbed, export subsidies to CMEA countries were curtailed, with the exception of the Soviet

Union, which was guaranteed special treatment.[7] Another important factor in the decline of east Germany's exports to its former CMEA trading partners has been the fact that most east German products, particularly those of a high-tech nature, had been experiencing a relative market loss in the most Western-oriented Central European countries, namely Hungary and Poland, during most of the 1980s and even earlier. External factors influencing the situation include radical import liberalization introduced in the reforming countries, increased competition in the import market, the collapse of CMEA trade agreements, and the well-known liquidity problems of the former Soviet economy.

For the Central and East European economies, the time gap between the decline of exports to and imports from eastern Germany has manifested itself in a serious trade deficit. In 1990 this deficit reached TR 9.8 billion with the European CMEA countries.[8] About two-thirds of this deficit was accumulated by the former Soviet Union. Czechoslovakia's trade deficit with eastern Germany was TR 480 million, with another TR 200 million from tourism and services. The Polish deficit reached TR 630 million in a few months after the currency union, and Hungary had accumulated a deficit of TR 571 million by January 1991.

Bilateral negotiations are under way to settle these deficits. Germany's position is that the deficit must be financed in deutsche marks at the official exchange rate of DM 2.34 to one TR, the rate used in transactions between the former East Germany and the ex-CMEA countries. Using this exchange rate, Poland and Czechoslovakia owe Germany about DM 1.5 and 1.6 billion, respectively, and Hungary DM 1.3 billion. However, all the countries involved are pursuing two lines of argument against the German claims. First, they emphasize that the exchange rate was chosen arbitrarily. Although it may be used for intra-German transactions, it does not reflect the market value of east German export products.[9] These countries argue that applying the ruble's financial market rate—1 ruble to DM 0.20 or DM 0.30 before the collapse of the Soviet Union—would be more realistic. In fact, this would reduce the outstanding deficits to one-tenth of their original level. Second, all the countries stress that their economies have been seriously affected by the nonfulfillment of bilateral treaties and the sudden loss of the east German market, developments for which they are not responsible. According to Hungarian calculations, German unification caused a loss of TR 885 million to Hungary (TR 250 million in unfulfilled commercial contracts and TR 635 million in market loss). Because this sum is substantially higher than the Hungarian deficit of TR 571 million, Hungary claims that Germany must make up the difference.

German experts not only fail to take into account the losses resulting from the dissolution of East Germany, but they also argue that, according to international law, this issue must be assessed in two separate parts. On the one hand, East Germany did not unite with West Germany; the East German Parliament dissolved the GDR and declared that the country had become a part of the Federal Republic of Germany. These experts argue that obligations such as long-term specialization agreements assumed by the former East Germany ended with the country's demise. On the other hand, losses and damages emerging from legally binding trade agreements, including delivery and purchase commitments, may be negotiated on the basis of private law.[10]

Although negotiations with all the affected countries opened in 1991, no agreement is yet in sight. Germany has proposed various options, including paying the deficit in cash, goods, or yearly installments. Some experts have suggested that Germany should give up its claims in recognition of the bold and often risky decisions on the part of several countries, which helped make unification possible. It is widely believed that negotiations on the expert level will not bring satisfactory results and that binding decisions must come from the political level. The unexpected costs of unification have raised concern that the German position will become more rigid as the country attempts to cope with its own economic problems. It is not unlikely that Germany sees the outstanding deficits as additional sources of income for its badly hit budget.

Medium-Term Implications

Economic developments in the united Germany have given rise to mixed medium-term expectations in Central and Eastern Europe. On the negative side, steadily increasing east German financial needs have raised fears of higher interest rates. In addition, investment capital is expected to be diverted from the reforming economies of Central and Eastern Europe to the former East German territory. On the positive side, an increased demand for imports and economic recovery in eastern Germany may improve conditions for sustainable export expansion.

Various projections have been made regarding the total costs of financing unification. According to an International Monetary Fund survey, raising the productivity, infrastructure, and living standards of eastern Germany to the current west German level by 2001 would cost between DM 1.5 and DM 1.9 trillion—seven times the current gross external debt of all Central and East European countries, including the former Soviet Union, at present exchange rates.[11] Other estimates range from DM 1 trillion to 2.7 trillion.[12] Based on the modest assumption that 50 percent of east German capital stock is outdated and must be replaced, new investments alone will amount to DM 600 billion during the 1990s.[13] Maintaining the present levels of west German capital intensity will require investments of DM 1.5 trillion, or an average yearly investment of DM 150 billion during the next decade.[14]

The costs of unification have clearly been seriously underestimated. State transfers reached about DM 100 billion during 1990. They are expected to climb to between DM 140 billion and DM 150 billion in 1992, and to at least DM 170 billion in 1993.[15] This means that state transfers to eastern Germany will equal two-thirds of the GNP of the former East German state, or DM 9,000 per inhabitant.[16] But the fundamental problem is not the huge volume of transfers. Much more troubling is the fact that the transfers are not financing new investments; instead, they are being used to maintain an unjustifiably high level of consumption, which is not supported by either economic efficiency or productivity gains, and to pay for the social costs of economic shock therapy.

Can western Germany continue to finance unification, and if so, at what price? West German experts offer several reasons for their confidence in the country's ability to cope with the increasing financial burdens. First, in 1989, the West German federal deficit was the lowest it had been in fifteen years, amounting to less than 1 percent of the GDP.[17] Second, West Germany accumulated a substantial foreign trade and current account surplus in the 1980s.[18] Third, west German saving rates have traditionally been high in comparison to those of other countries and are currently estimated to total about DM 3 trillion. Fourth, incomes from accelerated privatization are expected to provide additional budgetary resources. Finally, partial economic recovery in eastern Germany should reduce subsidies and raise tax revenues.

Despite these favorable expectations, current developments present a gloomy picture. Western Germany seems to be overly strained by exploding costs. The current account surplus has vanished, and, in September 1991, was replaced by a substantial deficit of more than DM 30 billion.[19] Public transfers will total some 5.5 percent of western Germany's GDP in 1991 and may be even higher in 1992.[20] Previously announced budget cuts—from DM 59 billion to DM 45 billion in 1991, based primarily on declining subsidies—did not materialize, and another increase in tax subsidies of about DM 1.8 billion has been announced for 1993.[21] The rapidly increasing costs of financing Treuhand, the east German state privatization agency, will push Treuhand's debt to DM 57 billion by the end of 1992.[22] Restitution claimed by earlier property owners, the financing of nonperforming debts made by former East German enterprises, infrastructural and environmental expenditures, as well as the huge costs of moving the German capital from Bonn to Berlin (estimated at between DM 50 billion and 100 billion), plus emergency payments that may have to be made to the former Soviet Union to forestall state bankruptcies or adverse political developments, add to the financial burdens. A realistic estimate suggests that transfers to eastern Germany will not fall below 4 percent of the west German GDP by 1995; earlier estimates had predicted the transfers would fall to 2.5 percent.[23] And higher wage claims, fueled in part by inflation but primarily by political considerations, will increase the economic problems of unification.[24]

Growing public sector indebtedness is also seriously limiting the chances for a healthier German budget in coming years, as interest payments on earlier budget-balancing credits amount to some DM 10 billion annually.[25] Higher taxes can only partially offset the substantial deficit. New income sources must be opened up within Germany and in international markets. This need to generate new income will have two immediate adverse effects on the Central and East European economies, which badly need a substantial influx of external resources to speed up the process of economic regeneration. First, Germany's own needs may drain the investment capital available for these countries. Second, interest rates, which have already risen sharply in Germany, are likely to rise elsewhere as well. Since most Central and East European countries are heavily in debt, they face the prospect of having to pay higher interest rates for both new and existing debts. An increase of 1 percentage point in the international interest rate would cost Poland some $320 million, Hungary $200 million, and Czechoslovakia $100 million. In the long term, another problem may result from Germany's current financial practices. Tight monetary and loose fiscal policies could produce more than a temporary increase in interest rates, predetermining as well the rates for long-term financing of growing deficits. This would delay the successful transformation of Central and East European economies or even make reform impossible, as most European countries would simply run out of resources, and growth, if any, would be sluggish.

One of the arguments supporting this pessimistic outlook for Germany's economic development involves the reluctance with which private capital, non-German and German, is moving to eastern Germany. Investments in the ex-GDR have been dominated by state-supported investments in infrastructure, as private capital has hesitated to make larger investments, in part because of the disastrous state of infrastructure. It is supposed that once a modern infrastructure is developed, one barrier to large-scale private investment can be eliminated. Also, the restitution law and legal uncertainties hinder private commitments. Most recently, there has been increasing private investment activity in the new Bundesländer in construction, the service sector, and banking, but very limited investment has taken place in manufacturing, with the exceptions of the automobile industry and Treuhand-led privatization. A cursory assessment also suggests that private west German capital may prefer the lower-cost countries of Central and Eastern Europe. In fact, western Germany is currently the major foreign investor in Czechoslovakia and Poland and one of the leading investors in Hungary, despite the modest amount involved (about $1.0 billion) for all three countries. In all of the countries undergoing economic transformation, additional German investment is considered a key factor in technological modernization, improved quality, and up-to-date management practices.

Two fears, however, have emerged concerning the future of German investment in Central and Eastern Europe. First, major German companies have currently adopted a wait-and-see attitude rather than making major investments in neighboring countries.[26] They are following closely the impact of both the substantial investments in the infrastructure of eastern Germany and the generous subsidies provided to investors in that area, which Central and East Europeans believe are likely to divert west German capital to eastern Germany, even if production costs are much higher there than elsewhere in the region.[27] The second fear is linked to Germany's foreign investment capacity, as the country's current account balance is in deficit. In the past, there has always been a clear link between the high current account surplus and the level of Germany's direct foreign investments, but it is unlikely that investment activity abroad can be maintained if its major financing source is depleted.

While German unification may have a negative impact on the financial market, raise interest rates, and limit direct investments, it is also expected to create favorable export opportunities for Central and Eastern Europe. Germany is, after the United States, the largest importer in the world, and it is likely to grow more dynamically than other import markets. With the collapse of east German production, imports (including deliveries from western Germany) now account for as much as 50 percent of consumption of the former East Germans. In addition, investments in the manufacturing sector and in the infrastructure of eastern Germany will require resources not only from western Germany but also from other foreign sources.

Although Central and East European exports to eastern Germany declined markedly in 1990 and 1991, exports to western Germany grew at spectacular rates. From 1989 to 1990, total German imports increased by 9.4 percent in DM value and by 27.3 percent in current U.S. dollar terms. Over the same period, Central and East European exports to Germany increased by 14.3 percent in DM value and 32.9 percent in U.S. dollars. This increase, however, was due exclusively to the boom in Polish and Hungarian imports. Poland showed the most growth of the major exporters to Germany, with an increase of 45 percent in DM value, followed by the People's Republic of China with 32.2 percent, Spain with 24.3 percent, and Hungary with 21.8 percent (table 9-3). In the first half of 1991, Czechoslovakia joined the two other Central European exporters, significantly increasing its exports to western Germany. Overall, European members of the now-defunct CMEA expanded their market share of western Germany's total imports from 3.6 percent in 1988 to

Table 9-3. *Import Demand of West Germany, January 1989–June 1991*[a]
Amounts in billions of deutsche marks

Country or area	Amount		Percent change	Amount, Jan.–June		Percent change
	1989	1990		1990	1991	
Total imports	506.9	554.5	9.4	263.0	317.3	20.6
OECD	409.2	446.1	9.0	n.a.	n.a.	n.a.
European Commun.	259.2	288.5	11.3	135.9	169.1	24.4
Belgium-Luxembourg	35.0	39.9	14.2	18.8	24.1	28.2
France	60.5	65.5	8.4	31.1	40.2	29.3
Italy	45.4	52.2	15.0	24.8	29.9	20.6
Netherlands	51.9	56.2	8.4	26.5	31.7	19.6
Spain	10.6	13.2	24.3	6.1	8.8	44.3
United Kingdom	34.7	37.2	7.1	17.4	20.8	19.5
Austria	21.0	24.0	14.6	11.5	13.2	14.8
Sweden	12.9	13.2	2.5	6.5	7.2	10.8
Switzerland	21.2	23.5	10.6	11.0	12.4	12.7
Yugoslavia	6.3	7.4	16.6	3.6	4.1	13.9
Japan	32.3	33.0	2.2	15.8	19.5	23.4
United States	38.4	37.0	−3.4	19.4	21.7	11.9
OPEC countries	12.4	14.4	15.6	6.1	7.1	16.4
Other LDCs	42.0	44.2	5.3	31.1	35.9	15.4
PR of China	5.9	7.8	32.2	3.4	5.3	55.9
Asian NICs[b]	17.2	18.6	8.6	8.6	10.6	23.3
European CMEA	19.2	21.9	14.3	10.1	12.4	22.8
Soviet Union	8.6	9.1	6.3	4.4	5.0	13.6
Poland	3.6	5.2	45.0	2.2	3.0	36.4
Czechoslovakia	2.5	2.7	9.4	1.3	1.8	38.5
Hungary	2.7	3.3	21.8	1.5	1.9	26.7

Source: Statistisches Bundesamt, *Aussenhandel,* Fachserie 7, Reihe 1 Zusammenfassende Übersichten für den Aussenhandel (Wiesbaden, June 1991); and OECD, *Monthly Statistics of Foreign Trade,* series A (Paris, November 1991), p. 68.

n.a. Not available.

a. Figures always refer to the old Federal Republic of Germany.

b. Newly industrialized countries: Hong Kong, Republic of Korea, Singapore, and Taiwan.

5 percent in the first half of 1991. The figure is modest, but the trend, after a long period of steady market decline, cannot be ignored.

In the long run, the sustainability of this new dynamism will depend partly on the pattern of exports. Final manufactured products (*Enderzeugnisse,* according to German product classification) accounted for 55.9 percent of west German imports in 1990. Of the European CMEA countries, only

Table 9-4. *Pattern of Final Manufactured Exports from Central and Eastern Europe to West Germany, 1990*
Percent of total CMEA exports[a]

Product	Bul-garia	Czecho-slovakia	Hungary	Poland	Romania	USSR
Total exports	1.8	12.4	15.0	23.7	5.1	41.9
Final manufactured goods	2.7	15.0	27.4	33.7	14.5	7.0
Clothing	5.1	11.5	25.1	37.6	20.4	0.3
Footwear	2.5	9.3	48.5	24.8	11.3	3.6
Wood products	0.8	12.7	12.9	38.2	31.5	3.9
Glassware	0.5	38.0	16.3	25.6	18.5	1.1
Metal manufactures	1.2	15.4	23.2	48.5	8.3	3.3
Machinery	2.8	19.0	38.1	27.0	5.1	7.9
Electrotechnical goods	1.3	11.4	43.9	36.6	1.5	5.3
Optical goods	3.7	14.8	33.6	37.6	3.0	7.3
Pharmaceuticals	5.3	35.0	29.0	7.9	2.6	20.2
Transport equipment	0.4	21.9	10.5	14.8	2.2	50.2

Source: Statistisches Bundesamt, *Aussenhandel,* Fachserie 7, Reihe 3: *Aussenhandel nach Ländern und Warengruppen (Spezialhandel),* vol. 2, *Halbjahr und Jahr 1990* (Wiesbaden, 1991).
a. East Germany is not included in the calculations.

Romania had a higher percentage of these goods among their exports: with 81.4 percent, while Hungary stood at 54.9 percent. On the other hand, only 41.3 percent of Polish and 37.9 percent of Czechoslovak exports consisted of final manufactured products.

The types of products that fall into the *Enderzeugnisse* category may provide further insights into the collective and individual export potential of Central and East European countries. Ten product groups have been identified in table 9-4. The European CMEA's share has been growing in all groups except pharmaceuticals. In the first half of 1991, 14.5 percent of western Germany's imports of wood manufactures, 7.3 percent of glassware, 6.2 percent of clothing, 5.6 percent of shoes, and 5.3 percent of miscellaneous metal manufactures originated from Central and Eastern Europe. Market positions improved, though not as dramatically, in some technology-intensive sectors such as machinery, transport equipment, and electrical appliances (see table 9-5).

According to 1990 west German trade figures on country specialization, Poland is the primary exporter of miscellaneous metal manufactures, shipping 48.5 percent of total European ex-CMEA exports in this category to Germany, as well as of wood products (38.2 percent) and clothing (37.6 percent). Czechoslovakia is the leading exporter of transport equipment (21.9 percent), glassware (38 percent), and pharmaceuticals (35 percent). In most technology-

Table 9-5. *West Germany's Imports from Central and Eastern Europe,*
1988, January–June 1991[a]
Percent of total imports

Product	1988	1991 (Jan.–June)
Wood manufactures	13.9	14.5
Glassware	5.1	7.3
Clothing	5.3	6.2
Shoes	3.9	5.6
Metal manufactures	3.1	5.3
Machinery	1.0	2.1
Transport equipment	0.4	1.7
Electrical appliances	0.8	1.6

Source: Statistisches Bundesamt, *Aussenhandel,* Fachserie 7, Reihe 3: *Aussenhandel nach Ländern und Warengruppen (Spezialhandel),* vol. 2, *Halbjahr und Jahr 1988* (Wiesbaden, September 1989); and vol. 1, *Halbjahr 1991* (Wiesbaden 1991).

a. East Germany is not included in the calculations.

intensive product groups, Hungary takes the lead. It exports 43.9 percent of total electrotechnical goods from the region to western Germany, 38.1 percent of machinery, and, with 33.4 percent of optical product exports, is a close second to Poland. Also, 48.5 percent of shoe exports have been marketed by Hungary (see table 9-4).[28]

Given that the global markets—including western Germany's—for technology-based products that rely on a highly skilled labor force expanded rapidly during the 1980s, and the likelihood that future German import requirements will focus on these goods, the Hungarian, Polish, and Czechoslovak economies seem to have the best chances of increasing their exports to the growing German market.

Despite these positive developments in the west German market, the prospects for recovery in eastern Germany seem to be much less rosy. Most of eastern Germany's consumer and investment goods will be supplied by western Germany. Direct sales on the east German market are further blocked by the disappearance of most traditional trading companies that had been engaged in importing from Central and Eastern Europe. Well-known Polish, Czechoslovak, and Hungarian products, for example, are being exported to eastern Germany by west German trading companies. Thus, achieving the desirable goal of participating in the economic restructuring and modernization of eastern Germany will require the Central and East European countries to work with and subcontract from leading west German firms.

Finally, there is the theoretical possibility that national or joint Polish-Czechoslovak-Hungarian companies could be established in east German territory, where they would enjoy the generous tax breaks granted to such ventures. These companies would offer better access to the local market and unrestrained access to the European Community markets through the united Germany. But on the national and regional level, such an approach would require substantial financial resources. Due to the strict anti-inflationary policies currently in place in the Central and East European economies and the precarious financial position of formerly CMEA-oriented enterprises, such ventures are unlikely in the near future.

Overall, then, trade between Central and Eastern Europe and Germany will be concentrated increasingly on western Germany. The net financial balance of unification can be calculated as the difference between these benefits from export expansion and the losses attributable to higher interest rates and diverted financial resources and investments. Poland and Hungary, for example, could compensate for a 1 percent increase in the international interest rate with export growth of 10 percent, Czechoslovakia with export growth of about 6 percent. Further calculations of potential benefits and losses may be complicated by shifts in the exchange rate between the deutsche mark and the U.S. dollar.

Some Strategic Issues

The course of German unification's success is a high-priority concern for all Central and East European countries, particularly after the collapse of the Soviet Union and the danger of a political and economic vacuum developing in the region. The consequences of unification, however, will extend beyond the short-term impact on trade and medium-term financial and trade developments. And while these short- and medium-term assessments will influence strategic decisions, they cannot provide a satisfactory substitute for comprehensive long-range planning. In this respect, it is important to consider six issues that will no doubt occupy the Central and East European countries for several years.

First, the likely scenarios of intra-German economic development must be assessed. Three potential development trends have been forecast for the former East German territory. Its economy could be based on the production of exports to Eastern Europe and the former Soviet Union; it could develop into a high-tech region as a result of substantial structural changes that allow the economy to start again from scratch; or it could become a deindustrialized Mezzogiorno with lasting social and economic problems.

The first scenario would require strong industrialization and competitive production in eastern Germany. At present, however, with west German private investors hesitant to invest in eastern Germany, with private non-

German capital largely absent, with the continuous exodus of skilled labor, and the horrendous pollution, major obstacles stand in the way of successful industrialization. Furthermore, the adoption of the west German deutsche mark exchange rate and subsequent salary raises made without considering the surprisingly low level of east German productivity have virtually assured the region's inability to compete in global markets. Current Polish, Czechoslovak, and Hungarian labor costs are a fraction of eastern Germany's, and it is unlikely that the situation will change significantly in the next decade. It is more likely that Germany's eastern neighbors will become increasingly appealing as potential investment locations, attracting German and non-German capital and expanding production to satisfy the needs of heavily subsidized east German consumers.

The question is not whether eastern Germany can exploit the Central and East European markets, but whether Central and Eastern Europe, with its many comparative advantages, will be allowed to exploit east German markets. This question raises two additional issues. First, sociopolitical conflicts may arise between German private capital interested in the lower production costs in Eastern Europe and German political parties interested in social peace in Germany. Second, economic conflicts may arise as advocates of free trade are challenged by lobbies interested in centrally supported industrialization and job creation backed by protectionist measures that would limit the competitiveness of Central and East European exports to high-cost eastern Germany. Private investors, exporters, importers, and many consumers are likely to support free trade.

The second scenario acknowledges that, if labor costs remain unreasonably high, industrial strategies for eastern Germany cannot rely on labor-intensive production. Yet the outlook for technology-intensive production is not much better. There is no international precedent suggesting that leading technologies flow into previously uncompetitive and largely deindustrialized areas. The considerably improved infrastructure and communications currently being implemented in Germany are a necessary but not a sufficient condition for attracting high-tech investments. Educating highly skilled and market-oriented workers is also important, but it takes a long time. Meanwhile, the skilled workers that would otherwise be available continue to leave for more developed western areas. But even if most of the necessary production factors existed in eastern Germany, high-tech industries are unlikely to relocate to the area. Such firms tend to remain near the parent company and within a highly developed economic region. Both these factors, therefore, favor western rather than eastern Germany.[29]

The third scenario posits a highly subsidized society living well above its levels both of productivity and international competitiveness. Beyond the domestic problems that financing this consumer society would create, this scenario would produce two major conflicts in Germany's relations with its eastern neighbors. First, Central and East Europeans would be producing goods for the east German market at production rates higher than those attained by those consuming the products. The Central and East Europeans could very well object to a living standard that is considerably lower than that of the relatively "unproductive" east Germans. Conflicts between subsidized east German tourists and Central and East Europeans are a real possibility. Second, the free movement of Central and East European—mainly Polish—workers willing to work for lower wages could provide a substantial impetus to industrialization in eastern Germany and break the cycle of high wages and low productivity that has developed there. Yet allowing such workers to enter Germany could spark protests against the loss of German jobs, even if German workers were unwilling to accept the low-wage positions being filled by the non-Germans. If Central and East European workers are not allowed into Germany, as is likely, then the conflicts will be externalized but not eliminated.[30]

The second strategic issue to consider is that Germany's economic influence is likely to increase in Central and Eastern Europe in the 1990s. Although the costs of unification have been much higher than expected and have placed a serious strain on Germany's budget, no alternative economic partner is available for the region. The collapse of the Soviet Union and the CMEA initiated or, as in the case of Poland and Hungary, reinforced the reorientation of existing trade relations, with the result that Germany has already become the leading trading partner for all countries in the region and will command some 30 to 35 percent of total trade by 1995. This is the equivalent of the Soviet share during the best years of the CMEA. Modest amounts of German capital have also started to flow to neighboring countries and in particular to the region of Bohemia in Czechoslovakia.[31] In addition, for obvious geographic reasons, the improved infrastructure so badly needed in Central and Eastern Europe requires German cooperation and even the use of German territory for such developments as oil and gas pipelines, electrical grids, highways, and railways. Deeply rooted historical and cultural tendencies reinforce this pattern of dependence.

As a third strategic consideration, Central and East European countries need to look for alternative economic partners to reduce the possibility of German dominance, without compromising ties with Germany. At the same time, Germany wants to coordinate its policy with those of other industrialized countries interested in cooperating with the new Central and East European democracies. It recognizes, moreover, the need to present German interests in a low-profile context, preferably as part of joint EC activities. Indeed, one solution would be to consider the Community the most important partner, particularly in light of the association treaties that have been signed with Poland, Czechoslovakia, and Hungary. All three countries may enjoy full

EC membership by the end of the 1990s. However, the behavior of other West European countries toward Eastern Europe has been inconsistent. A pronounced fear that Germany may dominate Central and Eastern Europe has not been accompanied by increased West European interest in Central and Eastern Europe. France, in particular, which seems to be the biggest loser after the Soviet Union in the reshaping of Europe, is attempting the impossible by behaving as if nothing has changed in Europe. Any attempt to prevent Germany from strengthening its position in Central and Eastern Europe instead of promoting active participation in the restructuring of the new democracies and their incorporation into the West European community will be self-defeating. Such a policy would not impede strong economic and eventually political relations between Germany and its neighbors to the east, but it would prevent other countries from benefiting from those contacts.

The association treaties with the EC, at least in their present form, reflect the European realities of 1989–90 and not those of 1991–92. The treaties are expected to have a modest impact on diversifying economic relations. First, more than 50 percent of Poland, Czechoslovakia, and Hungary's trade with the community is with Germany alone.[32] Second, this trade has been developing rapidly, with all three countries showing significantly more trade with Germany than with the rest of the EC since 1988.[33] Third, the commodity pattern of trade with Germany is substantially more developed than it is with other EC member countries. For example, approximately two-thirds of Hungary's machinery exports to and imports from the EC involve Germany. Fourth, and partly as a consequence of this more developed commodity pattern, exports to Germany include a smaller share of politically sensitive goods such as agricultural products, steel, and textiles. The importance of the ties between Germany and its eastern neighbors can also be observed on the German side. Germany is the only major EC country for which trade with Poland, Hungary, and Czechoslovakia is more important than trade with the former Soviet Union.[34]

Germany has always supported improved economic relations between the EC and Central and Eastern Europe. Together with the United Kingdom and some smaller North European member countries, it has been the champion of free trade. Germany has always carried a great deal of weight in the struggle against a more protectionist EC, as favored by France and the South European member states, but this policy may now be changing. In the medium term, however, Germany's position may be challenged by intra-German developments. If industrial recovery in eastern Germany is seriously hindered by social concerns and wage disputes, more protectionist German trade policies may develop. This would not only hamper export growth in Central and Eastern Europe but increase the economic and social costs of establishing well-functioning market economies in the region. Central control is necessarily increasing in the eastern part of Germany as bureaucratic interventions take the place of market mechanisms that have not yet developed. More state intervention may give rise to some protectionist tendencies in Germany. A more protectionist Germany would also become a significant factor in converting the EC into a European fortress (with or without the associated countries). Although this is not the most likely scenario in the coming years, growing German opposition to improved market access for some Central and East European products cannot be ruled out. Relations between Germany and Eastern Europe could be particularly strained if the Polish question re-emerges and Germany supports full EC membership for Czechoslovakia and Hungary but not Poland.

The fourth strategic question involves the extent to which the Central and East European countries can and will diversify their external economic relations as they develop their market economies. For reasons of economic efficiency, Germany will remain the most important trading partner for all countries in the region and will account for a growing share of foreign direct investment above its already high level. At the end of May 1991, for example, 85 percent of the registered value of foreign investment in Czechoslovakia had come from Germany, and, by the end of 1990, some 30 percent of such investment in Poland. But in Hungary, the country with the highest rate of foreign investment in the region, Germany's share was less than 22 percent, while the United States was responsible for more than 40 percent and the Far Eastern countries for almost 20 percent. The possibility of counterbalancing economic dependence on Germany with direct investments from other countries in order to diversify external economic relations seems to be more feasible for Hungary. It is less likely for Czechoslovakia and perhaps also for Poland. But it must be stressed that the small Central and East European countries are hardly in a position to shape their economies to the most desirable pattern by themselves; they need considerable support from the West and Far East. Such cooperation is not one sided, as substantial Western and Far Eastern interests are also at stake. The best chances for non-German investors to establish firm positions in Central and Eastern Europe are probably limited to the period in which Germany is still fundamentally absorbed in intra-German issues. Once these problems have been settled, at least in economic terms, and a new, dynamic Germany emerges in Europe, German influence in Central and Eastern Europe will increase rapidly if other interested countries do not establish themselves in the region beforehand.

Fifth, Germany's role in Central and Eastern Europe depends largely on developments in the former Soviet Union. For reasons of security, Germany wants to maintain good relations with the new independent republics. As of October 1991, about 225,000 troops deployed by the Soviet Union remain in eastern Germany, and as the nearest Western country, Germany remains more exposed than others to the danger of nuclear accidents.[35] Nevertheless,

Germany is more interested in ensuring political and economic stability in its neighboring countries, particularly Czechoslovakia and Poland, which share a common border. But the new democracies cannot conceal their fear that, under certain circumstances, Germany may favor the former Soviet Union at their expense. In this case, the Central and East European area would become a highly unstable economic and political vacuum.

Last but not least, the Central and East European countries would like to be integrated into the international economy. For most of them, the way leads through Germany, particularly in the area of trade. What role Germany plays in the international economy during the 1990s is therefore of vital importance. If the present diversion of resources to eastern Germany is a short-term development that produces positive results in the near future, Germany could maintain or even strengthen its position in the world economy, prevent the rise of protectionism, and provide increasing opportunities for Central and East European economic development and modernization. If, however, resources continue to be diverted over the long term, new bureaucratic, interventionist, and protectionist patterns could emerge. As a result, Germany would see its competitiveness challenged or reduced, and the prospects for Central and Eastern Europe would be bleaker. Although the region would continue to receive some support from Germany for modernization, it could become the unwilling partner of an increasingly protectionist and globally uncompetitive Europe that failed to keep up with international developments—with serious implications for political and economic developments in the region.

Lessons from German Unification for Central and Eastern Europe

Besides having a direct impact on trade, finance, and investment in Central and Eastern Europe, German unification provides a series of important lessons about transforming a more or less centrally planned economy into a market economy. The treatment applied to the former East Germany has its unique features and in some ways differs substantially from policies applied to other countries of the region; thus, two sets of useful experiences are available. The first includes the failures that have been and are still being made by all reforming countries. The second includes some problems specific to Germany that should be avoided by the Central and East European economies. The east German experience is not a good indicator of how to accelerate the transition process, but it is a valuable indicator of what should be avoided in order to maximize chances for successful transformation.[36] Some of the major lessons are listed below.

—Privatization is a long and expensive process, even if a lot of money is available. Although a number of mostly small- and medium-sized companies have been privatized, the number of companies still waiting to be privatized has decreased very little because, as the first step in privatization, large enterprises were split into smaller units. In addition, privatization did not produce the expected net income of DM 14 billion for the already delicate German budget. On the contrary, it resulted in a substantial loss, and increasing subsidization of the privatization process now seems unavoidable. Treuhand's losses in 1991 and its expected deficits in 1992 will be at least twice as high as Hungary's total gross debt. Unfortunately, the reforming Central and East European countries do not have access to the financial resources necessary to foster the privatization process or link it to efficient restructuring.

—State agencies controlling privatization can help avoid some of the pitfalls of the transformation process—such as extremely cheap sales of state-owned enterprises—but the costs of maintaining a huge and steadily increasing bureaucracy seem to be several times higher than the potential savings. In addition, such interventionist activities appear to multiply, increasing costs still further.

—Issues of ownership and rules regarding restitution, however politically desirable they may be, hinder the smooth and rapid transformation of an economy by spreading insecurity and weakening the confidence of potential investors.

—A successful transformation must begin with heavy investments in infrastructure. This is the economic framework that reduces investment costs and transmits the right psychological signals to potential investors. However, infrastructural projects have generally been financed by domestic savings and long-term international loans, and only partially (as in the case of telecommunications) by foreign direct investment. In eastern Germany, the federal German budget provides the majority of such investments, while the Polish, Czechoslovak, and Hungarian infrastructures lack crucial financial assets due to the strict anti-inflationary policies currently in place. If Europe does indeed unite, future infrastructural investments should be prioritized and linked, both in implementation and financing, to the projects currently under way in eastern Germany.[37]

In several areas, however, the economic lessons of German unification are discouraging and, in general, not applicable to the Central and East European countries.

First, Western experience with basic economic and political change has been sporadic and has taken place in completely different historical and cultural settings. Frequent exposure to Western ambiguities neither encourages the new democracies nor adds credibility to suggestions offered by the West. The most radical reforms are frequently proposed by countries that are absolutely unable to implement even minor changes in their own political and economic systems, claiming that insurmountable obstacles stand in the way of such changes.

Second, one of the primary reasons why German unification will cost several times more than expected is that economic, institutional, and educational goals were not pursued before unification. While political developments certainly shortened the preparation period for unification, it should have been taken into account that East Germany not only had one of the most orthodox centrally planned economies in the European CMEA but was also one of its least flexible and market economy-minded societies. The decline of east German industrial production, the spectacular collapse of what was alleged to be the world's tenth-largest industrial power, and a frightening unemployment rate of 17 percent are hardly examples to be followed by any country.

Third, the currency union revalued many already uncompetitive east German products by about three times. Even the most competitive economies would have been devastated by this measure. Independent exchange rate policy, including periodic devaluations, is an important economic instrument during the transition from a centrally planned to a free market economy; east Germany did not have this tool after the currency union.

Fourth, the economic shock therapy applied to eastern Germany has resulted in a number of grave social consequences that will have to be paid for by western Germany for some time. This therapy cannot be used in other Central and East European countries because domestic resources for financing the social consequences of transformation are limited and external resources almost nonexistent. At the same time, members of these relatively homogeneous societies are able to identify with the successes and failures of the painful transformation process in a way east Germans—whose market economy has been imposed from above and outside—cannot. The issue of integrating east German society into the west German system and the social and possibly the political costs of integration remain problematic. Certainly, this unification will take much longer than economic unification.

The most important lesson, however, should be addressed to those members of the international community interested in or affected by developments in Central and Eastern Europe. Eastern Germany does not provide a useful model for transforming a planned economy into an efficient market economy. Nevertheless, this experience demonstrates that substantial international cooperation and financial support are needed to sustain the transformation process. The high level of external debt and debt servicing; the continuing resource transfers; the highly negative growth rates; the forced overnight reorientation of foreign economic relations; and the mounting social problems need not only a careful analysis but, more urgently, immediate international attention.

It would be misleading to assume that the large sums of money that have been transferred and are still to be channeled to eastern Germany will be required by other economies in the region that are better prepared than eastern Germany for the transition. The Central and East European countries— especially Hungary, with its two decades of preparation for a market economy—will require a fraction of the money invested in eastern Germany. In addition, the populations of these countries will not suffer from the comparison of their living standard with that of affluent west Germans. The approximately DM 250 billion that has been invested in eastern Germany since the unification equals the gross external debt accumulated since the early 1970s by the East and Central European countries, including the former Soviet Union. By using part of this money to support the transformation in other countries of the region, western Germany could have helped both to create successful market economies and to stabilize the region without abandoning its political union with eastern Germany. Political motivations caused western Germany to make a different decision.

Conclusion

German unification has had and will have a substantial impact on the Central and East European economies. The ramifications of unification come during a crucial period of radical economic and political transformation in the region. Some developments support the transformation process, but some hinder it and may distort or delay desirable policy measures by, in part, greatly increasing the costs of adjustment.

The spectacular collapse of the east German economy was a significant economic loss for all ex-CMEA countries. The high costs of unification raised international interest rates and, to a large extent, depleted the external financial resources available for the basic tasks of modernization and restructuring in the new democracies. At the same time, booming German demand supported exports by Central and East European economies and contributed to the success of export-oriented economic policies, mainly in Poland, Hungary, and, in 1991, Czechoslovakia.

Because Germany is the most important economic partner in the region, and because the region is of growing importance to the unified Germany, a strategy is needed for developing bilateral relations and determining their place in both the EC and the world. The main pillars of such a strategy will not be determined exclusively by the successes, failures, and costs of intra-German relations or the trends in the Central and East European countries, including the former Soviet Union. Other countries with international political and economic influence that are interested in the future of Central and Eastern Europe can and should help shape this strategy. The issue is a particularly timely one, as political and economic reforms have entered a critical stage, and the future of a stable, reliable and internationally open Europe has become a pressing question on the international agenda.

Notes

1. Even so, intraindustry trade did not represent more than 60 percent of these bilateral trade flows, in comparison with shares well above 80 percent among developed market economies (Detlef Lorenz, "Konsequenzen für den deutschen Aussenhandel aus der Integration West- und Ostdeutschlands," in E. Kantzenbach, *Schriften des Vereins für Sozialpolitik*, Autumn 1991). Neither was this trade always based on terms of economic efficiency and international competitiveness.

2. In addition, employment possibilities in East Germany, mainly used by Polish workers, were sharply reduced.

3. George A. Akerlof and others, "East Germany in from the Cold: The Economic Aftermath of Currency Union," in *Brookings Papers on Economic Activity, 1:1991*, pp. 1–87.

4. András Inotai, "Competition between the European CMEA and Rapidly Industrializing Countries on the OECD Market for Manufactured Goods: Facts, Trends and Economic Policy Implications," *Empirica Austrian Economic Papers*, no. 1 (Vienna, 1988), pp. 189–204.

5. Akerlof and others, "East Germany," p. 30.

6. From among the forty-five state-owned foreign trade companies only fifteen are expected to be privatized, while ten companies have already been liquidated. Their staff fell from 12,000 to 5,000 in one year, but it is unlikely that more than 1,000 people remain employed in this area. (Deutsches Institut für Wirtschafts- forschung—Institut für Weltwirtschaft an der Universität Kie), "Gesamtwirtschaftliche und unternehmerische Anpassungsprozesse in Ostdeutschland," *DIW Wochenbericht*, 39–40 (September 26, 1991), p. 569.

7. Continuing subsidies to the former USSR included generous Hermes export credits, which, according to German Chancellor Helmut Kohl, admittedly have little to do with economic considerations and which "the average company could only dream of." Helmut Kohl, "Vortrag," in Forum für Deutschland. Die Rolle Deutschlands in Europa, Maerz 13–15, 1991, Die Welt, 1991, p. 16. For special details see Federal Republic of Germany, *Doing Business in Germany's New Federal States* (Cologne: Federal Office of Foreign Trade Information, 1991), pp. 157–58.

8. Benedikt Thanner, "Nachfolgeorganisation für den RGW nicht in Sicht," *IFO- Schnelldienst*, nos. 8–9 (March 21, 1991), pp. 7–14.

9. German officials consider even the exchange rate of DM 2.34 to be a compromise. Their original position was an exchange rate of DM 2.63 to 1 TR.

10. Hans-Dieter Kuschel, "Die Einbeziehung der ehemaligen DDR in die Euro- paeische Gemeinschaft," *Wirtschaftsdienst*, no. 2 (February 1991), pp. 80–87.

11. Leslie Lipschitz and Donogh McDonald, eds., *German Unification: Economic Issues*, IMF Occasional Paper 75 (Washington, December 1990).

12. H. Lutz, "Integrating the East German States into the German Economy: Opportunities, Burdens and Options," Berlin, 1990.

13. Horst Siebert, "The Economic Integration of Germany," Kiel Discussion Papers, no. 160 (Kiel: Institut für Weltwirtschaft, May 1990).

14. See Lipschitz and McDonald, *German Unification*.

15. Federal Office of Foreign Trade Information, *Doing Business*, p. 19; "The West German Economy under the Impact of the Economic Unification of Germany," *Monthly Report of the Deutsche Bundesbank* (October 1991), p. 17; and Helmut Schmidt, "Deutschlands Rolle im neuen Europa," *Europa-Archiv*, no. 21 (November 10, 1991), pp. 616–17.

16. "IMF to Criticise Size of German Deficit," *Financial Times*, November 18, 1991, p. 16.

17. M. Aho, "Global Economic Rivalry: New Perspectives on the European Community, Japan, and the United States," Washington, 1990.

18. The trade surplus rose from DM 63 bn in 1982 to DM 85 bn in 1985 and to the record level of DM 135 bn in 1989.

19. This is equal to a deterioration of DM 108 bn between the end of 1990 and September 1991. The major factor behind this development is that huge trade surpluses practically disappeared. Against the West German trade surplus of DM 135 bn in 1989 and of DM 105 bn in 1990, nine-month figures for 1991 show a very modest surplus of DM 10 bn. More important, in April and in May 1991, foreign trade balance indicated deficits, the first ones after May 1951. See "Zahlungsbilanzstatistiken," *Statistische Beihefte zu den Monatsberichten der Deutschen Bundesbank,* Reihe 3, no. 11, Frankfurt, November 1991.

20. "The West German Economy under the Impact of the Economic Unification," p. 19.

21. "Abbau von Steuersubventionen war ein Reinfall," *Süddeutsche Zeitung*, November 28, 1991, p. 33, and "Bundestag Verabschiedet den Haushalt für 1992," November 30–December 1, 1991, p. 2.

22. "Die öffentlichen Schulden Explodieren Formlich," *Süddeutsche Zeitung*, November 27, 1991, p. 33.

23. Martin Wolf, "German Express Slows Down," *Financial Times*, November 12, 1991, p. 22.

24. It is planned that, irrespective of productivity, east German wages should reach west German levels by 1994. This target has not been approved by east German inhabitants only, but strongly fought for by west German trade unions that consider this measure as the only effective one in order to prevent lower-paid east German workers from getting employment in western Germany, and, as a consequence, crowd out higher-paid west German labor.

25. Even worse, public sector indebtedness will reach DM 1,500 bn by the end of 1992, or a 62 percent increase compared with the mid-1990 figure, before economic reunification started (*Süddeutsche Zeitung*, November 27, 1991).

26. As an exception, growing activity of a few large West German companies in the western part of Czechoslovakia (Volkswagen, Siemens), and of a number of middle-sized companies both in Czechoslovakia and Hungary can be mentioned.

27. Volkswagen, Mercedes-Benz, and BASF are among the most active German multinational firms, having announced major investment projects in eastern Germany.

28. It was particularly interesting that Hungary's exports of machinery to Germany were twice as high as those of Czechoslovakia in 1990. In the first half of 1991, however, Czechoslovak machinery exports started to increase very dynamically.

29. It does not rule out, however, that some development poles will be established in the eastern states, particularly in and around Berlin. However, their spillover effects are likely to be modest, without involving underdeveloped areas in modern economic activities, and thus accentuating economic and social differentiation within eastern Germany.

30. Free movement of workers, as foreseen by the EC 92 project, has been excluded from the association treaties recently signed between Poland, Czechoslovakia, and Hungary, on the one hand, and Brussels, on the other. Yearly quotas will be determined by EC member countries, in order to protect their domestic labor markets from potential low-wage workers coming from Central and Eastern Europe. For Hungary, Germany has granted a quota of 14,000 people in 1992 (as against 10,000 job opportunities in 1991).

31. The effects of the Volkswagen-Skoda deal are already visible. Volkswagen, Siemens, and several other large German firms, along with hundreds of small- and medium-sized enterprises (primarily from Bavaria), have been establishing themselves in Bohemia recently. Surprisingly, they have not invested in the new German states—Thuringia or Saxony, for example—but in a geographic area that has clear cost advantages and can serve as a bridge between the developed southern and the underdeveloped east German states.

32. In 1990, the export and import figures for Poland were 48 and 52 percent, for Czechoslovakia 49 and 58 percent, and for Hungary 53 and 57 percent. Taking into account that another 14 percent of the three countries' EC trade is with Italy, with some exaggeration, the association agreement can be qualified as a treaty with Germany and Italy.

33. Between 1988 and 1990, West Germany's share of Hungary's exports to the EC increased from 49.9 to 52.7 percent. The same figures for Poland were 41.1 and 48 percent, and for Czechoslovakia 47.8 and 49.2 percent. Similar trends can be observed in imports from the EC. Here, Germany's share increased from 50.5 to 51.8 percent for Poland and from 55 to 58 percent for Czechoslovakia, with the Hungarian share remaining constant at 56.5 percent. Between 1989 and 1990, the EC's share of total Hungarian exports to the OECD grew from 64.3 to 67.3 percent; Polish exports from 71.3 to 75.5 percent; and Czechoslovakia's exports from 68.6 to 70 percent. Simultaneously, in all Central and East European countries, the growth of German market share surpassed that of the total EC market, so that the whole dynamism of exports to the EC was supported by Germany alone. From 1989 to 1990 Germany's share in Hungarian exports to the OECD rose from 31.6 to 35.5 percent, in Polish exports from 31.1 to 36.3 percent, and in Czechoslovak exports from 31.9 to 34.4 percent. For detailed information see András Inotai, "Assoziierungsabkommen: Schritte zur Reintegration ostmitteleuropaeischer Staaten," *Integration*, vol. 15 (January 1992), pp. 33–34.

34. In 1990, the share of Poland, Czechoslovakia, and Hungary in German exports to the European ex-CMEA countries amounted to 48 percent, and in German imports to 51 percent. The corresponding Soviet figures were 44 and 42 percent. On the contrary, the Soviet Union clearly dominated the Eastern trade of France (53 and 65 percent vis-à-vis 35 and 27 percent for the three Central Eastern European economies), Italy (55 and 63 percent vis-á-vis 36 and 28 percent) or the United Kingdom (50 and 57 percent vis-á-vis 39 and 37 percent). For detailed information, see Inotai, "Assoziierungsabkommen: Schritte zur Reintegration ostmiltteleuropaeischer Staaten," pp. 33–34; and Organization for Economic Cooperation and Development, *Monthly Statistics of Foreign Trade,* Series A (Paris, September 1991).

35. "Borisov Journal; German Prefabs Await an Unwelcome Red Army," *New York Times*, October 17, 1991, p. A4.

36. For a different view see Günther Storch, "Germany's Role in a Changing World Economy," *Deutsche Bundesbank, Auszüge aus Presseartikeln*, no. 50 (July 4, 1991), p. 9.

37. Ambitious plans and huge infrastructural projects are taking place in the

former East Germany. In the planning stage, at least some of these projects should be based on regional considerations. At present, one of the major obstacles to long-term export-led growth and higher competitiveness among the Central and East European economies is the underdeveloped state of physical infrastructure. This situation is also becoming a major barrier to more intraregional trade among Poland, Czechoslovakia, and Hungary. The modernization of east German infrastructure could be linked to all-European projects, and international financing should be sought for this kind of investment.

TEN

Security Problems Facing Central and Eastern Europe after German Unification

Slawomir A. Dabrowa

THROUGH THEIR ideas and actions, the countries of Central and Eastern Europe have made significant contributions to the changes that have taken place in Europe. They are also among the countries most affected by these changes. Strategically situated between Germany and the former Soviet Union, they must closely observe developments in their two powerful neighbors and assess the ways in which their security is affected in order to formulate and implement policies that best meet their needs.

The purpose of this chapter is to discuss the security problems facing Central and Eastern Europe in general and Poland in particular during this turbulent period in European history.[1] Past and present perceptions of the security dilemma and the policy responses of the new democracies in Central and Eastern Europe will be considered.

Unification and the Security of Central and Eastern Europe

Clearly the European political and strategic landscape has changed completely from what it was only two or three years ago. The most fundamental alterations have been in the central and eastern part of the continent, and while these changes have been significant, they should not be regarded either exclusively or predominantly as security threats. Such an approach would clearly be one sided.[2] The new situation, including German unification and the disintegration of the Soviet Union, creates opportunities to promote security in Central and Eastern Europe as well as in the whole of Europe.

German unification must be analyzed within the context of the broader transformation of Europe during the 1990s. While it occurred during the same historical period as the disintegration of the Soviet Union, the countries of Central and Eastern Europe hold distinctly different attitudes toward the two events. Unification was anticipated—albeit at a later date—but not necessarily welcomed because of the uncertainties involved. On the other hand, the un- expected disintegration of the Soviet Union was welcomed despite the uncer- tainties it created. This difference in attitudes can be explained by the fact that, forty-five years after World War II, fewer and fewer Central and East Europeans remember the period of German dominance, while all are familiar with Soviet rule. Neither of the two events was a stated goal or the result of a specific policy by a Central or East European country.

Chances for Improved Security

Unification has created three important opportunities for Central and Eastern Europe: the chance to settle finally the question of Germany's borders, the possibility of "shortening" the geographic distance between the region and Western Europe, and the prospect of joining a united Europe.

THE ISSUE OF BORDERS.   The only remaining unsettled problem concerning borders during the final stage of the German unification process involved the Polish-German frontier along the Oder and Neisse rivers. Though it had been internationally recognized in the Zgorzelec Agreement between Poland and the former East Germany signed on July 6, 1950; in the Warsaw Treaty between Poland and the Federal Republic signed in December 1970; and in the Helsinki Final Act of 1975, in which European and North American governments recognized the inviolability of existing borders, unification could have raised questions about the legal status of this border. Bonn's official position had been based on the legal fiction that Germany continued to exist within its 1937 borders. According to this definition, one-third of Poland could have been considered part of Germany, and for domestic reasons Chancellor Helmut Kohl reiterated this position during the debate on uni- fication.[3]

The objective of Polish foreign policy at that time was to secure the integrity of its western border by convincing other countries that Germany's legal and political recognition of the border represented a key component of the new European framework. Although the border was not endorsed before unification because Germany insisted that only the new, sovereign German state could make such a decision, Poland did win three major concessions.

First, the Four Powers and the two Germanies invited Poland to the Two plus Four negotiations in Paris on July 17, 1990, to participate in a discussion of the security needs of Germany's neighbors. This opportunity to present its views was important for Poland; the country had not forgotten those times when decisions on its fate were made without consulting the Poles themselves.

Second, Poland secured the support not only of the Four Powers but of the other European states for its argument that unification could and should not take place while an issue of such magnitude as that of the Polish border remained unresolved. As a result, Article 1 of the Treaty on the Final Settlement with Respect to Germany (known as the Two plus Four Treaty), signed in Moscow on September 12, 1990, stipulated that "the united Germany and the Republic of Poland shall confirm the existing border between them in a treaty that is binding under international law."[4]

Third, Germany promised that the issue would be resolved soon after unification. This promise has been fulfilled. On November 14, 1990, Germany and Poland signed a treaty in Warsaw confirming the present border and their mutual commitment to unreservedly respecting its inviolability. This treaty opened the way to Polish-German reconciliation, which is as important to European unity as reconciliation between France and Germany was to the process of West European integration.[5]

Only somebody inside the circle of negotiators could reveal the extent to which Poland's success on these issues was due to the justice of its cause, Germany's reasonable position, support from other countries, or the diplomatic skill of the Polish representatives. These successes may also have been influenced by the fact that the Polish negotiations were conducted by the Solidarity government formed after the June 1989 elections—the first noncommunist government east of the Elbe in many decades. Perhaps the West felt a special affinity for Polish democracy, because Poland was one of the first countries to set the process of European change in motion. It was also one of the first to speak out against German neutrality during the discussions on unification.

The Soviet Union's position on the issue of the Oder-Neisse frontier is also worth noting here, since the Soviets must have felt somewhat ambivalent. On the one hand, the USSR was almost certainly interested in obtaining the united Germany's confirmation of the existing borders, for without it, the status of the Kaliningrad district could have been called into question. (The district, a Russian enclave on the Baltic coast that once formed the northern portion of German East Prussia, was taken over by the USSR in 1945; the rest of the territory was granted to Poland.) On the other hand, since World War II the Soviet Union had assumed the self-declared role of "guarantor" of the Polish western frontier. This role had given the Soviets additional leverage in Poland and had been willingly accepted by Poland's communist governments. Germany's confirmation of the borders deprived the Soviet Union of this leverage, but to the credit of the Soviets, all official statements supported the Polish position.

CLOSER ASSOCIATION WITH THE WEST. The second opportunity raised by German unification should bring Western Europe closer to its Central and East European neighbors. Hopefully, proximity to the united Germany will make it easier for the new democracies to join Western institutions such as the EC and NATO. Had East Germany survived, it would have constituted a major barrier to both membership in such organizations and enhanced cooperation in general with the West. Poland, in particular, cannot ignore the importance of Germany as a gateway to the West.[6] At the same time, Poland's importance to Germany has been recognized. As Theo Sommer points out,

> The Germans hurled Europe into the great war with their invasion of Poland 50 years ago. Now they have the opportunity—again in Poland, as fate will have it—to help lay the foundations of a new European order.[7]

THE PROMISE OF EUROPEAN INTEGRATION. Together with the dissolution of the Warsaw Treaty Organization (WTO), German unification prevented the petrification of the postwar order established at Yalta and Potsdam and raised the prospect of European integration. Thus, shortly after unification, thirty-four European and North American countries could declare in the Charter of Paris, signed on November 21, 1990, at the summit of the Conference on Security and Cooperation in Europe (CSCE) that one of their goals was "a united, democratic Europe."[8] This could not have been achieved without German unification. As Czechoslovak President Vaclav Havel said, "It is hard to conceive of a united Europe with a divided Germany. Likewise difficult to conceive of a united Germany in a divided Europe." Polish Minister of Foreign Affairs Krzysztof Skubiszewski echoed this view at a press conference in Paris on July 17, 1990, "There is no question of a united Europe without a united Germany and vice versa."[9]

This argument explains why Central and Eastern Europe had relatively little difficulty recognizing the right of the German people to live as one nation, despite the problems unification causes for the region. German unification was considered an acceptable price to pay for European integration, despite the line taken by previous communist governments that the division of Germany was central to European security.

Challenges to Security

What conceivable hazards or threats does German unification pose for Central and Eastern Europe? If one applies the rule formulated by Mikhail Bakunin that "every State must conquer or be conquered," territorial or political expansionism is one of them. To the same category of threats belongs an alliance between Germany and Russia at the expense of Central and Eastern Europe. Another threat could come from an excess of German military power that undermines the Central and East European framework. But of all the theoretical hazards, only one seems likely to develop into a reality: German economic dominance over the region.

Poland, and no doubt other Central and East European countries, believe that unification has fulfilled Germany's primary strategic goal and national aspirations. It is assumed that the talents of the German people will now be directed at raising the east German standard of living, promoting pan-European integration, and strengthening peace and security in Europe and elsewhere. Germany has an important role to play in the construction of the new European and international order. Fortunately, unification has not made expansion of the European Community or pan-European cooperation within the framework of the CSCE more difficult, nor has it hampered the formation of new ties between Western Europe and the Central and East European region. These developments provide further explanations for the relative ease with which Central and Eastern Europe accepted unification.[10]

A revival of an expansionist German policy with German domination as its goal—the infamous *Drang nach Osten* (push eastward)—is highly unlikely but nevertheless worthy of consideration. As such it would be a catastrophe for Europe. Europeanizing Germany by anchoring it in the EC and NATO is seen as the best means of protecting against this possibility. For this reason, the Central and East European countries strongly favor the process of Western European integration and vehemently support cooperation between Germany, Western Europe, the United States, and Canada within the framework of NATO and the CSCE. For the same reason, these countries speak out unreservedly in favor of an American military presence in Europe. Despite all the changes that have affected their military role, the political function of U.S. troops in Europe remains. As one American observer noted, "as long as U.S. troops are in Germany, Poland has no need to fear Germany, since the type of Germany that welcomes U.S. troops will not be a belligerent one."[11] One could imagine a Europe without American armed forces, but before that happens, an effective all-European system of collective security that includes U.S. and Canadian support must be put in place.[12]

The second hypothetical menace stems from a rapprochement between Germany and Russia that deliberately excludes Central and Eastern Europe. This fear of a new Rapallo, or a Berlin-Moscow axis, is particularly strong in Poland, which has suffered more than most from collusion between Germany and the Soviet Union/Russia over the last few centuries. Fortunately, the present political situation in Europe is unlikely to yield such a result, as Germany's relations with Russia and the rest of the former Soviet Union complement its relations with Western Europe and the United States rather than supplants them. The United States and Western Europe are the allies Germany will have to choose between if such a choice becomes necessary.

The real risk for Central and Eastern Europe lies not in a potential Rapallo but in the possibility that an economically powerful Germany could literally buy concessions from a weak Russia that might be harmful to other countries. The Kaliningrad district again serves as an example. Germany could provide

Russia with financial incentives to resettle ethnic Germans from the Volga region and Kazakhstan in this area, in effect creating an ersatz East Prussia. With German economic influence also expected to grow in Lithuania, Latvia, and Estonia, Germany could eventually dominate the Baltic region.[13]

The possibility that German military power might destabilize the security of Central and Eastern Europe is also unlikely, given the legal constraints the country has willingly accepted. In Article 3 of the Two plus Four Treaty, Germany reaffirmed its renunciation of nuclear, biological, and chemical (NBC) weapons. Under the terms of the Paris Treaty on Conventional Armed Forces in Europe (CFE) of November 19, 1990, Germany also undertook unilaterally to reduce its armed forces to 370,000 in three to four years, with no more than 345,000 ground and air troops.[14] When these reductions have been made, German military strength will be one-half that of the former West and East Germanies combined.

While the economic consequences of unification for Central and Eastern Europe are too extensive to be covered completely in this chapter, those linked directly to security need attention. In the past, the region's economic dependence on the Soviet Union had numerous consequences for security. For example, strategic raw materials had to be purchased from the former Soviet Union, which also licensed the production of military equipment. Replacing Soviet with German influence would simply replicate this earlier situation with a different partner. A Polish scholar has pointed out that the risk of Poland becoming dependent on Germany is high not because of the strong Bundeswehr, but because of the strong deutsche mark—especially when compared to the zloty. Another opinion holds that ". . . German economic influence in Poland [is] becoming so vast it could ultimately lead to German demands for a peaceful revision of the border."[15]

A middle course must be found between the possibility that German economic influence will become excessive and the possibility that Germany will become so absorbed with the problems of the former GDR, the EC, and Russia that it ignores Central and Eastern Europe. All the countries of the region badly need foreign capital to carry out economic reforms and make the transformation from centrally planned to free market economies. And in all likelihood, German capital will be the most available.

The Disintegration of the Soviet Union and the Security of Central and Eastern Europe

The disintegration of the Soviet Union has shifted interest from the German question to the "Soviet" question, which has more important implications for the region's security. While the effects of German unification on regional security will become apparent only in the long term, the disintegration of the

Soviet Union has had an immediate impact, including raising the threat of nuclear proliferation. In addition, German unification occurred only after negotiations that resulted in a detailed treaty and under the strict control not only of the Four Powers but of the Germans themselves. In contrast, the dissolution of the Soviet Union, which was accelerated by the short-lived military coup in August 1991, was much less manageable.[16] Concern in Europe about Germany has therefore been replaced by concern about the successor states of the Soviet Union. The disintegration of the Soviet Union into many sovereign entities has raised several issues that have important implications for the security of Central and Eastern Europe.

The first is the question of borders. The frontiers of the newly independent states are far from settled, and it will be some time before they enjoy universal recognition. Three factors complicate this problem. The first is residual distrust. For example, between the two world wars, the capital of Lithuania was Kaunas; the historical (and present) capital, Vilnius, belonged to Poland. Today, despite Poland's assurances, Lithuanians are not entirely convinced that the Poles have really become reconciled to the new situation. Second, the issue of borders is inseparable from the problem of national and ethnic minorities. Moldova, annexed by the Soviet Union from Romania in 1945, is one such case among the former Soviet republics. Conflict has erupted between its Russian-speaking minority, which seeks independence, and the ethnic Romanian majority. Romania, moreover, unlike Poland and Germany, has not renounced its historical rights to its former eastern territories. And third, new countries tend to keep the question of borders open for a period of time, either to ascertain that no reciprocal territorial claims will be made or to use as an instrument of policy—for example, to extort diplomatic recognition in exchange for the renunciation of territorial claims.

It is encouraging, however, that progress is being made to head off potential problems in some areas. Poland, for example, which shares borders with Lithuania, Russia, Ukraine, and Belarus, has affirmed that it has no territorial claims on its neighbors. Concurrently, it has requested respect for the rights of Polish minorities living on neighboring territories.

Just as serious for the whole of Europe is the threat of the proliferation of nuclear weapons if Ukraine, Belarus, and Kazakhstan refuse to return former Soviet strategic nuclear warheads to Russia. The total number of Soviet strategic nuclear warheads before START reductions is usually given as 25,000–30,000. Of this total, an estimated 65 percent are deployed within Russia, with the remaining 35 percent spread throughout Ukraine, Kazakhstan, and Belarus.[17] Thousands of Soviet tactical nuclear weapons were distributed throughout the country, but it is assumed that those in other republics have been recently removed to Russia.

Still another threat is the possibility that a civil war or famine in Russia or other successor states of the Soviet Union could send waves of refugees westward. The likely scope of this negative phenomenon would exceed the ability of the Central and East European countries to cope efficiently, if only for economic reasons. It is better to admit in advance that such a development would be a problem shared equally by Eastern, Central, and Western Europe.

If this discussion of the impact of the dissolution of the Soviet Union on the security of Central and Eastern Europe were limited to threats only, it would not accurately reflect feelings in the region. But the recent changes have also occasioned hopes and expectations. Poland was once the traditional frontier of Soviet/Russian westward expansion; now the danger of such expansionism and interventionism has decreased. And while the danger of nationalism in Lithuania, Belarus, Ukraine, and even Poland has increased, new possibilities have been created for countries of the region to diversify their previously uniform Ostpolitik and develop separate policies for each of their eastern neighbors, as Poland is doing. New opportunities have opened up for Poland, in particular, to act as a kind of middleman in economic cooperation between Eastern and Western Europe and to share its experience and knowledge of international cooperation.

Asked about the consequences of the withdrawal of Soviet security guarantees and disintegration of the Soviet Union, many Poles would answer that their external security is certainly better now than it was before if Berlin in 1953, Budapest in 1956, Prague in 1968, and to some extent Poland in 1981 are taken into account. However, some West European and, not surprisingly, former Soviet experts differ from their Central and East European counterparts on the consequences of the end of the Cold War on European security in general. As a rule, Western authors stress the deficiencies of the previous bipolar European order but also point out that it at least had the advantage, in spite of the political antagonism it engendered, of assuring stability. They argue that the high tension/high stability bipolarity of the Cold War has been replaced with low tension and correspondingly low stability. But experts from Central and Eastern Europe argue that the so-called stability of the previous era was enjoyed by the West and not by Central and Eastern Europe. For the East, it represented stalemate and stagnation and constituted a kind of "cemetery stability." In fact, the entire continent was less stable because of the deep division of Europe.[18]

New Security Policies of the Central and East European Countries

The recent changes, both international and domestic, have required the Central and East European democracies to formulate new foreign and security policies. The new security policies are based on three principles. First, they reject the previous order of European security established in Yalta and

Potsdam, which accepted the permanent division of Europe as well as Soviet dominance in Central and Eastern Europe. Second, they dismiss neutrality as an alternative, despite geographical proximities—the relative attractiveness of Finnish and Swedish neutrality to Poland, and Austrian neutrality to Hungary and Czechoslovakia, for example—and the suggestions volunteered by several leading Western politicians.[19] Third, they put forth the "European option" as a priority of their foreign policy, including the closest possible security links with Western Europe.

This European option is the natural consequence of the fact that the new democracies do not want to be in any intermediate security zone that might exist between Western and Eastern Europe. They want to be part of Western Europe. They have initiated Western-style parliamentary democracies, even if, during this present transitional period, their governments are still a mix of the precommunist, postcommunist, and democratic systems. They have declared their commitment to the rule of law and full respect for human rights. They have adopted the principles of a market economy. They are developing relations with Western countries and trying to coordinate foreign policy with them.

In Poland, the European option in foreign policy has replaced the traditional dilemma between the "German option" and the "Russian option" that had long been inseparable from the country's geopolitical location. Another question is often asked now in connection with the new domestic and foreign policy: how can unity with Europe be achieved without the loss of national and cultural identities?[20] Pope John Paul II and Polish President Lech Walesa have said that Poland does not need to return to Europe, because it has always been in Europe and shares the European system of Christian values.

The question of whether there is a place for an "American option" in foreign policy has also been raised. But here the answer is easier, since Poland, and Central and Eastern Europe in general, do not need to choose between a European and an American option. The United States, with its membership in NATO, military presence in Europe, and participation in the CSCE, is as much a European as it is a North American power. Thus, developing relations with the United States is also a part of the European option for Central and Eastern Europe.

The new security policies of the Central and East European countries are characterized by unilateral decisions, bilateral arrangements, regional initiatives, and broader pan-European security cooperation.

Unilateral Decisions

The first task of the Central and East European governments has been to regain control of their armed forces and decrease their military expenditures. Military doctrines have been revamped to reflect the new international situation and those elements that served the former WTO's coalition doctrine have been abandoned. The new Polish military doctrine provides a good example of the now strictly defensive approach.[21] First, no a priori enemy is defined; no country is recognized as overtly hostile to Poland. In turn, Poland does not want to be perceived as a threat to any of its neighbors. Second, the new military doctrine is based on the principle of defensive sufficiency, which stipulates that Poland must have enough forces to defend itself from any quarter without being capable of waging offensive operations. The primary function of Polish forces is to defend national borders, although Poland will also participate in international peacekeeping missions. Third, the level of forces, their deployment patterns, and the composition of weapons will be unambiguously defensive. Fourth, Poland will not possess or use weapons of mass destruction.

The changes in Poland's military doctrine are reflected in the planned changes to its armed forces. The main component of the armed forces will be operational forces, including rapid deployment units. These will be supported by regional defense units, which are not expected to be used outside their assigned territories. The new armed forces will be modernized and equipped according to general European standards, and procurement plans anticipate purchasing equipment from the West. Troops will also be relocated from the western part of the country to central and eastern Poland.[22] Heavily armored formations, missile brigades, pontoon-bridge units, and large logistic formations have been either dissolved or reduced in strength and number to cut back on offensive capabilities.[23] Overall, the peacetime strength of the Polish armed forces, in 1991 about 300,000, will be reduced to just over 200,000: 140,000 in the army, 46,000 in the air and air defense forces, and 17,000 in the navy. In time of war, troop strength could be increased rapidly to 750,000 from Poland's population of more than 38 million. According to military sources, "the number of tanks will be reduced by over 1100; armoured combat vehicles by over 220; artillery pieces by nearly 700; combat aircraft by 60; combat ships by over 31."[24] Ceilings for some types of armaments and equipment are fixed by the CFE treaty, but the actual numbers will probably be lower in some categories.

The reform of the armed forces, to be completed by 2000, also envisions combining air force and air defense into a single service, dividing the country into more military districts, reorganizing the command and control system, and reducing the central administration. The general staff will be the only central command of the armed forces. The ministry of defense, until now a predominantly military structure, will be transformed into a civilian department of the government.[25] As in Hungary and Czechoslovakia, the minister of defense is now a civilian. This is a break from Polish military tradition, demonstrating the priority attached to securing civilian control over the armed forces and remaining in step with Western standards.

Bilateral Arrangements

Although bilateral security agreements still play a role in countries such as Korea, Israel, and Cuba, they are unlikely to be revived in Europe. In the western part of the continent, multilateral structures such as NATO, the Western European Union (WEU), and the EC predominate. The Central and East European countries want to disengage from their former military alliances and move closer to these Western institutions. However, one dimension of military security is political security, and in this realm bilateral arrangements are still useful, particularly since the recent changes. Thus, Central and Eastern Europe is developing bilateral links within and outside the region. As a rule, the new treaties of cooperation envisage regular political consultations on security matters.

The treaties between Poland and Germany and Poland and the successor states to the Soviet Union deserve special attention. Although Poland cannot change its geographical location, it is trying to change its geopolitical situation. Discarding both the prewar principle under which "equal distance" was maintained and the postwar policy under which Poland worked together with the Soviet Union against Germany, Polish foreign policy has recently introduced the concept of "equal proximity and friendship."

Both Poland and Germany have made efforts to create a climate favorable to a reconciliation between the two countries. Poland welcomed unification, and the problem of the Polish-German border has been solved. The rights of the German minority in Poland and the Polish minority in Germany have been guaranteed. The last contentious issue between the two countries— compensation for some victims of Nazi persecution in Poland—has also been negotiated to the satisfaction of both governments. Germany has became Poland's most important trade partner, occupying the place that for decades belonged to the Soviet Union. On June 17, 1991, the Polish-German Treaty on Good-Neighborliness and Cooperation was signed, closing one chapter of Polish-German history and opening another, but this time characterized by a community of interests that will soon become an important element of the process of pan-European integration.[26]

In 1991, Poland and the Soviet Union entered negotiations on a treaty of good neighborliness and cooperation to replace the 1965 treaty on friendship, cooperation, and mutual assistance. Four issues complicated the negotiation process, three of them security related.

The first concerned Soviet troops in Poland. After the withdrawal of troops from Hungary and Czechoslovakia and the initial withdrawals from Germany, Poland found itself in the uncomfortable position of being the only Central European country with Soviet troops on its soil and no agreement on their withdrawal. Negotiations throughout 1991 made little progress because of a disagreement on the final date for withdrawal of all troops; Poland insisted on 1992, while negotiators for the Soviet Union argued for 1993. Finally, it was agreed that combat units will be withdrawn by November 15, 1992, but that several thousand noncombatant troops doing liaison work could remain until the end of 1993. An agreement initialed in Moscow on October 26, 1991, by representatives of the Soviet Union and Poland was signed in Moscow on May 22, 1992, by representatives of Russia and Poland, together with protocols on property, financial, and environmental matters related to the deployment of Soviet forces in Poland.

The second major obstacle to concluding a new treaty between Poland and the Soviet Union developed when the two sides were unable to agree on the transport across Poland of former Soviet forces being withdrawn from Germany to Russia. The Soviet-German agreement on troop withdrawal had been concluded without consulting Poland. Germany believed that the troop withdrawals concerned only Germany and the Soviet Union, while the transport issue concerned only Poland and the USSR. Poland and the Soviet Union were for some time unable to reach a satisfactory agreement, but nevertheless Poland allowed former Soviet forces to travel eastward across Polish territory without a formal agreement and despite overdue payments for the costs of the move. The relevant agreement was finally initialed in December 1991 with the Soviets and signed on May 22, 1992, with Russia as the successor state.

The third obstacle resulted from the Soviet insistence on including in the treaty a so-called security clause forbidding either party to join any alliance hostile to the other. This clause was modeled after a similar clause in the Finnish-Soviet Treaty of 1948. A few years ago, Central and Eastern Europe could only dream of achieving a security status similar to that of Finland in relation to the Soviet Union, but in 1991, such a status was no longer enough. Only Romania completed an agreement with the Soviet Union containing this type of clause in March 1991. Poland, Czechoslovakia, and Hungary rejected the demand, which they considered tantamount to giving the Soviet Union *droit de regard* in security policy and reestablishing a kind of Soviet security zone in the region. The new democracies argued that, in the Helsinki Final Act, all CSCE countries had explicitly acknowledged their right to join or not to join any alliance of their choice. After the coup in Moscow failed and foreign policy returned to the line put forward by former Soviet Foreign Minister Eduard Schevardnadze, the Soviet negotiators ceased to insist on the security clause.

The final obstacle was linked to the situation in the former Soviet Union, because doubts had been raised about whether the existing central government was entitled to conclude internationally binding agreements in the absence of a union treaty. Further developments in the former Soviet Union—in particular the December 1991 agreement establishing a new Commonwealth of Independent States (CIS)—were evidence that these doubts were justified.

Hungary, however, signed a treaty on friendship and cooperation with the former Soviet Union only a few days before the republics created the CIS. A similar treaty between the Soviet Union and Czechoslovakia had been initialed in October, and a treaty between the Soviet Union and Poland was initialed in December, but neither was signed due to the collapse of the Soviet Union. However, the treaty between Poland and the Russian Federation on Friendly and Neighborly Cooperation was signed on May 22, 1992. Poland concluded similar treaties with Ukraine on May 18, 1992, and with Belarus on June 23, 1992.

Regional Integration

The trend toward integration has dominated West European foreign policy for several decades. It is based on the recognition that freedom, prosperity, and security are no longer attainable within the confines of the nation-state. However, in Central and Eastern Europe and especially the Soviet Union, the trend has been toward disintegration. The two trends could collide, with potentially dangerous effects for Europe as a whole. To avoid such a collision, Poland, Czechoslovakia, and Hungary decided to strengthen their mutual relations. On April 9, 1990, in Bratislava, leaders of the three states met for the first time, with the foreign ministers of Austria, Italy, and Yugoslavia as observers. The presidents of Poland and Czechoslovakia and prime minister of Hungary met again in Budapest on February 15, 1991, to sign in the nearby town of Visegrad a declaration pledging to coordinate efforts in seeking membership to Western institutions.

On this modest foundation, the members of the Visegrad Triangle have agreed to cooperate on political, economic, humanitarian, and environmental matters. Foreign and security policy are now coordinated by the foreign and defense ministers and expert advisers. As a consequence, delegations from the three countries now submit common proposals in the United Nations, CSCE, and other international bodies. In this manner, they coordinated their negotiations with the former Soviet Union and, following the coup attempt, met to discuss their response. On October 5, 1991, before the Visegrad summit in Cracow, the foreign affairs ministers of the three countries also issued a joint statement on cooperation with NATO. While the Visegrad Triangle is not a security alliance and has specifically rejected the idea of creating a military bloc, its members are eager to identify common security interests and coordinate policies.

In November 1989 Austria, Italy, Yugoslavia, and Hungary initiated what became the so-called Pentagonal group to promote cooperation in the areas of transportation, the environment, and culture, among others.[27] On July 27, 1991, Poland joined what then became the Hexagonal group; in 1992 the group became the Central European Initiative (CEI). In principle, the group does not discuss security matters, but after the August coup attempt, representatives of all member countries met in Warsaw to review the situation in the Soviet Union and its impact on Europe. This interesting development was unfortunately interrupted by events in one of the member countries, Yugoslavia.

The reemergence of independent Lithuania, Latvia, and Estonia has also opened up the possibility of greater cooperation among Baltic states. With this goal in mind, Poland and Sweden sponsored a conference of all the Baltic states at Ronneby, Sweden. On September 3, 1990, the prime ministers attending this conference adopted the Baltic Sea Declaration, which covers primarily environmental and transportation issues.[28] Initially, political and security issues were not matters for discussion among the Baltic states. However, the foreign ministers met in Copenhagen on March 5–6, 1992, and established the Baltic Council, which will have annual meetings of foreign ministers as well as working groups.

The foreign ministers of Poland, France, and Germany also met at Weimar on August 28–29, 1991, and adopted a joint statement on security matters in Europe. They decided to continue meeting annually, and more often if necessary. The Weimar gathering was the first trilateral meeting of those countries forming a belt of land from the Atlantic to the border of the former Soviet Union. The second meeting took place at Tremolat, France, on April 24, 1992. The next one will be held in Poland in 1993.

Taken together, these regional initiatives constitute an increasingly important part of the new European politics. The experience is a particularly novel one for the Central and East European countries, since under Soviet rule their foreign relations were predominantly with Moscow. While the "new regionalism" in Central and Eastern Europe has been strongly encouraged by Western countries, the successor states of the Soviet Union must still be convinced that it will not work against their interests.[29]

European Security Cooperation

In parallel with the dissolution of the WTO and the Soviet Union, the Central and East European states have sought closer ties with NATO and the WEU, while also supporting further institutionalization of the CSCE. From the regional point of view, the measures envisaged by NATO, the WEU, and the European Community to develop relations with Central and Eastern Europe are mutually complementary and serve the interests of pan-European cooperation and security.

The interest the three countries have shown in moving under the NATO umbrella is quite natural, considering their general interest in closer cooperation with Western institutions and NATO's attractiveness as the only viable security system in Europe. Initially, the Central and East European countries considered two means of affiliating themselves with NATO. The first entailed rapprochement between NATO and the WTO. It is likely that Western politicians initially preferred this approach, as indicated by the Joint Declaration of Twenty-Two States, signed in Paris on November 19, 1990. The declaration states that the members of NATO and the WTO "solemnly declare that, in the new era of European relations which is beginning, they are no longer adversaries, will build new partnerships and extend to each other the hand of friendship."[30]

The second, preferred by the Central and East European countries, assumed that disbanding the WTO would promote rapprochement between its members and NATO. Western politicians who feared the Soviet reaction to such a sudden shift in allegiances responded accordingly. As late as February 1990, German Foreign Minister Hans-Dietrich Genscher stated at a conference in Potsdam that "in setting out to design the future structures for Europe, especially its security structure, we must clearly define the future role of the two alliances. . . . They will become elements of the new co-operative security structures in Europe, by which they will be increasingly overarched and into which they can ultimately be absorbed."[31] In Western political thinking, the WTO could have existed without Poland, Czechoslovakia, or Hungary as a "residual WTO."[32] To give these opinions their due, similar views were being expressed in Poland. And, as Genscher suggested, one alliance—NATO—would indeed become an element in the new pan-European security structure being built through the CSCE process.

With the formal dissolution of the WTO's military structure on March 31, 1991, and of its political arrangements on July 1, 1991, NATO has taken several initiatives to foster cooperation with former members.[33] Building on the London Declaration on a transformed North Atlantic Alliance, issued by the North Atlantic Council at its meeting on July 5–6, 1990, the council issued the Copenhagen statement on June 6–7, 1991, on Partnership with the Countries of Central and Eastern Europe, which declares that the security of NATO countries "is inseparably linked to that of all other states in Europe."[34] And following the Moscow coup, NATO countries issued a statement after their meeting in Brussels on August 21, 1991, expressing their solidarity with the new democracies of Central and Eastern Europe and their intention to strengthen their contribution to political and economic reform in the region.

These declarations of intent have enabled Central and East European countries to begin forming their own ties with NATO. Poland, for example, established diplomatic contacts with NATO in August 1990. Within the framework of this diplomatic liaison, Manfred Wörner, the Secretary-General of NATO, visited Poland on September 13, 1990, and the Polish ministers of foreign affairs and defense visited NATO Headquarters in Brussels. Civilian and military study missions were exchanged. Finally, President Lech

Walesa, visiting NATO Headquarters on July 3, 1991, noted that Poland shares NATO's credo and political goals and does not believe that cooperation with the alliance constitutes a threat to any country.

Proposals for further developing relations between NATO and Central and Eastern Europe were outlined in the joint statement by U.S. Secretary of State James Baker and Genscher on October 2, 1991, in Washington, D.C. This statement contained a proposal to establish a North Atlantic Cooperation Council (NACC) that would include the NATO countries, Central and Eastern Europe, and the Soviet Union. The presidents of Poland and Czechoslovakia and the prime minister of Hungary, meeting in Cracow in October 1991, responded quickly and positively to the statement and expressed their willingness not only to strengthen relations with NATO but to institutionalize them. The ministers of foreign affairs of the three countries stated in a declaration on their relationship with NATO (adopted in Cracow in October 1991) that existing diplomatic ties should be broadened to create conditions favorable to direct participation in NATO activities.

In the Declaration on Peace and Cooperation, adopted on November 8, 1991, in Rome, leaders of sixteen NATO countries submitted to eight Central and East European countries (Bulgaria, Czechoslovakia, Estonia, Hungary, Latvia, Lithuania, Poland, and Romania) and the Soviet Union proposals intended to further institutionalize consultations and cooperation on political and security issues. The proposals included annual and other meetings with the North Atlantic Council at the ministerial or ambassadorial level; and regular meetings, at intervals to be agreed upon, with NATO committees, including the political, economic, and military committees and, under the direction of the latter, other NATO military authorities. These proposals were accepted by the foreign ministers of twenty-five countries at a meeting in Brussels on December 20, 1991. The declaration adopted at that meeting marks a new era of partnership between NATO and Central and Eastern Europe. By mid-1992 the NACC was already well established, having held three sessions at the ministerial level.

The possibility that NATO will extend its protective umbrella and security guarantees to the Central and East European countries is now being increasingly discussed.[35] Such a move would be welcome but is not expected in the immediate future. No country of the region has formally requested membership, although none has formally rejected the concept, either; rather, options have been left open. One option would be to adopt only the first four articles of the North Atlantic Treaty signed in Washington on April 4, 1949, excluding the mutual defense provisions of the fifth article.[36] Under such a plan, the countries involved would be obligated only to consult with one another should a party to the agreement be threatened.

In strengthening their relations with NATO, the countries of Central and Eastern Europe have been careful to emphasize their desire not to be forced to choose between the alliance and the WEU. The Polish minister of foreign affairs, for example, explained in his address to the Extraordinary Session of the Parliamentary Assembly of the WEU in Luxembourg on March 22, 1990, that the Central and East European countries want to develop cooperation with both NATO and the WEU.[37] They welcomed the intentions expressed in the communiqué of the foreign and defense ministers of the WEU member countries, issued in Bonn on November 18, 1991, to enhance the dialogue on security and cooperation between the WEU and the countries of Central and Eastern Europe, including the Baltic States and the former Soviet republics. The communiqué states that "the Foreign and Defence Ministers of Bulgaria, Czechoslovakia, Hungary, Poland, and Romania will be invited to participate in a special meeting with the members of the [WEU] Council; seminars in these countries [will be] organized by the WEU Institute for Security Studies." The WEU Institute's scholarship program will also be expanded, and the presidency and secretary-general of the WEU may conduct fact-finding missions to the former Soviet republics and the Baltic States. Further development of this relationship will reflect decisions made about the WEU's future role.[38]

With the door to NATO and the WEU not yet entirely open, the countries of Central and Eastern Europe have turned to the CSCE in their quest for improved security. It is as difficult to overestimate the importance of the twenty-year-old CSCE process to the whole of Europe as it is to imagine the all-European house without the Helsinki Final Act of 1975 or the meetings on political, economic, cultural, and other matters that are regularly convened within the CSCE framework. The CSCE has neither prevented nor solved all conflicts (Cyprus and Yugoslavia are good examples), but without it more conflicts might have developed. Five aspects of the CSCE process relating to the security of Central and Eastern Europe deserve attention.

The first is the security dimension of the CSCE process, which has come a long way from the modest confidence- and security-building measures (CSBMs) included in the Helsinki Final Act (such as notifications of military maneuvers) to the ambitious measures (such as on-site inspections) of the Vienna CSBM accords and the Supplement to the Charter of Paris, both adopted in Paris on November 21, 1990. (The charter and supplementary document established the Conflict Prevention Center in Vienna.) New possibilities have been opened for joint efforts in military security, such as crisis management, conflict prevention, and peaceful settlement of disputes. A document on CSCE monitoring and peacekeeping forces was submitted by Poland at the session of the CSCE Committee of Senior Officials on October 22, 1991, in Prague.[39]

The second involves institutionalizing the CSCE through such permanent centers as the Conflict Prevention Center in Vienna, the Secretariat in Prague, and the Office for Free Elections in Warsaw, as well as through political bodies such as the Council of Ministers for Foreign Affairs and the Committee of Senior Officials. Although this institutionalization is not an end in itself, it enriches the structures of European security.[40]

Third, the favorable change of the U.S. position on the CSCE benefits the development of the process. Fearing that the security institutions created within the CSCE framework could weaken NATO or that CSCE members (several dozen of them) would begin disregarding American interests, the United States initially responded with reserve. Now, however, that reserve is being replaced by the conviction that the CSCE process is beneficial to relations between Europe and North America and that the development of the CSCE structures further legitimizes the American presence in a future system of pan-European security.

Fourth, the role of the CSCE in the Europeanization of Central and Eastern Europe through multiple contacts with Western Europe has been particularly important to the promotion of greater openness and mutual confidence. It has been necessary to convince Soviet generals that replacing traditional military secrecy with openness and transparency will benefit the security of all of Europe, including the former Soviet Union. But to a large extent, the CSCE process has ensured that no fears of Western aggression have been voiced in the former republics of the USSR, despite the internal turmoil.

Finally, the CSCE has played an important role in the region in promoting the international standards of behavior (including respect for human rights) set forth by the Helsinki Final Act. In doing so, the CSCE helped diminish the postwar division of Europe without sanctioning it. As the Polish minister of foreign affairs declared at the Second Meeting of the Conference on the Human Dimension of the CSCE on June 6, 1990, in Copenhagen, "The essence of European security is to gradually establish a community of democratic nations rather than merely apply various measures relating to military confidence-building and arms reduction."[41]

The efforts made by the countries of Central and Eastern Europe to use the CSCE to improve their security fall into two stages. The first, in 1990 and the first half of 1991, can be described as a period of fascination with the alleged security possibilities of the CSCE. So profound were the changes taking place in the region at that time that it was tempting to believe in a fundamental change in the CSCE as well. Many thought that German unification would be a catalyst for the creation of a cooperative security system in Europe within the framework of the CSCE, which would quickly change from a mere forum for debate to a decisionmaking body.

The second stage began once the war in Yugoslavia erupted in the summer of 1991 and the CSCE institutions and procedures proved inadequate to the task of ending the hostilities. Far from underestimating the CSCE's role in trying to resolve the crisis, however, the Central and East European countries realized that the CSCE process does offer some avenues for action but is not yet a satisfactory alternative to existing Western security structures such as NATO.

Future Security Problems in Central and Eastern Europe

As the Yalta and Potsdam order fades into the past, the nature of international security will be fundamentally different in Europe.[42] Traditional threats to security have diminished considerably or even disappeared, and a war between East and West in Europe is no longer conceivable. However, the civil war in Yugoslavia and the disintegration of the Soviet Union have brought home the realization that Europe is not yet a stable region. Both events testify to the fact that security in this part of the continent is still very fragile and not yet assured.

At the very top of the inventory of threats to the peace and security of Central and Eastern Europe must therefore be placed not external threats but dangers emerging from within distinct states, such as nationalistic and ethnic conflicts, cross-border minority problems, territorial claims and separatism. The inventory is not complete, however, without the addition of the unrest caused by unfulfilled expectations about the victory over communism, which, it was believed, would automatically create a better standard of living. Ecological dangers should also be mentioned, in particular those posed by the Chernobyl-type nuclear plants that continue to function in Eastern Europe.

The danger of such destabilizing events is especially acute in the territory of the former Soviet Union. It is a paradox of historical dimensions that, after the German problem has been solved for Europe, the Russian question has emerged. Another irony of history is that the Soviet Union disintegrated not because of any of the external menaces or hostile activities that had been feared for so long; it simply imploded. A Russian author wrote, "Looking into the future, one can see that most of the military-political challenges for the security of the Soviet Union will be generated not in the West, but either within the country itself or from the South."[43]

Whatever entity or entities replace the Soviet Union, the following elements are predictable: first, of all the former republics, Russia will remain the strongest military power in Europe. Although its role in and influence on pan-European security cannot be as decisive as the former Soviet Union's, a new European order without Russia is inconceivable. It is in the interests of Western, Central, and Eastern Europe not to isolate Russia but to bring it closer to Europe, particularly in pan-European security cooperation. A policy that deliberately excludes Russia would be dangerous for Europe, as it would push the Russians aside and encourage them to form an alliance of poor against rich. This outcome would be especially ominous since the alliance would have nuclear capabilities.

Besides Russia, Ukraine is becoming a new and very important subject of European relations. Ukraine has three significant foreign policy options: closeness with Russia, a rapprochement with Western Europe much like that of its western neighbors, or a middle course. In all three cases, because of its size, population and military potential, Ukraine's role will be critical to the future not only of Central and Eastern Europe but of the continent as a whole. Characteristically enough, Poland, Russia, and Hungary, Ukraine's neighbors to the west and east, were the first three countries to recognize the former republic's independence almost immediately after it had been proclaimed by popular referendum on December 1, 1991, and to extend diplomatic recognition.

In the area of security policy, Ukraine had originally planned to use three ex-Soviet military districts and the Black Sea Fleet as the basis of a force of more than 400,000 soldiers.[44] A considerably smaller number of troops than the estimated 1.2 million Soviets recently deployed in Ukraine, it was still greater than the anticipated troop strength of the unified Germany, which has been set at 370,000. There were conflicting declarations in Ukraine concerning Soviet nuclear weapons, both strategic and tactical, deployed in that country. This vagueness may have been due to the nuclear ambitions of Ukraine, but it could also have resulted from tactical considerations aimed at extracting diplomatic recognition from other countries. It took some six months to convince Ukraine, as well as Belarus and Kazakhstan, that they should not attempt to become true nuclear powers. In May 1992 the United States and Russia, as parties to the START Treaty, together with Ukraine, Belarus, and Kazakhstan, agreed that within seven years all nuclear weapons will be removed from the territory of the former republics, with the exception of Russia.

The domestic stability of Germany and its good relations with the rest of Europe and the United States will help the Germans to perform an important function in promoting sustained development and stability in Central and Eastern Europe. Germany's role in this part of the continent should involve bringing Central and Eastern Europe nearer to Western Europe. Russia should be included in this assimilation with the West, but the pace of rapprochement need not be identical in both cases.

The role that Germany can play in dealing with the economic problems facing Central and Eastern Europe is not considered in this chapter, but one aspect closely linked to security cannot be ignored, and it depends greatly on Germany: equalizing, as far as possible, the standard of living in both parts of Europe. This task must be completed before the division of Europe can be truly overcome rather than just pushed further east. The frontier between the rich Europe and the poor Europe is no more acceptable than was the Iron Curtain or the Berlin Wall and is equally unwelcome on the Elbe, Oder, or Bug. The ministers of foreign affairs of France, Germany, and Poland, in their statement issued after the meeting in Weimar on August 28–29, 1991, declared that "Europe must not be carved up by new borders between poor and rich."[45] If this is not avoided, Europe will soon have its own North-South conflict on an East-West axis.

Conclusion

There is no better way to ensure the security of Central and Eastern Europe than to foster security for Europe as a whole. Today, the essence of European security is no longer based on the balance of forces between East and West, the WTO and NATO, and the Soviet Union and the United States. The old system of security is gradually being replaced by a new system worked out within the framework of the CSCE. It is important that NATO and the WEU be given a place in this new system of cooperative security, which will replace the somewhat passive system of common security that characterizes the present state of European development.[46] At a later stage, a more active cooperative security system, as delineated at the Helsinki CSCE follow-up meeting in July 1992, should be conducive to the creation of a pan-European collective security regime.

It is assumed that the territorial scope of the cooperative security system would extend from Vancouver to Vladivostok. The idea of this vast Euro-Atlantic Community was officially proposed by Secretary of State Baker in his address to the Aspen Institute on June 18, 1991, in Berlin. It quickly gained more popularity in Central and Eastern Europe than the idea of a European Confederation proposed by President François Mitterrand on December 31, 1989, largely because the French proposal would most likely have precluded U.S. participation. The proposed system would comprise three primary geographical areas: the Atlantic, incorporating the United States and Canada; the European, which would include Western, Central, and Eastern Europe; and the Euro-Asiatic, including Russia and the other successor states of the Soviet Union. These three areas should be able to work closely together and be free of conflict. No buffer, neutral, grey, or special security zones would be needed, and security would be shared equally.[47]

The Charter of Paris set forth the idea that security is indivisible: the security of every state participating in the CSCE is inseparably linked to that of every other. This noble principle should now be forged into a new system of European security. Those who consider such an idea utopian should remember the words of Walter Hallstein: "Anyone who does not believe in miracles in European affairs is no realist."

Notes

1. This chapter is based mostly, but not exclusively, on the experience of Poland. Security preoccupations of several other Central and Eastern European countries, including the former Soviet Union, are presented by the authors from those countries in Armand Clesse and Lothar Rühl, eds., *Beyond East-West Confrontation: Searching for a New Security Structure in Europe* (Baden-Baden, Germany: Nomos Verlagsgesellschaft for the Institute for European and International Studies, Luxembourg, 1990), in particular pp. 386–445. Security policies of some Central and Eastern European countries just before the great changes in Europe are described in Sverre Lodgaard and Karl Birnbaum, eds., *Overcoming Threats to Europe: A New Deal for Confidence and Security* (Oxford University Press for Stockholm International Peace Research Institute [SIPRI], 1987).

2. Such an approach is presented in Ronald D. Asmus and Thomas S. Szayna, with Barbara Kliszewski, *Polish National Security Thinking in a Changing Europe: A Conference Report*, report R-4056-FF (Santa Monica, Calif.: Rand, 1991).

3. For a more detailed examination see William E. Griffith, "German-American Relations 1989–1990," in Clesse and Rühl, eds., *Beyond East-West Confrontation*, pp. 474–75.

4. Text of the Treaty on the Final Settlement with respect to Germany, in Adam Daniel Rotfeld and Walther Stützle, eds., *Germany and Europe in Transition* (Oxford University Press for SIPRI, 1991), p. 184.

5. Prerequisites of the German-Polish reconciliation are examined in Marion Gräfin Dönhoff, *Polen und Deutsche. Die schwierige Versöhnung. Betrachtungen aus drei Jahrzehnten* (Frankfurtam Main: Luchterhand Literaturverlag, 1991).

6. Polish journalists who have studied the statements made by leading Polish politicians during visits to various Western countries observed the following differences. According to the minister of foreign affairs, the road to closer ties with the West leads through France; according to the prime minster, through Germany; and according to the president, through the United States.

7. Theo Sommer, "Germany's Long Shadow of Guilt and Shame," *Observer*, September 3, 1989, p. 16.

8. Charter of Paris for a New Europe, signed November 21, 1990, in Paris at CSCE Summit (Washington: Commission on Security and Cooperation in Europe, 1990), p. 4.

9. Havel is quoted in an address by Hans-Dietrich Genscher, minister for foreign affairs of the Federal Republic of Germany, "German Responsibility for a Peaceful Order in Europe," given at SIPRI/IPW Conference in Potsdam, February 8–10, 1990, printed in Rotfeld and Stützle, eds., *Germany and Europe in Transition*, p. 20. Skubiszewski is quoted in "Two-plus-Four results," Paris, July 17, 1990, transcript of the July 17, 1990, press conference following the Two plus Four meetings in Paris, printed in Rotfeld and Stützle, eds., *Germany and Europe in Transition*, p. 177.

10. Recent public opinion polls in Poland showed that 62 percent of the population did not fear unification; only 35 percent felt "somewhat threatened." This reflected a tremendous shift in Polish public opinion: only two years earlier, the percentages had been reversed (Adam Daniel Rotfeld, "The Future of Europe and of Germany: Conference Summary," in Rotfeld and Stützle, eds., *Germany and Europe in Transition*, p. 83).

11. Asmus and Szayna, with Kliszewski, *Polish National Security Thinking*, p. 17.

12. This issue is thoroughly analyzed in Jane M. O. Sharp, ed., *Europe after an*

American Withdrawal: Economic and Military Issues (Oxford University Press for SIPRI, 1990).

13. Marek Ilnicki and others, "Security and Politico-Military Stability in the Baltic Region," PISM Occasional Paper 21 (Warsaw: Polish Institute of International Affairs, 1991), p. 4.

14. Text of the treaty in Sergey Koulik and Richard Kokoski, *Verification of the CFE Treaty,* A SIPRI Research Report (Stockholm: SIPRI, October 1991), pp. 99–112; German declaration, pp. 2–3.

15. Wojciech Lamentowicz, "Niemcy" [The Germans], in Janusz Stefanowicz, ed., *Polityka europejska rzeczpospolitej polskiej—oceny i wskazania* [Polish European Policy—Opinions and Suggestions] (Warsaw: Instytut Studiów Politycznych Polskiej Akademii Nauk, 1991), p. 82; and Asmus and Szayna, with Kliszewski, *Polish National Security Thinking*, p. 15.

16. For a more detailed examination of the implications of the putsch see Marek Thee, "Disintegration of the Soviet Empire: Dangers and Opportunities," paper prepared for SIPRI Conference, Saltsjöbaden, Sweden, November 12–14, 1991.

17. Signe Landgren, "Developments in the Soviet Union," paper prepared for SIPRI Conference, Saltsjöbaden, Sweden, November 12–14, 1991, appendix B.

18. See Burton Yale Pines, "The New World Order: Sense or Nonsense?" in Kim R. Holmes and Burton Yale Pines, *George Bush's New World Order: Two Assessments*, Heritage Lectures 333 (Washington: Heritage Foundation, 1991), p. 7. See also Lothar Rühl, Jerzy Nowak, and Vladimir Shustov, quoted in "Annex B: Excerpts from the Discussions at the Conference," in Clesse and Rühl, eds., *Beyond East-West Confrontation,* pp. 586–89; and Adam Daniel Rotfeld, "Changes in the European Security System," in ibid., p. 121.

19. For further details see Jerzy M. Nowak, "Rethinking the European Security System: A Polish Perspective," in Clesse and Rühl, eds., *Beyond East-West Confrontation*, p. 360.

20. For a more detailed examination of this issue see Antoni Kukliński, ed., *Poland—the Quest for New Identity and Competitive Advantage*, Globality versus Locality 2 (Warsaw: Polish Association for the Club of Rome and European Institute for Regional and Local Development of the University of Warsaw, 1991), and in particular the chapter written by the former rector of the Catholic University in Lublin, Mieczyslaw Albert Krapiec, "On Some Foundation of Polish National Identity," pp. 23–38.

21. This section is based on two statements delivered by Polish military officials: Janusz Onyszkiewicz, deputy minister for defense, "Statement" at Second Seminar on Military Doctrines, Vienna, CSCE Conflict Prevention Center, October 8, 1991; and Maj. Gen. Zdzislaw Stelmaszuk, chief of general staff of the Polish armed forces, "Presentation" to Second Seminar on Military Doctrine, Vienna, CSCE Conflict Prevention Center, October 11, 1991.

22. Hungary and Czechoslovakia made similar decisions to redeploy a certain portion of their armed forces from Western parts of their territories closer to their eastern borders.

23. Onyszkiewicz, "Statement," p. 7.

24. Stelmaszuk, "Presentation," p. 3. See also Onyszkiewicz, "Statement," p. 9; and Stelmaszuk, "Presentation," pp. 3–5.

25. These planned reforms are outlined in Stelmaszuk, "Presentation," and Onyszkiewicz, "Statement."

26. Stephen Kinzer, "Germans and Poles Pledge Mutual Help," *New York Times*, June 18, 1991, p. A3.

27. Czechoslovakia joined the group on April 20, 1990, and the Pentagonal Group was formally launched on April 27, 1990. See Adrian G. V. Hyde-Price, *European Security beyond the Cold War: Four Scenarios for the Year 2010* (London: SAGE Publications for the Royal Institute of International Affairs, 1991), p. 104.

28. See the Baltic Sea Declaration, reprinted in Rotfeld and Stützle, eds., *Germany and Europe in Transition*, pp. 164–66.

29. See TASS's criticism of the Visegrad Declaration, reported in Jane M. O. Sharp, "Security Options in Central and South-Eastern Europe," paper prepared for SIPRI Conference, Saltsjöbaden, Sweden, November 12–14, 1991, p. 6. TASS claims that in establishing a new regional grouping, Poland, Hungary, and Czechoslovakia "had ignored the interests of the Soviet Union." On the other hand, a Soviet diplomat has observed that such tendencies are welcome as elements supporting the institutionalization of the Helsinki process: Vladimir Shustov, "From Interbloc Confrontation Towards a New Peaceful Order in Europe," in Clesse and Rühl, eds., *Beyond East-West Confrontation*, pp. 444–45.

30. Text of the Joint Declaration of Twenty-Two States, reprinted in Rotfeld and Stützle, eds., *Germany and Europe in Transition*, p. 217.

31. Genscher, "German Responsibility for a Peaceful Order in Europe."

32. See Albrecht A. C. von Müller, "A Tripolar Security Structure for Europe," in Clesse and Rühl, eds., *Beyond East-West Confrontation*, pp. 264–73.

33. On July 1, 1991, a protocol was signed in Prague on the termination of the Treaty of Friendship, Cooperation, and Mutual Assistance signed in Warsaw on May 14, 1955. The protocol's preamble gives four reasons for terminating the earlier treaty: the changes in Europe, the Joint Declaration of the Twenty-Two States of November 19, 1990, the agreement reached at the CSCE summit in Paris to build pan-European security structures, and the intention of all parties to the protocol to develop bilateral and possibly multilateral relations. Article 1 of the protocol stipulates that the Warsaw Treaty is terminated on the day the protocol goes into effect. In Article 2, the parties declare that they have no property claims against each other resulting from the WTO. Article 3 envisages ratification of the protocol, and Article 4 enters it into force. The text was signed by such disparate persons as Lech Walesa, Vaclav Havel, and G. I. Janajev six weeks before the August coup attempt. See "Protocol on the Termination of the Treaty of Friendship, Cooperation and Mutual Assistance Signed in Warsaw on May 14, 1955," signed in Prague on July 1, 1991.

34. Thomas L. Friedman, "NATO Tries to Ease Security Concerns in Eastern Europe," *New York Times*, June 7, 1991, p. A1.

35. See, for example, Wojtek Lamentowicz, "Evolution des structures politiques de l'Europe: Un point de vue polonais," *Politique Étrangère*, no. 1 (Spring 1991), pp. 146–48; Sharp, "Security Options in Central and South-Eastern Europe," pp. 2–4; and Janusz Stefanowicz, "Modele bezpieczeństwa europejskiego—opcje Polski" [Patterns of European security: Options for Poland] in Janusz Stefanowicz, ed., *Polityka europejska rzeczpospolitej polskiej—oceny I wskazania* (Warsaw: Instytut Studiów Politycznych Polskiej Akademii Nauk, 1991), p. 62.

36. Option envisaged by Hans Binnendijk, "NATO Can't Be Vague about Commitment to Eastern Europe," *International Herald Tribune*, November 8, 1991, p. 6.

37. Ireneusz Lukasik, "Skubiszewski Addresses WEU Parliament," Warsaw PAP, March 23, 1990, printed in *Foreign Broadcast Information Service, Daily Report:*

East Europe, FBIS-EE4-90-057, March 23, 1990, pp. 65–66. Poland, Czechoslovakia, and Hungary also signed association agreements with the European Community in December 1991. The three countries were successively admitted into the Council of Europe after meeting the condition requiring free elections. They also entered into cooperation with the European Free Trade Association (EFTA) and the Organization for Economic Cooperation and Development (OECD).

38. WEU Council of Ministers, "Communique," Bonn, Western European Union, November 18, 1991, p. 3.

39. Polish delegation, "Monitoring and Peace-keeping Forces under the Auspices of the CSCE," Committee of Senior Officials, Fourth CSO Meeting in Prague, Communication 162, Secretariat of the Conference on Security and Cooperation in Europe, Prague, October 22, 1991.

40. See Adam Daniel Rotfeld, "New Security Structures in Europe: Concepts, Proposals and Decisions," *SIPRI Yearbook 1991: World Armaments and Disarmament* (Oxford University Press for SIPRI, 1991) pp. 585–600; and Adam Daniel Rotfeld, "New Structures of European Security," paper prepared for SIPRI Conference, Saltsjöbaden, Sweden, November 12–14, 1991.

41. Krzysztof Skubiszewski, minister of foreign affairs of the Republic of Poland, Opening Statement at the Second Meeting of the Conference on the Human Dimension of the CSCE, Copenhagen, June 6, 1990, p. 4.

42. For a comprehensive assessment of the changes in this respect, see Volker Heise and Zdzislaw Lachowski, "Military Dimensions of European Security," paper prepared for SIPRI Conference, Saltsjöbaden, Sweden, November 12–14, 1991; Rotfeld, "Changes in the European Security System," in Clesse and Rühl, eds., *Beyond East-West Confrontation*, pp. 103–23; and Gerhard Wachter and Axel Krohn, eds., *Stability and Arms Control in Europe: The Role of Military Forces within a European Security System*, A SIPRI Research Report (Stockholm: SIPRI, July 1989).

43. Sergei A. Karaganov, "The Soviet Union and the New European Architecture," in Clesse and Rühl, eds., *Beyond East-West Confrontation*, p. 432.

44. On November 30, 1991, Ukranian officials announced that they had revised plans for their army and estimated future manpower at 90,000. See Francis X. Clines, "Ukraine Reduces Plans for an Army," *New York Times*, December 1, 1991, p. 1. Higher force levels have again been discussed in 1992.

45. "Joint Statement Adopted," Hamburg DPA (wire service), August 29, 1991, printed in Foreign Broadcast Information Service, *Daily Report: West Europe*, FBIS-WEU-91-169, August 30, 1991, p. 2. Polish minister of foreign affairs Krzysztof Skubiszewski stressed the same fact in "'Nicht alle haben dasselbe Gefühl der Sicherheit': Polen besorgt über wirtschaftliches und soziales Gefälle in Europa," *Der Tagesspiegel*, June 19, 1991, p. 5.

46. This concept is discussed thoroughly by Jerzy M. Nowak in "The Cooperative Security System in Europe As Seen from the Perspective of the Vienna Talks in 1991," unpublished paper prepared for SIPRI, January 1992. See also Adam Daniel Rotfeld, "Europe at the Crossroads: The Transformation of the Continent's Security System," in Karl E. Birnbaum, Josef B. Binter, and Stephen K. Badzik, eds., *Towards a Future European Peace Order?* (Basingstoke, Hampshire, Great Britain: Macmillan Academic and Professional Ltd. in association with the European University Centre for Peace Studies, Schlaining, Austria, 1991), pp. 25–44; and Hyde-Price, *European Security Beyond the Cold War*.

47. It is, for instance, in this new spirit that negotiations were conducted in Vienna in 1991 and 1992 aimed at concluding a treaty on Open Skies. When the Open Skies

regime of aerial observations enters into force, for the first time the present CSCE territorial scope from the Atlantic to the Urals will be extended to cover the whole ex-Soviet territory. It should be added that the area beyond the Urals, that is from the Urals to Vladivostok, is even bigger than the area between the Atlantic and the Urals. The territories of the United States and Canada are also included in the Open Skies Treaty, as well as the entire Asiatic territory of Turkey. The Open Skies Treaty was signed in Helsinki on March 24, 1992.

ELEVEN

Implications of German Unification for the Former Soviet Union

Sergei A. Karaganov

IT IS ONLY PARTLY true that a love-hate relationship has always existed between Russia—the former Soviet Union—and Germany. Before the reign of Peter the Great, the relationship between the two nations oscillated between cooperation (as with the Hansa traders) and confrontation (exemplified by the Teuton Order). But neither the love nor the hate ran particularly deep, and neither left a lasting impression.

Then followed two centuries of close and virtually uninterrupted multilayered cooperation that, by modern standards, could be termed friendly. During these years, Germans attained positions of authority in Russia, married into the royal family, taught in the universities, and played a significant role in the nineteenth-century industrialization of the country. Except for a brief interval during the Seven Years War, the Russian empire and various German states (especially Prussia) were for these two centuries geopolitical partners, although they were almost never allies. Russia's return to Europe, in both the political and material sense, came about largely because of the country's connections with Germans and the German states. This period of Russian-German relations could be described as amicable.

The element of "hate" was added by a single historical mistake—World War I—which pitted the two countries against each other and paved the way for the two different kinds of totalitarianism that preceded World War II. It was this war, which brought the Nazis and their inhuman doctrine to the territory of the USSR and cost close to 30 million Soviet lives, that solidified Russian mistrust and fear of Germans. The postwar confrontation in Europe and the division of Germany between military alliances, each of which perceived the other as threatening, did little to dispel this mistrust.

Between World War II and unification, Soviet policy toward Germany

The author thanks many Soviet and German politicians, scholars, and diplomats for information valuable to the analysis. The interviews were granted on condition of anonymity.

passed through three stages. During the first, which lasted until the second half of the 1950s, the Moscow leadership more or less consistently supported German unification, but with the goal of keeping the country outside the U.S.-led military and political coalition. Most historical data show that the phrase "a peaceful, democratic, and neutral Germany" was used genuinely enough, though it was sometimes grossly overplayed for propaganda purposes. Very probably the Moscow leadership would have accepted a united Germany even at the price of capitalism, much as it accepted that solution for Austria.[1]

This conclusion is also supported by geopolitical logic—perhaps the only kind that Stalin mastered, albeit crudely.[2] Keeping Germany—even a capitalist Germany—out of NATO would have offered several benefits. Without Germany, NATO could have never become such a powerful military alliance. The "buffer zone" beyond the western borders of the Soviet Union, which embraced not only countries from the socialist camp but also Austria, would have been much wider, and the Soviet Union's economic isolation from the West would not have been so complete. And, last but not least, a Germany free from alliances could have been counted on as a partner for a new Rapallo-like rapprochement, ending any possible political isolation as well.

The second stage began with the incorporation of West Germany into NATO and East Germany into the Warsaw Treaty Organization (WTO). The theme of German unification started to fade from serious political deliberations but was kept alive in the sphere of propaganda, where it won some public relations points for the Soviet Union and also provided the idea with a certain legitimacy, giving Soviet diplomacy more room to maneuver. Meanwhile, real Soviet policy toward Germany was moving in the opposite direction. On a deeper level, as East Germany became an increasingly valuable client, certain mental attitudes developed among groups in the Soviet leadership with vested interests in preserving the status quo.

The logic of East-West confrontation also affected German-Soviet relations. While Moscow purported to be seeking ways to ameliorate relations with the West, the necessity of keeping WTO clients and allies under control pushed Soviet policies in the opposite direction. This tendency became especially obvious after the change of government in Bonn and the formation of the Kissinger-Brandt coalition, with its much more flexible policies toward Central and Eastern Europe (though not yet toward the Soviet Union). The rhetoric directed at West Germany by the Soviet leadership grew more strident, and the parallel objectives of "American imperialism" and "German revanchism" were constantly stressed, as was the "aggressiveness" of the Bonn-Washington "axis."[3] In its efforts to maintain discipline within the Eastern bloc, the Soviet Union had to act—or at least sound—more belligerent than it might have preferred to otherwise.

The advent of the third stage, at the beginning of the 1970s, was marked by an almost complete loss of flexibility in Soviet policy toward Germany. In addition to those factors already mentioned, the period of détente made U.S.-Soviet relations a priority, pushing European issues, including the German question, to the back burner. The changes in the military and, in particular, the nuclear balance of power may also have made the Soviet leadership less worried about the "German menace" and more concerned about the threat of a NATO attack spearheaded by the United States and West Germany.

But the main reason for this loss of flexibility lay in the beginning of a period of conservative stabilization that was later termed the "era of stagnation." The early successes of this era, such as détente and the comparative normalization of relations with the West, left the makers of Soviet foreign policy feeling secure enough not to undertake new radical initiatives, adding to the inertia from the previous period. But this policy contained several internal contradictions. The methodical accumulation of military power that resulted from the World War II-vintage idea that bigger is better, latent ideological instincts, an uncontrolled defense industry, and the belief that the imperialists had changed their policies toward the Soviet Union because of the shift in the military balance of power were bound to clash with the genuine desire for political rapprochement and economic cooperation with the West. This two-track policy, combined with a proclivity (also inherited from the 1960s) to try to fill every vacuum and grab anything available in the Third World, gave many Westerners the impression that the Soviet Union had a Machiavellian long-range plan aimed at luring Western countries into a false sense of security and tipping the balance of military and political power to such an extent that they could be intimidated into submission. Fortunately for the world, no such plan existed. But unfortunately for professional Soviet policymakers, neither was there any game plan.[4]

While Soviet policy toward Europe in the 1970s could be characterized as inertia interrupted by occasional movement and some notable successes, such as the signing of the Helsinki Act of 1975, Soviet policy toward Germany seemed to go into hibernation after the August 1970 Moscow Treaty with West Germany and the Four Power Berlin Agreement. Soviet diplomacy fully embraced the concept, propagandized by the East German leadership, of two separate German nations. This concept was not just blatantly unrealistic; it also robbed Soviet policy of room to maneuver and of many of its bargaining chips.

Gradually the idea of unification became a heresy, and a dangerous one. The East German leadership's growing influence with the administration of Leonid Brezhnev brought about what was almost a right to censor even

internal Soviet debates. The careers of some Soviet officials even suffered
when their challenges to the orthodox line became known to the East German
leadership, which then demanded that the authorities in Moscow punish the
heretics. All in all, it was the sad story of a totalitarian tail wagging a
totalitarian dog.

Thus the debate on Germany almost faded away.

The consequences of this twenty-year absence of open debate were far
reaching and help explain what occurred in Soviet policy prior to and
immediately after the fall of the Berlin Wall. The absence of debate and lack
of serious study of the German question, the general orientation toward East
Germany's ruling elite, and the very scarce contacts (if any existed) with
opposition circles meant that Moscow was largely uninformed on the real
state of affairs and unprepared for the events that started to unfold in East
Germany. To be sure, there had been some attempts—rather awkward and
crude in the late 1970s and early 1980s and timid at the end of the 1980s—
to play the "German card." But in the first case—during negotiations on
the agreement on Intermediate-Range Nuclear Forces (INFs)—they largely
backfired. In the second—after several high-level Soviet statements indicated
that Gorbachev might entertain the idea of the unification or confederation
of Germany—they were too ambiguous to bear significant results.[5]

The general guidelines influencing Soviet policy toward the two German
states during this period were the perceived necessity of deterring any
aggressive Western movements and some rather ambivalent anti-Americanism. While the Soviet leaders wanted to get the United States out of Europe,
they were also following a deep and never clearly formulated instinct favoring
a U.S. presence in Europe, if only to keep Germany down. There was also
a perfectly logical interest in maintaining the maximum amount of room to
maneuver and fomenting discord within the Western alliance. However, this
strategy was not balanced by an appreciation of the fact that the Soviet Union
also benefited from stability in the Western system and that direct attempts
to fuel discord would be mostly counterproductive.

But for all Moscow's lack of ingenuity, Soviet-German policy and Soviet-
German relations yielded some positive results. Soviet-East German economic
relations and personal contacts expanded steadily. The relatively friendly
relations with "our Germans" contributed to the healing of the wounds of
World War II that had caused so much hatred and mistrust. Soviet-West
German relations also expanded, though more gradually. The bitter fight that
surrounded the INF issue, while resurrecting some of the old fears, also
showed how far West German society had progressed beyond its Cold War
image. Extensive contacts with peace movements, the Social Democrats, and
other liberal elements of the ruling elite helped to create a more favorable
image of Germans and to open up Soviet political circles to many of the
ideas that crystallized a few years later as the New Political Thinking.

Prior to Unification

When Mikhail Gorbachev and his circle came to power, they recognized that the Soviet social system was in a deep crisis and that Soviet foreign policy, including its key European component, was caught in a blind alley. There is no need to describe in detail the bleak situation in which the Soviet Union found itself in 1984 and 1985. Suffice it to say that politically, economically, and socially it was in semi-isolation; the ongoing arms race was producing only negative political effects and progressively destabilizing the strategic situation. But in the debates unfolding in Moscow, larger issues were starting to be discussed. The postwar settlement, with its two-bloc system, came more and more to be perceived as a Pyrrhic victory that not only was unfair but worked against real Soviet interests. This settlement left the USSR with weak and unreliable allies, compelled to contain and balance a coalition consisting of virtually all the industrially advanced countries. The two-bloc system also cut the Soviet Union off from the achievements of science and technology—the driving spirit of human civilization—even more so than in the 1930s. The semblance of success achieved in spreading the Soviet model of development to Central and Eastern Europe and the ensuing Western policy of containment, aimed at isolating and pressuring the Soviets, only bolstered Stalinism and its conservative supporters while delaying reforms.[6]

The process of reassessment in Moscow also moved on to such sacred cows as the usefulness of the Central and East European "defensive buffer" in the nuclear environment. Questions of this kind were reinforced by realpolitik analyses of the costs of the empire in Central and Eastern Europe, as well as by growing feelings of moral guilt over the imposition of an unwanted system on the peoples of this region. There was some hope that, freed from direct Soviet control, Central and East Europeans would opt for "socialism with a human face" and a loose security bond with the USSR. Looking back, it seems that most Soviet thinking on this subject seriously underestimated the degree to which the Central and East European peoples would reject the old system. This failure was the result of the same blindness that kept the supporters of *perestroika* from acknowledging at the outset that the system they had inherited was so completely rotten that it could not be reformed but would have to be changed wholesale.[7]

One more element figured in these considerations: the growing understanding in many circles of the elite that the Soviet Union had achieved a level of military security unparalleled in its history and therefore had a window of opportunity, at least until the beginning of the next century, to restructure the country and the economy that formed the base of its political and military strength. One theory postulated that the accumulated surplus of military might could be traded for political benefits. Although not everyone shared this view, especially within the military, this was the view that eventually prevailed.

It is important to note here that, contrary to what is widely believed in the West, the Soviet Union did not change its security policies because of the Reagan challenge, with its implicit threat of an unwinnable arms race. In fact, increased American military expenditures provided one of the strongest arguments put forth against changes in Soviet military policies and patterns of procurement, even after general foreign policy began to change. Changes in Soviet military policy began to be implemented only at the end of 1987, two years after the advent of the New Political Thinking.[8]

It is clear that the Soviet leadership wanted to break out of the system of containment and confrontation. It feared that the country was losing the competition not just because its social system was uncompetitive (nor, it should be added, was it viable) but also because the terms of this competition were unfair. But the military argument was only one among many, and it worked in both directions. The driving force behind the policy conducted under the banner of the common European house was to open Europe and the Soviet Union to each other politically, economically, and socially. In particular it aimed at doing away with the USSR's "Western front," thereby creating favorable conditions for transforming the society and the economy, and ultimately for returning the country to the European civilization where, it was felt, it largely belonged and had only partially left.

Some Soviet foreign defense policymakers of the late 1980s have claimed that when the Soviet Union embraced the "freedom of choice" policy for Central and Eastern Europe and put forward the idea of withdrawing all foreign troops, Soviet leaders were fully aware of the possible consequences.[9] Perhaps some elements in the Soviet leadership knew what could and would happen, but it was not common knowledge in the foreign policy community. Virtually nobody predicted the speed with which events finally unfolded, especially in East Germany. And it is hard to imagine that any Soviet leader would have openly proposed a policy that within a year would do away with the Soviet Union's most valuable ally.

When the debate on Germany resumed in the late 1980s, the issue of unification was undoubtedly put back on the agenda. Four positions crystallized. The first was that unification was in the Soviet interest and that the Soviet Union should promote it. The second favored active bargaining with West Germany on the fate of East Germany with the aim of eventually selling out the East Germans. The third, a milder variation of the second, held that a sellout would be immoral and unrealistic but that bargaining over the terms and schedule of rapprochement between the two German states would be useful. The fourth position took a no-bargaining, no-discussion stand and offered unconditional support for Erich Honecker's regime. My experience with the discussions on Germany at the time suggests that the first position was held by very few people, perhaps only one or two specialists in academic circles. The second was a bit more popular and was also propagandized by a few academics. Only the last two positions were influential among policymakers. The proponents of the fourth position were in the majority; they occupied key positions in the Ministry of Foreign Affairs and were well represented on the Central Committee of the Communist party, which still formulated policy.

Gorbachev himself toyed very timidly with the third position when he began to argue that in "a hundred years history will decide." But immediately after making this remark, he attacked "those who pretended that the German question remained open."[10] He went further, acknowledging in the Soviet-West German Joint Declaration signed in June 1989 "the right of all peoples and states" to determine freely their destiny and mandating "respect for the right of peoples to self-determination."[11] While this acknowledgment meant a great deal from the West German point of view, in the political parlance of Soviet New Thinking it was regarded largely as a clever diplomatic move rather than as acquiescence to the idea of German unification. But while Gorbachev played the German card, most of the bureaucracy adhered to the fourth position and refused even to question the position of East Germany's gerontocratic leadership or to discuss the possibilities of unification.

Partly because Gorbachev and the Soviet leadership were in general preoccupied with the internal situation and attempts to mend relations with the West, and partly because they sincerely adhered to the new policies of "freedom of choice" and nonintervention in the internal affairs of other countries, Moscow did not pay sufficient attention to what was happening in East Germany until the situation began deteriorating into a crisis. Only in October 1989, during Gorbachev's visit to Berlin, did the Soviet leader try to persuade Honecker to undertake reforms. But during the October 7 meeting with Honecker and the full Politburo of the Central Committee of the East German Communist party (SED), Gorbachev's arguments were rebuffed by the East German leader, who said, "Do not teach us how to live, when there is not even salt in your shops."[12] It became clear then that his regime could not survive.

The effects of the lack of serious Soviet debate on Germany during the preceding two decades or so began to show.[13] The Soviet leadership was unprepared, and an air of panic began spreading among some of those concerned. The ensuing policy was awkward and largely contradictory.[14] The government spoke with different voices, which could, in principle, have been an asset, but in reality reflected genuine contradictions and confusion that weakened rather than reinforced the Soviet negotiating position.

The Soviet Union put forward several proposals, including some that were relatively extreme, such as suggesting that a referendum be held among all Europeans on the external and security aspects of German unification. Other ideas included giving Germany the same status in NATO as France, so that, in effect, it would be a member of the political alliance but not the integrated military command; some kind of continuation of the rights of the Four Powers in the united Germany; the creation of a center in Berlin to monitor all the military activities on German territory; and double membership for Germany in NATO and the WTO. Most of these proposals were put forward after May 1990. During the preceding six months, however, the Soviet Union had stuck with one position—that of German neutrality. This old idea, taken directly from the 1950s, could have provided a good starting point, but only a starting point. In retrospect, it seems highly plausible that, had the Soviet Union not used this proposition as the centerpiece of its policy toward Germany— suggesting, for instance, in December 1989, or even January or February 1990, that Germany leave the military but remain within the political organization of NATO, or even that a united Germany remain a full NATO member while simultaneously holding a seat in the political organization of the then-functioning WTO, it could have negotiated a better deal. For at that time, the Western position had not yet crystallized. Washington had not yet developed the diplomatic strategy aimed at keeping Germany in NATO that would in the end prove successful. And in Bonn as well as in many other Western capitals, serious doubts existed about the feasibility of keeping a united Germany in NATO.[15]

To make things worse, advocating German neutrality was one of the least advantageous positions the Soviet Union could have adopted. The Soviet intransigence isolated the country and caused some damage to its prestige. To be precise, the question of neutrality was not as pressing for the Soviet Union as it was for almost all the other European nations. Moscow, with its nuclear superiority, could not have been as afraid as the European countries of a resurgence of German nationalist feeling or even of the resurrection of German military power. But from most other points of view, the position was counterproductive.

The Soviet intransigence, which occurred in spite of criticism from abroad and also from something close to a majority of nongovernment experts, can be explained by several factors.[16] The Soviets were, of course, initially unprepared for such a rapid movement toward unification—more so than most other countries, for the reasons mentioned earlier. This unpreparedness was the key reason why the Soviet Union was unable to work out at least a superficially coherent diplomatic strategy during the first months after the fall of the Berlin Wall. Other factors influencing Soviet policy that explain its relative intransigence as well as some of its vacillations are listed below in ascending order of importance.

Disagreements were evident within and between bureaucracies, especially between the Ministry of Foreign Affairs, where most of the in-house specialists were advocating the harshest possible policies, and the Central Committee, which supported Gorbachev and which had, in addition, split into several factions. Academic specialists were also divided, though in general they advocated a more flexible line. But things were moving so fast that it is hard to say whether these views exerted any significant influence, apart from legitimizing for the public the Soviet Union's eventual approval of a united Germany within NATO. Not surprisingly, there were also the usual disagreements between the Ministry of Foreign Affairs and the Ministry of Defense. Over such a touchy issue and against a background of increasing political tension in the country, these disagreements played a bigger role than usual.

Soviet insistence on German neutrality could also be and was to a certain extent justified as a negotiating tactic aimed at extricating more concessions from the other side, especially concerning the reform of NATO and the size of the armed forces of a united Germany. The Soviet government was playing for time in order to try to synchronize unification with the development of new all-European security structures designed to provide Moscow with political leverage to replace what had been given away and to sugarcoat unification.

The rigidity of the Soviet position can be attributed in part to the influence of some Western countries, especially France, that had latent fears of Germany. These countries were willing to postpone unification—with the assistance of the Soviets—and at the same time complicate Soviet-German relations, precluding a Rapallo-type arrangement. But the relatively tough position maintained by Gorbachev and Foreign Minister Eduard Shevardnadze had another cause. The Soviet people needed time to adjust to the idea of unification.[17] Concerns existed about the feelings of those Soviet citizens who saw Germany as a threat, a united Germany as a greater threat, and a united Germany within the NATO alliance as the greatest threat of all. In retrospect, these concerns may or may not have been justified, but they were real enough at the time.

Such concerns were exacerbated by the fact that, by the autumn and winter of 1989–90, the policy of *perestroika* was being belligerently challenged by powerful interest groups threatened by the changes. As one of their targets for criticism, they chose foreign policy—previously one of Gorbachev's primary assets—to undermine his and other reformers' positions on the more central internal issues.[18] Of course, some in these groups were also genuinely concerned about the collapse of the security order they had grown used to and considered indispensable. But the critics were also playing somewhat shamelessly on the fears of the general population. Concentrated mostly in the party apparatus and the military, they supported conservative forces in East Germany, fearing that the demise of such forces there would pave the way for their own. Together these pressures created a very dangerous situation for the Soviet Union and international stability in general, especially since a "military solution" was probably one of the options suggested by those opposed to unification.[19]

Despite all these contradictions, it is possible to discern some of the goals Soviet policy was trying to achieve after the unification process began and during the Two plus Four talks. There were, most probably, two agendas: one open, one hidden.

The open agenda had several objectives.

—First, to the credit of top Soviet policymakers, they did not try to prevent unification but looked on the Germans' desire for unity as legitimate and logical. In a conversation with Genscher, Shevardnadze said that he had intuitively believed since the beginning of his diplomatic career that Germany would eventually unite.[20] The Soviet Union was trying, above all, to create a legal and political framework that could prevent the remilitarization of Germany and the acquisition of nuclear weapons.

—The second goal was to build an international framework for unification that would strengthen rather than challenge European stability. Here the question of the legitimacy of existing borders was of paramount importance.

—The third objective of the Soviet Union was to limit the economic damage that would be incurred with the loss of the East German market. There were hopes, which proved to be unrealistic, of gaining some economic benefits from unification.

—The fourth aim was to influence NATO policies and strategies in a way that would strengthen Soviet security and weaken potential military and political challenges from the Western alliance.

—Finally, the Soviet Union was also interested in tying down the new Germany with as many institutional arrangements as possible, primarily within the Economic Community and the Conference for Security and Cooperation in Europe (CSCE). All in all, the primary goals of the open agenda were to create a close relationship with the new Germany and to lay the foundation for a new security system in Europe based on the CSCE process.[21]

As for the possible hidden agenda: it looked as if some policymakers were thinking of trying to impose a peace treaty that would have made Germany pay reparations to countries that had suffered from Nazi aggression. Another possibility is that the concept of neutrality was supported by some who hoped that severing West Germany from NATO (or even just from its military organization) would inflict damage on the alliance and compensate, at least in part, for the inevitable loss of the WTO. Without Germany, the integrated military command would most likely have been badly crippled. But these last goals, if they indeed existed, never made it to the top of the Soviet agenda for the Two plus Four diplomatic process.

Consequences of German Unification

By summer 1990, many observers in Moscow felt that the Soviet Union was on the brink of a major political defeat. The Two plus Four talks had reached what looked like an impasse. The fact that the Soviet Union had never had any leverage it could use to influence the situation, except for the untenable military option, was becoming increasingly clear and even developing into a matter of intense debate.[22] Virtually the only effective leverage that Moscow had was the interest of the West—especially Bonn—in the continuation of the Gorbachev regime and its policies.

In fact, it was this leverage, together with Gorbachev's tactical genius, that helped the Soviet Union literally to steal victory from the jaws of defeat. On July 16, 1990, during the meeting in the northern Caucasus, the Soviet President and the German Chancellor reached an agreement on the external aspects of German unification and on the main elements of future Soviet-German relations. This agreement paved the way for the signing on September 12, 1990, of the Treaty on the Final Settlement with Respect to Germany and, in the fall of 1990, a set of Soviet-German treaties.[23]

These treaties included the following:

—An acknowledgement of the definitive nature of Germany's borders, to be recognized by appropriate changes to the constitution, or Basic Law;

—Germany's reaffirmation that only peace will emanate from German soil;

—Germany's reiteration of its earlier promise not to manufacture or acquire nuclear, biological, or chemical (NBC) weapons;

—Germany's obligation to cut its armed forces to 370,000 within three to four years;

—The Soviet Union's obligation to withdraw its troops from German territory by 1994;

—An agreement that foreign armed forces and nuclear weapons will not be stationed in the former East Germany once the Soviet troops are withdrawn;

—The stipulation that, until all Soviet troops are withdrawn from East German territory, no German troops under NATO command may be deployed there;

—A set of guarantees aimed at preventing any resurgence of Nazism;

—Germany's adherence to the treaties signed by both East and West Germany.

In addition, the treaties require Germany to fulfill existing East German economic obligations to the Soviet Union. Some 15 billion marks have also been allocated to help finance the Soviet troops remaining on German territory, as well as their transportation back to the Soviet Union, housing in their homeland, and retraining for civilian work.

There were and still are those who believe that the Soviet Union could have done better financially, demanded more reductions in the Bundeswehr, and negotiated a better deal on the question of Germany's NATO membership. That may be true. But taking into consideration the dangers that were avoided—especially the risk of complicating long-term relations with the European nation most important to the economic, political, and security interests of the Soviet Union and its successors—the deal was more than palatable.[24]

One of the most obvious results was the increase in the goodwill and even gratitude of the German political establishment and people. This goodwill cannot be relied on indefinitely, but together with the obvious geopolitical, economic, and other interests that tie Germany to the former Soviet Union and make it deeply interested in the stability and welfare of the successor states, this goodwill had and still has the chance of developing into an important influence in long-term bilateral relations, as has already been demonstrated. Germany is much more active than most Western countries in its efforts to provide a friendly external environment for the former Soviet Union and to involve the West in the process of restructuring the centrally planned economy. This was especially evident just before and after the G-7 meeting in London to which Gorbachev was invited.[25]

Another intangible but nevertheless significant result of the deal between the two countries was the visible acceleration, after the treaties were signed, of the process of changing the traditional Soviet distrust toward Germans and Germany into something more positive. This process continues. Germans are showing themselves to be in fact new Germans—reliable, benevolent, and even compassionate. The massive flow of food parcels into the Soviet Union in the winter of 1990 and spring of 1991 may have been humiliating, but the overall aftertaste was much more sweet than sour, and the humanitarian aid that arrived in the winter of 1991–92 was met mostly with gratitude. Media reporting on Germany has become predominantly positive. At least on the surface, the feelings of distrust and fear are hardly visible. All in all, the process of declaring a political truce of historic significance between two great nations and peoples has been set into motion.

The Paris CSCE charter, the Treaty on Conventional Forces in Europe (CFE), the various Soviet-German agreements, and the withdrawal of Soviet troops from the countries of Eastern and Central Europe and eventually from Germany itself have eliminated military confrontation as the major obstacle to Soviet/Russian-German and, even more broadly, Soviet/Russian-Western relations. In retrospect, it is becoming more and more clear that this posture, which not only bred fears and suspicions but provoked the development of offensive military doctrines, was one of the most tragic consequences of the Cold War. The military disengagement currently under way will eliminate this constant irritant. And last but not least, unification has done away with yet another political irritant—the revisionism of one of the major European powers. Germany now seems content with its status in Europe, at least for the time being.

On the whole, the treaties of July–December 1990 have laid a solid political, legal, and social foundation for positive developments between Germany and the former Soviet Union and could even foster a return to the normalcy of earlier times, with close partnerships and intermingling societies. These new developments offer Germany the chance to play a role similar to the one it played in the much earlier history of Russia.[26] To achieve this, however, it will be necessary to respond adequately to many complex challenges and avoid many dangerous pitfalls that have arisen since unification, principally as a result of events in the former Soviet Union. These challenges are much more trying for Germany than for any other European country, except of course for the successors to the Soviet Union.

Germany and Possible Developments in the Former Soviet Union

The August 1991 coup attempt speeded up almost all the developments it was allegedly aimed at preventing. Antimarket and antidemocratic forces connected primarily with the Communist party apparatus were dealt a severe if not a mortal blow. Conservative, backward-looking forces were pushed out of the bureaucracies where they had been holding on to key positions, especially in security and defense agencies. Many of these bureaucracies, mostly the all-union ministries, were emasculated or simply wiped out. New people with a clear sense of the desperate necessity of radical reforms assumed positions of power in Russia, though not in most of the other republics. The path of reform in Moscow was cleared. But at the same time the putsch gave added impetus to many destabilizing tendencies and exacerbated the country's crisis.

Of the many consequences of the putsch, two cause the gravest concern. One is the disintegration of the country. The radical weakening of the center cleared the way for those forces in the republics, especially Ukraine, which had been planning for a long and inconclusive struggle for independence through some form of weak federation or confederation. These forces seized the moment to win complete formal independence immediately. The acceleration of the movement in Ukraine toward complete independence brought into question the necessity for Russia to maintain more than perfunctory, confederative links with other republics, most of which are weaker economically and could become a drain on already scarce resources. Some of the former republics are alien to the Russian culture as well as politically conservative. And history has shown that a confederation, especially a weak one, is in most cases a very unstable and only transitional structure.

On the whole, the territory and peoples of the former USSR are moving through a historic period of nation-state building. This period, as history also shows, is far more dangerous and unstable than the process of decolonization or the breakdown of colonial empires. We are witnessing the breakup not only of the Soviet empire but of the core of historic Russia itself. Many of the new countries now being formed on the territory of the former USSR, including Ukraine and to a certain extent even the Russian Federation, have little historic legitimacy. Their internal borders are almost totally artificial and lack long-standing recognition.

Another cause for concern is the fact that promarket, democratic forces in Russia came to power unexpectedly, without a clearly formulated program or people with managerial experience. These democrats and free marketers must now implement the most unpopular reforms, especially the liberalization of prices. In hindsight, it is clear that it would have been much more politically profitable for the Russian leadership to come to power after the previous government had put some of the reforms in place. And in fact it is known that the Yeltsin group's strategy had been to come to real power later. The sudden necessity to govern caught the new leaders off guard, explaining in part the indecisiveness and fluctuations of the Russian leadership in September and October of 1991. The program of reforms was not ready until December, and by then much of the goodwill and enthusiasm both within and outside the country had been lost.

At the time of this writing, four scenarios for the development of the former USSR look plausible. The first involves the rise of neofascism in the successor states. The second scenario envisions another attempt at a coup by forces similar to those that made the attempt in August 1991. The third posits the country's slide into a series of conflicts and civil wars along the lines of those in Yugoslavia, with further disintegration of the major states into yet smaller units. This scenario would have major repercussions for the military (considering the distribution of weapons of mass destruction) and would lead to the total breakdown of order in and eventual "lebanization" of the former Soviet Union. The fourth scenario ends with the former republics becoming independent states and Russia muddling through, avoiding civil war and neofascism while moving slowly from crisis to crisis along the road to social and economic modernization. To be sure, this fourth, relatively optimistic scenario would most probably include some elements of the previous three. But real catastrophes would be avoided. Unfortunately, at this juncture, there is no realistic fifth, more optimistic scenario.

The sections that follow will try to outline the main features and foreign policy implications (especially for relations with Germany and Europe) of the first three scenarios. The fourth scenario is also described, but its external implications will be dealt with largely in the concluding section of the chapter.

The First Scenario: Neofascism

For the purposes of this analysis, the term "neofascism" means the emergence in the political arena and eventual rise to power in some republics of forces and leaders propagandizing ultraright nationalist or national-socialist ideologies and practices.

If the situation in the Soviet Union prior to August 1991 can be described as pre-Weimar, the putsch and the events that followed transformed it into a clearly Weimar one. The cumulative effects of soaring inflation during the whole of 1991 and the liberalization of prices have wiped out people's savings, while the rapid deterioration of living standards has pushed more and more people into poverty—all this before the truly massive unemployment that will likely result from the radical economic reforms takes effect.

To make things worse, the breakup of the country has created a sense of insecurity and even national humiliation among the citizens of the former republics. Many members of society now labor, both psychologically and socially, under what can be termed a defeated-country syndrome. While the former Soviet Union has never been defeated and has in fact been able to begin the long process of overcoming its totalitarian heritage with remarkable success, its disintegration has created psychological, political, and economic aftereffects of dangerous proportions.

The growing economic deprivation could provide fertile ground for populist and outright fascist ideologies, especially considering the absence of responsible political parties that could represent and channel the grievances of the most disaffected groups, particularly the blue collar workers. The most obvious gap in the political spectrum is now on the left, which is completely devoid of any representatives of social democracy. Most of the parties and groups that claim to espouse social democratic ideals are indistinguishable from liberals or even conservative liberals. This gap could be filled by either left- or right-populist groups, which are also virtually indistinguishable from one another.

These trends will not automatically bring about a return to totalitarianism, however. Offsetting factors do exist. Political safety valves such as freedom of the press, elections, and some parliamentary and municipal democracy are already functioning. The citizens of my country are known for their legendary perseverance. And the leaderships of most of the former republics, including Russia, are considered legitimate by the population. Also, significant groups of the elite have not yet staked their hopes on a national-socialist regime. The groups that allegedly supported the neofascist leader Vladimir Zhirinovsky lost their power base after the August coup attempt.

Neofascism will not automatically develop, but a combination of bad luck, grave mistakes by political leaders, rising resentment that the former republics are being treated unfairly by the outside world, and, above all, mistreatment of the national minorities that constitute close to one-third of the population of the former Soviet Union could make it unavoidable. Any significant internal migration will form a social milieu that will almost certainly encourage neofascist political movements made up of the urban poor and other disgruntled citizens. Hunger or severe malnutrition among large segments of the population, especially in urban areas, could exacerbate the situation in the next two or three years. Hopefully, after that the agricultural sector will begin to improve and the people will have adapted to the new conditions.

The international implications that would result if a fascist movement came to power in Russia with the support of conservative military elements are obvious. Even if the inevitable chauvinism, xenophobia, imperialistic tendencies, militaristic ideology, and disregard for basic human rights were relatively mild, the Western policy of containment would almost certainly be revived. As a result, two Iron Curtains, one on the border of the former Soviet Union and the other on the border of Russia, could be created. The former republics in the West would most probably be used as a buffer zone supported by but not belonging to the Western security system. The Central and East European countries would most likely make up a second buffer zone within the Western security system.

The ensuing partial remilitarization of European politics would inevitably diminish Germany's influence and increase America's. The European Community, which, judging by its current situation, would not be ready to act as the political and security leader of the West, would have to yield much of its influence to NATO. At least for a time, the European political union would be slowed down, if not reversed, as national differences intensified.

Russian-German relations would also be dealt a severe blow, with potential long-term consequences. The inevitable anti-foreign and perhaps specifically anti-German propaganda would sour public opinion and damage goodwill toward the Russians. The economic blockade that would be part of the new containment policy would further undermine the already shrinking trade between Germany and the former Soviet Union. Even the speedy overthrow of a fascist regime probably could not restore hopes for a rapprochement, and Germany would strengthen its Western orientation.

A more complex situation could occur if a totalitarian or a violently nationalist regime came to power in Ukraine. Russia would then become the obvious geopolitical ally of Eastern, Central, and Western Europe. An additional special link would be created between Moscow and the West European capitals, especially Bonn. But in general, the creation of such a regime on the European territory of the former USSR would cause disillusionment throughout Europe and especially in Germany, where hopes have been high for a relatively smooth transition to a stable democracy and viable economy in the former Soviet Union. Such a regime would also contribute to the gradual isolation of Russia for at least a decade, during which it would be struggling to overcome its internal problems. It would also mean the loss of the current momentum of Russian-German relations.

The Second Scenario: A Military-Political Coup

A coup along the lines of the August 1991 attempt could become a reality if some current tendencies are not corrected and the Russian government commits certain political mistakes. Among the negative tendencies that could raise the threat of a possible coup are the progressive weakening of the mechanisms governing society and the deterioration of the food situation, which together could provoke riots and other types of civil disorder. The chances for a coup will increase markedly if the current process of disintegration spreads to the military and the troops turn on each other, or if antimilitary pressure continues in some former republics, primarily the Baltics. New political leaders could make things worse by failing to work constructively with the military. Potentially, the most vulnerable of the former republics are Ukraine, which has the largest concentration of military personnel; Russia; and probably some of the Baltic countries. The coup would be justified as necessary to restore law and order and prevent further geopolitical disintegration that could lead to civil war. Under such a banner, a second coup could initially command more support than the first attempt.

The prospect of a large-scale, well-organized coup whereby the military and allied political groups assume control of large parts of the country is still not likely. Having pushed out the most reactionary of the forces within its ranks, the military has shown that it respects basic democratic values. In fact, it is more law abiding and disciplined than other parts of the elite, and it is also not united in the belief that it can deliver a better life. What is more likely than a single well-organized coup attempt is a series of semi-coups that occur as different governments turn to the military for help to stay in power or maintain order. The price, of course, will be yielding greater political influence to the military. This process has already begun in Russia and Ukraine.

The international consequences of a coup will probably be very close to those described in the previous scenario, but with one significant variation. It seems possible that the opportunities for the West to cooperate with such a regime would be somewhat greater than with a purely reactionary, neofascist leadership, particularly on nuclear security and related matters. Concern already exists in Russia that some Western politicians, faced with deepening chaos in the former Soviet Union, would not be willing to make the heavy political and economic investments required to offset it and might offer only perfunctory condemnations of a coup they would eventually learn to accept and live with.

The Third Scenario: Civil War and/or "Lebanization"

Unfortunately, this scenario is already becoming a reality, even without the rise of neofascism or a military coup. Relatively small-scale low-intensity conflicts—almost civil wars—are already in progress on the territory of the former USSR, so far mostly in the Caucasus. But the problem is spreading, and the conflicts that have already begun in Moldova and elsewhere are gradually but very visibly undermining any hope for democratic development and economic recovery in the affected areas in the foreseeable future. However, such conflicts have so far had only marginal effects on the fate of the key republics.

But what is most important for the stability of the former Soviet Union, as well as for international peace and security in general, is the future relationship between Russia and Ukraine. If historical analogies—such as Yugoslavia—can be used as a basis for a prognostication, the chances for conflict between these two newly emerging countries appear far from negligible. An analysis of the current political and economic trends involving Ukraine and Russia supports such a conclusion.

Both republics are beginning the process of nation-state formation, and both are enduring radical social transformations and internal crises. Under such circumstances, elite groups often evoke an external threat to solidify national feeling. The borders of Ukraine and Russia are almost completely artificial, and the two countries have very few, if any, permanent conflict prevention mechanisms to resolve disputes between them.

In addition, economic reforms in the two former republics are developing at different speeds and will probably create tension on issues such as protectionism and price adjustments, exacerbating political relations. Political self-assertion will further hamper economic ties. Ukraine will continue to encounter problems trying to nationalize those parts of the military on its territory. There is also the intangible but potentially dangerous psychological discomfort of most Russians and Ukrainians, who once lived together in a unified country and suddenly find themselves separated.

This list of problems is incomplete. But it clearly shows that, in order to live through the transitional decade peacefully, political leaders of both former republics must demonstrate unusual ingenuity, flexibility, and, above all, wisdom. The new revolutionary leaders are by and large not expected to display such traits. Yet the situation is not as ominous as might be implied, for the two republics are so economically interdependent that their economic ties, at least, cannot be completely broken. Even the most diehard separatists will have to learn this fact. The question, of course, is what the price of this learning process will be. Fortunately the two peoples do not have a history of wars and hatred such as that of the Serbs and Croats. With good luck, wisdom, and help from the outside, conflicts and wars can be avoided, though the possibility of trouble remains.

If tension should escalate into open conflict, the disintegration first of Russia and then Ukraine would no doubt be accelerated. The process of "feudalizing" the entire territory of the former USSR would immediately raise the question of who controlled the weapons of mass destruction, including chemical agents and nuclear energy plants. The West would be faced with the excruciating dilemma of deciding whether to seal off the former Soviet Union or to actively intervene to influence events, possibly even playing the former republics against each other. Judging by recent Western behavior, the first instinct would probably be to try to isolate the "sick man of Europe." But gradually, as the conflicts deepened and spread to neighboring countries, the West would be sucked into attempts to regulate the situation.

Under these circumstances, the still relatively fragile European political union would start to crumble and NATO, which has a more robust machinery, especially on military-political matters, would regain some lost ground. Given the high stakes involved, it is hard to say whether the West would be able to organize a cohesive policy even within the framework of the alliance. It seems probable that only a few countries would try to play an active role, among them the United States (as the nuclear custodian of the West) and Germany (as the country most affected).[27] International interference in an internal conflict would inevitably involve taking sides and would undoubtedly create not only friends but bitter enemies.

If the former Soviet Union lives through a civil conflict during which a large part of the country is reunited by force, future relations between Germany and the new entity will depend on whether Germany supports the winner or loser during the conflict. However, civil wars are so inherently unpredictable that all attempts to assess the outcome or its implications are futile. It is just as likely, for instance, that a civil conflict would lead to the complete disintegration of the former USSR into dozens of smaller units, as has already been suggested.

The Fourth Scenario: "Muddling Through"

While muddling through and gradual modernization would no doubt involve elements of the previous three scenarios in a milder form, the consequences would be far less tragic. The former Soviet Union has been moving along the lines envisioned by this scenario since the late spring of 1991. If this scenario does continue to develop, it will entail several waves of market-oriented reforms that gradually create a more propitious economic, social, and psychological environment for the modernization of the economy.

Politically, however, this scenario will mean continued instability; frequent changes of governments; a combination of the regionalization of Russia, Ukraine, and some other republics; and increasingly authoritarian methods of government. In fact, a certain level of at least mild authoritarianism seems virtually unavoidable; the question is only one of degree and depends largely on whether some democratic mechanisms will be preserved as checks on the executive. If they are not, this authoritarianism will degenerate into some form of dictatorship.

Riots and local putsches will very probably be part of the political picture. One likely development is the further growth of the military's political influence. Already one of the greatest barriers to the expansion of separatist tendencies is the fear of a military backlash. Additionally, this scenario entails a slowdown and some stabilization of the process of political fragmentation and the creation of new countries. Within such a framework, however fragile it might be in the long run, some sources of tension may be eliminated and others kept from escalating.

The "muddling through" scenario is the only one that allows for the planning of a coherent foreign policy toward the former Soviet Union and its successors. It is also the only scenario that permits relatively accurate predictions of the outcomes of such policies. Under the "muddling through" scenario, the foreign policy positions of the successors to the Soviet Union would probably be characterized by several features.

—Further relative loss of international influence.

—A less global, more regional, and increasingly economically oriented foreign policy. Europe and Germany would inevitably climb higher on the ladder of foreign policy priorities; other countries that could receive higher priority include China, Turkey, Iran, and Japan.

—Gradual demilitarization of national security policy, though with some reversals, and a reduction in military activities. At the same time, military power might be needed as a symbol of prestige in this period of weakness. The probable outcome of such a development would be an increase in political reliance on nuclear weapons, much like France and Britain.

The process of formulating and implementing foreign policy would become even more chaotic, in part due to the inexperience of the new ruling elites. This scenario may pose difficult problems for the West. The outside world would be faced with neither a relatively stable and predictable partner (such as the USSR under Gorbachev) nor a clear-cut enemy, but with several new, unknown partners. It could also be hard to swallow some of their relatively unpleasant traits. At the same time, it would be clearly counterproductive to react to the unpleasant aspects of the new reality with a policy of ostracism and isolation. Equally dangerous would be a policy that condoned nondemocratic and antireform moves made by the new regimes.

Another complicated issue the outside world would face is the inevitable growth of Russian self-consciousness and even nationalism. This growth is not only inexorable but also arguably necessary for the moral revival of the Russian people. Without it, the country cannot be rebuilt on the economic and ideological ruins of totalitarianism. So far the rise of Russian nationalism and patriotism has been delayed, and what has emerged is taking mostly civilized forms; the ugly manifestations of nationalism have clearly been the work of marginal groups.

When Russian nationalism becomes more evident, the West will have to devise a reasonable policy. The tendency to label every manifestation of Russian nationalism imperialistic and to condemn it on that basis will only strengthen xenophobic and anti-Western tendencies. Attempts to overlook or to placate such tendencies could be equally counterproductive.

Russia and Germany: Foreign Policy Challenges

Despite all its vagueness—and in part due to it—the concept of the common European house served the former Soviet Union well when the task at hand was to break out of the old political and security paradigm.[28] But the developments in Central and Eastern Europe, Germany, and the USSR itself between 1989 and 1991 radically altered existing Soviet foreign policy agendas in Europe and elsewhere.[29] The full implications of the momentous events have not yet been grasped or placed in their new political context. The disintegration of the Soviet Union, impelled by the August 1991 coup attempt, and the secession of Ukraine make it unlikely that the USSR will be resurrected in any form in the foreseeable future. Thus, this section is written from a Russian rather than a Soviet vantage point, although the interests of some other republics are also taken into account.[30]

As the old dangers and postwar structures fade away and the tragic social experiment that was the Soviet Union ends, Europe is returning to a situation much like that which existed before World War I. As before, this situation is fraught with all kinds of dangers, such as the resurgence of traditional nationalist feelings and possible shifts in the balance of power politics, despite the fact that certain factors make the current situation much less prone to destabilization. At the same time, the situation is complicated by the presence of several new countries that are undergoing revolutionary or postrevolutionary transitions.[31] These challenges call for new policies and levels of diplomacy difficult for the former republics to achieve, given their internal problems.

The overriding foreign policy challenge during the last years of the USSR was to create a favorable international climate for the country's painful social transformation. But today the most important foreign policy challenges facing Russia and the other republics are different. The successor states must avoid civil wars and totalitarian backlashes while simultaneously ensuring a peaceful transition to a new community of countries. They must do this, moreover, while carrying out major economic and social reforms. The international environment does matter, but the challenges it poses are clearly diminishing in significance in the light of the mounting threats emanating from within the former USSR.

Russia and other republics still want a favorable international climate, but their definition of the term "favorable" has changed. If previously it meant peaceful, friendly, and conducive to various kinds of cooperation that would increase political and economic influence, it now means something more. It has become increasingly clear, especially to foreign policy experts in Russia, that the former Soviet Union will have very little chance of surviving this period of transformation and societal reform peacefully without outside assistance. Not only economic aid but also direct political involvement is needed, and the most obvious partners are the United States, especially on nuclear matters; Germany, on economic and political matters; the CSCE; the European Community; and NATO. The former republics will now surely judge the outside world—both individual countries and other international institutions—in terms of what they can do to help in managing the current internal reforms and transformations. As a consequence, traditional international priorities will to a large extent become secondary as the domestic agenda becomes internationalized.

This shift to what I would call the "provincialization," or internalization of the foreign policy and security agendas most probably will not result in self-imposed isolationism. Most of the new leaders coming to power are outward looking and seek global recognition and economic aid. Although the "muddling through" scenario would from time to time see xenophobia or isolationism surface, internationalism would be the prevailing tendency.

Nevertheless, the current economic crisis and political instability are rapidly curtailing economic ties with the outside world. Internal turmoil, bureaucratic rivalries, and struggles between the republics have effectively tied down diplomacy on key issues in which the Soviet Union used to play a significant role. The slowing down of foreign policy initiatives and loss of influence are only partly compensated for by the activities of the new republican governments. Most contacts currently being made are perfunctory in nature or required by protocol and deal primarily with bilateral matters. In addition, the secession of the Baltic republics and especially of Ukraine could presage geopolitical and even cultural isolation for Russia.

The "muddling through" scenario implies that, even under the most favorable of circumstances, the successor states of the USSR will have to live through several crises. Although it is relatively unlikely, some of these crises might spill over into the territories of Western neighbors. If so, this would raise genuine concerns and fears among East and Central European countries and could be used to bolster the arguments for immediate admission to the Western security system. However, if NATO or even the Western

European Union (WEU) were to formally embrace the countries of Central and Eastern Europe and provide official guarantees, the possibility of a direct military threat to Russia or the other former republics would probably not increase significantly. Nevertheless, for many in Russia the military situation would undoubtedly feel more threatening, especially since it would add to the already existing sense of economic and social isolation. The fear of being isolated and locked out was one of the reasons why, in late 1991, some members of the Russian government began to entertain publicly the idea of an independent Russia within NATO.

The internal turmoil and concern with becoming isolated are exacerbated for both Russia and Ukraine by the emergence near the western and especially southwestern borders of the former Soviet Union of a group of states whose development, for all its variety, will be characterized in the coming years by internal weakness and instability. Threatened by the emergence of a relatively powerful Ukraine, some countries of Central and Eastern Europe could try to forge a classic geopolitical alliance with the more distant Russia; in fact, calls for such a union are already being heard in Poland and Czechoslovakia. As a consequence, the geopolitical map of Europe from the Oder to the Urals has started to shift in unexpected ways.

Another problem is the security vacuum in Central and Eastern Europe, which NATO has so far declined to fill by offering full membership to the countries in the region. Unless it is filled in a mutually acceptable manner, it will continue to be a constant irritant, creating suspicions and tension. To make matters worse, this vacuum has expanded. The Central and East European countries are no longer alone; Moldova, Ukraine, the Baltic states, and even to a certain extent Russia are feeling something of the same insecurity. The North Atlantic Cooperation Council (NACC) is a welcome development, but it clearly cannot fill the emerging "geostrategic gap."

From Moscow's viewpoint, the situation in Eastern and Central Europe harbors yet another danger. If the conflict in Yugoslavia spreads, or a similar conflict develops in neighboring countries, the attention as well as the political and economic resources of the West and especially of Germany will be diverted, further hampering Western participation in the revival of Russia. Another danger lies in the possibility that Germany and other parts of the West might close themselves off to Eastern Europe because of uncontrollable instability and waves of refugees. Such action would probably put an end to the hopes of the Central and East European countries for a relatively speedy economic recovery. A belt of permanently unstable states would be created as a consequence.

There is, of course, further concern over the likely German domination of Central and Eastern Europe. In a way, greater German influence is inevitable and will simply have to be accepted. Bonn's preoccupation with the restructuring of the former East Germany, however, will delay and perhaps soften the impact. The real danger, however, is not German domination but the previously mentioned possibility that Central and Eastern Europe and, consequently, the former republics could become isolated due to domestic turmoil, violent crises, social stagnation, and waves of refugees. In such a case, Germany could turn toward the West or even further inward.

Military-political developments also present the Soviet military with a radically new situation. From the traditional point of view, the change in the balance of power has been much greater than Soviet political and military leaders envisioned when they agreed to the principle of equal ceilings in the CFE agreement. At least four developments, in addition to the unequal reductions stipulated by the CFE agreements, provide those who adhere to this traditional viewpoint with reason for concern: the demise of the WTO; the situation in the Baltic republics, which occupy key geopolitical positions; the secession of Ukraine, home to many of the elite troops; and the effects of the general social and economic crisis on the readiness and morale of the armed forces.

These concerns could be overcome as some of the positive repercussions of the military-political changes become more evident—especially when, as planned, NATO countries reduce their armed forces far below the levels stipulated in the CFE treaty, or when it becomes clear that NATO will not penetrate into Central and Eastern Europe, or when the Russian security establishment fully understands that creating a non-nuclear semi-demilitarized corridor to replace the WTO is not a loss but a net security gain. But these adjustments will take time. The concerns are exacerbated by the difficult situation in which the military, the political elite, and the workers dependent on the military-industrial complex have found themselves. Virtually all assessments agree that the military-industrial complex forms the core of Soviet industry, if not the industry itself, and most of those affected by the current downsizing have not yet found a new place in the new world. The desperate state of the military and the military-industrial complex is becoming a separate social, political, and even security problem, with illegal arms sales, the use of mercenaries, possible social unrest in the cities, and domination by the military industry.

Of course, some traditional military concerns remain: on the southern flank of the former USSR, where the Gulf War and severe instability in the Caucasus have deepened the military imbalance; and on the northern flank, where the balance of naval forces has tipped due to the rejection by the United States (and, much less adamantly, by other NATO countries) of naval arms control.[32] On the "central front," which includes Germany, analysis conducted by the Institute of Europe in Moscow has thus far demonstrated that, even if it were advisable to reduce NATO's military preponderance, full-scale CFE-like reduction talks are counterproductive, if only because of the increasingly obvious artificiality of the principle of parity and the political danger associated with regional arms reduction schemes. Also, unless political tension returns, the residual imbalances will lose their significance in the eyes of all but the most devoted arms controllers.

It appears that the main objects of future arms control talks will be greater transparency, other confidence- and security-building measures (CSBMs), and adjustments to the military posture and doctrine of the participating countries. In principle, these talks could be supplemented by narrower negotiations. The emergence of new security challenges calls for new goals in the arms control process. One primary objective should be the social re-integration of former Soviet soldiers, many of whom have been left in a desperate position. Much is already being done on both the national and international level, but there is no coordinated, comprehensive approach to the problem. Most of the efforts, especially on the international level, affect only a relatively narrow strata of the military. Another possible focus of arms control should be the coordination of the conversion of military industries.

Recent, fast-moving political events, however, have left virtually no time even to consider the desirability of such talks. Under the circumstances, the only possible approach is to make parallel unilateral reductions, despite the well-known shortcomings of this type of arms control. Gorbachev and Bush have in fact already taken such steps with the nuclear cuts announced in September and October of 1991. But considering the increasing ungovernabil-ity of the former Soviet Union, it is still too early to say whether the proposed cuts will be implemented on their current rather grand scale.

The former Soviet Union, however, should not be interested in rapidly and drastically reducing its nuclear arsenal. Recent political and military developments—specifically, the drastic change in the military balance and Russia's increasing economic and social weaknesses—strengthen the argu-ment against this. However, the changing landscape of the former Soviet Union calls for radical reductions and withdrawals of theater nuclear weapons. Even land-based tactical nuclear weapons (TNFs) are rapidly becoming useless and politically dangerous, as they create problems among the former republics and have the potential to complicate relations with the countries of Central and Eastern Europe. In addition, they could be potentially deadly if serious destabilization occurs in Russia or elsewhere.

Russia's changing foreign policy and security priorities call for a re-evaluation of attitudes and policies toward the European institutions. Moscow has already gone from advocating a position of reserved partnership with NATO to desiring the closest possible cooperation. Clearly, changes in Moscow's strategic policies, as well as the fear of isolation mentioned earlier, influenced this development. Some in Moscow's strategic community also perceive NATO as a useful counterbalance to the increasingly influential European Community, which in effect is merging with the WEU. The presence of two competing political and security institutions increases

Moscow's room to maneuver. Some pro-NATO (but not anti-EC) leanings are also being caused by the EC and WEU's tendency to regard the former Soviet Union and its successors as second-class partners, while considering other member countries of the former WTO, especially Poland, Hungary, and Czechoslovakia, as first-class partners.

The re-evaluation of attitudes toward NATO is also being influenced by the understanding that other institutions alone or even together are clearly inadequate to deal with the challenges faced by Europe and the former Soviet Union. The CSCE is far from being an effective tool for pan-European management, as the crisis in Yugoslavia has demonstrated. The EC, for all its newly acquired economic muscle, has also failed to organize a coherent, effective common foreign policy in one crisis after another—the Gulf War and the conflict in Yugoslavia, especially its early stages, are good examples. The greater political cooperation within the EC has yet to prove its ability to function well under stress. Under these circumstances, NATO is seen not only as a fact of life that makes any opposition to it counterproductive but as an increasingly valuable element in European stability. It is also considered by many to be one of the guarantors of the continued process of democratization in Central and Eastern Europe and beyond. In addition, NATO is showing its usefulness as a means of keeping the United States in the European security system. Moscow is more than ever interested in this presence, if only to balance and regulate Germany's influence. And NATO is useful as a means of soothing concerns over the rather improbable possibility of German remilitarization.

The increase in German influence and the concerns it is causing—rightly or wrongly—provide Moscow with an additional incentive to overcome its residual ambivalence to the other institutions that could serve as counter-weights. These include NATO and, of course, the EC, which is the most effective instrument in terms of absorbing and diluting this influence. Even the Central European Initiative (CEI) (the former Pentagonal group, now composed of Austria, Czechoslovakia, Hungary, Italy, Poland, and Yugo-slavia) and the Visegrad Triangle (Czechoslovakia, Hungary, and Poland) could eventually be viewed more positively if they do not develop any visible anti-Russian potential, which seems improbable.

All in all, the German factor, developments in Europe, and general uncertainty about the future are pushing Russia toward reliance on the interlocking institutions that make up the architecture of the European house. This trend, which can be traced back to Soviet foreign policy thinking in 1991, does not preclude continued emphasis on the CSCE framework. Quite a few political interests are involved in Russia's continued support of the CSCE, principally the desire to avoid isolation and the need to engage the new Germany constructively. Russia's stake in the CSCE could even increase due to the very probable need that all-European instruments will be required to manage relations between and within the former Soviet Union, particularly on such issues as human rights, minorities, and borders. The CSCE could provide a framework of legitimacy for outside involvement in such cases.

In the development of the CSCE process, Germany is the most active and influential partner of the former republics and, in particular, Russia. Apart from having more than the usual interest in reassuring Moscow, Germany is more dependent than other Western countries on stability in Central and Eastern Europe and the former USSR. For this reason, it stands to gain the most politically from strengthening the all-European institutions.

There are grounds to believe that bilateral political relations between Russia and Germany, as well as cooperation in multilateral institutions, could develop relatively smoothly. Due to turmoil in the former Soviet Union, however, some political and economic possibilities will no doubt be lost. Russian-German relations will probably never acquire anything close to a special status, as the turmoil in the former USSR is pushing Germany further away from bilateralism toward greater reliance on multilateral institutions, primarily the EC. In addition, Germany's preoccupation with the former GDR has caused Bonn to concentrate primarily on its own political and economic problems.

Other issues could complicate relations, such as the remaining Soviet garrisons, the ethnic Germans in the former USSR, and the potential anti-Sovietism of some east Germans. Another irritant could be generated by German policy toward immigrants from the former Soviet Union if this policy is either too restrictive or too liberal toward young, skilled workers. Larger problems could be created if Germany begins flexing its newly acquired muscle without concern for the sensitivities of other countries. Any such behavior would inflate latent fears about Germany. But the most serious potential problem for Russian-German relations could be engendered by separate German policies toward the former republics, especially if conflict breaks out between them. The historic legacy of distrust and fear will be revived if Germany shows any sign of taking sides. Currently, the German interest in Russia seems to be declining, in part because of the turmoil there and in part because, for the first time in recent history, the former Soviets are not a direct threat.

These are only short-term concerns, however. The long-term danger is that the former Soviet republics will fall into semi-isolation. It is still not clear whether Germany will continue to act as a bridge between Russia and Europe after the Kohl/Genscher generation is gone and new, Western-oriented leaders, less intellectually and emotionally attached to Eastern policies, come to power. Much will depend, of course, on developments in the former Soviet Union itself. If the former republics begin to emerge from the current crisis within the next few years, this problem may not arise. But this could take more than just a few years.

Finally, the issue of economic relations with the outside world, including Germany, obviously was a very high priority on the Soviet foreign policy agenda and has become even more important to Russia. Most of the elite, whatever their ideological differences, understand that economic welfare and continued democratization are impossible if the economy is not opened to the outside world and integrated into the global economy. But thus far such integration remains in the theoretical stage. Painful and contradictory efforts at implementing market reforms are opening the country a bit and making dealings with the outside world somewhat easier, but domestic economic failures and political instability are drastically reducing the possibilities. The situation is further complicated by the shortage of available capital on the world market due to the economic situation in the United States and Germany.

Both sides had expected Soviet-Western economic interaction to rise sharply after the end of the Cold War. East Germany had been expected to provide a new market for the EC, and it was widely believed that Germany would save the Soviet Union economically as the two countries helped create a common economic space from the Rhine to the Urals.[33] But just the opposite has been happening. The decline in economic interaction is the result of several factors: accumulated debt, political uncertainty, and the absence of a legal framework to accommodate foreign investment and credits.[34] Energy exports have decreased due to aging facilities and a shortage of capital in the oil and gas industries. The primary reasons, however, lie in the collapse of the former Soviet domestic market and the indecisiveness of those leaders who for several years were unable to embrace the necessity of completely overhauling the centrally planned economy rather than just reforming it. This indecision only exacerbated the economic problems, and Yeltsin's reform package was introduced too late; political instability had already undermined whatever willingness to invest existed.

Special emphasis was placed on continuing the extensive trade between the Soviet Union and eastern Germany,[35] particularly since the German government had agreed to support the obligations of former East German firms. Nevertheless, by the end of 1991, Soviet-east German trade was showing signs of collapse as well. In addition to those reasons already given for the general decline in economic relations, this collapse resulted from the decrease in production levels brought about by restructuring and from the switch to hard currency payments, which allowed both east German and Soviet firms to look for new, mostly Western partners. Because the redirected trade patterns will probably be permanent, unification—for the time being at least—has damaged rather than helped Russian-German trade, in spite of generous government-backed financial support and continued credit lines.

Medium- to long-range prospects appear brighter, however. Germany, as well as other West European countries, remains interested in the potentially enormous market of the former USSR. Economically as well as politically,

Germany is also keen on developing Russia's energy and resource base. Nobody—and particularly not Germany—will benefit if the former USSR disintegrates completely, relapses into totalitarianism, or slides into civil war. Several assessments that have already been made and used extensively in political struggles argue that Ukraine, with its relatively well-developed machine-building and manufacturing industries and agriculture, will benefit the most from trade with the West.[36] However, most products of the former Soviet manufacturing industries are not globally competitive, and the market for agricultural products is very narrow. In the next few years, the former Soviet Union will probably have only one type of marketable commodity to offer—natural resources and energy. And here Russia occupies the predominant position.

Recommendations

This section is divided into two parts. The first offers recommendations for Russian policy, the second for Western.

Recommendations for Russian Policy

The current and future challenges facing the former Soviet Union call for a reformulation of the conceptual base underlying policy toward Europe, which could include the following goals.

The first priority of both internal and external policy should be to make the transformation of the former USSR as peaceful as possible. Since this will almost certainly require outside help, Russia will have to learn to deal with external involvement and possible interference in its domestic affairs.

The second priority is working out a new modus operandi for relations between the former republics. Without it, Western and other countries could exploit the situation and even play the new countries against each other, or alternatively, refuse to deal with countries that cannot cooperate with each other in a civilized way.

The third priority should be to fill the security vacuum that exists in Central and Eastern Europe between the Oder and the Urals. Otherwise, the area will remain a constant irritant and may sooner or later explode. There are several ways to accomplish this, including developing a general CSCE collective security commitment that would allow Western countries and alliances to extend security guarantees outside their formal structures. At the same time, Moscow should make perfectly clear its desire not to be excluded from any offers of formal security guarantees by NATO and the WEU to members of the former WTO.

The fourth goal should be to avoid creeping isolationism by creating as many institutional and cooperative links as possible between the former republics and Western Europe, the United States, Canada, and Japan. The growing strategic concord with the West should be continued and intensified.

Fifth, relations with Germany should be developed quickly in order to settle certain outstanding issues, including the status of the German minority in the former USSR. Otherwise, the positive trends could gradually diminish. Considering Germany's importance, Russian-German relations in general should be given a higher priority. At the same time, Moscow should not try to make Germany the centerpiece of its European policy but should work to improve relations with other countries.

Specialized relations with multilateral institutions should also be given priority. For example, ties with NATO should be developed in order to foster international security, arms control, and military-to-military contacts. The European Community, on the other hand, should be the main focus of economic relations, particularly with Central and Eastern Europe. Out-of-area challenges could be discussed with the Community, the WEU, and the United States, among others.

Finally, Russia should continue to work toward strengthening the CSCE process to make it the foundation of the new European house. The CSCE is one of the very few legitimate international mechanisms that could be used to regulate severe internal crises.

Recommendations for Western Policy

The West needs a major readjustment of its policies as well. First, it is important to move beyond the recent Western parochialism. Strengthening the EC, renovating and defining a new role for NATO, finding a new balance between the EC, NATO, and the WEU, and integrating Germany are all goals worth pursuing. But most of the real challenges for the security of Europe lie outside this framework. While these institutions provide a useful base, by themselves they are not sufficient, as their general ineffectiveness in preventing crises in Central and Eastern Europe and the former USSR has demonstrated.

Now that the Western institutional framework has been strengthened, latent distrust and skepticism toward the CSCE can and must be overcome, and the West should agree to provide real muscle so the EC and the CSCE can work jointly to prevent and regulate conflicts. At the same time, NATO can continue to provide hard-core military support and gradually become the security arm of the CSCE.

While economic and financial assistance represent the primary means of helping the successor countries to the Soviet Union, these efforts could take years to bear fruit. In the meantime, every effort should be made to engage Moscow in political and security affairs to prevent isolationism. Its security community, including the military and the military-industrial complex, should be involved in both European and global initiatives. The concept of a Vladivostok-to-Vancouver (or even a Tokyo-to-Vancouver) strategic alliance is promising in this respect.

During this century, Germany has twice been in a situation similar to the one the former Soviet Union—especially Russia—finds itself in now. The first time it was abandoned; the second time it was helped. Today, the international community is offered the historic opportunity to bring Russia and the other successor states to the Soviet Union into the new world order.

Notes

1. For official accounts of Soviet-German policies see G. V. Fokeyev, ed., *Istoriya mezhdunarodnykh otnosheniy i vneshney politiki SSSR, 1945–1970* (The history of international relations and foreign policy of the USSR, 1945–1970) vol. 2 (Moscow: Mezhdunarodnyye otnosheniya, 1987), pp. 170–95.

2. Very few Western analysts have so far agreed to such an assertion. For a rare example, see F. Stephen Larrabee, "The View from Moscow," in F. Stephen Larrabee, ed., *The Two German States and European Security* (MacMillan, in association with the Institute for East-West Security Studies, 1989), pp. 182–205. For a recent Soviet treatment of this issue, see I. Maksimychev, "V dvukh shagakh ot ob"yedinënnoy Germanii" (Two steps from a unified Germany), *Mezhdunarodnaya Zhizn'*, no. 9 (1990), pp. 37–44.

3. *Otchetnyy dokald Tsentral'nogo Komiteta KPSS XXIII. S"yezdu Kommunis-ticheskoy Partii Sovetskogo Soyuza, 29 marta 1966 goda. Doklad pervogo sekretarya tovarishcha L. I. Brezhneva* (Report of the Central Committee of the CPSU to the XXIII Congress of the Communist party of the Soviet Union: Report of the first secretary of the Central Committee L. I. Brezhnev) (Moscow: Politicheskaya Literatura, 1966), pp. 30–42, especially pp. 34–36; and N. Polyanov, "obuzdat' agressorov, obespechit' mir" (To restrain aggressors, to provide peace), *Kommunist*, vol. 2 (July 1966), pp. 89–97.

4. I, at least, am sure of that, for neither I nor anyone I know in Soviet foreign policy circles has ever heard of it. For a similar argument, see Igor Maksimychev, "Germaniya i my" (Germany and us), *Mezhdunarodnaya Zhizn'*, no. 8 (1991), pp. 37–44.

5. See on the latter attempts Larrabee, "The View from Moscow," pp. 201–03.

6. I provided this kind of argument at length in Sergei Karaganov, "Pobedit li sebya Sovetskiy Soyuz? Pobediv vo vtoroy mirovoy voyne, SSSR, po suti dela, proigral poslevoyennyy mir. Segodnya est' shans ego vyigrat'" (Will the Soviet Union survive? Having achieved victory in WW II, the USSR, in essence, lost the postwar peace. Today there is an opportunity to win it), *Novoye Vremya*, no.13 (1991), pp. 22–24.

7. See an interesting exchange of opinions on the economic costs of the empire among members of the Commission of the Central Committee of the CPSU on International Affairs, "Peremeny v Tsentral'noy i Vostochnoy Evrope: S zasedaniya Komissii *TsK KPSS* po voprosam mezhdunarodnoy politiki (Changes in Eastern and Central Europe: From the Meeting of the Commission of the CC of the CPSU on International Policy), *Isvestiya TsK KPSS*, no. 10 (1990), p. 104.

8. I almost never heard this argument in the Soviet Union in the years between 1983 and 1987. Those who used this argument in the Soviet Union did so mostly with tongue in cheek, trying to outdo the hardliners in quasi-confrontational rhetoric by maintaining that the Reagan administration's policy was not to achieve a military advantage but simply to impose a new arms race. To defeat this policy, the theory went, it would be necessary to avoid engaging in the military buildup toward which the United States was pushing the Soviet Union.

9. For such an assertion, see the two-part interview with Counselor to President Mikhail Gorbachev, Marshal S.F. Akhromeev, "Vse razumnoye dostatochno? Na voyne kak na voyne. No i posle voyny kak posle voyny. . . Kakova rol' armii posle 'kholodnoy voyny'?" (Is everything reasonable sufficient? During the war like during the war. But after the war, like after the war. . . . What is the role of the army in the aftermath of the 'Cold War'?), *Novoye Vremya*, no. 14 (April 1991), pp. 14–19, and "Armiya Zashchishchayet Sebya?" (Is the army defending itself?) no. 15 (1991), pp. 12–17.

10. "Vstrecha M. S. Gorbacheva s R. fon Vaytszekkerom" (The meeting between M. S. Gorbachev and R. von Weizsäcker), *Pravda*, July 8, 1987, pp. 1–2.

11. "Sovmestnoye zayavleniye" (Joint declaration), *Izvestiya*, June 15, 1989, pp. 1–3.

12. "Peremeny v Tsentral'noy i Vostochnoy Yevrope" (Changes in Central and Eastern Europe), *Izvestiya TsK KPSS*, no. 10 (1990), p. 103.

13. My own observations and experience strongly suggest that most of the specialists who advised the politicians on Germany did not believe that unification was inevitable even in the days immediately before and after the fall of the Berlin Wall. The prevailing view was that opening East Germany to the West would provide a safety valve and that most East Germans would still opt for a separate country, though one closely tied to West Germany in a kind of confederation.

14. For an excellent expose of the Soviet policy toward German unification, see Hannes Adomeit, "Gorbachev and German Unification: Revision of Thinking, Realignment of Power," *Problems of Communism*, no. 4 (July–August 1990), pp. 1–23.

15. Applying the "French solution" to Germany was a possibility entertained by at least some of the West German leadership and was in fact put forward by Foreign Minister Hans-Dietrich Genscher. Some members of the West German leadership told me later that it would have been extremely hard for them to reject such an initiative if it had been put forward by the Soviet Union relatively early.

16. For Soviet criticism of neutrality, see, for example, S.Ye. Blagovolin, "Opasno li ob"yedineniye Germanii?" (Is German unification dangerous?), *Tochka Zreniya*, no. 1 (1990), pp. 57–59; and S. Smol'nikov, "Novaya logika yevropeyskogo razvitiya" (The new logic of European development), *MEiMO*, no. 6 (1990), pp. 21–22.

17. See Eduard Shevardnadze, *Moy vybor. V zashchitu demokratii i svobody* (My choice: In defense of democracy and freedom) (Moscow: Novosti, 1991), p. 225.

18. For an overview of politically motivated criticisms of Gorbachev and Shevardnadze's German policies, see Adomeit, "Gorbachev and German Unification," pp. 20–22. For a professional Soviet analysis of the dangers—real or imaginary—of unification, see General-Colonel A.A. Danilevich "Voyenno-strategicheskiye aspekty ob"yedineniya Germanii" (Military-political aspects of German unification), *Tochka zreniya*, no. 1 (1990), pp. 60–67. See also N. Pavlov, "Germanskiy vopros i 'obshcheyevropeyskiy dom' (o balanse sil i uchëte interesov)" (The German question and the Common European home [about the balance of forces and the calculation of interests]), *MEiMO*, no. 6 (1990), pp. 5–17.

19. For indirect but nevertheless transparent hints at these calls, see the speech of Politbureau member Alexander Yakovlev at the June 15, 1990, meeting of the Commission on International Affairs of the CC of the CPSU in "Peremeny v Tsentral'noy i Vostochnoy Evrope," p. 113. Shevardnadze said that one of these calls suggested deploying Soviet rear-guard divisions to seal off the GDR again. See Shevardnadze, *Moy Vybor*, p. 228.

20. Shevardnadze, *Moy Vybor*, p. 223.

21. For an authoritative description of the aims of Soviet policy during the process of German unification, see Eduard Shevardnadze, *Moy Vybor*, pp. 228–31.

22. See, for example, the exchange of opinions at the meeting of the International Affairs Commission on June 15, 1990 ("Peremeny v Tsentral'noy i Vostochnoy Evrope," pp. 108–09).

23. "Vneshnepoliticheskaya i diplomaticheskaya deyatel'nost' SSSR (Noyabr' 1989-Dekabr' 1990). Obsor MID SSSR" (The foreign policy and diplomatic activity of the USSR [November 1989–December 1990]. A survey by the USSR Ministry of Foreign Affairs), *Mezhdunarodnaya Zhizn'*, no. 3 (1991), pp. 41–43. For the original September 12 treaty, see Paul B. Stares, *Allied Rights and Legal Constraints on German Military Power* (Brookings, 1990).

24. For official Soviet assessments of the treaties with Germany and the response to the critique of the treaties, see two interviews with the main Soviet architect of the treaties, First Deputy Foreign Minister Yuliy Kvitsinskiy, "Dogovor dorozhe deneg. Ob"edineniye Germanii bylo neizbezhno. Sovetskaya diplomatiya tol'ko priznala evropeyskiye real'nosti." (The treaty is more valuable than money. The unification of Germany was inevitable. Soviet diplomacy merely recognized European realities), *Novoye Vremiya*, no. 12 (1991), pp. 18–20, and "Dogcvory, kotorym suzhdeno stat' istoricheskimi. Interv'yu zamestitelya ministra inostrannykh del SSSR Yu. A. Kvitsinskogo diplomaticheskomy korrespondenty TASS (Treaties that are bound to become historical. Interview with the Deputy Minister of Foreign Affairs of the SSSR, Yuliy Kvitsinskiy, conducted by the diplomatic correspondent of TASS.) *Izvestiya*, February 15, 1991, p. 5.

25. A similar observation has been made by W. R. Smyser in "USSR-Germany: A Link Restored," *Foreign Policy*, no. 84 (Fall 1991), pp. 132–34.

26. On hopes for a new Soviet-Germany rapprochcment, see, for example, Daniel Proektor, "My, Germaniya i budushcheye" (We, Germany, and the future), *Literaturnaya Gazeta*, February 27, 1991, p. 4.

27. One can already detect some indications that a special relationship is being formed between Washington and Bonn on questions relating to the policy toward the former Soviet Union.

28. For an interesting and largely accurate account of the Soviet common European house policy in conjunction with Germany, see Eugene B. Rumer, "The German Question in Moscow's 'Common European Home': A Background to the Revolutions of 1989," Rand Note N-3220-USDR (Santa Monica: Rand, 1991), pp. iii-19.

29. I tried to assess the Soviet policy agenda in Europe in 1989 and 1990 in two previously published articles. S. Karaganov, "Problemy evropeyskoy politiki SSSR" (The problems of Soviet European policy), *Mezhdunarodnaya Zhizn'*, no. 6 (1990), pp. 85–94; and S. Karaganov, "Budushcheye Yevropy stavit voprosy (Questions facing the future of Europe), *Mezhdunarodnaya Zhizn'*, no. 4 (1991), pp. 49–57.

30. The changes in the Russian foreign and security policy agenda were analyzed at length in S. Karaganov, "Vneshchnaya politika posle putcha" (Foreign policy after the putsch) *Nezavisimaya Gazeta*, September 21, 1991, p. 5.

31. For in-depth analyses of the stabilizing and destabilizing features of the present

political situation in Europe, see Stephen Van Evera, "Primed for Peace: Europe after the Cold War," *International Security*, no. 3 (Winter 1990/1991), pp. 7–57; Stanley Hoffmann, Robert O. Keohane, and John Mearsheimer, "Back to the Future. Part Two: International Relations Theory and Post-Cold War Europe," *International Security*, no. 2 (Fall 1990), pp. 191–99.

32. One logical measure that has attracted support is the creation of zones free of antisubmarine weapons (ASW) operations.

33. See, for example, Smol'nikov, *Novaya logika*, p. 28.

34. The recent IMF-OECD study indicates that in 1990 the Soviet Union had a current account deficit of more than $10 billion (gold was not included). Only three years before, the country had an almost $7 billion surplus. See International Monetary Fund, International Bank for Reconstruction and Development, Organization for Economic Cooperation and Development, and the European Bank for Reconstruction and Development, *The Economy of the USSR. Summary and Recommendations: A Study Undertaken in Response to a Request by the Houston Summit* (Washington 1990), p. 10. In 1991 the situation deteriorated further, and different rescheduling schemes came under discussion.

35. The Soviet Union was and is still Germany's most important Eastern trading partner. Its share in German exports to the region in 1990 was 52 to 54 percent, its share of imports 48 to 49 percent. See Deutsche Bank, Economics Department, *Rebuilding Eastern Europe* (Frankfurt, March 1, 1991), pp. 102–03.

36. Jürgen Corbet and Andreas Gummich, *The Soviet Union at the Crossroads* (Frankfurt: Deutsche Bank, Economics Department, May 1991), pp. 24–25.

TWELVE

Implications of German Unification for Japan

Hideo Sato

THE NEWS OF German unification, which became a reality on October 3, 1990, drew a favorable response from various groups in Japan, including the media, the business community, and the government. Some Japanese, however, did express concern and caution.

Yomiuri Shimbun, Japan's largest newspaper with a daily circulation of several million, said in an editorial:

> "The partition of Europe," which has lasted since the end of World War II, finally comes to an end. The United States, Britain, France and the Soviet Union— the four victorious nations of the war—have relinquished their rights and obligations over Germany, thus bringing to an end "the postwar period in Europe." We wish to congratulate the German people heartily for restoring full sovereignty and fulfilling their earnest wish for unification. . . . One has to point out, however, that West Germany's move for achieving the unification, having been so swift, is apparently creating some apprehension among its neighboring countries.[1]

Nihon Keizai Shimbun emphasized that the new Germany would come to occupy a central place, not only in the European Community but also in Europe as a whole. At the same time it noted that Chancellor Helmut Kohl's hurried maneuver could cause a rift in the relationship of trust built up with other European countries since the days of Konrad Adenauer, West Germany's first chancellor. The paper, cautioning Germany not to become an arrogant nation, suggested that Germany and Japan (which had learned a lesson in the futility of military adventurism in the last world war) should cooperate with each other and assist the United States in the shaping of a new world order.[2]

The business community responded enthusiastically at the time. "With the expanded economic influence of the new Germany," said Saburo Yuzawa of the Japan External Trade Organization (JETRO), "Germany, Japan, and the United States will become three nuclei for the world economy, thus increasing the need for expanding a direct dialogue between Japan and Germany" (as well as between Japan and the United States).[3] At the time of unification several Japanese banks and trading companies, believing that Berlin would shortly become the center of German economic activities, opened or planned to open branches or representative offices there. These establishments included the Bank of Tokyo, Sumitomo Bank, Nomura Securities, C. Itoh, Mitsubishi Corporation, and Nissho-Iwai. Mitsui and Company announced it would move the headquarters of its German subsidiary from Düsseldorf to Berlin. Minoru Murofuse of C. Itoh said, "Many Japanese manufacturers will also invest in the unified Germany, looking for new business opportunities."[4] According to another business source, Japanese companies were likely to invest in the old East German territory by concluding tie-ups with German companies, just as Mitsubishi Corporation had forged its link with Daimler-Benz AG in spring 1990. Still another source said it would be too costly to rebuild industrial bases there.[5]

Banking sources made a somewhat cautious response. They said that, as a result of the unification, the deutsche mark would virtually become the key currency for all Europe, including Central and Eastern Europe. That would lower the relative position of the yen, which had been gradually rising in international financial markets. "The German mark may weaken a little for a little while because of the economic problems accompanying unification," said a Bank of Tokyo executive, "but in a few years it will become an extremely strong currency, establishing a dominant position in Europe even more than before and threatening to destabilize a delicate balance among the dollar, the yen, and the mark."[6]

The Diplomatic Blue Book of the Japanese Foreign Ministry wrote of German unification: "Since the Berlin Wall virtually fell on November 9, 1989, the movement (for unifying the divided states of Germany) has progressed at an unexpectedly high tempo, culminating in the realization of German unification on October 3, 1990. This symbolically demonstrates a historical transition in the European order from one of conflict to one of cooperation."[7] A Foreign Ministry source believed that Germany would have to bear heavy financial burdens for reconstructing the economy of the old East Germany. However, as an outstanding economic power in the European Community, Germany's importance in assisting Central and Eastern Europe would be undeniable. Therefore, the Japanese government would like to strengthen its cooperative relationship with the new Germany in providing economic assistance to Eastern Europe through the Group of 24; it would also like to work closely with Germany in the Uruguay round trade talks.[8] Finance Ministry officials noted that through close geographical, historical, and cultural linkages, the unified Germany would play a crucial role in assisting the economic development and the shift toward a market economy in the former Soviet Union and Central and Eastern Europe, while holding a key to the future of European integration and that of the world economy.[9]

The Role of Germany in EC-Japan Relations

As we have seen, Japan has great expectations for, as well as some apprehension about, the new Germany, whose economic and political importance in Europe has increased. Consequently, a consensus has occurred among the Japanese that Tokyo would do well to maintain good and close relations with this European power, not only for the sake of the bilateral relationship but also for the purpose of strengthening the Japanese-European relationship—often called "the weakest link" in the triangle consisting of the United States, Japan, and the European Community. With the inclusion of the old East German territory and population, the Community has significantly expanded its size, and it will probably achieve greater internal integration after 1992. Tokyo believes that "the EC will ultimately bring the six countries of the European Free Trade Association (EFTA), as well as many of the Eastern European countries, into a more formal relationship with the 12 existing members of the Community."[10] Consequently, Tokyo attaches greater importance than before to the improvement of relations with the EC in Brussels, which it sees as "the Gateway to the new Europe," and Japan wants "to enter into a broader and more mature dialogue with the EC—one that goes beyond the realm of dealing with trade frictions."[11] Indeed, conflicts over trade, and, more recently, over investment, have too often beset EC-Japan relations. But one cannot simply bypass these economic conflicts to improve and expand Japan's relations with the Community.

Improving Economic Relations

Some EC member countries, particularly France and Italy, have maintained very protectionist policies toward Japan. To this day, these countries control imports of cars from Japan as well as a number of other products through formal agreements. France, Italy, and some other EC members limit several other goods through voluntary restraint agreements. By contrast, West Germany was a driving force for free trade within the Community. Therefore, one might hypothesize that the emergence of the larger and more influential Germany may help the Community accelerate its process of trade liberalization with extraregional trading partners, thus making a significant contribution to the betterment of EC-Japan relations.

Table 12-1. *Japan's Trade with the European Community and Selected EC Members, 1986–90*

Values in millions of dollars; change in percent

Region or country	Exports		Imports		Balance	
	Value	Change	Value	Change	Value	Change
European Community						
1990	53,510	11.7	35,063	24.6	18,447	−6.6
1989	47,908	2.2	28,146	16.9	19,761	−13.3
1988	46,873	24.3	24,071	36.2	22,802	13.9
1987	37,693	22.9	17,670	26.3	20,023	20.0
1986	30,675	53.3	13,989	57.3	16,686	50.0
Great Britain						
1990	10,782	0.4	4,765	6.7	6,017	−4.1
1989	10,741	1.0	4,466	6.5	6,275	−2.5
1988	10,632	26.5	4,193	37.2	6,439	20.5
1987	8,400	26.4	3,057	−14.4	5,343	73.8
1986	6,647	40.7	3,573	96.6	3,074	5.8
West Germany						
1990	17,777	11.7	11,487	27.7	6,290	−9.2
1989	15,920	0.8	8,995	10.9	6,925	−10.0
1988	15,793	23.1	8,101	31.8	7,692	15.1
1987	12,833	22.5	6,150	43.1	6,683	8.2
1986	10,477	51.0	4,298	46.8	6,179	54.1
France						
1990	6,124	15.6	7,586	26.8	−1,462	489.5
1989	5,298	6.3	5,546	28.6	−248	. . .
1988	4,986	24.2	4,313	50.2	673	−41.1
1987	4,014	27.3	2,871	54.8	1,143	−11.9
1986	3,152	51.3	1,855	40.1	1,297	70.9

Trade

Japan and Germany are the world's second and third largest economic powers, and before October 3, 1990, the two countries had maintained relatively good and close trade relations. Germany is Japan's largest European trade partner, while Japan is Germany's second largest trade partner outside Europe. The two countries also have similar trade structures, exporting mostly industrial manufactured goods. Consequently, one might expect Germany to have considerable sympathy for and empathy with Japan's trade problems.

In 1987, Andreas van Agt, then head of the European Community's delegation in Tokyo stated, "There was a time when our relationship could be said to have revolved almost exclusively around our anxiety over the avalanche of Japanese car exports to Europe, then videotape recorders, ball

Table 12-1. *(Continued)*

Region or country	Exports		Imports		Balance	
	Value	*Change*	*Value*	*Change*	*Value*	*Change*
Italy						
1990	3,410	22.5	5,007	31.6	− 1,597	56.1
1989	2,783	− 0.0	3,806	31.6	− 1,023	847.2
1988	2,787	32.5	2,895	35.5	− 108	237.5
1987	2,103	22.1	2,135	42.8	− 32	. . .
1986	1,723	54.3	1,495	42.4	228	240.3
Denmark						
1990[a]	883	16.5	1,046	− 12.8	− 163	− 63.0
1989	758	− 4.3	1,199	5.0	− 441	26.0
1988	792	− 13.6	1,142	21.0	− 350	1,196.3
1987	917	− 7.3	944	20.9	− 27	. . .
1986	989	30.5	781	34.9	198	10.6
Netherlands						
1990[a]	5,521	8.0	1,071	− 4.5	4,450	11.5
1989	5,112	1.1	1,122	12.7	3,990	− 1.7
1988	5,054	24.1	996	31.6	4,058	22.5
1987	4,071	24.8	757	31.2	3,314	23.5
1986	3,261	57.5	577	31.4	2,684	64.5
Spain						
1990[a]	1,895	− 2.4	736	32.4	1,158	− 16.4
1989	1,941	4.4	556	3.5	1,385	4.7
1988	1,860	38.5	537	50.4	1,323	31.2
1987	1,343	24.8	357	20.2	986	26.6
1986	1,076	77.9	297	− 15.1	779	205.5
Greece						
1990[a]	746	29.1	145	− 18.1	601	49.9
1989	578	28.2	177	29.2	401	27.7
1988	431	1.1	137	98.6	314	− 16.7
1987	446	− 20.8	69	− 4.2	377	− 23.2
1986	563	− 2.4	72	14.3	491	− 4.5

Source: *JEI* Report, no. 10a (Washington: Japan Economic Institute, March 15, 1991), p. 4.
a. January–November 1990; percent change based on the same period of 1989.

bearings, copiers and again more cars. Meanwhile, the EC was painstakingly, and with little response, asking Japan to open its market, while the Japanese surplus with the EC got bigger and bigger. During the past year, things have started to change. We are both now exporting more to each other than ever before."[12] What van Agt said remained true until recently. Exports and imports between Japan and the EC expanded through the end of 1990 (table 12-1). Partly because of the breakup of the so-called bubbles in the Japanese economy, Japanese imports have greatly declined in 1991. As a result, Japan's January–August 1991 trade surplus with the European Community jumped 62.9 percent over the same period a year earlier.[13] Moreover, Japan and the EC still haggle over trade in automobiles.

In EC-Japan economic relations, three different channels of interaction have been used: those between Japanese and European industry representatives, those between the Japanese government and individual EC member countries, and those between the Japanese government and the Community (or the European Community). As evidenced by interaction on past automobile trade issues, which one of these channels was used or not had important implications for the resolution of particular issues.

In Japan's auto trade issue with Great Britain (November 1974–March 1978), negotiations were largely done by Japanese and British industry representatives. The role of the two governments was ceremonial. The interindustrial agreement to keep Japanese auto imports within about 10 percent of the British market led to a relatively amicable settlement of the issue.[14] Unlike the Anglo-Japanese auto issue, Japan's auto trade conflict with France (summer 1977–September 1981) mostly involved French and Japanese government officials. Because France maintained the very rigid position that Japan's auto imports should not exceed 3 percent of France's domestic market, there was little room for bilateral negotiations, and the Japanese side could not get France to make any important concessions in expanded import quotas for Japanese-made cars. The issue did not become unnecessarily complicated, however, partly because Japan did not entertain any optimistic expectations about significant concessions from France.[15]

Since around 1980, the European Commission has gradually gained control over automobile negotiations with Japan. As the commission has increased its leverage over negotiating and coordinating policy, it has become correspondingly easier for Japan to negotiate over autos and other trade issues. While individual countries like France and Italy have maintained aggressive and protectionist postures in their bilateral negotiations with Japan, other EC members more oriented toward free trade have not been in a position to influence such negotiations. The commission, however, has exerted a moderating influence on negotiation outcomes because it is in a position to strike a balance between free-trading and protectionist EC members.[16] In any case, it is a good thing that the EC has come to negotiate (or at least try to negotiate) a unified position on autos and other issues with both its members and Tokyo. Japan expects Germany to influence this process in the direction of freer trade.

Most recently, after a year of talks, Japan and the EC concluded an informal agreement on July 31, 1991, limiting the number of Japanese cars exported to and built within the EC. "Under the informal accord EC member nations will drop their individual controls on the import of Japanese cars on

January 1, 1993, and adopt a community-wide annual limit of 1.2 to 1.3 million made-in-Japan cars through the end of 1999. Five EC countries that currently impose tight restrictions on Japanese car imports will retain individual (though more generous) import ceilings during the transition period: 190,000 for Great Britain, 150,000 for France, 138,000 for Italy, 79,000 for Spain, and 23,000 for Portugal. A gentlemen's agreement also will allow the output of the EC subsidiaries of Japanese automakers to rise to as much as 1.2 million units a year by the end of the seven-year transition period; these vehicles are to be classified as domestic products."[17] The agreement was a product of bargaining among Tokyo, hard-line EC members, and free trade-oriented EC members.

Direct Investment

Japan's investment in Europe in recent years has grown rapidly, and the rate of expansion of Japanese investment flowing into Europe has outpaced that headed toward the United States (table 12-2). Some people in Japan have suspected that Japanese companies have increased investment in Europe in anticipation of 1992; they have tried to expand production bases within the Community for fear that the EC after 1992 may become more discriminatory toward imports from Japan and other non-European countries. In 1990, the Japan External Trade Organization (JETRO) conducted a survey of 529 Japanese companies in Europe by asking, among other things, why they have invested in Europe. Popular responses were as follows:

—To make one of the steps toward a globalized business strategy (179 companies, plural answers allowed).

—To convert to local production to meet increasing demands in Europe (97 companies).

—To meet specific needs of European consumers (91 companies).

—To avoid import restrictions on goods made in Japan (48 companies).

—To cope with possible protectionist policies and measures to be taken by EC countries after 1992 (45 companies).[18]

The responses show that a large majority of Japanese companies have decided to invest in Europe in anticipation of more favorable, rather than more unfavorable, business environments. It could also mean that Japanese investment in Europe might keep growing, almost regardless of favorable or unfavorable business environments. According to one observer, "Western Europe will account for as much as one third of Japan's overseas commitments by the end of the decade."[19]

In the past, Japanese companies were criticized for building relatively unsophisticated "screwdriver" plants in Europe, which assembled parts usually imported from Japan. But from now on, Japan will increasingly invest in

Table 12-2. Japan's Foreign Direct Investment by Country, Fiscal Years 1985–89, March 1990
Values in millions of dollars; shares in percent

Region or country	1985			1986			1987		
	Cases	Value	Share	Cases	Value	Share	Cases	Value	Share
United Kingdom	85	375	3.1	142	984	4.4	178	2,473	7.4
Netherlands	38	613	5.0	60	651	2.9	71	829	2.5
Luxembourg	12	300	2.5	16	1,092	4.9	18	1,764	5.3
West Germany	48	172	1.4	59	210	0.9	50	403	1.2
France	60	67	0.5	52	152	0.7	99	330	1.0
Spain	8	91	0.7	15	86	0.4	24	283	0.8
Italy	11	32	0.3	18	23	0.1	26	59	0.2
Ireland	5	81	0.7	4	72	0.3	5	58	0.2
Portugal	..	..	..	..	..	..	..	..	..
Switzerland	15	60	0.5	7	91	0.4	22	224	0.7
Other Europe	31	139	1.1	31	99	0.4	44	71	0.2
Total Europe	313	1,930	15.8	404	3,469	15.5	537	6,576	19.7
United States	921	5,395	44.2	1,232	10,165	45.5	1,816	14,704	44.1
Hong Kong	105	131	1.1	163	502	2.2	261	1,072	3.2
China	118	100	0.8	85	226	1.0	101	1,226	3.7
Total	2,613	12,217	100.0	3,196	22,320	100.0	4,584	33,364	100.0

Table 12-2. (Continued)

Region or country	1988			1989			Cumulative, March 31, 1990		
	Cases	Value	Share	Cases	Value	Share	Cases	Value	Share
United Kingdom	211	3,956	8.4	285	5,239	7.8	1,864	15,793	6.2
Netherlands	105	2,359	5.0	112	4,547	6.7	642	10,072	4.0
Luxembourg	13	657	1.4	13	654	1.0	143	5,383	2.1
West Germany	67	409	0.9	119	1,083	1.6	1,053	3,448	1.4
France	148	463	1.0	168	1,136	1.7	1,157	2,899	1.1
Spain	32	161	0.3	58	501	0.7	277	1,546	0.6
Italy	26	108	0.2	47	314	0.5	255	684	0.3
Ireland	12	42	0.1	11	133	0.2	90	565	0.2
Portugal	4	7	0.0	10	74	0.1	44	114	0.0
Switzerland	27	454	1.0	19	397	0.6	288	1,829	0.7
Other Europe	47	500	1.1	74	730	1.1	656	2,639	1.0
Total Europe	692	9,116	19.4	916	14,808	21.9	6,469	44,972	17.7
United States	2,434	21,701	46.2	2,668	32,540	48.2	20,657	104,400	41.1
Hong Kong	335	1,662	3.5	335	1,898	2.8	3,499	8,066	3.2
China	171	296	0.6	126	438	0.6	694	2,472	1.0
Total	6,077	47,022	100.0	6,589	67,540	100.0	57,373	253,896	100.0

Source: JEI Report, no. 10A (March 15, 1991), p. 12.

advanced technology, research and development, and plants using local supplies, thus posing new competitive threats to European companies.

Indeed, European companies are hypersensitive to high-technology competition from Japan, as well as from the United States. In November 1990, Fujitsu purchased 80 percent of the British computer giant, International Computers, putting Fujitsu in a close race with Digital Equipment Corporation for the number two spot in a global information services market. This transaction, which other European companies viewed as "an unpatriotic sellout," triggered controversy in Europe, especially because it meant possible Japanese participation in joint European research projects that had previously been closed to non-EC members, including some projects organized by ESPRIT (the European Strategic Program for Research in Information Technologies, a roundtable of twelve European computer makers formed in the late 1970s) and JESSI (Joint European Submicron Silicon Initiative). International Computers participated in both ESPRIT and JESSI projects. Tension with Japan is also exemplified in a project aimed at developing the next generation of advanced televisions. EUREKA (European Research Coordination Agency), another exclusively European joint research program started in 1985 to develop commercial technologies, is in competition with the Japan Broadcasting Corporation, which has been developing its own version of high-definition television. But although the Japanese corporation had been working on high-definition television (HDTV) since the 1960s, the Europeans managed to delay a 1986 vote on international standards proposed by the Japanese corporation, giving European firms time to pool their resources to propose a different HDTV system.[20]

Whether this kind of technonationalism or "techno-Europeanism" is good for the Europeans in the long run is questionable, since it wastes precious time and resources for high-technology research and development. Some Europeans, however, may argue that they have an inherent right to try to develop their own high technology if only to minimize dependence on Japan or the United States in the future.

Lately, however, a noteworthy development has occurred. The West German Electric Industry Association, consisting of television makers in the old West German region, approached European subsidiaries of Sony, Matsushita, and Hitachi for capital assistance of about 30 million deutsche marks to be used for promoting EUREKA's television systems called MAC, an improved version of the current television system but still a step behind high-definition television. In some parts of France, MAC is already being used, but German television broadcasters were lukewarm about EUREKA's system. They have been in conflict with the German government, which had been promoting the MAC system. Under these circumstances, it seems that the German government, eager to use MAC in German television broadcasting as soon as possible, prevailed upon the electric industry association to ask the Japanese companies (as well as Philips and other European companies) for capital assistance.[21] Whatever the real motive may have been, the German industry took a step in the right direction by approaching the Japanese companies for cooperation.

As Japanese companies increasingly target investment strategies on high-technology manufacturing and service industries, "the thrust of investment will switch from Britain (and the Benelux) countries to Germany and France, which the Japanese now see as the best springboards for dominant positions" in these industries.[22]

Expanding Political and Security Relations

Japan has long wanted to broaden relations with Europe beyond trade and investment. It would like to develop political and security relations because, as one Japanese diplomat put it, "The security of the Western alliance is not separable: Japan and Europe too are involved."[23] For instance, Japanese officials believe that "Soviet weapon redeployment—especially from the European theater to the east of the Urals—is very much a subject for Japanese-European discussion."[24] But such Japanese views are not yet widely shared in Europe, where Germany enjoys an enhanced political status in the wake of its unification. In this context, Takashi Inoguchi of Tokyo University writes:

> German unification has been accompanied by two other major tasks of German diplomacy—further embedding the country in the European Community and NATO while achieving rapprochement and friendship with the Soviet Union. Because Germany shares some similarities with Japan—its role in the Second World War, its status as a semisovereign country since then, and its increasing economic and perhaps political influence—Japan cannot but help pay special attention to it. Furthermore, the 1990 Conference on Security and Cooperation in Europe has left Japan feeling lonely, since it is the only major country in the northern hemisphere that has not been part of the CSCE.[25]

Because of its legacy of militarism most other countries, particularly other Asian countries, do not want Japan to exercise significant military power in the world. Neither do most Japanese people. Germany is in a similar situation. Other countries, especially other European countries, do not want Germany to become an independent military power divorced from the context of NATO. Consequently, these two countries' security contributions to the world would have to be largely nonmilitary in nature.

In fact, this viewpoint would be perfectly in tune with the dictate of the post-Cold War world because, as Richard H. Solomon said in a recent address, "We now face a future in which technological and commercial capabilities more than military strength are the significant determinants of state power and influence." He also said, "National security is ever more reckoned in terms of economic and environmental concerns."[26] In short, what Richard Rosecrance calls "the military-political world" is giving way to "the trading world."[27] Japan and Germany might be able to make useful contributions to international security, broadly defined, as "trading states" or, in Hanns W. Maull's words, "civilian powers."[28] Perhaps Germany would make the most of its increased political influence with the Community in persuading other EC members to invite Japan to participate in various political and security discussions in Europe, including those held in the context of the Conference on Security and Cooperation in Europe (CSCE).

Some progress in the right direction has already taken place, as reflected in the joint declaration worked out between Japan and the European Community immediately following the successful July 1991 London summit of leaders from the major industrial democracies. The declaration, which is similar to an accord signed by the EC and the United States in 1990, "laid out a broad framework to smooth bilateral frictions and improve cooperation on political, as well as economic, matters. For instance, the EC and Japan reaffirmed common values for freedom, democracy, the rule of law, human rights, etc., and specifically called for cooperation on nonproliferation of missile technology and international arms sales," as well as on "transnational challenges," including environmental pollution and destruction, energy and resource conservation, and international drug dealing and other crimes. One must point out, however, that some doubt and skepticism has been exposed in official circles about the effectiveness and weight of this declaration.[29]

New Challenges to German-Japanese Relations

One could assume that Japan and Germany would be able to maintain good, amicable relations in the future simply because Japan and West Germany maintained such relations up to October 3, 1990. But one cannot afford to be too optimistic because changing circumstances present new challenges to German-Japanese relations. Several possible problems may stand in the way of a smooth bilateral relationship.

An Inward-Looking Germany

First of all, the new Germany could turn inward for some time because of the economic and social problems resulting from the absorption of the old East Germany. In that case, the unified Germany could slow down, instead of speeding up, the process of European integration for the time being. Under such circumstances, German influence within the Community would not substantially increase, and Germany would not be especially interested in taking initiatives on behalf of Japan.

While arguing that the situation will change during this decade, Michael H. Haltzel wrote in April 1991:

> The primary focus of German attention . . . is understandably riveted on the economic and social turmoil in the five new federal states and East Berlin, which used to comprise East Germany. Officials fear that unemployment and underemployment there may rise to 30–40 percent by summer. Whole sectors of the economy—ship-building, for example—are being eliminated, and several others are finding it extremely difficult to compete. Unaccustomed to the competitiveness of a free-market economy, most newly unemployed Easterners are at a loss [as to] how to secure a job, and government retraining programs will require time to yield results.[30]

In fact, the German economic situation has not been improving and may even worsen. While West Germany achieved an economic growth of 4.5 percent in 1990, Germany's growth rate for 1991 is estimated at 2.5 percent to 3 percent. More worrisome to officials in Bonn and Frankfurt is the prospect that inflation will surge. Labor costs and import prices are rising by nearly 5 percent this year. The inflationary effects of giving east Germans one deutsche mark for every ostmark they held may yet take place.[31]

Germany's possibly inward-looking attitude was reflected in the sudden shift in its position on the proposed European monetary union (EMU). At the EC summit held in Rome in October 1990, it was decided by eleven EC member countries (minus Great Britain) to establish the Community's central bank in January 1994 with a view to creating a truly unified European currency as soon as possible. Only several months later, however, the German federal government and the Bundesbank suddenly became cautious, unwilling to go along with the earlier decision by the EC summit. This change in the German position temporarily created a rift in the "French-German coalition" for the EMU. German officials then explained that if the Community should make haste in creating the monetary union without seriously considering substantial interest-rate differences among its members, it would end up repeating the very mistake of the recent German monetary union. Rightly or wrongly, some people suspect that Germany wants to delay the EMU until it further strengthens the deutsche mark and virtually gains control over other European currencies. Recently, German control has somewhat softened.[32]

A Germany Fully Committed to the EC

Consider another possibility. Suppose Germany should become fully committed to European integration, either before or after resolving most of its domestic economic and social problems. What then would happen to German-Japanese relations? In its eagerness to build consensus and solidarity within the Community, Germany might become less interested in supporting Japan's views or the views of any other non-EC member countries. Yuya Ishihara, an astute observer of EC-Japan relations, writes: "EC member-countries will increasingly come to speak in one voice as the integration progresses. Germany will be more like the EC (in its policy orientation) and will be forced to respect 'lower common denominators' in its give-and-take relations with other EC member-countries in intra-EC discussions on Japan. [Germany] will also find it more difficult to defend the principle of free trade as consistently as before."[33] In other words, in regard to Japan and international trade, Germany could conceivably end up taking positions somewhat closer to those of France and Italy.

New Tensions in Bilateral Economic Relations

As mentioned earlier, Japan's bilateral economic relations have been basically good and smooth. Despite its relative large bilateral trade deficit with Japan, Germany has thus far maintained a magnanimous attitude toward Tokyo, perhaps partly because Germany, like Japan, has been achieving relatively high economic growth and has been accumulating trade surpluses globally. But, as noted, Germany's economic growth is slowing down, and the country is faced with difficult domestic economic (as well as social) problems. As a result, Germany may become less patient and less generous with Japan over its trade deficit, which, while leveling off at around $6 billion annually for the last several years, constitutes as much as 30 percent of the Community's total annual trade deficit with Japan (see table 12-1).

More important, Germany is now being seriously challenged by Japan in several industries, including automobiles and electronics, which have long been sources of German pride. Some even say that Japan has already taken over the lead in these industries, and the perception of Japan as an economic competitor, rather than an economic partner, seems to be growing in Germany.[34] For Japan and Germany, the auto industry has been the lead export industry. According to table 12-3, the number of Japanese auto exports to the West increased from 274,705 in 1981 to 467,279 in 1990. The number of Japanese auto imports from West Germany increased from 24,945 to 137,442 during the same period. Although Japanese auto imports from Germany have been increasing more rapidly than Japanese auto exports to Germany, the number of the exports was still 3.4 times the number of imports. Some Germans would be wary of this situation. At the same time, some Japanese would be wary because, in 1990, for the first time the value

Table 12-3. *Automotive Trade between Japan and West Germany*
Number of cars

Year	Japanese exports to West Germany	Japanese imports from West Germany
1981	274,705	24,945
1982	198,507	26,698
1983	274,436	26,787
1984	320,288	32,634
1985	324,470	40,157
1986	379,326	53,916
1987	436,034	74,289
1988	461,361	91,648
1989	470,722	120,293
1990	467,279	137,442

Sources: For exports see *Jidōsha Yushutsu Gaikyō, 1981–90* (Tokyo: Japan Automobile Manufacturers Association, various editions); for imports, statistics from the Japan Automobile Importers Association, Tokyo, were used.

of German cars exported to Japan exceeded the value of Japanese cars exported to Germany. Japanese auto imports from Germany include many luxury cars. In any case, the German-Japanese competition in auto trade will only intensify in the future.

Some Germans are becoming extremely sensitive to the Japanese challenge in high-technology industries. Representing this sentiment, Konrad Seitz, who headed the planning division of the German Foreign Ministry, emphasized the following points found in the concluding chapter of his recent study:

—Competitiveness in high technology is important for the future of the European economy.

—It is better for the EC to strengthen ties (at governmental and industrial levels) with the United States, rather than with Japan, because of similar cultural backgrounds.

—The EC should apply the reciprocity principle (as incorporated in the U.S.-Japan Semiconductor Agreement) in dealing with Japan because Japanese society is not amenable to GATT's free-trade rules and principles.

—Regardless of the final outcome of the Uruguay round, there will be a tripolar power structure in high technology involving Europe with the EC as its nucleus, the North American Free Trade Area, and the Yen Economic Zone in East and Southeast Asia. Regionalism (as well as the reciprocity principle) is an answer to the Japanese challenge.

—Germany's economic policy is too conservative and too irrational because the government is historically opposed to the idea of subsidizing high-technology industries while retaining subsidy programs for agriculture and coal mining. The government tends to neglect high-technology industries and does not fully understand the Japanese threat.

International competition in high-technology industries does not simply mean competition for the concerned. It means competition for the country, its social system, and its culture.[35]

As just suggested, Japanese direct investment in Germany, particularly by high-technology industries, will increase in the future, and this development could create bilateral conflicts unless such investment can prove mutually beneficial. Increasing transnational industrial collaboration, such as has occurred between Mitsubishi and Daimler-Benz, may be one answer.

Lack of Japanese Investment in the Former East Germany

Although Japanese investment in Germany as a whole will increase, it is uncertain whether enough Japanese companies will invest in the old East Germany. Chancellor Kohl has asked the Japanese government to encourage Japanese companies to invest there to help Germany reconstruct and revitalize the eastern states. Helmut Muller, who heads the German Productivity Center, expressed a similar hope on his visit to Japan at the time of the unification. Despite generally enthusiastic reactions to the news of German unification noted at the beginning of this paper, the Japanese business community has become very cautious about investing in eastern Germany. Many Japanese banks and trading companies did open offices in Berlin, mainly because they thought Berlin would become the capital city for the whole Germany. But the oft-reported news about the economic and social turmoil in the five new federal states has discouraged many Japanese companies that might have invested there. Apparently, even German companies have been finding it unexpectedly difficult to make viable investments in eastern Germany for several reasons, including lower productivity of labor, rising wages, various administrative barriers, land ownership problems, the difficulty of obtaining financing, and uncontrolled environmental conditions.[36]

Japan, attending to its foreign policy, has at least three reasons to invest in the new federal states. First, the German government wants investment, and for the sake of good relations Japan would do well to accommodate Germany's hopes. Second, the sooner Germany can reconstruct the economy of eastern Germany, the more attention it can pay to other matters, including German-Japanese relations. Last but not least, through a greater economic presence in the eastern part of Germany, Japan can build a base for improving and expanding relations, not only with Germany and Western Europe but also with Central and Eastern Europe and the former Soviet Union. Here the logic of economics and the logic of foreign policy do not seem compatible, at least in the short run.

Germany would also appreciate greater Japanese involvement in developing the economies of the Central and East European countries. Basically for similar reasons, the Japanese government has been more interested than the Japanese business community in assisting Central and Eastern Europe. During a January 1990 tour of Europe, Prime Minister Toshiki Kaifu pledged a package of nearly $2 billion in assistance to Hungary and Poland. The Japanese government announced in April 1991 that it would provide roughly $6.3 million to establish a fund for the region within the European Bank for Reconstruction and Development. "By showing support for Eastern Europe through foreign aid," says a JEI Report, "Tokyo has expected the business community will pick up on its lead and become more involved in the region."[37] That expectation has turned into a disappointment. Japanese business, after taking a close look at Central and Eastern Europe, concluded that the region is too risky and has politely decided against making large investments. This decision is quite unfortunate because the amount of money given through foreign aid is relatively small compared with the amount of money the private sector can channel through investment. "Hungary has received the region's biggest share of Japanese corporate investment, about $12 million and twelve joint ventures (as of April 1991). In contrast, U.S. and West European companies have funneled more than $1 billion into Hungary and formed several thousand joint ventures."[38]

The Japanese government would be required to provide attractive trade and investment insurance programs to induce larger Japanese private sector involvement in eastern Germany and Central and Eastern Europe. One wonders if it is wise for Japan to resign itself to accepting that "Europe is for the Europeans so far as reconstructing the continent goes."[39]

Disagreement over Aid to the Former Soviet Union

The views of Japan and Germany on joint economic assistance to the former Soviet Union diverged widely at the time of the 7 + 1 London summit of July 1991. Germany was one of the strongest supporters for economic assistance to the Soviet Union, in part because Chancellor Helmut Kohl was indebted to former President Mikhail Gorbachev for making German unification possible. But, more important, Germany wanted to increase aid to Moscow because it believed the Western support for perestroika in the Soviet Union would contribute to peace and security in the world. Starting before unification, Germany provided about $33.7 billion in economic assistance up to July 1991, including export insurance programs. This sum is not simply the price of German unification. If economic reforms should fail and should large-scale political and economic chaos shake the former Soviet Union, the economic and security implications for Germany and

Europe as a whole would be serious. To give just one example, many refugees would flood into the region.[40]

At the London summit, Japan was most cautious and most reluctant about economic assistance to the Soviet Union, arguing that the Soviet Union should first get its reforms going. By asking the Soviet Union to apply its "new thinking" to Asia, Japan put pressure on Moscow to concede on the pending issue of the Northern Islands. If Japan should maintain too rigid a stand on economic assistance to Moscow, then serious strains could develop in its relations with Germany. Since the abortive coup in the Soviet Union in August 1991, however, the Japanese position has softened and Japan's relationship with the successor states of the Soviet Union, particularly with the Russian Republic, has significantly improved.

We have discussed a number of possible challenges to German-Japanese relations. Indeed, unless the two countries can effectively cope with these and other challenges, the bilateral relationship, which has largely proved amicable and uneventful, may become unnecessarily conflictual, boding ill for EC-Japan relations as well.

Japan and Germany in the Shaping of a New World Order

German unification was in a way a by-product of the ending of the Cold War in Europe. Moreover, the unification became a reality when the United States had already ceased to enjoy economic hegemony in the world. At the height of the Cold War, the United States had a strong foreign policy incentive to create and maintain a stable international political and economic order, and it had sufficient economic capabilities to maintain the order practically by itself. Now with the ending of the Cold War and the relative economic decline of the United States, Washington has become less willing and less able financially to bear the cost of maintaining peace and the liberal economic order that has brought enormous prosperity to Japan and Germany. In this concluding section, I briefly examine the possible roles of Japan and Germany in the shaping of a new world order.

In an earlier study, I discussed four scenarios for a new world order: namely, the restoration of Pax Americana, Pax Nipponica, competing economic blocs, and a system of joint leadership by major powers, with the United States acting as first among equals. The conclusion was that the first three scenarios would be impossible, undesirable, or both.[41] Hanns W. Maull came to a similar conclusion about Pax Teutonica.[42]

To the extent that the United States is no longer willing and able to bear alone the cost of maintaining a stable international economic and political order, the nations of the world may have to depend on a system of joint leadership, in which Japan and the European Community will exercise strong leadership, along with the United States. Others have expressed similar ideas. C. Fred Bergsten has called for a "Big-Three Steering Committee" for the world economy, including the United States, Japan, and Europe.[43] Stanley Hoffmann advocates "a deal to redistribute power—now still largely in the hands of the United States—among the main actors in the international financial and economic organizations, the United States, Japan and the European Community."[44] Robert Kuttner has suggested that

> In some respects, a U.S.-dominated grand alliance was simpler and stabler than a plural system. But, for better or worse, a plural system is where we are headed. America cannot afford to "bear any burden, pay any price" to defend liberty and safeguard its interests—at least not singlehandedly. Rather than going broke resisting that reality, the United States should seize the moment and work to build a stable, plural world order.[45]

In July 1990, Jeane Kirkpatrick suggested that George Bush seemed to have "a trilateral vision of Japan and Germany in starring roles alongside the United States."[46] As early as 1984, Ronald McKinnon proposed the idea of a tripolar monetary system, with the United States, West Germany, and Japan coordinating their money supply in order to control destabilizing fluctuations in the global supply of money. The three major centers of economic power, accounting for nearly two-thirds of the industrialized world's output, would agree on and set a target for the growth of the world's money supply. Each would direct its domestic monetary policy toward exchange-rate stabilization, expanding and contracting the money supply as necessary to maintain monetary values. Together, these three "hard currency" countries would in effect impose a rule of global monetary growth on the rest of the world liquidity.[47] At the International Monetary Fund meeting in September 1990, Ryutaro Hashimoto, finance minister of Japan, proposed a new currency system based on policy coordination among the United States, the EC, and Japan.[48]

All the above proposals point out the importance of better and closer policy coordination among the trilateral countries. Some people may argue that the Commonwealth of Independent States, or Russia, and China should be included in the joint leadership system.

Whatever form a system of joint leadership might take, it would not be easy to institutionalize a viable and effective mechanism of multilateral policymaking and policy coordination. For some time to come, the United States will remain reluctant to share power and influence while asking for greater financial burden sharing by other countries. Japan is not sufficiently ready to exercise international leadership, even as part of a plural leadership system. The European Community will for some time be preoccupied with the problem of European integration.

There is still a danger of creating competing economic blocs. Apart from Europe 1992, the United States has been implementing the U.S.-Canada Free Trade Agreement and has now advanced the Enterprise for the Americas Initiative by successfully concluding a North American Free Trade Agreement (NAFTA) with Mexico and Canada. A Japanese Foreign Ministry official reportedly observed that "if European or North American countries should be tempted to create regional trading blocs, then Japan 'might be forced to join similar types of cooperation in Asia,'" perhaps alluding to the East Asian Economic Grouping proposed by Malaysia.[49] Instead of taking such a reactive posture, Japan would do well to take positive measures to prevent mutually exclusive regionalism from taking root.

Among other things, Japan will have to promote through self-initiation further liberalization of the domestic market for trade, investment, and services, including financial services. As noted earlier, some in the Japanese banking community were afraid that the strengthened deutsche mark after German unification might lead to the relative decline of the Japanese currency in the international monetary market. But the real problem is that the role of the yen in international economic transactions has not been allowed to expand as much as it should have, at least enough to match the share of Japan's GNP in the world because Japan's own financial and capital markets have not been sufficiently opened up yet. At the end of 1988, the U.S. currency's share of world reserves was 63.3 percent, far above the share of the American GNP in the world, which was 21.3 percent. The deutsche mark's share of reserves was 16.2 percent, still much above the German GNP share of 5.3 percent. By contrast, Japan's share of reserves was only 7.2 percent (8.1 percent in 1989), far below its GNP share of 12.5 percent in 1988.[50] If the yen can achieve a higher profile, Japanese policymakers will inevitably consider international repercussions more seriously.

Moreover, while helping other Asian countries sustain relatively high economic growth by acting as a greater "import absorber," Japan will need to make sure that Asia is kept open to other regions, including Europe and North America, by expanding close networks of transnational and intergovernmental contacts. Japan can also see to it that the European Community be invited to attend future Asian Pacific Economic Cooperation (APEC) meetings.

As mentioned earlier, how Germany will behave from now on will greatly influence the process of European integration and the character of an integrated Europe. The new Germany would continue to be a driving force in the EC for multilateral free trade and an important civilian power in maintaining peace and stability in the international relations of a Europe that includes Western, Central and Eastern Europe, and the former Soviet Union. Japan could play a similar role in Asia as another civilian power.

Notes

1. *Yomiuri Shimbun*, October 3, 1990, p. 3.
2. *Nihon Keizai Shimbun*, October 8, 1990, p. 1.
3. *Yomiuri Shimbun*, October 4, 1990, p. 6.
4. *Yomiuri Shimbun*, October 4, 1990, p. 6.
5. *Yomiuri Shimbun*, October 4, 1990, p. 6.
6. *Yomiuri Shimbun*, October 4, 1990, p. 7.
7. Japanese Ministry of Foreign Affairs, *Gaiko Seisho* (Diplomatic Blue Book), (Tokyo: Finance Ministry Printing Office, 1990), p. 207.
8. *Yomiuri Shimbun*, October 4, 1990, p. 7.
9. Ministry of Finance, International Finance Bureau, Research Division, "Togo go no Doitsu ni tsuite" (On Germany after the Unification), *Boeki to Kanzei*, vol. 39 (July 1991), p. 37.
10. Anthony Rowley, "A Partnership of Equals," *Far Eastern Economic Review*, June 20, 1991, p. 58.
11. Rowley, "Partnership," p. 58.
12. Quoted in the *Japan Times*, October 28, 1987.
13. *Asahi Shimun*, September 30, 1991.
14. Hideo Sato, "Patterns of Interaction over Economic Conflicts: Japan, the United States, and the European Community," paper prepared for delivery at the IUJ-SAIS Joint Seminar in Washington, March 20, 1989, p. 15.
15. Sato, "Patterns of Interaction," p. 16.
16. Sato, "Patterns of Interaction," p. 17.
17. *JEI Report*, no. 30B (Washington: Japan Economic Institute, August 9, 1991), p. 11; Steven Greenhouse, "Issues Linger in Europe's Japan Auto Pact," *New York Times*, August 12, 1991, p. D1; and *EUROPE*, Agence Internationale d'Information pour la Presse, Luxembourg, July 26, 1991, pp. 5–6.
18. Japan External Trade Organization, *The Current Situation of Business Operations of Japanese Manufacturing Enterprises in Europe—The 6th Survey Report* (Tokyo: JETRO, March 1990), pp. 4, 22–24. This survey was discussed in Toshiro Tanaka, "The EC 1992 and Japan: Opportunity for Cooperation," paper prepared for ISA 32d Annual Convention, Vancouver, March 22, 1991, pp. 3–4.
19. Patrick L. Smith, "Tokyo's Money Will Reshape Europe," *International Herald Tribune*, May 29, 1990, p. 1.
20. The analysis in this section depends largely on *JEI Report*, no. 10A (March 15, 1991), pp. 13–14.
21. *Nihon Keizai Shimbun*, November 13, 1990, p. 1.
22. Smith, "Tokyo's Money," p. 1.
23. Rowley, "Partnership," p. 60.
24. Rowley, "Partnership," p. 60.
25. Takashi Inoguchi, "Japan and Europe: Wary Partners," *European Affairs*, (February–March 1991), vol. 1, p. 56.
26. Richard H. Solomon, assistant secretary of state for East Asian and Pacific Affairs, address to the University of California at San Diego, Graduate School of International Relations and Pacific Studies, "Asian Security in the 1990s: Integration in Economics; Diversity in Defense," October 30, 1990, official text, press office, United States Information Service, American Embassy, Tokyo, November 1, 1990, p. 2.
27. Richard Rosecrance, *The Rise of the Trading State: Commerce and Conquest in the Modern World* (Basic Books, 1986).

28. Hanns W. Maull, "Germany and Japan: The New Civilian Powers," *Foreign Affairs*, vol. 69 (Winter 1990–91), pp. 91–106.

29. *JEI Report*, no. 28B (July 26, 1991), pp. 3–4; *EUROPE*, July 17, 1991, pp. 9–10; and interviews with European and Japanese officials and academic experts, September–November, 1991.

30. Michael H. Haltzel, "Germany Remains Healthy Despite Its Sufferings," *Japan Times*, April 29, 1991.

31. Tony Catterall, "Germany Faced Some Harsh Realities in Its New State," *Japan Times*, October 3, 1991.

32. *Sankei Shimbun*, April 12, 1991; *Yomiuri Shimbun*, April 27, 1991; and *EUROPE*, September 12, 13, 25, 1991.

33. Yuya Ishihara, "Tsurugamine no Nichi-Oh Kankei: Dororu Iinchō Hōjitsu no Imisuru-mono" (Japan-Europe Reactions on Trial: The Meaning of Chairman Delors's Visit to Japan), *Gaiko Forum*, July 1991, p. 47.

34. Ishihara, "Tsurugamine no Nichi-Oh Kankei," p. 47.

35. Konrad Seitz, *Westpolitik 2000: Das amerikanisch-japanische Zeitalter als neue Gefahr für Europa* (World Politics 2000: The American-Japanese Era as the New Danger for Europe) (Bonn: Verlag Bonn aktuell, 1991). The Japanese Ministry of Foreign Affairs produced a summary sheet of this book's concluding section.

36. Ministry of Finance, "Togo go no Doitsu ni tsuite," p. 33.

37. *JEI Report*, no. 16B (April 26, 1991), pp. 10–11.

38. Peter Maass, "Japan Reluctant to Invest in East Europe," *International Herald Tribune*, April 10, 1991, p. 25.

39. Rowley, "Partnership," p. 60.

40. Shigeru Tsumori, "Doitsu Tōitsu go no Shinro o Yomu" (On the Course of Germany after Unification), *Gaiko Forum*, July 1991, pp. 31–32.

41. Hideo Sato, "Japan and the Changing Economic Order," *Pacific Review*, vol. 1, no. 2 (1988), pp. 109–18.

42. Maull, "Germany and Japan," p. 91.

43. Quoted in David Gergen, "For the Tripolar World—a Big Three Steering Committee," *International Herald Tribune*, May 7, 1990, p. 8.

44. Stanley Hoffmann, "A New World and Its Troubles," *Foreign Affairs*, vol. 69 (Fall 1990), p. 120.

45. Robert Kuttner, "The Former Free Riders Will Require a Say," *International Herald Tribune*, September 19, 1990, p. 8.

46. Jeane Kirkpatrick, "The Bush Vision Is of Japanese and Germans," *International Herald Tribune*, July 14–15, 1990, p. 4.

47. Ronald I. McKinnon, "An International Standard for Monetary Stabilization," in *Policy Analyses in International Economics* (Washington: Institute for International Economics, 1984), p. 75.

48. *Nihon Keizai Shimbun*, September 26, 1990, p. 5.

49. Rowley, "Partnership," p. 60.

50. Hideo Sato, "The Emerging Role of Japan in the World Economy," *International Spectator*, vol. 26 (July–September 1991), pp. 85–86; see also *Yomiuri Shimbun*, October 4, 1990, p. 7.

Contributors

Slawomir A. Dabrowa is the deputy director of the Department of European Institutions of the Polish Ministry of Foreign Affairs in Warsaw. A professional diplomat, he has held ambassadorial posts to the negotiations on Mutual and Balanced Force Reductions (MBFR) and the Conference on Security and Cooperation in Europe (CSCE). He has also been the head of several official Polish delegations to international conferences, most recently the Open Skies Conference in Vienna.

András Inotai is director of the Institute for World Economics of the Hungarian Academy of Sciences in Budapest where he has held several research and administrative positions since 1967 before assuming his current post. He has also been a visiting professor to San Marcos University in Lima, Peru, a visiting research fellow to the Kiel Institute for World Economy, and most recently in residence at the Trade Policy Division of the World Bank.

Sergei A. Karaganov is deputy director, Institute of Europe, Russian Academy of Sciences in Moscow where he is an expert on economic aspects of foreign policy, arms control, and Soviet-European relations. He has been a visiting researcher at the Brookings Institution, the Peace Research Institute Frankfurt, and Kings College, London.

Catherine McArdle Kelleher is a senior fellow in the Foreign Policy Studies program at the Brookings Institution. She was previously director of the Center for International Security Studies and professor in the School of Public Affairs at the University of Maryland. She also taught at the National War College, Columbia University, the Universities of Illinois and Michigan, and the Graduate School of International Studies in Denver. She has also served on the National Security Council staff and most recently was a visiting fellow at All Souls, Oxford.

Michael Kreile is a professor of International Policies at the University of Konstanz. He was previously assistant professor at the Institute of Political Science at Heidelberg University as well as a visiting professor at Georgetown University.

Hilmar Linnenkamp is director of the Department of Social Sciences at the Federal Armed Forces Command and General Staff College, Hamburg, where he was a lecturer on Conflict Research between 1988 and 1991. He was formerly counselor at the Planning Division of the Army Staff and, from 1979 to 1987, head of Section of the Planning Staff of the FRG Ministry of Defence.

Anne-Marie Le Gloannec is a research fellow at the Centre D'Études et de Recherches Internationales of the Fondation Nationale des Sciences Politiques, Paris, and also lectures at the Sorbonne (Paris 1). She has been a visiting fellow at the Woodrow Wilson Center, Washington; the Institute of East-West Security Studies, New York; the Johns Hopkins University Center in Bologna, Italy; and most recently the Stiftung Wissenchaft und Politik at Ebenhausen.

Harald Müller is director of International Programs at the Peace Research Institute Frankfurt (PRIF) and directs its nuclear nonproliferation program. He is also visiting professor at the Johns Hopkins University Center at Bologna. From 1984 to 1986 he was a senior fellow for security policy at the Centre for European Policy Studies in Brussels.

Wolfgang H. Reinicke is a research associate in the Foreign Policy Studies program at Brookings where he was formerly a research fellow. Before joining Brookings he was a research fellow at the Institute for the Study of World Politics, New York, and the Institute for Social and Policy Studies at Yale University. He has consulted for the National Academy of Sciences, the U.S. Agency for International Development, and the American Institute for Contemporary German Studies.

Hideo Sato is director of the Office of Educational Planning at the University of Tsukuba. From 1976 to 1982 he was an assistant and then associate professor in the Department of Political Science at Yale University and before that a research associate in the Brookings Foreign Policy Studies program.

Paul B. Stares is a senior fellow in the Foreign Policy Studies program at Brookings where he was previously a research associate and guest scholar. He has been a consultant to the U.S. Arms Control and Disarmament Agency and the United Nations Institute for Disarmament Research (UNIDIR). Before joining the staff of Brookings, he was a Rockefeller Foundation International Relations fellow and has held research positions at the Centre for the Study of Arms Control and International Security, Lancaster University, and the Science Policy Research Unit at Sussex University.

John D. Steinbruner is director of the Foreign Policy Studies Program at Brookings. He has held teaching and administrative posts at Yale and Harvard Universities as well as the Massachusetts Institute of Technology. He is a consultant and participant in many committees and organizations including the Committee on International Security and Arms Control of the National Academy of Sciences, the Defense Science Board, and the Aspen Strategy Group. He has also testified frequently before the U.S. Congress.

Index

391